D0138617

PSYCHOLOGY OF
EMOTION

PSYCHOLOGY OF
EMOTION

John G. Carlson

University of Hawaii

Elaine Hatfield

University of Hawaii

Harcourt Brace Jovanovich College Publishers

Fort Worth   Philadelphia   San Diego   New York   Orlando   Austin   San Antonio
Toronto   Montreal   London   Sydney   Tokyo

WINGATE COLLEGE LIBRARY

Publisher	*Ted Buchholz*
Acquisitions Editor	*Eve Howard*
Project Editors	*Clifford Crouch, Steve Welch*
Production Manager	*Kenneth A. Dunaway*
Manager of Art & Design	*Guy Jacobs*
Text Designer	*Geri Davis, Quadrata, Inc.*
Cover Designer	*Pat Sloan*

Library of Congress Cataloging-in-Publication Data

Carlson, John G.
    Psychology of emotion / John G. Carlson, Elaine Hatfield.
      p. cm.
    Includes bibliographical references and index.
    ISBN 0-03-055419-5
    1. Emotions. I. Hatfield, Elaine. II. Title.
BF511.C37 1991
152.4—dc20   91-13622
                                             CIP

Copyright © 1992 by Holt, Rinehart and Winston, Inc.

All rights reserved. No part of this publication may be reproduced or transmitted in any form or by any means, electronic or mechanical, including photocopy, recording or any information storage and retrieval system, without permission in writing from the publisher.

Requests for permission to make copies of any part of the work should be mailed to: Permissions Department, Harcourt Brace Jovanovich, Publishers, 8th Floor, Orlando, Florida 32887.

Special acknowledgments of copyright ownership and of permission to reproduce works included in this volume follow the index and constitute an extension of this page.

Address editorial correspondence to: 301 Commerce Street, Suite 3700, Fort Worth, TX 76102

Address orders to: 6277 Sea Harbor Drive, Orlando, FL 32887
                1-800-782-4479, or 1-800-433-0001 (in Florida)

Printed in the United States of America

2 3 4 016 9 8 7 6 5 4 3 2

This book is for the wellsprings of our *emotion:*

Betty and the children: Jared, Sarah, and Wende (JGC)

Dick and Kim (EH)

Contents in Brief

Preface   ix

1 Introduction and Overview   3

2 Traditional Approaches to Emotion   27

3 Motivational and Cognitive Theories of Emotion   63

4 Neurophysiological Theories of Emotion   101

5 Expressive Theories of Emotion   149

6 Facial Expression   181

7 Measures of Emotion   225

8 Sadness, Grief, and Depression   263

9 Happiness and Joy   309

10 Anger and Aggression   345

11 Passionate and Companionate Love   385

12 Fear and Anxiety   431

13 Emotions, Stress, and Physical Health   475

14 Dealing With Emotions   517

Preface

Humanity has always been intrigued by the emotions. Thousands of years of literature and art provide glowing evidence of artists' fascination with the passions. Scientific curiosity about emotion, however, began to emerge only recently. It was little more than 100 years ago that Charles Darwin first speculated about the origins of emotion. Exactly 100 years ago (as we write this), William James's *Principles of Psychology* ignited the interest of psychologists in the topic. And only within the past 15 to 20 years or so have modern-day psychologists begun to propose relatively comprehensive theories of emotion and conduct the research necessary to test their ideas. Courses on the psychology of emotion have begun to appear in college catalogues yet more recently. Why have psychologists become so captivated by this field of late?

One reason is that recent scientific advances have produced a surge of interest in the science of emotion. Advances in the study of the neurochemistry of brain function have contributed significantly to our understanding of central mechanisms of emotion. Recent technological advances in psychophysiology make it easier to measure emotional reactions throughout the body. Computers now make it possible to compare simultaneously a host of cognitive, physiological, and behavioral emotional reactions. Such advances lend scientific credibility to a topic once limited to anecdotes and common-sense accounts of human experience. Paradoxically, the current surge of interest in cognitive psychology, though seemingly at the other end of the spectrum from emotion, may also have contributed to recent interest in some aspects of this complex topic.

Perhaps an even more compelling reason behind the current popularity of the topic of emotion lies in the sweeping cultural changes that began in the United States in the 1960s. During that period of protest and social upheaval, some of America's youth vociferously criticized traditional values and models of government, experimented with drugs and altered states of consciousness, and styled themselves *flower-children* and *love-children*. At that time, a shift in society's self-awareness took place mirroring this shift in individual self-awareness. Carl Jung's *Modern Man in Search of His Soul* emphasized man's capacity for intuition, emotional expression, and sensitivity. And now, in the 1990s—as Jung might have predicted—many middle-aged former youths of the 1960s are increasingly interested in the "nondominant" aspects of their own personalities: their feelings, the non-rational, and the phenomenological aspects of emotion.

A book such as this is a natural consequence of this cultural context. Our subject is the contribution that modern psychology, with the help of other social and natural sciences, has made to our understanding of human emotion. This introductory book is our attempt to summarize, in a readable and precise way, a vast array of ideas and facts about the nature of emotion from the perspectives of human and animal neurophysiology, human behavior, and human experience, including cognitive processes and motivation. Through the use of some artistic and literary reference-points (which, we hope, add liveliness and a human aspect to the scientific presentation), we also attempt to remind the reader of the historical traditions of the study of emotion.

In many respects, the study of emotion appears to be in upheaval, with theories abounding and research sprawling from studies of cellular activity to surveys of social attitudes and behavior. We do *not* attempt in this book to add yet more theories of emotion to the literature. It is our view, rather, that what is needed at this time is more careful conceptual organization, description, and synthesis. From these efforts—by ourselves and others—we may all then progress to more comprehensive systems of thought and theory that will bring us to a deeper understanding of this difficult field.

This book is aimed at college undergraduates. Its topics, being many and varied, will be most easily handled by students who have completed more than a single course in general psychology. Completion of courses in learning theory, psychobiology, personality, social psychology, and abnormal psychology would be helpful, but are not necessary. The concepts here are explained thoroughly enough for a second-year undergraduate, but he or she may experience more difficulty in following the text than will an experienced major in psychology. This material is intended for presentation in a single-semester course.

Chapter 1 introduces the concept of emotion, definitions of it offered by others, and then our own working definition—namely, that emotion is *a genetic and acquired motivational predisposition to respond experientially, physiologically, and behaviorally to certain internal and external variables.* This definition provides us with the organizational framework for the chapters that follow. Thus in chapter 2 we review the traditional experiential, physiological, and expressive (behavioral) perspectives on emotion. In this chapter, the student will learn of Freud's and the psychoanalytic theorists' fundamental interest in human emotion, of James's and Cannon's classic debate on the nature of emotion, and of the contrasting focus on emotional behaviors in the evolutionary and more recent behavioral traditions.

In chapters 3 through 5 we take a longer look at more current theories of emotion. In these chapters we have selected the work of a relatively few eminent theorists to introduce the field through example. In chapter 3, we focus on motivational and cognitive theories, especially Carl Gustav Jung's analytic theory and the cognitive views of emotion of present-day theorists, including Richard Lazarus, Robert Zajonc, Gordon Bower, and Stanley Schachter. We turn in chapter 4 to two neurophysiological approaches to emotion—those of Joseph LeDoux and James Henry—in order to broadly survey the role of central and peripheral neural processes in emotion. In chapter 5, we discuss Robert Plutchik's evolutionary theory and J.R. Millenson's behavioral theory to illustrate the focus of some theorists on the role of actions, gestures, and facial expressions in emotion.

Because of the considerable interest current among psychologists in the role of the human face in emotional experience and expression, we devote an entire chapter (6) to this topic. Here left- and right-brain activity is explored, as well as the emerging field of social psychophysiology. Chapter 7 focuses on the measurement of emotion. In it we describe the methods researchers have devised to assess some common antecedents of emotion and measure the experiences, psychophysiological reactions, and behavioral expressions of emotion.

Thus, the first half of the text deals with the basics of emotion: its issues, theories, methods, and the most clearly established findings in the field. In the chapters remaining, these theories and techniques are seen in their application to some critical emotions: sadness, happiness, anger, love, fear, and serenity. The topical organization of these chapters reflects the oppositional view of emotions present in so many of the theories reviewed earlier. We survey research and theoretical analyses that provide insight into sadness, grief, and depression in chapter 8; their opposites, joy and happiness, in chapter 9; anger and aggression in chapter 10; and their complements, passionate and companionate love, in chapter 11. Fear and anxiety, about which so much has been written in the field of psychology, are reviewed in chapter 12. Their clinical opposites, calm and relaxation, are part of a larger discussion in chapter 13 of the impact of emotion in stress, disease, and pain.

The purpose of these later chapters is not to systematically review all that psychologists have had to say about every emotion, but to offer instead a sampler of the ways in which various theorists would have us look at specific emotions—for example, psychoanalytic and behavioral theorists on depression, experimental social psychologists on love and anger, health psychologists on anxiety and stress, and so forth. This allows for a review of the role of "mini-theories" in actual application to the field of emotion.

In the final chapter (14), we return to an issue, touched upon in chapter

1, that emerges as a significant problem for many students in their daily lives: dealing with emotion. Both clinical and everyday methods for controlling the cognitive, physiological, and behavioral manifestations of emotion are examined; also considered is the argument that—at least part of the time—some emotions are best left to their natural development and expression rather than control.

This book was designed to fill a significant need for texts in the study of emotion for undergraduate courses, as well as for supplemental reading in courses in which the emotions are an important, though secondary, focus— for example, in the study of motivation, personality, health psychology, behavioral medicine, abnormal psychology, and social psychology, among others. An introductory and comprehensive survey of emotion should open up a range of opportunities for presenting a rich and fascinating study of the topic. In contrast with other texts, which strive to develop a particular conceptual framework and narrowly define the field, this book surveys different perspectives, integrates them, and suggests new directions for understanding and research. In some respects, *Psychology of Emotion* thus poses many more questions for students than it attempts to answer. Yet the outcome may well be the further inspiration of scientific study—in our view, the best of all possible goals for an enterprise such as this.

J.G.C.
E.H.
June, 1991

Neuroendocrine Bases of Negative Emotions: Anger, Fear,
    and Depression   128
Neuroendocrine Bases of Positive Emotions: Serenity and Elation   138
Neurophysiological Patterns of Emotional Response
    and Archetypes   141

Summing Up   145

5   **Expressive Theories of Emotion**   149

Introduction   150

Plutchik's Psychoevolutionary Synthesis   151

Theoretical Postulates   151
The Structure of Emotions   153
Diagnostic Concepts of Emotion   158

Millenson's Behavioral Analysis   161

Three Ways of Thinking About Emotions   161
A Model of Emotion   165
Implications of the Model   171

Summing Up   177

6   **Facial Expression**   181

Introduction   182

The Universal and Cultural Bases of Facial Expression   182

Cultural Masks   184
Telling Lies   188

Left Brain/Right Brain   192

The Perception of Emotion   193
The Expression of Emotion   194
Studies With Neurological Patients   195

Facial Expression and Emotional Experience   197

Evidence on the Impact of Facial Feedback on Emotion   201
Facial Expression and ANS Activity   206

The Social Psychophysiology of Facial Expression   212

Social Psychophysiological Measurement   213
Theoretical Conclusions   219

Summing Up   221

7   **Measures of Emotion**   225

Introduction   226

Subjective (Self-Report) Measures of Emotion   227

Psychometric Principles   228
Popular Self-Report Measures of Emotion   233

Psychophysiological Measures of Emotion   238

The Basics of Psychophysiological Measurement   239
Studies Utilizing Psychophysiological Measurement   247

Behavioral Measures of Emotion   249

Measuring Emotional Behaviors in Animals   250
Measuring Emotional Behaviors in Humans   255

In Conclusion   259

Summing Up   260

8   Sadness, Grief, and Depression   263

Introduction   264

Emotional Development of Sadness and Other Emotions   264

Assessing Sadness   265
The Sequence of Emotional Development   268
Emotional Milestones   270
Individual Differences in Emotionality   272
The Caretakers' Contribution   274

Sadness and Grief in Adulthood   277

Sadness   277
Grief   280

Depression   287

Theories of Depression   289
The Treatment of Depression   303

Summing Up   306

9   Happiness and Joy   309

Introduction and Definitions   310

Happiness   312

The Nature of Happiness   312
The Experience of Happiness   313
How Happy Are Most People?   314
The Raw Materials of Happiness   317
The Relative Nature of Happiness: Is That All There Is?   322

Arranging for a Happy and Just Life   327

The Happy Life   327
Justice   328

Joy   329

The Experience of Joy and Ecstasy   329
The Anatomy of Joy   331
The Chemistry of Joy   332
Richard Solomon's Opponent Process Theory   336
Going With the Flow   339

Summing Up   341

10   Anger and Aggression   345

Introduction   346

The Roots of Anger   346

Who Incites Anger?   348
What Causes Anger?   349

Tha Anatomy of Anger   350

The Look of Anger   350
The Neuroanatomy and Neurophysiology of Anger   351
The Visceral Determinants of Anger   354
Expressions of Anger   354

The "Hard-Wiring" of Aggression   356

The Sociobiological Perspective   356
The Psychoanalytic Approach   358
The Great Catharsis Debate   359
The Frustration-Aggression Model   364
Against Whom Will Aggression Be Directed?   365
What Form Will Aggression Take?   367
The Frustration-Aggression Theory Revisited   369

The "Programming": Social Learning Theory   370

Observational Learning   370
Reinforcement Theory   377

Summing Up   381

11   Passionate and Companionate Love   385

Introduction   386

What Is Love?   387

Passionate Love   387

How Do I Love Thee?—Let Me Count the Ways   388
The Genesis of Love   390
Attachment and Adult Love   393
The Nature of Passionate Love   394

Emotional Interlinkages   400
Behavioral Evidence That Both Pleasure and Pain May
      Fuel Emotion   402
Who Knows How to Make Love Stay?   406

Companionate Love   408

Measures and Models   408
Stages of Relationships: Initiation and Maintenance   411
Stages of Relationships: Decline and Jealousy   421
Stages of Relationships: The End of the Affair   425

Summing Up   427

12   **Fear and Anxiety**   431

Introduction   432

Definitions   432

Anxiety Disorders   436

Whatever Happened to Good Old Neuroses?   436
Phobic Disorder   437
Generalized Anxiety Disorder   439
Panic Disorder   439
Obsessive-Compulsive Disorder   440
Post-Traumatic Stress Disorder (PTSD)   441
Some Words of Reassurance   443

Approaches to Fear and Anxiety   444

Psychodynamic Approaches to Fear and Anxiety   444
Physiological Approaches to Fear and Anxiety   447
Behavioral Approaches to Fear and Anxiety   453
Cognitive-Learning Approaches to Fear and Anxiety   457

Measuring Anxiety and Fear   459

Self-Report Measures   459
Psychophysiological Measures   460
Behavioral Measures   462

Other Perspectives on Fear   464

Cross-Cultural Aspects of Fear   464
Fear of Success   466
Controlling Fear   467

Summing Up   471

13   **Emotions, Stress, and Physical Health**   475

Introduction   476

Emotional Stress   477

Early Contributions to the Study of Stress   477
Sources of Stress   479

Emotional Responses to Stress   485

Physiological Responses   486
Behavioral Responses   488
Cognitive Responses to Stress   490

The Diseases of Emotional Stress   491

Ulcers   492
Cardiovascular Disease   493
Disease and Immunity   497

Coping with Emotional Stress   498

What It Means "To Cope"   498
Coping Resources   500

Pain and Pain Management   504

How Is Pain Transmitted to the Brain?   505
Brain Mechanisms for Pain   508
Pain and Cognition   510
Methods of Pain Control   510

Summing Up   514

14 Dealing With Emotions   517

Introduction: Sense or Sensibility?   518

Some Recollections and a Model for Emotional Control   519

The Cognitive Control of Emotion   522

Cognitive Therapies   522
Some Risks of Cognitive Therapies   528

The Physiological Control of Emotion   528

Biofeedback   529
Psychopharmacological "Therapies"   532

The Behavioral Control of Emotion   542

Behavioral Therapies for Emotional Control   543
Relaxation and Meditation   553
Exercise   554

Should You Try to Control Your Emotions?   556

Reasons for Sense *and* Sensibility   557

Emotions May "Transform" Us   560
Conclusion   562

Summing Up   563

References   565

Index   613

PSYCHOLOGY OF
EMOTION

*C*onceive yourself, if possible, suddenly stripped of all the emotion with which your world now inspires you. . . . It will be almost impossible for you to realize such a condition of negativity and deadness. No one portion of the universe would then have importance beyond another; the whole collection of its things and series of its events would be without significance, character, expression, or perspective. Whatever of value, interest, or meaning our respective worlds may appear endowed with are thus pure gifts of the spectator's mind. The passion of love is the most familiar and extreme example of this fact. If it comes, it comes; if it does not come, no process of reasoning can force it. Yet it transforms the value of the creature loved as utterly as the sunrise transforms Mont Blanc from a corpse-like gray to a rosy enchantment; and it sets the whole world to a new tune for the lover and gives a new issue to his life. So with fear, with indignation, jealousy, ambition, worship. If they are there, life changes.

WILLIAM JAMES

1

Introduction and Overview

Introduction

Defining Emotion
A Working Definition of Emotion
Defining Our Terms

Why Study Emotion?
Emotions Are a Part of All of Us
All Relationships Are "Emotional"
Emotional Conflicts Are Inevitable
People Want to Be Able to Manage Their Emotions

Notes on the State of Theory and Research on Emotion
But Where's the Theory?
Can Science Shed Light on the Emotions?

Issues in Emotion
How Many Emotions Are There? How Are They Organized?
How Long Do Emotions Last?
Can We Classify Emotions as Good or Bad? Functional or Nonfunctional?
How Important Is Emotion?
What Is the Role of Learning in Emotion?
Are Emotions Controllable? Should They Be Controlled?
What Else Is There to Know About Emotions?

Overview

Summing Up

FIGURE 1.1 *Dance* (first version). Henri Matisse. 1909, early. Oil on canvas, 8' 6½" x 12' 9½". Collection, The Museum of Modern Art, New York. Gift of Nelson A. Rockefeller in honor of Alfred H. Barr, Jr.

Introduction

What would you like to know about emotions? If you offer most people the chance to ask anything they would like, a flood of questions comes tumbling out. "What is an emotion?" "How do you know what you feel?" "Can people control their most passionate feelings?" "Can we really keep jealousy, hate, and fear in check?" "Do we want to?" In this text, we will try to answer these and a host of other questions.

To us, this is a perfect time to be studying what psychologists know about emotion. There are certain eras when we, as scientists, wish we had been alive, times when a series of new discoveries came together and changed the way people saw the world: The advent of the Industrial Revolution was one such time. The publication of Charles Darwin's *The Origin of Species* (1859) was another. For us, today is just such a time, as new discoveries about the brain change our conceptions of who we are as humans. In our adolescence, it never occurred to us that neuroscientists would discover how neurotransmitters are able to send messages to all parts of the brain; that psychophysiologists would discover how to detect emotions in the tiniest movements of the facial muscles or in drops of blood or urine. In this text, we will bring together the knowledge that many disciplines have painstakingly assembled about the psychology of emotions. Because we are presenting so many perspectives, this review will paint a rich, multilayered picture of emotions. Occasionally, some facts will not quite fit together. This text is intended to be a first word on emotion, not the last. In *Psychology of Emotion,* we catch the field of emotion as it is poised at the brink of a leap forward in the moments before a grand, unifying paradigm is proposed, before diverse perspectives are integrated. The most eminent scientists have begun to apply the most sophisticated methodologies to un-raveling the mysteries of emotion, after decades of neglect. Today's students may, in their academic and research careers to come, have a great deal to do with bringing about this integration.

In this chapter, we begin by defining emotion and explaining why we should be interested in the field of emotion. Then we proceed to discuss some of the issues that currently challenge researchers: How many emotions are there? How long do they last? Are emotions controllable? Should they be controlled? We review these and a potpourri of other questions that have fascinated researchers. Finally, we end this chapter by previewing what is to come in chapters 2–14.

Defining Emotion

A WORKING DEFINITION OF EMOTION

Some psychologists have concluded that it is still too early to craft a definitive definition of emotion. For example, George Mandler (1975b) contends, "An attempt to define emotion is obviously misplaced and doomed to failure" (p. 10). In spite of Mandler's pessimism, psychologists have crafted a number of useful working definitions of emotion (see Box 1.1).

In general, psychologists tend to define emotion in a way that emphasizes those aspects of emotions that interest them. In this respect, they are like the blind men who were asked to place their hands on an elephant and report what "an elephant" is like. Depending on which part they happened to touch, they insisted that an elephant was "really" shaped like a Greek column, a wall, or a snake. Thus, cognitive theorists generally focus on thoughts and evaluations when defining emotion, while physiologists focus on physiological reactions, behaviorists on emotional behavior, and so on. In this text, however, we must select a working definition of emotion that is broad enough to allow us to explore the work of all the psychologists who have studied the psychology of emotion. Thus, we define **emotion** as a genetic and acquired motivational predisposition to respond experientially, physiologically, and behaviorally to certain internal and external variables.

In the next section, we will explain what we mean by all these terms. This definition is designed to be balanced—to appropriately reflect the triumvirate of cognitive, physiological, and behavioral factors that comprise human experience. It is designed to appeal to psychologists who take a variety of approaches to understanding emotions—researchers who are experts in social psychology, personality, physiology, learning, or clinical psychology—and to scientists whose insights about the psychology of emotion come from other fields, such as physiology, neurology, biochemistry, psychiatry, sociology, and anthropology, as well as from literature, theater, art, architecture, or history.

BOX 1.1

Defining Emotion

Emotion is "a complex feeling-state involving conscious experience and internal and overt physical responses that tend to facilitate or inhibit motivated behavior." (Dworetsky, 1985, p. 301)

Emotion is defined in terms of subjective experiences or feelings, goal-directed behavior (attack, flight), expressive behavior (smiling, snarling), and physiological arousal (heart rate increases, sweating, defecation). (Hothersall, 1985, p. 232)

Emotions are organized, meaningful, generally adaptive action systems. . . . Emotions are complex functional wholes including appraisals or appreci-ations, patterned physiological processes, action tendencies, subjective feelings, expressions, and instrumental behaviors. . . . None of these features is necessary for a particular instance of emotion. (Fischer, Shaver, Carnochan, 1990)

An emotion is an inferred complex sequence of reactions to a stimulus and includes cognitive evaluations, subjective changes, autonomic and neural arousal, impulses to action, and behavior designed to have an effect upon the stimulus that initiated the complex sequence. (Plutchik, 1984, p. 217)

DEFINING OUR TERMS

We have defined emotion as "a genetic and acquired motivational predisposition to respond experientially, physiologically, and behaviorally to certain internal and external variables." Some of the terms in this working definition demand explanation. First, we assume that emotions are "genetic and acquired" predispositions. Emotions have their origins in people's genes, anatomy, physiology, and biochemistry. Emotions also become refined and develop through learning and life experiences. All theories of emotion acknowledge these two sources of human emotion.

Moreover, emotions are "motivational predispositions." What do we mean by motivation? Many psychologists, such as Arthur Reber (1985), define motivation this way: "an intervening process or an internal state of an organism that impels or drives it to action" (p. 454). Emotions, then, possess motivational energy and direction. (We discuss some of the distinctions between emotion and motivation in chapter 2.)

Emotions are defined as "predispositions" to respond, rather than as actual responses, for a reason. Often, people are tempted to react emotionally, but they automatically or deliberately suppress, transform, or deny their feelings. For example, a terrified deer and a terrified child may "freeze"; but this does not mean that the deer or the child are any the less emotional. Moreover, they are *potentially* likely to do a variety of things "in terror" besides freezing. An emotional state predisposes us to patterns of subjective, behavioral, and physiological responses, no one of which will adequately define the state.

The definition also makes explicit our tripartite view of emotion. Emotion is defined as "a predisposition to respond *experientially, physiologically* and *behaviorally.*" We assume that emotions include cognitive, physiological, and behavioral elements. One must understand all three aspects of emotion if one is to understand emotion. For example, if a therapist were trying to figure out how Pauline, a mother, feels about her rebellious daughter Sara, he might try to piece together several bits of emotional data. The more kinds of information he can collect, the better his detective work will be. For example, he might ask Pauline, "How do you feel about Sara?"

"She is a wonderful daughter; she has a lot of good qualities."

"What are her best qualities?"

"Well, it would be a lot easier on everyone if she were easier to get along with, and her room is such a mess." (So much for her "best qualities.")

Words, then (i.e., "She is a wonderful daughter") tell the therapist something, but not everything. He can detect more by observing mother and daughter as they talk. What do their faces portray? Are their expressions hard and distant or warm and receptive? Do they appear to be physiologically aroused? Some indicators of internal activity are hidden from view—mother and daughter would have to note aloud if their hearts were pounding and their stomachs churning. (Of course, if he had the right instruments, the therapist could measure some of these physiological responses.) But the therapist can spot some physiological symptoms of emotion—he can see if their faces redden, if their hands tremble, or if they perspire. Finally, he can observe behavioral sequences. When the father says he thinks they can afford to buy Sara a car, does Pauline touch his arm and smile, or does she stiffly walk out of the room, slamming the door?

If emotional indicators are inconsistent, and often they are, some high-level detective work is required. How do we make sense of it if Sara asks Pauline whether she is angry, and Pauline snarls, "What makes you think I'm angry? I'm not angry, I'm just sick and tired of never getting any help around the house, that's all." How do we interpret it if Pauline gives Sara lavish presents but pushes her away anytime she wants to talk; or if Pauline tells Sara to go away any time she does try to help around the house? Most people are fairly good at threading out the pattern from a crazy quilt of emotional cues. If everything points in the same direction, of course, detective work is easy. If not, we may simply look for the most common emotional signs. For this reason, we would assume that no single clue is necessary or sufficient in identifying an emotion; the more clues one possesses, the better.

Finally, emotion is defined as "a predisposition to respond to *certain internal and external variables*." Our working definition acknowledges that if researchers are to understand emotion, they must identify the kinds of internal and external stimuli that precipitate emotion. They must look at emotion in context. For example, in part, emotional experience depends on people's *internal* state: people whose MAOI (monoamine oxidase inhibitor, a neurotransmitter) levels are too high may become manic; those whose MAOI levels are too low may become depressed. *External* factors, too, play a crucial role. The person who is insulted, yelled at, or knocked around is more likely to become angry than someone who is treated with respect.

This working definition serves only as the the bare bones of a definition. It provides the backbone and organizational structure of this text and will be fleshed out by the theory and research to come.

Why Study Emotion?

Why are so many of us interested in the topic of emotion? Before we begin our review of this fascinating field, let us take a few minutes to think about the reasons we should study this topic.

EMOTIONS ARE A PART OF ALL OF US

Many students take courses in psychology because they hope to come to a better understanding of themselves. The only way we can understand ourselves is to understand why we think, feel, and behave as we do. The study of emotion is an indispensable pathway to self-knowledge.

Curiously enough, psychologists began to take an active scientific interest in the topic of emotion only recently. But humankind has felt a need to understand emotions for centuries—as evidenced in the myriad of paintings, songs, stories, poems, plays, legends, histories, manuscripts, and scholarly treatises concerned with human feeling. We are like our predecessors. Emotions are a part of our lives. Emotions bring us pain and euphoria, richness and trouble, hope and despair. To understand emotions is to understand ourselves and humankind.

ALL RELATIONSHIPS ARE "EMOTIONAL"

Whenever we encounter others—in intimate relationships, at school, in day-to-day business—we transmit and receive a crowd of emotional messages. Generally, we simply have vague "feelings" about the give-and-take of our encounters. Sometimes we have more powerful emotional reactions. Psychologists such as Gregory Bateson (1972) point out that all communications have two components. First is the direct message (Q: "Why don't you come to see me more often?" A: "I've been busy, studying.") Second, each message is accompanied by an emotional "meta-message"—a sort of nonverbal, play-by-play commentary on the speaker's and receiver's relationship. (In this example, "Q" might look vaguely irritated, with brow furrowed and lips pursed. "A" might look slightly sheepish.) In glance, tone, and gesture, people continually signal how they feel about each other and the situation in which they find themselves. Both direct messages and emotional meta-messages are processed simultaneously.

Family therapists have been especially interested in situations in which the two channels (the direct message and the meta-message) conflict and a person is put in a "double-bind." For example, Bateson (1972) cites the following case:

> A young man who had fairly well recovered from an acute schizophrenic episode was visited in the hospital by his mother. He was glad to see her and impulsively put his arm around her shoulders, whereupon she stiffened. He withdrew his arm and she asked, "Don't you love me any more?" He then blushed, and she said, "Dear, you must not be so easily embarrassed and afraid of your feelings." The patient was able to stay with her only a few minutes more and following her departure he assaulted an aide and was put in the tubs [a calming bath]. (p. 217)

The son, enmeshed in a complicated family ballet, was baffled by his conflicting feelings. He could only feel ill at ease and withdraw—and later flail around in confusion. Bateson, as his therapist, could do far better. Bateson had learned to use his thoughts, his intuition, and his own feelings as guides in decoding impossibly messy and complex encounters. He confronted mother and son. He taught them how to talk about the complex feelings that they had considered too dangerous to reveal: how frightened they were of hurting each other's feelings; the fact that sometimes they didn't really like each other;

the fact that sometimes they wanted to be left alone. They found that relationships simply go better when one has a knowledge of emotions and emotional communication.

We all believe, quite correctly, that men and women do better at both love and work if they are emotionally sensitive and emotionally skilled. Thus, a knowledge of emotions and emotional communication is indispensable.

Life is trouble.

KAZANTZAKIS

EMOTIONAL CONFLICTS ARE INEVITABLE

Sometimes the very people we love the most are impossible to deal with. For example, children are a source of great fun, but they are a source of enormous frustration, too. The same child who, at two years of age boosts our self-esteem by intoning, "My dad and I wear sweaters," with obvious pride, is bound to metamorphose into the painfully embarrassed 15-year-old who humiliates us by asking if we can't scrunch down in the seat when we drive him to school so his friends won't see us. "Please, Dad," he says, "Don't say anything. Just nod."

When close encounters are good, they are a source of fun, security, excitement, and energy. But when they are not, they are distracting (we cannot get our mind off our problems), and they burn up energy. People often try to shut off such feelings by taking an aspirin, a tranquilizer, or a drink. It is not surprising, then, that some people equate close relationships and the emotions they engender with trouble. They long to lead a "normal" life, a life of quiet reason, untrammeled by emotion. Most people enjoy love affairs, friendships, and family affairs and their surprises, but now and then, when things get too difficult, even they wish they knew how to control or manage their emotions.

PEOPLE WANT TO BE ABLE TO MANAGE THEIR EMOTIONS

Each semester, a professor begins a course on the psychology of emotion by asking students why they are taking the class. Each semester, the students come up with the same answer: About a third of the students feel they have very little control over their emotions. Most students hope to learn how to deal with their feelings.

This is no trivial concern. In a later chapter, we will see that Americans spend an enormous amount of time and money in the pursuit of emotional control. People pray, exercise, see therapists, study Zen, drink, and take antidepressants and tranquilizers, all in an effort to calm their emotions.

Clearly, emotional control is appropriate and necessary in some instances.

If someone giggles at a funeral or begins to cry in the middle of a boisterous party, we are likely to be surprised or irritated. Emotional displays are supposed to be appropriate in intensity, quality, and frequency. No wonder, then, that some people want to learn how to clamp a tight lid on their feelings. It is the socially appropriate thing to do. However, if people are to do well in their personal and professional relationships, they have to do far more than simply develop an off-switch for their feelings. Today, men and women expect intimates and friends to be able to talk about complex intellectual and emotional issues. They expect them to know what they feel and to explain themselves as well as be able to keep their feelings in check when necessary.

Couples often come to therapy with the complaint that "they can't communicate." Generally, they can't. Often the woman is fairly comfortable with the language of emotion. She enjoys unraveling the tangled threads of her feelings, and she is indignant that her partner is so reluctant to reveal his inner life to her. Such intimacy, she thinks, is the whole point of being together. The man sometimes has little idea of what he is feeling or has little practice in expressing his feelings. But, sometimes, when he does try to express his complicated reactions, he is brought up short when his partner begins to cry at the sharp cruelty of his words or explodes at his "unfairness." (She wanted to know what he felt, but she had no idea he felt *that* way!) Not surprisingly, the whole process of discussing feelings may make him extremely anxious. In therapy, people learn how to discuss their thoughts and feelings. When necessary, they can also learn how to carefully calibrate their emotional expressions—learning that they may choose to respond with tact and truth, to respond powerfully, or, when appropriate, to keep their emotions under tight control.

It seems obvious, then, that people would want to learn all there is to know about emotion and its expression and control. How much do psychologists know about that topic?

Notes on the State of Theory and Research on Emotion

After centuries of neglect, emotion has become a topic of interest for researchers from a variety of disciplines. The scientific revolution is so recent in human history, and science has mushroomed so quickly in the last few decades, that most of the researchers who have *ever* lived are living right now. Depending on your point of view, this is either an electrifying state of affairs or a profoundly discouraging one.

For us, this explosion of scientific insight is immensely stimulating. Almost day by day, scientists come up with answers to questions that philosophers have pondered for generations. It is an especially exciting time to be studying the nature of emotions. In most disciplines, researchers have been tilling their scientific gardens for so long that the ground is well worked over. A new researcher assumes that it will take most of a career merely to grasp what others have done. Only if she is very lucky will she be able to make a contribution to the field. Many of you may well conduct, or participate in, research on emotions. Should you decide to study emotions yourself, you will have the chance to make a real contribution. Here, you will be stepping into wilder territory. You may be able to mark off new territories and to clear wide areas of tangled underbrush in your lifetimes.

Sometimes, however, students find the "new frontier" aura of emotions research a bit unsettling. They bemoan the lack of a general theory; they see incompleteness, disarray, confusion, and arguments built on shifting sands and fragmentary research. Let us confront some of these problems.

BUT WHERE'S THE THEORY?

In any discipline, researchers long for a general theory, a theory that consists of some basic definitions and a few general principles; a grand theory that organizes a number of "minitheories." Ideally, each minitheory would, in turn, provide a fine-grained understanding of some portion of the phenomena under discussion. Unfortunately, science is rarely so orderly. Or, when it is, it is usually wrong.

It probably comes as no surprise, then, to learn that no grand theory of emotion exists. However, a number of elegant minitheories have been proposed: evolutionary theories, motivational theories, cognitive theories, neurochemical theories, and social theories. Each minitheory provides some fascinating insights into the nature of emotion. In this text, we try to provide some general organization for these minimodels. Perhaps those of you who plan to be psychologists will do even better in the next decade.

CAN SCIENCE SHED LIGHT ON THE EMOTIONS?

Senator William Proxmire once issued a blistering attack on the National Science Foundation for funding psychologists to study emotions such as love. Such emotions, he contended, cannot and should not be studied. They are too elusive to even try to study. And they should not be studied: "I believe that 200 million other Americans want to leave some things in life a mystery, and right at the top of things we don't want to know is why a man falls in love with a woman and vice versa. Even if they could give us an answer, we wouldn't want to hear it" (*Capitol Times*, 1975). The noted *New York Times* columnist James Reston (1975) fired back: "You have to assume he was kidding."

If people are unfamiliar with psychological research, it is easy to wonder how scientists go about studying emotions. How can they produce intense emotion in laboratory settings? Imagine sitting down to take a final examination in the psychology of emotion and confronting question 1: "Devise a laboratory experiment to produce passionate love. You have 30 minutes." You would probably appeal.

How do scientists get subjects to tell them about their innermost private feelings? Wouldn't subjects lie? Or at least have a hard time describing their inner lives? Subjects in experiments are simply not practiced in standing back, observing their feelings, and reporting them. Worse yet, wouldn't the very process of observing emotions change them? For example, an angry person who is assigned to push buttons labeled like the following may well calm down a bit in the process of calculating a response:

1. I am enraged.
2. I am quite angry.
3. I am slightly angry.
4. I am totally calm.

Finally, critics raise ethical problems: How can you study grief? What are you going to do—randomly assign 50 families (those in the experimental group) to lose someone they love and another 50 families (those in the control group) to go on as before? Is it right to cause pain in the name of science? To invade people's privacy?

Researchers who have had extensive research experience, however, are not put off by such worries. They have confidence that where there's a will, there's a way. Any time researchers push into new territories, at first it looks as if they are facing unique and insurmountable problems. In time, however, what once seemed impossible becomes routine. In this text, you will see how researchers from a variety of disciplines have investigated emotions. Their paradigms should give you some sense of the variety of ways that emotions can be explored. In fact, emotion research is currently undergoing a renaissance. Some intriguing questions that, until recently, seemed impossible to test can now be explored because of new discoveries in the neurosciences, social psychology, and social-psychophysiology.

Issues in Emotion

Social commentators have been asking questions about the nature of emotion for more than 150 years. Nonetheless, we still have no definitive answers to many critically important questions about emotion. Let us review some of the most common issues; they will help to focus the discussion to come.

HOW MANY EMOTIONS ARE THERE? HOW ARE THEY ORGANIZED?

In antiquity, Chinese doctors believed people experienced four basic emotions—anger, happiness, sorrow, and fear. These were thought to arise from activities of the liver, heart, lungs, and kidneys (Critchley, 1969). Today, researchers still disagree as to the number of basic emotions. For example, John B. Watson (1924) thought there were three—fear, rage, and love. Paul Ekman (1980) contends there are six—happiness, disgust, surprise, sadness, anger, and fear. Robert Plutchik (1980a), as we will see, thinks there are eight. Fischer, Shaver, and Carnochan (1990) propose a hierarchy of emotions, based on the way Americans use emotion terms. They contend that there are five basic emotions—two positive emotions (love and joy) and three negative ones (anger, sadness, and fear). However, because emotional experiences are also social constructions, there are actually an unlimited number of possible emotions.

Researchers also answer the question in very different ways: "How can emotions be classified?" Wilhelm Wundt's (1897) early attempts to classify emotions relied on people's reports of their experiential states. Wundt concluded that conscious emotional experiences could be classified along three dimensions: pleasantness–unpleasantness, calm–excitement, and relaxation–tension.

Behavioral psychologists have tried to classify emotional facial expressions, too. For example, the eminent experimentalist, Robert Woodworth (1938), reported that subjects' judgments of the emotions portrayed in photographs could generally be grouped into the following six categories: (a) fear, suffering; (b) anger, determination; (c) disgust; (d) contempt; (e) love, happiness, mirth; and (f) surprise—suggesting that perhaps these are "universal" human emotions. Later, Harold Schlosberg (1941) expanded on Woodworth's scheme by proposing that the emotions could best be understood on a circular scale, one axis representing Pleasantness–Unpleasantness and the other Attention–Rejection. Still later, Schlosberg (1954) proposed a third axis, Sleep–Tension, which yielded a cone-shaped model for the emotions. This early model is shown in Figure 1.2.

Wundt's original work and later, more statistically based research (such as that by Hastorf, Osgood, & Ono, 1966; Russell & Mehrabian, 1977; or Watson & Tellegan, 1985) convinced most researchers that emotions have at least two basic qualities: They have hedonic value (they can be classified as pleasurable or painful), and they arouse people and motivate them to act. These observations no doubt inspired Plutchik (1980a) and others to offer structural models of the emotions, which classify emotions along a number of dimensions. Plutchik proposes eight primary emotions—fear, anger, disgust, surprise, joy, sadness, acceptance, and expectancy. Plutchik suggests that the easiest way to understand his model is to imagine that the eight emotions are arranged on a circular color wheel; opposite emotions (love versus hate) are at opposite sides of the wheel (see Figure 1.3).

Currently, then, researchers differ somewhat in the number of basic emotions they think exist and the number of dimensions they use to classify them.

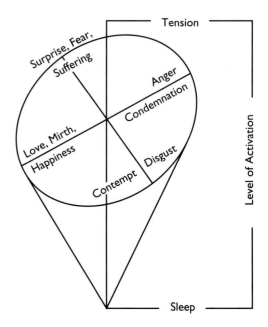

FIGURE 1.2 The Schlosberg model. On this solid figure, emotions are placed with respect to their maximum level of activation (sleep-tension); this is indicated on the ordinate. The top surface is sloped to show that anger and fear can reach higher levels of activation than can contempt. Emotions can also be placed on two other dimensions—pleasantness-unpleasantness and attention-rejection. Reprinted from H. Schlosberg, 1954. Three dimensions of emotions. *Psychological Review,* 61, p. 81.

*F*or violent fires soon burn out themselves; Small showers last long, but sudden storms are short.
SHAKESPEARE

HOW LONG DO EMOTIONS LAST?

Most emotional experiences, even quite intense ones, are short-lived. This is one way in which we distinguish emotional phenomena from, say, learning phenomena. When a person learns something, such as how to drive a car, the skill endures a lifetime. But when a person is emotional, we expect the state to change.

How long can emotions last? A few theorists contend that both positive and negative emotions *can* be intense and sustained. For example, Richard Lazarus and his colleagues (Lazarus, Kanner, & Folkman, 1980) argue that: "People experience intense hope, curiosity and joy, strong exhilaration, glee, passion, and ecstasy, and some of these states seem capable of being sustained quite as long as episodes of fear and anger" (p. 205). Probably most theorists assume that positive emotions are relatively weak and fleeting while negative emotions can be far more powerful and long-lasting.

Theorists also distinguish between emotional **states** (intense feelings of limited duration) and emotional **traits** (feelings that may be less intense but persist from one day to the next, and usually longer). For example, Charles Spielberger, Richard Gorsuch, and Robert Lushene (1970) distinguish two kinds of anxiety—state anxiety, precipitated by frightening events (such as examinations), and trait anxiety, which is a chronic, manifest, and persistent apprehensiveness.

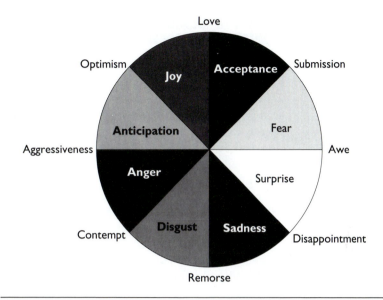

FIGURE 1.3 Plutchik's emotion wheel. This emotion "wheel" depicts the eight primary emotions and the dyads that result when adjacent primary emotions are mixed. For example, the primaries "fear" and "surprise," when combined, yield the dyad "awe," and joy mixed with acceptance leads to "love."

Normally, emotional states are transient. When people begin to experience frequent, intense emotions, especially when such emotions seem inexplicable, it is generally regarded as a tip-off that something is wrong; they have a psychological problem. They may be, say, depressed, manic, or both, or "neurotically" anxious.

Where do **moods** fit in this schema? Moods are more diffuse, mild, and longer lasting than emotional episodes. Interestingly enough, the terms psychologists use in describing people's personalities often are thinly veiled descriptions of mood. (We might say "She's good natured and energetic"; "he's a bit morose.") Sometimes, people use the term to complain about another's emotionality. ("Quit being so moody!")

Finally, psychologists and others may use the term **feelings** to refer to people's moment-by-moment evaluations of the events they encounter. (People move to a spot that "feels" cool; grab the warm sweater that "feels" right; or have a "feeling" that things are going to go well.)

Emotions, then, are generally intense but short-lived. Moods are less intense but longer-lasting. Feelings are barely noticeable, fleeting impressions.

*P*assion is a sort of fever in the mind, which ever leaves us weaker than it found us.

WILLIAM PENN (1644-1718)

CAN WE CLASSIFY EMOTIONS AS GOOD OR BAD? FUNCTIONAL OR NONFUNCTIONAL?

Emotions can be classified as "good" or "bad" in two vastly different ways. First, they can be classified as good or bad in a hedonic sense—that is, does it feel pleasant or unpleasant to experience that emotion? Most people can classify almost all emotions in this way. Most of us can agree that joy, passionate love, ecstasy, and exhilaration "feel good," while anger, grief, depression, and fear "feel bad." (Of course, exceptions abound. Sometimes, say, people enjoy working themselves up into a frenzy of self-righteous anger.)

In addition, emotions can be classified as good or bad in a functional sense—that is, is it beneficial or costly to possess such feelings? Here, classifying emotions becomes far more difficult.

Some theorists tend to think of *all* emotion as bad, as destructive remnants of a prehistoric past. They acknowledge that emotions may have had an important function once, somewhere in the evolutionary past, but now, like an appendix, they are just "appendages" with no apparent function. Except that, like a ruptured appendix, emotions might at times be painful or even dangerous. The problem, as such theorists see it, is that the body and its processes are slow to evolve, while the environment can change rapidly. Thus, the emotions that once had a clear survival function often become dysfunctional in our own "rational," technological society.

Other theorists take issue with that argument. They contend that things are not so different today as they might seem. They think of emotions as eminently functional, a source of reason, understanding, passion, and humanity. Robert Plutchik (1980a), for example, suggests that each of the primary emotions has a general function; each contributes to an individual's well-being. (We discuss Plutchik's theory in chapter 3.) Silvan Tomkins (1984a) takes an even stronger position. He argues that emotion (affect) is the "primary innate biological motivating mechanism." Its dictates are more powerful than pleasure, deprivation of fundamental needs, or even physical pain! Without emotion, nothing else matters. With it, everything else can matter. Its promptings are both urgent and general. "It lends its power to memory, to perception, to thought, and to action" (pp. 146–147).

Some psychologists have pointed out that the same emotions may be good or bad, functional or nonfunctional, for the individual at different times. They would classify fear as a negative emotion when it prevents a businessperson from boarding an airplane but as a positive emotion when it motivates a student to study for exams. Love is a positive emotion if it is shared; it becomes a dark, painful emotion when one's mate dies.

Carroll Izard (1977) argues that it is useless to try to classify either general or specific emotions as functional or nonfunctional. Instead, we must assess the value of various emotions in terms of whether they help or hinder us in securing the things that we value. Do they enrich our lives, our society, our own and other species, and the environment; or do they cause problems? The answers to those questions determine whether emotions should be classified as good or bad.

Today, then, theorists are divided as to how functional emotions are. In the future, theorists will have to develop models to answer such questions as: When are emotions functional, when not? Are some emotions more functional than others?

The next decade or so belongs to affect.
SILVAN TOMKINS

HOW IMPORTANT IS EMOTION?

Scientists disagree as to how important emotion is in people's lives. Western thought has seesawed from glorifying rational man to exalting the man of passion. For example, the eighteenth century claimed to be the "Age of Reason." It was the time of the Enlightenment, of Voltaire, John Locke, and Thomas Jefferson. Reason was enshrined and emotion disdained. Inevitably, this obsession with rationality led to a backlash. In the nineteenth century the passions were glorified. The Romantic era is associated with the emotional outpourings of poets such as Keats and Byron and the impassioned landscapes of Turner. It was a period alive with the turbulent sounds of Beethoven, the expressiveness of Chopin and Schumann, and the tempestuousness of Tchaikovsky. In the late nineteenth century, the seesaw tipped again. Science and technology became the new messiahs. Western cultures became supremely confident that science, using the twin tools of reason and technology, could come to understand and control virtually everything—both the rational and the irrational.

Psychology, too, has been buffeted by a dialectic between sense and sensibility. In the first half of this century, psychologists emphasized reason, thinking, problem solving, and behavior. They ignored the nonrational, emotive, and impulsive. Some even argued that the concept of emotion was not necessary for understanding human behavior; the notion of arousal would substitute nicely (Duffy, 1962). Others held that no inferred, hypothetical psychological events, including feelings, should serve as causes in theories of behavior (Skinner, 1953).

Now, we see the products of opposing views. Theorists have begun to elevate the concept of emotion to a prominent position. Richard Lazarus (1984), for example, argues that the "higher" mental processes of thought or reason are not superior to emotions. Emotions are, Lazarus insists, "a fusion of highly developed forms of cognitive appraisal with action impulse and bodily changes" (p. 213). Emotions are important to our health and survival. Positively toned emotions such as hope, curiosity, joy, strong exhilaration, glee, passion, and ecstasy serve important functions—they provide a breather, sustain us, and restore us. The negatively toned emotions such as fear and anger are, of course, critically important for survival.

Other theorists observe that emotions serve important roles in organizing and motivating behavior (Leeper, 1948; Izard, 1977). For example, Hobart Mowrer (1960) argues that:

> The emotions play a central role, indeed an indispensable role, in those changes in behavior or performance which are said to represent 'learning'.... The emotions are of quite extraordinary importance in the total economy of living organisms and do not at all deserve being put into opposition with 'intelligence.' The emotions are, it seems, themselves a high order of intelligence. (1960, pp. 307–308).

In this text we hope to steer a stable middle course, keeping humankind's rationality and emotional nature in proper perspective.

WHAT IS THE ROLE OF LEARNING IN EMOTION?

All theorists would agree that people's emotional lives are shaped by both their genetic background and their life experiences. What they argue about is how much of a contribution nature and nurture each make and to what extent people can manage their feelings.

Charles Darwin (1872) was one of the first researchers to argue that emotions have an unlearned or genetic basis. (We study Darwin's views in chapter 2.) He was most interested in the expressive aspects of emotions. He gathered evidence to show that all animals—including infants, adults, and wild animals—express their emotions in strikingly similar ways. Darwin also stressed the fact that emotional responses show commonality across cultures. Today, virtually all theorists would acknowledge that our genetic heritage shapes emotional expressiveness.

But there is little doubt that people also *learn* the "appropriate" way to express their feelings as well. Can you recall how you expressed your feelings when you were two or three years old? If not, perhaps your parents can fill you in. You may well have held your breath until you turned blue or lay on the floor kicking and screaming. Can you remember how you expressed your feelings when you were 10 or 11 years of age? Once a babysitter watched her nephews, who were 8 and 10, erupt in a bitter fight. One had shot the other in the head with a toy suction-cup dart gun. The victim retaliated with a slap. A fight broke out. The sitter remembers holding one child, his face contorted with hate, as he writhed around, lashing out like an eel. She understood, for the first time, Freud's contention that family relations are the most primitively passionate relations of all. She had never seen so much hatred bound up in small, warring people. Of course, today the boys are sedate college students, like you. People dramatically change the way they deal with emotions as they grow older.

It appears that although emotional experience has a definite genetic basis, cultural norms have a great deal to do with which emotions are emphasized, which are played down, and which subtle combinations of feelings seem to go together (Ekman & Friesen, 1967; Hatfield, Schmitz, Parpart, & Weaver, 1987; Harre, 1986). When children are blind from birth, at first they *express* emotion in the same ways as sighted children. As they get older, however, they become less expressive (Eibl-Eibesfeldt, 1973). Apparently, because they are unable to see their caretakers' facial expressions, unable to perceive their mother's smile of approval at their smiles, their father's frowns of displeasure at their frowns, these emotional signals tend to drop out of their behavioral repertoires.

Society also trains people in how they "ought" to display emotions. For example, in our culture, boys are taught at an early age not to cry; girls are encouraged to be emotionally expressive. Many cultures encourage both sexes to inhibit their emotional expressiveness. They encourage men and women to "be cool" by developing an inscrutable public face (or at least to wear sunglasses to mask the expressiveness of the eyes), by controlling gestures of the arms and hands, or by flattening their speech. People may also be taught to "mask" one emotion with another. The father who waits up late for his daughter to return from a date may erupt in rage on her return; beneath the anger may be intense anxiety or even jealousy.

The question as to what impact training people to express or suppress their emotions has on other aspects of emotion is a fascinating one. Do people actually feel less and show fewer physiological signs of emotion if they are trained to inhibit emotional behaviors? Are the most emotional people those who have been encouraged to act out? Can a culture, by emphasizing emotional expression in theater, literature, and the arts, and by valuing intimate emotional encounters, produce people who have an unusually rich, intense, and varied emotional life? Can it generate people who are more comfortable with feelings?

What impact do changes in cultural norms have? There is some evidence that Western culture is becoming ever more tolerant of emotional expression. How might that affect the average American's interior landscape? It also looks as if American values with respect to emotional expression are being adopted by some other more reserved cultures such as the Japanese (along with Western science and technology). Are the experiential and physiological aspects of their lives changing as well?

ARE EMOTIONS CONTROLLABLE? SHOULD THEY BE CONTROLLED?

As we mentioned earlier, students express considerable interest in learning how to control their emotions. This concern is not new. In the 1600s, René Descartes (1694) insisted that man differs from the rest of the animal world in possessing reason and the power to exert rational control over his "animal" nature. Descartes' dualistic view—that humans have both a mind and a body, and that the former is dominant over the latter—has had a great impact on the thinking of people in Western cultures down to the present day. Most of us come to early courses in psychology with unchallenged notions concerning the mind-body relationship. We are convinced that the mind, with its intellect, is superior to the primitive workings of the body, that the mind can generally voluntarily control bodily functions.

We tend to extend this dualistic conception to our commonsense understanding of emotions. We think that the more we can control our emotions, the better off we will be. If we had conscious control over our emotions, we would be able to feel love, joy, or delight and avoid fear, grief, or embarrassment as we chose. If we could manipulate our emotional displays, we could pretend to feel socially correct emotions. We could look sad when our cranky elderly aunt dies, even though (to our shame) we are rather relieved that she is gone. We could appear properly sad and repentant when our boss yells at us, knowing it will make him more likely to give us a second chance.

Of course, if we had full power over our feelings, we could also choose to express our real feelings with honesty and grace. It is not surprising, then, that most of us assume that the more methods we know for the control of our emotions, the happier we will be. In fact, we already do practice a considerable variety of methods in the attempt to alter our feelings. These include methods such as consuming a wide assortment of mood-altering drugs (tranquilizers and amphetamines, for example), seeking advice on our feelings (from friends, parents, therapists, and others), and engaging in a variety of emotion-altering behaviors (such as exercising, going to parties, or listening to music).

There seems little doubt that emotions are controllable. The issue does not appear to be whether emotional experiences, internal changes, and expressions can be modified in significant ways. More difficult questions have to do with just what methods are preferable, more effective, or more long-lasting. Still more serious is the issue of whether emotions should be modified at all. As we will see, in the view of one notable theorist, Carl Jung (whose work we discuss in chapter 3), overzealous attempts to gain rational control of ourselves may have costly long-term consequences.

WHAT ELSE IS THERE TO KNOW ABOUT EMOTIONS?

Researchers have asked many other fascinating questions about the nature of emotion. These include such questions as the following:

1. What causes emotions to occur?
2. How are the various components of emotion—the cognitive, physiological, and behavioral aspects—related?
3. Do people differ in how emotional they are?

4. Is there a universal "language" of emotion?
5. How do we "read" our own feelings? Those of other people?
6. Is emotion "contagious"? Do we get excited around happy people, depressed around sad ones? How does this process work?
7. Can we really hide our feelings, or can they always be detected by a sensitive observer?
8. Do lie detectors work?
9. Do other animals have emotions? How do we know?
10. Can we feel two emotions at the same time?

Of course, you might have a few questions of your own. For a list of still other questions psychologists have asked, see the work of Paul Ekman and Klaus Scherer (1984), Paul Ekman, Wallace Friesen, and Phoebe Ellsworth (1972), and Robert Plutchik (1980a).

Eminent thinkers and researchers have offered some surprising and illuminating answers to these questions; we will review their answers throughout this book.

Overview

In the pages that follow, our working definition of emotion will serve as an organizational framework.

In 1675, in a letter to Robert Hooke, Sir Isaac Newton observed: "If I have seen further (than you and Descartes) it is by standing upon the shoulders of Giants." Thus, we begin in chapter 2 by focusing on the past, by reviewing the ideas of psychology's giants. In this chapter, we review several traditional approaches to emotion, beginning with a review of Freudian theory, which emphasizes emotional experience—an approach that focuses on thinking, imaginal processes, and motives. Then, we outline the early physiological approaches of William James and Walter Cannon. Finally, we review the work of Charles Darwin, John B. Watson, and B. F. Skinner, who focus on emotional expressiveness, approaches that emphasize facial expression, gestures, and behavior.

Then, in chapters 3–5, we take a longer look at the present, sketching the work of some eminent modern-day theorists who, standing on these early foundations, are peering even further into the world of emotion. In chapter 3 we focus on Carl Gustav Jung's motivational theory and Richard Lazarus's cognitive theory of emotion. In chapter 4 we discuss Joseph LeDoux's and James Henry's physiological approaches to emotion. Then, in chapter 5, we discuss Robert Plutchik's evolutionary theory and J. R. Millenson's behavioral theory of emotion. This focused review is designed to give you a sense of how a few representative scientists think about the emotions, the way they pose questions, and how they go about conducting research to find answers.

This review will also give you a deeper understanding of the motivational, cognitive, physiological, and behavioral aspects of emotion.

In chapter 6, we discuss the importance of facial expression in decoding emotion. We will discover that people can gain some insight into the differences between what people feel and what they say they feel, by looking at the face.

In chapter 7 we examine the measurement of emotion. The chapter begins with a discussion of the scientific method. Then, we look behind the scenes to see how researchers use observation and experimental techniques to procure information. Finally, we describe the methods researchers have devised to: (a) assess some common antecedents of emotion, and (b) measure the experiences, bodily reactions, and behavioral expressions of emotion.

In a sense, the first half of this text is concerned with basic principles of emotion. In the second half of the text, we apply these theories to some representative emotions. Fischer, Shaver, and Carnochan (1990) concluded that the basic emotions were the positive emotions of love and joy and the negative emotions of anger, sadness, and fear. Thus, we review the "mini-theories" and state-of-the-art research which provide insights into such common emotions as sadness, grief, and depression (chapter 8) and their complements, joy and happiness (chapter 9), anger and aggression (chapter 10) and their complements, passionate and companionate love (chapter 11), and fear and anxiety (chapter 12). The complements of fear and anxiety, "calm and relaxation," are discussed in chapter 13. In all these chapters, we also touch on the psychopathological problems associated with these emotions. This text is too short to allow us to systematically review what psychologists from each of the major schools of psychology have had to say about each of the emotions. Instead, in chapters 8–12, we present a kind of "sampler" of the ways in which various theorists would look at one or another of the emotions. For example, in chapter 8 we begin by reviewing the way developmental psychologists look at emotions such as sadness. Next, we focus on what psychoanalytic and behavioral theorists have learned about the nature of depression. In chapter 10, we focus on what experimental social psychologists have discovered about anger, and so forth. This way, students can gain an in-depth understanding of how psychologists from a variety of persuasions think about emotion.

In chapter 13, we examine the role of emotions in physical health, especially the impact of emotions in stress and pain. Finally, in chapter 14, we return to a topic of serious concern to many students—dealing with their emotions. We discuss both time-tested and recently discovered techniques for managing the experiential, physiological, and behavioral components of emotion.

It may seem almost contradictory to use intellect, scientific methodology, and language—human qualities that many people consider diametrically opposed to emotion—in an attempt to understand emotion. However, it is our optimistic conviction that reason and comprehension can only enrich emotional experience. An understanding of the various scientific approaches to emotion and the vast research literature on emotion should broaden rather than limit appreciation and understanding of the passionate life. In the words of William James, whose insights into the significance of emotion prefaced this chapter, "Whatever of value, interest, or meaning our respective worlds may appear endowed with are thus pure gifts of the spectator's mind."

Summing Up

- Emotion is defined as "a genetic and acquired motivational predisposition to respond experientially, physiologically, and behaviorally to certain internal and external variables." This definition is designed to be a balanced one—to appropriately reflect the triumvirate of cognitive, physiological, and behavioral factors which comprise human experience. It is broad enough to permit coverage of the immense range of theory and research on emotion.

- We study emotion because we are all emotional beings, because emotions pervade our social lives, and because knowledge of the emotions helps us to deal with emotional conflicts and our personal emotional difficulties.

- The field of emotion is young and constantly changing as knowledge is acquired. There is no single, comprehensive theory of emotions, but rather a host of "minitheories" that emphasize cognitive and motivational, physiological, and behavioral dimensions of emotion.

- Social commentators have been asking questions about the nature of emotion for more than 150 years. One issue that has fascinated them is: "How many emotions are there and how are they organized?"

- Another issue is "How long do emotions last?" Different terms capture both differences in the intensity and duration of emotional experience—emotional states are limited in duration; emotional traits are more enduring; moods are less intense but more persistent than fleeting emotions; feelings are cognitive evaluations of our day-to-day world.

- Emotions can be classified as good or bad in two very different ways. It is easy to classify them in a hedonic sense—that is, whether it feels pleasant or unpleasant to experience a given emotion. It is harder to classify them as good or bad in a functional sense—that is, in terms of whether emotional behaviors are facilitative or disruptive—do they enrich our lives, our society, our own and other species, and the environment?

- Theorists agree that people's emotional lives are shaped by both their genetic background and their life experiences. What theorists argue about is the amount of contribution each makes. Different cultures differ in whether they encourage or attempt to suppress emotion.

- Our Western heritage and our social institutions, including legal systems, encourage us to adopt a dualistic conception of mind and body—to believe that the emotions must be controlled. People disagree, however, about how emotions should be controlled and which techniques are most effective and longest-lasting. Still more serious is the issue of whether emotions should be modified at all.

- Researchers have asked many other fascinating questions about the nature of emotion.

- The first half of this text deals with theories, principles, and methods in the study of emotion. The second half applies some of the most popular cognitive/motivational, physiological, and behavioral theories to a number of specific emotions as well as related psychological and physiological disorders.

2
Traditional Approaches to Emotion

Introduction

Experiential Approaches
Motives and Emotions
Freud and the Dynamic Tradition

Physiological Approaches
Psychophysiology
Neurological and Biochemical Approaches

Expressive Approaches
Evolutionary Approaches
Behavioral Approaches

Summing Up

FIGURE 2.1   *Dance of Life.* Edvard Munch. 1896. Lithograph. The Munch Museum and Oslo Kommune.

Introduction

In recent years, a number of popular books such as *Nutcracker, In Cold Blood,* or *Small Sacrifices* have appeared, providing painstaking accounts of sensational crimes of passion. In *Savage Grace,* in a psychiatric interview, Antony Baekeland tries to explain why he was forced to kill his mother and stab his grandmother. Obviously, something is very wrong with Antony. (Psychiatrists diagnosed him to be a paranoid schizophrenic.)

> My grandmother helped me and brought me back to New York. I spent one week with her but had a difficult time.... I kept hearing voices, including my grandmother talking in my head, but I couldn't hear her voice clearly because there was noise around and my voices kept bothering me. The voices are those of people I know and people I don't know. They sound like a machine. They talk back to me and it really bothers me a lot. The voices tell me that I'm a savior, that I'm Satan, that I'm an angel, that I'm royalty. Sometimes they say that I'm a dirty little man or a bad woman or a dog. They also give me helpful messages. I hear them all the time. I also hear music and the music lifts my soul.
>
> We were in my grandmother's bedroom but she wouldn't shut up. She kept talking and talking and talking and she wouldn't let me make the phone call. Then I threw the telephone across the room at her and she fell down. When she fell down, I felt very bad for her. I didn't want her to go to the hospital with broken bones and suffer more, so in order to help her I rushed to the kitchen, took a little knife from the drawer, went back, and stabbed her in the breast. I wanted to kill her so I could liberate her—not because I was angry, just to liberate her from the mistake I had made and from the suffering that she was experiencing at the time and from the time I was thirteen years of age.
>
> All this happened because I was denied physical contact with my grandmother and homosexual relations with anybody else.
>
> After I stabbed her, the nurse came to the door and she must have called the ambulance. (Robins & Aronson, 1985; pp. 415-416. Copyright © 1985 by Steven M. L. Aronson & Natalie Robins)

At first glance, Antony and his confused emotional state seem utterly foreign to us. His story makes no sense. But, as we learn more about him, the blurred image sharpens. First, we learn a bit about Antony's inner life—the way that he thinks and sees the world. Psychiatric reports provide clues as to his conscious thoughts and fantasies and his perhaps unconscious motives for the crimes. Next, we learn more about his physiological state at the time of the murder. There are some hints that the socially powerful Baekeland family may have been predisposed to schizophrenia. We learn something about Antony's physical state at the time of the murder. He was not eating or sleeping. He was "high" on a potpourri of drugs. We discover that Antony had a history of violent behavior. He had learned that all he had to do to get what he wanted was to threaten. His weary family would do almost anything to keep him quiet.

To understand Antony and his emotions, then, we must focus on his emotional experience, physiology, and expression. In chapters 2–6, we will discover that we can use the same strategy we used to understand Antony's emotional life in understanding what theorists have learned about the way people in general think, feel, and behave, emotionally (see Table 2.1).

Let us now consider the work of theorists who have been primarily interested in emotional experience. Note that when we say that a theorist has *focused* on emotional experience, physiology, or behavior, we certainly do not mean to imply that he or she has been interested only in that aspect of emotion. Almost all emotions theorists have *something* to say about almost every aspect of emotion. We have simply classified theorists as to their major interest for the sake of clarity.

Experiential Approaches

Sigmund Freud was one of the early theorists who explored the conscious and unconscious thoughts and fantasies that add richness to our emotional lives. He and his colleagues are called **psychodynamic** or **motivational** theorists. (Today, cognitive theorists have even more to say about the links between thought and emotion, but a review of such modern-day work must wait until chapter 4, when we discuss current theorists who take an experiential approach.) Before we outline Freud's psychodynamic theory, however, let us discuss exactly what psychologists mean by "motivational theories of emotion."

MOTIVES AND EMOTIONS

What is a motivational approach? You may recall that Reber (1985) defines motivation as an internal state that impels an animal to action. The notion

Table 2.1   Traditional Approaches to Emotion

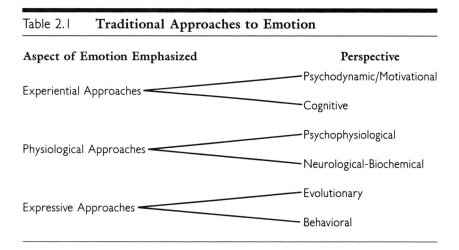

Aspect of Emotion Emphasized	Perspective
Experiential Approaches	Psychodynamic/Motivational
	Cognitive
Physiological Approaches	Psychophysiological
	Neurological-Biochemical
Expressive Approaches	Evolutionary
	Behavioral

that people are motivated to behave in certain ways makes common sense. The terms *motives, impulses, forces, instincts, drives, needs,* and the like are part of everyday language. You will probably recall from your other psychology courses that learning theorists have had much to say about the so-called primary drives (such as hunger, thirst, pain, or sex) and psychosocial motives (such as the need for power, achievement, or intimacy) that shape human behavior. Many learning theorists agree that motives energize behavior. Some insist that motivational states are merely *generalized* energizers; they prod the organism to do something, but nothing in particular. Others insist that motives *energize, direct,* and *select.* They argue, for example, that a thirsty animal is motivated to look for water (a saltine cracker will not do) and is not satisfied until it finds it.

Theorists differ in how tightly linked they consider emotion and motivation to be. Some theorists have attempted to draw a sharp distinction between emotion and motivation. In an early view, William James (1890) suggested that "emotional reaction usually terminates in the subject's own body," while motivation "is apt to go farther and enter into practical relations with the exciting object" (Vol. 2, p. 442). James believed that we "feel" emotions but that we "express" our needs. Later theorists have drawn still other distinctions between the two (see Table 2.2). They suggest that motives (such as hunger) often arise from a state of need (food deprivation) and give rise to specific actions (raiding the refrigerator) aimed at reducing this need and its accompanying sense of internal tension or discomfort. Motives are "active." Emotions seem more "passive"—people may have a strong emotional reaction to the things that happen to them without feeling compelled to express their feelings in any way or to move toward goal satisfaction. People are sometimes said to "suffer" emotion.

Other "motivational" theorists such as Sigmund Freud, Carl Jung, John Bowlby, Sandor Rado, and Robert Leeper see things very differently. They contend that emotion and motivation are tightly linked, that they cannot be distinguished so tidily as Table 2.2 implies. They argue that the angry woman

---

Table 2.2   Motivation versus Emotion: Some Traditional Distinctions

Motives	Emotions
Stimulus generally unobserved	Stimulus often apparent
Often cyclical (e.g., recurring hunger)	Not normally cyclical
Energize, direct, and sustain activity	May interfere with everyday activity
Responses are goal-directed	Responses are "inner-directed"
Experienced as "motives"	Experienced as "feelings"
Active	Passive

is impelled to action. (She can barely restrain herself from lashing out.) The embarrassed boy is motivated to hide. Robert Leeper (1948) provides an evolutionary explanation for why emotion and motivation should be so inextricably entwined. He contends that in the course of evolution animals were forced to evolve emotional and motivational reactions to ensure their survival. The emotions, as motives, arouse, direct, and sustain activity. (When we are frightened of prowlers in the night, for example, we prick up our ears. We edge to the side of the bed and begin to calculate whether we should pick up a shoe and threaten the intruder or make a run for it.) The more intense the emotion, the more powerfully it arouses and directs behavior. This means that when people are in a highly emotional state, their behavior becomes unusually focused and goal-directed. Leeper takes the position that all emotions, positive or negative, are generally functional. For example, anger provides the passion necessary to change things. Depression allows us to "save our energy" and "lie low" when things are hopeless. Leeper takes issue with theorists who think of emotions as disorganized and disorganizing.

Arthur Reber (1985), too, assumes that emotion and motivation are tightly linked:

> . . . the topic of motivation is intimately intertwined with that of emotion. Emotional states tend to have motivational properties and the energizing elements of a motivational disposition often have a strong emotional tone to them. Moreover, the physiological structures identified in one context tend to be implicated in the other. (p. 455)

In general, then, a motivational theory of emotion is one that emphasizes an emotion's energizing properties and/or its importance in selecting and guiding behavior.

FREUD AND THE DYNAMIC TRADITION

Sigmund Freud (1856–1939) was born in Freiberg, Moravia (now Czechoslovakia) in 1856. When he was three years old, his family immigrated to Vienna. Freud joined the University of Vienna medical faculty in 1873 and then began to work at the Vienna General Hospital as a resident physician. In 1885, he went to Paris to study with neurologist Jean Martin Charcot, who was interested in hysteria and hypnosis. Charcot had observed that after a traumatic event some people began to develop "hysterical" symptoms—for example, they might lose all sensation in a hand or their arm would become paralyzed. From a medical point of view, nothing was wrong with them. Freud came to the conclusion that they were unconsciously trying to repress disturbing memories and feelings, which surfaced in these bizarre forms.

Freud began to explore several techniques for helping patients work through their tangled feelings. He tried hypnosis, prodding patients to relive painful experiences until eventually their feelings came flooding out. His colleague Josef Breuer called this process "catharsis." Freud tried free association, dream analysis, and simply listening. Eventually, this "talking cure" developed into psychoanalysis. All these techniques seemed to help alleviate patients' symptoms. Eventually, Freud came to the conclusion that **repression** —pushing unacceptable wishes or emotionally charged memories into the unconscious—was the basis for all neurotic symptoms. During this period, some of the psychoanalysts' central ideas—the fact that conscious and unconscious thoughts, emotions, and motivations guide behavior, the importance of childhood sexual experiences in shaping adult personality, and the fact that people use a variety of defense mechanisms to protect themselves from thoughts and emotions that are too painful to endure—were developed. The reaction to Freud's new work was decidedly cool. Many people were repelled by the idea that humankind is motivated by unconscious and sexual desires. Things were to get worse.

Every man has reminiscences which he would not tell to everyone but only to his friends. . . . But there are other things which a man is afraid to tell even to himself.

DOSTOEVSKY

The Unconscious

Freud was fascinated by the workings of the conscious versus the unconscious mind. He saw the conscious mind as a bastion of reason and logic. Things were ordered in time and space. The unconscious was fundamentally different. It was a murky world of infantile sexuality, Oedipus complexes (love for mother and hatred and fear of father), primitive guilt, and devouring hatred of rivals, among other demons. You see an example of primitive thinking in the Baekeland quotation that began this section. Freud presented these early ideas in *The Interpretation of Dreams* (1900/1953). Not surprisingly, Freud's assault on human rationality aroused a storm of protest.

Freud argued that unconscious processes often guide behavior: Sometimes people cannot bear to admit their real motives, even to themselves. They simply cannot admit that they are greedy, silly, small-minded, passionate, or violent. Today, of course, owing to Freud's influence, the notion that people are sometimes propelled by motives they do not understand or refuse to admit seems obvious. It is hard to understand what all the fuss was about.

None so blind as those that will not see.

MATHEW HENRY

The Defense Mechanisms

According to Freud, the conscious mind possesses a variety of **defense mechanisms** that allow it to shield itself from painful unconscious information.

How does this work? Essentially, the conscious mind clamps a lid down when it spots threatening ideas and feelings trying to escape from the dark regions of the unconscious. In Freud's conception, the conscious mind simultaneously knows and does not know what is in the unconscious. It vigilantly defends itself against painful unconscious instincts. Freud's daughter, Anna Freud (1966), elaborated these ideas. (Interestingly enough, today social-psycho-physiologists have a renewed interest in unconscious processes. They make it clear that although people can be conscious of what is motivating some of their behavior, other nonconscious parts of the the brain control a great deal of behavior (see Brody, 1987; Cacioppo & Petty, 1983; or Wilson, 1985).

Since Freud's time, theorists have identified literally dozens of defense mechanisms (See Table 2.3). The generic term for the variety of defense mechanisms is *repression* (one of the specific defense mechanisms is labeled "repression," too). People use repression to keep material out of consciousness, to ward off anxiety, and to protect themselves from behaving inappropriately.

In the years since Freud's work, psychologists have confirmed people's readiness to engage in self-serving self-deceptions. For example, theorists interested in social justice, or "equity" (see Hatfield, Walster, & Berscheid,

---

Table 2.3   Defense Mechanisms

Controlling	Attempting to ward off anxiety by keeping a tight rein on people and events
Compensation	Attempting to cover up weakness in one area by going overboard in another area (of greater strength)
Denial	Refusing to see what one does not wish to see
Displacement	Rather than expressing pent-up feelings directly, picking a safe target (for example, the man who is angry at his boss may shout at his cat)
Fantasy	Daydreaming; satisfying frustrated desires in imagination
Identification	Identifying with a powerful person or institution in order to boost one's self-esteem
Isolation	Splitting off affect from content, or keeping incompatible attitudes in logic-tight compartments
Projection	Attributing one's own unacceptable desires to others
Rationalization	Providing "rational" reasons for attitudes, emotions, or behavior that in fact have darker motivations
Reaction Formation	Keeping down dangerous impulses by endorsing opposing attitudes and behavior
Regression	Retreating to an earlier stage of development to avoid the anxieties of adulthood
Repression	Preventing painful thoughts from entering consciousness— the most basic of the defense mechanisms

1978), have studied the techniques that people who insult, exploit, and hurt others use to justify their harsh behavior. They found that people use a variety of defense mechanisms to justify such actions: They deny responsibility for the victims' suffering, blame them, and minimize their suffering. There is no doubt that we often make ourselves feel better by justifying our actions.

The Instincts

World War I was a time of hardship for Freud and his colleagues. In 1915, a dispirited Freud published *Thoughts for the Time on War and Death*. Freud concluded that humankind's instinctive nature was a serious obstacle in the way of peace. (Today, Freud's "instincts" would be translated as "drives" or "motives.")

Freud's ideas on people's instinctive nature evolved over time. In his later writings, he divided the personality into three parts—the **superego** (a harsh, unconscious, parental and social conscience), the **id** (the unconscious, which is guided by the "pleasure principle"), and the **ego** (a conscious structure, which is guided by the "reality" principle). The ego tries to mediate among the conflicting demands of the punitive superego, the selfish id, and the relentless forces of society. Freud envisioned the id as a primordial reservoir of undifferentiated energy. This "psychical soup" is composed of two primitive instincts, sex and aggression. The unconscious is driven by these urges. Freud thought of the instincts as chemical, biological, or mechanical processes with psychological consequences.

The desires of the superego, ego, and id may well conflict with one another and with the demands of the outside world. People invoke the defense mechanisms we described earlier to protect them against the anxiety associated with conscious awareness of these conflicts. (Conflict between the ego and the id may lead to **neurotic anxiety;** between the ego and the superego, to **moral anxiety;** and between the ego and the world, to **reality** or **objective anxiety.**) We see, then, that people's conscious and unconscious minds have a powerful impact on their emotional lives.

In his later writings, Freud began to speak of two main categories of instincts—the life (Eros) and the death (Thanatos) instincts. Life instincts include the urge for self-preservation and creative forces. The death instincts may be directed inward (their energies focused on self-destruction) or outward (in aggression and hatred).

How are instincts expressed? According to Freud (1959), an instinct may be "altogether suppressed, so that no trace of it is found, or it appears in the guise of an affect of a particular qualitative tone, or it is transformed into anxiety" (Vol. 3, p. 92). We will see exactly what that means in the next section.

The Emotions

In the Freudian system, emotion and instinct are tightly linked. People possess a dazzling array of emotions; their reactions are subtle, complex, delicate, ever changing. According to Freud, however, our conscious ideas and emotions are actually carefully pruned and trimmed versions of the "real thing." They are mere representations of our dark, subterranean instincts.

For humans, things are not necessarily what they appear to be. We all see "through a glass, darkly." We all think of our ideas as objective and assume that we are in touch with our emotions. But we are wrong. Our beliefs are often self-serving. The "civilized" emotions we feel are pale shadows of the fiery instincts that lie beneath the surface. In Freud's view, one's rich emotional life is the result of conscious distortion and repression of the primary drives.

For most of us, most of the time, this process works. We possess as much self-knowledge as we can bear. Our conscious ideas, or representative forms, necessarily distort the unconscious form of the instinct. Any greater awareness of instincts, and the resulting affect would be unbearably painful. As Freud (1970) put it, the goal as well as the result of repression is to prevent the development of experienced pain.

According to Freud, emotions are always conscious. It is not correct to speak of an unconscious feeling or emotion. It is the instincts that are unconscious. Sometimes, however, the conscious mind catches a glimpse of raw instinct. "In that case, the affect always has the character of anxiety" (Russell, 1970, p. 343). That glimpse into the cauldron of the id sparks anxiety. Presumably, the instincts are like "hot" atomic energy. We can trace their paths by observing the anxiety they leave in their wake as they bombard the conscious mind. In Freud's view, the discharge or release of the energy of a drive, directly from its unconscious form into consciousness, always takes the form of anxiety.

Freud points out that sometimes, when repression completely fails and people come face to face with the dark forces of the id, they confront terror or madness. Novelist Joseph Conrad (1947) provides a classic, chilling description of one man's experience in *Heart of Darkness*:

> I tried to break the spell—the heavy, mute spell of the wilderness—that seemed to draw him [Kurtz] to its pitiless breast by the awakening of forgotten and brutal instincts, by the memory of gratified and monstrous passions. This alone, I was convinced, had driven him out to the edge of the forest, to the bush, towards the gleam of fires, the throb of drums, the drone of weird incantations; this alone had beguiled his unlawful soul beyond the bounds of permitted aspirations.... But his soul was mad. Being alone in the wilderness, it had looked within itself, and by heavens! I tell you, it had gone mad. (pp. 585–586)

The task of psychoanalysis is to carefully guide patients to recognize that their conscious thoughts and feelings may be shielding them from anxiety and to recognize the unconscious motives that drive them. In therapy, patients' complicated and disturbing feelings can be worked through. Freud discusses these procedures in *The Psychopathology of Everyday Life* (1949b) and *Introduction to Psychoanalysis* (1949b).

Freud's last years were a time of adulation. They were also years of bitter hardship. In 1933, the Nazi persecutions began. Because Freud was a Jew, his writings were burned in a public bonfire, and his supporters were forced to flee. He died in 1939.

Freud, then, had several insights about the cognitive aspects of emotion: He proposed that there is both conscious and unconscious processing of emotional information, that what we think we feel may not be what we "really" feel at a deeper level, that people use a variety of defense mechanisms to protect themselves from information that is too emotionally painful to bear, and that people may experience intense anxiety when they become aware of some of their more unacceptable motives.

Thus far, we have focused on Freud's experiential perspective on emotion. In the next section, we examine the work of three other intellectual giants—William James, Walter Cannon, and Paul MacLean, who pioneered the study of the physiological processes associated with emotion (see Table 2.1). Later, in chapters 4 and 6, we review the work of modern-day theorists who are currently exploring the physiology of emotion.

Physiological Approaches

The notion that the various emotions are associated with specific physiological reactions occurred to scientists early on. In ancient Greece, most physicians from the time of Hippocrates (c. 460–357 B.C.) to Galen (A.D. 130–201) believed that people's temperaments depended on which of four bodily fluids or "humors" were dominant:

Types	Humors
Choleric (angry)	Yellow bile
Phlegmatic (slow and lethargic)	Phlegm
Melancholic (sad and brooding)	Black bile
Sanguine (joyful and good-natured)	Blood

Today, psychologists have adopted two strategies in attempting to understand more about the physiology of emotion: They have placed their bets on *psychophysiological* versus *neurochemical* methods. Box 2.1 reviews the procedures involved in both types of research.

PSYCHOPHYSIOLOGY

Theorists who have taken a psychophysiological approach to emotion include William James and Carl Lange, Marion Wenger, Paul Young, and Elizabeth Duffy. In the earliest traditions of psychology, two Americans—William James and his son-in-law Walter Cannon—battled for preeminence. In some respects, James became the star of the psychophysiological tradition, Cannon the luminary of the neurobiological tradition.

BOX 2.1

Research Methods

Psychophysiological techniques for measuring biological processes are generally noninvasive means for measuring a variety of functions—they do not require penetration of the skin or organs of the body. Such methods include some of the techniques you have seen your family doctor employ—blood-pressure measurement (with the familiar cuff device) and heart-rate measurement (with the electrocardiograph), as well as less familiar brain-wave measurement (with the electroencephalograph), muscle-tension measurement (with the electromyograph), and still other techniques we describe in later chapters. Because they are painless, psychophysiological methods are especially useful with human subjects.

Naturally, psychologists are interested in comparing the various components of emotion. They want to compare experiential measures (such as self-report or questionnaire responses) with measures of physiological activity. Psychophysiological techniques are ideal for this sort of study. For example, studies of the relationship between reported anxiety or distress and heart rate confirm that both processes are involved in fear (Lang, Melamed, & Hart, 1970).

By contrast, **neurological or neurochemical methods** for physiological measurement are invasive, in the sense that penetration of the skin (as well as deeper structures) is often required. Physiological psychologists or neuropsychologists who use these techniques experimentally almost always focus on the emotional reactions of animals. Their surgery is simply too painful and too dangerous to be used on humans. Neuropsychologists generally focus on the activity of the brain, the spinal cord, and other central nervous system structures. Using electrodes or "cannulas" (tiny tubes through which chemicals may be injected into neural tissue), they may stimulate the brain or destroy brain tissue in an effort to determine its role in emotional behavior. For instance, it was through such methods that researchers discovered that the brain structure called the amygdala was involved in aggressive and other emotional reactions (Kling, 1986).

Because their methods are so demanding, physiological psychologists are rarely able to explore self-report/physiological relationships. On rare occasions they have been able to observe people who have suffered brain injuries or disease or who have had electrode implants for a variety of medical reasons. Such cross-species comparisons have been extremely helpful in discovering the function of various brain structures.

William James (1842–1910) was an American psychologist and philosopher. James first studied art but made little progress. Next, he studied medicine, but because of failing health he was unable to practice; instead, in 1872, he began his long association with Harvard as an instructor in physiology, anatomy, and hygiene. He was fascinated by the relationship between psychology and physiology and, in 1876, established the first laboratory for psychological research in the United States at Harvard. His book, *Principles of Psychology* (1890), did much to establish psychology as an independent science. Although *Principles* was enormously popular, in his later years almost all of James's work was in philosophy.

James's views on the nature of emotion are still influential. One of the oldest debates concerns "Which comes first—the experience of emotion or physiological arousal?" In the late nineteenth century, writers argued commonsensically (as some cognitive theorists do today) that our perceptions of a situation trigger our emotions, which, in turn, motivate us to act. James (1890) took the opposite tack—he argued that we know what we feel by monitoring bodily cues. In his words:

> ... *the bodily changes follow directly the perception of the exciting fact, and ... our feelings of the same changes as they occur is the emotion.* Common sense says we lose our fortune, are sorry, and weep; we meet a bear, are frightened, and run; we are insulted by a rival, are angry, and strike. The hypothesis here to be defended says that this order or sequence is incorrect, that the one mental state is not immediately induced by the other and that the bodily manifestations must be interposed between. The more rational statement is that we feel sorry because we cry, angry because we strike, afraid because we tremble, and not that we cry, strike, or tremble, because we are sorry, angry or fearful, as the case may be.... If we fancy some strong emotion, and then try to abstract from our consciousness of it all the feelings of its bodily symptoms, we find we have nothing left behind, no "mind stuff" out of which the emotion can be constituted and that a cold and neutral state of intellectual perception is all that remains. (pp. 449–451)

Note that in his writings James emphasized both visceral ("gut") reactions (such as a churning stomach) and overt bodily (motor) reactions (such as trembling, running away, or striking out) as central to emotional states. Independently, a Danish physiologist, Carl Lange, proposed a theory similar to that of James. However, Lange emphasized vascular changes (notably, changes in blood pressure) as central to the process. Since then, the view that emotion is the perception of bodily changes has been called the **James-Lange theory of emotion** (Lange & James, 1922).

For most people, common sense suggests that when we perceive something (a bear), we become frightened, and *then* our hearts begin to pound, our stomachs churn, and we start to run (see Figure 2.2). However, after a little thought, it becomes clear that sometimes the sequence proposed by James and Lange does occur. A car careens toward us, and we somehow swerve out of the way and slam on the brakes. Only later, when we begin to realize what might have happened ("I could have been killed!"), does the full impact of the incident hit us, and we become sick with anxiety. The James-Lange theory seems especially appropriate for the coarse emotions such as grief, fear, rage, and love. In situations involving these primitive emotions, we sometimes react instinctively. Later, we may have to stop to figure out why we reacted as we did.

Consider, for instance, a hiker recounting an incident several years ago in which he was cornered by a grizzly bear while hiking in an area of fallen timber in Yellowstone National Park. Years later, he can still give a second-by-second account of his thoughts, feelings, and reactions as the event unfolded. The experience is etched in his memory. He vividly remembers hearing the bear in the distance, spotting it coming at him, and then running,

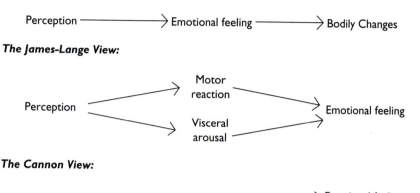

The Commonsense View:

Perception ⟶ Emotional feeling ⟶ Bodily Changes

The James-Lange View:

Perception → Motor reaction / Visceral arousal → Emotional feeling

The Cannon View:

Perception ⟶ Thalamic arousal → Emotional feeling / Bodily changes

FIGURE 2.2 The sequence problem: traditional views.

tripping over a fallen tree, and finally jumping halfway up one of the few standing trees in the area. But he does not remember being "afraid" until after the experience was over. Only later, when he was sure the bear had gone, did the sensation of naked terror sweep over the hiker.

Some therapists use Jamesian techniques in psychotherapy to help their clients sort out their feelings. At times clients' emotions are so deeply buried that they have no idea what they are feeling, even though it is obvious from their agitated manner that they are feeling something. "I don't really know," they might reply, with interested puzzlement, when asked how they felt when someone insulted them. To help them do detective work on their emotions, therapists must often resort to asking them to pay careful attention to their bodily sensations: Are they dizzy? Sweating? Is their pulse racing? Do they feel numb? Our language is filled with such mind–body connections. For example, when we feel nervous we say our "throat feels dry." Africans say they have a "cold stone" in their stomachs. When we are frightened, we say "our blood ran cold." When we are angry, we "get hot under the collar." When we are ashamed, we "blush."

Researchers have offered a potpourri of evidence for the contention that emotional intensity depends on vascular and visceral changes. For example, George Hohmann (1966) studied 25 paraplegics and quadriplegics confined to the Spinal Cord Injury Service of the Veterans Hospital at Long Beach. The patients were divided into five groups, each varying in the amount of visceral sensation they were still capable of perceiving (the higher the lesion, or separation in the spinal cord, the less visceral sensation they had). If James and Lange are correct, if we "feel" emotions by observing bodily cues, then the higher the spinal cord damage, the less intense emotional experience should be. Hohmann's data for the states of fear and anger are plotted in Figure 2.3. It can be seen that the higher the lesion (and the less the visceral sensation), the more precipitously fear and anger decline in intensity. Precisely the same relationship holds for the states of sexual excitement and grief.

If we look at how the patients described their feelings, we see again that those with cervical lesions describe themselves as feeling less intensely emotional than they had before receiving their injuries. For instance, one patient who suffered a serious spinal cord injury near the brain reported:

> Now, I don't get a feeling of physical animation, it's sort of a cold anger. Sometimes I act angry when I see some injustice. I yell and cuss and raise hell because if you don't do it sometimes, I've learned people will take advantage of you, but it doesn't have the heat to it that it used to. It's a mental kind of anger. (pp. 150–151)

It seems plausible, then, to conclude that sometimes emotion follows physiological arousal. On the other hand, it is hard to believe that things always work that way. It simply sounds wrong to say that "After I ran up to her and flung my arms around her, I realized that I loved her," or "After I threw coffee in his face, I realized I must hate him." Sometimes it seems more natural to speak as if love or hate, which occur first, cause vascular or visceral sensations and action. Theorists now believe that all of the emotional

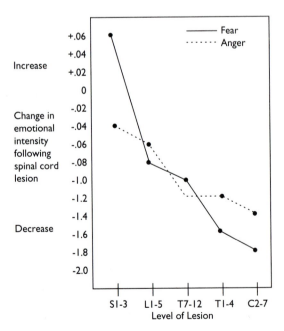

FIGURE 2.3   The impact of spinal cord lesions on changes in emotional intensity. (Adapted from Hohmann, 1966)

sequences depicted earlier in Figure 2.2 can occur under different circumstances. For example, some have suggested that if one reacts emotionally to a sudden and immediately threatening event, the James-Lange sequence is the most appropriate description of the process. However, if the emotional event occurs regularly, or the emotion has a chance to build more slowly, the commonsense view—feeling precedes action—may more accurately describe the sequence. (Note that in either case, however, we need not take a stance on this issue, "Do feelings *cause* actions?" We need to know much more than which comes *first* in order to decide what causes the emotions' various manifestations.)

Perhaps James's most lasting contribution is the interest that his views sparked in the relationship between cognition and bodily processes. Even today, as we will see, health psychologists are searching for links between emotions in the form of stress, anxiety, or arousal and certain autonomic responses (i.e., the relatively automatic reactions of internal organs such as the heart, blood vessels, and glands).

One of the first studies in the psychophysiology area was conducted by Marion Wenger during World War II. Wenger (1948) interviewed more than 2,000 Air Force cadets and aviation students. Wenger assumed that emotional men would make poor combat pilots, navigators, or bombardiers; he reasoned that the Air Force could predict which men would be overly emotional in combat by weeding out those with autonomic "imbalances" such as unusually high heart rates, fast respiration, and unusual skin conductance (a measure of sweat gland activity). He developed a battery which measured "symptoms" of emotionality. Wenger's initial interviews with flight surgeons and instructors increased his confidence that "balanced" men would do better in combat.

Wenger's research yielded a fascinating finding. He found that those cadets who were easily aroused in the original battery of tests were especially prone in later life to **psychosomatic disorders,** physical disorders which appear to have no known organic cause.

Recent technological advances make it possible to precisely, inexpensively, and noninvasively assess a wide range of physiological processes. It is not surprising, then, that today psychophysiologists are investigating a wide range of issues concerning the impact of the autonomic nervous system on emotion. We review some of this research in chapters 5 and 6.

NEUROLOGICAL AND BIOCHEMICAL APPROACHES

Figures such as Walter Cannon, Paul MacLean, Jose Delgado, and others have taken a "deeper" approach to the physiology of emotion—they have looked to the brain and other central portions of the nervous system for their answers to the causality of emotion.

Walter Cannon (1871–1945) was born in Wisconsin and attended Harvard, where he studied medicine. After graduation, he took a position there

lecturing, consulting, and performing research in physiology and endrocri-
nology. He remained at Harvard for 42 years.

Cannon developed a sweeping theory; he assumed that people's bodies
are programmed to try to maintain an ideal "adaptation level." When they
experience powerful emotions, stress, or tissue need, their bodies automatically begin to make a series of adaptive adjustments designed to bring things
back to the status quo. He presented his hypotheses in the brilliant book
Bodily Changes in Pain, Hunger, Fear, and Rage (1929). Basically, Walter
Cannon and Philip Bard—in what is labeled the Cannon-Bard theory of emotion—argued that emotions signal an emergency; they cause the body to react
with the resources needed to cope.

Cannon took issue with the theories of William James, and the debate
between the Jamesians and Cannon generated some classic research. What
were Cannon's objections? Since James's proposition equates emotion with
bodily changes, it follows that: (a) different emotions must be accompanied
by recognizably different bodily states; and (b) emotions can be manipulated
by drugs or surgery that alter bodily states in appropriate ways. Researchers
soon began to test these notions. As the facts accumulated, Cannon (1929)
was led inexorably to what was considered by many to be a devastating critique
of the James-Lange theory. Cannon's case rested on the following arguments:

1. Very different emotional states are associated with identical visceral
    changes.
2. The internal organs (the viscera) are relatively insensitive structures.
    They cannot provide the subtle and complex kinds of information that
    would permit people to distinguish one emotion from another.
3. Emotion is not necessarily produced by experimental stimulation of the
    viscera. People do not usually feel emotional when they exercise vig-
    orously or are injected with adrenaline, even though they experience the
    bodily changes typical of strong emotion.
4. Visceral responses are too slow to be a source of feeling. (Typically, it
    takes the viscera several seconds to react.) How could the viscera be the
    source of sudden emotion?
5. Separation of the viscera from the central nervous system through surgery
    does not alter emotional behavior.

Cannon argued that if people cannot rely on information from the viscera
to alert them to what they are feeling, they must, therefore, rely on some
other source of information. Cannon concluded that it is the brain itself,
specifically the thalamus, which is the control center for emotional behavior
(see Figure 2.4). In his view, the activation of this brain structure produces
both the experience of emotion and the bodily effects associated with it.
Cannon surgically removed various parts of cats' brains. He found that when
the cerebral hemispheres were ablated, cats generally displayed "sham rage."
This display consisted of internal reactions (i.e., increases in epinephrine and

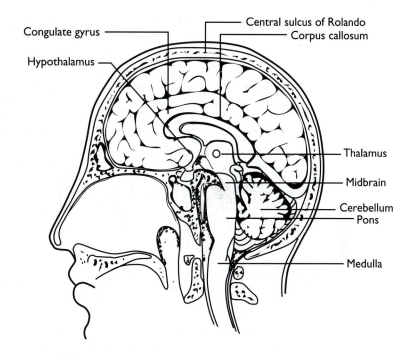

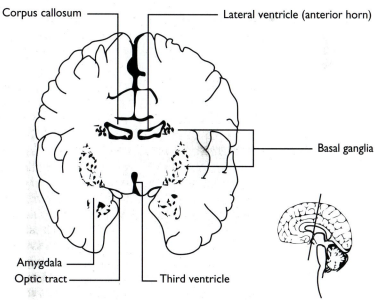

FIGURE 2.4 The brain and its structures.

blood sugar levels) and aggressive behaviors (muscle tension, clawing, snarling, and attempts to bite).

As we will discuss in chapter 4, it now appears that some of Cannon's criticisms were not valid. For example: (a) There is evidence that severing the spinal cord does alter some aspects of the experience of emotion (Fehr & Stern, 1970); and (b) it has been found that it is possible to make physiological distinctions between certain emotions. Anger, for instance, is generally associated with an increase in gastric activity, fear with an inhibition of gastric function. Albert Ax (1953), Stewart Wolf and Harold Wolff (1947), and more recently Paul Ekman, Robert Levenson, and Wallace Friesen (1983) all claim to have discovered autonomic nervous system markers for a wide variety of emotions. However, different people do show different patterns of such responses, and their responses can vary from situation to situation (Lang, Rice, & Sternbach, 1972).

Today, most researchers would conclude that both Cannon and James were each, in part, correct. Cannon was right that brain structures play an important role in emotion. James was right in contending that people read their emotions, in part, by observing bodily changes.

Since Cannon's original formulation, neurologists have discovered that many parts of the brain play a significant role in emotion. Evidence has been found that the so-called limbic system (including the hypothalamus, the amygdala, and the hippocampus), the temporal lobe, the cingulate gyrus, and even the neocortex itself, among other brain structures, all have something to do with emotion (Plutchik & Kellerman, 1986). Figure 2.4, which depicts two views of the brain and its structures, may be of some help in locating some of the areas we have just mentioned.

Cannon made a major contribution to the psychology of emotion. He has taught us much about its physiology, and more importantly, he gave the neurological approach to emotion a bright start. Let us now round out our discussion of the role of brain mechanisms in emotion by reviewing Paul MacLean's research.

For thousands of years, researchers have tried to understand the brain. Recently, they have begun to make some impressive strides. From **evolutionary biology,** we are learning when the different parts of the brain evolved. From **neuroanatomy,** we are discovering how the structures of the brain were first assembled. From **neurophysiology,** we are beginning to understand how the brain functions chemically. MacLean advanced these efforts in a major way.

Paul MacLean (b. 1913) has proposed one of the most fascinating neurological theories with relevance to emotion. Recently, evidence to support MacLean's and other neurological models of emotion has been summarized in a series of state-of-the-art papers (Plutchik & Kellerman, 1986). MacLean observes that in the course of evolution, humans have ended up with a forebrain that is a "triune structure." In a sense, the brain consists of three different types of brains, with different anatomical structures and chemical processes layered one upon the other. The oldest type of brain is basically reptilian; the second, the neo-mammalian, is inherited from the early mammals, and the third, the late mammalian/early primate, from the late mammals and early primates.

In their primer, Robert Ornstein and Richard Thompson (1984) provide a simple description of this layering process (see Box 2.2).

MacLean (1986) points out that the reptilian brain was primarily concerned with preservation of the self and the species. Its primitive structures

BOX 2.2

The Amazing Brain

Ornstein and Thompson (1984) observe: "The brain is like an old ramshackle house that has been added on to over the years in a rather disorganized fashion."

The brainstem:

The brainstem is the oldest part of the brain. It evolved more than 500 million years ago. Because it resembles the entire brain of a rep-

tile, it is often referred to as the reptilian brain. It determines the general level of alertness and warns the organism of important incoming information, as well as handling the basic bodily functions necessary for survival—breathing and heart rate. (p. 4)

The cerebellum:

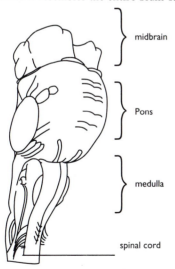

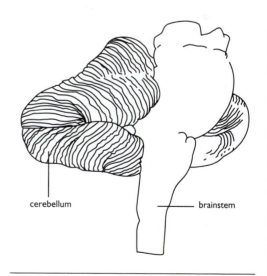

FIGURE 2.5   The brainstem.

FIGURE 2.6   The cerebellum.

(continued)

BOX 2.2 *(continued)*

The cerebellum, or "little brain," is attached to the rear of the brainstem. Among other functions, the cerebellum maintains and adjusts posture and coordinates muscular move-

ment. . . . It now appears that memories for simple learned responses may be stored there. (p. 6)

The limbic system:

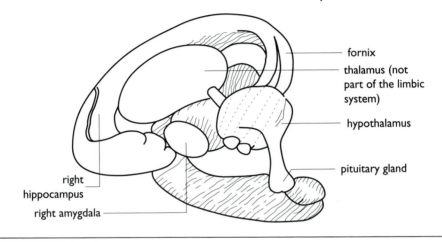

FIGURE 2.7   The limbic system.

(continued)

were designed to guide the reptile in the processes required for obtaining food and mates (search, angry attacks, self-defense, and feeding or sexual activity).

In the neo-mammalian brain, three new patterns of behavior emerged through evolution. These were primarily designed to facilitate mother-child relationships. MacLean contends that such affects as desire, fear, anger, dejection, depression, ecstasy, and affection all derive from activities in the limbic system. He observes that the limbic system "derives information . . . in terms of affective feelings that guide behavior required for self-preservation and preservation of the species" (p. 62). Not until the neo-cortex evolved in the late mammalian/primate period did symbolic or verbal information become important in shaping primate emotional experience or expression.

Thus, MacLean (1986) attributes both emotional behaviors and a variety of natural behaviors (the "preservation" behaviors) to activities of the central nervous system. Emotion and adaptive behavior are thus locked together. MacLean (1986) reviews more than 40 years of clinical and experimental

BOX 2.2 *(continued)*

The next structure on the totem pole is the limbic system. Ornstein and Thompson note:

> The limbic system is the group of cellular structures located between the brainstem and the cortex. It evolved sometime between 300 and 200 million years ago. Because the limbic system is most highly developed in mammals, it is often called the mammalian brain. In addition to helping maintain body temperature, blood pressure, heartbeat rate, and blood sugar levels, the limbic system is strongly involved in the emotional reactions that have to do with survival. (p. 8)

The cerebrum:

> The largest part of the human brain is the cerebrum. It is divided into two halves, or hemispheres, each of which controls its opposite half of the body. The hemispheres are connected by a band of some 300 million nerve cell fibers called the corpus callosum. Covering each hemisphere is a one-eighth-inch thick, intricately folded layer of nerve cells called the cortex. The cortex first appeared in our ances-

tors about 200 million years ago, and it is what makes us uniquely human. Because of it, we are able to organize, remember, communicate, understand, appreciate, and create. (p. 12)

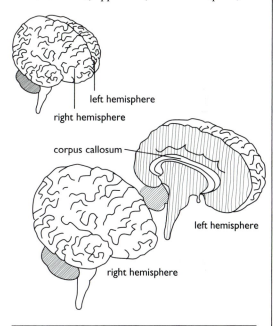

Taken from Ornstein & Thompson (1984, pp. 3–12)

FIGURE 2.8   The cerebrum.

findings in support of his contention that it is not cognition but emotion that guides the behavior required for self- and species-preservation.

MacLean's theory gives us insight into two types of phenomena that have puzzled psychologists: (a) Emotions such as anger and desire or fear and rage often flicker and alternate through consciousness in a bewildering way; and (b) emotions and adaptive behavior are tightly linked. The fact that the brain structures and the neural connections for these processes are in such close proximity and are so interconnected helps explain the links among various emotions and between these emotions and behavior. The facts of evolution account for the adaptive value of the emotions.

In summary, William James and Walter Cannon offered early insights into the physiology of emotion. Whereas James was particularly concerned with the relationship between bodily responses and the experience of emotion, Cannon located the control center of emotion in the brain, notably the thalamus. These two approaches initiated the psychophysiological and neurophysiological traditions in the field of emotion. In more recent years, Paul MacLean expanded on the role of the brain in emotion, distinguishing between older structures and the late mammalian brain, including the neo-cortex. Complex interactions among the "layers" of the brain underlie the complexities of emotional experience, physiology, and behavior.

Expressive Approaches

Finally, a number of theorists have focused on the **expressive** aspects of emotion (see Table 2.1). They have focused on the observable, measurable, aspects of overt emotional behavior. In this last section of the chapter, we will highlight the pioneering work of giants Charles Darwin, John Watson, and B. F. Skinner on emotional expression. (In chapter 5, we focus on modern-day scientists who similarly use evolutionary or behavioral principles to explain emotional expression.)

Those who take an evolutionary approach to the origins of emotional behavior provide detailed observations of the multitude of ways that emotion is expressed by all animals, from the lowest to the highest in the evolutionary chain. They argue that emotional expression evolved over time and is adaptive. It is functional in that it increases the chances that the species will survive. Where evolutionary theorists leave off, the learning theorists begin. They describe the principles by which individual animals, man included, learn to shape their emotional expression according to environmental rewards and punishments. That is, the emotions are seen to play a functional role in the individual's survival.

Even insects express anger, terror, jealousy, and love.
CHARLES DARWIN

EVOLUTIONARY APPROACHES

Charles Darwin (1809–1882) was born in Shrewsbury, England, and from his youth he was fascinated by natural history. In his day, boys with such interests studied medicine. Thus, he attended both the University of Edinburgh and Cambridge University, where he developed an interest in botany and geology. After graduation, Darwin took the post of naturalist on the HMS Beagle and spent four years circumnavigating the globe. During the voyage, he sailed the coast of South America, taking inland trips from the various ports. He was dazzled by the extraordinary variety of animal life he observed. On the cliffs of Patagonia, he traced the fossils of gigantic extinct creatures and then spent five weeks among the Galapagos Islands. These experiences made a profound impression on Darwin. He was struck by the fact that in the various geographic regions animals were related, yet very different. Why was there such an array? How did these animals come to be so exquisitely suited to their environments? Darwin began thinking through a theory of evolution, a topic that occupied his mind for the rest of his life.

Darwin became convinced that natural selection could account for the fact that most animals fit their ecological niche. He spelled out how this process might operate. Individuals and species vary in how well adapted they are to their environment. Those that fit best in their environment are likely to survive and reproduce. Those that are too tall or too short, too fast or too slow for the world they inhabit will perish. Over the vast spans of time involved in evolution, species come to be well adapted to their environments.

Darwin's ideas were clear; the next step was to gather data. Darwin was a methodical researcher, and for the next 22 years he observed and experimented in secret. The years of preparation came to an abrupt end in June of 1858, when he received a manuscript from a young naturalist, Alfred Russell Wallace. Wallace, too, had independently come upon the concepts of the survival of the fittest. Darwin was forced to prepare an abstract of his own ideas and began writing his momentous work, *On the Origin of Species by Means of Natural Selection* (1872/1964). Researchers immediately recognized the importance of this work. It sold out on the day of publication, and in scientific circles the new ideas gained almost instant acceptance. Nonetheless, Darwin's ideas sparked a violent clash between religious fundamentalists (who believed in a literal interpretation of the book of Genesis) and those who were able to accept the discovery that evolution is a slow and continuous process.

Darwin's Principles

It was another 13 years before Darwin detailed his views of the *Expression of the Emotions in Man and Animals* (1872/1965). This text has provided the framework for all subsequent evolutionary approaches to emotion. Darwin was convinced that animals and humankind expressed emotions in many of the same ways. These facial and postural expressions had evolved because they worked; they increased the chances of survival. (The dog that bares its teeth when angry is prepared to attack. The rabbit that pricks up its ears at the scent of trouble is prepared to run to its burrow at the first sound of trouble.) Darwin proposed that emotional expression was shaped by three main principles: the principle of **serviceable associated habits,** the principle of **antithesis,** and the principle of **direct action of the excited nervous system.**

Principle I. The Principle of Serviceable Associated Habits. Often, our thoughts and feelings can be read in our behavior. Unconsciously, we perform those actions that we (individually or as a species) have previously used to our profit in similar circumstances. For example, when we are riding with someone who is driving much too fast, we might try to look cool, but terror will win out. We keep applying the brake, futilely, on the passenger side.

Darwin provides a host of such examples. For instance:

> A man . . . who vehemently rejects a proposition, will almost certainly shut his eyes or turn away his face; but if he accepts the proposition, he will nod his head in affirmation and open his eyes widely. The man acts in this latter case as if he clearly saw the thing, and in the former case as if he did not or would not see it. I have noticed that persons in describing a horrid sight often shut their eyes momentarily and firmly, or shake their heads, as if not to see or to drive away something disagreeable; and I have caught myself, when thinking in the dark of a horrid spectacle, closing my eyes firmly. (pp. 32–33)

Darwin noticed that even when we try to hide our feelings, they creep out. When we check one habitual movement, it requires other slight movements; these movements then serve as a means of expression. Emotion will be expressed.

For example, imagine a woman who comes from a very nervous family. At the first hint of trouble, voices begin to rise in panic. Her mother and aunts are worriers. "Don't stand too near the curb. Someone may push you into the street." "Don't go for a walk alone in the woods; you might get eaten by a pack of wild dogs." It is not surprising, then, that early on she decides to become an extremely calm person in an effort to counter such hysteria. She practices meeting challenges with a low voice and measured tone. Soon after she receives her Ph.D., she is working with a colleague on a grant proposal. Things keep falling apart; they become more and more angry and frustrated. Once, in answer to a question, her colleague says with irritation, "Don't you use that sweet, reasonable tone with me!" The colleague is exactly right. She knows her friend is angry. The tone isn't just reasonable; it is infuriatingly reasonable. It might fool people who don't know her very well, but not a friend.

Principle 2. The Principle of Antithesis. Principle 1 stated that thoughts and emotions spark an array of adaptive (or once adaptive) behaviors. Darwin points out that when we are feeling a directly opposite state of mind—love instead of hate, fear instead of rage—we have a strong involuntary tendency to perform movements of a directly opposite nature, even though these actions may have no particular adaptive advantage. Darwin (1965) observes:

> When a dog approaches a strange dog or man in a savage or hostile frame of mind he walks upright and very stiffly; his head is slightly raised, or not much lowered; the tail is held erect and quite rigid; the hairs bristle, especially along the neck and back; the pricked ears are directed forwards, and the eyes have a

fixed stare [see Figure 2.9]. These actions . . . follow from the dog's intention to attack his enemy, and are thus to a large extent intelligible. . . .

Let us now suppose that the dog suddenly discovers that the man he is approaching is not a stranger, but his master; and let it be observed how completely and instantaneously his whole bearing is reversed [see Figure 2.10].

. . . Not one of the above movements, so clearly expressive of affection, are of the least direct service to the animal. They are explicable, as far as I can see, solely from being in complete opposition or antithesis to the attitude and movements which, from intelligible causes, are assumed when a dog intends to fight. (pp. 50–51)

Principle 3. The Principle of Direct Action of the Excited Nervous System.

Finally, Darwin reviews an array of emotions—anxiety, grief, dejection, despair, joy, high spirits, love, sulkiness, and others—and attempts to show how their expression follows from action of the nervous system.

Darwin's book is a joy to read. No wonder it caused a sensation. He reviewed a staggering array of data in support of his theses. He assembled evidence from infants, the insane, artists, and anthropologists. Clearly, he spent a lifetime meticulously observing the most minute forms of bodily expression—from raised eyebrows to trickles of perspiration on the palm—and attempted, with infinite patience, to trace those forms of expression back to their origins.

Since Darwin's time, anthropologists and biologists have collected considerable evidence that some aspects of emotionality are biologically based. For example, in one study, Melvin Allerhand (1967) asked identical twins, fraternal twins, and siblings to describe the way they experienced affection, anger, delight, disgust, excitement, fear, sadness, and worry. Identical twins (who have exactly the same genetic makeup) have more emotional similarities than do fraternal twins or normal siblings. Such data suggest the possibility of a hereditary factor in emotional experience and expression.

One of the most frequently cited pieces of evidence supporting the proposition that emotional expression has biological underpinnings is Florence Goodenough's (1932) study of a 10-year-old girl who was born deaf and blind. Since this little girl could not have learned emotional expressions by observation, Goodenough assumed that her expressive behavior was "the nearest approach to 'native' reaction-patterns, freed from the influence of any social milieu, which can be observed in a civilized state of society" (p. 328).

This child seemed remarkably similar to most 10-year-olds in the way she expressed her feelings. Some examples:

The girl, deaf and blind, living in poverty, untaught, had invented "dance". . . . The dance is clearly an expression of pleasure. It is usually accompanied by laughter and sometimes breaks up in wild peals of such violent laughter as to prevent her continuing. It may occur spontaneously when she is in good spirits, apparently as an expression of general joie de vivre, or it may sometimes be stimulated by giving her a bit of jelly or some other simple treat. (p. 331)

FIGURE 2.9   Dog approaching another dog with hostile intentions. By Mr. Riviere. Reprinted from Darwin, C., *The Expression of the Emotions in Man and Animals.* The University of Chicago Press, Chicago and London, copyright 1965, p. 52.

FIGURE 2.10   The same in a humble and affectionate frame of mind. By Mr. Riviere. Reprinted from Darwin, C., *The Expression of the Emotions in Man and Animals.* The University of Chicago Press, Chicago and London, copyright 1965, p. 53.

The girl also showed anger in characteristic ways.

Mild forms of resentment are shown by turning away her head, pouting the lips, or frowning.... More intense forms are shown by throwing back the head and shaking it from side to side, during which the lips are retracted, exposing the teeth which are sometimes clenched. This is accompanied by whimpering or whining noises, rising at intervals to short high-pitched staccato yelps. (p. 331)

Goodenough concluded that the expression of human emotion is essentially built on innate tendencies that have been altered by a social veneer. Later studies of handicapped children have supported this conclusion.

Probably the strongest evidence that biological factors play an important role in the expression and interpretation of emotion comes from cross-cultural research. In chapter 6, we will see that people in most societies often communicate emotions in much the same way.

Adaptation

Since Darwin, evolution-oriented emotions theorists such as Robert Plutchik, Carroll Izard, Edward O. Wilson, and others have argued that emotions and emotional behavior are adaptive. What does this mean? When psychologists argue about whether or not something is adaptive, they may be taking one of three very different positions: (a) Emotions benefit individuals themselves; they increase a person's happiness or ability to fit in (this is, of course, *not* what Darwin meant by "adaptive"); (b) emotions increase the likelihood that members of a given species will survive and reproduce; or (c) emotions are simply outdated remnants of another time (that is, they were *once* adaptive).

Consider one emotion—passionate love. Is passion adaptive? How? Certainly, passion does not always contribute to an individual's happiness or ability to "fit in." In Somerset Maugham's (1953) *Of Human Bondage,* the hero, Philip, is baffled by the fact that he is so passionately attached to Mildred, a woman he doesn't even like. (See Box 2.3.)

Philip's obsession leads to ruin, so is it adaptive in any sense of the word? In Philip's case, it is certainly hard to see the advantage it bestows. However, followers of Freud (who was greatly influenced by Darwin's notions) might insist that, even for Philip, passion has some advantages. Perhaps he has an unconscious need to be punished. Perhaps his love for Mildred enables him to avoid responsibilities that he finds overwhelming. Sometimes, then, when people debate whether or not emotions are adaptive, they are speaking in a psychological rather than an evolutionary sense.

Darwinians, of course, would point out that in the vast reaches of time, it is not really important whether an individual is happy; what matters is survival and reproduction. Paul Rosenblatt (1967) takes just such a position. He argues that passionate love functions, in primitive societies and our own, to keep couples together for two or three years. This gives them enough time to establish a family and to develop other sources of solidarity. Passionate

BOX 2.3

Of Human Bondage

When he lay in bed it seemed impossible that he should be in love with Mildred Rogers. Her name was grotesque. He did not think her pretty; he hated the thinness of her; only that evening he had noticed how the bones of her chest stood out in evening-dress; he went over her features one by one; he did not like her mouth, and the unhealthiness of her colour vaguely repelled him. She was common. . . . He remembered her insolence; sometimes he had felt inclined to box her ears; and suddenly, he knew not why, perhaps it was the thought of hitting her or the recollection of her tiny, beautiful ears, he was seized by an uprush of emotion. He yearned for her. He thought of taking her in his arms, the thin, fragile body, and kissing her pale mouth: he wanted to pass his fingers down the slightly greenish cheeks. He wanted her.

He had thought of love as a rapture which seized one so that all the world seemed spring-like, he had looked forward to an ecstatic happiness; but this was not happiness; it was a hunger of the soul, it was a painful yearning, it was a bitter anguish, he had never known before. He tried to think when it had first come to him. He did not know. He only remembered that each time he had gone into the shop, after the first two or three times, it had been with a little feeling in the heart that was pain; and he remembered that when she spoke to him he felt curiously breathless. When she left him it was wretchedness, and when she came to him again it was despair. (p. 158)

love may simply be part of a design to ensure that people's genes survive. (Too bad for Philip.)

Still others might argue that emotions such as passionate love may once have had a purpose, but that purpose is no more. Evolution is slow; societies can change rapidly. Plutchik (1980a) points out that evolution is "ultraconservative." Emotions that were once useful may continue to exist, pointlessly, for centuries and longer. Perhaps passionate love has become "useless" in an already overpopulated world.

We can find other examples in which emotions seem out of date. Think, for example, of fear. We have seen television episodes in which a soldier assigned to dismantle a bomb freezes, or worse yet, cannot stop shaking in terror. Is his fear functional? Obviously not. Yet that same predisposition to "stop in our tracks" when we are frightened or to be filled with too much energy no doubt spared many of our ancestors' lives as they successfully avoided danger.

Thus far, we have considered emotional behaviors that have evolved to help us deal with the environment. Essentially, such wired-in behaviors equip us to deal with yesterday. To the extent that yesterday matches today, we are fine. Unfortunately, sometimes today's world is very different from that of the past. Then, we are in trouble. Let us now consider the learning theorists, who study the process by which emotional expressiveness adapts itself to current realities.

BEHAVIORAL APPROACHES

Some theorists have assumed that the best way to understand emotion is to focus on emotional behavior. Theorists such as John Watson, B. F. Skinner, J. R. Millenson, and O. Hobart Mowrer have been especially interested in how people *learn* to behave emotionally.

When we begin to discuss what the behaviorists have to say about emotion, many people are brought up short. Most of us vaguely remember from our introductory psychology courses that it was the behaviorists who attacked the study of cognition and emotion as unscientific. For example, consider John Watson's (1924) scathing critique of Freud and James:

> . . . The belief in the existence of consciousness goes back to the ancient days of superstition and magic.
>
> The great mass of people even today has not yet progressed very far away from savagery—it wants to believe in magic. The savage believes that incantations can bring rain, good crops, good hunting, that an unfriendly voodoo doctor can bring disaster to a person or to a whole tribe. . . . These concepts—these heritages of a timid savage past—have made the emergence and growth of scientific psychology extremely difficult. (pp. 2–3)

John Watson (1878–1958), despite his attacks on the scientific validity of conscious experiences, nevertheless had much to say about emotional expression. Watson (1919) argued that children have in them three innate emotions, roughly equivalent to fear, rage, and love, each one elicited by a surprisingly few stimuli. Fear is elicited by loud and unexpected sounds and loss of support, as when an infant is dropped or its covers are suddenly jerked beneath it. Fear responses are characterized by "a sudden catching of the breath, clutching randomly with the hands . . . sudden closing of the eye-lids, puckering of the lips, then crying" (p. 200). Rage is produced by hampering the infant's movements, for example, by holding its arms tightly to its sides. Then "the body stiffens and fairly well-coordinated slashing or striking movements of the hands and arms result; the feet and legs are drawn up and down; the breath is held until the child's face is flushed" (p. 200). Finally, love is sparked by tickling, shaking, gentle rocking, patting, turning on the stomach, or stroking the erogenous zones. Love responses vary: "If the infant is crying, crying ceases, a smile may appear, attempts at gurgling, cooing, and finally, in older children, the extension of the arms, which we should class as the forerunner of the embrace of adults" (p. 201).

As nearly as Watson could tell, these few stimuli and corresponding emotional responses constituted all that was innate about emotional responding. Everything else was the result of conditioning (or learning).

Watson conducted experiments to demonstrate that emotions can be learned and then extinguished (i.e., unlearned). In your course in introductory psychology, you may have heard the classic story of how Little Albert was trained to fear white rats and, eventually, anything that even reminded him of a rat. Each time the infant Albert would reach for a tiny white rat, Watson would sneak up behind him and clang a large gong. Not surprisingly, Albert soon learned to be afraid of rats. In fact, in time Albert even learned to generalize: Soon he cringed when he encountered rabbits, dogs, seal-skin coats, cotton wool, human hair, and false faces.

Peter, a little boy, was deathly afraid of rabbits. Watson set out to demonstrate that even such deeply ingrained fears can be extinguished. In a variation on "Peter and the Wolf," Watson and his co-worker, Mary Cover Jones, devised a "reconditioning" plan. They started by placing a white rabbit quite a distance from Peter while the boy was eating lunch. Each day, the rabbit was moved closer, inch by inch, as Peter ate. Eventually, the once fearful Peter could hold the rabbit on his lap (see chapter 14). Such research convinced Watson that people's emotions are mostly learned. What has been learned can be unlearned.

Watson (1928) counseled parents on rearing children. He recognized that children had to be inculcated with fear in order to establish a "certain kind of conformity with group standards" (p. 62). He was much more uncertain about the need for any positive emotions. He contended that "mother love is a dangerous instrument" (p. 87). Children should never be hugged or kissed, never be allowed to sit in a mother's lap; shaking hands with them is all that is necessary or desirable. More recent behaviorists have obviously taken a very different approach: They assume that reward should be used lavishly, punishment stingily, to shape children's behavior.

B. F. Skinner (1904–1990), a professor at Harvard University, is considered one of the most influential psychologists of our time. He, too, was critical of psychologists who are interested in emotion as it is traditionally understood. In his book, *Science and Human Behavior* (1953), he warned:

> The "emotions" are excellent examples of the fictional causes to which we commonly attribute behavior. We run away because of "fear" and strike because of "anger"; we are paralyzed by "rage" and depressed by "grief." (p. 160)

Skinner insisted that emotions are not causes of human activity; rather, they *are* human activities. To attribute causality to an emotion—for example, to explain a behavior such as striking out by saying it was caused by anger—is circular and not an effective explanation at all. The causes of emotional behaviors are to be found in the individual's environment or in the individual species' history, not in the emotion itself: "The behavior observed during an emotion is not to be confused with emotion as a hypothetical 'state,' any more than eating is to be confused with hunger" (1953, p. 168). Skinner's general position has been labeled **radical behaviorism;** he insisted that both "private events" (thoughts, feelings, sensations, and the like) and more "public" activities (walking, talking, and moving one's hands) must be considered behavior, the causes for which are to be discovered.

Skinner (1953) defined emotion as a "state of strength or weakness in one or more responses induced by any one of a class of operations" (p.166); or, in everyday language, an emotion is a person's predisposition to behave in certain ways at certain times. Emotional responses may be of two different types: they may be relatively simple **reflexes** (innate or learned), such as crying in pain, or they may be **operants** (complex learned behaviors), such as trying to placate someone you love when that person is angry. In everyday language, we often refer to operants as "voluntary" behaviors. Examples of operant emotional behavior would be avoiding dark alleys or learning to smile in response to others.

Like many learning theorists, Skinner (1953) argued that emotional patterns of responding may arise from two very different sources. First, the evolutionary history of the species may favor certain unlearned, or unconditioned, responses. "For example, in some species biting, striking, and clawing appear to be strengthened during anger before conditioning [that is, learning] can have taken place" (p. 164). In short, we may strike out in anger simply because we are "wired" that way. Second, some emotional behaviors are learned. For example, an angry child may have been conditioned to react by "teasing the other child, taking toys away from him, destroying his work, or calling him names" (p. 164). The child has learned that such irritating behavior causes his enemies to cry or run away.

According to Skinner, people identify emotions in part by observing their consequences. We conclude that someone is angry if he is "all worked up" or if he lashes out at another. Whether unlearned or learned, emotional patterns develop because of their consequences. In the case of innate behaviors (such as instinctive anger), the history of the species guaranteed that emotional behavior would be practical (i.e., it would generally increase the animal's chance of survival). Those patterns of anger behavior that fostered survival (such as biting or clawing one's enemies) came to be wired in—for example, we still tend to clench our teeth when we are furious. Reactions that were inappropriate or ineffective dropped out.

Presumably, learned emotional behavior continues because it is reinforcing. Angry outbursts work if they cause the timid to give you what you want (**positive reinforcement**) or at least to quit causing you trouble (**negative reinforcement**).

What of feelings themselves in the behavioral view of emotion? Cognitive psychologists, among others, may say that behaviorism has nothing to say about feelings. Skinner (in press), countered that "they [cognitive psychologists] themselves have done very little in the field," and he went on to argue that this is because neither approach is appropriate for the study of feelings. Rather:

> in the case of feeling, both the conditions felt and what is done in feeling them must be left to the physiologist. What remains for the behavior analyst are the genetic and personal [learning] histories responsible for the bodily conditions the physiologist will find.

In other words, psychologists should not waste their time studying people's inner lives. Those subjective, internal, experiences are, in Skinner's terms, "out of reach of the instruments and methods of the behavior analyst." The behaviorist can, however, study the "genetic" and "personal" conditions that predispose animals to react physiologically and behaviorally in emotional ways. Knowledge of these conditions is important because "feelings are most easily changed by changing the settings responsible for what is felt."

How much have behaviorists contributed to the understanding of emotion, in general? Not surprisingly, they have contributed little to our understanding of the cognitive or physiological aspects of emotion (as Skinner readily admitted). They have taught us a great deal about emotional expression and also how to apply their behavioral insights in practical settings. No group of therapists is more skilled than behavior therapists at carefully ferreting out why people do the things they do—and then developing concrete plans to teach them other, more productive, ways of behaving.

In some respects, the behavioral and evolutionary approaches overlap. All behaviorists appear to pay homage to evolutionary principles in one form or another. Also, as we have seen, both learning and evolutionary theorists emphasize adaptation to the environment. However, behaviorists such as John Watson have emphasized learning mechanisms, while evolutionary theorists, such as Charles Darwin himself, have emphasized inherited biological processes. Finally, both groups are particularly interested in the expressive aspects of emotion; they emphasize gestures, movements, facial expressions, or other overt activities. These are the aspects of emotion that interact with the environment directly and that play an immediate role in adaptation.

In this chapter, then, we have reviewed traditional approaches to the ways people experience, react, and express their feelings. First we considered the pioneering work of Sigmund Freud, a psychodynamic and motivational theorist who was especially interested in emotional *experience*. Freud was fascinated by the discovery that both conscious thoughts and unconscious processes produce emotional behavior. He illustrated how the defense mechanisms protect people from self-knowledge too painful to endure. Then we turned to the work and early theorizing of William James, Walter Cannon, and Paul MacLean, who were especially interested in the *physiology* of emotion. Cannon and MacLean maintained that the control center for the emotions is in the brain, in the limbic system. James argued that people's emotional reactions are primarily influenced by their visceral and motor reactions. Finally, we explored the early work of Charles Darwin, J. B. Watson, and B. F. Skinner, who were primarily interested in emotional *expression*. Darwin found that emotions evolved because they were adaptive: They increased the species' chances to survive and reproduce. Watson and Skinner continued from there, arguing that people will learn to express their emotions in ways that work in the current environment, and that emotional reactions can be learned or extinguished.

These theorists have ignited some brush fires which illuminate the terrain to be explored. In the next four chapters, we see what modern theorists, with more penetrating lights, have had to say about these topics.

Summing Up

- Emotion has been defined as "a motivational predisposition to respond experientially, physiologically, and behaviorally to certain internal and external variables."

- Theorists such as Freud, Jung, Bowlby, Rado, and Leeper take a motivational approach to explaining emotional experience. Freud argued that emotion is fueled by the instincts and that unconscious processes often guide our behavior. The mind utilizes a variety of defense mechanisms to shield itself from painful information. These include repression, regression, rationalization, and projection.

- Psychologists who are interested in physiological aspects of emotion have utilized both psychophysiological and neurochemical methods.

- William James argued that "bodily changes follow directly the perception of the exciting fact, and . . . our feelings of the same changes as they occur is emotion." The James-Lange theory argued that motor and visceral reactions are of critical importance.

- Walter Cannon argued that people are programmed to try to maintain an ideal "adaptation level." He pointed out that we cannot explain emotions by referring to visceral changes—they are simply too slow, too diffuse, too undifferentiated, too independent of emotion. He proposed that the brain, particularly the thalamus, is the control center for emotions.

- Paul MacLean argued that, in the course of evolution, humans have ended up with a forebrain that is a triune structure. The oldest type of brain is reptilian; the second is inherited from the early mammals; and the third from the late mammals/primates.

- Theorists have also focused on the expressive aspects of emotion. Charles Darwin proposed three principles for understanding emotional expression: (a) the principle of serviceable associated habits; (b) the principle of antithesis; and (c) the principle of direct action of the excited nervous system.

- Theorists who have emphasized a behavioral approach to emotion are John Watson, B. F. Skinner, J. R. Millenson, and O. Hobart Mowrer. Watson argued that there are three innate emotions: fear, rage, and love. He conducted a series of experiments to demonstrate that emotions can be learned or extinguished.

- Skinner argued that emotions may be reflexes or operants whose origins are in evolutionary or current consequences of behavior. This approach has led to therapies that emphasize modification of emotional behaviors.

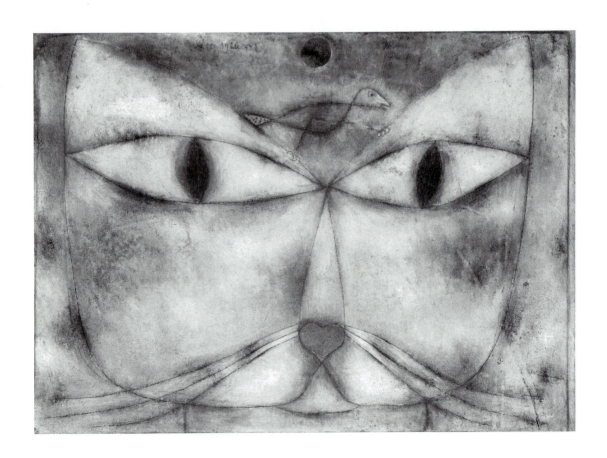

3
Motivational and Cognitive Theories of Emotion

Introduction

Jung's Analytical Psychology
The Structure of Personality
Psychological Types: The Dimensions of Personality
Feeling: Function versus Affect (Emotion)
Critique of Jung

Cognitive Approaches
Attribution Theory
Richard Lazarus
Stanley Schachter
Robert Zajonc
Gordon Bower

Conclusion

Summing Up

FIGURE 3.1   *Cat and Bird.* Paul Klee. 1928. Oil and ink on gesso on canvas, mounted on wood. 15 inches by 21 inches (38.1 cm by 53.2 cm). Sidney and Harriet Janis Collection Fund and gift of Suzy Prudden and Joan H. Meijer in memory of F. H. Hirschland. Museum of Modern Art, New York.

Introduction

*G*reat thoughts come from the heart.

LUC DE CLAPIERS,
MARQUIS DE VAUVENARGUES

One day, Carolyn called a friend in tears. Carolyn's husband, Bart, was a happy-go-lucky rascal. He was good looking, good natured, and a great deal of fun. Unfortunately, Bart had a dark side, too. He drank too much, flirted outrageously with other women at parties, and lost job after job. Carolyn had decided that his drunken gaiety at a party the night before was the last straw. "Look what he's done to me. I can't stand the humiliation. I feel terrible. I spent all last night crying. I'm dizzy. I have no energy. I'm sick. I hurt all over. I can't go on with this marriage." Two days later, Carolyn called again, this time in a cheery mood. "Oh, I'm not worried about Saturday night anymore. That's just Bart," she said. "It turns out that it wasn't Bart that was making me miserable. I have the flu." She was vastly relieved.

Examples of this sort illustrate the powerful role that cognition plays in emotion. Our fantasies about what ought to be, our clear-eyed perceptions of what is and what will be, all play a role in shaping our emotional lives.

A number of eminent researchers have been fascinated with the links between motivation and emotion or cognition and emotion. In chapter 2, we reviewed the pioneering work of Sigmund Freud and his insights into the unconscious processes that shape emotional experience. This chapter focuses on the work of a second motivational theorist, Carl Gustav Jung. His review of the unconscious forces that shape emotion is a mixture of poetry, metaphor, and science. Jung's approach (like Freud's) has been labeled "psychodynamic" or "motivational." These terms merely indicate that he is interested in the ways that unconscious mental processes guide and motivate emotional behavior. Then we turn to the more recent work of cognitive theorists—Richard Lazarus, Stanley Schachter, Robert Zajonc, and Gordon Bower. These researchers focus on the cognitive, and generally conscious, steps that people follow in perceiving, processing, and dealing with emotional information. Together, these views of the unconscious and conscious bases of emotion represent the experiential perspective in our tripartite model of emotion.

Jung's Analytical Psychology

Carl Gustav Jung (1875–1961) was born in a small village in Switzerland. His autobiography, *Memories, Dreams, Reflections* (1961), is surprisingly candid. In it, he discusses the personal experiences that shaped his intellectual vision. Jung was a solitary, bookish, introverted child. He spent his free time alone, exploring mountains, woods, and swamps. He worried over religious and philosophical questions. His spiritual life was a world of dreams and visions. He had a sickly mother and an irritable and difficult father. The village boys thought him a bit odd. Nonetheless, they liked him.

As a young physician, Jung studied with a variety of eminent psychiatrists. Early in his career, Jung began corresponding with Sigmund Freud, who was to have a powerful impact on his life. The two became fast friends; Freud called Jung his adopted eldest son, his crown prince, and his successor. In 1910, with Freud's encouragement, Jung was elected the first president of the International Psychoanalytic Association.

Despite the fact that Freud and Jung were so close, they eventually found themselves at odds. Jung was too independent to be a "crown prince." He disagreed with some of Freud's ideas (for example, whether sex was central or just another instinct) and knew he had to follow his own star. He suspected that Freud was an authoritarian who would not be able to accept such heresy and that independence would threaten their friendship. It did. In 1913, Jung broke with Freud. Jung observed, "I could not accept Freud's placing authority above truth" (Jung quoted in Campbell, 1971, p. xx). The break was painful for both men. Jung was left confused and uncertain, unable to read, write, or do research. He resigned from the University of Zurich and as president of the association. The next three years were times of reflection and preparation for change. Eventually, Jung began to develop his own "analytical theory." He traveled to India, Ceylon, Africa, and the United States. When he retreated to his summer house—a tower of stone he built for himself on the shores of Lake Zurich—he began to think and write on an enormous array of topics. His interests were to include Eastern and Western religions, mysticism, the occult, mythology, alchemy, and theories of the human psyche. In 1948, he founded the first C. G. Jung Institute, which is still in Zurich. He died in 1961.

Jung was interested in all aspects of personality. He was not primarily a theorist of emotion. However, unlike most twentieth-century theorists, Jung gave the same theoretical status to feelings as he gave to thinking (cognitive processes). Of all the theorists in the psychodynamic tradition, Jung has the most to say about the motivational consequences of emotion.

THE STRUCTURE OF PERSONALITY

Let us begin by briefly reviewing Jung's general theoretical model, which he termed **analytical psychology**. This will help us to understand what he has to say about affect (emotion) and feeling. Box 3.1 contains an outline of Jung's model. You might check your memory by referring to this "scorecard" now and again. (For convenient collections of Jung's theoretical views, see Joseph Campbell [1971], Violet deLaszlo [1959], or Jung [1909–1960] *Collected Works, Part I,* Volumes 7, 8, and 9.)

BOX 3.1

The Structure of Personality

The personality or *psyche* is an integrated whole. It consists of three parts—the conscious, the personal unconscious, and the collective unconscious.

1. *The Conscious:* People are able to process conscious information in four ways—thinking, feeling, sensing, and intuiting.

2. *The Personal Unconscious:* This structure consists of material that has been stored away in memory. People's unique history is organized into complexes—personally meaningful thematic cores.

3. *The Collective Unconscious:* The species' collective wisdom is recorded here. The species' history is organized into archetypes, collectively meaningful images and symbols.

The Psyche

Jungians contend that personality is an integrated whole, the **psyche.** The psyche includes all thought, feeling, and behavior, conscious or unconscious. The psyche consists of three parts—the conscious, the personal unconscious, and the collective unconscious.

Consciousness. Children possess consciousness from birth onward. Their consciousness expands as they become aware of their parents, toys, and the world around them. In time, children become conscious that they are individuals, different from everyone and everything around them. This process is called **individuation.** People are able to possess conscious information in four ways—thinking, feeling, sensing, and intuiting. Different people tend to rely on one technique more than others. For example, scholars may prefer to think through a problem; artists may try to feel their way to the right answer.

According to both Freud and Jung, a person's ego is made up of all his or her conscious perceptions, thoughts, feelings, and memories. The ego is a strict gatekeeper. Each day, people are bombarded with an infinite amount of material. The ego determines which stimuli they will even notice, how they will evaluate such experiences, and what they will choose to remember. Of course, extremely powerful stimuli are more likely to ram through the gates of the ego than are weak stimuli. A person's identity and sense of continuity comes from the ego.

People cling to their conscious perceptions; that is, after all, all that is available to them. Nonetheless, the psyche is like an iceberg. The conscious processes are the visible tip, but beneath the surface loom the the personal and collective unconscious. They possess the real power to shape the fate of men and women.

The heart has its reasons which reason does not know.

PASCAL

The Personal Unconscious. According to Jung, the **personal unconscious** (which roughly corresponds with Freud's preconscious) is a sort of attic, filled to overflowing with material that has been stored away. Each individual's personal unconscious is unique. It is stuffed with thoughts too painful to remember, personal conflicts, unresolved problems, subliminal perceptions, and perceptions so trivial they never even reach consciousness. (For example, "What color is the cover of this book?" Probably you don't care, but perhaps the information is stored.) Nothing is ever given away or lost. Someday it might be needed, and then it can be retrieved from a dusty corner, brushed off, and used.

Steady traffic goes on between the conscious and the personal unconscious. The conscious mind can easily retrieve that friend's name that is on the tip of your tongue. It simply sorts through the files and pulls it out. This stored material spills out, sometimes in a disorderly array, in dreams. For some reason, in old age, early memories come flooding back in vivid clarity.

In the personal unconscious, perceptions, thoughts, emotions, and memories tend to clump together in patterns or "constellations." These are called **complexes.** This term has become a part of everyday language. When we speak of people who have an inferiority complex, a mother complex, or a "hangup" about sex, we mean that they are so preoccupied with themselves, their mothers, or sex that they can hardly think of anything else. As Jung observed, "A person does not have a complex; the complex has him." Complexes are thematic cores. The person's unique history has been organized into personally meaningful categories.

At this point, Freudian and Jungian theory diverge. Jung concluded that there is yet another level to the human psyche—the collective unconscious. This aspect of his theory has the most to say about the nature of human emotion.

The things we know best are those we have not learned.

LUC DE CLAPIERS, MARQUIS DE VAUVENARGUES

The Collective Unconscious. Jung's proposition is a controversial one: Evolution provides a blueprint for the psyche as well as for the body. He argued that people possess a **collective** or **transpersonal unconscious.** This collective unconscious contains the archetypes. All our prehistoric ancestors' experiences are genetically coded into these preexistent forms. As Jung (1959) states:

My thesis, then, is as follows: In addition to our immediate consciousness, which is of a thoroughly personal nature . . . there exists a second psychic system of a collective, universal, and impersonal nature which is identical in all individuals. This collective unconscious does not develop individually but is inherited. (p. 43)

Jung argued that just as an individual's history is recorded in the personal unconscious, a species' accumulated wisdom is recorded in the collective unconscious. We have inherited primordial images from our animal and pre-historic ancestors, the tendency to see the world as they once did. For example, Jung observed that people do not have to be painstakingly taught to fear the dark or snakes. They inherit their primitive ancestors' predispositions to fear them; the latent images of fear are engraved in their brains. All it takes is the slightest hint of danger to bring out these primitive fears.

Although humankind is born with predispositions (or forms) for thinking, feeling, and behaving in certain ways, whether these forms ever develop into clear ideas, images, dreams, or behavior depends entirely on the individual's experiences. Duane Schultz (1976) observes: "It is important to note that we do not inherit these collective experiences directly. We do not, for example, inherit an actual fear of snakes. Rather, we inherit the potentiality or pre-disposition to fear snakes. . . . Whether the predisposition becomes a reality depends on the specific experiences the individual encounters" (p. 125). We will come to fear snakes, then, only if we have at least one unpleasant en-counter with them.

The collective unconscious has a powerful impact on people's person-alities and on their thoughts, emotions, actions, and memories; it is all-con-trolling.

The Instincts and the Archetypes

Like Freud, Jung took it for granted that all animals are programmed to behave in certain ways. He observed that "we use the word 'instinct' very frequently in ordinary speech" (1960, in Campbell, 1971, p. 48). For Jung, instincts "are impersonal, universally distributed, hereditary factors of a dynamic or motivating character. . . . Moreover, the instincts are not vague and indefinite by nature, but are specifically formed motive forces which . . . pursue their inherent goals" (1959, in Campbell, 1971, p. 61). Today, the notion that both heredity and environment shape behavior seems fairly commonsensical. The red squirrel instinctively buries nuts as winter approaches, the robin builds a nest each spring, and newborns suck when a nipple is put to their mouth. A person who lived a completely instinctual life would eat when hungry, drink when thirsty, flee when frightened, and strike out when annoyed. Of course, people can be taught to do otherwise.

In the first half of the twentieth century, psychologists influenced by theories of learning—which represented a large segment of American psy-chology—believed that the human mind was more or less a *tabula rasa* (blank slate) at birth and that almost all human behavior was learned. To believe otherwise was considered unscientific and counterproductive. Thus, Jung's views were ridiculed or ignored. In recent years, however, even learning theorists have begun to document the impact of heredity on personality and behavior (Seligman, 1970). Thus, the scientific community, including neuroscientists interested in brain-behavior relationships, has become a bit more receptive to views such as Jung's (Henry, 1986).

Although Freud and Jung may have agreed that men and women are propelled by instinctive forces, they disagreed as to the nature of these forces. Freud thought of the instincts as an amorphous reservoir of raw energy; the instincts provided the power for behavior, but they gave neither distinct form nor direction to it. Childhood experiences determined how instinctive energy was channeled. Jung, of course, thought instincts provided relatively detailed blueprints for behavior.

Today, we sometimes hear echos of the Freud-Jung debate when we listen to theorists argue about the nature of emotion. Some theorists take the Freudian-like position, arguing that emotions are tied to general arousal. (See, for example, Duffy, 1957 or Schachter, 1966.) Others take a Jungian-like position that emotions provide distinct shapes to behavior. For example, Plutchik (1980a) contends that the emotions are "prototypes," which motivate an integrated and complex set of subjective, physiological and behavioral responses.

Closely related to the issue of the instinctual forms of behavior is the concept of archetypes. In Jung's theory, the instincts are stored in the collective unconscious in the form of images or symbols termed **archetypes.** Jung (1959, in Campbell, 1971) observes: "There is good reason for supposing that the archetypes are unconscious images of the instincts themselves, in other words, that they are *patterns of instinctual behavior*" (p. 61). An archetype is a "prototype," "primordial image," or "mythological image." Presumably, in the course of evolution, our ancestors replayed the same scenes and experienced the same emotions over and over in the same situations, generation after generation. The archetype is, however, not a specific memory; rather it is a representation of those experiences. In particular, it is a "subjective emotional reaction to or remembrance of previously experienced significant events in the history of the species" (Jung, 1953, cited in Monte, 1987, p. 249).

Jung spent more than 40 years investigating the archetypes. The number of archetypes has no theoretical limit because the history of the species contains unlimited significant experiences. Among those Jung identified are birth, death, rebirth, God, the hero, power, the earth mother, the demon, the giant, and the child. Archetypes also include natural objects (such as the sun, the moon, wind, rivers, trees, fire, and animals) and man-made objects such as rings and weapons. The archetype, then, is not a fully developed photograph.

Rather, it is more like a negative that has to be developed using the material of conscious experience.

Jung described several archetypes in detail. A few of these are especially important in understanding his view of emotion—the persona, the anima and animus, and the shadow.

The Persona. Greek and Roman actors wore a persona, a mask over the face to indicate their role. The **persona** is the face we put on in front of others. (In chapter 6, we discuss the fact that societies' "display rules" provide strict guidelines for how emotion should be expressed.) In Jung's (1953) terms, "It is, as its name implies, only a mask of the collective psyche, a mask that *feigns individuality,* making others and oneself believe that one is individual, whereas one is simply acting a role through which the collective psyche speaks" (p. 158). During the day, people put on one persona after another. At work, they may play the part of the serious young executive—possessing the style, manner, dress, and speech that is appropriate to that role. At night, they may play the role of the smooth "macho man"; their dress, manner, and speech might be quite different. The persona is the archetype of conformity. Obviously, everyone has to play a role a good deal of the time. But people can overdo it. If any one archetype, such as the persona, is allowed to dominate the personality, things get out of balance. In Jung's (1953) words, "Whoever builds up too good a persona for himself naturally has to pay for it with irritability" (p. 193)—and perhaps worse. People who are on stage all the time eventually wake up and realize they have wasted their lives. They may be successful, but they feel emotionally lonely, empty, and depressed.

The Anima and Animus. The psyche's outward, conforming face is the persona. One of the psyche's inward, hidden faces is the **anima** (in males) or **animus** (in females). Naturally, men and women are a unique blend of masculine and feminine. (Today, we know that men and women are surprisingly similar psychologically, physiologically, and behaviorally. They are far more similar than the Victorian scientists of Jung's time believed.) Jung (1961) argued that both men and women embrace an archetype of the opposite sex, owing to the thousands of past generations of living together and taking on one another's characteristics. In Jung's words, "I came to see that this inner feminine figure plays a typical, or archetypal, role in the unconscious of a man, and I called her the 'anima.' The corresponding figure in the unconscious of woman I called the 'animus' " (p. 186). Normally, a man's natural masculinity is softened by the anima; a woman's femininity is strengthened by the animus. If men and women try to deny their natures, terrified of being called a "sissy" or a "tomboy," they will succeed only in becoming rigid caricatures, denying their complex natures.

The fact that men and women eternally carry within themselves an image of the "perfect" man or woman has a profound effect on their romantic choices and feelings (see Johnson, 1986 a and b). Jung (1954b) observes: "Since this image is unconscious, it is always unconsciously projected upon the person of the beloved, and is one of the chief reasons for passionate attraction or aversion" (Vol. 17, p. 198). Some men are afflicted with the quest for the "perfect woman." They know exactly what she will look like (warm brown eyes, honey colored hair, and tall), think like, what her personality will be like (warm, soft, yielding, but independent), and how she will feel and act. Again and again, a man thinks he has found her, only to be disappointed. If only he were better looking, richer, taller, he knows he could find her. The real women he encounters are fine, but not quite right, somehow.

In time, most men adapt to reality. But some men can never give up the dream. They keep spotting the perfect embodiment of their anima—just out of sight, just over the horizon. Women, too, seek the animus. They search for the man who is heroic, intellectual, artistic, and athletic. Modern men and women have pinned their hopes on finding Mr. and Ms. Right, only to be confronted with reality. Real people are imperfect. It is not surprising, then, that many couples are disillusioned, frustrated, and lonely and complain that they cannot communicate.

The Shadow. This archetype represents humanity's basic animal nature. It is the source of what is worst and best in people. Those who have an overstuffed persona are too civilized and conforming. Their shadow is crushed and spiritless. They lack insight, spontaneity, creativity, or passion, and they have cut themselves off from the wisdom of their instinctual natures. Of course, if the shadow were allowed to run amok, people would be selfish, cruel, vicious, animalistic, and crude. In Bertolt Brecht and Kurt Weill's *The Threepenny Opera,* petty criminal MacHeath (Mack the Knife) is a shadowy figure. His similarity to the lower orders of animals is evident:

> Oh the shark has pretty teeth, dear.
> And he shows them pearly white.
> Just a jackknife, has MacHeath, dear.
> But he keeps it out of sight.

Note the ever-present theme of oppositional forces in Jung's archetypes; the source of considerable psychic energy derives from the conflicts created by the archetypes in the depths of the unconscious. Once again, balance is called for. It is important every now and then for an innocent Little Red Riding Hood to run with the wolves.

In summary: Deep within the structure of the psyche lies the collective unconscious. The collective unconscious is the powerful center in which the archetypes, the emotions, and instinctual energy reside. Because we are primarily interested in the emotions, it is important to remember that the archetypes, the "primordial images" of the instincts, are not pictures, but *emotional forms* that predispose people to perceive the world and react to it emotionally and behaviorally. Lawrence Stewart (1987) proposes that Jung was uncertain as to which came first, emotion or archetype. He concludes that in Jung's writings chronologically, "first came the affect [emotion], then the archetype. The archetype then takes precedence over the affect, yet is inseparable from it: where there is an archetype there is an affect" (p. 36). Thus, in the end, the archetypes and the emotions are inseparably linked.

PSYCHOLOGICAL TYPES: THE DIMENSIONS OF PERSONALITY

To place Jung's "feeling" construct into proper perspective, we will find it helpful to see how it relates to the other functions of conscious life in his theory. In 1921, Jung published *Psychological Types*. In this book, to use current terminology, Jung began by pointing out that people perceive and process information about the world in very different ways, according to their type. As a consequence, people possess very different personalities and characters. Let us outline Jung's typology.

The Attitudes

Jung (1953) observed that people—from Sigmund Freud and Alfred Adler (the colleagues he knew best) to great historical figures—differed markedly in attitude. Some (like Adler) were shy and introverted, while others (like Freud) were outgoing and extraverted. **Introverts** possess a "subjective attitude." They focus their psychic energy (libido) inward. They think their own thoughts, sometimes trying to catch inner rhythms they can barely sense. They are "hesitant, reflective and retiring." Others sometimes see them as aloof, antisocial, and reserved and preoccupied. They seek answers from themselves. **Extraverts** possess an "objective attitude." They focus their psychic energy outward and are interested in people and things. They are "outgoing, candid, and accommodating." They seek information from objective reality. These two attitudes are incompatible; one cannot look inward and outward at the same time; the two can, of course, alternate. People are never totally introverted or extraverted. The secretary who seems so introverted at the office may "break out" on the dance floor every weekend. Generally, however, people will be primarily one or the other. Most of us can probably make an educated guess as to how we and our friends would rate on this dimension.

The Functions

A **function** is a "form of psychic activity that remains theoretically the same under varying circumstances" (Jung, 1938, p. 547). Theoretically, people can "function"—that is, obtain and process information—in four ways: by sensation, intuition, thinking, or feeling. We will examine only two of these in more detail—thinking and feeling.

Thinking. People use two functions, thinking and feeling, to make judgments about their worlds. We can think about facts—naming, categorizing, organizing, analyzing, and synthesizing them—or we can feel about them—judging how good or bad, pleasant or unpleasant, acceptable or unacceptable things are, and the like. Both thinking and feeling are equally valid ways for evaluating the raw data that people obtain from their senses and intuitions. Of course, thinking and feeling are different methods of information processing; each may yield a different form of answer.

In **thinking,** people form concepts, manipulate ideas, try to assess the truth of various ideas, solve problems, and understand things. Thinking involves the analytical, logical, sequential processing of information, the "linking up of representations by means of a concept, whereas in other words, an act of judgment prevails" (Jung, 1938, p. 611).

Feeling. By contrast, **feeling** is a "process that takes place between the ego and a given content, a process, moreover, that imparts to the content a definite *value* in the sense of acceptance or rejection ('like' or 'dislike')" (Jung, 1938, p. 543). Feelings tell one whether something is agreeable or disagreeable, "what a thing is *worth* to you" (Jung, 1968, p. 12).

Jung (Jung & von Franz, 1964) summarizes the four functions of the psyche very neatly:

> These four functional types correspond to the obvious means by which consciousness obtains its orientation to experience. *Sensation* (i.e. sense perception) tells you that something exists; *thinking* tells you what it is; *feeling* tells you whether it is agreeable or not; and *intuition* tells you whence it comes and where it is going. (p. 61)

Interestingly enough, although most people tend to deal with the world in repetitive, stereotyped ways corresponding to their personality type, that is not the ideal in Jung's view. If people are too extraverted (or introverted) or too obsessed with thinking (to the exclusion of feeling), they cut themselves off from the range of possibilities of human experience. For the psyche, the ideal is **equilibrium.**

FEELING: FUNCTION VERSUS AFFECT (EMOTION)

Let us now integrate these various aspects of Jung's theory with our general discussion of feelings and emotions. In Jung's typology, feelings have two important roles: (a) People have the ability to use feelings as an important guide to their likes and dislikes; and (b) the emotions are made up of feelings. Let us summarize Jung's view of these two very different types of feelings.

"Feeling" as Function

First, Jung argues that people's conscious perceptions can be shaped by either thinking or feeling. Jung differs dramatically from other theorists in his insistence that both thinking and feeling should be classified as equally important functions, in the trust he places in people's intellects *and* feelings, and in the attention he lavishes on trying to understand both. (Many psychological theorists, of course, have generally idealized thought and dismissed feeling as a way to process important information.) In Jung's system, conscious feelings are an enormously significant function. Without feeling there can be no appreciation of the moment, other people, or the world. There can be little differentiation between the individual ("me") and the environment, no evaluation, and no adaptation to the inner or outer world. In history, few scientists have treated feeling with such respect.

"Feelings" as Affects (Emotions)

In the European tradition, both Jung and Freud used the term affect to indicate what we now term emotion. In Jung's theory, emotions are shaped by feelings. Jung (1938) stated that although feeling is "primarily a process," it can also be "isolated in the form of 'mood', quite apart from the momentary contents of consciousness or momentary sensations" (p. 543). According to Jung, when a person's conscious feelings become intense, they begin to produce physiological effects and are transformed into full-blown affective or emotional reactions. This quotation from Jung (1938) summarizes this important distinction and gives us some of the flavor of this eloquent theorist's writing:

> On practical grounds, however, it is advisable to discriminate affect from feeling, since feeling can be a disposable function, whereas affect is usually not so. Similarly, affect is clearly distinguished from feeling by quite perceptible physical innervations, while feeling for the most part lacks them, or their intensity is so slight that they can only be demonstrated by the finest instruments, as for example the psycho-galvanic phenomenon [sweating]. Affect becomes cumulative through the sensation of the physical innervations released by it. (pp. 522–523)

To summarize: Usually, feelings as conscious functions are relatively tepid. Feelings provide a running commentary on moment-by-moment sensations/intuitions. Such evaluations determine whether various events are significant. These feelings usually have little emotional impact—they are "disposable." Sometimes, however, feelings become intense. Psychic energy excites ("innervates") a series of physiological responses, which give rise to emotion. Jung proposed that conscious and physiological events are "cumulative" and "reciprocal." Emotion is produced by the interaction of the two. Presumably, the more people feel, the more physiologically "innervated" they will be. In turn, the more physiologically excited they are, the more they will feel. Jung makes it clear that he does not take a James-Lange view. The source of emotion is "psychic" energy, not physiological processes. Physiological processes are simply the precursors of emotion, not the cause. Psychic and physiological processes combine to form the stuff of emotion.

Implications

Jung's views on feelings and affect have several interesting implications for the psychology of emotion (see Hillman, 1970). First, since feelings may appear both in the form of functions as well as contents of the mind, this expands the notion of feeling beyond our usual sense—feelings are not just "moods" or "emotions." People can also use feelings in their struggles to make sense of their chaotic impressions, not only by thinking things through but also by feeling them through. As James Hillman (1970) states, "We may feel our thoughts, discover their value, their importance" just as we may "feel . . . feelings," that is, have feelings about our feelings (p. 129). For instance, how do you "feel" about being angry? About falling in love? For Jung, every aspect of the personality is potentially colored and shaped by feeling.

Second, people differ in how skilled they are at using intellect and feeling to evaluate information. For example, some people know full well what they think. What they have trouble with is knowing what they *feel*. (Thinking is their dominant function; feeling an inferior one.) Other people are quite skilled at using both of these processes to deal with information. For example, clinicians are trained to use both their minds and their emotions to figure out what is going on with a client. On occasion, therapists start to feel anxious as they listen to their clients. The untrained therapist will look inward for an explanation. "Did I say something gauche? What should I do next? Maybe they should see a *real* therapist. I'm too young for this line of work!" The experienced therapist knows enough to probe further. The client may look calm, but the therapist knows it is time to do a little detective work. What is the client thinking about? What is he feeling? Generally, in such situations, clients report that they are feeling uneasy (Hsee, et al., in press).

Hillman (1970) suggests that underdeveloped "feeling botches up values and makes the wrong feeling-judgments. . . . Its timing is off. It does not inform the person how he feels about this or that, whether he likes or loves, whether he is adaptively related to what is taking place outside or inside. . . . His work-world has no feeling (moral or social) consequences. Even such positive feelings as love, joy, or giving may be handled inadequately" (p. 129).

In other words, underdeveloped feelings (as functions) may lead to inappropriate behavior or cognition. In this society, some people must learn how to think more clearly. Most, however, probably need to learn how to feel more clearly. People who can do both have closer and more fulfilling relationships with others and are more effective in shaping their world.

Third, Jung's work suggests that people can be educated. Their feeling function can be strengthened. Some shifts in the dominance of functions happen as people age. In middle age, many people get better at integrating thought and feeling. People who are thinking-dominant can be taught how consciously to perceive and accept their feelings: "to like what one likes, to feel what one feels, to refuse what one truly cannot abide" (Hillman, 1970, p. 130). Of course, this is exactly what psychotherapists try to do. They try to teach people to know what they think and feel and use all that information in making decisions about their lives.

Perhaps at this point, you may be beginning to feel a little uneasy. People surely want to be fully aware of their positive feelings, but what about negative ones? "Negative feelings are those either inwardly experienced as bad and painful, such as guilt, boredom, fear, or as socially condemned, such as hatred and envy" (Hillman, 1970, p. 129). Do people really want to become sensitive to those feelings? Jung would answer, "Yes." He points out that the problem is not that people possess negative feelings, but that they are poor at knowing what to do about them. When people's attitudes and functions are in balance, they possess a rich array of techniques for dealing with overpowering emotion. In Western cultures, however, people tend to idealize a narrow band of attitudes and functions: extraversion, sensing, and thinking. Most people tend not to cultivate the remaining attitudes and functions: introversion, intuition, and feeling. Since many people possess little emotional knowledge and even less experience in dealing with it, they tend to make major emotional mistakes—they may lash out at the wrong person, in the wrong way, at the wrong time. Things are not dealt with calmly; problems repeat themselves. What causes problems are not emotions per se, but an inability to deal with them. Thus, in Jung's view, societies would do well to educate people not just to think, but to think *and* feel.

Measuring Emotion

Jung's theory also had implications for the study of associative and physiological processes in emotion. Early in his career, Jung had been interested in using word associations to get a glimpse into the unconscious. He noticed that when he read through a list of words and asked his clients to blurt out the first thing that came to mind, clients could generally speed along until they came to an emotionally significant word. Then they had trouble. Jung and his colleague, Franz Riklin, began to investigate this phenomenon in a more systematic way. They constructed the Word Association Test, a list of 100 words—including such items as *head, death, table, angry, tree, money, white, anxiety,* and *abuse*. Some terms (such as *table*) were relatively neutral; others (such as *death*) had powerful emotional connotations (Jung, 1973). The experimenter recited the words, one at a time. Clients were to say the first thing that popped into their minds.

Jung used several techniques to assess how much emotion the meaningful versus the neutral words aroused. First, he systematically recorded the presence or absence of 11 "diagnostic signs" of emotionality: such as, did the subject take an unusually long time to respond to a word; fail to respond altogether; make a superficial response (say, responding with a homonym, such as bear/bare); or display other signs of nervousness, such as laughing, twitching, stammering, or slips of the tongue. It was Jung's belief that this method revealed the symbolic bases undergirding the patterns of ideas and affect, the complexes.

Jung also assessed emotionality via several surprisingly modern physiological measures, including respiration rate and the galvanic skin response (GSR), a measure of the resistance of the skin that was introduced in chapter 2. Jung saw the GSR as a "window to the unconscious processes" (Hassett, 1978, p. 33). On the basis of this research, Jung concluded that one could spot complexes that were powerful for people by observing which words aroused emotion and which did not. He found that if one word (say, inferiority) aroused emotion, related words (say, shame, or humiliation) would, too. From this he reasoned that ideas, emotions, and memories must cluster together in complexes of the unconscious.

CRITIQUE OF JUNG

At first, readers may be slightly taken aback to find Carl Jung's work included in a chapter on current motivational and cognitive theories. He was, after all, the "number two" man, after Freud, in the hierarchy of psychodynamic theorists. Nonetheless, he had a great deal to say about emotion.

In the early 1900s, American psychologists were not very receptive to Jung's ideas. He seemed too mystical, too metaphorical, too vague. Worse yet, he later expressed interest in such taboo topics as alchemy, astrology, spiritualism, seances, visions, and dreams. No wonder he was generally ignored. Critics remain sharply divided as to the value of Jung's ideas. Some assume that his theorizing about, say, the antecedents of feeling and emotion is clear, consistent, and original. Others rip into his ideas. They criticize him for a lack of a systematic approach, "inconsistencies and contradictions" (Schultz, 1976, p. 137).

Today, however, a variety of social changes make Jung's theorizing more acceptable. In a new age, in which we read about millions of Westerners aligning their chakras, consulting shamans, ringing Tibetan bells, meditating, and drinking Ayurvedic teas, Jung's ideas don't seem so strange anymore. As Calvin Hall and Gardner Lindzey (1970) stated, with these "growing trend[s] in Western society, especially among young people . . . Jung will come to be recognized as the spiritual and intellectual leader of this revolutionary movement" (p. 112). Moreover, it has been pointed out that "artistic expression of Jung's theories can be seen in many contemporary films, plays, and novels" (Papalia & Olds, 1985, p. 493).

More importantly, Jung's theorizing seems to be consistent with some recent discoveries in the neurosciences, physiology, and learning theory. We will discuss these in detail in chapter 4. For now, let us consider some examples and additional criticisms:

1. In his day, Jung's distinction between conscious and unconscious processes seemed suspect. Today, however, neuroscientists know that people are aware of only a bit of what goes on in their own minds. Conscious

awareness, analytical thought, and language are involved in only a small portion of the brain's activity. Most information is processed automatically, out of awareness, in other areas, especially those below the neocortex. (We are never conscious, for example, of the fact that our brains are signaling our hearts to beat or our lungs to breathe. We are not aware of the complex programming that it takes to walk, one step at a time, across the room.)

2. Researchers also know that the brain's left hemisphere (which is primarily concerned with linear thought and language) and right hemisphere, (which is primarily concerned with spatial perception, imagery, and certain emotional experiences) process different kinds of information. Thus, as we will see in chapter 6, the various parts of an emotional experience are stored, maintained, and activated in very different parts of the brain. For example, emotional stimuli may be recognized in one center and labeled in another, the neurochemicals involved in emotion triggered in another, and the signals for a facial response processed in still another portion of the brain (Le Doux, Wilson, & Gazzaniga, 1977).

3. Supporters argue that perhaps Jung was correct in proposing a connection between archetypal forms, images, and affect. All three may have an anatomical basis in, say, right hemisphere activity. Of course, cynics would disagree. They would add that the fact that the brain stores information in different ways in different centers provides no evidence that information is stored in archetypes. There is no evidence that any of Jung's archetypes—the persona, anima and animus, the shadow, or others—exist. It is clear that Jung's ideas will become more acceptable only if they can be translated into neurobiological language and survive the researchers' analyses.

4. Jung argued that feelings are as important as thoughts (cognitions) in processing information. The most primitive part of the psyche, the archetypes, are imaginal and "affect laden." As we will see in the next section, today's cognitive and learning theorists sound much like Jung when they acknowledge the importance of emotion and feeling in information processing.

5. Finally, certain of Jung's ideas have begun to find echoes in contemporary views on evolutionary mechanisms. For example, Louis Stewart (1987) recently suggested that Jungians should try to identify a system of "archetypal affects." These might include such affects as terror, anguish, rage, and disgust/humiliation. Interestingly enough, these archetypal affects parallel Silvan Tomkins' (1962, 1963) basic inherited emotions (see also Plutchik, 1980 a and b). When contemporary Jungians such as Stewart link the archetypes to affect, they are identifying the dynamic motivation which propels people to action. Just how such evolutionary programming is translated into specific forms of action is yet to be established.

Cognitive Approaches

In chapter 1, we defined emotion, in part, as "a predisposition to respond *experientially* to certain variables." As we have seen, in the early 1900s, Freud, Jung, and and a host of other psychodynamically oriented theorists had something to say about the unconscious processes that shape emotional experience. However, much of what we know about the cognitive aspects of emotions has been learned very recently—from theorists such as Richard Lazarus, Stanley Schachter, Robert Zajonc, and Gordon Bower, who have focused more on conscious processes.

Cognitive approaches gained prominence in the 1960s, as psychology began to break out of narrow behavioristic paradigms. Psychologists began to rediscover the important role of cognition, beliefs, expectations, thought, and information processing, in guiding human behavior. Essentially, a cognitive approach takes into account the "individual phenomenal (that is, experiential) world of the behaving organism" (Swenson, 1980). It focuses on *molar* behaviors such as purposes, plans, strategies, skills, and goals. Most recently, cognitive theorists have begun to emphasize the importance of cognitive appraisal in shaping emotions. Joseph Campos and Craig Sternberg (1981) observe:

> The recent history of the study of emotion has been dominated by approaches stressing cognitive factors. In theories of adult emotional response, cognitive appraisal now functions as the central construct. (p. 273)

No single theorist best represents the cognitive position. We introduce the cognitive approach by discussing attribution theory, which provides a general framework for understanding how people make sense of the world around them. Then, to get a perspective on this rapidly developing area, we focus especially on the work of Richard Lazarus as well as on the views of his critics, Stanley Schachter and Robert Zajonc. Finally, we review Gordon Bower's *state dependent memory theory* and another model, termed the *continuous feedback loop* view of the role of cognitions in emotion.

ATTRIBUTION THEORY

Attribution theory analyzes the way people go about making judgments about themselves and others. Attribution theorists share several assumptions (Jones et al., 1971):

> I. The individual attempts to assign a cause for important instances of his behavior and that of others; when necessary, he seeks information that enables him to do so.
>
> II. His assignment of causes is determined in a systematic manner.
>
> III. The particular cause that he attributes for a given event has important consequences for his subsequent feelings and behavior. (p. xi)

Fritz Heider (1980), the first attribution theorist, was interested in "naive psychology"—the cause and effect analyses of behavior made by the "man in the street." He pointed out that people tend to attribute people's behavior to either internal causes (for example, their personalities) or external causes (for example, their situations). For example, take the case of an elderly woman who had long been engaged in a bitter dispute with a group of "hippies" who lived next door. They invaded her jungle hideaway with blaring radios and a yard full of junked cars. One day, she had had enough of sweet reason. She strolled over to their front door, completely naked, and said that she wasn't moving until they shut off their radio and cleaned up their yard. They moved. Her children attributed her bizarre behavior to a manic-depressive personality—the problem was in her. She insisted that she was merely trying to shock her young neighbors into action—the problem was in them. (Probably it was a bit of both.)

Some attribution theorists have suggested that people generally use the same clues to figure out their own emotions as they would use if they were trying to figure out what others were feeling. For example, Daryl Bem (1972) argues that people come to "know" what they and others think and feel in this way: They observe how they (and others) are acting and the circumstances in which they find themselves, and they put two and two together. From such bits of evidence, they infer what they (and others) must be feeling. He observes:

> Thus, to the extent that internal cues are weak, ambiguous, or uninterpretable, the individual is functionally in the same position as an outside observer, an observer who must necessarily rely upon these same external cues to infer the individual's inner states. (p. 2)

The ancestor of every action is a thought.
RALPH WALDO EMERSON

RICHARD LAZARUS

Richard Lazarus (b. 1922) is a theoretician/researcher in the field of emotion, stress, and coping. He has taught at Johns Hopkins and Clark University, where he was the director of clinical training. Since 1957, he has been at the University of California, Berkeley.

Lazarus contends that cognitive appraisals are critically important in emotional experience. Generally, the first step in an emotional sequence is a cognitive appraisal of the situation (Lazarus et al., 1980) .

Cognitive Appraisal

People make three kinds of appraisals. In the process of **primary appraisal,** they try to decide what consequences impending events may have for their well-being. Is the dark figure approaching in the twilight likely to be **benign-positive** (the lover they were hoping to meet), **irrelevant** (just another jogger), or **stressful,** involving challenge, threat, or loss (members of the Bloody Angels gang)?

Once individuals have assessed the situation, they must proceed to a **secondary appraisal.** Here they must decide what they should and can do about the situation. Do they have the skills to make the most of their opportunity? Can they endure the troubles that are about to befall them? Avoid them? Ignore them in the hope that they'll go away?

After people perceive and react, the environment counterreacts. People, in turn, must appraise these reactions. People never stop making evaluative judgments about themselves and the world around them. The process of appraising again, **reappraisal,** highlights the interactive nature of people's encounters with other people and with the world.

Emotions

The appraisals people make determine which emotions—joy, love, anxiety, guilt, jealousy—they will feel and how intensely they will feel them.

In chapter 1, we found that some theorists think of emotions as sources of organized behavior. Other theorists think of them as disturbing elements. For Lazarus (1977), emotions are "complex disturbances." They interrupt ongoing activity, produce a disturbed state of arousal, and mobilize coping activities to the exclusion of other behaviors. We can detect such emotional disturbances in a variety of ways. We can look at subjective indicators of emotion (we can ask, "Are you angry?"), physiological indicators ("Does her face flush beet red?"), or action impulses ("Does he take a swing at his opponent?"). Lazarus points out that these three aspects of emotion are not always in synchrony:

> . . . the three components correlate very poorly with each other: an individual might report no distress, yet exhibit strong physiological reactions, or the behavioral responses signifying anger or fear might be inhibited as a result of social or internal pressures. (pp. 69–70)

A person may say one thing and do another. For example, when a motorist is pulled over by a traffic officer, his face may flush an angry red, but he will fearfully and submissively accede to all requests.

Coping

In Lazarus's theory, **coping** processes are a "central feature of the emotional state" (1977, p. 77). People who are emotionally "disturbed" when confronted with a challenging opportunity or a threat can utilize one of two coping strategies for dealing with the emotional situation: They can focus on changing their own feelings about the situation, or they can try to actually change the situation itself. Coping may take the form of palliation or direct action.

In **palliation**, individuals try to alter their own reactions to emotional events. They resolve to worry about problems "tomorrow," convince themselves that things will change "somehow," or shrug troubles off. "There's no use crying over spilt milk." There are two kinds of palliation. In the first, **intrapsychic palliation,** people can use a variety of cognitive strategies to avoid painful confrontations with reality. The strategies Lazarus describes parallel the Freudian defense mechanisms we listed in Table 2.3 (denial, projection, repression, and so forth). Lazarus (1977) observes:

> We have long recognized a large variety of such modes of coping; denial, intel-lectualized detachment, and attention deployment (trying not to think of the threat or focusing attention on nonthreatening features or tasks) are among the most common. (p. 81)

By contrast, in **somatic palliation,** people try to modify their physio-logical reactions to emotional events. They may meditate, jog, drink, or take drugs. Lazarus (1977) notes that when faced with the threat of final exams, an occasional student "uses tranquilizers, drinks to control his/her disturbed bodily state, takes sleeping pills . . . diverts attention for a time, or tries other techniques designed to quiet the heightened arousal" (p. 81).

Palliative forms of coping may be desirable or undesirable, depending on the circumstances. For example, Chuck Yeager (Yeager & Janos, 1985) is a World War II flying ace and the first man to fly faster than the speed of sound. In his autobiography, he describes the intrapsychic techniques he used to stay calm, cool, and collected in the face of death (see Box 3.2).

Such defensive techniques helped Yeager survive. Sometimes, of course, the rigid use of palliative techniques can be dangerous. People who toughen themselves may lose a sense of their own humanity. They may come to disdain those who have chosen to deal with reality in a more clear-eyed way. They may fail to take the precautions they need to stay alive. (If a frog is placed in a beaker of water that is gradually heated, instead of jumping out, it will adapt and adapt to the uncomfortable heat. Finally, it can adapt no more; it is dead. Some people seem to behave like that.)

Generally, however, people can shape their lives. They can engage in another form of coping, **direct action**. As Lazarus (1977) states, they can choose, plan, postpone, avoid, escape, or demolish. To some extent, they can even select their environments. People who hate confrontation can choose friends who are sweet, agreeable, and very timid. People who can't bear boredom can choose friends who are eccentric, fiery, and just a bit mad. In direct action, then, people attempt to regulate their emotions not by changing themselves, but by altering their circumstances.

Some coping reactions may be biological in origin. For example, the frustration-aggression link may be wired in. It seems natural, though futile, to kick the vending machine that swallows our quarter, gives us a trickle of soda, and belatedly supplies a cup. Other coping actions may require more conscious processing: For instance, planned avoidance (deciding to snub a

BOX 3.2

Dealing with Death

"Crash" is not a word pilots ever use. I don't really know why, but the word is avoided in describing what happens when several tons of metal plows itself and its pilot into the ground. Instead, we might say, "He augured in." Or, "He bought the farm." However you chose to describe it, we were doing it. . . .

A gruesome weeding-out process was taking place. Those who were killed in Nevada were likely to have been the first killed in combat. But those of us who did survive the training were rapidly becoming skilled combat pilots and a cohesive team. I turned my back on lousy fliers as if their mistakes were catching. When one of them became a grease spot on the tarmac, I almost felt relieved: it was better to bury a weak sister in training than in com-

bat, where he might not only bust his ass, but do something (or more than likely, fail to do something) that would bust two or three other asses in addition to his own.

But I got mad at the dead: angry at them for dying so young and so senselessly; angry at them for destroying expensive government property. . . . Anger was my defense mechanism. I've lost count of how many good friends have augured in over the years, but either you become calloused or you crack. . . . Some losses, of course, tore into your guts as if you'd been shot. Then there was nothing left to do but go out and get blind drunk. . . . Those who couldn't put a lid on their grief couldn't hack combat. They were either sent home or became a basket case. (pp. 20–21)

---

rival's party), premeditated aggression (placing a bomb in an airport), or inhibiting expression (being a "good sport" about losing the biology prize) require complicated plans.

The impact of the cognitive approach on current-day understanding of emotion cannot be overemphasized. We will bump into Lazarus's ideas again and again in this text.

Lazarus and His Critics

A number of theorists have objected to one or another aspect of Lazarus's paradigm. For example, one critic argues that cognitive appraisals do not precede emotional arousal but rather come later. Another argues that conscious cognition and affect can be processed separately. Still another emphasizes the interaction between the cognition and affect to a greater extent than does Lazarus. Let us turn to these approaches. First, we consider the theories of Stanley Schachter, who argues that cognitive appraisals do not precede emotion but follow it. Then we review the work of Robert Zajonc, who contends that emotion can exist without cognition. Finally, we review the work of Gordon Bower, who argues that emotion has a powerful effect on memory.

STANLEY SCHACHTER

Stanley Schachter (b. 1922) received his B.A. and M.A. degrees from Yale University and his Ph.D. from the University of Michigan. Most of his career has been spent at Columbia University. He received the American Psychological Association's Distinguished Scientific Award in 1969.

Mind and Body

Schachter (1971) argues that two components, mind and body, make a critical contribution to emotional experience. First, people's semiconscious assumptions about what they should be feeling in a given situation have a profound impact on what they do feel in that situation. A person learns—from society, parents, friends, and personal experience—which emotions, if any, it is appropriate to feel in various settings. She knows that she should feel joyous excitement when an old friend drops into town. He knows he should feel anxiety when a surly cowboy challenges him to meet him in the alley. (The untutored may well experience the very same physiological feelings on both occasions, a sort of "hyper" state.) According to Schachter, our assumptions as to what it is appropriate to feel have a critical impact on what we do feel.

*A*s Louis XVI said, when surrounded by a fierce mob, "Am I afraid? Feel my pulse." So a man may intensely hate another, but until his bodily frame is affected, he cannot be said to be enraged.

CHARLES DARWIN

Schachter argues that all emotions have a second, indispensable component: intense bodily arousal. People can experience an emotion only if they have some "feelings"; that is, they must be aroused physiologically. What did Schachter mean by arousal? In chapter 2, we discussed the James-Lange theory, one of the earliest, most famous, and most controversial of all the theories of emotion. According to this view, the emotions we feel are the results of messages we receive from our bodies as they react to emotion-producing aspects of the environment. For example, if you encounter a snarling dog, your body reacts first—you tremble, you sweat, your heart pounds. These physical changes, in turn, precede the experience of fear. Schachter was convinced that, in part, the James-Lange theory was correct. He believed that when people are emotional, their sympathetic nervous systems pump out adrenalin. People experience an undifferentiated state of high activation. Joy, anger, passion, envy, and hate all are accompanied by telltale symptoms—a flushed face, a pounding heart, trembling hands, accelerated breathing.

Delightful experiences—such as making love or simply talking with someone who loves and understands you—are physiologically arousing. Extremely painful experiences—such as fear, jealousy, anger, rejection, or total confusion—are arousing, too. Thus, either delightful or painful experiences (or a combination of the two) should have the potential for fueling a passionate experience. According to Schachter, both cognition and sympathetic arousal make an indispensable contribution to emotion. Cognitive factors determine the specific emotion that people feel. The degree of sympathetic activation determines whether they feel any emotion at all.

Note that Lazarus and Schachter disagree about the order in which appraisal and activation occur. Lazarus assumes that cognitive appraisals cause emotional arousal and behavior. Schachter argues that the sequence is quite the opposite. When people become aroused, a quick appraisal of the situation allows them to find an appropriate label for their feelings.

Interestingly, novelist Thomas Mann (1969), in *The Magic Mountain*, anticipated such a link between emotion and physical symptoms, when describing Hans's reactions to some symptoms he thought signaled tuberculosis. (In actuality, Hans was undoubtedly experiencing the effects of high altitude at the sanitorium in Switzerland where he was residing.)

> "If I only knew," Hans Castorp went on, and laid his hands like a lover on his heart, "if I only knew why I have palpitations the whole time—it is very disquieting; I keep thinking about it. For, you see, a person ordinarily has palpitations of the heart when he is frightened, or when he is looking forward to some great joy. But when the heart palpitates all by itself, without any reason, senselessly, of its own accord, so to speak, I feel that's uncanny. . . . You keep trying to find an explanation for them, an emotion to account for them, a feeling of joy or pain, which would, so to speak, justify them." (pp. 71–72)

The Classic Schachter and Singer Experiments

Stanley Schachter and Jerome Singer (1962) tested their theory in an ingenious series of experiments.

Manipulating Physiological Arousal.

According to Schachter and Singer, people experience emotion only when they are physiologically aroused. Thus, their first step was to inject some subjects with the drug "Suproxin" (actually adrenalin), which produced a pounding heart, trembling hands, and accelerated breathing. They injected other subjects with a placebo.

The authors did this in the following way: They claimed medical researchers were exploring the effect of a vitamin supplement, "Suproxin," on vision. They began by giving all subjects an injection of Suproxin. In reality, half the students (those in the "Unaroused" group) received a placebo, namely a saline solution. The remaining students (those in the "Aroused" group) received an arousing drug, epinephrine (adrenalin). (Epinephrine is an ideal drug for producing a state of intense excitement. Its effects mimic the natural discharge of the nervous system in states of emergency. Shortly after people receive an epinephrine injection, they experience palpitations, tremor, flushes, and accelerated breathing. In short, they experience the same physiological reactions that accompany a variety of natural emotional states. These effects usually begin within 3–5 minutes after the injection and last anywhere from 10 minutes to an hour.)

Manipulating an Appropriate Explanation. According to Schachter and Singer, people feel what is appropriate to feel. If everyone around you is euphoric—caught up in a wild, abandoned water fight, enjoying a Rose Bowl victory, or celebrating a friend's engagement—it seems appropriate to feel happy. If everyone around you is furious—your roommate got stuck with the dishes again or a close friend has been told there will be a surprise quiz two days before Christmas—it seems appropriate to be angry. On the other hand, if you are in a doctor's exam room and he asks you to describe your symptoms, you will probably tend to think about your symptoms in physical terms (Pennebaker, 1982). In the second phase of the experiment, then, Schachter and Singer attempted to manipulate subjects' explanations of any arousal they might experience. Subjects were assigned to one of three experimental conditions: "Epinephrine Informed," "Epinephrine Ignorant," or "Epinephrine Misinformed." In the "Informed" condition, subjects were alerted to exactly what they would feel (physiologically) and why. In the "Ignorant" condition, subjects were given no explanation for whatever feelings they were to experience. And in the "Misinformed" condition, they were told they would experience symptoms very different from those they in fact were to experience. (They were told their feet would feel numb, they would have an itching sensation over parts of their body, and they would get a slight headache.) In the first condition, then, subjects had a perfectly good explanation for what was about to happen to them. In the second two conditions, they did not. They had to look to their own thoughts and the external setting for clues.

Producing an Emotion. Next, the experimenters arranged for students to be placed in a setting in which it was easy to "catch" either a euphoric or an angry emotion at the time the drugs or placebo began to take effect. They did this in the following way: In the "Euphoria" condition, subjects were assigned to interact with an actor who acted giddy and silly. In the "Angry" condition, subjects interacted with an actor who acted angry and resentful.

In the "Euphoria" condition, the subject and the actor were told to sit and wait for 20 minutes until the Suproxin took effect (so that the vision tests could begin). The waiting room was in a mild state of disarray. Paper, pencils, rubber bands, and trash were scattered about. The experimenter left the room ... and the fun began. First, the actor-clown crumpled up some paper and entered into an energetic game of "basketball" with the wastebasket. Next, he began making paper airplanes, exclaiming, "This is one of my good days. I feel like a kid again. I think I'll make a plane." After several other antics, including slingshooting and hula-hooping, he finally sat down, and the experimenter entered the room.

In the "Anger" condition, the experimenter asked the "subjects" to use the 20 minutes filling out questionnaires. The questionnaires were designed to drive anyone crazy. As soon as the experimenter was gone, the actor began leafing through the questionnaire. "Boy, this is a long one," he grumbled. His comments started off innocently enough. But as the questions got worse and worse, he became more and more irritated. By Question 9, "Do you ever hear bells? How often?" the actor was angry. "How ridiculous can you get? I hear bells every time I change classes." Finally, the actor reached Question 28: "How many times each week do you have sexual intercourse?" "The hell with it," he yelled. "I don't have to tell them all this." He ripped his questionnaire to shreds, shouting, "I'm not wasting any more time. I'm getting my books and leaving," and he stomped out. The questionnaire went on for eight more questions, the last one being: "With how many men (other than your father) has your mother had extra-marital relationships?" (The smallest number the subjects could indicate was "4 and under.")

Assessing Emotion. Schachter and Singer measured their subjects' emotional states in two ways: First, they asked subjects to complete a standard self-report measure. They were asked how euphoric or angry they felt and whether they had experienced heart palpitations or tremor. Second, while all this had been going on, observers had been watching the subjects from behind a one-way mirror. They rated how euphoric or angry the subjects acted.

The results of the Schachter and Singer study supported their two-component theory. The students who had everything going for them—those who were in a setting in which it was appropriate to feel euphoria or anger *and* who were physiologically aroused—experienced the most intense emotions. On the basis of this research, the authors concluded that both appropriate cognitions and physiological arousal are indispensable components of a true emotional experience. Additional evidence for the two-component theory of emotion comes from Stanley Schachter and Ladd Wheeler (1962) and from George W. Hohmann (1966).

Schachter (1971) could have interpreted these data in a relatively conservative way. He could have been content with arguing: a) that both cognitive and physiological factors contribute to emotion; b) that sometimes, cognition may *follow* physiological arousal: c) that people assess their emotional state, in part, by observing how physiologically stirred up they are. Had Schachter stopped with these conclusions, his theory would have been subject to very little criticism.

But Schachter went further than that. He made a number of controversial assertions, arguing, for example:

1. Cognition *always* follows physiological arousal.
2. Cognition and physiological arousal are *indispensable* aspects of an emotional experience.
3. Neurochemical differences between emotions are nonexistent or unimportant.
4. *Any* emotional label can be attached to a given state of arousal. Which one is attached depends on the situation.

These bold proposals were to come back to haunt Schachter in the decade to come. We will review some of these criticisms at the end of this section.

Problems with Schachter's View

Two decades later, most psychologists would agree with Schachter's main thesis—both cognition and physiological arousal are critical to emotion (see Candland et al., 1977). (We would assume that the behavioral component is important, too.) However, many psychologists would no longer agree with his other conclusions.

For example, Schachter assumed that neurochemical differences between emotions are nonexistent or unimportant. We now know that different emotions are often associated with very different neurochemical and visceral responses. (We discuss this research in chapters 4 and 6. See Ekman et al., 1983.) Schachter thought generalized arousal was everything; we now know that its contribution to emotion varies depending on many factors (Henry, 1986). Schachter insisted that physiological arousal always precedes cognition. We now know that the question, "Which comes first, cognition or physiological arousal?" pulls theorists into a futile debate. Cognition, physiological, and behavioral responses occur in different sequences in different contexts; inevitably they interact. (We close this chapter with a discussion of that point.)

Schachter argued that people could easily be led to label their stirred-up states in a variety of ways. Theorists such as Gary Marshall and Philip Zimbardo (1979) and Christina Maslach (1979) quickly spotted the flaw in that argument. Some emotions, namely negative emotions, seem to "fit" with the discovery that we are aroused for some unknown reason. They argue that when we find our heart pounding or our hands shaking, we are more likely to assume that something terrible is happening—we are anxious, angry, or just plain sick—than anything else.

In spite of all these criticisms, Schachter's experiments remain a catalyst for research. His theory was intriguing. It excited a generation of young researchers. His experiments were daring and ingeniously crafted. The fact that his formulation has been revised by young researchers is as much a testimony to the importance of his work as anything else (see Box 3.3).

Let us now turn to the work of a second theorist who has taken issue with Richard Lazarus's contention that cognitive appraisal precedes physiological arousal. Recently, Robert Zajonc has argued that cognition and emotion can be two very different processes.

ROBERT ZAJONC

Robert Zajonc (pronounced "zye-ons") is interested in the relationship between thinking and feeling. By *thinking,* Zajonc means the higher order processes people use in processing information (Zajonc, Pietromonaco, & Bargh, 1982). In cognitive processing, people encode information, store it, and make

BOX 3.3

False Feedback in Emotional Responding

In another classic study, Stuart Valins (1966) demonstrated that, in formulating their own thoughts and feelings, people are even influenced by the reactions they *think* they are having. Valins recruited college men ostensibly to determine how they would react physiologically to sexual stimuli. The men were told that their heart rate would be amplified and recorded while they viewed ten semi-nude *Playboy* centerfolds. Actually, the feedback they received was false and experimentally controlled. Men were led to believe that when they examined slides picturing some of the women, their heart rate altered markedly; when they examined others, they presumably had no reaction. (Valins assumed that the men would interpret any alteration in heart rate, either a marked speed-up or a precipitous "standing still," as enthusiasm for the woman, and no change in heart rate as disinterest.)

The men's liking for the arousing versus unarousing slides was assessed in three ways: (a) they were asked to rate how attractive and appealing each of the women was; (b) they were offered a photograph of a woman in remuneration for participating in the experiment; and (c) a month later, in a totally different context, they were interviewed and asked to rank the attractiveness of the women. On all measures, the men markedly preferred the women they thought had aroused them—those who made their pulses race or their hearts stand still—to those they thought had not. It appears that we do come to feel what we think we feel.

Subsequent research reveals how this fascinating process works. When people perceive that they are sexually excited (i.e., when they are told their heart is racing or standing still), their body begins to actually respond that way (e.g., Hirschman, 1975). Have you ever begun to worry that you might be having a heart attack? As you haul out your *Medical Guide* and begin to work your way through the checklist of symptoms, things get worse and worse. You begin to notice that you are experiencing all the relevant symptoms: Are your fingers tingling? So they are. Is there a pain in your right arm? So there is. Actually, of course, nothing is wrong; you merely overdosed on Mexican food the night before. (See Pennebaker, 1982, for an analysis of this process.) As in Valins's experiment, people may come to feel erotic attraction because they think their heart is racing, or they may feel aroused because their heart is in fact racing via suggestion.

a high-level comparative judgment before deciding, "I have seen this widget before." By *feeling*, Zajonc (like Jung) means a simple affective reaction, the sort of judgment involved in the gut reaction, "I like that widget." Zajonc acknowledges that cognition plays some role in people's lives, even in their emotional reactions: "There can be no pride, guilt, jealousy, or disappointment without some cognitive participation" (p. 211). (These subtle emotions seem to cry out for complicated calculations of what one wants and what one is getting.) So thinking is important, but feeling is even more important. Zajonc (1980) observes:

> There are practically no social phenomena that do not implicate affect in some important way. Affect dominates social interaction, and it is the major currency in which social intercourse is transacted. The vast majority of our daily conversations entail the exchange of information about our opinions, preferences, and

evaluations. And affect in these conversations is transmitted not only by the verbal channel but by nonverbal cues as well—cues that may, in fact, carry the principal components of information about affect. It is much less important for us to know whether someone has just said "You are a friend" or "You are a fiend" than to know whether it was spoken in contempt or with affection. (p. 153)

Zajonc observes that most contemporary theorists assume that affect is post-cognitive (recall our discussion of Lazarus's theory, for instance). That is, a great deal of information has to be processed before people can decide what they feel about something. Not so, says Zajonc. It often takes a long time to figure out what we think. Generally we know immediately what we feel. Zajonc (1980) suggests some reasons why this might be so. He speculates that in humankind's evolutionary history, thinking was less important than feeling. Only humans and other primates possess a cortex. Only they possess language or cognition. All animals, however, possess a brain stem and emotion. Usually, that is enough. (If a rabbit is confronted by a snake, it does not bother to think through the situation and calculate the costs/benefits of running, freezing, or negotiating. It simply runs in terror. Its primitive brain stem directs the rabbit to run.) Zajonc (1980) observes that affect is basic, primary, and inescapable. "Affective reactions can occur without extensive perceptual and cognitive encoding, are made with greater confidence than cognitive judgments, and can be made sooner" (p. 151). We know instantaneously what we like, even though it may be difficult to verbalize the reasons for our attraction or repulsion.

In fact, Zajonc argues that under some circumstances, thinking and feeling involve two entirely different systems. Cognition and affect are separable, parallel, and partially independent systems. They are often processed in entirely different parts of the brain. Thinking is centered in the higher brain centers; feeling in the lower brain centers (see chapters 5 and 6). Thus, it is not surprising that cognition and affect often function independently. Zajonc (1980) adds:

> If affect is not always transformed into semantic content but is instead often encoded in, for example, visceral or muscular symbols, we would expect information contained in feelings to be acquired, organized, categorized, represented, and retrieved somewhat differently than information having direct verbal referents. (p. 151)

Zajonc et al. (1982) cite a variety of experiments to support their assertion that thought and feeling are two separate systems. They present experimental evidence demonstrating that reliable affective discriminations (ratings of like-dislike) can be made in the total absence of recognition memory (old–new judgments). For example, in an early study, Richard Littman and Horace Manning (1954) studied smokers of Camels, Chesterfields, and Lucky Strike cigarettes. They asked smokers to try some unmarked cigarettes and to (a) see whether they could distinguish their favorite brand from the others; and

(b) indicate how much they liked the cigarettes. Although smokers had trouble telling one brand from another, they knew what they liked. On the basis of such research, Zajonc concluded that cognition and affect can function quite independently.

Recently, Zajonc has proposed a controversial idea as to the nature of emotion. He proposes that as the brain processes information, its metabolic activity heats up the brain. Continuous cooling is required. Zajonc speculates about how such cooling generally occurs: Hypothalamic cooling depends on the temperature of the arterial blood supplying it. The arterial blood that supplies the brain is cooled by air flowing into the cavernous sinus. Anything that cools the brain (via the cavernous sinus) is pleasurable; anything that inhibits cooling is unpleasant. Zajonc attempted to demonstrate that those facial muscle actions and those breathing patterns that bring cool air to the cavernous sinus (say, the opened nose of a smile, sucking one's thumb, or kissing, which forces nasal breathing) increase people's feelings of happiness. Anything that stops up the nose, and makes it more difficult for cool air to enter the cavernous sinus (say, the pinched nose of anger, a hot day, or a bad cold) increases people's misery (Zajonc, Murphy, & Inglehart, 1989; Zajonc, 1990).

Finally, let us review the work of Gordon Bower, who has had a great deal to say about the links between emotion and memory.

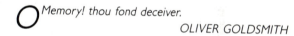

Memory! thou fond deceiver.
OLIVER GOLDSMITH

GORDON BOWER

Gordon Bower has been interested in the interaction of cognition and affect (Bower & Cohen, 1982). He contends that people's feelings have powerful effects upon their cognitive processes. He has investigated the impact of emotion on perception, judgment, thinking, and memory.

Bower's theoretical model is a fairly complex one. Essentially, Bower argues that, in the brain, events tend to be grouped according to the emotions associated with them. It is as if people have a separate bulletin board in their minds for every emotion they experience. As an event enters consciousness, it is automatically tacked up on the relevant board. "Ah, this is an example of joy"; "and this is anger." This system of organization accounts for the tight link between cognition and emotion. According to Bower's theory of **state-dependent memory,** the information that people acquire in one state of emotion is easiest to recall later when in that same state of emotion. It is as if the messages people learn when in one mood are easiest to read off the appropriate bulletin board when people are in the same mood later on.

In a series of experiments, Bower and his associates (see Bower, 1981; or Bower & Cohen, 1982) have studied the link between cognition and such emotions as joy, sadness, anger, and fear. They have found that our thoughts and our emotions do tend to hang together.

The heart hath its own memory, like the mind.
LONGFELLOW

Selective Filtering

When people are in a given mood, they tend to focus on events that are consistent with that mood. In one experiment, for example, Bower and his colleagues selected subjects who had been found to be highly hypnotizable. After hypnotizing them, the experimenters suggested that they try to recall either a happy scene (one associated with a moment of success or personal intimacy) or a sad scene (one associated with failure, loss, or rejection). Once subjects were in the mood, the experimenters asked them to read a story about two college chums, Andre and Jack, who had gotten together to play tennis. Andre was ecstatic—everything was going well for him; Jack was miserable—his life was falling apart. The two men's emotional reactions were vividly described. After completing the story, students were asked who the central character was. Students identified more with the character whose mood was similar to their own. They assumed that the story was about him and thought the story contained more statements about him. People tend to selectively perceive events, then, emphasizing those that fit with their current emotional state.

What happens when students cool down? The next day, when subjects were in a neutral mood, they were asked to recall the text. Those who had been sad the day before remembered more about the sad character. Yesterday's happy readers recalled more about the happy character. It is clear that information had been selectively stored in memory.

Selective Retrieval

Emotion influences not only what is stored in memory, but also how easily records can be accessed from memory. Bower's (1981) theory of state-dependent memory predicts that when people are happy they will find it unusually easy to recall good times. When they are sad, their lives will seem like an endless collection of dismal experiences. Bower proposed that people can best retrieve emotional memories by reinstating the emotion they were experiencing at the time they originally stored it. A variety of experiments documents the existence of such state-dependency effects.

For example, Bower et al. (1978), as before, recruited college students who were easily hypnotizable for this study. After hypnotizing them, the researchers asked them to get into a happy or sad mood by imagining or remembering a scene in which they had been "extremely happy" or "miserably sad." Often, the happy scene was a moment of personal success or of close intimacy. The sad scenes were of personal failure or the loss of a loved one. After getting into the right mood, subjects performed a learning task for 20–30 minutes. Subjects learned one list of 16 words when they were happy. They learned a similar list of 16 words when they were sad. Later, when they were either in the same mood or in a very different mood from the mood they had been in when they learned the lists, they were asked to recall the words on both lists. Bower and his associates found strong evidence for state-dependent memory. Happy people were best at retrieving the words they had learned when they were happy. Sad people were best at recalling the words they had learned when they were sad.

> *The mind is always the dupe of the heart.*
> *FRANCOIS, DUC DE LA ROCHEFOUCAULD*

In later research, Bower et al. (1978) found evidence that state-dependent memory operates in natural settings as well as in laboratory ones. Some examples:

Remembrance of Things Past. Students were asked to keep a diary in which they recorded all the emotion-arousing events that happened to them for one week. A week later, the students were hypnotized and put in a happy or sad mood. All were asked to recall every incident they could remember of those recorded in their diaries the week before. People in a happy mood recalled a greater percentage of their recorded pleasant experiences than of their unpleasant experiences. The results were exactly the opposite for people in a sad mood.

After subjects had finished recalling, the researchers asked them to rate the current emotional intensity of the incidents they recalled. Subjects rewrote history. If they were feeling happy, the recalled incidents seemed more pleasant than before. If they were feeling sad, the recalled events seemed blacker than before. Here we see the optimist's rose-colored glasses and the pessimist's dreary outlook in action.

Snap Judgments. The experimenters asked subjects to give thumbnail personality sketches of familiar people in their lives (a cousin, uncle, teacher). Some subjects described these acquaintances while they were happy, others while they were angry. Their judgments were strongly influenced by their passing mood. The authors conclude: "Angry judges are merciless, faultfinding; happy judges are charitable, loving, generous" (p. 302).

Social Judgments. Judgments about interpersonal actions are often subjective. Is our fellow student independent and iconoclastic or pigheaded? Is that man a free spirit or morally loose? Bower and Cohen (1982) find that social judgments are distorted by the mood of the judge. They note:

Happy people tend to be charitable, loving, positive in their interpretation of others. Depressed people are quick to notice any signs of flagging friendship, to exaggerate the slightest criticism, to overinterpret remarks as personal, denigrating, and pitying. Angry people have a chip on their shoulder, tend to be uncharitable, ready to find fault, to take offense. (p. 304)

Joseph Forgas and his colleagues (cited in Bower & Cohen, 1982) found that college students see themselves and others very differently when they are in a good versus bad mood. To test this hypothesis, the authors invited students in for a two-day experiment. On the first day, students were interviewed, two at a time, about some deeply personal topics. The interviews went on for 20 minutes and they were videotaped. Then, students were taught how to score videotapes for positive (social) and negative (antisocial) behaviors. Smiling, leaning forward, and contributing friendly remarks were considered to be positive social behaviors. Frowning, looking away, and grimacing were considered to be negative, antisocial behaviors. They practiced scoring conversations such as they had engaged in. They rated both participants at 10-second intervals.

The next day, subjects were hypnotized. Half of them were asked to recall a success, a time when they performed spectacularly well and felt good about themselves. Half were asked to recall a moment of social failure, when they were embarrassed and socially rejected because of something awkward or shameful they had done. Finally, subjects were asked to maintain their happy or sad mood while they scored the 20-minute videotape that they and their partner had made the day before. This study is impressive because subjects were not asked to recall how they felt about themselves or others. Instead, they were being asked to make moment-by-moment judgments of themselves and their partners. The authors found that subjects' ratings were affected by their moods, positive or negative. Happy subjects saw themselves and their partners through rose-colored glasses. Unhappy subjects saw themselves and others through a blacker lens. The researchers conclude: "It appears that social behavior is almost a blank canvas onto which perceivers project a picture according to their moods" (p. 307).

What about more complex emotions? What effect is there on cognition when we are angry *and* afraid? In love *and* furious? We do not know. Sometimes, Bower and Cohen assume that the effects of the emotions cancel each other out ("happiness is decreased by a sad or frightening event" [p. 311]). Sometimes they assume that cross-magnification effects operate ("Anger may intensify one's depression" [p. 311]). Clark (1982) argues that both processes operate.

Of course, Bower and Cohen are not without critics. For example, recently Paul Blaney (1986) reviewed the voluminous research that investigates the role of elation and depression in biasing memory. Blaney distinguishes between two related concepts—state-dependent memory and mood congruence. He defines **state dependence** this way:

State dependence implies that what one remembers during a given mood is determined in part by what one has learned (or focused on) when previously in that mood. (p. 229)

If memory is "state dependent," then what counts is not whether the material students are learning is pleasant or unpleasant but the mood they are in when they first learn it compared with the mood they are in when they attempt to remember it later. For example, Bower and his colleagues could have designed an experiment in which students were required to learn an extremely sad poem at a time when they were extremely happy (they had just won a starring role in the school play). If they were asked to recite the sad poem again, later, when they were still happy, the poem should be especially easy to remember. For, in state-dependent memory, it is not the content of the poem that is important but the similarity between the mood people are in when they learn versus the mood they are in when called upon to recite the poem.

Blaney defines **mood congruence** this way:

Mood congruence assumes that some material, by virtue of its affectively-valenced content, is more likely to be stored and/or recalled when one is in a particular mood; concordance between mood at exposure and mood at recall is not required or relevant. (p. 229)

This means that people should find it easier to learn and to recall happy material when they are in a good mood and to learn and to recall negatively valenced material when they are in a bad mood. Note that in mood congruence, it should not matter what mood people are in when learning that material. All that matters is whether the emotional content of the material matches (or is opposed to) the mood you are in when you are trying to recall it. When you are in a good mood, you are not necessarily more likely to remember everything you learned in that mood. You are simply more likely to remember the positive things you learned at one time or another.

Thus, Blaney is making a clear distinction between state dependence and mood congruence. In the studies we have described, the two processes varied together. Bower and his associates were studying how people responded to happy (or sad) material that they learned when they were happy (or sad) and were asked to retrieve when they were happy (or sad). Blaney finds that the evidence for state dependence is "mixed," while the evidence for mood congruence is "impressive in its size, consistency, and diversity" (p. 229).

Blaney also suggests that people probably find it easier to recall happy things (positively valenced material) than sad things (negatively valenced material). The average person tends to dwell on positive events, despite experiencing the normal ups and downs of daily life. The depressed person tends to recall neutral, rather than unhappy material (see chapter 8).

The several theories we have reviewed in this section deal in their own ways with the sequence of cognition and physiological arousal in emotion. In Box 3.4, we see yet another alternative—the possibility of mutual interactions of all variables in a continuous feedback loop.

BOX 3.4

The Continuous Feedback Loop

Since the time of William James, emotion researchers have been plagued with the sequence problem—which comes first, cognition or arousal? Are the two separate? Do they interact? Researchers kept trying to find out. Recently, researchers such as Douglas Candland (1977) and Ellen Berscheid (1983) have observed that the controversy is hardly worth all the effort that has been lavished on it. For example, Candland (1977) observes:

> There is no special advantage in assuming that there is a temporal sequence among the three processes [cognitive appraisal, emotional experience, and physiological reaction], and much waste has come from believing that the appropriate way to untangle our confusions about emotion is to sort out the temporal sequence. We have created a monstrous problem by assuming that explanation requires uncovering a temporal sequence: perhaps the monster can be made more presentable by changing our perception of its features. (p. 66)

Candland offers a sensible way to tame the monster. He proposes that emotional stimuli (sensations) quickly elicit both a cognitive and a physiological response. Neither emotional element comes before the other. Both are activated at roughly the same time. The two elements combine to produce an emotional experience. Each of the three elements (cognitive appraisal, physiological reaction, and emotional experience) is an indispensable part of a **continuous emotional feedback loop** (see Figure 3.2). Each element modifies and

is modified by the others. Each is both a stimulus and a response. Initially, emotional stimuli spark both a cognitive appraisal and a physiological response. These, in turn, shape one's emotional experience. In the next instant, the situation can change. The person's cognitive appraisals shape and are shaped by their physiological reactions. Their experience feeds back and shapes their perception of the eliciting stimuli. The various aspects of emotion continually feed back on one another, affecting the course of an emotional experience. We assume, of course, that emotional stimuli generate cognitive, physiological, and behavioral responses, and that all three should form part of this feedback loop.

Ellen Berscheid (1979) agrees that Candland's model has many virtues.

> ... the continuous-loop proposition has been generally accepted: most contemporary theories of emotion propose some version of a continuous feedback loop between the physiological and the cognitive, running from sensory input to attention, comparison with past events (memory), prediction of future events (meaning), and emotion (with the latter reverberating to influence all processes in the loop and resulting in behavioral output we would classify as "emotional" as well as other types of behavior). (pp. 34–36)

She notes that Candland's model has one additional virtue. It allows theorists and researchers to redirect their attention to other, more potentially profitable lines of inquiry.

Conclusion

In this chapter, we have reviewed the work of a number of theorists and researchers who have explored the link between conscious and unconscious experience and emotion. These included such theorists as Carl Gustav Jung, Richard Lazarus, Stanley Schachter, and Robert Zajonc. Jung was most interested in the structure of personality. He provided a poetic, metaphorical

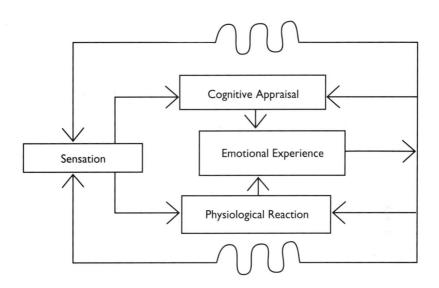

FIGURE 3.2   A flow chart of the continuous feedback loop responsible for emotion (proposed as a solution to the "sequence problem").

account of the ways in which the conscious, the personal unconscious, and the collective unconscious silently guide our emotional lives. Modern-day cognitive theorists have taken a more rigorous and experimental approach to understanding emotions. They have speculated about the important role of cognition, beliefs, expectations, thought, and information processing in guiding human emotional behavior. Many of these theorists have debated the exact nature of the relationship between thinking and feeling. Lazarus was convinced that cognitive appraisals usually preceded an emotional experience. Schachter, on the other hand, was equally convinced that cognitive appraisals were, in fact, motivated by states of ambiguous physiological arousal. Zajonc thought that thinking and feeling were quite often independent processes. In the end, Candland provided a sensible resolution to this debate. He proposed that emotional stimuli elicit both a cognitive and a physiological reaction. Each of these elements contributes to an emotional experience as part of a continuous feedback loop, in which each element can affect and is affected by the others.

Summing Up

- In Carl Jung's psychodynamic view, the psyche includes all thought, feeling, and behavior. It includes the conscious ego, the personal unconscious, and the collective unconscious.

- The ego is made up of all one's conscious perceptions, thoughts, feelings, and memories. The personal unconscious is a kind of "attic" filled with material that has been stored away and includes the complexes. (A person's perceptions, thoughts, emotions, and memories are organized in ways that have meaning for them. These patterns or constellations are called complexes.) The collective unconscious contains the archetypes and the instincts. Among the most important archetypes are the persona, anima and animus, and the shadow.

- Jung outlines some basic personality types. They may obtain information from either sensation or intuition, and they may process it either by thinking or feeling.

- In Jung's view, feelings may be either "functions," in the sense of moment-by-moment evaluations of one's environment; or feelings may become more intense, with physiological accompaniments, in which case they are referred to as "affects" (emotions).

- People differ in their preferences for thinking versus feeling, but the feeling function can be strengthened through emotional education.

- Jung measured emotion through word-association tests and even certain physiological responses, including the GSR.

- Despite indications that Jung's views may be becoming more acceptable and are finding some neurobiological and other forms of theoretical translation, Jung continues to have his critics.

- Richard Lazarus argues that the first step in an emotional sequence is a cognitive appraisal. There are three kinds of appraisals. In the process of primary appraisal, people try to assess the consequences of events. In secondary appraisal, they decide what they can and should do about events. In reappraisal, they reconsider their appraisals in light of new information. The appraisals people make determine which emotions they will feel and their intensity.

- People can utilize two strategies for coping with a situation. They can change their own reactions or change the situation itself.

- Stanley Schachter argued that both mind and body make a critical contribution to emotion. Cognitive factors determine the specific emotion that people feel; sympathetic activation determines whether they feel any emotion at all. Lazarus and Schachter disagree about the order in which appraisal and activation occur. Lazarus assumes that cognitive appraisals cause emotional arousal and behavior. Schachter argues that the sequence is just the opposite.

- Robert Zajonc argues that cognition and affect are separable, parallel, and partially independent systems.

- Gordon Bower suggests that in the brain, events tend to be grouped according to the emotions associated with them. Bower and his associates have studied the link between cognition and such emotions as joy, sadness, anger, and fear. They find that states of emotion produce selective filtering and selective retrieval and have an effect on remembrance of things past, snap judgments, estimates of future events, and social judgments.

- Candland proposes that emotional stimuli elicit both the cognitive and physiological elements of an emotional experience concurrently; each of the elements of emotional experience is part of a continuous feedback loop.

4

Neurophysiological Theories of Emotion

Introduction

LeDoux's Neurophysiological Theory of Emotion
The Peripheral Nervous System in Emotion
The Central Nervous System in Emotion
Summary

Henry's Neuroendocrine Theory of Emotion
The General Model
Neuroendocrine Bases of Negative Emotions: Anger, Fear, and Depression
Neuroendocrine Bases of Positive Emotions: Serenity and Elation
Neurophysiological Patterns of Emotional Response and Archetypes

Summing Up

FIGURE 4.1   *Consolation*. Edvard Munch. 1894. Drypoint and aquatint. The Munch Museum and Oslo Kommune.

Introduction

In the seventeenth century, French philosopher René Descartes visited the quiet country village of St. Germain, just outside Paris. The queen's fountaineers had constructed a set of mechanical statues that were cleverly engineered, so that they moved in lifelike ways: The statues were placed in six dimly lit grottoes. When spectators approached the statues to get a closer look at them, they unknowingly stepped on a hidden floor plate. This set the whole machinery into action. A device began to pump water through a series of pipes and valves in the statues' interiors, and the statues began to move. As tourists approached the statue of the goddess Diana bathing, for example, Diana slowly retreated into the recesses of the grotto. As tourists continued their approach, a statue of Neptune was set in motion. He strode forward, waving his trident menacingly. These statues suggested a startling hypothesis to the young Descartes. Perhaps people's bodies worked the same way! Descartes quickly worked out a model. The brain cavities are filled with "animal spirits," a pure fluid. Perhaps the brain is nothing more than a complicated system of tubes and valves, which shunt the animal spirits in various directions. These spirits then travel through the nerves into the muscles. People are jerked to and fro, like puppets on a string.

Descartes proposed that the mind and the body are distinctly different entities. The mind/consciousness/soul, he said, was a spiritual essence. The brain/body was a physical entity, governed by natural law. Descartes contended that only humans possessed a soul, consciousness, reason, or passion. Only humans could love, hate, feel pity, or despair. Other animals were like mechanical toys. The instant their brains received a sensory message, they automatically evaluated it and (when it was appropriate) mechanically triggered "vital spirits" that rushed through the nerves leading to the glands and muscles, initiating an appropriate reaction. Descartes insisted that the entire sequence was purely mechanical. In his charts, one can literally hear cogs whirring and gears grinding. Animals, like other mechanical toys, could feel no emotion, no pain. They merely responded like automatons when prodded or poked.

People were different. Initially, they too perceived, evaluated, and mechanically responded to sensory signals. But it didn't stop there. Humans possessed a soul (consciousness) and reason. The mind and the body could act upon each other via the pineal gland, which hung precariously on a slender stalk between soul and brain. The mind felt passion when the soul was touched by bodily sensations. The conscious, rational mind was in control; it could rein in the body. Lower animals possessed neither soul, mind, reason, nor passion. They were at the mercy of their whirring, clanking machinery.

Descartes is more important for what he began than for what he completed. His fanciful theory was the first neurophysiological theory. It was soon shredded and replaced by more sophisticated models. In this chapter, we closely examine the approaches of two modern-day theorists who take a physiological approach to understanding emotion—Joseph LeDoux and James Henry. Both are neurophysiologists; they are primarily interested in the workings of the brain and other parts of the nervous system. However, these theorists focus on two different aspects of the physiology of emotion. LeDoux emphasizes the role of the central and peripheral nervous system in emotion. Henry emphasizes the role of neuroendocrines (hormones) in emotion. These two men are representative of the many neuroscientists who have explored emotion. By the time we have outlined the work of these researchers, you should possess up-to-the-minute knowledge of what neurophysiologists know about emotion.

LeDoux's Neurophysiological Theory of Emotion

Joseph E. LeDoux (b. 1947) is a professor in the Department of Neurology, Cornell University Medical College. His neurobiological approach focuses on two physiological systems as bases for the emotions, the peripheral nervous system and the central nervous system (especially the brain). He is also concerned with the cognitive, expressive, and experiential aspects of emotions, believing that any physiological theory must deal with all the components of emotion. LeDoux surveys recent discoveries as to how the brain and peripheral nervous system operate and how they influence emotional evaluation, expression, and experience. In the end, he proposes an integrative model of brain/periphery functioning in emotion.

THE PERIPHERAL NERVOUS SYSTEM IN EMOTION

Structures and Organization: Traditional Views

Since the time of the great Greek physicians, Hippocrates and Galen (2,000 years ago), physicians have been theorizing about the brain and peripheral nervous system (see Figure 4.2). To understand LeDoux's approach, let us review some of the work on which his theorizing rests.

The **central nervous system (CNS)** and the **peripheral nervous system (PNS)** are made up of billions of nerve cells, or **neurons.** These neurons transmit information throughout the nervous system. The CNS consists of the brain, brain stem, and spinal cord (see Figure 4.2a). The PNS consists of all the rest of the neurons. The PNS transmits information from the periphery of the body to the CNS and back again (see Figure 4.2b and Table 4.1).

1. **Afferent** nerve impulses transmit sensory information toward the CNS (they "affect" the CNS) from the periphery. Sensory receptors in the eyes, ears, and so on **(exteroceptors)** provide information about the external world. Receptors located in the skeletal muscles and joints **(proprioceptors)** provide information about the position, location, orientation, and movement of the body. Receptors located in the smooth muscles

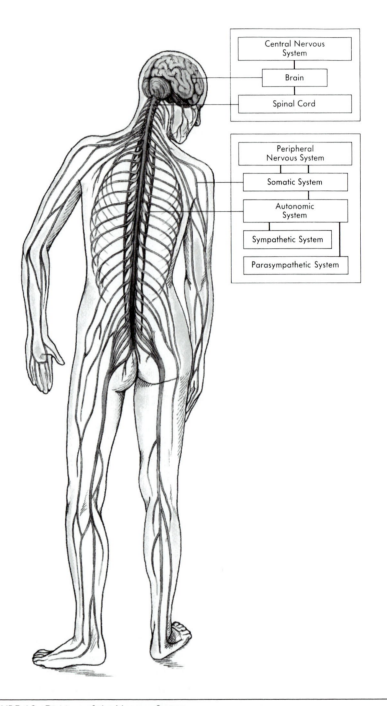

FIGURE 4.2 Divisions of the Nervous System

Table 4.1   **Functional Classification of Peripheral Nerves**

Peripheral Nerve Group	Origin	Termination	Example
Exteroceptive afferent	Peripheral receptor tuned to external environment	CNS	Nerves transmitting visual impulses to brain
Interoceptive afferent Somatic afferent	Receptors located in striated muscle	CNS	Nerves transmitting proprioceptive input from muscles
Visceral afferent	Receptors located in smooth muscle and internal organs and glands	CNS	Nerves transmitting input from brain (i.e., afferent limb of vagus nerve)
Somatic efferent	CNS	Striated muscles	Nerves carrying impulses to muscles from brain
Visceral efferent	CNS	Visceral tissues	Nerves innervating heart and blood vessels

LeDoux (1986), p. 308

and internal organs (**interoceptors**) provide feedback as to what is happening within the body itself: sensations of hunger, thirst, nausea, or visceral sensations. All this information is transmitted to the CNS via afferent pathways.

2. By contrast, **efferent** nerve impulses carry information from the CNS to the periphery (i.e., they allow the brain to have "effects" upon the muscles, organs, and glands). These descending pathways are commonly called efferent, or motor, pathways.

We see, then, that the brain can use two kinds of internal information—somatic and visceral information—in making emotional judgments. Receptors in the skeletal muscles and joints (such as in the face, arms, or legs) generate stimuli which are transmitted to the brain by somatic afferent nerves. Receptors in the smooth muscles and internal organs (such as the stomach and intestines) generate stimuli, transmitted to the brain by visceral afferent nerves. By these means, the brain comes to possess information about facial muscle movements, internal activity, internal distress, position of the limbs, and so forth. By these mechanisms, the emotional person becomes aware that his brow is knit, her teeth are clenched, he has "butterflies in his stomach," or she is breaking out in a "cold sweat."

The peripheral nervous system can be divided into two main parts—the somatic and the autonomic nervous system. The **somatic nervous system** consists of neurons which travel to and from the sensory and motor organs (such as the skeletal muscles). The **autonomic nervous system (ANS)** consists of neurons that regulate smooth muscle, cardiac muscle, and glands (autonomic means "self-governing"). The ANS innervates the cardiovascular system, respiratory system, digestive system, and endocrine (glandular) system—including the adrenal glands (about which we will have more to say), the ovaries, and the testes. The ANS, which is especially important in emotional expression,

> is so named [autonomic] because its functions are, for the most part, outside of conscious direction. While we can willfully control skeletal muscles, voluntary control over smooth and cardiac muscles is difficult to achieve. The involuntary nature of autonomic function allows for the internal housekeeping chores of the body to be performed without necessitating any conscious decision making. Thus, for example, the rate of the heart's pumping action, the constriction and dilation of arterial beds, the secretion of digestive fluids, pupillary adjustments, and so forth, are automatically controlled by the ANS. (LeDoux, 1986, pp. 308–309)

It is lucky that the ANS is "automatic." If—whether awake or sleeping—we had to remind ourselves to breathe every few seconds, remind our heart to beat every one or two seconds (as well as to speed up when "fight or flight" was necessary and to slow down when the crisis was over), remind our stomach to digest its food, and so on, we would soon be overwhelmed. "If, in fact, these internal systems were under our everyday control, we would have precious little time for anything but the complicated business of keeping ourselves alive" (Hassett, 1978, p. 12).

The ANS itself consists of two divisions. In the **sympathetic nervous system,** neurons lead from the spinal cord (in the middle, or thoracic and lumbar, portions) to a wide variety of organs, such as the heart, salivary glands, lungs, liver, and others. In the **parasympathetic nervous system,** neurons lead from the brainstem or the very lowest levels (sacral portions) of the spinal cord largely to the same organs—heart, lungs, stomach, bladder, and so forth. Figure 4.3 depicts the major pathways and organ end-points of the neurons in the sympathetic and parasympathetic systems.

One other distinction between these two systems lies in the nature of their **ganglia** (a ganglion is a collection of neurons) and their **neurotransmitters** (the body's chemicals that help transmit information from one neuron to another). Nerves from the spinal cord lead first to ganglia and then from the ganglia to the end organ. In the parasympathetic system, the ganglia are typically located at the end organ itself, so that the postganglionic neurons (those neurons after the ganglia) are very short. In the case of the sympathetic system, the ganglia lie between the spinal cord and the organ, as shown in Figure 4.3. In both systems, the substance *acetylcholine* (ACh) facilitates neural transmission up to the ganglia (that is, in the preganglionic nerves). In the sympathetic system only, *noradrenaline* (or *norepinephrine*) facilitates neural transmission in the postganglionic nerves. (This neurotransmitter is mentioned in connection with emotional arousal many times throughout this text.)

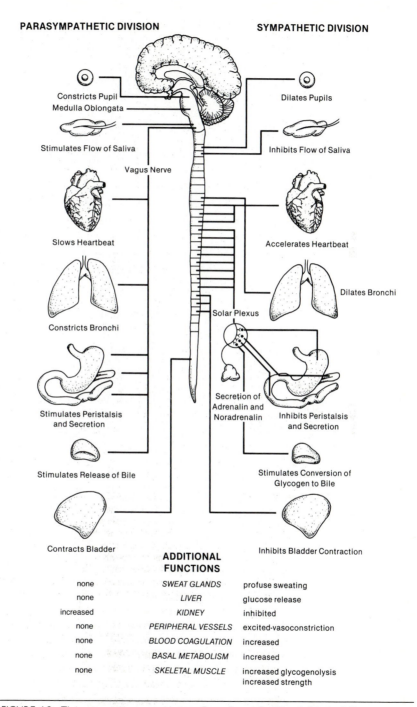

PARASYMPATHETIC DIVISION

SYMPATHETIC DIVISION

Constricts Pupil

Dilates Pupils

Medulla Oblongata

Stimulates Flow of Saliva

Inhibits Flow of Saliva

Vagus Nerve

Slows Heartbeat

Accelerates Heartbeat

Dilates Bronchi

Constricts Bronchi

Solar Plexus

Secretion of
Adrenalin and
Noradrenalin

Stimulates Peristalsis
and Secretion

Inhibits Peristalsis
and Secretion

Stimulates Release of Bile

Stimulates Conversion of
Glycogen to Bile

Contracts Bladder

Inhibits Bladder Contraction

**ADDITIONAL
FUNCTIONS**

none	*SWEAT GLANDS*	profuse sweating
none	*LIVER*	glucose release
increased	*KIDNEY*	inhibited
none	*PERIPHERAL VESSELS*	excited-vasoconstriction
none	*BLOOD COAGULATION*	increased
none	*BASAL METABOLISM*	increased
none	*SKELETAL MUSCLE*	increased glycogenolysis increased strength

FIGURE 4.3 The autonomic nervous system. From Ernest R. Hilgard, Rita L. Atkinson, and Richard L. Atkinson, 1979. *Introduction to Psychology.* Harcourt Brace Jovanovich, Inc. Reprinted by permission of the publisher.

For these reasons, the parasympathetic system is said to be *cholinergic* in nature, while the sympathetic system is *adrenergic*, referring specifically to the nature of postganglionic neurotransmission.

Another important point is that the sympathetic system has nerve endings in a gland called the *adrenal*, located at the top of each kidney, as shown in Figure 4.3. This gland plays a profound role in the operation of the sympathetic nervous system. When the central (medulla) portion of the adrenal is activated, it begins to produce both noradrenaline (the same neurotransmitter that appears in the sympathetic postganglionic nerves) and *adrenaline* (or *epinephrine*). (Adrenaline is a chemical that Walter Cannon identified as important in the release of glycogen from the liver into the bloodstream, thus providing extra energy for the bodily tissues in emergencies). These neurotransmitters enter the bloodstream and may produce effects—including continuing the activation of sympathetic neural transmission—that last longer than the effects of the neurotransmitters generated within the nerves themselves. In effect, once the sympathetic system is activated, its activity is for a time self-perpetuating (because the adrenals continue to pump out adrenaline.) Moreover, epinephrine and norepinephrine from the adrenals and circulating in the blood may themselves directly activate the end-organs. If you saw the movie *Platoon*, you saw the effects of combat soldiers' surges of adrenaline. In battle, their hearts pounded, sweat poured from their bodies, their hands trembled so badly that they could hardly aim their automatic weapons. Sometimes they simply went wild—leaping out from their jungle hideaways to pursue the enemy, oblivious of their own safety.

Another important point is that in the sympathetic nervous system, relatively few sympathetic ganglia activate a great many end-organs (see Figure 4.3). This means that sympathetic activation will produce parallel changes in several organs. For example, if an emotional event causes someone's heart to race, we might also expect the pupils to dilate, respiration to increase, digestion to be inhibited, and so forth. The parasympathetic system's effects are much more specific; even after the heart begins to slow, the person's pupils may remain dilated and the chest may continue to heave. Evolutionarily, this makes sense. In emotion, as in emergency ("fight or flight") situations, sympathetic activation of the entire body is required. Almost every system needs a rapid flow of blood and oxygen (and glucose). Once the emotional situation or emergency disappears and the person begins to settle down, there is no particular reason why the parasympathetic nervous system should slow down the action quickly and uniformly.

Changing Views of the ANS. Recently, LeDoux and many other neuroscientists have taken a look at the accumulating evidence and begun to alter their views about the way the ANS functions. For example, traditional theorists noted that, in general, the sympathetic and parasympathetic systems act in opposition to each other—the sympathetic system speeds things up, and the parasympathetic system slows things down. There are a number of exceptions to this rule, however. Sometimes, only the sympathetic system has an effect on a given organ. Sometimes both systems have a similar effect. For example, the sweat glands (eccrine glands) and the small blood vessels in the surface of the body (peripheral arterioles, which are important in the regulation of blood pressure), as well as blood vessels in the abdomen and musculature, are stimulated by the sympathetic system. You may have experienced the sort of "cold sweat" this process produces if you have ever had to deliver a speech in class. However, the action of these structures is *not* reversed by the parasympathetic system (see Figure 4.3). Conversely, both sympathetic and parasympathetic stimulation produce parallel functioning in the liver: Parasympathetic stimulation causes the liver to synthesize glycogen; sympathetic stimulation causes it to release glucose (Guyton, 1981).

Neuroscientists have even begun to challenge the notion that sympathetic activation produces simultaneous, parallel changes in the various organ systems! LeDoux (1986) argues that the degree of activation may vary from one organ to the next. Similarly, John and Beatrice Lacey (1970) point out that some emotional stimuli may spark the same ANS changes in almost everyone. However, these emotion-arousing events may not spark parallel changes in the various sympathetic indicants of emotion. For example, when students are shown gruesome photographs of an autopsy, their heart rates slow down (rather than speed up), but their electrodermal activity increases (they perspire more). The Laceys also point out that different people show different patterns of sympathetic responding. People show **individual response stereotypy.** A person may display the same profile of physiological responses to a wide variety of eliciting situations. Different people display different profiles. One person's heart may pound at the first hint of trouble. They may respond to every emotional event by moaning "Oh my heart!" Another person may respond to any upsetting event by developing cramps. For example, in his candid autobiography, the eminent film director Ingmar Bergman (1987) reports that he has always suffered from "nervous stomach." Since childhood, whenever he is emotionally upset, he is seized with a violent attack of stomach cramps and begins to defecate. "School was an unremitting misery. Suddenly shitting in your trousers is a traumatic experience. It does not have to happen often for it to become a constant worry" (p. 62). Bergman finds it so painful to have to keep dealing with such problems that he has decided to abandon the stressful business of making films.

The discovery that different emotional stimuli may be linked to different patterns of ANS response has had a profound impact on how scientists think about the relationship between emotion and ANS arousal. For instance, until very recently, most emotion researchers have assumed that Walter Cannon was right—that ANS arousal is "all or nothing." If this is so, then there is no way people can tell which emotion they are feeling by focusing on their own ANS activity. They will be able to tell only whether or not they are emotional (aroused). On the other hand, some psychologists, such as Paul Ekman and his colleagues (1983), argue that each basic emotion may be linked to a unique pattern of ANS arousal. For example, LeDoux (1986) points out:

> Different patterns of autonomic activity accompany different emotions, as dictated by the unique demands imposed on the organism by the emotional state itself and by the somatomotor activities [muscle movements] that constitute the behavioral expression of emotion. (p. 315)

If this is so, people may well be able to tell what they are "really" feeling by getting in touch with their pattern of ANS arousal. People could use cues from the ANS to draw inferences about their feelings. Recently, then, scientists have been rethinking their assumptions about the link between emotion and ANS arousal.

Scientists have also uncovered receptors in the ganglia that seem to be sensitive to substances other than acetylcholine. This opens up the possibility that the ANS may respond to a variety of emotional neurotransmitters, with obvious implications for the potential complexity of emotional activation and inhibition. However, as LeDoux points out, researchers must now begin to explore the functions of such receptors.

Additionally, the possibility exists for yet a third ANS division—the **enteric nervous system.** The enteric nervous system seems to control the workings of the intestinal system independently of the other ANS systems. Evidence that such a third system does exist comes from several converging sources (Langley, 1921; Gershon, Dreyfus, & Rothman, 1979). Unfortunately, the implications of this finding have not yet been thought through.

Evidence for the Role of the ANS in Emotion

Generalized Effects. LeDoux (1986) contends that it is too early to know whether we will discover that each of the various emotions is associated with a specific pattern of ANS response. Although compelling data fall on both sides of that controversy, considerable evidence points to the fact that, in general, strong emotions do spark a generalized ANS response. In LeDoux's words, "Diffuse sympathetic activation accompanies many states of acute, intense aversive emotional arousal . . . [and] prepare the organism to face adversity over the short run" (p. 321).

The evidence supporting LeDoux's contentions comes from many sources. Let us describe a bit of the research LeDoux culls to illustrate his points. There is considerable evidence that many emotional states are accompanied by widespread sympathetic arousal. For example, in one early laboratory study, Walter Hess (1935) found that when cats' brains are electrically stimulated, they display a typical **defense response.** They hiss, snarl and arch their backs, their body hair stands on end, and they attack. A distinct pattern of sympathetically mediated internal responses accompanies these reactions.

These include increased blood flow to the muscles (owing to vasodilation), decreased blood flow to the viscera (owing to vasoconstriction), increased heart rate and blood pressure, and other of the responses outlined in Figure 4.3 (Hilton, 1966). These internal changes may occur even if the animal is anesthetized and, therefore, unable to respond expressively.

As we will see in chapter 5, when animals are warned of an impending electric shock by a signal, such as a light or noise, they may show conditioned emotional responding (fear). As Cannon's emergency hypothesis would predict, the fear stimulus produces increases in animals' heart rate, blood pressure, and blood flow to the skeletal muscles. These ANS changes occur in spite of the fact that the animals can do nothing about the coming shock. They can only stand and wait. LeDoux (1986) points out that animals' ANS reactions come in two waves in such situations. The first, immediate reaction comes as the sympathetic nerves withhold blood from the viscera and send it instead to the skeletal muscles. In the second slower, but longer-lasting, wave, the adrenal medulla (in the central portion of the adrenal glands) releases epinephrine. These changes, too, are consistent with the emergency model of emotion. They evoke a host of reactions in the heart, lungs, stomach, and other organs (as we described earlier).

If cats experience sympathetic arousal in the conditioning setting, it seems reasonable that people might become similarly aroused by mental stress even when there is nothing they can do, behaviorally, about the situation. In a study by J. Brod, V. Fencl, Z. Hejl, and J. Jirka (1959), subjects were asked to engage in mental arithmetic. (They were asked to count backward from 1,194, subtracting 17 every two seconds.) As predicted, subjects responded to this stressful task by displaying decreased blood flow to the viscera and increased blood flow to the skeletal muscles. This research illustrates that a purely psychological stressor (arithmetic) may spark an autonomic reaction, even if very little physical activity is required to deal with the problem. Moreover, it is psychogenic emotional factors, that is, *perceived* stress, not motor activity, that determine whether or not arousal will be maintained. When ancient, dark fears wrap a chilly hand around the human heart, the heart responds, whether or not this pattern of responses parallels the energy or physical demands of the body.

Neuroscientists have also assembled a cascade of evidence supporting Hans Selye's (1974) view that under conditions of sustained or chronic stress, the body responds with a generalized alarm reaction. If a person is trapped in stressful circumstances, after several hours (or days), the surface (cortex) portion of the adrenal glands begins to pour out adrenocortical hormones, which help sustain the ANS emergency reactions. If such chronic stress is allowed to continue, it can lead to such reactions as sustained high blood pressure and a breakdown in immune responses. These general stress reactions may lead to a variety of human problems—hypertension, gastrointestinal disease, and cancer. We discuss this research in chapter 13, when we look at the effects of emotions on physical health.

Specific Effects. By contrast with the general activating effects of the ANS, investigators have also assembled some evidence to suggest that various emotions may be associated with different patterns of physiological response. In a classic experiment, Albert Ax (1953) found that fear and anger were associated with different physiological reactions. In his study, subjects were connected to a variety of electrodes. They were told to lie quietly as a nurse took their blood pressure once each minute. In the "Fear" condition, the experimenter gradually increased a shock to the subject's finger. Suddenly, the experimenter acted alarmed and cautioned the subject to remain still. He pressed a button that caused sparks to emerge from the equipment. Naturally, subjects were terrified. In the "Anger" condition, the experimenter soon began acting in an obnoxious and arrogant manner. He criticized the nurse. He blamed the subject for not cooperating and handled him roughly. Naturally, subjects were furious. Ax found that fear was associated with high levels of epinephrine, anger with a combination of epinephrine plus norepinephrine. Ax's research and conclusions were roundly criticized, however. Critics pointed out that Ax may have been comparing subjects who differed both in type and degree of emotion. Thus, it is impossible to tell whether the differences Ax secured between fear and anger were due to differences in the *type* of emotion subjects felt or in its *intensity* (more about this later).

Recently, however, other researchers have come to believe that the various emotions are, in fact, distinguished by unique patterns of physiological response (see Cacioppo & Petty, 1983). Chief among these are Paul Ekman, Robert Levenson, and Wallace Friesen (1983). They asked people to "put on" a facial expression characteristic of such emotions as anger, fear, sadness, or surprise, while the researchers monitored their heart rates and peripheral (skin) temperatures. They found clear evidence of emotional patterning. For instance, when subjects mimed anger, fear, or sadness, their heart rate increased. When they mimed surprise, heart rate decreased. When subjects displayed anger, their skin temperature increased dramatically. When they showed fear, sadness, and surprise, their temperature showed little change or decreased slightly (see chapter 6). Critics have yet to challenge these unexpected findings.

Evidence such as this led LeDoux to conclude that the various emotions may be associated with specific ANS markers. It is known that as emotions become more intense, they activate more and more ANS reactions. Thus, regardless of the emotions people are experiencing, the level of ANS activity provides some information as to their emotional intensity.

Evidence for the Role of Feedback in Emotion

People have been speculating about the nature of their physiological reactions in emotion for thousands of years. As William Grings and Michael Dawson (1978) state:

The idea that bodily reactions are intimately involved with emotions can be found in the writings of the ancient philosophers and poets. Even today, our language is replete with references to this relationship. For example, we use phrases like: "red with rage," "butterflies in the stomach," "cold sweat," "trembling with fear," and the like to describe emotional distress. (p. 2)

Different theorists have proposed radically different ideas about the link between the brain, emotion, and peripheral feedback (i.e., sensory information from the face, viscera, touch, and so forth). For example, as we have seen, William James assumed that the very basis of emotional experience was visceral and skeletal muscle feedback. Later, Stanley Schachter (1975) argued that people use both cognitive and physiological information in labeling their feelings. People label their feelings in ways that they think are "appropriate." (We expect to be "nervous" when we give a speech but "excited" when we are skiing.) They rely on peripheral feedback to tell them whether they are feeling anything at all. (They assume they must be emotional if they feel their heart pounding or assume they are calm, cool, and collected if "nothing" is happening.)

In any case, LeDoux points out that the brain has two ways of securing information about the viscera. First, a network of sensory receptors is located in the viscera. Thus, some feedback can be telegraphed to the brain via afferent nerves (in the same way as the optic nerve transmits retinal information to the CNS). Unfortunately, the visceral afferent system has received little experimental attention and is thus little understood. The second major source of visceral feedback is the endocrine system, under the control of the ANS, which releases hormonal substances into the blood. Some of these blood-borne hormones influence the CNS directly, stimulating receptor sites in the brain. For example, steroids released from the ovaries, testes, and adrenal cortex have specific CNS sites of action (LeDoux, 1986).

Other substances affect the CNS only indirectly. Normally, epinephrine does not cross the protective blood-brain barrier. This and other hormones cause a reaction in one organ or another. In turn, the brain then receives feedback via afferent neurons as to changes in that organ. Thus, in emotional states, feedback from these sources may provide specific cues that underlie experiences ("this feels good" or "that makes me mad") as well as the energy (arousal) that we experience as excitement or distress. We take a closer look at how emotions are shaped by complex hormonal interactions when we discuss Henry's work later in this chapter.

How can scientists find out how emotions and visceral feedback are related? One way is to study how emotions are affected when the brain is unable to receive any information from the periphery. If people's emotional experiences are perfectly normal, it suggests that peripheral information is unimportant. If emotions are markedly altered, we have information as to the importance of peripheral feedback. Numerous studies have been performed on the effects of blocking or disrupting visceral feedback through surgical procedures (especially, *sympathectomy*—separation of the sympathetic nervous system from the brain) or through the use of drugs.

LeDoux (1986) argues that this research generally supports three conclusions:

1. It is difficult to be certain when the sympathetic nervous system is completely separated from the brain. In most studies it is probably best to refer to "feedback reduction rather than elimination" (p. 324). Moreover, the more we learn about the nervous system, the more it appears that there are multiple means by which the brain might be influenced by activity in other parts of the body including, as we have said, the direct effects of hormones in the blood.

2. It appears that the intensity of an emotional experience is reduced when peripheral feedback is blocked.

3. It is uncertain whether the quality of emotional experience or reactions are influenced by the reduction of feedback. People's emotional experiences and reactions sometimes seem to remain unchanged even when feedback is markedly reduced.

In support of the last point, for example, George Hohmann (1966) studied military men with spinal cord injuries (discussed in chapter 3). The higher the damage to the spinal cord, the more the brain is cut off from the sympathetic nervous system, and the less the men were capable of experiencing intense emotion (be it anger, fear, or happiness). Interestingly enough, the amount of damage did not seem to affect which emotion was experienced or how soldiers dealt with it. The men's behavior remained normal. Such evidence suggests that, at the very least, the intensity of emotional experiences is shaped by peripheral visceral feedback.

Recently, however, Kathleen Chivalisz, Ed Diener, and Dennis Gallagher (1988) have taken issue with Hohmann's conclusions. They, too, interviewed men and women who had suffered spinal cord injuries. However, they found that even patients with extremely serious spinal cord injuries were capable of intense emotion. One man with a high and nearly complete cervical lesion reported being so angry at one of his instructors that he wanted to "run over him a few times" with his wheelchair. In their view, many factors may contribute to emotional intensity. Theories that "maintain that the perception of autonomic arousal is an essential component of emotion and that the experience of emotion cannot occur without it" are just plain wrong (p. 825).

Researchers, then, seem to agree that emotional intensity is shaped to some extent by ANS arousal. They disagree, however, as to how important a role such arousal plays. Only further research will determine how big a role such feedback plays in emotion.

THE CENTRAL NERVOUS SYSTEM IN EMOTION

In searching for the source of emotional experience, James and Lange focused on the organs of the body peripheral to the brain. Cannon focused on the central nervous system (CNS) itself. In recent years, neuroscientists have directed their attention to the portion of the brain called the **limbic system,** a lobe that lies above and includes parts of the thalamus (identified by Cannon as the seat of emotion) and other brain structures that we will discuss later. Jon Franklin (1987) has observed that "in the architecture of the primate brain, [we see] the indelible footprints of several hundred million years of evolution" (p. 221). The limbic system is an amalgam of the so-called old reptilian and mammalian brains. The neocortex is the newest brain structure. The locations of some of the brain structures that will be referred to in the following material are illustrated in Figures 4.4 and 4.5.

Central Nervous System Structures and Functions: Traditional Views

Early theorists disagreed on how important CNS structures were in emotion. William James rejected the idea that the brain possessed special emotional centers. He assumed that the sensory and motor areas of the brain simply

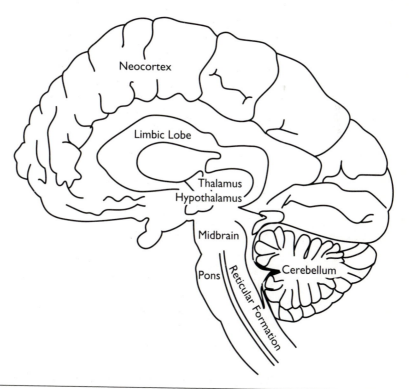

FIGURE 4.4 Structures of the brain. Reprinted with permission of Macmillan Publishing Company from W. B. Webb, *Sleep: An Experimental Approach.* New York: Macmillan. Copyright © 1968 by Macmillan Publishing Company.

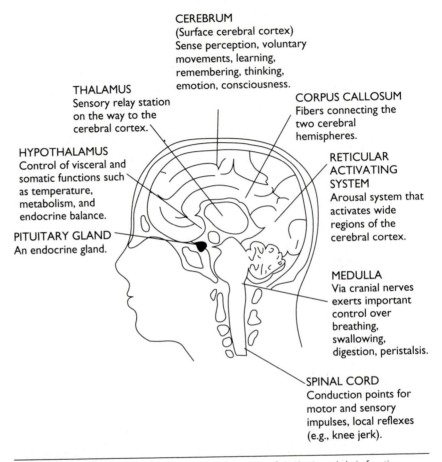

THALAMUS
Sensory relay station
on the way to the
cerebral cortex.

CEREBRUM
(Surface cerebral cortex)
Sense perception, voluntary
movements, learning,
remembering, thinking,
emotion, consciousness.

CORPUS CALLOSUM
Fibers connecting the
two cerebral
hemispheres.

HYPOTHALAMUS
Control of visceral and
somatic functions such
as temperature,
metabolism, and
endocrine balance.

RETICULAR
ACTIVATING
SYSTEM
Arousal system that
activates wide
regions of the
cerebral cortex.

PITUITARY GLAND
An endocrine gland.

MEDULLA
Via cranial nerves
exerts important
control over
breathing,
swallowing,
digestion, peristalsis.

SPINAL CORD
Conduction points for
motor and sensory
impulses, local reflexes
(e.g., knee jerk).

FIGURE 4.5   Cross-section of the brain. Major structures of the brain and their functions. From Ernest R. Hilgard, Richard C. Atkinson, and Rita L. Atkinson (Eds.), *Introduction to Psychology, Sixth Edition.* Copyright © 1975 by Harcourt Brace Jovanovich, Inc., and reproduced with their permission.

recorded emotional information from the periphery like they did any other information. Early physiological studies cited by LeDoux (1986) challenged such notions; they confirmed that the sensory and motor cortex were not essential to emotional experience and response. Cannon's studies showed that cats without brain cortex would exhibit signs of rage when their brains were electrically stimulated. He identified the thalamus as the structure that was important in emotion (see Figure 4.4). Later, Bard concluded that the hypothalamus, a small structure below the thalamus, was more important in emotional expression (e.g., Bard & Rioch, 1937). LeDoux feels, however, that it was James W. Papez who gave the greatest boost to the role of the hypothalamus in emotion. The Papez "loop" plays an integral role within LeDoux's theory.

The Papez Loop. In 1937, Papez outlined a theory linking brain structures in the "old brain" and the cortex—the Papez "loop." Papez's insight poured fuel on the early flames of brain-behavior research. Scientists rushed to their laboratories to see whether his ideas made sense; they seemed to. LeDoux (1986) observes:

> Papez drew upon clinical observation and scant anatomical facts and suggested that at the thalamus afferent pathways split into three routes: to the cortex, to the basal ganglia, and to the hypothalamus. While the cortical route represented the "stream of thought" and the projection to the basal ganglia the "stream of movement," the input to the hypothalamus constituted the "stream of feeling." (p. 328)

In Papez's view, input from the environment is gated through the thalamus to the hypothalamus in a neuronal "stream of feeling" (see Figure 4.6). From there, emotional stimuli are transmitted in two directions: downstream toward the peripheral nervous system and upstream toward the cortex.

1. Sometimes, the "stream of feeling" is shunted directly from the hypothalamus to the brain stem and spinal cord, and then to the peripheral nervous system. Thus, sometimes emotional stimuli directly spark emotional behavior.
2. Sometimes, however, the "stream of feeling" is shunted from the hypothalamus to the cortex. In this view, the cingulate cortex is the receiving area for emotional information. Thus, emotional stimuli may trigger cognitive involvement—perceptions, thoughts, attitudes, and the like become important.
3. Finally, information can be transmitted from the cortex back to the hippocampus, and thence to the hypothalamus. It is this pathway that allows the "mind" (the cortex) to shape peripheral reactions. This circuit completes the Papez "loop."

For example, if a stimulus (say, an old love song) activates the association cortex, a person might be reminded of someone he once knew. Such memories might activate the hippocampus and the hypothalamus and then discharge through the peripheral nervous system. The person, touched by bittersweet memories, may begin to cry. Thus, sometimes a purely psychological process may, in and of itself, spark a complex sequence of emotional reactions (LeDoux, 1986, pp. 329–330). In *Remembrance of Things Past* (see Box 4.1), Marcel Proust (1928) poetically illustrates this point.

Changing Views of the CNS in Emotion. The brain structures in the Papez "loop" are closely related to those once called "the great limbic lobe." Paul MacLean (1949) proposed that the limbic lobe and related subcortical structures constituted a functional system, the limbic system. This system was also termed the visceral brain, referring to the important role it played

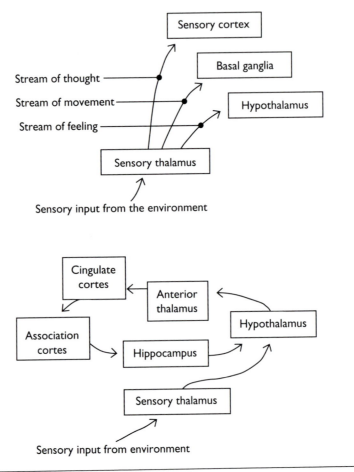

FIGURE 4.6   The Papez Loop. From LeDoux, 1968, p. 329. Reprinted with the permission of Cambridge University Press.

in regulating visceral activity in a wide variety of emotional settings. MacLean argued that the neo-mammalian limbic system evolved from a more primitive brain structure, the rhinencephalon which plays a significant role in smell (olfaction) in lower animals. In lower animals, the sense of smell triggers a variety of adaptive behaviors—including food getting, mating, and the location of predators. In higher animals, the sense of smell is relatively weak and unimportant. Nonetheless, these primitive structures are probably as important as ever. These ancient structures have evolved into the complex limbic system, which triggers the same visceral reactions that have always been a part of our primitive patterns of behavior. The limbic structures remain the seat of emotion, regulating the most profound of human behaviors.

LeDoux points out that different theorists have slightly different ideas as

BOX 4.1

Remembrance of Things Past

Many years had elapsed during which nothing of Combray . . . had any existence for me, when one day in winter as I came home, my mother, seeing that I was cold, offered me some tea, a thing I did not ordinarily take. . . . I raised to my lips a spoonful of the tea in which I had soaked a morsel of the cake. No sooner had the warm liquid, and the crumbs with it, touched my palate than a shudder ran through my whole body. . . . An exquisite pleasure had invaded my senses. . . . Whence could it have come to me, this all-powerful joy? . . . And suddenly the memory returns. The taste was that of the little crumb of 'madeleine' which on Sunday mornings at Combray . . . my Aunt Leonie used to give me, dipping it first in her own cup of real or of lime-flower tea. . . . Immediately the old grey house upon the street rose up like the scenery of a theatre . . . and just as the Japanese amuse themselves by filling a porcelain bowl with water and steeping in it little crumbs of paper which . . . stretch and bend, take on colour and distinctive shapes, so in that moment all the flowers in our garden and in M. Swann's park, and the water-lilies on the Vivonne and the good folk of the village and their little dwellings and the parish church and the whole of Combray and of its surroundings, taking their proper shapes and growing solid, sprang into being, town and gardens alike, from my cup of tea. (pp. xii–xiii)

to the brain structures that should be included in the limbic system. All theorists include structures that are proximate to one another and that have overlapping functions. Figure 4.7 depicts the structures that MacLean believed made up the visceral brain. It includes such cortical areas as the cingulate gyrus and hippocampal gyrus and such subcortical areas as the amygdala, hypothalamus, anterior thalamus, and so forth. From MacLean (1949) to James Henry (1986), whose work we review in the next section, many neuroscientists have identified the hippocampus as the "place of visceral and environmental sensory integration and thus . . . the seat of emotional experience" (LeDoux, 1986, p. 330). The cingulate gyrus in Papez's (1937) early theory performed the same "feeling" function that the hippocampus does in MacLean and Henry's model—it is the cortical receiving area for emotion. It coordinates internal and external stimuli and provides an evaluation for the hypothalamus. The brain and body become prepared to act.

LeDoux (1986) cites considerable evidence to support the view that the limbic system is a receiving area for sensory input. The limbic system consists of a tangled maze of connections and interconnections, linking the sensory receptors to the limbic structures and these structures to one another. Recently, for example, the sensory thalamus has been found to contain areas that receive visual and auditory information and to transfer signals to the hypothalamus and amygdala. There is even evidence to suggest that neural connections run directly from the eyes to the hypothalamus and the hippocampus, thus allowing for the direct receipt of visual emotional stimuli by

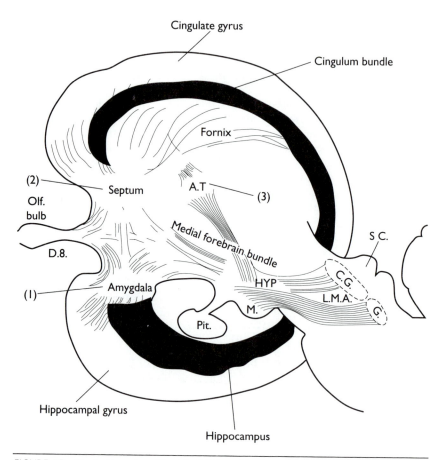

FIGURE 4.7   The limbic system. Plutchik, 1980a, p. 52. Copyright © 1980 by Robert Plutchik. Reprinted by permission of Harper & Row, Publishers, Inc.

the midbrain limbic system. In turn, clear evidence has arisen that the hypothalamus and amgydala receive information directly from visceral inputs and transmit directly to the brainstem and spinal cord. In short, if an emotional center exists, the midbrain is ideally suited to serve that function. LeDoux (1986) observes: "Limbic regions are richly interconnected, thus supporting the notion that limbic areas function as a system" (p. 333). The limbic system is designed to receive and transmit precisely the kind of information which would allow it both to initiate and to regulate emotional events in the brain and throughout the rest of the body.

On the other hand, the notion that the limbic system is the seat of all emotion has its critics. The role of the hippocampus is by no means clear, and it is possible that other brain structures play a significant role in emotional events. On the flip side, certain limbic structures have a role in higher mental processes—for example, the hippocampus in memory and the cirgulate cortex in perception. Moreover, "to say that emotion is a limbic function only transfers our ignorance from a field called brain and emotion to a field called limbic system function" (LeDoux, 1986, p. 334). Thus, LeDoux proposes that the neuroscientist's best strategy is to try to map out the the physiological linkages involved in each emotion, rather than allowing assumptions about the role of the limbic system in emotion to dictate the direction of theory and research for all emotions. Nevertheless, until a better theory is postulated as to how the CNS controls emotional reactions and experiences, the limbic system will continue to receive considerable attention.

The Physiology of Emotional Stimulus Evaluation, Emotional Expression, and Emotional Experience

In chapter 2, we observed that when researchers express an interest in emotion, they may be talking about very different things—emotional experience (including cognition), the physiology of emotion, or emotional behavior. LeDoux, too, acknowledges that a neuroscientific model of emotion must be able to account for the different aspects of emotion. The three aspects of emotion which he attempts to explain in neurophysiological terms are stimulus evaluation (a cognitive event), emotional expression (behavior), and emotional experience (feelings). Historically, researchers who tried to tease out the neural foundations of emotion ended in a tangle of confusion when they failed to distinguish between say, fear as a conscious state versus fear as indicated by such overt behaviors as freezing, defecation, and so forth. In an earlier section, we reviewed the peripheral nervous system and its powerful impact on emotional experience and expression. In this section, we discover that the CNS has a special role in the cognitive evaluation of incoming stimuli, that is, in the assignment of affective value to stimuli.

The CNS Physiology of Stimulus Evaluation.

LeDoux (1986) defines **stimulus evaluation** as "a process by which sensory input is compared with stored information or knowledge. . . . Such knowledge can be bestowed by either experience or inheritance" (p. 341). In invertebrates and lower vertebrates, animals' judgments are guided by ancient instincts. Stimuli that have signaled danger for millennia (the smell of rotten food; the shadow of a predator) activate prewired neural circuits, which trigger preprogrammed adaptive behavioral patterns. In humans and higher animals, only a few emotional assessments are entirely instinctive. For instance, a few ancient unconditioned stimuli (food, warmth, loud noises, falling) call out primitive positive or negative emotional reactions. Usually, information must be acquired through experience. As we discover in chapter 5, through association and in other learning experiences, an infinite variety of stimuli may come to trigger evaluative reactions.

In LeDoux's view, the brain mechanisms for stimulus evaluation reside, in part, in the temporal lobe, especially the amygdala (see Figure 4.7). LeDoux cites a study in which researchers produced lesions in the amygdala area of laboratory monkeys' brains (Jones & Mishkin, 1972). The investigators found that the animals showed "a dissociation between the sensory-perceptual and affective qualities of stimuli" (LeDoux, 1986, p. 341). In other words, after their operations, the monkeys could still see perfectly well, but they did not react normally (emotionally) to what they saw. The animals suddenly lost their fear of human observers, they now ate a variety of formerly repugnant objects, and they attempted to copulate indiscriminately (approaching members of their own sex or even animals of other species). In short, some sort of coupling mechanism that had previously enabled the monkeys to associate stimuli with an emotional label ("good" or "bad") had been destroyed. Jones and Mishkin traced the problem to neuron pathways from the cortex to the amygdala. It appears to LeDoux that the amygdala "assigns meaning to cortically processed visual information" and guides behavior by its pathways to the hypothalamus and other brain structures (p. 342).

Much less is known about how the brain processes information from other exteroceptors (such as, the nose, ears, etc.). There is some evidence, however, that pathways run to the amygdala as well from the cortical areas that receive information from these senses. (Throughout this discussion, it may help to recall that the structures we are describing are all part of the Papez "loop" shown in Figure 4.6.) Also relevant, LeDoux and his co-workers (LeDoux, Sakaguchi, & Reis, 1983) found that rats were unable to learn a fear response if critical areas of their brains (those relaying information to the thamalus and the amygdala) were destroyed.

More than one limbic structure may have a role in stimulus evaluation. The cortex also has sequential connections with the hippocampus (see Figure 4.6). Sensory information may pass through the hippocampus on the way to the hypothalamus. Since, as we have noted, the hippocampus also has functions in memory and spatial perception, neuroscientists are currently investigating whether this limbic area might play a role in stimulus evaluation (Poletti, Kliot, & Boytim, 1984).

Neuroscientists have suggested an intriguing possibility. Perhaps the brain possesses a system of parallel processing for evaluating the meaning of various stimuli. Sometimes, a subtle, complex assessment of a situation is required. (For example, although we know we can generally trust our actor friend, we may know that if a part in a play is involved, we had better watch out. He may be dangerous. He'd sell us out in a moment.) When such complex discriminations are required, the brain may find it necessary to route information via the neocortex to the limbic system. The neocortex possesses the brain's most sophisticated processing capabilities. It enables us to make subtle discriminations. On the other hand, sometimes only a relatively simple and crude stimulus evaluation is required. (All we may need to know about ice cream is "Do I like it?") In such cases, information may be routed via projections directly from the thalamus to the limbic system.

Often, the two forms of processing work in concert. When sensory input reaches the thalamus, it is routed through the primary projection systems to the cortex for further analysis. It is simultaneously relayed via the adjunct systems to subcortical areas. LeDoux (1986) observes that there may be method in this seeming madness. First, only a few emotional stimuli are so important and so complicated that they require conscious attention. Most things can be handled routinely, out of consciousness. The suggestion that the limbic system may function independently of the neocortex to trigger emotional reactions without conscious processing is intriguing. This would provide a central, neurological basis for the role of the "unconscious" in emotional expression. Second, even when conscious processing is required, there is a real advantage to a two-step process. Initially, the limbic system may function as an emotional filter, shaping people's quick, rough-and-ready initial reaction to events (alerting them to something good or bad, warning them to approach or avoid something). Shortly thereafter, the neocortex comes through with a more carefully processed, detailed, deeper impression of the situation. (Recall Proust's cup of tea, which first gave "shudders" of joy, then colors and shapes, characters and gardens, in Box 4.1.)

Stimulus Evaluation and Reward. In an early experiment, James Olds and Peter Milner (1954) discovered, somewhat by chance, that if electrodes were implanted in the limbic system and certain other areas of a rat's brain and these areas were electrically stimulated, the rats acted as if they were receiving a tremendous reward. They behaved like drug addicts. They seemed willing to perform any task, for any length of time, just to get their reward. For example, the rats would expend monumental energy repetitively pressing a lever in order to obtain a small jolt of current in this brain area. Since then, psychologists have carefully charted a number of such reward centers in the brain (Olds, 1977).

How do these reward centers work? Edmund Rolls (1976) hypothesizes that one of the functions of the limbic system, particularly the amygdala, is to associate environmental events with rewards and punishments. He contends that connections from the medial forebrain bundle system (especially the hypothalamus) provide the amygdala with information as to whether or not reward or punishment has occurred. The amygdala sends back information as to which sensory events were associated with the reward. The animal then develops an association which can guide behavior. In studies such as Olds and Milner's, rats had an unusual opportunity to "short-circuit" the usual pathways. They could press a lever and receive direct stimulation of their limbic systems. The limbic system would send out a message: There is an association between the stimuli generated by the lever pressing and the rewards of "pleasure center" stimulation. Not surprisingly, the animals pressed the lever for more.

In sum, LeDoux speculates that the chain of events involved in a typical emotional sequence looks like this. An emotional stimulus appears. Mother is baking chocolate-chip cookies. Their sweet smell wafts through the kitchen. We watch her scrape them off the hot metal baking pan and place them on a cool plate. Our senses pick up the cookies' sights, sounds, and smells and telegraph them to the brain. This information is evaluated in certain forebrain areas, such as the amygdala, in the the limbic system. The simple verdict comes in: "Smells good!" The amygdala sends information to the brain stem areas via the hypothalamus. This area sends a message to the ANS. We begin to salivate, and we approach the plate of cookies.

Despite what is known in general terms about these brain areas and pathways, however, LeDoux emphasizes that considerably more research is needed. For example, we have little knowledge of how the system determines the emotional significance of information in different sense modalities, such as visual, auditory, and touch.

The Brain in Conscious Emotional Experience. Today, the neurosciences still know very little about the nature of consciousness, subjective experience, or emotional feelings. Such misty concepts are difficult even to define. Even harder is determining how to study them. Nonetheless, LeDoux contends that neuroscientists must try. LeDoux (1986) defines feelings as a class of "conscious experiences having to do with the individual's welfare" (p. 350). At first glance, such a definition seems reasonable enough. On second glance, we are confused. We seem to have substituted one vague term (consciousness) for another (feelings). How, then, does LeDoux define consciousness?

For LeDoux, consciousness (self-awareness) and language are closely allied. In support of his view, LeDoux cites several observations, among them: (a) The same organisms that possess conscious self-awareness (humans) possess language. (b) In most people, the left side of the brain contains Broca's area, the so-called "language center." Split-brain patients (whose brains' left and right hemispheres have been surgically separated) seem quite conscious of what their left brains are up to. The workings of their right brains remain more or less a mystery to them (LeDoux, 1986, p. 350).

LeDoux takes the position that if language is not the same thing as conscious awareness, it is still a "first approximation." But what about infants, who seem to possess self-awareness but are unable to understand language? LeDoux handles such objections by proposing a second definition: "Consciousness is not so much a function of language as of the cognitive *capacity* to speak or understand speech" (pp. 350–351). What about other animals? Do they possess consciousness? Lower animals and humans possess very different neurocognitive mechanisms; they differ enormously in their ability to produce and process language. Thus, although other animals may possess some primitive forerunner of consciousness, their sense of self and experience is likely to be distinctly different from our own, both qualitatively and quantitatively.

In general, the left hemisphere of the brain specializes in tasks involving language. LeDoux identifies a posterior (rear) portion of the neocortex, the inferior parietal lobule (IPL), a small lobe of the brain, as the area primarily responsible for understanding the meaning (semantics) of linguistic information. This area is somewhat toward the rear but in the same hemisphere in which the speech production and grammatical center (Broca's area) is located. (A corresponding area is also located in the right hemisphere.)

LeDoux proposes that our conscious emotional experiences (or feelings) can be based on two very different kinds of information. Sometimes, our conscious perceptions are powerful and relatively direct. Our conscious emotional language includes information which has come to us directly from connections with the all-important limbic system. In addition, the IPL may receive incoming information from the five senses and feedback from the viscera and the muscles. It can rely on an abundance of information in coding feelings. When people have such a wealth of information, their assessments are likely to be accurate.

Sometimes, however, people are forced to make inferences about their feelings on the basis of insufficient information. The IPL is short-circuited. Sensory information is relayed directly to the limbic system; the limbic system sends a message directly to the ANS, and a relatively unconscious emotional response occurs. In this case, people have a great deal more trouble figuring out what they feel. They have no information from the limbic areas, only feedback from the viscera and the muscles. They must rely on a calculation of what a normal person might reasonably feel in such circumstances. Here, the chances for self-deception are great, and we are reminded of Stanley Schachter's model (chapter 3). Schachter proposed that people cognitively assess environmental stimuli to decide what it is appropriate to feel when their physiological responses signal that they should feel something. LeDoux seems to provide a neurobiological analogue of Schachter's two-component model. Under these circumstances, people might conclude that they feel a wide variety of emotions when all they have to go on is a knowledge that they are aroused and in a certain situation. Interestingly, since such cognitive detective work is based on inference rather than on direct limbic input, LeDoux points out that "it will often be imprecise or wrong" (1986, p. 353).

Sometimes people have no conscious experience of feeling emotional even though others insist they are behaving emotionally. (Sometimes we are totally unaware that we are angry until we hear ourselves snarling, "Angry, what do you mean, angry? I'm not angry!" Then, we realize to our amazement that we are.) Again, in such cases, LeDoux might speculate that sensory information has not reached the IPL. Instead, it has gone directly from the limbic system to the ANS. A relatively unconscious and automatic emotional response has occurred.

In short, conscious emotional experiences (or feelings) are due either to linguistic processing of (a) information directly from the limbic system, the brain's subcortical emotional system, or (b) information about the link between emotional stimuli and environmental events. In the first case, when people have immediate and direct feedback about their bodies, their assessments are likely to be accurate. (We are reminded here of Freud's and Jung's insistence that people must get in touch with their unconscious if they are to gain insight into their emotional inner life.) In the second case, people rely on the process of inference in decoding their feelings. Here, the difficulty of pinpointing the cause of such emotions is much greater.

SUMMARY

To summarize, LeDoux provides us with a useful review of existing knowledge concerning the functions of the peripheral and central nervous systems and their roles in emotional stimulus evaluation, emotional expression, and experience. His updates on the changing views of the ANS and CNS make it clear that what we once thought we knew about the physiology of emotion is being constantly revised as research continues. Clearly, we still have much to learn. LeDoux's revival of notions concerning parallel processing of emotional information at the cognitive and visceral levels is intriguing. It may lead to neurological solutions to the continuing problems of the relationships among feeling, the unconscious, and the bodily accompaniments of emotion. Finally, his views of the possible role of the parietal lobules in the consciousness of emotion is a bold proposal for further research on the "language of emotion."

We are far from finished, however. While LeDoux so nicely outlines the structures and functions of the nervous systems, let us now turn to the work of James Henry, who emphasizes the role of hormones in emotion.

Henry's Neuroendocrine Theory of Emotion

James P. Henry (b. 1914) is a professor of psychiatry at Loma Linda University in California. He has presented his ideas in a variety of books and papers, most notably, *Stress, Health and the Social Environment* (1977) (with Patricia M. Stephens). Henry focuses on the role of the cortex, the limbic and neuroendocrine systems, and the brainstem in emotion. In his theorizing, he draws heavily upon the work of neurologist Paul MacLean and others. When reviewing LeDoux's work, you learned a number of neuroscientific terms and a great deal about the role that the cortex, the limbic system, and the brainstem play in emotion. Thus, in our review of Henry's work, we can focus on the functions of the neuroendocrine system in emotion. Of necessity, we will provide a highly simplified explanation of these processes. More knowledgeable readers, with an extensive background in physiological psychology, should read Henry and Stephens (1977) for an in-depth description of this fascinating field of research.

Henry is a creative, perhaps fanciful, theorist. His ideas are on the cutting edge of research into emotional neurophysiology. Such ideas are likely to stimulate future research ... and criticism. As more and more information accumulates, many of Henry's ideas will surely have to be revised. Nonetheless, it is exciting to peer in and catch a glimpse of the possible future.

THE GENERAL MODEL

Let us begin by outlining Henry's general model of the physiological processes involved in emotion, and then fill in the details. According to Henry, in emotion, the sequence of events that commonly occurs is shown in Figure 4.8. At point A, psychosocial and environmental stimuli impinge on the individual. At point B, these stimuli are fed into a **psychobiologic program**. Genetic factors determine the program's "hard-wiring" (the anatomical, biological, and physiological structures that determine how people can respond to emotional stimuli). Early experiences provide "soft-wiring" or "programming" (which determine how individuals do respond to emotional stimuli). The output from these two sources is processed in the neocortex and the limbic system at point C. Next, at point D, the CNS telegraphs specific directions to the periphery. Emotions are associated with specific patterns of neuroendocrine and behavioral responses. These typical patterns of neurophysiological and hormonal responses may produce certain structural and functional changes; these, in turn, may produce emotion-related diseases (at points E and F). In this chapter, we focus on the neurophysiological mechanisms of emotion (points C and D in the figure) and reserve the discussions of the role of emotions and stress in mental and physical health for other chapters.

Consider a real-life example of the emotional sequence depicted in steps a-f: (a) Bus drivers have extraordinarily stressful jobs. They have to deal with cranky passengers, hectic traffic, and impossible schedules. (b) In part, how

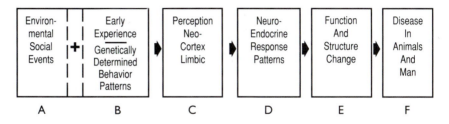

FIGURE 4.8   Henry's general model. Based on Henry and Stephens, 1977, p. 17. Permission of Academic Press.

they stand up to this pressure is determined both by their genetic heritage and by their acquired personalities. For instance, drivers who have friends with whom they can vent their frustrations do better than those who keep their daily frustrations all inside. (c and d) In circumstances perceived as stressful, the brain generates higher levels of certain hormones (such as cortisol) and lower levels of others (testosterone). (e) In the short run, these changes help drivers deal with stress. (f) If stress continues too long, however, sooner or later the pressure takes its toll, and drivers develop physical problems. For example, 100% of bus drivers who stay on the job until age 60 develop symptoms of essential hypertension (high blood pressure) (see Henry, in press).

Henry (1986) argues that the emotions of fear, anger, depression, and elation or relaxation are associated with different experiences, different patterns of neuroendocrine response, and different behaviors. For example, Figure 4.9 shows the specific brain structures and patterns of neuroendocrine responses involved in three of these emotions—anger, fear, and depression. (Henry considers these to be basic emotions.) When people are angry, their norepinephrine and testosterone levels show a dramatic rise. They feel like "fighting." When people are fearful, their epinephrine levels rise. They are motivated to "flee." When people are depressed, their ACTH and cortisol levels rise precipitously. They may behave like "subordinates" (rather than aggressive "dominants"). They barely feel like moving.

Henry argues that the two positive emotions—elation and relaxation (serenity)—are also associated with distinctive experiences, neuroendocrine patterns, and behavior. As shown in Figure 4.10, when people are most serene, their catecholamine levels decline. Such states may occur when people are meditating or relaxing. When people are elated, their testosterone levels increase. Such reactions happen when people are in love or feeling "in control."

Let us examine these distinctive patterns of central, neuroendocrinal, and behavioral responses associated with the various emotions in greater detail.

NEUROENDOCRINE BASES OF NEGATIVE EMOTIONS: ANGER, FEAR, AND DEPRESSION

*D*espair and confidence both banish fear.
        WILLIAM ALEXANDER

The Perception of Control

According to Henry (1986), one of the most important factors in determining which emotions people and animals display in various settings is how much control they feel they have over other events. According to Henry and Stephens (1977), the brain (specifically, the frontal cortex) is unusually good at analyzing which sort of emotion will work in a given situation. For example, when people are challenged, "if it is perceived that the challenge can be

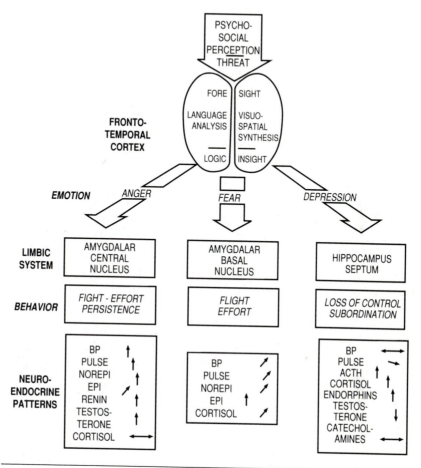

FIGURE 4.9 The neuroendocrinology of anger, fear, and depression. Henry, 1986, p. 40. Permission of Academic Press.

mastered, an attempt is made to master the threat by fight, effort, and persistance [sic], and the subjective feeling will be anger" (Henry, 1986, p. 41). When people feel in charge of things, threats lead to anger and effective coping. Sometimes, however, people are not in charge. Anger would be counterproductive. Here, sensible people get frightened and beat a hasty retreat, knowing that they can thereby "live to fight another day." Of course, sometimes the situation is hopeless. Slaves, for example, can neither fight nor run. Under such conditions, people have a reason to be depressed. Nearly all they *can* do is submit and save their energy. In a sense, the brain chooses which emotions and reactions are appropriate, depending on the situation.

In the brain, the hypothalamus and the pituitary gland (a small endocrine

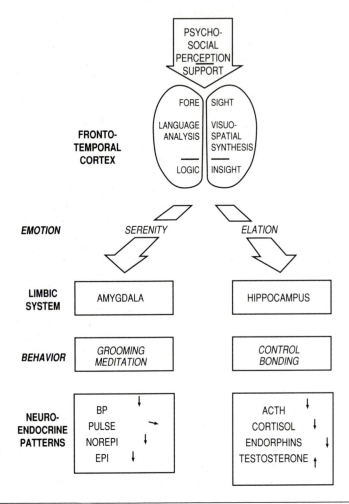

FIGURE 4.10   The neuroendocrinology of serenity and elation. Henry, 1986, p. 40. Permission of Academic Press.

gland located approximately in the center-lower part of the brain, beneath the hypothalamus) trigger the specific neuroendocrine responses associated with each of the emotions. These, in turn, shape the person's or animal's physiological and behavioral reactions. As Henry and Stephens (1977) state:

> Together, the hypothalamus and the pituitary form the crucial outflow for the control of the neuroendocrine apparatus by converting nerve impulses into hormonal responses, thus linking the brain to the regulatory mechanisms. (p. 118)

People (and animals) who believe they are in control of a situation react cognitively, behaviorally, and physiologically in different ways from those who do not (Carlson, 1982). (See Box 4.2.)

BOX 4.2

The Neuroendocrine Effects of the Perception of Control

In an early demonstration, Jay Weiss (1972) documented the powerful effect that the ability or inability to control an important event has on rats' physiological responses. Weiss placed a trio of rats in an apparatus. The rat on the left and the rat in the middle were electrically shocked on their tails at exactly the same time. However, at a signal (tone) that preceded the shock, the rat on the left (avoidance–escape rat) was permitted to turn a wheel that turned off the shock or prevented it from being turned on at all. The middle rat (whose fate was linked, or "yoked," to that of the avoidance–escape rat) could not turn its wheel (it was locked in a fixed position) and had no control over its fate. In other words, the avoidance–escape rat could con-

trol the shock, while the middle, yoked rat could not. Both received the same number of shocks. The rat on the far right received no shock at all; it merely sat in the apparatus. Weiss found that whether or not rats had control over the events in their lives had a profound impact on their physiological reactions. Avoidance–escape rats (who had control over the shock) showed few physiological signs of stress; they reacted much as did rats who had received no shock. However, the yoked rats, who found it impossible to control any of the events, showed signs of severe emotional distress, including ulceration, increases in plasma corticosterone levels, and loss of body weight.

Henry suggests that ancient neuroendocrinal "programs" guide animals to react one way when they are in power and in quite another way when they are helpless. In prehistory, animals evolved instinctive reactions to guide their interactions with the social and physical world. If animals were generally successful in acquiring social and physical resources (food, water, etc.), they would react to threats of loss of control with a standard set of active coping reactions—with the "fight or flight" responses described by Walter Cannon. If they suddenly lost control (as in the Weiss experiments), they would react with subordination and withdrawal, the responses of a "depressed subordinate" in a social group (Weiss & Stephens, 1977, p. 119). In a monkey troop, both dominant and subordinate monkeys have clearly defined roles vis-à-vis one another. Eventually, even the dominant monkeys must assume a subordinate role such as the old monkey who loses status and suffers a painful loss in resources, mating opportunities, and territorial rights (Bernstein & Gordon, 1974). When this happens, his physiology and behavior change, along with his status.

Humans are often forced to switch roles as they move from one setting to another. Consider this real-life personality sketch of Major General X. On the military base, his word was law. All his friends were powerful community, business, or military leaders. He couldn't be bothered with "riff-raff." He had a relentless need to control his family's every act. He insisted that his wife organize the cupboards the "right way"; that his 15-year-old son share his ideas about music; that his 2-year-old daughter wear a sweater when *he* felt cold. ("You're not going to win this struggle, old girl," he announced to the toddler. "I'm bigger than you are.") Unfortunately for him, they weren't willing to play along. When he behaved this way, his wife half-jokingly addressed him as "Your Way-Way-Up-Thereness." His daughter took to saying "No" with a ferocity to match his own. At first, he was enraged. He tried everything he could to turn things around. He got sick. He bellowed and threatened. Finally, he gave up. Eventually, he learned to enjoy simply being another member of his family. When last seen, he was down on his knees, playing with his daughter, pretending to be a horse. Henry and Stephens (1977) echo the importance of learning to play different roles in different settings:

> The capacity to switch from an aggressive self-confident demeanor of one in a control position to that of a modest deferential subordinate is particularly necessary in human society where activities fall into different categories. A leader in a game or sport, such as chess or skiing, may have far lower status at work or at home. (p. 25)

When animals are threatened, they differ in the extent to which they perceive they are in control. Centrally, in Henry's view, the main difference between powerful and powerless animals seems to be in the role the various brain structures—the frontal association areas, the amygdala, and the hippocampus—play in emotion. In turn, the various brain structures give rise to distinctive neuroendocrinal, physiological, and behavioral responses.

*A*nger is an expensive luxury in which only men of a certain income can indulge.
GEORGE WILLIAM CURTIS

Anger and Fear

Henry (1986) observed that under normal circumstances, when people are threatened or challenged, if they feel competent to deal with a threat, they will experience anger. They will have a powerful physiological reaction and will attempt to master the threat by fight, effort, and persistence. (In chapter 10, we examine different types of anger. For now, let us consider only the physiological underpinnings of the simplest forms of anger.)

When the threat appears, a message is sent to the frontal cortex in the association areas for processing (see Figure 4.9). Soon, the central amygdala and the hypothalamus (in the limbic system) are activated. They signal the ANS to release norepinephrine. In addition, sympathetic neural innervation of the adrenal medulla occurs, stimulating increases in an enzyme that synthesizes additional norepinephrine. People's hearts begin to pound, their breathing becomes fast and shallow, their blood pressure rises. When people are angry, another hormone, testosterone, is produced owing to an outflow of the gonadotrophic hormone, one of the secretions of the pituitary, from the anterior portion of this gland. Testosterone, of course, plays a powerful role in sexual behavior (especially in male sexual behavior), but it has also been identified as an accompaniment of anger.

In an article in *Sports Illustrated,* South Carolina lineman Tommy Chaikin described what happened to his mind and body when he began "chemical warfare" and started taking massive doses of anabolic steroid (testosterone) injections. He became more self-confident. His weight climbed from 210 to a lean 235 pounds. His arm, chest, and leg muscles began to bulge. He became fiercely aggressive.

> I was developing an aggressiveness that was scary. That summer I was work-ing as a bouncer at this bar in D. D., and one night a Marine bumped into a girl I was dancing with. Words were exchanged, then I followed him to where he was sitting and said, "I didn't appreciate that." He put his beer down and came up hard under my chin with his hands, and a slice of my tongue about an inch long went flying out of my mouth. I didn't even notice it. I saw red. I felt an aggression I'd never felt before. I hit him so hard that he went right to the floor. He was semiconscious, and I got him in a headlock and started hitting him in the ribs and kneeing him in the back. I wanted to hurt him real bad. I could literally feel the hair standing up on the back of my neck, like I was a wolf or something. If I hadn't been on steroids, I would've walked away in the first place. But I had that cocky attitude. I wanted to try out my new size. I was beginning to feel like a killer. (Chaikin & Telander, 1988, p. 90)

Unfortunately, Chaikin's steroid use also took him out of football. He eventually developed psychotic anxiety, headaches, edginess, high blood pres-sure, a "whooshing" in his ears, and vision problems. His conclusion: "Ste-roids screwed me up pretty good" (p. 102).

To demonstrate the link among anger, stimulation of the amygdala, and ANS arousal, G. Stock, K. H. Schlor, H. Heidt, and J. Buss (1978) conducted an experiment with cats. In this study, cats received electrical stimulation in the central portion of their amygdala. The researchers recorded the changes in the cats' cardiovascular output and their behavior. The animals showed the kinds of reactions generally associated with anger. Their ears flattened, and they prepared for attack. Their heart rates, blood pressure, and peripheral vascular resistance (which increases as the blood vessels near the surface of the body constrict) all rose. Note in Figure 4.9 that anger is accompanied by relatively higher levels of norepinephrine than epinephrine. In fact, this is hypothesized to be one way in which anger differs from fear. (In fear, the ratio is the reverse.)

Recently, psychologists have found that angry, aggressive people (like angry cats) tend to have relatively greater amounts of norepinephrine in their system. Researchers can get an estimate of how much norepinephrine/epi-nephrine people are secreting by taking urine samples. They have found that men and women who are identified via personality tests as angry, irritable, and resentful possess a higher ratio of norepinephrine to epinephrine in their urine samples (Kadish, 1983).

Fear gave wings to his feet.

VIRGIL

Thus far, we have focused primarily on the neuroendocrinology of anger. Let us turn now to fear. (Again, see Figure 4.9.) Sometimes a small boy is too timid to stand up to a bully. Sometimes a shy girl is afraid to speak in class. Henry (1986) observes that when people are threatened but know they cannot manage the threat, the "feeling of fear-anxiety predominates." In fear, "the response involves basal amygdalar activation with a predominance of epinephrine" (Henry, 1986, p. 41). Such a response makes sense. In fear and anxiety, people's bodies must be primed to expend a great deal of mental and physical energy as they race to escape. Epinephrine (from the adrenals) activates a wide range of necessary internal adjustments, as you learned earlier in this chapter. In addition, if anxious or frightened people feel helpless to alter their circumstances, they will begin to show a rise in the distress hormone adrenocorticotropin, ACTH (Henry, 1986, pp. 41–42). Let us detail some of these reactions.

When an animal encounters a threatening or stressful situation, the frontal cortex makes an assessment: Is it better to fight or flee? If to flee, a message is again sent to the amygdala—this time to its base. The animal quickly mobilizes for action. Initially, it shows alarm. The medullary (internal) portion of the adrenal glands is activated, and the ANS is aroused. In this aroused state, the fearful animal is well prepared for the intense mental and physical activity required to escape from the situation. These reactions involve the sympathetic adrenal-medullary system. If the threat is repeated or chronic, the animal begins to show a second-stage response. The hypothalamus activates the pituitary gland; the pituitary, in turn, activates another portion of the adrenal glands (the cortex, or surface). The adrenal cortex, in its turn, releases a number of cortisone-related hormones, including cortisol. (It may come as no surprise, then, that neuroscientists who wish to measure fear or anxiety often measure cortisol levels in the blood, urine, or saliva.) If frightened, animals are forced into a long-term retreat, and the cortisone-related hormones provide certain biological advantages. For example, they help maintain the body's production of, and sensitivity to, epinephrine, and they suppress certain immune reactions, such as swelling of the joints, which might interfere with escape.

In Truman Capote's *Breakfast at Tiffany's* (1958), the heroine, Holly Golightly, describes what such "mean reds" (generalized anxiety) feel like: "... the mean reds are horrible. You're afraid and you sweat like hell, but you don't know what you're afraid of. Except something bad is going to happen, only you don't know what it is" (p. 40).

Thus, Henry theorizes that in some ways, angry and fearful animals are similar. Both must be prepared to expend enormous energy in sustained fighting or fleeing. But their physiological reactions may well differ. For example, in the amygdalar region of the brain, anger is linked to central activity; fear to basal activity. In anger, there may be more norepinephrine secretion; in fear, more epinephrine secretion. In anger, testosterone makes a contribution; when fear is sustained, cortisol and other hormones keep the action going.

Depression

The preceding scenario has yet another variation. Sometimes, when animals are threatened, they experience a profound loss of control. They can neither fight nor flee; they experience a sense of fearful helplessness. Ultimately, they may become depressed (see Figure 4.9). They become despondent, sad, and unable to act. For example, take a couple who are considering divorce and seeking therapy. The wife is buoyant and filled with energy. She is fed up with her husband. He is boring. At home, all he does is eat, sleep, and sit staring at the television. They rarely have sexual relations.

He, on the other hand, is depressed. As a child and adolescent, he had been intensely religious. His life was tightly controlled. When he met her, everything changed—everything seemed possible. He went wild. He began to drink and take drugs, but he couldn't handle it. He began an affair with a local thug's wife and "borrowed" money from his employer's firm. Eventually, he sobered up and recognized what could happen to him if he were caught. He could be divorced, fired, imprisoned, or killed. At first, he was paralyzed with fear. Then, he sank into depression. Now, papers keep piling up at work, and he just sits and stares at them. The Internal Revenue Service is threatening to imprison him if he does not file his tax returns for 1980–1989.

Usually, when people are depressed, they require at least some talk therapy. He does not. All he needs are anti-depressant medications. After two weeks, his mood and behavior have altered completely. He is good natured when he comes home at night. He talked to his boss and has worked out a pay-back plan for the money he borrowed. Now he can tackle his work with enthusiasm. He contacted the IRS and has worked out an arrangement so that he can pay off his back taxes over a 10-year period. His is a case of a biologically based depression, triggered by fear and anxiety and, eventually, exhaustion. An antidepressant changed his life.

In many ways, fear and depression are similar. Both are associated with increased pituitary activity and high adrenal corticoid hormone levels. In depression, there may also be especially high levels of a substance secreted by the pituitary (see Figure 4.9). ACTH stimulates the cortex tissue of the adrenals to activity; this, in turn, increases the level of cortisol and related hormones. (In Figure 4.9, Henry probably should have reported the fact that ACTH may also be elevated in chronic fear.)

However, Henry notes that in other ways, fear and depression (fearful helplessness) are very different. When animals are initially frightened, the amygdala and the sympathetic adrenal-medullary system are activated. As fear turns to depression, the hippocampus and the pituitary-adrenocortical system become involved. To some extent, these two systems have opposite physiological and behavioral effects. Generally, in fear, the animal's reactions are speeded up. In depression, they are slowed down.

In theory, the role of the hippocampus is to provide a cognitive "map" of the animal's relationship to the world. For example, it may give an animal a sense of its hierarchical place in the pecking order. It may tell the animal that it should have a dominant or a subordinate position. It also gives an animal a sense of its location in physical space. Henry and John Meehan (1981) speculate that the hippocampus is activated whenever the animal perceives a mismatch between its perception of how things are and its stored representations of how things ought to be. This comes into play when usual patterns of responding fail to pay off (and control is lost). Then, the animal stops responding in the old, unprofitable ways. Sometimes, the animal is able to come up with new, more effective ways of dealing with change. Sometimes, however, nothing works, and the animal simply quits doing much of anything at all.

At the human level, consider, for example, what happens to the powerful executive when the stock market crashes and his company fails. Suddenly, he experiences a loss of control over the resources that he once took for granted. He once could hire and fire people at will. Now he is looking for a job. He has no secretary to take his letters. He can't pay his bill at the health club. At first, he may feel anger or fear. Eventually, he may begin to be depressed. His hippocampus alerts him that the old patterns will no longer work. He must try something new, but what? When there is a failure to overcome challenges, the pituitary begins to release ACTH, which, in turn, produces a series of bodily effects (such as adrenocortical responses) and behavioral effects. While the fearful executive's heart raced and his blood pressure soared, the depressed executive's heart rate and blood pressure may actually decline. Interestingly, once the executive becomes depressed, endorphin levels in his brain may rise. Endorphins are the brain's natural opiates. This explains why people, like other animals, may become less sensitive to pain in situations in which they have lost control. In chronic depression, a kind of numbness sets in.

In summary, Henry's approach differentiates two forms of fear—fear itself (fear–anxiety) and depression (fear–helplessness). Fear is associated with activity in the basal amygdala. A fearful person is motivated to flee or take cover. Depression is associated with activity in the hippocampus. A depressed person is motivated to remain in place. Depression is accompanied by a sense of powerlessness, helplessness, insensitivity, and inactivity.

Studies by Marianne Frankenhauser confirm that how frightened/depressed persons respond physiologically will depend on how much control they believe they have over the situation. For example, Marianne Franken-hauser, Ulf Lundberg, and Lennart Forsman (1980) demonstrated that when students were given a pleasant task on which they could self-pace, their epinephrine levels increased. However, when the task involved considerable attention and distress, their cortisol levels increased. Similarly, when monkeys were permitted to control an intense noise, they did not show increases in blood plasma cortisol levels. When the monkeys were not able to turn off the noise, they did show cortisol increases. Moreover, these neurophysiol-ogical responses associated with helplessness were also associated with be-havioral disturbances and withdrawal from social contact (Hanson, Larson, & Snowdon, 1976).

When animals are depressed, then, they show what we might call a *hippocampal-pituitary-adrenocortical* reaction. What function can such a re-sponse possibly serve, since depression seems to lead to withdrawal from social interaction, helplessness, submissiveness, and a host of other ineffective behaviors? Henry (1986) proposes that, for our prehistoric ancestors and for ourselves, the tendency to react to impossible situations by "sitting and star-ing" may have some real functions. The paleolithic man who lost a big battle and hid out in the weeds, immobile, frozen, gave his wounds a chance to heal. The exhausted father who sits and stares at the cracks in the ceiling has a chance to replenish his energy and enthusiasm. Further, this conservation-withdrawal reaction may ensure that we, like our ancestors, are forced to learn new, more adaptive patterns of behavior. For example, if the elderly shaman, whose prestige and powers wane becomes despondent and submis-sive, the other tribe members may be able to "push him around" and force him to learn his new role. The divorced man who is depressed at the failure of his marriage, may become motivated to take a new hard look at himself. Because our ancestors were involved in more violent conflicts with man and nature than we are today, the habit of "sitting this one out" when things became too difficult may have served an even more important function then than now. Nonetheless, Plutchik (1980a) and others observe that these ancient neural-hormonal patterns endure (see chapter 5). Probably, they are still more functional even today than they seem at first glance.

Now that we have considered three basic negative emotions—anger, fear, and depression, let us consider two basic positive emotions—serenity and elation.

NEUROENDOCRINE BASES OF POSITIVE EMOTIONS: SERENITY AND ELATION

According to Henry (1986), the positive and negative emotions are opposites in many ways. They are associated with very different neuroendocrine re-actions and very different behaviors. If you take a look at Figure 4.11, you will be able to trace some of these differences.

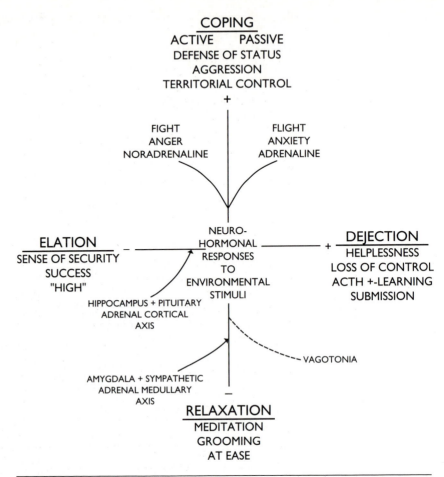

COPING
ACTIVE   PASSIVE
DEFENSE OF STATUS
AGGRESSION
TERRITORIAL CONTROL
+

FIGHT   FLIGHT
ANGER   ANXIETY
NORADRENALINE   ADRENALINE

ELATION   −   NEURO-   +   DEJECTION
SENSE OF SECURITY   HORMONAL   HELPLESSNESS
SUCCESS   RESPONSES   LOSS OF CONTROL
"HIGH"   TO   ACTH +-LEARNING
                           ENVIRONMENTAL   SUBMISSION
                           STIMULI
HIPPOCAMPUS + PITUITARY
ADRENAL CORTICAL
AXIS

                                                    VAGOTONIA

AMYGDALA + SYMPATHETIC
ADRENAL MEDULLARY
AXIS   −

RELAXATION
MEDITATION
GROOMING
AT EASE

FIGURE 4.11 Emotions as polar opposites. This diagram contrasts two emotional response patterns—the "pituitary adrenal-cortical" system (see the horizontal axis) and the "sympathetic adrenal-medullary" system (see the vertical axis). *Dejection* (on the far right) is associated with loss of control. (Here, the adrenal-cortical system generates cortisol.) *Elation* (far left) is associated with high control (and lower cortisol levels). *Coping* versus *Relaxation* responses are contrasted on the "sympathetic adrenal-medullary system" (vertical) axis. In anger and fear, as people try to cope (and maintain control), the sympathetic system is activated—adrenaline and noradrenaline are produced. Relaxation occurs once people achieve control. It is associated with low cortisol levels. Henry, 1982, p. 371. Copyright 1982, Pergamon Press.

According to Henry (1986), serenity–relaxation is the polar opposite of anger–fear. Serenity and relaxation are associated, in animals with grooming behavior, in man with states such as meditation. (Anger and fear, of course, are associated with the opposite, fighting or fleeing.) Similarly, elation is vastly different from depression and helplessness. "Elation accompanies a sense of control and the perception of bonding, nurturance, and grooming" (p. 44).

(Depression, as we have seen, is associated with helplessness and loss, including the loss of attachments.) We now consider these positive emotions in more detail.

*S*erene amidst the savage waves.
WILLIAM OF ORANGE'S MOTTO

Serenity

We all know what serenity feels like. We feel serene contentment when we come home wet and exhausted and sink into a tub, when we look up from a good book and see the sun setting through the trees, or when the children finally troop off to bed. The left side of Figure 4.11 depicts the events which shape a serene or relaxed emotional response. The first step in central processing of environmental input takes place in the fronto-temporal cortex. The amygdala is critically involved in this processing. Serenity is associated with decreased activation of the sympathetic adrenal-medullary system. Specifically, a significant decline occurs in both catecholamine (epinephrine and norepinephrine) levels and cardiovascular activity (such as pulse rate). Herbert Benson (1975) describes the physiological changes that constitute the relaxation response. When one is relaxed, breathing slows, oxygen consumption decreases, blood pressure falls, and muscle tension decreases. This suggests that in serenity, there is a general shift in the ANS to parasympathetic dominance and a corresponding decrease in catecholamines. Similarly, Chandra Patel and her co-workers (Patel, Marmot, & Terry, 1981) have demonstrated that when patients are instructed to meditate and utilize a variety of other relaxation techniques, their blood pressure begins to fall and their heart rate slows. For some time, medical researchers have suggested that if patients can learn to relax, the neuroendocrine changes that occur will counteract the negative effects of chronic fear and anger (and the neural and hormonal effects they bring about—see chapter 13). Henry's proposal suggests an explanation for how this process might work.

*J*oy makes us giddy, dizzy.
GOTTHOLD LESSING

Elation

Experientially, elation is at the opposite pole from depression. Henry suggests that depression follows from the perception of loss of control in the face of threat. Elation, by contrast, results from the perception of control accompanied by environmental support. Although there is little related evidence, Henry (1982) suggests that elation may be defined centrally in terms of hippocampal activity, in particular, "selective activation of high-voltage slow waves in the hippocampal septal system" (p. 372)—a match rather than a mismatch. In elation, people are reassured that the strategies they have always used for dealing with the world are working. Theoretically, this activity is accompanied by a suppression of the pituitary-adrenocortical response: There is a decrease in ACTH, cortisol, and the endorphins and an increase in testosterone (again, producing a neuroendocrine pattern opposite to that involved in depression).

Henry cites some fascinating evidence in support of the possibility that the adrenal cortex is relatively inactive when a person has the perception of control and support. Peter Bourne (1970) kept medical records on medical corpsmen flying dangerous helicopter rescue missions in Vietnam. Often they were under heavy fire. He monitored the men's plasma corticosterone levels both on flying days and off-duty days. Surprisingly, he found no difference! In fact, the men's corticosterone levels were actually below that expected of a civilian population not under any particular stress. Similarly, low levels of this hormone were found in expert special forces troops, in a camp surrounded by the Viet Cong. The special forces officers and radio operators, however, showed signs of fear and anxiety. It was these men who had the higher plasma corticosterone levels.

Bourne points out that the medical corpsmen and special forces troops had two things in common—the (inaccurate) perception that they were in control and the (accurate) recognition that their fellows supported the work they were doing. The medical corpsmen were a tight, cohesive group. The troops they rescued were naturally grateful for their heroic rescues. They received extra pay and medals. They had no doubt that their missions were socially valuable. They did, however, deny that the missions were dangerous, a perception belied by high casualty rates. The special forces were also a tight band. They were not introspective; they simply didn't think about the risks of mutilation or death. ("It can't happen to me.") They kept themselves furiously busy maintaining equipment and fortifying their positions. Such activity bolstered their sense that they were in control. Their commanding officer and radio operators, by contrast, felt far less in control. Their superiors frequently sent radio messages that were unreasonable and inconsistent, too little, too late. They had no other work to distract them. They were less in control and felt the effects.

The same results, suppressed corticosterone levels, were found in the Gemini astronauts in space flight (Lutwak, Whedon, Lachance, Reid, & Lipscomb, 1969). They, too, felt in control. They were a cohesive group. They received a great deal of approval, both from their fellow astronauts and from the American public. Also, the astronauts had a considerable array of tasks to perform, many of which directly and successfully controlled their flight. (*Columbia* astronaut Bob Parker recalled, a bit chagrined, that he had been so busy activating a manually operated tape recorder that he had forgotten to look out the window as he hurled out into space.) Interestingly, astronauts' corticosterone levels returned to higher baselines after completion of the flight.

Figure 4.11 diagrams the processes just described. Here the poles of the vectors define the four patterns of response—coping (anger/fear) versus relaxation, and elation versus dejection. The various brain structures and neuroendocrine responses, which mediate these responses, are also outlined.

NEUROPHYSIOLOGICAL PATTERNS OF EMOTIONAL RESPONSE AND ARCHETYPES

In chapter 3, we reviewed Carl Jung's work. Jung believed that the instincts are stored in mankind's collective unconscious in the form of archetypes. Jung believed that these primeval images silently guide thought, emotion, and behavior and give shape and direction to human activity. What brain structures could be involved in such biological programming? MacLean (1975) and others have concluded from their research that the higher cortical structures do not play an essential role in guiding lower animals' purposive, goal-directed behavior. Higher structures do not guide play, maternal behavior, feeding, or nest building. Thus, Henry concludes that it must be the lower brain structures (the brainstem and the limbic system) and the neurotransmitters they control that guide these ancient behaviors. Perhaps a modern way to understand archetypes, then, is to understand the brain structures and neuroendocrine patterns that underlie primitive emotional behavior patterns. As Henry and Stephens (1977) state:

> The biogrammar or archetype can be seen as a vital but prerational element of behavior dependent on subcortical structures. It might be termed the language of psychologic programs that originate from the structures of the brain stem and limbic system. (p. 4)

Henry argues that archetypal programming influences most socially significant behavior—from gender differences in behavior to sexual preferences, territorially, and aggression. Henry (1986) observes that an "extensive body of new data persuade[s] us of the existence of sexual differentiation of instinctual or archetypal behavior patterns in man and lower animals" (p. 50). If these prewired archetypal neurohormonal patterns are altered, the instinctive, complex, emotional behaviors they guide will be dramatically altered as well. But how can ancient archetypes be altered? Henry suggests one way. If an embryo does not receive correct hormones at the right stage of prenatal development, its behavior might be altered from childhood through adulthood. Or, adult hormonal influences on an embryo might similarly alter behavior.

Henry cites a raft of evidence in support of the contention that archetypal neuroendocrine patterns shape emotional behavior. For example, Ingeborg Ward and Judith Weisz (1980) found that male fetal rats normally receive a surge of testosterone on the eighteenth and nineteenth days of gestation. If rat mothers are psychologically stressed during that critical period, when their male offspring reach adulthood, they may not respond to female rats in heat in sexually appropriate ways. Recall that levels of testosterone are suppressed when control is low during threat—perhaps it is this imbalance that affects the embryo. It is also believed that higher levels of ACTH may adversely impact on the testes of the fetus, resulting in a deficiency in critical testosterone levels.

Henry suggests that even something as complex as human sexual preferences may rest on an archetypal or instinctual base in neurohormonal patterns. Also, he proposes that variations in the sex hormones may affect aggressive behavior. Katharina Dalton (1977) suggests that a few women become tense and aggressive at certain phases in their menstrual cycle, when their progesterone levels are unusually low. She cites several studies indicating that such schoolgirls are more likely to cause discipline problems and such women to engage in criminal activities and in disorderly conduct in prison. Dalton contends that 40% of women are affected by the cyclical hormonal swings of menstruation. She calls this reaction *premenstrual syndrome.* Henry agrees, maintaining, "It appears that the hormonal changes of menstruation may make some individuals less amenable to discipline, more tense, and less alert" (1986, p. 51).

Recently, a great deal of evidence has been collected to explore the impact of women's menstrual cycles on their emotional behavior. However, the data suggest that the facts of the matter are more complex than Henry and others have believed (see Box 4.3).

Mother-infant bonding, too, may be mediated by instinctive, hormonally based mechanisms. Such archetypal mechanisms can be disrupted by life events. In research cited by Henry (1986), mothers who are allowed to hold their newborns immediately after birth quickly develop a strong maternal attachment to them. Mothers who are separated from their newborns for hours or days seem to have unusual difficulty forming such bonds (Klaus & Kennel, 1982). Similarly, if premature infants are separated from their mothers, they, too, may have unusual difficulty in bonding (Klaus, 1970). Recently, however, child psychologists have begun to collect evidence that humans are amazingly resilient. Even children who suffer severe deprivation during the first few years of life (children who are orphaned, left in refugee camps, or placed in isolation in hospitals) seem able to form deep, loving relationships thereafter (McGraw, 1987). It seems, then, that Henry may have overstated his case.

Henry (1986) sketches evidence from a variety of other sources to document his contention that the emotional patterns of neuroendocrine response underlie the archetypes. He contends that in the human brain, in the dark regions below the huge association cortex, hormone-driven neuronal complexes mediate the emotional behaviors critical for self- and species-preservation. He attempts to demonstrate that such archetypal hormonal patterns

BOX 4.3

Premenstrual Syndrome (PMS) and Mood

For decades scientists have debated whether women's changes in personality and mood are caused by fluctuations in the hormones associated with the phases of the menstrual cycle. According to cultural stereotypes, in the premenstrual period, some women are tense and disagreeable. A few years ago, Dr. Edgar Berman, Vice President Hubert Humphrey's physician, argued that women were unfit to hold public office or participate in the space program because of their "raging hormones" (Hyde, 1986, p. 98). Since then, astronaut Sally Ride's successful voyages have squashed that notion. What effects, if any, does a woman's menstrual cycle have on her mood?

Sex researchers have found that immediately before some women ovulate (in the middle of their cycle), they sometimes experience an unusual sense of well-being, a higher energy level, heightened sexual interest, and a general increase in visual, auditory, and olfactory sensitivity, as well as a decrease in sensitivity to pain. In contrast, in the premenstrual phase and in the first days of their period, they may experience lowered self-esteem as well as some depression, tension, and irritability (McCauley & Ehrhardt, 1976; Rossi & Rossi, 1980).

Most women do not really experience cyclical changes in mood, however. Daniel Cox (1983) asked college men and women to participate in a study that a medical school was conducting to find out how common various symptoms were among college students. They were asked to keep a record every day for a month of their emotional and physical symptoms. Were they irritable? Depressed?

Tense? Was their face broken out? Did they have cramps? They found that men and women were equally even tempered throughout the month. Women were not more emotional before, during, or just after their periods. Men's and women's reports differed in only one way. When women were menstruating, they were especially likely to report bloating, stomach pains, and cramps.

Given that fact that most men and women experience roughly the same feelings throughout the month, why has the myth that women's mood changes dramatically throughout the month endured for so long? It may be that the myth benefits both men and women. For example, Carolyn Sherif (1980) observes that many women use menstruation as an excuse for avoiding work or sexual interactions they don't like. Men, too, may have a vested interested in thinking of women as emotional beings, especially during their periods. For example, take the case of a couple who were professional graphic artists. The husband was good looking, kind, and impossible to live with. He would forget to empty the trash in his private workroom for months at a time. (The wife was forbidden to touch it.) When he was chilly, he would wander into her room (because it was closest) and grab her favorite silk shirt. Months later the shirt would turn up in his car. His cat had used it as a litter box. At any rate, he was convinced that her complaints were due solely to the fact that it was "that time of the month." That way, he didn't have to deal with her complaints. Because it was *always* either before, during, or after her period, it was impossible to prove him wrong.

shape young children's friendship choices, their language (especially grammatical and syntactic patterns [Eimas, 1985]), facial expressions (see chapter 6), and romantic love (Liebowitz, 1983). (In chapter 11, we discuss the fact that passionate love's obsessional quality may be caused by the endorphins, epinephrine, and norepinephrine that swirl through lovers' bodies.)

When it comes to specific fears (phobias), Henry proposes that humans may be prewired to acquire phobic reactions to certain stimuli rather than others. There is evidence that infants naturally fear snakes crawling on the floor (Torgerson, 1979). As Jung suggested, there may also be a natural tendency to fear spindly-legged creatures, such as spiders or centipedes. Such predispositions certainly make sense from an evolutionary point of view. Our prehistoric ancestors had to learn to avoid large and dangerous prototypes of many current-day insects and arthropods if they were to survive. It would be biologically advantageous for them to be prewired to treat such insects with respect. In Henry's view, "phobias may be a further example of innate archetypal machinery at work. . . . The fact that phobias more commonly occur to objects and events that our hunter-gatherer ancestors would also fear suggests that inherited patterns may be involved" (1986, p. 53; see also Seligman, 1971). It should be noted that even theorists who believe that people are genetically predisposed to fear certain things disagree about how this process might work. Some argue, for instance, that people may inherit a tendency to become fearful under certain perceptual conditions, rather than inheriting fears of specific objects. Richard McNally (1987) suggests that we might be especially likely to fear objects that move quickly or that are very different from ourselves (such as cockroaches); he doubts that we are predisposed to fear specific classes of organisms. In short, if people are genetically predisposed to certain phobias, we are not quite sure how this process operates.

To summarize, Henry offers us a broad conceptual scheme for understanding the neuroendocrinology of emotion. He contends that five basic emotions—anger, fear, depression, serenity, and elation—are derived from specific patterns of cortical, limbic system, and hormonal activity. He cites a wide range of data in support of his speculations. Of course, his critics can cite contrary evidence. One of Henry's controversial notions is that specific patterns of behavior in emotion have biological bases ("biogrammars") that parallel Jung's archetypes. The possibility is intriguing that such widely disparate activities as sexual preferences, facial expressions, women's nurturant attachments, phobias, and other behaviors with powerful emotional components are based in primitive structures of the brain, such as the amygdala and hippocampus, and in ancient neurotransmitters. Henry also speculates that in the left hemisphere of the brain (which is primarily involved in tasks requiring language, reason, and empirical analysis), the archetypes may be "clothed in technical and dogmatic expression" (Henry & Stephens, 1977, p. 265). But in the right hemisphere of the brain (which is primarily involved in spatial perception and emotional expression), these primitive bases for behavior, the archetypes, can appear in dreams, myths, and symbols. We are only at the beginning of research and conceptualization of the role of the neurophysiological and endocrine processes in emotion. Henry and LeDoux surely take us to the very edges of the frontiers of that knowledge.

Summing Up

- Joseph LeDoux and James Henry take a neurophysiological approach to the study of emotion. They focus on the central nervous system (CNS), peripheral nervous system (PNS), and neuroendocrines.

- In LeDoux's view, the CNS functions in stimulus evaluation and makes a contribution to emotional experience and expression. The PNS also makes a special contribution to emotional experience and expression.

- The somatic nervous system consists of neurons to and from the sensory and motor organs. The autonomic nervous system (ANS), with centers in the brain and spinal cord, consists of neurons leading to internal organs in the cardiovascular, respiratory, digestive, and endocrine systems.

- The sympathetic portion of the ANS, with centers in the thoracic and lumbar portions of the spinal cord, functions in general arousal. Its neurotransmitters include epinephrine and norepinephrine. Owing in part to patterns of sympathetic ganglia, the sympathetic nervous system tends to excite parallel responses in a variety of organs.

- The parasympathetic nervous system includes neurons from the brain stem and sacral portions of the spinal cord, which innervate individual organs, usually in directions opposite of sympathetic responses. Acetylcholine is the predominant neurotransmitter throughout this system.

- In recent years, views of the autonomic nervous system have undergone changes, some of which challenge Cannon's views: The two branches do not always operate in strict opposition; different patterns and levels of end-organ responses occur during sympathetic activation; synapses may respond to other neurotransmitters; and yet another branch of the autonomic nervous system may exist.

- The limbic system or visceral brain—consisting of the amygdala, thalamus, hippocampus, hypothalamus, cingulate cortex, and other areas—has been traditionally and more recently identified as an important center for central nervous system activity in emotion. LeDoux feels that identifying the limbic system as the seat of emotion may oversimplify the neurophysiology of emotion.

- LeDoux suggests that the amygdala (and possibly the hippocampus) functions in stimulus evaluation, assigning meaning to information from the cortex. In theory, the thalamus may permit parallel processing of evaluative properties of stimuli, at once preparing the organism for a general affective reaction ("good" versus "bad"), while transmitting input to cortical areas for more sophisticated processing.

- LeDoux speculates that input to the inferior parietal lobule in the left and right hemispheres may be responsible for assigning emotional meaning, which contributes to the conscious experience of emotion.

- Henry suggests that environmental and psychosocial stimuli, combined with a "biogrammar," converge on the neocortex and limbic system. There, different neuroendocrine response patterns are initiated which define the individual emotions, including specific functional and behavioral patterns.

- The negative emotions, anger, fear, and depression, develop in part because of different perceptions of perceived control over the environment. Anger and fear are emotions demanding effort for fight or flight (and heightened cardiovascular responding) when control over threat is possible. Depression appears under circumstances of loss of control under threat; cardiovascular responding may decline.

- Anger and fear may be differentiated in terms of relative activity in different parts of the amygdala; the central nucleus may function in anger, the basal portion in fear. Anger and fear differ hormonally in terms of relative amounts of circulating catecholamines—anger is correlated with greater amounts of norepinephrine, fear with epinephrine—and testosterone levels are greater with anger; cortisol levels may be elevated with chronic fear.

- Depression is distinguished hormonally by increases in ACTH, with resulting elevations of cortisol and other adrenocorticoid hormones. In addition, elevations of endorphins in the brain and decreases in the catecholamines differentiate depression from other emotions during threat.

- Positive emotions, namely serenity and elation, develop when one perceives psychosocial support in the environment. When the amygdala is involved, catecholamine levels and cardiovascular functioning decline, defining states of relaxation or meditation (serenity), the polar opposite of anger and fear.

- When the hippocampus is involved, ACTH and the adrenocorticoid hormones, as well as endorphins, decline. Testosterone levels may increase. During these periods, the perception of control ("elation"), the polar opposite of depression, occurs.

- These neurophysiological and neuroendocrinal substratum of the emotions may parallel Jung's notion of the archetypes—complex patterns of innate activities and experience that form the bases for the instincts.

5
Expressive Theories of Emotion

Introduction

Plutchik's Psychoevolutionary Synthesis
Theoretical Postulates
The Structure of Emotions
Diagnostic Concepts and Emotion

Millenson's Behavioral Analysis
Three Ways of Thinking About Emotions
A Model of Emotion
Implications of the Model

Summing Up

FIGURE 5.1   *Separation*. Edvard Munch. Lithograph. The Munch Museum and Oslo Kommune.

Introduction

Recently, the Unitarian church invited their singles group to get together to discuss "dealing with 'hot' emotions in a love affair." As men and women recounted their fumbling attempts to make relationships work, it became increasingly clear that it is often difficult to figure out how to act in a new relationship. It is hard to know when you should bite your tongue and keep your feelings to yourself and when you should express your deepest feelings, letting the chips fall where they may. For example, one young woman, Rose, said that early in her marriage, her husband, Bob, had said he hated conflict. Thus, in the first years of her marriage, she had struggled to be a model of rationality. She had learned to speak softly, smile, be patient, and try to work things out. Their marriage had been going swimmingly. Then, three months ago, Bob left her. He had fallen in love with his secretary, a flirt who drank too much, talked too much, and was always caught up in some sort of trouble. She was in constant conflict with her alcoholic parents and brutal boyfriends. Her life just didn't work. What could Bob possibly see in this emotional wreck? All he could say was that she was "spontaneous" and that she needed him.

Others pointed out that it didn't always pay to be spontaneous, however. Several men and women reported that they had just gotten "burned out" by constant "hassles." What they were looking for was a little peace and quiet. Often, it is difficult to figure out the right way to behave emotionally. In this chapter, we focus on what modern-day theorists know about the factors that shape men and women's emotional behavior or expression. Later, in chapter 14, we consider some of the consequences of choosing one or another strategy for dealing with our emotions.

In chapter 2, we introduced the approaches of theorists Charles Darwin, John B. Watson, and B. F. Skinner, who speculated about why people behave as they do. Darwin proposed that people are genetically programmed to respond in ways that were appropriate and adaptive in their species' evolutionary history. Watson and Skinner pointed out that people also are capable of learning to express their feelings in ways that are appropriate in the world of today. This chapter, focuses on the theories of two modern-day researchers—Robert Plutchik and J. R. Millenson. Plutchik (like Darwin) is interested in the ways in which people's emotional reactions are shaped by their evolutionary heritage. Millenson (like Watson and Skinner) is interested in the fact that men and women learn to express their emotions in ways that "pay off." Both Plutchik and Millenson assume that the best way to understand emotion is to focus not on what people think or feel, but on what they do. Both are interested in emotional expression.

Plutchik's Psychoevolutionary Synthesis

Robert Plutchik (b. 1927) is a professor of psychiatry and psychology at Bronx Municipal Hospital Center in New York. He received his Ph.D. in experimental psychology from Columbia University. Since then, he has taught and conducted research at such institutions as Hofstra University, Columbia University, and the National Institute of Mental Health. Plutchik has outlined his ideas in *The Emotions: Facts, Theories and a New Model* (1962) and *Emotion: A Psychoevolutionary Synthesis* (1980). Let us review Plutchik's psychoevolutionary theory—its fundamental postulates, its taxonomy of emotions, and the structural model.

We may affirm absolutely that nothing great in the world has been accomplished without great passion.

GEORGE WILHELM FRIEDRICH HEGEL

THEORETICAL POSTULATES

Plutchik begins by proposing 10 postulates. In the first four, he points out that emotion, evolution, and behavior are inextricably linked.

The Evolutionary Postulates

These postulates represent the evolutionary aspect of Plutchik's **psychoevolutionary synthesis**:

1. The concept of emotion is applicable to all evolutionary levels and applies to all animals as well as humans.
2. Emotions have an evolutionary history and have evolved various forms of expression in different species.
3. Emotions serve an adaptive role in helping organisms deal with key survival issues posed by the environment.
4. Despite different forms of expression of emotions in different species, there are certain common elements, or prototype patterns, that can be identified. (Plutchik, 1980a, p. 129)

Plutchik (1962) argues that the emotions must be considered from a broad evolutionary point of view. At every phylogenetic level (from the lowest single-celled organism, to reptiles, to mammals, up to the highest primate), organisms face the same problems—they must find food, avoid injury, and procreate if they are to survive and reproduce. Emotions developed in the first place, were shaped and reshaped over the millennia, and continued to survive because they were adaptive. They helped the species survive and reproduce. Emotions are inherited, adaptive patterns of behavior. These adaptive reactions include **protection responses** (flight, avoidance, hiding, and playing dead), **destruction responses** (clawing, biting, and hitting), and **reproduction responses** (courting, copulating, and egg laying). Emotions evolved, then, because they were adaptive for the species.

But prehuman primates first appeared 25 million years ago. It has taken that long for the basic emotional patterns to evolve. In many ways, the prehistoric world was very different from our own. Plutchik points out that evolution is ultraconservative—organisms may continue to transmit genetic material for millions of years after its adaptive advantage has disappeared. Thus, it should come as no surprise if an emotional response that once was supremely functional is maladaptive in today's different world. (Today, we may feel like snarling, advancing on our computer, and smashing it against the wall when a power surge destroys a day's work. That is not, however, an adaptive response.)

One other point: It is easy to see why Plutchik and other evolutionary theorists are interested, not in a species' emotional thoughts and feelings, but in its behavior. An animal's inner life can have little effect on survival. Only emotional behavior can be adaptive or nonadaptive, functional or nonfunctional, increasing or decreasing the species' chances of survival. Only when the tiger in anger expresses itself by striking out can natural selection occur.

Primary Emotions Postulates

The next three postulates propose a limited number of emotions (functional patterns of expression):

5. There is a small number of basic, primary, or prototype emotions.
6. All other emotions are mixed or derivative states; that is, they occur as combinations, mixtures, or compounds of the primary emotions.
7. Primary emotions are hypothetical constructs or idealized states whose properties and characteristics can only be inferred from various kinds of evidence. (Plutchik, 1980a, p. 129)

Theorists disagree as to the number of basic emotions. Watson (1930) argued that there were three innate emotions—fear, rage, and love. Raymond Cattell (1957) calculated 10 emotional *factors* (sex-lust, fear, loneliness, pity, curiosity, pride, sensuous comfort, despair, sleepiness, and anger). Plutchik maintains that there are eight **prototype emotions:** fear, anger, joy, sadness, acceptance, disgust, expectancy, and surprise. All the other emotions are built upon them. We will return to this point later.

Structural Postulates

In Postulates 8–10, Plutchik attempts to describe the structure of emotion. (These postulates represent the psychological aspect of Plutchik's psychoevolutionary synthesis.)

8. Primary emotions can be conceptualized in terms of pairs of polar opposites.

9. All emotions vary in their degree of similarity to one another.
10. Each emotion can exist in varying degrees of intensity or levels of arousal. (Plutchik, 1980a, p. 129)

Plutchik's ideas—that the primary emotional dimensions can be conceptualized in terms of pairs of polar opposites and that emotions vary in similarity and intensity—all seem to make common sense. This view is also shared by many other theorists in the field of emotion.

Consider Plutchik's contention that emotions come in pairs of opposites:

Joy	versus	Sadness
Acceptance	versus	Disgust
Fear	versus	Anger
Surprise	versus	Anticipation

Presumably, the emotional pairs (say, joy versus sadness) feel like opposites, are associated with different physiological reactions (heart rate may speed up versus slow down), and lead to incompatible behaviors (dancing for joy versus collapsing in a heap). Theorists from a variety of perspectives agree that emotions come in pairs. In early factor analytic studies (Cattell, 1946), bipolar dimensions often emerged. Richard Solomon and John Corbit (1974) proposed that "opponent processes" shape many addictive behaviors. Psychiatrists have long observed patients who have bipolar affective disorders swing from mania to depression; somehow, these opposite emotions seem entwined. Plutchik believes that polarities are inherent in the structure of emotion.

Plutchik also proposes that emotions vary in similarity. At the most basic level, one can categorize emotions as positive or negative. Within these broad categories, one can continue to sort out emotions into still other, more subtle categories. For example, Jack Block (1957) found that college students felt that "pride, elation, love, and contentment" had much in common. They thought that "worry, humiliation, guilt, and grief" had much in common, too. But they felt that the first set of (positive) emotions was very different from the second (negative) set. People can easily sort emotions into categories on the basis of similarity or dissimilarity.

Finally, emotions differ in intensity. People can easily distinguish between tepid liking and intense passion, between slight unease and panic, and between sadness and intense grief. For example, people can easily assess whether they are merely pensive (a weak form of sadness), sad, or experiencing grief (an intense form of sadness).

THE STRUCTURE OF EMOTIONS

Plutchik (1980a) proposes a taxonomy (or orderly classification system) for classifying emotions. In the previous section, we noted Plutchik's observation that emotions can be classified along three dimensions—**bipolar quality** (whether the emotion is positive or negative), **similarity** (how similar emotions are to one another), and **intensity.** Plutchik's problem was to design a three-dimensional figure that would allow him to illustrate his classification scheme. Luckily for Plutchik, some time ago, artists and color experts found a way to do just that. They had to figure out how to classify the primary hues (red, blue, and yellow) and color blends when these colors could vary in purity (saturation) and intensity. First, color experts developed the color wheel (you might take a look at Figure 1.3 to remind yourself what such a two-dimensional color wheel looks like) and the three-dimensional color solid. (This time take a look at Figure 5.2.)

The "Emotion Solid"

Plutchik's postulates—that emotions are bipolar and vary in similarity and intensity—are incorporated in Figure 5.2, the **emotion solid.** Each level in this three-dimensional model looks much like a simple color wheel. The prototypic emotions (grief, amazement, etc.) circle the wheel. Emotions that seem very similar (grief and amazement) crowd in on one another; emotions

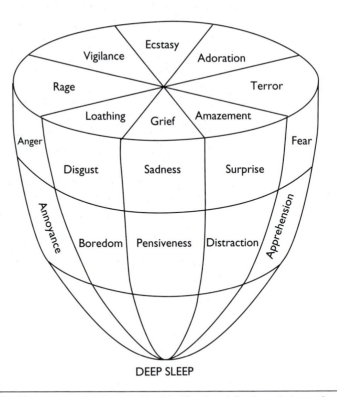

FIGURE 5.2   The emotion solid. From R. Plutchik, *Emotion: A Psychoevolutionary Synthesis*, p. 157. Copyright © 1980 by Robert Plutchik. Reprinted by permission of Harper & Row, Publishers, Inc.

that are opposite in feel (grief versus ecstasy) are directly opposite one another. As one moves from top to bottom (from grief to sadness to pensiveness to deep sleep), the emotional experiences become less and less intense, finally ending in deep sleep.

Now that you have a basic understanding of how Plutchik arranges emotions on the emotion solid, let us proceed to a more fine-grained understanding of how Plutchik chooses the emotional terms to be included in his taxonomy, how he decides which emotions are similar and which not, and how he assesses emotional intensity.

The Language of the Emotions

People can talk about emotions in a variety of languages. Plutchik (1980b) observes:

> Since an emotion is a complex sequence of reactions, one may describe different aspects of the sequence in different terms, or in different languages. Thus, there is a language for describing the stimulus events that produce emotions, a separate language for describing the inferred cognitions that interpret these events, still another language for describing the feeling states, and a language of behavioral reactions. The function of each emotion can be described in yet another way. (p. 15)

Consider the sequence of emotional events depicted in Table 5.1. A man walking in New York's Central Park late at night spots a stimulus (a mugger) emerging from the shadows; he makes a quick cognitive appraisal of the situation ("Is he kidding?" The answer is "No"). Terrified, the man runs. His quick overt reaction serves an important function, that of protection.

People can describe each event in the sequence in very different languages—subjective, behavioral, or functional, as shown in Table 5.2. People use a **subjective language** when they describe their personal feelings (Why did you run? "I was scared"). They use a **behavioral language** when they describe their reactions (What did you do? "I ran"). Finally, they use a **functional language** when they describe the outcome of their acts (What happened? "I got away").

Plutchik maintains that there are eight primary or prototype emotions. In subjective terms these are fear, anger, joy, sadness, acceptance, disgust, expectancy, and surprise (see Table 5.2). But other languages are possible,

---

Table 5.1   **The Sequence of Events in Emotion**

Stimulus Event	→	Cognitive Appraisal	→	Subjective Reaction	→	Behavioral Reaction	→	Function
Sight of Predator		"Danger"		"Fear"		"Run"		"Protection"

After Plutchik (1980a), p. 155

Table 5.2   Three Languages That May Be Used to Describe Emotional States

Subjective Language	Behavioral Language	Functional Language
Fear, terror	Withdrawal, escaping	Protection
Anger, rage	Attacking, biting	Destruction
Joy, ecstasy	Mating, possessing	Reproduction
Sadness, grief	Crying for help	Reintegration
Acceptance, trust	Pair bonding, grooming	Incorporation or affiliation
Disgust, loathing	Vomiting, defecating	Rejection
Expectancy, anticipation	Examining, mapping	Exploration
Surprise, astonishment	Stopping, freezing	Orientation

Plutchik (1980a), p. 154.

too. Table 5.2 gives examples of how the prototype emotions could be described in behavioral or functional languages. Plutchik's structural model attempts to organize the multifaceted language of emotion.

Of course, each primary emotion may be experienced more or less intensely. English is a rich language, and it possesses an array of terms to express subtle differences in emotional intensity. For instance, "fear" can range from wariness to terror; anger may vary from mild annoyance to fury. Emotional behaviors can vary in intensity as well. Expressions of anger can range from a black look to a vicious stabbing.

In Figure 5.2, Plutchik uses subjective, everyday language ("grief," "anger") to sort out the emotions in the emotion solid because this is the language with which people are most familiar. He points out that if he had chosen instead to use a behavioral or functional language, the emotional space would have looked somewhat different. For example, when Plutchik is categorizing subjective reactions, perceived similarity determines how close emotions are to one another. If he were categorizing behavioral reactions, objective similarity would determine the placement of emotions. Currently, we have a rough idea of how the various emotions should be placed on the emotion solid. A few problems still remain to be worked out, however. What is the appropriate emotional language (subjective, behavioral, or functional) to use in a given situation? Are all the languages equivalent? Sometimes it is hard to say just how similar various emotions are. Luckily, it is far easier to say how intense they are. Today, where emotions are placed depends on how researchers have measured emotional similarity and intensity (i.e., with a verbal report, measures of physiological state, or overt behavior). With additional research, the emotion solid will probably be standardized.

A Dictionary of Emotions: Emotional Mixtures

Plutchik asserts that the subjective emotions people experience may be mixed, just as colors can be mixed. A mixture of two primaries is called a dyad. A mixture of any three primaries, a triad. According to Plutchik, when a stimulus event evokes two primary emotions, say both fear and surprise, people experience an intermediate, mixed emotion. Plutchik assumes that emotions combine much as colors do. Just as blue and yellow produce green, fear and surprise would produce alarm. What if a stimulus evokes two emotions that are bipolar opposites (such as fear and anger)? In that case, the person will not experience a distinct emotion. Instead, the person will experience either two conflicting tendencies ("I didn't know whether to laugh or cry") or will be immobilized. (The angry-frightened child may not know whether to hit or run. Instead, of doing either, he may stand stock still, frozen.) "Just as opposite colors when mixed in equal intensity act to neutralize one another to produce gray, so too do opposite emotions when occurring simultaneously in equal intensity act to inhibit or neutralize each other" (Plutchik, 1980a, p. 1963).

Plutchik observes that the English language may or may not possess a term for such combinations:

> The problem is in a way similar to that faced by chemists at the beginning of the nineteenth century. Their task was to find ways of determining the elements present in any given compound. . . . Even today, chemists do not know the exact formulas for many complex organic substances. It may take psychologists a long time to determine the components of all mixed emotional states. (1980a, p. 161)

In other words, simply because the English language does not yet have a name for a hypothesized emotion does not mean that such an emotion does not exist. A language may have to be developed to express such feelings. Plutchik points out that soon after an international color system was adopted, researchers named a number of newly discovered colors. Their work may provide a model for the task of naming newly discovered emotions.

Recently, Plutchik set out on a fascinating quest: to find out how people would label the various emotional mixtures. He began by asking judges to identify the primary emotions involved in a long list of emotional mixtures. He found that often, people could agree on a name for the various mixtures. Some examples:

- joy + acceptance = love
- surprise + sadness = embarrassment
- disgust + anger = scorn
- joy + fear = guilt
- joy + surprise = delight
- surprise + anger = outrage

In a few instances, people could not find the right term to describe an emotional mixture. (What, for example, is surprise + disgust? What is disgust + joy? Or anger + acceptance?) Plutchik's endeavor reminds one of the efforts of the structuralist psychologists in the 1800s to extract the elements of color from subjects' color sensations. Plutchik's exercises are designed to develop an emotional language and taxonomy in which there is agreement as to the "hue" (specific emotion), the "saturation" (the purity of the emotions involved in an emotional mixture), and the "brightness" (intensity) of a given emotion. If no appropriate terms exist, Plutchik suggests that they should be coined so that a true language of the emotions can emerge.

Emotions and Personality Traits

Plutchik (1980a) has suggested that personality traits are really emotional descriptions in disguise. Because observers draw conclusions about personality by observing people's complex emotional reactions in social encounters, Plutchik asserts that personality traits and emotions are one and the same. In Plutchik's words, "In this sense, a trait is simply a tendency or disposition to react to interpersonal relations with certain consistent emotional reactions" (1980a, p. 173). People are said to have an angry and hostile personality if they are snide, short tempered, and cruel in social interactions. They are said to be loving and affectionate if they generally have a kind word for everyone.

Plutchik (1980a) goes a step further in attempting to explain the persistence of personality traits. He points out that, in a sense, when people display a personality trait (when they are hostile, or cooperative, or timid), their behavioral repertoire is stereotyped—their behaviors replay, like an endless cassette tape. The hostile person isn't angry only sometimes, like the rest of us. He is angry so often that people consider it part of his personality. They cannot help but notice. Plutchik suggests that people are most likely to get stuck, or "frozen," when their emotions are mixed and in conflict. When people are ambivalent , they are "caught." For example, it is when we both love and are irritated by our loved ones that we become obsessed with them. We can't leave them—we love them too much to do that. But we can't stand their rudeness, their irresponsibility, their irritating habit of drumming on the table with their knuckles. So we think and think about them. On the basis of such reasoning, Plutchik proposes that personality traits reflect the conflicts between two or more emotions. People with mixed emotions are torn between two or three different, conflicting, actions: "Thus, a person who is *spiteful* has an impulse to *reject* someone as well as an impulse to *attack*. A person who is *docile* has an impulse to *accept* as well as to *run*" (p. 173). Perhaps people's personality traits really describe the conflicts they face, again and again. If such personality traits and emotional conflicts become too serious and too pervasive, people may be said to have a personality disorder. Plutchik (1980a) has attempted to match up personality traits with the two or three basic emotions with which they were most closely associated (see Box 5.1).

DIAGNOSTIC CONCEPTS AND EMOTION

Finally, Plutchik observes that the terms psychiatrists and clinical psychologists use in categorizing patients, terms for personality traits, and emotional

BOX 5.1

Personality Traits or Emotional Descriptions?

Plutchik and his colleagues (1980a) tried to identify which personality traits are associated with the various emotions. To do this, Plutchik asked a group of clinical psychologists, public school teachers, and college students to look at a list of 66 personality traits and decide which of the eight primary emotions was most associated with that trait.

Once they had made their first selection, he asked them to choose the primary emotion which seemed next most associated with that trait (from the seven remaining primary emotions). A listing of some common personality traits and the emotions on which these traits are based is presented in Table 5.3.

Table 5.3   **Personality Traits and Their Emotional Components**

Trait	Emotional Components	
	First Choice	**Second Choice**
Affectionate	Accepting	Joyful
Cautious	Timid	Expectant
Cooperative	Agreeable	Satisfied
Courageous	Expectant	Joyful+
Cruel	Rageful	Disgusted
Curious	Expectant	Surprised+
Forlorn	Sad	Timid
Friendly	Pleased	Agreeable
Gloomy	Sad	Annoyed
Greedy	Angry	Expectant+
Grouchy	Disgusted	Annoyed
Guilty	Afraid	Sad+
Happy	Joyful	Accepting
Jealous	Angry	Afraid
Passive	Timid	Sad+
Pessimistic	Sad	Expectant+
Romantic	Pleased	Accepting+
Sentimental	Pensive	Joyful+
Shy	Timid	Expectant
Suspicious	Watchful	Afraid+

+ The "plus" sign after a word indicates that at least one additional component is present.

Plutchik (1980a), p. 175

labels have a great deal in common. Clinicians use a manual called *DSM III-R (Diagnostic and Statistical Manual No. III: Revised)* (American Psychiatric Association, 1987) in order to sort patients into categories so that they can devise a treatment plan. Patients may be labeled as having a serious problem (as being schizophrenic or manic-depressive) or as having a mild personality disorder (as being dependent, antisocial, avoidant, and so forth). Plutchik observes that the labels we assign to such mental problems are, like personality traits, really emotional descriptions in disguise. For example, paranoia is associated with distrust and criticalness; a schizoid personality with detachment, inhibition, and passivity.

Plutchik has collected compelling evidence in support of that contention. For example, Earl Schaefer and Robert Plutchik (1966) asked a group of psychotherapists to try to match up the basic psychiatric disorders with personality and emotional traits. Subjects were asked to take a look at a given mental disorder (the paranoid disorder) and to indicate whether a person having that disorder would possess certain personality traits ("Would they be kind, assertive, suspicious, passive?"). They were also asked to indicate whether such a person would tend to experience certain emotions ("Would they tend to be joyful, angry, disgusted, sad?"). Clinicians found it easy to match the standard diagnostic categories with appropriate personality traits and appropriate emotions. For example, a paranoid person is usually suspicious, distrustful, and critical (character traits) as well as angry (an emotion). Plutchik (1980b) found that the three sets of terms were virtually interchangeable: ". . . these diagnoses represent extremes or exaggerations, of certain personality traits, which in turn, represent mixtures of basic emotions" (p. 24).

Relatedly, Plutchik (1965, 1970) developed the **Emotions Profile Index (EPI)** to assess people's personalities and emotional styles. Test-takers are told to indicate which of two emotional words best describes them. (Are you more quarrelsome or shy? Are you more adventurous or affectionate?) All in all, test-takers are really indicating how typical 12 terms, arranged in 62 pairs, are of themselves. Respondents' profiles on the eight basic emotions indicate which prototypic emotions, personality traits, or pattern of emotional conflicts most powerfully shape their lives. (We describe the EPI in greater detail in chapter 7, when we discuss measures of emotion.)

In sum, because Plutchik's work is so grand in scope, it has attracted attention and criticism. Most theorists simply threw up their hands when confronted with the task of developing a taxonomy of emotion. J. R. Millenson (1967) wryly observed that there is a "resistance to systematic integration" in the field (p. 433). Plutchik simply waded in and set about organizing and synthesizing the field. His impressive taxonomy and structural model provide a starting point for research that is yet to be done.

Education makes the man.

JAMES COWTHORN

Millenson's Behavioral Analysis

J. R. Millenson (b. 1932) received his Ph.D. from Columbia University. Early in his career he taught at York University in Toronto. Today, he is a professor of psychology at the University of Brasilia, Brazil. Millenson's theory is rooted firmly in a behaviorist tradition. Like B. F. Skinner and others with his behavioral perspective, Millenson is interested in applying an "experimental analysis of behavior." Traditionally, psychologists with this philosophical approach have insisted that people's inner lives, their thoughts and feelings, are of little interest as causal factors. What is important is behavior. The hallmarks of this approach include a respect for behavioral observation and for the role of the external environment in behavior. On those rare occasions when such theorists do touch on such psychological concepts as emotion, instead of using the taboo "E" word, they tend to substitute concepts such as "discriminative stimuli," "Pavlovian (or respondent) conditioning," "reflex elicitation," "operant conditioning," "incompatible" or "disruptive behaviors," or "contingencies of reinforcement." It may, therefore, seem a little surprising to find that in his text, *Principles of Behavioral Analysis* (1967), and in its revision (Millenson & Leslie, 1979), Millenson provides a formal analysis of emotion. This treatment provides the basis for our discussion.

THREE WAYS OF THINKING ABOUT EMOTIONS

Scientific breakthroughs often occur when researchers finally figure out how to ask the right questions. Emotions researchers have had a difficult time figuring out exactly how to pose the many questions they have about the nature of emotion. Millenson suggests three conceptual steps, three ways of thinking about emotions that he hopes will make them easier to understand. He discusses the difficulties of exploring the emotions as private events, the fact that emotions are generally best thought of as patterns of reflexive responses, and the fact that emotions involve widespread changes in behavior.

Emotions Should Be Thought of as Public Events

Most traditional theorists have been interested, in part, in private events—emotional feelings that can be known only by the person experiencing them. James (1890) observes the fascination of such events:

> What kind of an emotion or fear would be left if the feeling neither of quickened heart-beats nor of shallow breathing, neither of trembling lips nor of weakened limbs, neither goose-flesh, nor of visceral stirrings, were present it is quite impossible for me to think. Can one fancy the state of rage and picture no ebullition in the chest, no flushing of the face, no dilation of the nostrils, no clenching of the teeth, no impulse to vigorous action. . . ? In like manner of grief, what could it be without its tears, its sobs, its suffocation of the heart, its pang in the breastbone? (pp. 435–436)

In Millenson's view, private events are so compelling, so vivid, in part, "simply because overt emotional behavior is frequently accompanied by intense and widespread visceral (stomach, heart, lungs, etc.) and glandular changes" (1967, p. 437). In addition to their intensity, unfortunately, these events are private and remain forever so.

Such private events confront researchers with a dilemma. Science must deal with phenomena that can be observed and measured. Yet, researchers hesitate to simply dismiss people's interior landscapes as inappropriate for investigation. Many are more captivated by the shadings of thought and emotion than anything else. Still, it is hard for researchers to know the best way to explore such events. No way is possible to pluck out an emotional experience, hold it in one's hand and gaze at it, touch it, prod it, or poke it.

Millenson suggests two resolutions: In the first case, scientists may not be able to explore emotional experience directly, but they can gain some understanding of what people think and feel by (a) examining physiological reactions and (b) learning the bases for verbal descriptions of feelings. Both these activities are observable. In the first case, Millenson and Leslie (1979) note that "the inaccessible private events we call feelings are correlated with particular physiological states which are accessible to observation, given the necessary instrumentation" (p. 417). Of course, scientists who study the physiological correlates of emotion are interested in exactly these reactions.

In the second case, both Millenson (1967) and Skinner (in press) contend that, at base, any language of emotion is in fact a language of emotional behavior and this has implications for parents and peers. Currently, parents and other educators teach people how to talk about emotions—the "community shape[s] our verbal repertoire of 'emotion' words" (Millenson & Leslie, 1979). Of course, this is done in a rather haphazard way: "Come on, don't be shy; come out here and meet Susan," a big sister says to the toddler hiding behind the sofa, or "Don't you get mad at me," an aunt says to the little boy who threatens her with his small fist. But how can parents and teachers possibly know that their small charges are feeling shy or angry? They can't. All they can do is guess at what children are feeling by observing their emotional behavior—what they say and what they do. Children are taught to link their self-descriptions with their private experiences by way of the visible physiological reactions (blushing, blanching) and overt behaviors (frowning, kissing, cuddling, slapping) which parents can read.

Generally, this process works; sometimes, it does not. Sometimes, when people say they are "sad," or "angry," or "pleased," they are describing personal experiences that other people might label quite differently. When a teacher says, "I'm only doing this for your own good. You know it hurts me more than it hurts you," as she raps our knuckles, we sometimes suspect that she has overstated both her affection for us and her suffering at seeing us hurt.

There are several reasons why people might have trouble accurately communicating their feelings to others. For instance, sometimes, for reasons of their own, parents try to mislead children about the proper label for their emotions. ("Of course you don't hate your little brother; you love him; now give him a kiss," the earnest mother says to the little boy whose despised younger brother has just ripped up his coloring book.) Sometimes, parents simply have trouble reading their children's emotions; they assume that children are sad when they are merely tired, wild when they are simply excited, and so forth. It is hard—but clearly not impossible—to teach people to become aware of their feelings, to help them talk about their inner lives, when in the strictest sense, the teacher of emotional language cannot feel what the student feels and must rely upon other, more overt cues. The problem is something like looking into a microscope and trying to describe what is seen based upon reports that are given by someone else—who cannot look into the microscope at the same time. It is not surprising, then, that people often have such difficulties communicating.

Emotions Should Be Thought of as Reflex Patterns

Millenson, then, argues that scientists should not be primarily concerned with people's private emotional feelings. In his terms, "Since the actual feelings are not measurable or directly manipulable, whether they come before, after, or at the same time as [emotional] behavior is not of critical interest to us" (1967, p. 437). Instead of focusing on thoughts or feelings, then, Millenson focuses on emotional behavior. He defines emotions as special patterns of responses. The questions Millenson finds most interesting are: (a) Which emotional responses are innate? and (b) How are the other emotional responses learned? In fact, Millenson's approach to emotions is much like that of John B. Watson's.

In chapter 2, we discussed the fact that Watson (1919) believed in only three innate emotional reactions—fear, rage, and love. Millenson's (1967) taxonomy is much the same—he considers anxiety, anger, and elation to be the basic emotions. It is from these three basic emotions that all other emotions are derived. Watson and Millenson both argue that initially, these three basic emotional responses are elicited by unconditioned stimuli. Consider fear. Watson (1919) found that initially, infants fear only two things—loud, sharp noises and the loss of physical support (such as when a baby is suddenly dropped). However, infants soon learn, through a process of **Pavlovian conditioning,** to be frightened of many other things. The process works this way: In infants, an **unconditioned fear stimulus** (UCS) provokes an **unlearned fear response.** (If, just as an infant is falling off to sleep, the blanket is suddenly jerked from under her, she will startle, pucker her lips, clutch her hands, and begin to scream.) If a **conditioned stimulus,** (CS) (a grinning brother) is routinely associated with the UCS , the infant will soon begin to howl the moment she spots the fiendish intruder. In Pavlovian terms, this is the learned or **conditioned response.** In Millenson's view, the study of emotion is essentially the study of the "complex effects of Pavlovian conditioning" (1967, p. 439). (For an up-to-date review of what is known about Pavlovian conditioning, see Rescorla, 1988.)

Emotions Involve Widespread Changes in Behavior

Thus far, Millenson has suggested that we can best understand emotions by thinking of them as publicly observable patterns of responses. But that is not enough. The primary emotions (anxiety, anger, and elation/love) are unconditioned response patterns. Many other reflexes, such as coughing, sneezing, allergic reactions, the panting and flushing of heavy exercise, in Millenson's view, "all involve complex patterns of respondents. Yet few would be disposed to call them emotions. What is special about the X, Y, Z reactions that they, rather than these other patterns, should be raised to special status and called 'emotions'?" (1967, p. 439).

Millenson suggests that the answer lies in the fact that emotions tend to markedly disrupt, enhance, or produce widespread, general changes in a person's activities. In other words, in emotional situations, people are more likely than usual to show emotional reactions and less likely than usual to go about their daily business. The "angry" man may stop and express his feelings (making sarcastic remarks and challenging everyone in the house to "step outside") rather than continue to plug along at his work. The "happy" child may squeal and literally jump for joy; she may forget to drink her milk before leaving the table or to finish her homework.

What generally produces emotions such as anxiety, anger, or elation and their widespread behavioral changes? Millenson suggests that emotion can be produced in two ways: (a) the presentation or withdrawal of strong primary reinforcers, and (b) the presentation of stimuli that have been associated with these events and that have taken on their properties through Pavlovian conditioning. In other words, the appearance (or loss) of such reinforcers as food, water, sex, or things associated with these events will spark strong emotional reactions.

Consider an example (see Table 5.4). Imagine Rosemary Chatauvert has worked for 30 years as an accountant for the TransPacific company. Suddenly, she hears through the grapevine that TransPacific may be sold. She is overcome with anxiety as she realizes that if TransPacific is sold, she is likely to be fired. (In the words of Millenson, she is "presented with a negative reinforcer.") Surely, Rosemary would have trouble eating, sleeping, or doing her job. She may well find herself unable to concentrate at the very time that it is essential that she look good. If Rosemary is not only fired but, to add insult to injury, also learns that terminated workers will not receive their pensions ("removal of positive reinforcers"), her anxiety may turn to anger. Now, she may spend her time filing a lawsuit, organizing other ex-employees, or fantasizing destroying company books and equipment. If the workers' threats

Table 5.4	**Disruptive Effects of Emotional Events**	
Emotion	**Stimulus**	**Disruptive Consequences**
Anxiety	Presentation of negative reinforcers	Avoidance, escape, defensive aggression
Anger	Removal of positive reinforcers	Forceful operant behavior; reinforcement of damaging and destructive responses
Elation	Presentation of positive reinforcers	Loss of appetite, focus on reinforcing stimulus

are effective and they are rehired, they may be elated (at the "presentation of positive reinforcers"). But so long as Rosemary's elation lasts, she may still have trouble getting back to normal. She may still have trouble eating and sleeping. Even though she wants to do her best so as to convince the new TransPacific owners that they made the right decision in keeping her, she may still have trouble concentrating. She may keep reliving her triumph, remembering the moment when TransPacific capitulated to the workers' demands.

Millenson also points out that in emotional situations, primary reinforcers become more (or less) potent than before. For example, people who are extremely depressed may lose their appetites and sexual desire and find it difficult to enjoy old, familiar things they liked. Lovers get so wrapped up in each other that they seem to "live on love"; they may have trouble eating or sleeping; the chance just to talk to the loved one may be worth almost any sacrifice. This indicates that the widespread behavioral changes seen in emotion are not simply due to overwhelming reflex activities but also to changes in patterns of reinforcement, which may discourage old behavior and encourage new activities.

In sum, it is Millenson's view that emotions have a powerful impact on behavior. This is not because emotional stimuli simply trigger powerful reflexes (say, as frustration may lead to aggression), nor because they profoundly disrupt all behavior, but because in emotion—as certain events become more reinforcing and others become less reinforcing—people's reflexive and operant (voluntary motor) behavior changes accordingly. We might add that when people experience deep emotion, their values and goals alter, and they can learn new ways of behaving.

A MODEL OF EMOTION

Assumptions

Millenson (1967) reviews the two historical ideas on which his model is based. First, like Robert Plutchik (1962), Millenson points out that: (a) Some emotions are basic emotions. Others are compounds of these fundamental emotions. (b) Some emotions are very similar to one another. They differ only in intensity. Other emotions are very different, differing in both similarity and intensity. We discussed Plutchik's work earlier in this chapter, so we need not repeat those same ideas here.

Secondly, Millenson adopts Watson's framework for understanding emotional development. That is: (a) He argues that the fundamental, unconditioned emotions are anxiety, anger, and elation; (b) the fundamental operations (unconditioned stimuli) which produce these emotions are the presentation or withdrawal of positive and negative reinforcers; and (c) emotions can be conditioned via Pavlovian conditioning (more about this later).

> A *burnt child fears the fire.*
>
> *PROVERB*

The Three Basic Emotions

At the heart of Millenson's model of emotional phenomena is his view of the three basic emotions.

Anxiety. In Table 5.4, we see that fear and anxiety are produced by negative reinforcers. What are negative reinforcers? Negative reinforcers are events that are so unappealing (a child's whining voice, a fly that keeps landing on our nose, a hot, humid day) that we feel delight when these things are eliminated from our lives. Negative reinforcers include events that we call "annoying," "uncomfortable," "painful," "unpleasant," "noxious," and so forth. Not surprisingly, when animals encounter negative reinforcers they try to escape in one way or another—they attempt to avoid, escape, or defend themselves. Millenson has been especially interested in the anxiety induced by negative reinforcers because it leads to **conditioned suppression.** Briefly, conditioned suppression refers to the fact that a stimulus (CS) that has been correlated with an aversive event (UCS) will disrupt ongoing behavior. Consider this typical experiment. A rat discovers that each time it presses a lever, it will be positively reinforced, say, with food. Soon, it is pressing the lever and receiving a steady supply of rewards. Then a CS is introduced: A (warning) tone is presented for five seconds, and at the end of that time the rat is shocked. The first time or two that the tone is presented, it has no effect. The rat keeps on pressing the lever and securing reinforcement. After several presentations, however, the CS begins to disrupt (suppress) performance. When the tone begins to sound, the rat begins to show signs of fear and anxiety. It crouches, trembles, or becomes immobile. Not until things become quiet again does the rat settle down and begin to resume normal activity. These fear reactions may even generalize to a CS similar to those involved in the original conditioning. (Rats so conditioned may come to fear whistles

or buzzers.) These generalized fear responses will, of course, be less pronounced than were the originals. Conditioned fear reactions are durable.
According to Millenson, they may persist for years. Interestingly enough,
such fear reactions in rats can be ameliorated by tranquilizers (Millenson &
Leslie, 1974) or electroconvulsive shock, the same treatments that reduce
anxiety's disruptive effects in people.

*Every normal man must be tempted at times to spit
on his hands, hoist the black flag, and begin slitting
throats.*

H. L. MENCKEN

Anger. As Table 5.4 indicates, Millenson assumes that anger is sparked by
the removal of positive reinforcers, the good things of life. When people are
told that the price of theater tickets has doubled, that gasoline is now being
rationed, or that their regular Saturday night date will be out of town on
prom night, they become angry and frustrated. Sometimes, angry, frustrated
people react aggressively, violently. In their classic monograph, *Frustration
and Aggression*, John Dollard and his Yale colleagues (1939) proposed a sweeping hypothesis: "Frustration always leads to some form of aggression," and
"Aggression is always a consequence of frustration" (p. 1). Frustration, said
Dollard and his colleagues, is anything that blocks goal attainment. It inevitably leads to aggression—fantasies of revenge, plans, or actions which are
intended to hurt another. Millenson's analysis fills out the Dollard et al.
formulation. Animals that are frustrated (i.e., have positive reinforcers removed) are disposed to anger as well as aggression.

In animals, anger generally fuels unusually energetic activity, some of
which is damaging and destructive. For example, in learning experiments,
Skinner (1938) has often trained rats to press a lever in return for pellets.
Their reinforcement schedule (the number of times they have to press before
they are rewarded) determines how fast they press the lever. Sometimes, the
rats are given a series of extinction trials. (No matter how often or how hard
they press, no reward is ever forthcoming.) Skinner has observed that when
the rats that have learned to press a lever in return for food are suddenly cut
off, they show an "extinction burst." They may frantically press the lever.
Interestingly, Georgiana Gates (1926) found that angry men and women act
in much the same way as the rats. In one study, she asked college women to
list the kinds of things that made them angry. The women reported that the
types of things that made them most angry were refusal of their reasonable
requests, having their friends arrive late, dialing a wrong number on the
telephone, having watches, pens, and typewriters that didn't work, waiting
on elevators or buses that were slow in arriving, or losing money. When
such frustrating things happened, the angry women found they were tempted
to react as Millenson predicts they might. Each of these situations produced

strong tendencies to make verbal retorts, physically harm someone else, damage objects, vigorously withdraw from the situation, and scream and swear.

An imaginative study by Nathan Azrin and his colleagues (1966) provides a demonstration of the link between loss of a positive reinforcer and forceful aggressive behavior. Pigeons were trained to peck at a key (a circular plastic disk mounted on the wall of the experimental chamber). Each time they pecked, they were rewarded with access to food. Then a "target" bird was introduced, a decoy shaped to look like a pigeon. This target was mounted on a movement-sensitive recorder. At first, the researchers collected base rate information. They found that as long as a bird's pecking was rewarded, it rarely touched the decoy. Then, extinction was begun. Pecking no longer led to reward since the food circuit had been switched off. At this point, the bird began strong aggressive attacks on the target, sometimes pecking it for as long as 10 minutes.

The pigeon's behavior reminds us of the Freudian defense mechanism of displacement, in which people displace their anger and hostility onto a "safe" target. Husbands and wives who have had a tough day at work come home and yell at their mates. The mates takes out their anger on the children. The children, in turn, are reduced to picking on the dog or cat. Everybody tends to displace their anger on someone who is less powerful than themselves, someone who is powerless to retaliate. In Millenson's terms, organisms show a tendency to transfer the emotions associated with one stimulus to new stimuli. We discuss anger and the displacement of aggression again in chapter 10.

*J*oy makes us giddy, dizzy.
                                   GOTTHOLD E. LESSING

Elation. Finally, as noted in Table 5.4, theoretically, joy and elation are aroused by the presentation of positive reinforcers. We are elated when we get an **A** we didn't expect, when someone shyly admits they love us, or when our favorite cat has a litter of cute kittens. Elation seems to include two very different effects on behavior: Usually, it facilitates and intensifies activity. However, sometimes elation, like anxiety, may lead to conditioned suppression. People may be so delighted by what has befallen them that they find it impossible to concentrate on the business at hand. In Millenson's (1967) words:

> Everyone has seen a child delighted by a promise of good things to come. Even the adult can be 'thrilled' by good news. The dog has a built-in mechanism, the tail wag, to indicate its enthusiasm when greeting its master or when about to be fed or petted. Such observations suggest that the effects of positive reinforcement are not confined to strengthening and maintaining operant behavior. (p. 448)

Like other positive reinforcing events, exceptionally good news can also be disruptive. The person who wins a lottery may have trouble buckling down to work. A child may be virtually immobilized with excitement on Christmas Eve.

In the laboratory, too, positive reinforcers may both heighten and dampen animals' responding, depending on the circumstances. In one experiment, R. J. Herrnstein and W. H. Morse (1957) illustrated the facilitative effects of so-called "conditioned elation." Pigeons were trained to peck at a plastic key in order to receive a contingent food reward. Suddenly, before the pigeon's eyes, the color of the key changed; this new stimulus signaled free food—whether or not the pigeons pecked, food became available. Surprisingly, the elated pigeons began to peck on the key even more often than before, even though pecking was now unnecessary!

Parallel evidence suggests that the anticipation of positive reinforcement ("joy") can also lead to disruption of operant behavior. Klaus Miczek (1973) demonstrated that when rats are presented with a stimulus that signals free food, they show conditioned suppression of lever pressing. (Perhaps this is for the same reason that the lottery winner stops working on the day the ticket number is announced—there are better things to do in preparation for the coming reinforcement than work!)

The point is that statements regarding the generally enhancing or disrupting effects of certain emotional events are not as useful as specifying the conditions under which each may be observed. While Millenson (1967) suggests that "fear, anger, and joy imply diffuse non-specific changes in the value of all reinforcers" (p. 441), the precise subjective, physiological, and behavioral changes that occur in emotion may vary greatly during positive or negative reinforcement.

An Emotional Coordinate System

On another tack, Millenson (1967) also suggests that the primary emotions of elation, anxiety, and anger can be seen as vectors in a geometrical model, similar to Plutchik's color wheel of emotion discussed earlier. (See Figure 1.3.) The primary emotions are most intense at the periphery. As one moves toward the center, the emotional terms begin to describe weaker and weaker feelings. (Ecstasy, for example, becomes merely pleasure.) At the absolute center, the emotions are so tepid that it may be impossible to discriminate between them. (This notion, too, is borrowed from Plutchik, 1962.) If an emotion does not appear along a vector, it is assumed to involve a mixture of primary emotions.

In one important respect, Millenson's model goes beyond that of Plutchik. Plutchik focuses on the emotional responses that people inherit. Millenson focuses on the way that people learn to respond emotionally. Thus, Plutchik assumes that conflict exists anytime people experience two or more basic emotions simultaneously, especially those at polar opposites. Millenson suggests that people may learn to experience conflicting emotions when a stimulus is successively paired with two or more unconditioned stimuli for primary emotions. Presumably, conditioning occurs via Pavlovian conditioning. For example, Millenson suggests that a child who steals a cookie will experience both responses because of the association between the pairings of the cookie with its good taste (a positive reinforcer) and its pairings with possible punishment, such as Mother's slap on the hand (a negative reinforcer). The cookie comes to evoke mixed emotional responses because of successive experiences of taste and Mother's wrath. The resulting mixture of emotion is generally termed guilt in our everyday emotional language.

People may come to experience mixed emotions in a second way. A stimulus may be paired with unconditioned stimuli which themselves simultaneously represent opposing tendencies. For example, wild river rafting may be associated at once with both elating (exhilarating) swift rides past rocks and over waves into areas of relative calm and safety *and* with anxiety-arousing plunges into walls of icy water that drench the rafter and threaten to tip over the craft. The mixture of emotions might best be described as "raw excitement," a "rush" or "high," or more colloquially as simply "awesome." In any case, Millenson suggests that the essence of such an emotional state is conflict, between, say, approach and withdrawal. The relative degree of learned elation or fear may determine whether the rafter returns to the river or seeks a safer thrill.

This mixture of emotions may give to an emotional experience a special kind of obsessive quality and persistence. Jules Masserman (1946) labeled his cats "neurotic" when they were unable to learn that it was safe to reapproach food (a reinforcement) that had once been paired simultaneously with a noxious blast of air, even when the air was turned off. Presumably, the mixed emotions lent such power to the aversive air blast experience that its effects persisted even when the food was safe. (Masserman also makes the interesting observation that the cats came to prefer milk "spiked" with alcohol after this hair-raising experience—small wonder.)

Review

Millenson argues, then, that in emotional situations, there is an abrupt change in stimulus conditions. These may produce strong emotions and widespread changes in the animal's reflexive reactions and overt operant behaviors. Emotions sometimes facilitate and sometimes disrupt everyday behavior. When we are emotionally stirred up, we are buffeted in two different directions. Our primitive, reflexive reactions compete with the graceful, complex, well-oiled routines we have learned for dealing with life's problems. Moreover, in emotional settings, people's values and the effects of reinforcers change. For example, one young theology student observed that when the question "Should young people engage in premarital sex?" was asked in class, his convictions were clear. He believed couples should wait until marriage to engage in sexual relations. At night, when he was with his fiancée and aroused, however, he found himself reciting arguments in favor of "free love." "God is love," he argued. "A marriage license is just a piece of paper. What matters is our commitment." What is rewarding when one is in love, or afraid, or angry may be quite different from what is rewarding or punishing when one is calm, cool, and collected.

Often, the emotional behaviors that seem so right in the short run are nonfunctional in the long run. In the heat of passion, people do things that they are sorry for later. Millenson attributes this lack of fit between behaviors and current reinforcements to the evolutionary origins of the emotions. He observes that in prehistory, our ancestor's emotional behavior was eminently practical behavior. It made good sense for our distant ancestors to engage in sexual relations whenever aroused or to pound smaller animals into submission when angry. These primitive emotion-behavior links were a part of the "hard wiring" of the central nervous system. The problem today is that, in our more civilized world, primitive reactions may not always be appropriate. Recall that Plutchik, too, argued that evolution is ultraconservative and that emotions may be vestigial remnants of previously adaptive behaviors. Philosophically, both theorists' ideas are rooted in the Darwinian tradition.

IMPLICATIONS OF THE MODEL

Emotion Control

As we observed in chapter 1, people are often eager to control their emotions. They want to calm themselves down enough to give a good speech. They want to love their children even though the children are driving them crazy right now. They want to snap out of their depression.

Traditional religions once urged people to control their thoughts, desires, and behavior. For example, Ann Landers once carried on a running theological debate in her advice column that illustrates the day-to-day confusion between thought, emotion, and behavior (see Angier, 1985). The feud started when a sex therapist suggested that an elderly couple could add some spice to their routine and boring sexual encounters by imagining they were doing deliciously wicked things with deliciously wicked people during sex. A religious fundamentalist was horrified at that advice. "It is just as bad to *think* of engaging in adultery as to do it. It is a sin to lust in your heart." (Clearly, this reader believed religious people can and should control thoughts and feelings as well as behavior.) A devilish reader was quick to challenge that advice on a sarcastic note: "If it is just as bad to think of sinning as to sin, why not go all the way? Why not have an affair and forget about it?" (Obviously this reader took it for granted that sexual thoughts are harder to control than sexual behavior—the two are very different things.)

Most psychologists, too, make an important distinction between thoughts, feelings, and behavior. For example, Millenson points out that emotions have a powerful reflexive (automatic) component. Certain stimuli generally ignite certain emotional thoughts and feelings. (For example, when we are deprived of enough sleep, we become irritable and crabby.) Such emotional reactions are fairly reflexive and nonvoluntary. It is probably neither desirable nor possible to keep them under control. But it is possible and profitable to control the most blatant expressions of our emotional feelings, that is, to control operant (voluntary) behaviors. And, sensibly enough, that is what most people try to do. We try to have a smile for everyone, regardless of our mood. We bite our tongue when our slightly addled friend says, "Oh dear. It looks like I've lost your class notes. Were they important?" We exert a great deal of effort trying to do what ought to be done and to avoid doing what ought not to be done. That is usually enough to keep us out of trouble with society.

Millenson's model raises a flurry of questions: How can people learn to control themselves if emotions are not under voluntary control? Are all efforts at emotional control doomed to failure? If so, what is the meaning of the expression emotional maturity? Indeed, Millenson suggests that people ordinarily can gain emotional control via three methods: adaptation (habituation), masking, and avoidance.

Adaptation and Habituation. These two terms essentially refer to the same thing: If the same stimulus is repeated again and again, people eventually stop perceiving or responding to it. They (or, more exactly, their reflexes) have adapted to it. For example, people who move next door to a freeway at first find the traffic noises, honks, and sirens unbearable. Sooner or later, however, they realize that they no longer notice the traffic. In fact, some people report that only when the noises stop, say, when an accident backs up traffic for miles, do they notice that something is vaguely wrong. When people are forced to deal routinely with emotion-provoking events, they tend to adapt to, habituate to, get used to, or learn to tolerate such events; they become less and less emotionally responsive.

As an emotional example, you meet someone and fall head-over-heels in love. You are passionately excited, tender and close. Then you get married. During the first year or two, you begin to notice that somehow, something has been lost. You still love your mate, but things are different—not so intense, not so passionate. You miss the closeness and the excitement of your early times together. Psychologists would say that adaptation has set in. In time, both passionate love and violent hate seem, somehow, to burn themselves out.

Adaptation can be deliberately used for the control of emotion—people can choose to expose themselves to the events that evoke emotional responses in order to diminish their intensity. We can train people to tolerate delays in reinforcement (delay of gratification) or to tolerate the loss of reinforcement (see Box 5.2).

A phenomenon closely related to adaptation is extinction. In fact, often

BOX 5.2

Adapting to Delay of Gratification

When children are hungry, they usually get irritable and crabby. They fidget, whine, and fight with one another. B. F. Skinner describes how children would be taught to control their frustration and other emotional behavior in his utopian *Walden Two* community:

> "...A group of children arrive home after a long walk tired and hungry. They're expecting supper; they find, instead, that it's time for a lesson in self-control: they must stand for five minutes in front of steaming bowls of soup.
> "The assignment is accepted like a problem in arithmetic. Any groaning or complaining is a wrong answer. Instead, the children begin at once to work on themselves to avoid any unhappiness during the delay. One of them may make a joke of it. We encourage a sense of humor as a good way of not taking an annoyance seriously. The joke won't be much, according to adult standards—perhaps the child will simply pretend to empty the bowl of soup into his upturned mouth. Another may start a song with many verses....
> "In a later stage we forbid all social devices. No songs, no jokes—merely silence. Each child is forced back upon his own resources—a very important step." (1962, p. 109)

Of course, tolerance training can go too far. Children can learn to expect too little from life.

Humorist Garrison Keillor (1986) describes the consequences in *Lake Wobegon Days*. One child adapted to a dry, harsh, and joyless life. When he returned home as an adult who had experienced the rich delights of the outside world, he nailed "95 complaints" about his Midwestern upbringing to the door of the local Lutheran church. Among them:

> You have taught me to value a good night's sleep over all else including adventures of love and friendship, and even when the night is charged with magic, to be sure to get to bed....
> Suffering was its own reward, to be preferred to pleasure. As Lutherans, we viewed pleasure with suspicion.... We were born to suffer. Pain was pooh-poohed. If you broke your leg, walk home and apply ice. Don't complain. Don't baby yourself. Our mothers ironed sheets, underwear, even in July. Our fathers wore out their backs at heavy, senseless labor, pulled their own teeth, lived with massive hemorrhoids. When Grandpa had his heart attack, he took one aspirin and went to bed early.... Punishment was good for you, deserved or not; if you hadn't done wrong, well, then it was for the last time.... (pp. 314–323)

The goal of adaptation training, then, is balance—between too much and too little.

it is difficult in practice to distinguish between the two. Adaptation occurs when a stimulus is repeated so often that people's reflexive responses, including unlearned or innate ones, begin to fade. In extinction, on the other hand, a stimulus occurs, and the person responds as he has learned to, but now, suddenly, no reward is forthcoming. Not surprisingly, the learned response begins to extinguish (or decline in strength.) This procedure often produces permanent changes in the behavior. Thus, extinction is the non-reinforcement of a learned response, which may lead to a decline in responding.

The distinction between adaptation and extinction is critically important.

Adaptation is reversible. After a period of time without the emotional stimulus to which we have adapted, our reflexes will recover in strength. Perhaps this underlies the old adage, "Absence makes the heart grow fonder." We should probably preface this with, "After repeated exposure and adaptation has made the heart less fond, ..." Extinction, however, may be forever—hence, the alternative adage, "Out of sight, out of mind." If emotions are learned, they can be unlearned. Consider the infant in the earlier example who learned to fear her brother who gleefully pulled the infant's blanket out from under her. If the infant learned to fear her brother via Pavlovian conditioning, theoretically, her parents could extinguish her fear by exposing the infant to the CS (her little brother's menacing face) unaccompanied by the UCS (the vanishing blanket). At first, the infant will jump each time she spots her brother, but eventually, the fear response would extinguish. Therapists can be remarkably effective in extinguishing fear using these methods. In chapter 14, we spend a great deal of time discussing these techniques. The most effective technique, then, for permanently changing an emotional reaction (i.e., for altering the strength of its reflexive component) is extinction.

Masking. People can gain emotional control via a second, more indirect technique—by covering up, or masking their emotions with operant behavior. Walter Cannon proposed that the point of emotions' bodily adjustments was to prepare man and animals for "flight" or "fight." Therefore, it should come as no surprise that emotions are expressed overtly. Millenson, too, assumes that emotional predispositions will be expressed in operant (voluntary) behavior. People reveal themselves in what they say, in their facial expressions, in gestures, and in movements.

When people wish to control their emotions voluntarily, they can utilize two different techniques—they can try not to express their feelings (to look relaxed when they are upset), or they can try to cover up their feelings by putting on a false front and engaging in incompatible behaviors. Often it is harder to do the former than the latter. For example, when small boys are hurt and embarrassed, they are often encouraged in our culture to try to hide their feelings. Since crying has operant (voluntary) aspects, they can usually manage to do so to some extent. Most find it fairly easy to restrain themselves from crying in the vocal sense. It is harder to control the potpourri of subtle indicators of hurt, however, hard to stop them from leaking out. Boys find it difficult to squeeze back their tears; their faces feel stiff, hot; their lips begin to quiver. At this point, they may revert to an easier strategy—they may try to mask their feelings. They harden their faces in a haughty, rigid, configuration; they glare. At some intuitive level, most people sense that others' "fake" expressions often are meant to disguise their opposites. Teenagers sometimes comment that they hate "sicky sweet" women; they are sensing the hostility behind the mask of sweetness. Adults catch the terror that lies behind "whistling in the dark." Most civilized people are generally able to mask their socially unacceptable feelings a good deal of the time. They are able to smile, wait patiently in lines, and engage in polite chit-chat, regardless of how they feel. As people's feelings become more intense, the task becomes harder. (A father can't help but be "lost in space" when he is worried about a missing child. A teenager who is in love may drive his family crazy as he monopolizes the telephone, forgets to pick up clothes at the dry cleaners, and obsesses endlessly about what kind of corsage, if any, his girlfriend would like best.)

Are private feelings changed by such public performances? It depends. Sometimes, Millenson observes, the more private aspects of emotion remain untouched; we still "cry a little inside" when we are hurt, even though we may learn to give an award-winning performance of reason and calm. Theoretically, however, the reflexive components of emotion can be influenced by the process of masking. It may work this way: Sometimes emotions are self-perpetuating. Once they begin, they seem to feed upon themselves. As our eyes puff up, we sob and wail, we feel out of control. We begin to think of all the terrible times we have had—the time Mother said we looked like a goof; the fact that we didn't get asked to the prom in spite of having prayed for six months for an invitation; the humiliations we've experienced in school. Things seem to get worse and worse. On the other hand, if someone yells "Stop it!" or does something else to sharply interrupt the action, we may find ourselves laughing at the absurdity of it all. At the very least, our feelings of self-pity may diminish abruptly.

Avoidance. Millenson suggests a third major technique by which people can control their emotions—simple avoidance. Emotional experiences are generally tied to identifiable stimuli. We fall in love when we are lonely, become irritable when over-tired, hurt when we are shouted at. Therefore, an unusually effective way to control emotions is by

> [avoiding] the situations that call out the emotional behavior. When we avoid an enemy who is likely to make us angry, or stop playing [frustrating] golf because we continually play poorly, or when we go to a [pleasing] restaurant where we have often had a good meal, we avoid or produce certain reinforcers; but as a by-product we may also escape or produce certain of our own emotional behaviors. (1967, p. 463)

It is easy to be agreeable and calm if your life is punctuated by an array of positive reinforcers (usually, pleasant events). It is almost impossible to stop yourself from being angry, petty, and churlish if your life is engulfed by negative reinforcers (aversive events). If we can arrange our lives so that we maximize positive reinforcers and minimize negative ones, we can shape our emotional predispositions by managing the stimuli that evoke our emotional responses.

The sum total of the results of the methods of control over their emotions that people come to use—adaptation, masking, and avoidance—define **emotional maturity,** "the usual change in emotional patterns from childhood to adulthood . . . characterized by greater increase in control over emotional behavior" (Millenson, 1967, p. 462).

Abnormal Emotional Behavior

In chapters 8–12, we discuss certain mental problems and their relationship to the various emotions. Millenson and Leslie (1979) ask: What causes abnormal emotional behavior? A century ago, the most common answer would have been "madness." Today, the answer may be "mental illness." Millenson and Leslie disagree with both views. They argue that the same basic principles generate and maintain all behavior—normal or not:

> We shall argue here that unusual abnormal behavior results either from prolonged punitive, oppressive, contradictory, and confusing contingencies, or from prolonged insufficient or inappropriate reinforcement in the history of the individual; and further, that these particular contingencies and reinforcer deficits can be identified and then changed or countered. (p. 464)

People can develop two types of emotional problems—they can be "flat" emotionally or develop emotions that are out of control. Some adults seem cold and distant. Stimuli that would normally produce happiness, joy, and sexual desire or, conversely, embarrassment, pain, and suffering produce no reaction. In such people, the link between eliciting stimuli and feelings, and normal reinforcement contingencies and emotional expression is somehow broken. Millenson (1967) describes one possibility: There are orphanages, foster homes, and families where children are neglected. Children's emotional needs for cuddling, attention, and comforting are not met. "If this affectionate stimulation is lacking during the first 6 months of life . . . the infants become dejected, detached, show stupor, lack of appetite, and retarded physical development. Such infants appear to lack the usual intensity of joy behavior as well as fear and anger behavior. In short, all their emotional behaviors appear to be highly attenuated" (p. 464). Infants who are deprived of emotional stimuli may be prone to an emotional life that is drab and dead; they may be predisposed to depression in adulthood.

For most people who are suffering from an emotional disorder, the problem is that they care too much. They are too depressed, too anxious, too angry to function. Why? Skinner (1953) sagely observes that in spite of all that psychologists know about the optimum conditions for learning—especially to maximize positive reinforcement—most societies provide innumerable forms of punishment and negative reinforcement for not behaving appropriately. Systems of punitive control are institutionalized—in police and military forces, in the courts, in the prison system, in schools. It is not surprising, then, that people are sad and depressed, tense and anxious, or angry a good deal of the time.

Physical Illness

In chapter 13, we review what is known about the links between emotions and physical illness. Emotional problems and stress can produce a range of psychosomatic disorders—from asthma, to cancer, to heart disease. Millenson (1967), too, points out that emotional problems also can lead to psychosomatic disorders and illness. The operations underlying the elicitation and conditioning of emotions "can, if implemented frequently, provoke acute pathological changes" (p. 456), including hypertension, asthma, headaches, and other disorders. Millenson explains how this process might work. Joseph Brady and his colleagues (Brady, Porter, Conrad, & Mason, 1958) contrasted "executive" monkeys with fellow monkeys that did not have the same responsibilities. The animals sat in restraining chairs. When a tone sounded, the "executive" monkeys could press a lever to turn off the electric shock. The other monkeys could do nothing about the shock; all they could do was sit there and take it. On the face of it, one might think that the executive monkeys who could control their fates were in a better position. Not so, said the Brady group. They were far more likely to develop duodenal ulcers than were the monkeys with no responsibilities.

In the 1960s, when Millenson wrote, this study was assumed to provide clear evidence that anxiety and the stress associated with decision making and high-level jobs produced ulcers. By the 1970s, however, the process was found to be more complex than the Brady group had supposed. For example, in 1972 Weiss found that "executive" animals actually get ulcers less frequently than do their powerless co-workers. These disparate results indicate that other factors must be taken into consideration; the issue of control over significant events is a persistent one in the understanding of emotion.

Thus, Millenson observes that we can best understand emotions and their control by considering them in a learning paradigm. Understanding the nature of emotions is crucial, in part, because of their effect on mental and physical health. The theory is an impressive one. It has the distinct advantage over many other theories in that it is closely tied to learning theory. Well-established principles of reflex and operant behavior are used to provide an understanding of the antecedents of emotion, the way emotions function in daily life, and what can be done to manage emotion. In many situations, the theory makes clear, compelling, and testable predictions.

Summing Up

- ■ Robert Plutchik's "psychoevolutionary synthesis" and J. R. Millenson's "behavioral analysis" stress the emotions' expressive (or behavioral) aspect.
- ■ Plutchik's Postulates 1–4 point out that emotion, evolution, and behavior

are inextricably linked. Emotions are inherited, adaptive patterns of behavior. They include protection, destruction, and reproduction responses. Evolution is ultraconservative; organisms continue to transmit genetic material long after its adaptive advantage has disappeared.

- Postulates 5–7 propose a limited number of primary emotions; the eight prototype emotions are fear, anger, joy, sadness, acceptance, disgust, expectancy, and surprise. All other emotions are mixtures or combinations of these.

- Plutchik's three structural postulates attempt to describe the structure of emotion. They state that the primary emotional dimensions can be conceptualized in terms of pairs of polar opposites and that emotions vary in similarity and intensity.

- People can talk about emotions in a variety of languages—a subjective ("feeling") language, a behavioral language (which describes the emotion's overt aspects), or a functional language (which describes the emotion's ultimate function).

- A three-dimensional emotion solid depicts the emotions' relationships to one another: The prototypic emotions circle the wheel. The more similar emotions are, the closer they are to one another; as one moves from top to bottom, the emotional experiences become less intense.

- Emotions may be mixed, just as colors can be mixed. A mixture of two primaries is termed a *dyad*; a combination of three, a *triad*. If one tries to mix polar opposites, the result is not a distinct emotion, but merely immobilization. The English language may not possess a term for all emotional combinations; such terms may have to be added to the language of emotions.

- Millenson points out that although scientists cannot directly explore private emotional events, they can gain some understanding of what people think and feel by examining physiological reactions and verbal behavior.

- He contends there are three basic emotions: anxiety, anger, and elation. Emotions can be conditioned in accordance with Pavlovian principles.

- Fear and anxiety are produced by negative reinforcers; they lead to avoidance, escape, and defensive aggression, as well as to conditioned suppression.

- Anger occurs when positive reinforcement is cut off. The animal displays emotional bursts in the extinction curve and destructive attacks on the source of deprivation and other convenient targets.

- Elation is aroused by the presentation of positive reinforcers. Joy both facilitates and intensifies activity or disrupts operant behavior.

- Emotions induce diffuse, nonspecific changes in the value of all reinforcers, resulting in widespread behavioral changes. Emotion differs from motivation in terms of abruptness of onset and effects on the value of reinforcers.

- The primary emotions can be seen as vectors in a geometrical model. The primary emotions are least intense at the vectors' centers, most intense at the periphery. If the three vectors converge, the emotions are at such a low level of intensity that it is impossible to discriminate among them.

- People possess mixed emotions anytime a stimulus is successively paired with two or more unconditioned stimuli for primary emotions. Presumably, conditioning of mixed emotions occurs via classical Pavlovian conditioning.

- Millenson suggests that people can gain emotional control through three methods: adaptation, masking, and avoidance. Together, their use constitutes emotional maturity.

- Millenson contends that abnormal behavior results from prolonged punitive, oppressive, contradictory, and confusing contingencies or from prolonged insufficient or inappropriate reinforcement in the history of the individual. Emotions may also be involved in physical illness.

6

Facial Expression

Introduction

The Universal and Cultural Bases of Facial Expression
Cultural Masks
Telling Lies

Left Brain/Right Brain
The Perception of Emotion
The Expression of Emotion
Studies With Neurological Patients

Facial Expression and Emotional Experience
Evidence on the Impact of Facial Feedback on Emotion
Facial Expression and ANS Activity

The Social Psychophysiology of Facial Expression
Social Psychophysiological Measurement
Theoretical Conclusions

Summing Up

FIGURE 6.1   *Jealousy.* Edvard Munch. 1896. Lithograph. 465 x 565 mm. The Munch Museum and Oslo Kommune.

Introduction

People care how others feel about them. When relationships are new, couples often spend a great deal of time trying to read each other's reactions from their faces, voices, and behavior. Take, for example, Laura, a nursery-school teacher. Laura was a pretty, shy, all-American type. She was timidly and uncertainly in love with a local actor, but she didn't know how he felt about her. Sometimes he seemed to be crazy about her. He would overwhelm her with compliments, send her roses, talk about their future together. Yet, sometimes he would ignore her in public and lavish attention on her friends. At those times, her friends would warn her that she was a fool to keep dating him. They had frequent scenes. He would express love, sadness, and intense anger, all in a confusing blend. What, she wondered, did he really feel for her? She studied his face and gestures, discussed his reactions with her friends, tried to piece together his behavior. Did he love her or didn't he?

For more than 100 years, psychologists have tried to determine whether people's inner lives are written upon their faces. They have explored a variety of questions concerning the link between emotion and facial expressiveness. Are people's emotions reflected in their faces? Are such expressions innate or merely learned? Is it possible to fake emotional expression? Can others detect such fakery? Only recently have psychologists begun to come up with definitive answers. In this chapter, we highlight the work of two researchers who have pioneered research on these exciting questions—Paul Ekman and John Cacioppo. First, let us review some of the research of Paul Ekman, and his insights into the universality of emotion. Ekman's work is in the tradition of Charles Darwin, who wrote a hundred years before (see chapter 2).

The Universal and Cultural Bases of Facial Expression

The face of man is the index to joy and mirth, to severity and sadness.
                                        PLINY THE ELDER (A.D. 62-113)

Casual observers probably have always assumed that facial and postural expressions differentiate emotional states. More than 2,500 years ago, actors at the Dionysian theatre in Greece wore masks from which the audience inferred the actors' emotional states. In the fifteenth century, Leonardo da Vinci, always deeply interested in human anatomy, sketched in his notebooks the *occipitofrontalis* (forehead), which he labeled the "muscle of sadness," the *corrugator supercilii* (brow) and *zygomaticus minor* (mouth), which he labeled the "muscle of anger," and a variety of other facial muscles (see Figure 6.2).

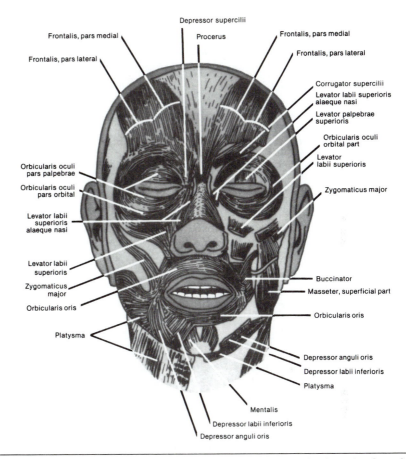

FIGURE 6.2 The facial muscles. Schematic representation of selected facial muscles. Overt facial expressions of emotion are based on contractions of the underlying musculature that are sufficiently intense to result in visibly perceptible dislocations of the skin and landmarks. The more common visible effects of strong contractions of the depicted facial muscles include the following: *Muscles of the lower face: depressor anguli oris*—pulls the lip corners downward; *depressor labii inferioris*—depresses the lower lip; *orbicularis oris*—tightens, compresses, protrudes, and/or inverts the lips; *mentalis*—raises the chin and protrudes the lower lip; *platysma*—wrinkles the skin of the neck and may draw down both the lower lip and the lip corners. *Muscles of the mid-face: buccinator*—compresses and tightens the cheek, forming a "dimple"; *levator labii superioris alaeque nasi*—raises the center of the upper lip and flares the nostrils; *levator labii superioris*—raises the upper lip and flares the nostrils, exposing the canine teeth; *masseter*—adducts the lower jaw; *zygomaticus major*—pulls the lip corners up and back. *Muscles of the upper face: corrugator supercilii*—draws the brows together and downward, producing vertical furrows between the brows; *depressor supercilii/procerus*—pulls the medial part of the brows downward and may wrinkle the skin over the bridge of the nose; *frontalis, pars medial*—raises the inner brows, producing horizontal furrows in the medial region of the forehead; *levator palpebrae superioris*—raises the upper eyelid; *orbicularis oculi, pars orbital*—tightens the skin surrounding the eye causing "crow's-feet" wrinkles; *orbicularis oculi, pars palpebrae*—tightens the skin surrounding the eye causing the lower eyelid to raise. (From Cacioppo, Martzke, Petty, & Tassinary, 1988. Copyright 1988 by the American Psychological Association. Reprinted by permission of the publisher and author.)

In the centuries that followed, early anatomists developed a fairly detailed knowledge of the facial musculature from dissections of cadavers (see Weaver, 1977.) Nonetheless, as late as 1840, physiologist Johannes Müller stated that "the bases of the relations of the facial muscles to specific emotions are completely unknown" (Cacioppo & Petty, 1979b).

Later, in an attempt to address the issue, Charles Darwin, in *The Expression of the Emotions in Man and Animals* (1872/1965), outlined a series of intriguing observations which were to guide research on facial expression and emotion for the next 100 years. He proposed the following: First, in all cultures, the various emotions are coupled to certain facial patterns suggesting a "universal language" of emotion. Second, the facial patterns of animals and humans are similar. Third, in both animals and humans, the pleasant versus unpleasant emotions are expressed via antithetical somatic patterning. And fourth, the somatic patterns associated with each emotion have functional significance. Darwin states, "Most of our emotions are so closely connected with their expression that they hardly exist if the body remains passive" (p. 257).

CULTURAL MASKS

Despite Darwin's powerful arguments, his thesis had little immediate impact. Anthropologists and psychologists such as Ray Birdwhistell (1963) and Otto Klineberg (1940) contended that "what shows on the face is written there by culture." They recounted anecdotes as to how differently emotions are expressed in different cultures. There could be no cultural universals, they argued. More recently, anthropologists have studied cultural **display rules,** societal expectations concerning the correct way of expressing emotions. For example, in our culture, a beauty contest winner is supposed to look startled at the decision and then immediately break into tears of joy. Her disappointed rivals are not supposed to break into tears; they are supposed to smile in empathy at her good fortune. These are the unwritten display rules.

Different cultural groups have different ideas as to how one "ought" to behave. For example, Elaine Hatfield and her colleagues (1987) interviewed European, Chinese, Filipino, Hawaiian, and Japanese students about their ideologies as to how one ought to behave in close relationships. They found that men and women of European descent were slightly more likely than members of other groups to think that intimates ought to be careful to express at least as much love, joy, or sexual interest as they are feeling. Members of the various ethnic groups did not differ in how they thought intimates ought to deal with negative emotions—everyone thought couples ought to eliminate, or at least minimize, the negative. It would not be surprising, then, that depending on their ideologies, people in different cultures would try to play up, play down, or shape their emotional expressions in some way.

Not until the mid-1960s did psychologists begin to resurrect Darwin's ideas. Silvan Tomkins (1962), Paul Ekman (Ekman & Friesen, 1971), and Carroll Izard (1971) proposed that both innate neural programs and cultural display rules shape emotional expression. If this is so, even infants should be able to communicate in the face's universal language. Recently, child psychologists have begun to carefully observe infants and their caretakers in an effort to test these notions. It is clear that Darwin was right. For example, in a series of studies, Jacob Steiner (1979) found that infants respond to sweet, sour, and bitter tastes by smiling, lip pursing, and making disgusted faces in the very first hours of life; observers have no trouble reading their feelings. To date, the emotional expressions identified in infants include those of surprise, happiness, fear, sadness, anger, disgust, and pain (see Klinnert, Campos, Sorce, Emde, & Svejda, 1983, for a review of this research). Moreover, not only adults can read infants' emotions. Infants appear to be equally good at reading their parents' feelings. In fact, when in doubt as to how to proceed, infants scan their parents' faces, apparently to see how the parents feel about the situation, and proceed accordingly. For example, Mary Klinnert and her colleagues (1983) have studied the process of **social referencing**— using others' emotional expressions to resolve the meaning of otherwise ambiguous situations. Consider a typical experiment by Klinnert (1981). The children in this study ranged from 12 to 18 months of age. Klinnert assembled a variety of toys that were novel but somewhat frightening in appearance: a remote-controlled spider and dinosaur and a model of a human head. The experimenter offered children each of the toys, one by one. The children were naturally somewhat wary. Was this fun . . . or dangerous? The children inevitably looked at their mothers' faces, as if to check things out. The mothers were part of the experiment. They had been trained to pose peak facial expressions, as described by Ekman and Friesen (1975). On each trial, the mothers posed a different expression: joy, fear, or a neutral face. They made no accompanying sounds or gestures. Infants approached the toys when their mothers smiled but avoided the toys and retreated to the mother when she pretended to be frightened. They showed mixed reactions when her face was neutral.

Recently, psychologists have uncovered compelling evidence that certain emotions are expressed in much the same way in all cultures. Of course, every culture possesses its own display rules. Recent research has demonstrated that, in part, facial expressions are innate and, in part, they are learned. For example, Ekman and Friesen (1971) studied members of the Fore group of the South East Highlands of New Guinea. They were chosen because they had had virtually no contact with the West and thus no chance to learn Western conventions of emotional expression. Would these tribesmen instinctively recognize Western expressions of such basic emotions as happiness, sadness, anger, fear, surprise, disgust, and interest? Could Westerners recognize the Fore's emotions? To find out, the authors selected 30 photographs depicting a variety of emotional expressions.

Tribe members were shown a trio of photographs and told a story. For example, "Sadness: His (her) child (mother) has died, and he (she) feels very sad." They were then asked to point to the face that seemed most appropriate to the story. The Fore's emotional repertoire seemed surprisingly similar to our own. For example, the Fore correctly selected the face as representing sadness 79% of the time. In Table 6.1 we see how easy it is for the Fore to read Western faces. Around the world, brows pulled down and inward, squinting eyelids, and pressed lips signal anger; a wrinkled nose signals disgust; and so forth.

American college students turn out to be equally good at decoding New Guineans' feelings. Ekman and Friesen (Ekman, 1971) asked the Fore to show how they would look if they were sad, happy, fearful, and so forth. When American college students who had never seen New Guineans were asked to judge the emotion that the tribespeople were expressing, they, too, were quite accurate.

Students were easily able to recognize happiness, anger, disgust, and sadness (see Table 6.2). They had a bit more trouble with fear and surprise. (Interestingly, these were the very emotions that the Fore had difficulty in discriminating.) Subsequent research provides clear evidence that emotional expression may well be universal and innate. People from a variety of cultures—Brazil, Argentina, Chile, the United States, and Japan—have been found to interpret the same facial expressions in much the same way (see Ekman, 1971, for a summary of this research). In Figure 6.3, Ekman depicts the extent to which the various cultures agree on the emotion depicted in photographs. Recently, Ekman and Friesen (1986) have concluded that contempt is also a pan-cultural facial expression. It is recognized by people in Estonia, Russia, Germany, Greece, Hong Kong, Italy, Japan, Scotland, Turkey, the United States, and West Sumatra.

Table 6.1   New Guineans' Percentage of Correct Judgments of Western Emotions

EMOTION	ADULTS	CHILDREN
Happiness	92%	92%
Sadness	79	81
Anger	84	90
Disgust	81	85
Surprise	68	98
Fear*	80	93
Fear**	43	—

*Distinguished from anger, disgust, or sadness
**Distinguished from surprise
Adapted from Ekman and Friesen (1971), p. 127

Table 6.2   **Percentage of Correct Judgments of New Guinean Emotions by U.S. Observers**

Emotion	Percentage
Happiness	73
Anger	51
Disgust/contempt	46
Sadness	68
Surprise	27
Fear	18

Ekman (1971), p. 275

These early studies dealt with posed emotions for experimental reasons. What about spontaneously occurring emotion? Are there cultural universals in that, too? It appears so. For example, Paul Ekman, Wallace Friesen, and Phoebe Ellsworth (1972) made a fascinating prediction. They proposed that in private, Japanese and American subjects should express their emotions in virtually the same way. In public, however, their emotional expressions should be shaped dramatically by cultural display rules. The authors were attracted to the idea of studying Japanese subjects because of the stereotype that the Japanese are inscrutable, that it is impossible to read much about their inner lives from their faces. The authors asked men and women from the United States and Japan to watch a film while they were seated alone in a room. One film was neutral (a travelogue). The other was stress inducing (the film, titled *Subincision*, showed tribesmen mutilating adolescent boys' genitals as part of a primitive puberty rite). Students knew that psychophysiological measures (skin conductivity and heart rate) were being recorded. What they did not know was that their facial expressions were being videotaped as well. Later, American and Japanese observers were asked to view the videotapes and guess which emotions the subjects were feeling. In addition, the subjects' facial displays were scored via Ekman and colleagues' Facial Affect Scoring Technique, or FAST (cf. Ekman & Friesen, 1975), which measures each movement of the face within each of three facial areas (brows/forehead, eyes/lids, lower face). This measurement procedure yields both frequency and duration scores for each of six emotions—happiness, anger, sadness, surprise, fear, and disgust—for each of the three areas of the face. As predicted, in private, American and Japanese students expressed their emotions in much the same way. In private, their faces were equally expressive in registering happiness, sadness, fear, and so forth.

When Japanese and American viewers were in public, however, cultural influences increased. After the subjects saw the stressful film, an interviewer questioned them about their experiences. Wallace Friesen (1972) measured

Country	Photo A	Photo B	Photo C	Photo D	Photo E	Photo F
U.S.A. (N=99)	97% Happiness	92% Disgust	95% Surprise	84% Sadness	67% Anger	85% Fear
Brazil (N=40)	95% Happiness	97% Disgust	87% Surprise	59% Sadness	90% Anger	67% Fear
Chile (N=119)	95% Happiness	92% Disgust	93% Surprise	88% Sadness	94% Anger	68% Fear
Argentina (N=168)	98% Happiness	92% Disgust	95% Surprise	78% Sadness	90% Anger	54% Fear
Japan (N=29)	100% Happiness	90% Disgust	100% Surprise	62% Sadness	90% Anger	66% Fear

FIGURE 6.3 Judgments of emotion in five literate cultures (percentage agreement in how photograph was judged across cultures). P. Ekman, *Darwin and Facial Expression: A Century of Research in Review.* New York: Academic Press, 1973, p. 206. By permission of Academic Press.

facial behavior in the interview and found that in these circumstances, Japanese and American students' faces sent very different, culturally prescribed messages. During the interview, the Japanese masked their feelings. When their Japanese interviewer asked them about their experiences, they presented a happy face. As they talked with their American interviewer, American students did not bother to disguise their negative feelings. Such research makes it clear that, while culture can have some influence on when, where, and how people express their feelings, some universals are evident in the way people express their feelings. (For a summary of research in this area, see Ekman, 1982.)

TELLING LIES

The cruelest lies are often told in silence.
ROBERT LOUIS STEVENSON

So far, we have focused on spontaneous, honest expressions of emotion. But people are far more complex than that—sometimes they try to lie about their feelings. Sometimes they try to put on a face that depicts a completely different emotion from the one they are feeling. As Ekman (1985) relates:

The late president of Egypt, Anwar Sadat, wrote about his attempts as a teenager to learn how to control his facial muscles: "... my hobby was politics. At that time Mussolini was in Italy. I saw his pictures and read about how he would change his facial expressions when he made public addresses, variously taking a pose of strength or aggression, so that people might look at him and read power and strength in his very features. I was fascinated by this. I stood before the mirror at home and tried to imitate this commanding expression, but for me the results were very disappointing. All that happened was that the muscles of my face got very tired. It hurt." (pp. 138–139)

From time to time, we long to read others' minds: Did President Reagan know about the Iran-Contra affair? Can the auto dealer really go no lower on this car? We wish we knew. Psychologists provide some techniques as to how we might find out.

Sigmund Freud (1905) observed, "He that has eyes to see and ears to hear may convince himself that no mortal can keep a secret. If his lips are silent, he chatters with his finger-tips; betrayal oozes out of him at every pore" (p. 94). Unfortunately, a master clinician like Freud may be able to read clues that are invisible to the rest of us. Parents often pretend to children that they can spot a liar every time. They stare at their children through skeptical, narrow eyes. The children blush, stammer, and confess. A mother, for instance, observes that she can still tell when her son, now 21, is lying. When he was a little boy, anyone could spot his lies. His stories were so fantastic that no one was fooled. When he asked how she always caught him, she jokingly replied, "When you lie, your ears turn bright red." Today, she remarks, when he is lying ("Really, mom, I was out all night studying"), he still automatically covers his ears with his hands!

In fact, Ekman has discovered, most of us are not very good at detecting lies. We are apt to believe the daring child or the used car salesman who looks us in the eye. In a series of experiments, Ekman attempted to find out exactly how people telegraph that they are lying. In his book, *Telling Lies* (1985), he reviews a myriad of ways that we can make educated guesses about the honesty of others. Following are some of Ekman's conclusions.

1. If people come to believe their own lies, it may be impossible to detect their deceptions. After all, they believe they are telling the truth.
2. When people know they are lying, however, they generally feel some sort of strong emotion—guilt, fear of detection, or even the smugness of knowing that they are putting something over on someone. Liars may try to hide these telltale emotions, but they are likely to leak out.
3. The more emotion the lie arouses, the more likely it is to leak out.
4. Facial expressions offer clues to deceit. The face often contains two messages—what the liar wants to reveal and what the liar hopes to conceal. Most people have considerable ability to disguise their feelings. Parents teach their children to control their expressions. ("Don't you give me that high and mighty look!" "Don't look so bored." "Wipe that smile off your face.") These display rules become deeply ingrained habits. In part, then, people generally look like they are supposed to. Nonetheless,

when people try to disguise their emotions, they are likely to unintentionally betray their true feelings. If one is to ferret out the truth, the first step is to know what to look for—to ignore unreliable indicators (which can easily be faked) and to concentrate on reliable clues to emotion (telltale signs which cannot be produced at will, inhibited, or squelched).

One can smile and smile and still be a villain.
WILLIAM SHAKESPEARE

General Facial Cues to Lies

The facial muscles differ greatly in their ease of control. For example, a smile is often used to disguise negative emotions—fear, anger, distress, disgust. People have a great deal of practice in smiling regardless of how they feel. For that reason, the simple presence or absence of a smile does not provide much information and is thus an unreliable indicator. (More detailed analysis is necessary to separate happy smiles from those that hide secret unhappiness. Ekman and his colleagues [1988] found that in spontaneous smiles, the cheeks move up, and the muscles around the eyes tighten, making "crow's feet." If the smile is broad enough, the skin around the eyebrow droops down a bit toward the eye. In false smiles, however, the face reveals traces of the sadness which lurks behind the smile—for example, a slight furrowing of the muscle behind the eyebrows can be seen apart from the supposed expression of pleasure.) Unlike often-practiced smiles, some indicators are extremely reliable; they occur only when people are sad. For example, only about 10% of people can deliberately pull the corners of their lips downward without moving their chin muscle. Yet people inevitably do this spontaneously when they feel sadness, sorrow, or grief. Thus, spotting this movement is a tip-off that the person is sad. Ekman (1985) provides a compendium of such telltale movements, too many to enumerate here. A sampling of some other facial indicators of emotion follows.

The Eyes. People's pupils seem to dilate when they are emotionally aroused—when they are excited, angry, or afraid. Since people cannot voluntarily dilate their pupils, others can be certain that when someone's pupils dilate, he or she is emotionally aroused. Unfortunately, this clue does not indicate which emotion one is feeling.

Blushing. When people are emotionally aroused, the autonomic nervous system produces visible changes in the face—blushing, blanching, and sweating. These clues are difficult to alter.

"Crooked" Expressions. According to Ekman, one extremely important clue to whether people are telling the truth is whether their facial expressions are symmetrical or asymmetrical. Ekman points out that spontaneous (involuntary) expressions of emotion and faked (voluntary) expressions should involve very different neural pathways. When one is expressing one's honest feelings, facial expressions may be triggered by the lower, primitive areas of the brain (the brain stem and limbic system). When one is consciously trying to "fake it," the cerebral cortex is involved. Because both the right and the left hemispheres of the brain are guiding the faked emotional expression, the timing is a bit off, and the expression is a bit lopsided. Thus, Ekman contends, true expressions are relatively symmetrical; insincere expressions are not. Hence the importance of symmetry versus asymmetry in detecting lying. Emotions that are displayed slightly more strongly on one side of the face than on the other may be an important clue that the person is pretending to feel something not truly felt—feigned surprise, for example. (In the next section, we see that not all researchers agree with Ekman. Some neuroscientists believe that even spontaneous emotions are processed in different hemispheres of the brain. At present, we simply do not have enough information to say who is correct, Ekman or the neuroscientists, or even to understand exactly why they secure such different results.)

Micro-expressions. When a person is "putting on" a face, the fake facial expression may be interrupted now and then by a fleeting expression, a micro-expression, that flickers across the face for less than a quarter of a second. These expressions are at distinct odds with the expression that is fixed upon the person's face. Moreover, these micro-expressions may provide a more full picture of the concealed emotion. In ordinary conversation, most people are unaware of these micro-expressions. They can only consciously spot the distinct movements if the conversation is filmed, slowed down, and examined. However, experienced clinicians may not need slow motion, having learned to detect micro-expressions because of their importance in therapy. Thus, therapists may sense such messages both in normal conversation and when viewing a film at full speed. Herein may lie some of the art of the clinician's practice.

Such micro-expressions can send powerful messages to us. For example, imagine a colleague of yours who drops by to say hello. His body is casually draped over your doorway, and he stays only a minute. Nonetheless, as soon as he leaves, you are filled with enormous apprehension. You feel you have said the wrong thing, done the wrong thing . . . yet nothing has happened. A day later, this colleague is hospitalized for having had a psychotic episode. Later, after you are an experienced therapist, you will learn to tune into your feelings a bit better. You will be aware that your inexplicable feelings are really valuable clues to another's emotions. You will be able to read clients' emotions in their faces, tones, and postures. The people we encounter often send us powerful messages about their emotional states in these ways.

Timing. Timing includes onset (the amount of time it takes a facial expression to appear), duration (the amount of time it lasts), and offset (the amount of time it takes to disappear). All three variables can provide clues to deception. For example, Ekman observes that expressions of long duration, say five seconds or more, are likely to be false.

Ekman cautions that observers should never try to rely upon only one clue to deceit. Only the existence of many facial clues provides convincing evidence that someone is lying. Furthermore, these clues should be confirmed by cues from the voice, words, or bodily gestures. (For other clues to lying, see the work of Miron Zuckerman, Bella DePaulo and Robert Rosenthal [1981].) In addition, neuroscientists have argued that another factor must be taken into account when trying to understand the link between emotion and facial expression—the fact that emotional information is processed somewhat differently by the left and right hemispheres of the brain.

Left Brain/Right Brain

Neuroscientists have known for some time that the left and the right sides of the brain differ in the way that they process emotional information. Originally, researchers thought simply that in most people, the left brain was the seat of reason (specializing in language and linear thought) and the right brain was the seat of emotion (specializing in intuition, emotion, and global spatial perceptions). In part, this was based on the knowledge that Broca's area (the speech center) is located in the left hemisphere in most people (see chapter 4). We now know that brain hemisphere functions are much more complex. Specifically:

1. Both sides of the brain are involved in emotional perception. Actually, this is not surprising because the two hemispheres can communicate through the *corpus callosum* and the other *commissures* —the neurons that interconnect the two sides of the brain.

2. Nonetheless, it appears that the different sides of the brain are differentially involved in specifics of the perception, experience, and expression of emotion. The left brain specializes in tasks involving language. The right brain specializes in visuo-spatial tasks, such as those involving facial recognition and in the perception, experience, and expression of emotion (see Springer & Deutsch, 1981).

3. The left brain may be slightly more involved in the processing of such positive emotions as joy, the right brain in the processing of such negative emotions as fear and anger.

4. Posed emotion and spontaneous emotion may well be guided by different parts of the brain.

We now consider some of the recent research that leads to these conclusions, keeping in mind that research into brain functioning is still in its infancy. Often we will have far more questions about the nature of emotion than can be answered. Now and then, theorists' ideas about emotion will conflict, but resolution of these dilemmas will have to await future research.

THE PERCEPTION OF EMOTION

Studies by Philip Bryden, Robert Ley, and their colleagues (Bryden & Ley, 1983; Ley & Bryden, 1982) found that the right hemisphere of the brain plays a more important role than does the left in the comprehension of emotion. These researchers have used a standard paradigm to study hemispheric differences in visual recognition. Subjects place their chins on a sort of headrest. They are asked to stare straight ahead, focusing on a fixed point. At that point, the researchers flash a stimulus on the screen via a tachistoscope, an instrument that flashes visual images extremely quickly. In this experiment, subjects do not have time to move their eyes. (In reviewing these studies, it is important to know that each hemisphere receives information from the contralateral side of the visual field. For example, when a person looks directly ahead, visual stimuli to the left of the fixation point [as seen with both eyes] are transmitted to the right hemisphere. Stimuli to the right of the fixation point are transmitted to the left hemisphere. Of course, the hemispheres exchange information by means of the interconnecting corpus callosum, but the information directly received by a hemisphere is more powerful than that which is merely exchanged.)

Many studies document that the left hemisphere is better than the right at recognizing words, including emotional words or descriptions of emotions (see Bryden & Ley, 1983) . However, when a person is required to discriminate among different whole patterns (called gestalts), including emotional faces, the right hemisphere performs far better than the left.

In one study, for example, Ley and Bryden (1979) prepared cartoon drawings of five different men, each displaying one of five facial expressions, ranging from extremely positive to extremely negative. They flashed these cartoon faces briefly in the right or left visual field (that is, to the left or right of the fixation point) one at a time. After each presentation, they showed the same face or a different one in the center of the visual field (to both hemispheres) and asked the subjects to guess whether the emotional expressions of the two faces were the same or different. The results indicated that the right hemisphere is more intimately involved than is the left in recognizing, responding to, and/or processing emotional stimuli.

Ley and Bryden (1982) also investigated perception of tone of voice. Subjects were told that they would hear two sentences played in competition with each other, one to the right ear and one to the left. They were told to attend to one or the other ear and ignore the material on the other channel. They were also alerted to the fact that each sentence would be spoken in one of four emotional tones: happy, neutral, sad, or angry. Subjects were asked to identify both the verbal content and the emotion of the speaker. Some 90% of the subjects were more accurate in identifying the verbal content of the message presented to the left hemisphere; 77% were more accurate in detecting the emotional tone of the voice presented to the right hemisphere. The results suggested that when a message is heard, the left hemisphere assesses the meaning of the words, while the right hemisphere assesses the emotional expression of the voice.

Similarly, Stuart Diamond and Linda Farrington (1977) fitted subjects with special contact lenses that allowed the investigators to present films exclusively to subjects' left or right visual fields. They found that films that generated positive emotions had a greater impact (as measured by heart rate) when they were presented to the right visual field (left hemisphere). Films that elicited negative emotions had a greater impact when presented to the left visual field (right hemisphere). Such studies lead to the conclusion that the left hemisphere is specialized for processing positive affective information, while the right hemisphere is specialized for processing negative affective information.

THE EXPRESSION OF EMOTION

For generations, artists and sculptors assumed that the human face is symmetrical. In 475 B.C., perhaps for the first time, an unknown sculptor captured the asymmetry of the human face in emotion in *The Charioteer*. Researchers have long been intrigued as to why the face should be "lopsided." Werner Wolff (1933) proposed that the right side of the face is public, that it reflects the emotions we want others to see, while the left side of the face is more private. Wolff's suggestions may well be valid. In general, recent evidence suggests that when people spontaneously display emotion, their expressions are often fairly symmetrical. When people self-consciously pose emotional expressions, however, facial asymmetry is more pronounced. In posing, the left side of the face expresses far more feeling.

Harold Sackheim and Ruben Gur (1978) asked Ekman and Friesen (1975) to lend them the photographs—depicting happiness, surprise, fear, sadness, anger, and disgust—used in their early cross-cultural studies of emotion. Sackheim and Gur then prepared composite photographs: They cut the photographs in two, prepared mirror images of each half, and reassembled them. Finally, they asked students to look at the composites, identify the emotion depicted, and rate how intense each emotional depiction seemed. They found that people do seem to express their emotions more intensely on the left sides of their faces. For example, students thought the man in a photograph made up of a composite of the left side of his face (and its mirror image) appeared more disgusted than the same man in the same photograph using a composite of the right side. The right hemisphere of the brain (which sends messages to the left side of the face) seems to be most powerfully involved in the production of emotional expression.

Sackheim and Gur, however, admit that their conclusion that the right hemisphere is most involved in producing *all* emotional expression requires caution. They conducted a separate analysis in which they compared peoples' faces when posing positive emotions (happiness and surprise) versus negative ones (sadness, disgust, fear, and anger) and found that the positive emotions are revealed more intensely on the left side of the face only 45% of the time. On the other hand, the negative emotions are displayed more powerfully on the left side of the face 73% of the time. This suggests that, as in the case of the processing of emotional information, hemispheric control over emotional expression may be determined by the type of emotion being expressed.

Researchers have also studied naturally occurring emotions—the emotions people express when recounting emotional experiences and the emotions they spontaneously display in restaurants, conversations in the park, and so forth. For example, in one experiment, Morris Moscovitch and Janet Olds (1982) observed passersby in Israel, the United States, and Italy. They recorded whether their grins, raised eyebrows, quick sneers, or flickering smiles were stronger on one side of the face or the other. They found that although most expressions are symmetrical, when they are not, they are stronger on the left side of a person's face. In a second study, they collected snapshots of personalities—John Wayne, Elvis Presley, Clark Gable, Marilyn Monroe, and the like. They found that 80% of the time, the stars' expressions are more pronounced on the left sides of their faces.

STUDIES WITH NEUROLOGICAL PATIENTS

Early on, neuroscientists observed that patients often react quite differently when they have unilateral left-hemisphere damage versus unilateral damage to the right hemisphere. For example, M. J. Babinski (1914) observed that when patients suffer from unilateral right-hemisphere damage, they often understand their plight intellectually, but they fail to react appropriately emotionally. They may be indifferent about their dire straits or even euphoric— they joke and laugh with apparent unconcern. Neil Carlson (1986) reports a typical case:

> I once examined a man who had sustained a right hemisphere stroke. Even though his left arm and leg were paralyzed, he was cheerful and indifferent to his disability. He even attempted several times to walk down the stairs although he did acknowledge, when asked why he was in a wheelchair, that he could not move the left side of his body. He was alert and intelligent and received superior scores on the verbal components of an intelligence test, so his failure to react emotionally to his deficit cannot be explained by a simple comprehension deficit. (p. 674)

On the other hand, patients with unilateral left-hemisphere damage exhibit "catastrophic reactions"—they are pessimistic about the future as well as anxious, fearful, and depressed (Goldstein, 1948).

Neuropsychologist Marcel Kinsbourne (1981) provides a straightforward explanation for these perplexing findings. He contends that the brain's left and right hemispheres specialize in different kinds of emotions. The left hemisphere is associated with positive feelings and their expression—joy, love, and excitement. The right hemisphere is involved with negative feelings and their expression—sadness, anger, guilt, and fear. If the left hemisphere of the brain is damaged by injury, surgery, or epilepsy, leaving the right hemisphere in command, patients are likely to suddenly develop a generally gloomy outlook on life. For example, they may burst into tears without really knowing why. When the right hemisphere is damaged (and the left must take charge), the patient suddenly becomes elated, cheerful, and surprisingly indifferent to the abnormal state.

The Perception of Emotion

Considerable evidence has amassed that damage to the right hemisphere markedly impairs the recognition of others' emotions. Steven DeKosky and his colleagues (1980), for instance, compared patients with left- versus right-hemispheric damage to a control group (neurology patients with no hemispheric damage). They found that patients with left-hemisphere damage and control subjects did far better than those with right-hemisphere damage in discriminating among the facial expressions associated with such emotions as happiness, sadness, and anger, as opposed to indifference.

Similarly, Kenneth Heilman, Robert Scholes, and Robert Watson (1975) studied patients who had temporo-parietal lesions in the left versus right hemisphere. They asked them to listen to neutral sentences (such as, "The man is showing the boys the dog food"), which were recited in a happy, sad, angry, or indifferent tone of voice. Patients with left-hemisphere damage did far better in judging the emotion being expressed. Again, this confirms the notion that the right hemisphere is critical in the perception of emotion.

The Expression of Emotion

Left-hemisphere lesions do not usually impair the expression of emotion. For example, neurologists often study patients who have had an injury (lesion) in some part of their brain. As a consequence, they have become aphasic (they have partially or completely lost their ability to use language). Dozens of varieties of aphasia exist, depending on exactly where in the brain the injury is. For example, Wernicke's aphasia occurs when patients have a lesion in Wernicke's area in the left hemisphere of the brain. (Broca's aphasia occurs when patients have a lesion in Broca's area, again in the left hemisphere of the brain.) Carlson (1986) observes that patients with Wernicke's aphasia are able to modulate their voices according to mood. Even patients with Broca's aphasia, who have trouble expressing themselves in words, can laugh and express emotions by tone of voice when uttering expletives. (When a Broca's aphasic swears he sounds as if he means it.) However, right hemisphere lesions do impair expression of emotion, both facially and by tone of voice.

Heilman, Watson, and Bowers (1983) asked patients with unilateral (one-sided) brain lesions to pose expressions of emotions. They found no differences between patients with right versus left lesions. They point out that people with Broca's aphasia often exhibit facial and oral apraxia—that is, they have difficulty making particular movements and sounds on command. They may find it difficult to respond to the request to smile, but they smile spontaneously when they are told a joke. Thus, the authors propose that they may have detected stronger right-brain versus left-brain differences had they studied the spontaneous expression of emotion. In support of this view, Ross Buck and Robert Duffy (1980) showed emotion-arousing slides to patients with damage to the right or left hemisphere and to control subjects. The investigators found that patients with left-hemisphere damage reacted spontaneously in a normal way. Those with right-hemisphere damage revealed muted facial and emotional expressions.

Differences in patients' emotionality is not limited to facial expression. Lisa Morrow, Bart Vrtunski, Youngjai Kim, and François Boller (1981) presented patients with right- versus left-hemisphere lesions and control subjects with emotion-arousing slides. The authors assessed autonomic nervous system functioning as indexed by skin conductance and respiration. Again, they found that patients with left-hemisphere damage exhibited more intense emotional reactions than did those with right-hemisphere damage.

Although little research yet indicates whether positive emotions, such as joy, may be processed somewhat differently than negative ones, such as sadness, fear, and anger, there is some evidence that they might be. Sackheim et al. (1982) reviewed 109 cases of pathological laughter and crying. They found that left-sided lesions were more frequently associated with crying and right-sided lesions with laughing.

The preceding evidence, then, leads us to several conclusions: Both sides of the brain are involved in emotional perception. Nonetheless, there are differences in the importance of the right and left hemispheres in the perception, experience, and expression of emotion. The left brain specializes in language, including emotional language. The right brain specializes in facial recognition and in the perception, experience, and expression of emotion. The left brain may be a bit more involved in the processing of positive emotions and the right brain in the processing of negative emotions. Spontaneous emotion may be sparked primarily by lower brain structures, such as the brain stem and limbic system. Posed emotion may involve more cortical processing and right-hemisphere dominance.

Facial Expression and Emotional Experience

In the preceding section we found that people's emotions spark appropriate facial expressions. But what about the reverse? What happens when we pretend to feel something we do not? For example, people are always telling others to "smile." If a crabby person smiles, how does this affect that person's mood? Does he somehow begin to cheer up as his eyes crinkle and his mouth shapes into a smile? Or does he get doubly irritated when he is forced to smile, although he feels like snarling? In this section, we see that most of the existing evidence suggests that we will come to feel happy if we put on a happy face or sad if we frown. However, a bit of evidence suggest that sometimes if we work too hard at controlling emotional expression, it begins to take an emotional toll.

Earlier, we argued that the mind integrates many pieces of evidence before it issues an emotional "print-out." People's emotional experiences include their thoughts, their conscious or semiconscious awareness of their facial expressions (see Box 6.1), ANS reactions, and emotional behaviors. Emotional experience probably does not depend entirely on any one of these emotional components—people can probably experience emotion even if one of the components, the cognitive, the physiological, or the behavioral, is dampened or absent. Generally, however, the various components of emotion each contribute something special to the experience. The belief that you are in love can generate a thrill of excitement. If you blush each time an appealing woman walks by, you may realize that you care more about her than you had thought. When your boyfriend points out that your face is contorted with hatred and your neck muscles are straining, you may rethink your protestation that you are not angry.

Many theorists have observed that emotional experience depends, at least in part, on **facial feedback.** (When our brain receives information that our brow is furrowed, our mouth is tightly pursed or tilted upward, etc., we say

BOX 6.1

Emotional Experience and Facial Feedback

Photographer Cecil Beaton, who designed the sets and costumes for *My Fair Lady,* thought in visual images. The only way he could figure out what he felt was by observing his own reactions! His biographer provides an example:

> On 3 May Peter Watson suddenly died. . . . As always on hearing bad news Cecil "let out a moan that was like that of a bull in agony, a great volume of grief." . . . Peter was dead and lost to Cecil forever. In his grief, as again so often, Cecil judged the effect of the shock by

his own visual image caught by chance in the looking-glass [now quoting from Beaton's diary]:

> The shock was enough to want to make me die as well, for my face was contorted, swollen, mauve, my hair white, untidy and almost bald. I looked like the most terrible old man, and it was appalling that this terrible old man was grieving for the love of his life. (Vickers, 1985, pp. 396–397)

it is receiving facial feedback.) Theorists argue that people's emotional re-actions are then influenced by such information. This is not a new idea. For example, Charles Darwin (1872/1965) observed:

> The free expression by outward signs of an emotion intensifies it. On the other hand, the repression, as far as is possible, of all outward signs softens our emotions. He who gives way to violent gestures will increase his rage; he who does not control the signs of fear will experience fear in a greater degree; and he who remains passive when overwhelmed with grief loses his best chance of recovering elasticity of mind. (p. 365)

Similarly, recall that philosopher/psychologist William James (1892/1961) proposed that people infer their emotions by observing their visceral, glandular, and muscular responses: "We feel sorry because we cry, angry because we strike, and afraid because we tremble" (p. 243). (People probably rely most heavily upon facial and postural feedback in decoding their emotions. As discussed in chapter 2, the glands and viscera generally have been thought to be too undifferentiated in their actions to provide much information about the type of emotion people are experiencing. Of course, these organs can provide information about emotional intensity.) James (1890/1984) concluded, "If our hypothesis be true, it makes us realize more deeply than ever how much our mental life is knit up with our corporeal frame, in the strictest sense of the term" (p. 138).

Today, most theorists agree that our emotions are influenced to some extent by facial feedback. However, they disagree about how important such feedback is—is it necessary, sufficient, or merely a small part of an emotional experience?—and exactly how the two are linked (see Lanzetta & McHugo, 1986). Many theorists take the position that emotion and facial feedback are tightly linked. For example, in the 1960s, Silvan Tomkins (1962, 1963) proposed that emotional experiences depend heavily on facial feedback. He observed:

> Just as the fingers respond both more rapidly with more precision and complexity than the grosser and slower moving arm to which they are attached, so the face expresses affect, both to others, and to the self, via feedback, which is more rapid and more complex than any stimulation of which the slower moving visceral organs are capable. . . . It is the very gross and slower moving characteristic of the inner organ system which provides the counterpoint for the melody expressed by the facial solo. (1962, pp. 205–206)

Tomkins believed that each emotion is associated with a different array of facial expressions. Joy feels different from sadness because smiling feels different from frowning. People know what they are feeling by tuning in to their facial expressions. They know how intensely emotional they are by tuning in to their ANS reactions. For Tomkins, then, emotional experience was necessarily linked to facial feedback. Over the decades, Tomkins has modified his theory, but he still believes that facial feedback is a critically important determinant of subjective experience (Tomkins, 1980).

Similarly, Carroll Izard (1971) reasoned that emotion results from the interaction of three separate components: subjective experience, neural activity, and voluntary muscle activity (chiefly that of the face). He thought that facial expression is generally of prime importance, although all three components make some contribution to emotion; all three can augment or attenuate emotion. Ernst Gellhorn (1964) contended that the emotional experience is shaped by both facial expression and the balance of ANS sympathetic/parasympathetic activity. He argued that emotions can be controlled by the willed action of the skeletal musculature. He might argue, for example, that an actor playing King Lear will become angry himself as he plays his part—cursing fate and shaking his fist at the heavens will stimulate angry feelings.

Attribution theorist Daryl Bem (1972) contends that emotional experience is influenced by a variety of factors; facial feedback is only one of those factors. Bem's proposal is, in fact, a bit startling. Most theorists assume that people have a great deal of information about their own inner lives. Bem, however, insists that in real life, people often have not the vaguest idea as to what they feel, that they are as confused as anyone else about their emotions. In such cases, people may read their own emotions in exactly the same way as they go about deducing others' emotions. Bem argues that people use a variety of clues in deciding what they feel. Facial feedback is simply one more clue:

> Individuals come to "know" their own attitudes, emotions, and other internal states partially by inferring them from observations of their own overt behavior and/or the circumstances in which this behavior occurs. Thus, to the extent that internal cues are weak, ambiguous, or uninterpretable, the individual is functionally in the same position as an outside observer, an observer who must necessarily rely upon these same external cues to infer the individual's inner states. (p. 2)

Of course, not all theorists agree that the face plays an important role in shaping subjective emotional experience. Carl Lange (1885/1922) and Marion Wenger (1950) argued that emotional experiences and feelings are not directly influenced by facial feedback. They believed that the emotions are shaped by visceral reactions. Only if facial feedback somehow influenced people's visceral reactions could it have any impact on emotion. (For example, if people snarled in anger and waved their arms around so wildly that it caused their hearts to race and their breathing to become labored, presumably that might shape emotion.) For them, then, emotional experience was influenced only indirectly, if at all, by facial and other bodily feedback. George Mandler (1975a) contends that any link at all between subjective experience and facial expression is merely "epiphenomenal" (an accessory to the expression but not a causal factor).

EVIDENCE ON THE IMPACT OF FACIAL FEEDBACK ON EMOTION

Considerable evidence, however, suggests that emotional experience, physiology, and expression do mutually influence one another. The literature overflows with anecdotes illustrating the powerful link between our inner lives and our actions (see Box 6.2).

A considerable number of experiments support the contention that emotional experience and facial feedback are coupled (Lanzetta & McHugo, 1986). This evidence comes from three sources: (a) Some researchers have studied the emotional lives of actors, who pretend to be happy, sad, or angry. They document that actors often come to feel the emotions they pretend to feel. (b) Some researchers take the opposite tack. They carefully avoid alerting subjects that they are manipulating their facial expressions. They document that when people are made to frown, smile, and so forth without realizing they are doing so, their emotions follow their unconscious patterns of expression. (c) Other researchers have documented that we tend to "catch" other

BOX 6.2

A Leg to Stand On

In *A Leg to Stand On,* Oliver Sacks (1983), a neuroscientist, describes what he learned about thought as his body changed the signals it sent his brain as a consequence of a serious accident and the healing process. On a climbing trip, Sacks fell and badly tore the muscles and tendons in his left leg. The injury took a long time in healing. When his cast was finally removed, Sacks was horrified to discover that he could not move his leg. Somehow, the link between the will to move and the fact of movement had been broken. At first, Sacks was well aware that he desperately wanted to move his leg but that he could not do so. He bore down, sweated, strained; nothing happened. But as he continued to try, to no effect, a puzzling change occurred. Although Sacks knew intellectually that he was trying with all his energies, somehow he began to perceive that he was not willing movement, in spite of all evidence to the contrary. At other times, he felt convinced that his leg was not his; it was merely a shriveled lump horrifyingly attached to his body. Somehow, Sacks observed, his perception of will had been determined by feedback from his skeletal muscles.

Sacks's experiences also graphically illustrate the fact that different portions of the brain produce voluntary versus spontaneous movements. Try as he might, Sacks could not will his leg to move. In desperation, his physical therapist, who had often dealt with this problem, hired a lifeguard to toss Sacks in a pool. Sacks, in the excitement, began to swim spontaneously, effortlessly, and gracefully. Once he had experienced how it felt to move, he could walk again—haltingly, ungracefully, but he could walk.

This anecdote, of course, illustrates the link between conscious perceptions and muscular feedback of the leg. We might expect, however, that the same sort of interdependence might exist between the experience of an emotion and facial feedback.

people's emotions, when we unconsciously mimic their facial and postural expressions. Let us now consider some of this research.

Acting the Part

Actors have long observed that they sometimes have difficulty separating their own feelings from those of the characters they play. In his autobiography, *The Ragman's Son*, Kirk Douglas (1988) reports that he tended to get confused:

> I was close to getting lost in the character of Van Gogh in "Lust for Life." I felt myself going over the line, into the skin of Van Gogh. Not only did I look like him, I was the same age he had been when he committed suicide. Sometimes I had to stop myself from reaching my hand up and touching my ear to find out if it was actually there. It was a frightening experience. That way lies madness. . . . I could never play him again. (Lehmann-Haupt, 1988, p. 10)

Paul Ekman, Robert Levenson, and Wallace Friesen (1983) asked scientists who study the face and professional actors to try a bit of method acting. They were asked to try to relive times they had experienced a variety of emotions—surprise, disgust, sadness, anger, fear, and happiness. As scientists and actors relived these earlier emotional experiences, not only were their remembrances reflected in their faces, but they began to experience the inner turmoil characteristic of these emotions. This should come as no surprise. Theorists such as Stanislawski (Moore, 1960) have observed that actors sometimes come to feel the emotions they portray. Stanislawski speculated as to how this process works: People's emotional experiences are stored in an "emotional memory." There they remain as "distilled essences" of emotion. "Emotional memory stores our past experiences; to relive them, actors must execute indispensable, logical physical actions in the given circumstances. There are as many nuances of emotions as there are physical actions" (pp. 52–53). We relive our own emotions, then, anytime we engage in a variety of small facial and other actions that were once associated with these emotions.

John Lanzetta and his colleagues (1976) found that men and women who were asked to pretend they were receiving intensely painful shocks (to deceive a fellow subject), rated the rather mild shocks they actually received as more painful than did subjects who were asked to try to hide their feelings. The subjects' pretended emotions had an effect on autonomic arousal as well. Those who exaggerated their emotional reactions ended up being more aroused autonomically (as measured by skin conductance) than were those who hid their feelings. Robert Kleck and his colleagues (1976) found that when people knew others were observing them, they automatically tried to react coolly to impending shock. As a consequence, they seemed to experience less pain and less ANS arousal (again as measured by skin conductance) than did control subjects (who believed they were unobserved). We see, then, that people's emotional experiences often do come to reflect the emotions they portray.

Arranging Facial Patterns

James Laird (1984) proposed that people's subjective experience of emotion is influenced by their self-attributions (the explanations they give as to why they are responding as they are). He proposed that people use two bits of data in decoding their emotional states: (a) patterns of expressive behavior, and (b) level of physiological arousal.

> In more colloquial terms, I am angry rather than euphoric or frightened because I am frowning, clenching my fists, and gritting my teeth, and I am angry rather than just annoyed because my heart is pounding, I have butterflies in my stomach, and I feel flushed. (p. 476)

To test his notions concerning self-attribution, Laird conducted an experiment. He carefully avoided alerting his subjects to the fact that he was manipulating their emotional expressions. Instead, he told them that he was interested in studying the action of facial muscles. The experimental room contained apparatus designed to convince anyone that complicated multi-channel recordings were about to be made of facial muscle activity. Silver cup electrodes were attached to the subjects' faces between their eyebrows, at the corners of their mouth, and at the corners of their jaws. These electrodes were connected via an impressive tangle of strings and wires to electronic apparatus (which, in fact, served no function at all).

The experimenter then proceeded to arrange the subjects' faces. He arranged them into either a smile or a frown by asking subjects to contract various muscles. In the "Angry" condition, they were told to contract the muscles between the eyebrows (to draw them together and down) and to contract the muscles at the corners of the jaw (i.e., to contract them by clenching their teeth). In the "Happy" condition, the subjects were asked to contract the muscles near the corners of their mouth (to draw the corners of their mouth back and up). Laird found that emotional attributions were shaped, in part, by changes in the facial musculature. Subjects in the "frown" condition were angrier, and those in the "smile" condition were happier than usual. The subjects' comments give us some idea of how this process worked. One man said, with a kind of puzzlement:

> When my jaw was clenched and my brows down, I tried not to be angry but it just fit the position. I'm not in any angry mood but I found my thoughts wandering to things that made me angry, which is sort of silly I guess. I knew I was in an experiment and knew I had no reason to feel that way, but I just lost control. (p. 480)

The same experimental manipulations produced differences in recall of sad versus happy memories (Laird et al., 1982).

In another experiment, Ekman, Levenson, and Friesen (1983) used much the same procedure. They asked scientists and professional actors to twist this muscle up and that one to the side, and to hold the expression. In fact, unbeknownst to the subjects, the researchers were arranging their faces in the expressions associated with surprise, disgust, sadness, anger, fear, or happiness. For example, in the "Fear" condition, subjects were told, "Raise your brows and pull them together. Now raise your upper eyelids. Now stretch your lips horizontally back toward your ears." Subjects were required to hold these poses for 10 seconds. The authors found that both the scientists and the actors experienced intense emotion when they simply followed orders and mechanically moved their muscles.

Researchers have used a variety of other ingenious techniques to produce smiles or to inhibit them without subjects' awareness. For example, Fritz Strack, Leonard Martin, and Sabine Stepper (1988) led subjects to smile by requiring them to fill out a series of rating forms with a pen held in their teeth. (Try it. You will see that when you hold a pen in your teeth, your facial muscles are shaped into a smile.) In other conditions, subjects were inhibited from smiling. (They were required to fill out forms with a pen held in their lips.) The researchers also found that people's emotional experiences are shaped by the unconscious tilt of their faces. Students rated cartoons as funnier when they held a pen in their teeth than when it was held in their lips or in their hand.

Emotional Contagion and Motor Mimicry

Evidence that emotional experience and facial feedback are intimately linked comes from yet another source—research on **emotional contagion** (the tendency of people to "catch" other people's emotions) and **motor mimicry** (the tendency of people to imitate others' facial expressions, gestures, postures, and so forth). Psychologists have long observed that therapists tend to "catch" their clients' feelings, mothers and fathers transmit their feelings to their infants and vice versa, and lovers "resonate" to each other's moods. Most people tend to perk up when their associates are elated or become depressed when their colleagues are depressed and angry when they are angry. Such contagion seems to exist even if these other people are doing their best to hide their joy, anger, or depression. How does this process work? Surely a variety of reasons explains why people who spend a great deal of time together end up experiencing the same emotions. Happy people may add sparkle to our lives in a dozen different ways; miserable people may drain our energies in an equal number of ways. But theorists have proposed that people tend to catch one another's emotions in yet another way. Unconsciously, people engage in motor mimicry—they automatically imitate other people's facial expressions, gestures, postures, and so forth. As a consequence, they come to feel, as well as to look, as others do.

For centuries, social commentators have observed that people tend to imitate the facial expressions, voices, postures, and reactions of those around them. For example, in 1759, Adam Smith observed, "When we see a stroke aimed, and just ready to fall upon the leg or arm of another person, we naturally shrink and draw back on our leg or our own arm" (1759/1966, p. 4).

Smith felt such imitation was immediate and "almost a reflex." Gordon Allport (1961) observed that a person automatically "felt oneself into" another's mind and emotions in the process of such imitation. An example of motor mimicry appears in Figure 6.4.

Janet Bevin Bavelas and her colleagues (1987) translate Smith's and Allport's observations into modern terms:

> This is elementary motor mimicry, overt action by an observer that is appropriate to or mimetic of the situation of the other person, rather than one's own. The observer acts as if in the other's place to the point of wincing at his pain, smiling at her delight, or (as Smith described) trying to avoid that person's danger. (p. 317)

Since the 1700s, scientists have collected considerable evidence that people do tend to imitate the facial expressions, postures, voices, and behaviors that they see and hear. Consider this potpourri of research: When babies open their mouths, mothers tend to open theirs, too. This is an unconscious reaction on their part (O'Toole & Dubin, 1968). People tend to mimic the expressions and postures of those around them, especially if they care for the others (Elman, cited in Schmeck, 1983; Scheflen, 1964). In one experiment, for example, Katherine Vaughan and John Lanzetta (1980) filmed subjects as

FIGURE 6.4 An example of motor mimicry. From Allport, 1961, p. 535.

they observed another (bogus) subject grimacing in pain as he received severe electric shock. They also recorded subjects' EMG (muscle) responses as the model winced in pain. They found that the subjects grimaced, too, as they observed the model grimace in pain. Soon after the subjects observed the actor's look of shock and pain, the subjects' medial frontalis, masseter (jaw), and orbicularis oculi muscles showed increased activity. (These muscles are depicted in Figure 6.2.)

Bavelas and her colleagues (1987) provide a survey of the many experiments documenting the existence of motor mimicry. She finds that people imitate others' expressions of pain, laughter, smiling, affection, embarrassment, discomfort, disgust, stuttering, and so forth.

Ekman (cited in Schmeck, 1983) contends that people's emotions may be shaped by such mimicry. He points out that this may be one reason why smiling faces at parties or those of grief at a time of mourning are infectious. "The perception of another face is not just an information transfer," contends Ekman, "but a very literal means by which we feel the sensations that the other feels" (p. 1). Psychologists are just beginning to explore how emotional contagion and motor mimicry operate, however. As yet, we know very little about these intriguing processes.

To sum up, 20 or so studies have demonstrated that emotional experience is influenced by changes in facial musculature (see Laird, 1984). Most researchers have argued that emotional experience is influenced directly by facial expression. A few have argued that emotional experience is only indirectly linked to facial expression. They contend that changes in facial expression may induce changes in respiration, general muscle tension, and movement. These ANS changes, in turn, affect emotional experience. Some evidence in support of this contention comes from biofeedback studies, which demonstrate that people's emotions change (they become more relaxed and calm) as they learn various techniques to quiet their muscle tension, slow their breathing, or increase the temperature in their fingers (see chapter 12).

FACIAL EXPRESSION AND ANS ACTIVITY

Thus far we have considered evidence that emotional experience and facial expressions are tightly linked. In this section, we consider evidence that facial expression and ANS activity are linked as well.

In the novel *Smiley's People,* author John LeCarré (1980) describes a technique of "spycraft" that George Smiley used in interrogation. This technique was designed to intensify the anxiety levels of the Soviet agents he interrogated. The technique was total impassivity. See Box 6.3 for LeCarré's description of this process.

It is clear what impact Smiley's preternatural calm had on those he interrogated—it drove them crazy. But what effect did it have on Smiley? Some might argue that when people force themselves to act calmly, they become

BOX 6.3

The Power of Impassivity

Smiley, with an air of official regret, opened a notebook on his lap ... and gave a small, very official sigh: "You are Counsellor Grigoriev of the Soviet Embassy in Berne?" he asked in the dullest possible voice.

"Grigoriev! I am Grigoriev! Yes, well done, I am Grigoriev! Who are you, please? Al Capone? Who are you? Why do you rumble at me like a commissar?"

Commissar could not have described Smiley's manner better: it was leaden to the point of indifference....

Once again, Toby insists on bearing witness here to Smiley's unique mastery of the occasion. It was the strongest proof yet of Smiley's tradecraft, says Toby—as well as of his command of Grigoriev altogether—that throughout Grigoriev's protracted narrative, he never once, whether by an overhasty follow-up question or the smallest false inflection of his voice, departed from the faceless role he had assumed for the interrogation. By his self-effacement, Toby insists, George held the whole scene "like a thrush's egg in his hand." The slightest careless movement on his part could have destroyed everything, but he never made it. (pp. 335–336)

calm. A popular song from the musical *The King and I* expresses this sentiment: "While shivering in my shoes, I strike a careless pose/ And whistle a happy tune, and no one even knows I'm afraid. The result of this deception is very strange to tell/ For when I fool the people I fear, I fool myself as well."

Others might contend that the heroic effort required to keep every flicker of emotion out of one's face would result in a headache, a pounding heart, and a churning stomach. Smiley was probably a regular user of aspirin and antacids.

The Relationship Between Emotional Experience and ANS Arousal

What impact does either spontaneous or posed facial feedback have on ANS responses? To answer this question, let us first examine the link between emotional experience, facial expression, and ANS activity and then focus on the link between facial feedback and ANS activity.

Is each basic emotion linked to a specific pattern of ANS response? Until 1984, most psychologists would have agreed that the answer to that question is "Probably not." Today, we are not so sure. The question as to whether or not each emotion produces the same pattern of ANS activity is an old one. As we have seen, in the early days of psychology, William James (1890), then later Albert Ax (1953), as well as others contended that each emotion is linked to a characteristic pattern of ANS activity. Bits and pieces of evidence supported this contention. For example, in 1822 a young French-Canadian trapper named Alexis St. Martin was accidentally wounded when a musket discharged. It blew a hole the size of a fist in his stomach. Physician William

Beaumont assumed the wound was fatal but patched up St. Martin as best he could. By some miracle, St. Martin recovered and went on to live an almost normal existence. The only odd thing was that the hole in the wall of his stomach never closed. For the rest of his life, St. Martin possessed a gastric fistula (a window through which the inside of his stomach could be seen). This accident enabled Beaumont (1833), who was primarily interested in digestion, to learn a bit about the link between such emotions as anger and fear and activity in the gut. Now and then, when St. Martin reported for an experiment, he was in a disagreeable mood. Normally, the inner coating of the stomach is of a light or pale pink color. When St. Martin was angry or afraid, however, the lining of his stomach changed color. When St. Martin admitted he was angry, the inner coat became bright red, and his digestive system began to secrete unusual amounts of bile. When he acknowledged he was afraid, the lining turned white. Not only St. Martin's face but the lining of his stomach turned "red with rage" and "white with fear."

Unfortunately, however, later researchers were unable to find a one-to-one correspondence between emotions and ANS activity (see Lacey, 1967). By the 1960s, most researchers agreed with Cannon (1929), Schachter and Singer (1962), and others who believed that the various emotions were not associated with specific patterns of ANS arousal. They believed that all emotions seemed to stimulate the same kind of diffuse, generalized arousal. Autonomic activity was a guide not to the kind of emotion a person was feeling, but merely to its intensity.

Recently, however, Ekman, Levenson, and Friesen (1983) made a surprising proposal. They suggested that James and Ax may have been right, after all. On the basis of their research, they concluded that each emotion is associated with a distinct pattern of facial expression and that each pattern of facial expression is associated with a distinct pattern of ANS activity. As yet, no one knows whether their speculations will prove to be correct. However, let us review this intriguing research.

The authors asked scientists and professional actors to produce six emotions—surprise, disgust, sadness, anger, fear, and happiness. They were asked to do this in two ways: (a) Sometimes they were asked to try to relive times they had experienced such emotions in the past, and (b) sometimes they were told to follow instructions, which told them how to arrange their expressions, muscle by muscle. For example, in the "Fear" condition, they were told only, "Raise your brows and pull them together. Now raise your upper eyelids. Now stretch your lips horizontally back toward your ears." They were required to hold these poses for 10 seconds. During both tasks, the authors assessed subjects' second-by-second responses on five physiological measures: heart rate, left- and right-hand temperatures, skin resistance, and forearm flexor muscle tension. On the basis of this research, the authors came to the following conclusions:

1. When people were asked to relive earlier emotional experiences, their feelings were reflected on their faces, and they experienced the inner turmoil characteristic of these emotions. When actors simply followed orders and mechanically moved their muscles (thus strongly reflecting their feeling on their faces), their ANS arousal levels were even stronger.

2. The act of reliving emotional experiences or flexing facial muscles into characteristic emotional expressions produces effects on the autonomic nervous system that would normally accompany such emotions. Thus, facial expressions seem to be capable of generating appropriate ANS arousal.

3. The most startling finding, however, was that the six basic emotions Ekman has identified seem to be associated with both distinctive patterns of facial activity and distinctive patterns of physiological arousal. The researchers found a clear link between six basic emotions and the type of ANS arousal subjects displayed (see Figure 6.5). Positive and negative emotions produced very different patterns of autonomic activity. (For example, heart rate increased more in anger and fear than it did in happiness. Left- and right-finger temperatures increased more in anger than they did in happiness.) Important differences were also measured among the negative emotions. When subjects were asked to relive an earlier emotional experience, psychologists could distinguish between sadness and fear, anger, and disgust on the basis of changes in skin resistance. When subjects were asked to arrange their muscles in certain ways, the researchers were able to distinguish three subgroups of emotions on the basis of heart rate and finger temperature differences (see Figure 6.6). Ekman (cited in Schmeck, 1983) reports that by using a larger battery of measurements, researchers are able to distinguish each of the six specific emotions. This finding challenges emotion theories that have assumed that autonomic activity is undifferentiated.

If Ekman and his co-workers are correct, how do they explain that all

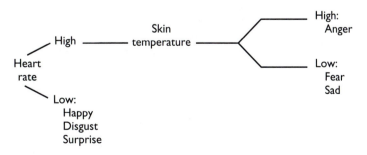

FIGURE 6.5 Decision tree for discriminating emotions in facial action task. From Ekman et al., 1983, p. 1209.

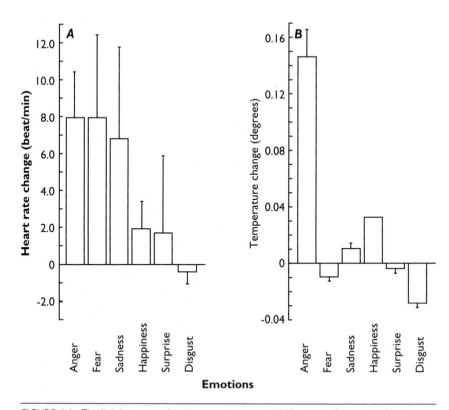

FIGURE 6.6   The link between subjective experience and ANS activity. Changes in (a) heart rate and (b) right-finger temperature during the directed facial action task. For heart rate, the changes associated with anger, fear, and sadness were greater than those for happiness, surprise, and disgust. For finger temperature, the changes associated with anger were significantly different from those for all other emotions. From Ekman, Levenson, and Friesen, 1983. Copyright 1983 by the AAAS.

previous attempts to demonstrate emotion-differentiated patterns of ANS activity failed? Ekman (1984) suggests that previous experiments possessed three critical flaws: First, they studied only one or two emotions and two ANS measures. Ekman studied six emotions and used four ANS measures. Second, subjects probably were embarrassed and ill at ease in all emotional conditions. Having electrical leads attached to various places on one's body does not make one feel at ease. Perhaps the ANS responses associated with embarrassment masked more subtle reactions. Third, perhaps psychologists were not measuring pure emotions. In real life, people typically experience blends of emotions. (We are guilty *and* a bit resentful; in love *and* a bit nervous). If this were the case in the experimental setting, it could account for the subjects' undifferentiated ANS activity.

Poets may have anticipated Ekman in recognizing that facial expressions give us a powerful view into another's emotional life. For example, Edgar Allan Poe, in "The Purloined Letter," revealed that when he wanted to find out how wise, stupid, good, or evil a person was or what a person was thinking at the moment, "I fashion the expression of my face, as accurately as possible, in accordance with the expression of his, and then wait to see what thoughts or sentiments arise in my mind or heart" (p. 227).

The Opposition Speaks

The preceding evidence would lull us into believing that the relationship between emotional experience, physiological arousal, and facial feedback is a straightforward one. It leads us to believe that all indicators of emotion go hand in hand and that the more emotion we feel, the more emotion we reflect on our faces and the more "churned up" we are inside. Not everyone agrees with that position, however. A few researchers have, in fact, argued that people who wear their hearts on their sleeves, will actually be less physiologically aroused than people who are more restrained. At first glance, such reasoning seems paradoxical. Nonetheless, a number of reasons might negatively correlate facial expression and ANS activity.

First, James Henry (in press) argues that throughout humans' long evolutionary history, dominant males were allowed to spontaneously express their emotions, especially their angry feelings. Subordinate males had to suppress their anger. Such suppression necessarily takes a toll. Henry presents evidence that even today, men who try to hide their feelings for personal or professional reasons (men who fail to disclose, repress their feelings, or deny their distress) are at risk for a variety of diseases, including essential hypertension. Their faces may be calm, but their blood pressure is rising.

Second, Sigmund Freud (1921/1946), as you learned in chapter 2, proposed a sort of "pressure cooker" model of emotional expression. If emotions were blocked from normal forms of expression (if people were afraid to express their emotions verbally or facially), sooner or later an explosion would occur, and people would reap serious physiological consequences. In recent times, some psychologists have echoed Freud's warning. For example, Ross Buck has argued that the more people try to hide their emotions from the world, the more upset they will feel inside. Buck (1986) observes that from infancy until about three and a half years of age, boys and girls both express their emotions quite openly. Soon, however, boys learn to hide their feelings. This does not mean the feelings disappear, however. People who show little in the way of facial expression do show large ANS (heart rate and skin conductance) reactions to emotional stimuli. Ross Buck (1980) observes that "blank-faced" people who appear to be feeling nothing actually show large internal reactions to emotional stimuli. In general, men tend to show an internalizing pattern of small overt but large physiological responses, while women tend to show the opposite, externalizing pattern of response.

Finally, it may be that different people express their feelings in different ways. Some people like to talk things out, others smile or frown, and still others' hearts pound or blood pressures rise.

Note that the results discussed in this section are not necessarily contradictory. If we are looking at a single person, the person who exaggerates (or plays down) his or her facial expression may have a stronger (or weaker) ANS response. On the other hand, in considering the differences between different people, we may find that the person who expresses emotions facially is not necessarily the same person who responds to emotional situations with a strong ANS response.

In summary: In this section we have seen that emotional experience, facial feedback, and ANS activity are tightly linked and seem to influence one another. Specifically, we have found that facial feedback shapes both emotional experience and ANS activity. Each emotion seems to be directly linked to a specific pattern of facial response. Whether these same emotions are directly linked to specific patterns of ANS activity or merely linked to a generalized state of arousal is not yet known.

The Social Psychophysiology of Facial Expression

Recently, a demonstration was conducted at the University of Iowa's summer program on social psychophysiology. An undergraduate who worked in John Cacioppo's laboratory was wired to electrodes designed to measure facial EMG, heart rate, breathing rate, and skin conductance. He was instructed to think about anything he wished. Some trainees watched the student on a television monitor. All they saw was a blank, relaxed, impassive face. Others watched the monitoring equipment's print-outs on a 10-channel Grass polygraph recorder. Now and then dramatic changes could be spotted on the print-out. For example, at one point, the electrodes connected to the corrugator supercilli muscle showed a sudden jump. "What are you thinking about?" the trainees asked. "An argument with my roommate." Later, there was a powerful movement around the orbicularis oris. It was so powerful that it interfered with all the other readings. Several people looked at the television monitor to see what the student was doing but could detect no sign of movement. "What is going on?" they asked. "I've just thought of a great argument," the student answered. "Well, quit it," said the observers. "Just imagine you are listening to what your roommate has to say." He did and the pens immediately quieted down (Hatfield & Rapson, 1990).

Darwin (1872/1965) complained, "The study of expression is difficult, owing to the movements being often extremely slight, and of a fleeting nature" (p. 12). Until recently, emotions researchers have been plagued by the same problem. In the past few years, however, researchers have begun to overcome this problem. New discoveries in neurochemistry concerning the workings of the somatic nervous system and effectors, coupled with new technological developments, have made it possible to measure even the most subtle or fleeting of emotions. **Social psychophysiologists** (social psychologists who use psychophysiological techniques in their research) can easily record fleeting amplitude changes in facial muscle action potentials too slight to be caught by the naked eye.

In this section, we review what social psychophysiologists such as Ohio State University psychologist John Cacioppo and his colleagues Richard Petty and Louis Tassinary have to say about the link between subjective/somatic and visceral indicators of emotion, review how they go about measuring facial muscle activity, and describe some already classic studies which demonstrate that positive versus negative emotions differ markedly in the type of muscle activity they engender.

SOCIAL PSYCHOPHYSIOLOGICAL MEASUREMENT

As people think about things, their faces and bodies silently reflect their thoughts. As they think through what they will say next, the orbicularis oris (the muscles around the mouth—see Figure 6.2) invisibly sounds out their unspoken words. When they think about writing, small muscle movements in their fingers and arms trace their ideas. Although these incipient movements are invisible to the naked eye, scientists can easily detect them via electromyographic, or EMG, recordings. (These record the very small electrical impulses that trigger muscle flexion.) Scientists now possess a fairly detailed map of the facial muscles (again, see Figure 6.2). If investigators attach small electrodes to the face, directly above these muscles, they can detect minute electrical changes in each individual facial muscle. (These changes are termed **facial EMG responses**). The changes can be picked up on a polygraph—an instrument that measures several physiological responses at once and depicts them on a graph or transmits the information to a computer (see Figure 6.7). Such incipient EMG movements are of enormous interest to psychologists. People's most fleeting thoughts and feelings are reflected in the rise and dip of the pens tracing their facial, ANS, and behavioral reactions. One can detect extremely subtle reactions via psychophysiological techniques. Not until these thoughts and feelings become extremely intense, however, can they be publicly read in people's facial expressions. Even then, people's public performances are likely to be influenced both by what they really feel and what they want others to think they feel. See Box 6.4.

Now that we know how social psychophysiologists go about measuring covert facial muscle movements, let us review some of their discoveries.

Measuring Positive Versus Negative Emotions

Clear experimental evidence exists that people's emotional experiences spark a continuous series of invisible, minute, facial muscle movements. Both pos-

FIGURE 6.7 A polygraph. Thanks to John Cacioppo (right) and Louis Tassinary (left) for providing this photograph.

itive and negative emotional states and the intensity of those states can be assessed by observing facial EMG activity. Emotions can be read in these tiny, covert reactions long before they can be detected in either people's overt facial expressions or the activity of their autonomic nervous systems.

In one experiment, for example, John Cacioppo and Richard Petty (1979a) recruited students to participate in a study of "biosensory processes." After subjects had adapted to the laboratory setting, researchers unobtrusively recorded their base-rate EMG activity—they measured changes in the zygomaticus major (cheek) and depressor (jaw) muscles (which seem to reflect happiness) and the corrugator supercilli (brow) muscles (which seem to reflect unhappiness). Then, the researchers warned students that they would soon be listening to a persuasive message that either supported or opposed their most cherished beliefs (i.e., tuition should be raised to $500 a semester or left as is) or to a neutral communication, which described an obscure archaeological expedition. (Actually, students seemed to find both the supportive and the neutral messages equally appealing; it was the counterattitudinal message they disliked.) Researchers measured the students' EMG activity for 60 seconds (while they sat quietly waiting for the messages to begin) and again for 120 seconds (while they actually listened to the messages).

The students' emotions can be detected in the printed EMG record. In

BOX 6.4

Choosing a Site for Facial EMG Measurement

How do psychophysiologists go about choosing an appropriate site for their electrodes? How precise do they have to be in making their selections? John Cacioppo, Richard Petty, and Louis Tassinary (in press) provide some guidelines:

1. Individual psychological processes are reflected in certain centers of somatic activity. Cacioppo et al. observe:

   For instance, a student who closes her eyes and vividly imagines watching a professor pace back and forth across the room during a lecture might show localized electromyographic (EMG) activity over the *orbicularis oculi (periocular)* muscle region [which circles the eye] . . . as if the student were actually visually scanning back and forth across the room to follow the pacing professor.

2. Psychological processes can either excite or inhibit EMG activity. Again, Cacioppo et al. observe:

For instance, in the preceding example the act of imagining one was watching a professor pace back and forth across the room led to an increase in *periocular* EMG activity; however, if the student were to imagine that the professor stood motionless and speechless in the middle of the room, this stationary image could actually lead to a diminution of *periocular* activity.

3. Changes in somatic activity are patterned both spatially and temporally:

Thus, consider the case in which a professor was pacing back and forth during her lecture but who during the course of making a point slowed and then stopped; a student who is imagining this scenario should show predictable changes in EMG activity over the *periocular* muscle region across time *(temporal specificity)*—and these changes would be localized rather than expressed generally across somatic sites *(spatial specificity)*. (Cacioppo et al., in press)

Figure 6.8, it is clear that students who expect to hear an appealing versus unappealing message show very different patterns of covert facial EMG activity both before and during the message. Those who expect to hear an appealing message show a great deal of zygomaticus major (cheek) and orbicularis oculi (muscles surrounding the eye) activity and very little corrugator supercilii (brow) activity. Those who expect to hear an unpleasant message show the opposite pattern—a great deal of corrugator activity and very little zygomaticus or orbicularis oculi activity. In short, people have a tendency to smile (even if the smile is invisible to the naked eye) when they hear information that supports their ingrained beliefs and to frown (again, even if the frown is invisible) when hearing information that opposes their beliefs.

In a second experiment, John Cacioppo, Jeffrey Martzke, Richard Petty, and Louis Tassinary (1988) explored the possibility that the best way to measure transient emotions was to focus on one type of EMG activity ("clus-

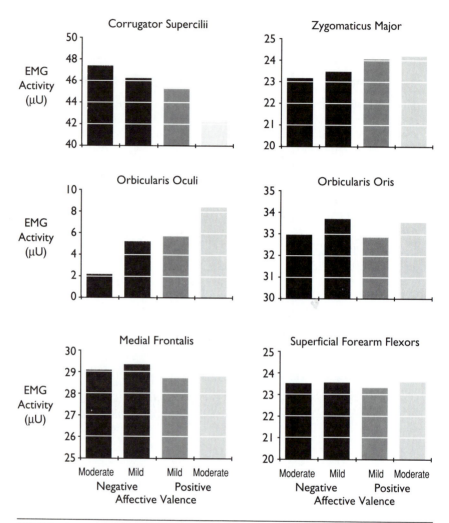

FIGURE 6.8 Reading emotions from the face. Average EMG amplitude over the brow (upper left), cheek (upper right), ocular (middle left), perioral (middle right), forehead (lower left), and forearm (lower right) muscle regions as a function of affective valence and intensity. Adapted from Cacioppo, Petty, Losch, and Kim, 1986, by permission of the author. Copyright 1986 by the American Psychological Association.

ters" of response) rather than on other types. (We describe what these specific types look like on an EMG recording below.) To test their notions, the authors recruited 15 undergraduate women to participate in a clinical-type interview.

The women were seated in a dimly lit room. They were asked to talk a bit about themselves—trying to be as frank, honest, and self-disclosing as possible. The interviewer was an advanced clinical psychology student. From time to time, he asked a question or two—ranging from the most superficial

("Where are you from? What's your major? What color are your eyes"?) to the most intimate ("What are your strengths?" "What are your weaknesses?" "Have you ever had a traumatic experience?") As the women described their thoughts, feelings, and lives, the experimenter videotaped and audiotaped the entire session. In addition, the women's facial EMG muscle activity was recorded throughout the experiment.

As the interview progressed, two assistants scanned the EMG print-out, in order to identify exemplars of four types of EMG responses: (a) a **cluster** (flurries of EMG activity), (b) a **mound** (a more sustained rise in EMG response), (c) a **spike** (a sharper, quicker rise in EMG response), and (e) **control responses** (periods of at least 10 seconds in which subjects showed very little EMG activity). The authors thought that clusters would be the best indicator of transient emotions and that subjects' emotional reactions would not be associated with the occurrence of mounds, spikes, or control reactions.

The next step was to find out what ideas and feelings were flickering through women's minds at various points in the experiment. Immediately after the interview, the women were invited to watch a videotape of their interview. They were told to try to recapture their thoughts, feelings, ideas, and images as they viewed the videotape. Then the tape was played again, and a videotape reconstruction was attempted. The women were told that whenever the tape paused, they should try to describe any thoughts, images, or feelings that had gone through their minds at that time. As the tape played, it was paused at five randomly selected exemplars from each of the four facial EMG response forms. These 20 recollections constituted the verbal protocols. Next, the women were asked to examine their verbal protocols and to rate the emotions they were feeling at the 20 pause points. They were to indicate on the Differential Emotions Scale (Izard, 1977) the extent to which they were feeling, for example, "merry/gleeful/amused," "irritated/angry/mad," or "tense/anxious/nervous" on a 7-point scale. (Possible alternatives ranged from 1 = not at all to 7 = very strongly.)

In Figure 6.9, you can see that negative emotional experiences were associated with very distinct types of EMG facial responses. As predicted, painful emotional revelations (remembrances of fearful, sad, disgusting, tense, irritating, or contemptuous feelings) were associated with clusters of EMG responses over the corrugator supercilii muscle region. They were not associated with mounds, spikes, or control EMG forms. Positive revelations (remembrances of merry and warmhearted feelings) were not associated with any type of corrugator activity. This study, then, provides clear support for the notion that clusters of EMG activity over the brow region can serve as a marker of negative affect. (Interestingly enough, trained observers who analyzed the videotapes were not able to distinguish subjects' emotional reactions simply by observing their overt facial expressions.)

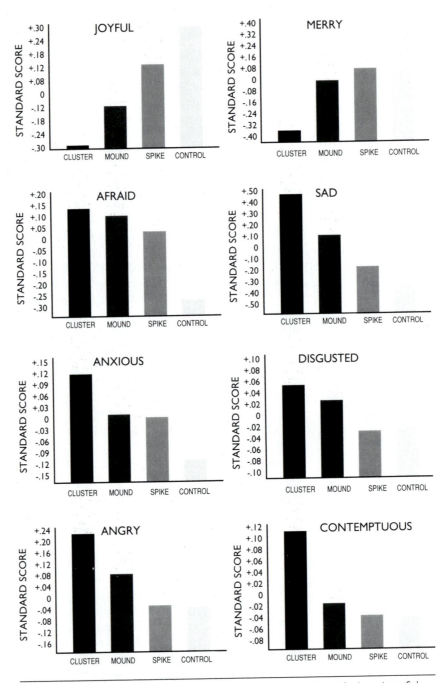

FIGURE 6.9   Subjects' emotional reactions at important moments during the interviews. Subjects were questioned about times in which they were discussing their feelings and displaying one of four types of EMG responses over the *corrugator supercilii* muscle region. From Cacioppo, Martzke, Petty, and Tassinary, 1988, p. 589.

Measuring Emotional Intensity

Laboratory research has also shown that an emotion's intensity will be reflected in the magnitude of the facial EMG response, provided that the stimulus for the emotion itself is not too intense (Ekman, Friesen, & Ancoli, 1980; Fridlund & Izard, 1983; McHugo, 1983). For example, John Cacioppo, Richard Petty, Mary Losch, and Hai Sook Kim (1986) showed women slides of moderately unpleasant, mildly unpleasant, mildly pleasant, and moderately pleasant scenes. (The pleasant scenes depicted mountain cliffs, ocean beaches, and the like. Unpleasant scenes depicted bruised torsos, polluted roadways, and the like.) Subjects viewed each slide for five seconds and then rated how much they liked the scene, how familiar it was, and how much it aroused them. Subjects were videotaped as they viewed the slides. Observers were unable to detect any visible changes in subjects' facial expressions. Nonetheless, both the women's emotional reactions to the scenes and the intensity of those reactions were evident from the type and direction of EMG activity over the brow (corrugator supercilii) and around the eye (orbicularis oculi). In general, the more the women liked the scenes, the less corrugator activity, and the more periocular and zygomatic major activity they showed. This and related research makes it clear that positive and negative emotions activate very different facial muscles. Within limits, the more intense the emotion, the larger the EMG response. It is equally clear that the various emotions are not simply fueling all sorts of somatic activity. For example, positive versus negative stimuli do not spark differential reactions in either the orbicularis oris (the area around the mouth) or in the peripheral muscles (i.e., the forearm flexor muscles).

THEORETICAL CONCLUSIONS

On the basis of their research on facial activity in emotion, John Cacioppo and his colleagues have come to some intriguing conclusions. First, according to Cacioppo, Petty, and Tassinary (in press), whether people are or are not conscious of their feelings depends on their personalities, where they direct their attention, and the amount of time they have to devote to processing their inner experiences.

> *Only in rare cases can an act of cognition be absolutely free from emotion . . . no emotion can be absolutely free from cognition.*
>
> SPENCER, 1890, p. 474

Second, Cacioppo and Petty (in press), in a tradition dating back to Spencer, argue that whether or not people are conscious of it, cognitive information almost always carries with it an emotional message. The face is a critical source of this emotional information. It is the site of four of the five major senses (vision, olfaction, audition, and gestation) and of the major linguistic output (speech). It is a multisignal, multimessage response system capable of tremendous flexibility and specificity. Cacioppo and Petty (1979) observe:

> . . . the mechanisms by which emotional tone is imputed to information processing are not well understood. Visceral and glandular reactions are too slow and undifferentiated to provide the kind of *continuous* neural coding of affect that is implied in these theories. But . . . feedback from the skeletal musculature, particularly in the face, can distinguish between the basic affects and may serve as a mechanism by which this information is recycled to the brain. The brain then may integrate the various affect-specific and cognitive-specific proprioception it continuously receives and thereby alters the subsequent efferent flow and the experience. (p. 180)

Cacioppo and Petty's argument assumes that the face's covert emotional patterning can occur with incredible speed, and the evidence supports the face's capability of such rapid-fire, moment-to-moment changes. For example, while scanning films of psychotherapy interviews, Ernest Haggard and Kenneth Isaacs (1966) found that many unique facial expressions appear and disappear within the span of 125–200 milliseconds! The researchers note that "occasionally the expression on the patient's face would change dramatically within three to five frames of film (as from smile to grimace to smile), which is equivalent to a period of from one-eighth to one-fifth of a second" (p. 154).

Third, psychologists traditionally assumed that one could not distinguish positive versus negative emotions on the basis of physiological measures; they assumed one could determine only how intensely subjects feel (from measures of ANS activity). The preceding studies provide compelling evidence that the various emotions do generate very different patterns of EMG activity. This discovery is especially exciting since these covert changes usually are not evident to the naked eye.

Fourth, EMG measures are probably most useful in detecting small emotional changes. The authors point out that typically, people respond to mild to moderate stimuli in a physiologically differentiated fashion. Once stimuli become too powerful, however, people begin to respond in a fairly stereotypical fashion. Interestingly enough, early researchers did not fully understand the implications of this "law." They purposely chose to study extreme emotions—rage rather than slight irritation, terror rather than unease, passionate love rather than tepid liking—in an effort to maximize their chances of finding emotions' expressive and visceral markers. This procedure inadvertently may have made it impossible to detect the very discriminators they sought. When emotions are too strong, all systems are "go."

Finally, Cacioppo and his colleagues (in press) assume, as we do, that subjective experience, autonomic, and somatic/expressive reactions all influence one another—interacting in a complex series of actions and reactions.

They assume that the first messages come from the central nervous system (e.g., the limbic system, thalamus, and connections to frontal and other brain areas—see chapter 4). Next, the peripheral systems begin to respond—people show their feelings in their faces, postures, and the like. But soon things become extremely complicated as these peripheral and overt expressions of emotion begin to send feedback to the brain. At this point, everything begins to affect everything else. Just how these systems interact is the question now facing emotions researchers. These authors assume that social psychophysiology may well help provide some answers. They observe: "Social psychophysiology represents a meta-theoretical orientation in which there is a joint consideration of the inherent bio-psycho-social nature of mentation, emotion, and behavior, and a goal of formulating integrated accounts of these phenomena" (Cacioppo, Petty, & Tassinary, in press).

Summing Up

- Charles Darwin argued that certain facial expressions are preprogrammed, universal, similar in humans and animals, and functionally significant.

- Steiner found that infants respond to sweet, sour, and bitter tastes with smiles, lip pursing, and disgusted faces during the first few hours of life. Observers have no trouble reading their feelings.

- Infants, in the process of social referencing, scan their parents' faces to see what they feel about the situation and proceed accordingly.

- Ekman and other psychologists have uncovered compelling evidence that six basic emotions are expressed in much the same way in all cultures.

- In *Telling Lies,* Ekman reviews a variety of techniques which people use to distinguish honest expressions from deceptive expressions of feeling. Important clues include pupil dilation or constriction, symmetrical or crooked expressions, and micro-expressions. He cautions observers to use a battery of indicators in their attempts to detect lying.

- Neuroscientists have discovered that the left and the right sides of the brain differ in the way that they process emotional information. Originally, they thought simply that the left brain was the seat of reason and that the right brain was the seat of emotion. Now researchers know things are more complex than this. Posed versus spontaneous emotions may be guided by different parts of the brain, the latter without hemispheric dominance. In addition, joy may be processed on the left side, negative emotions on the right.

- Compelling evidence suggests that emotional experience depends, in part, on facial feedback. Some theorists (such as Tomkins) assume that feedback is necessary to produce emotion. Others, such as Izard, reason that emotion results from the interaction of subjective experience, neural activity, and voluntary muscle activity. Attribution theorist Bem contends that emotional experience is influenced by a variety of factors, including external cues.

- Evidence that emotional experience and facial feedback are coupled comes from three sources. Researchers find that: (a) Actors often come to feel the emotions they pretend to feel. (b) When people are made to frown, smile, and so on, without realizing they are doing so, their emotions follow their unconscious patterns of expression. (c) People tend to "catch" other people's emotions and to unconsciously mimic others' facial and postural expressions.

- Recently, Ekman and his colleagues have argued that each emotion is associated with a distinct pattern of facial expression and a distinct pattern of ANS activity.

- As people think, their faces and bodies silently reflect their thoughts. Although these incipient movements are invisible to the naked eye, scientists can easily detect them via EMG recordings. Researchers now possess a fairly detailed map of the facial muscles.

- People's emotional experiences spark a continuous series of invisible, minute, facial muscle movements. Both positive and negative emotional states and the intensity of these states, can be assessed by observing facial EMG activity.

- The zygomaticus and depressor muscles seem to reflect happiness; the corrugator muscle reflects unhappiness.

- EMG measures are probably most useful in detecting small emotional changes. People usually respond to mild stimuli in a physiologically differentiated fashion. Once stimuli become too powerful, people begin to respond in a fairly stereotypical fashion.

7

Measures of Emotion

Introduction

Subjective (Self-Report) Measures of Emotion
Psychometric Principles
Popular Self-Report Measures of Emotion

Psychophysiological Measures of Emotion
The Basics of Psychophysiological Measurement
Studies Utilizing Psychophysiological Measurement

Behavioral Measures of Emotion
Measuring Emotional Behaviors in Animals
Measuring Emotional Behaviors in Humans

In Conclusion

Summing Up

FIGURE 7.1   *Lovers.* Edvard Munch. 1896. Lithograph. The Munch Museum and Oslo Kommune.

Introduction

Recently, a clinical psychologist at the Center for Student Development telephoned an applied psychophysiology laboratory. The therapist wanted to refer Gary M. to the laboratory. Gary was suffering an anxiety reaction related to public speaking and his therapist thought Gary might benefit from relaxation training.

During an intake interview, Gary revealed that his problems began while he was working on his master's degree in business at the University of Southern California. He was called on in class and asked to give a brief report on his thesis topic. He panicked. He was not prepared, he couldn't find words, and he could do nothing but leave the room. Soon after that, Gary left USC for medical reasons; he was developing a stress ulcer. A year later, he reentered school at the University of Hawaii in a different field. When he was asked to give a talk in his public speaking class, his anxiety returned.

When Gary arrived at the psychophysiology laboratory the following week, the first step was to discover the kinds of things that precipitated his anxiety and to assess the severity of his various fears. Gary was asked to indicate on a 10-point scale those events that caused "no anxiety" at all (these were to be placed at position 1 on the scale), some anxiety, on up to those that caused him "extremely severe" anxiety (these were to be placed at position 10). One thing that caused no anxiety was "Lying in a beach chair on the beach listening to music and reading." Placed above the middle (at position 7) was "Being called on in class." At the top of the scale (10), he placed "Standing in front of a class—without notes, lectern, or desk—discussing an unfamiliar topic, with strangers [present], in total silence—tiled or cement floor, room is big (can accommodate more than 20 people); can see the faces of the people in the class."

Once Gary's "hierarchy" of anxieties had been determined, therapy could begin to teach him to control those anxieties. He was scheduled to come to the laboratory once a week. When he arrived, he sat in a comfortable reclining chair. Electrodes were attached to his face and fingers; they monitored both facial muscle tension and sweat gland activity. Thus, the therapist had a running record of Gary's anxiety level from two different physiological indicators. In the first session, the therapist merely monitored Gary's anxiety level. In subsequent sessions, the therapist would be interested in how Gary's anxiety level changed. Gary also wore a set of headphones. In the next sessions, Gary was given a form of feedback. Through the headphones, Gary could hear a clear tone. Its pitch indicated how tense Gary's facial muscles were—the higher the tone, the more tense Gary knew he was. Gary's task was to learn to relax, and thus lower the tone's pitch. (We discuss this biofeedback technique in greater detail in chapter 14.) Gary could try to relax by thinking of the scene at the beach, other pleasant events, or anything else that made him relax.

If one looks at Gary's responses during his first five sessions in the lab, at first his level of facial tension was quite high. But during the course of biofeedback training, his tension level began to fall, both during the sessions and from one session to the next. His muscle tension levels were lowest at the end of each session. Gary's sweat-gland activity (or electrodermal response level) also declined during biofeedback training sessions. It is interesting to note that Gary's electrodermal response levels showed a temporary increase at the beginning of his third biofeedback session. He reported on that day that he was busy preparing for a speech he had to give in class the following week. (Gary's training lasted about three months. By the end of his therapeutic sessions, which involved psychotherapy as well as biofeedback training, he was able to speak in class with no more than a usual amount of "stage fright.")

We have chosen Gary's case because it illustrates the fact that researchers, therapists, and others who are interested in determining what another person is feeling often search for a variety of clues. The husband who is worried that his wife may be in love with someone else may ask her about her feelings ("Do you still love me? Are you sure there isn't someone else?"), wonder whether she looks more dreamy and animated than usual, and spy on her at parties to see whether she seems to be just a little too interested in his supposed rival. In Gary's case, the therapist used a multimodal technique to measure anxiety: First, Gary filled out a self-report questionnaire (he rated how anxious he felt in various situations.) Then, measures were made of his physiological arousal level (Gary's facial muscle tension and sweat-gland activity). Finally, the therapist observed Gary's behavior (whether or not he could manage to speak in class). Such multimodal assessments are common in psychophysiological laboratories. Psychophysiologists are interested in the linkages between the various dimensions of emotion—subjective experience, physiological responses, and overt behavior.

Generally, of course, theorists and researchers focus on only one aspect of emotion. This makes perfect sense. Often, psychologists take a lifetime simply to learn a little about one dimension of emotion. If they tried to take on more, they would probably end up being overwhelmed, learning nothing at all. As a consequence, researchers generally select or develop a specific measure of the single aspect of emotion in which they are most interested. In this text, we are searching for a more complete view of emotion. Thus, in this chapter, we examine the ways in which emotional experience, physiological responses, and behavior have been measured. We cannot, of course, survey every measure that has ever been used. We can, however, provide some typical examples of the kinds of measures that have been found to be especially reliable and valid.

Subjective (Self-Report) Measures of Emotion

In our everyday encounters, we often try to find out how our friends are feeling simply by asking, "How are you? Are you okay? You look kind of down." They then give us a verbal report: "No, I'm fine, just kind of tired." The most popular self-report measures do exactly the same thing. They ask a straightforward question and hope for an honest answer. Of course, their questions are more carefully crafted than our everyday queries. (The most likely response to "How are you?" is "Fine, thank you"—and that would tell us nothing. **Psychometricians** (psychologists who specialize in the development of tests) have used sophisticated assessment techniques to ensure that their questions and scales are both reliable and valid. In this section, we review some of the general principles of scale construction that have guided these measures. Then, we describe a sampling of the most common and most effective self-report measures of emotional experience.

PSYCHOMETRIC PRINCIPLES

Elizabeth Barrett Browning asked, "How do I love thee?" and proceeded to count the ways. Psychometricians who tried to do the same thing, to quantify emotional experience, had a harder time of it. They possessed no calipers which would allow them to measure the "height and depth and breadth a soul can reach." Neither calculator nor computer permitted them to quantify the following statements and figure out who loves the most: "I love thee with the breath, smiles, tears, of all my life!" (surely worth at least 10 units of love); compared with a less poetic person's awkwardly muttered, "You're okay, I guess" (5.5 units of love); or compared with a more flamboyant "ILUVKC," recently spotted on a license plate (3 units of love). Fortunately, although the measurement of self-reported emotion is not easy, it is possible.

In this section, we review some of the techniques psychometricians have devised to measure emotion. Much of this discussion is taken from work by Ellen Berscheid and Elaine Hatfield (1978). In our brief discussion, we will focus on one emotion, interpersonal attraction, to illustrate our points. The same logic, however, applies to the measurement of any emotion.

Scales

Nominal Scaling. Psychometricians can use four different kinds of scales to measure emotion. These scales range from simple nominal scaling through ordinal scaling to the more complex interval and ratio scales. A **nominal** scale is the most primitive form of measurement. In nominal scaling, psychologists simply name the emotion people are feeling. For example, if child psychologists wanted to assess parents' feelings for their children, they could record all parental messages to their children over a 24-hour period. They would end up with a large collection of messages such as "You drive me out of my mind," "Don't forget to bring your lunch money to school today, honey," and "Do you remember where you left your socks?" Psychologists could then sort such parental statements into various categories: (a) expressions of joy;

(b) expressions of anger; (c) expressions of sadness; and (d) expressions that are difficult to classify. A statement such as "You drive me out of my mind" would surely be tossed into category 2—expressions of anger. In nominal scaling, then, psychologists simply sort responses into categories. The numbers they assign to the various categories (1, 2, 3, etc.) are really labels rather than numbers. Statisticians cannot order or add the numbers assigned to the different categories in any way (e.g., a score of "4" does not represent four times as much joy as a score of "1").

Ordinal Scaling. An **ordinal** scale tries to rank people. When people say, "I think Fred is nicer than Sam," they are using an ordinal scale. Psychologists who use ordinal scaling are able to say that people like Person A more or less than Person B, but they cannot say how much "more than" or "less than" they like Person A.

Interval Scaling. In **interval** scaling, psychologists are able to say both who is liked more and "how much more" or less they are liked. On interval scales, numerically equal distances represent equal amounts of the property being measured—such as attraction. It is difficult to devise interval scales. Nonetheless, when people discuss their feelings they often talk as if they had exactly such a scale in mind. Anytime people make a statement such as, "I think Bill is a fool for sticking around; he loves Sue so passionately and she couldn't care less for him," they imply that they can rate Bill's and Sue's feelings for each other on the same equal-interval scale. Moreover, if one states, "I am much more anxious today than I was two days ago," again the implication is that the emotion is quantifiable, but only in relative terms.

Ratio Scaling. The highest level of measurement is the **ratio** scale. (A thermometer is one example.) In addition to possessing the advantages of nominal, ordinal, and interval scales, a ratio scale has an additional advantage—the zero point on the scale is an absolute or natural zero. (On a very useful thermometer, though not on our everyday thermometers, 0 could represent an absence of any heat at all.) If people rate a 0 on such an emotion scale, they are saying that they have none of the property being measured (they feel no love, no joy, no anger). Since ratio scales possess a 0 point, mathematicians can conduct any arithmetic operations on the numbers that they wish, including multiplication and division. Unfortunately, psychologists, including those in the field of emotion, almost never are able to devise ratio scales. If we possessed such scales, we would truly be able to say, "I love you twice as much as you love me."

People sometimes claim that it is not possible to measure feelings. For example, in 1975, United States Senator William Proxmire made political hay by denouncing social scientists who were so foolhardy as to try to study love. He stated: "No one—not even the National Science Foundation—can argue that falling in love is a science. . . . The impact of love on the heterosexual relationship [is a] very subjective, nonquantifiable subject matter. Love is simply a mystery," he concluded; "it is a waste of time and money to try to study it." The senator is, of course, wrong. Not only is the quantification of interpersonal attraction not impossible, but it is a procedure on which people will, on occasion, expend great effort. Berscheid and Hatfield (1978) provide an example of such quantification in Box 7.1.

Scaling Procedures

Investigators have devised several techniques for securing ordinal, interval, and ratio scales of emotion.

The Likert Scales. Perhaps the most common way to measure emotion is via Likert self-report scales. Rensis Likert (1932) proposed a simple procedure for measuring attitudes. Subjects are shown a series of statements and asked to indicate the extent to which they agree with each statement. Likert scales have frequently been used to assess people's emotional reactions toward various minorities. In the 1930s, for example, social psychologists measured people's racial feelings by asking them whether they agreed or disagreed with statements such as this:

Where there is segregation, the black section should have the same equipment in paving, water, and electric-light facilities as are found in the white districts.

(5)	(4)	(3)	(2)	(1)
Strongly Approve	Approve	Undecided	Disapprove	Strongly Disapprove

People's ratings on the various items were simply summed. In the preceding example, the lower a person's total score, the more prejudiced the person would be said to be.

A number of researchers have developed Likert scales of attraction. For example, Zick Rubin (1970) used a version of the classical Likert scales to measure liking and romantic love.

Liking Scale

1. I think that ———————— is unusually well adjusted.
2. I would highly recommend ———————— for a responsible job.
3. In my opinion, ———————— is an exceptionally mature person.

Romantic Love Scale

1. I feel that I can confide in ———————— about virtually everything.
2. I would do almost anything for ————————.
3. If I could never be with ————————, I would feel miserable.

Respondents were asked to indicate how they felt about the other on the following scale:

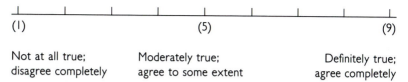

(1) Not at all true; disagree completely

(5) Moderately true; agree to some extent

(9) Definitely true; agree completely

Rubin found that couples' scores on the Liking and Love scales were good predictors of how much they seemed to like or love each other and whether they remained simply good friends or eventually married.

A New, Improved Ratio Scale. In spite of the popularity of the Likert scaling technique, researchers have not given up on the attempt to construct a ratio scale for measuring emotions. Recently, Gunnar Borg (1982) proposed a promising new technique for measuring emotion. The psychometric underpinnings of this scale are complex, but the scale itself is easy to understand.

Subjects are simply asked a question such as, "How strong is your liking (or anger, or joy, etc.)?" They try to gauge their feelings on the following psychophysical scale:

0	Nothing at all
0.5	Extremely weak (just noticeable)
1	Very weak
2	Weak
3	Moderate
4	Somewhat strong
5	Strong
6	
7	Very strong
8	
9	
10	Extremely strong (almost maximal)
*	Maximal
	(p. 31)

This scale is designed to reflect a psychological reality. Psychologists have found that people find it fairly easy to chart the intensity of their emotions as long as their feelings are tepid. As their feelings become more passionate, however, slight changes in feeling become increasingly difficult to detect. Things tend to blur together. The Borg scale reflects that reality.

This type of ratio scale has been found to be both reliable and valid in a series of studies. Borg concludes, "The new scale makes possible direct comparisons of intensity *'levels'* like those obtained with most category scales and also comparisons of *'ratio relations.'* The simplicity of the scale should make it applicable in many different kinds of situations where estimates of

Box 7.1

Measuring Liking and Loving

The following dialogue illustrates the "fancy footwork" that untrained psychometricians can perform when motivated to do so. It can be heard, with some variation, almost anywhere, but especially between couples whose relationship is developing in intensity:

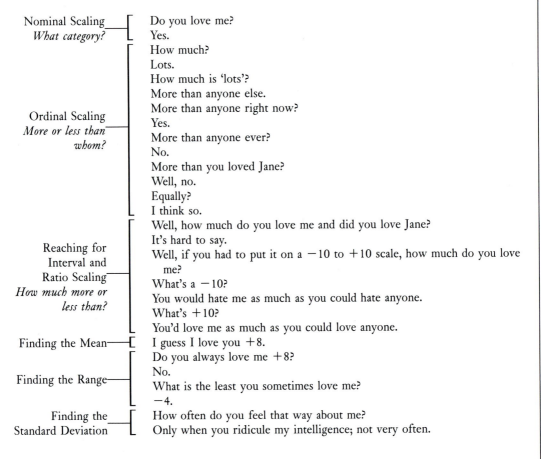

Nominal Scaling
What category?
[Do you love me?
  Yes.

Ordinal Scaling
More or less than whom?
[How much?
  Lots.
  How much is 'lots'?
  More than anyone else.
  More than anyone right now?
  Yes.
  More than anyone ever?
  No.
  More than you loved Jane?
  Well, no.
  Equally?
  I think so.

Reaching for Interval and Ratio Scaling
How much more or less than?
[Well, how much do you love me and did you love Jane?
  It's hard to say.
  Well, if you had to put it on a −10 to +10 scale, how much do you love me?
  What's a −10?
  You would hate me as much as you could hate anyone.
  What's +10?
  You'd love me as much as you could love anyone.

Finding the Mean
[I guess I love you +8.

Finding the Range
[Do you always love me +8?
  No.
  What is the least you sometimes love me?
  −4.

Finding the Standard Deviation
[How often do you feel that way about me?
  Only when you ridicule my intelligence; not very often.

Berscheid and Hatfield (Walster) (1978), p. 8. Permission granted from both the authors and Random House, Inc.

subjective intensities are needed" (p. 33). Borg's scaling technique seems promising. Whether this promise will be fulfilled is yet to be seen.

Now that we have reviewed the types of scales that are available—from nominal to ordinal, interval, and ratio—let us review a sampling of the scales that emotions researchers have actually used in their research.

POPULAR SELF-REPORT MEASURES OF EMOTION

Researchers generally use one of two types of self-report measures to assess emotion. Sometimes, researchers focus on a single emotion (say, anxiety) and ask subjects how anxious they feel "right now" or how anxious they "usually feel." A fine example of such a scale is the State-Trait Anxiety Inventory, or STAI (Spielberger, Gorsuch, & Lushene, 1970), which is designed to measure both momentary (state) anxiety and enduring (trait) anxiety. Let us look at some examples of the State and Trait items on the STAI (see also chapter 12). The state anxiety measure contains 24 items. They look like this:

SELF-EVALUATION QUESTIONNAIRE

Directions: A number of statements which people have used to describe themselves are given below. Read each statement and then circle the appropriate number to the right of the statement to indicate *how you feel right now,* that is, *at this moment.* Use the following key.

Key

0 = Not At All
1 = Somewhat
2 = Moderately So
3 = Very Much So

*I feel calm	0	1	2	3
I am tense	0	1	2	3
*I feel at ease	0	1	2	3
I am jittery	0	1	2	3
I feel "high strung"	0	1	2	3
I feel nervous	0	1	2	3

*Scored in reverse direction.

The trait anxiety measure has 16 items. They look like this:

Directions: A number of statements which people have used to describe themselves are given below. Read each statement and then circle the appropriate number to the right of the statement to indicate how you *generally* feel. Use the following key.

Key

1 = Almost Never
2 = Sometimes
3 = Often
4 = Almost Always

I feel like crying	I	2	3	4
*I feel rested	I	2	3	4
*I am "calm, cool and collected"	I	2	3	4
I feel that difficulties are piling up so that I cannot overcome them	I	2	3	4
I lack self-confidence	I	2	3	4

*Scored in reverse direction.

Another popular type of self-report questionnaire asks subjects not only about one or another emotion (anxiety *or* joy *or* fear), but about how joyous *and* angry *and* sad *and* fearful they usually feel (or feel at the moment). Such scales provide a sort of emotional profile. This chapter focuses on two types of instruments—self-report questionnaires and adjective checklists. These two types of instruments differ, in part, in their approach. Self-report questionnaires are usually designed to assess relatively enduring personality characteristics or emotional predispositions. They ascertain how often and how intensely people feel various emotions. Adjective checklists, on the other hand, are designed to determine subjects' current emotional states. They assess how intensely subjects are experiencing a variety of emotions right at the moment.

Multiple Emotional Assessment with Self-Report Questionnaires

An often-used technique for measuring emotions is Robert Plutchik and Henry Kellerman's (1974) Emotions Profile Index. Recall that Plutchik's (1970) psychoevolutionary theory of emotion contends that people are pre-wired to experience eight basic emotions—fear, anger, joy, sadness, acceptance, disgust, expectancy, and surprise. The Emotions Profile Index is designed to measure how typical of various people these emotions are.

The EPI is a forced-choice test. Subjects are simply asked which of two paired words best describes them. Are they more quarrelsome or more shy? More adventurous or more affectionate? More brooding or more resentful? Altogether, they must choose for 43 pairs of items. Researchers score the EPI by noting and recording which of the basic emotions is reflected by each choice. Does it reflect anger-fear, surprise-expectancy, sadness-joy, or acceptance-disgust? Subjects receive a score on each of the eight emotional dimensions. Plutchik (1980a) points out that the EPI has several advantages. For one, it provides a profile of subjects' chronic emotional states. (Some researchers have also used the EPI to profile momentary emotional experiences.) For another, the EPI allows researchers to compare the emotional profiles of different types of people and different groups. For yet another advantage, since it is not intuitively obvious what a given choice means (is it better to be quarrelsome or shy, for example?), the test has a projective quality—it is not obvious how one would "fake it." For example, since the alternatives are often equally appealing, people cannot bias the test by selecting the socially desirable alternative.

In several studies, researchers have compared the profiles of normal men and women with those of patients suffering from manic-depressive disorders. Normal men and women seem to be relatively high in joy, acceptance, and expectancy. Manic-depressives are high in sadness and perhaps anger, and low on joy and acceptance (i.e., they tend to shy away from affiliating with others).

One study of hospitalized patients (Platman, Plutchik, & Weinstein, 1971) yielded a fascinating, unanticipated finding. One woman, diagnosed as manic-depressive, had an EPI profile that seemed to be a bit different from that of the typical manic-depressive. Normally, as we have said, manic-depressive profiles are high on sadness, fear, and anxiety, and sometimes anger. Her profile was also high on depression (sadness) and anger. Her level of fear, however, was unusually low. The very day after testing, the patient made an unsuccessful suicide attempt. The investigators speculated that her particular constellation of emotions—anger, depression, and low anxiety or fear—may provide an early warning that a suicide attempt might occur. Perhaps, generally, it is their high levels of anxiety that protect many manic-depressive patients from desperate, suicidal acts.

Because the EPI is able to discriminate between normal and patient populations so neatly, it would seem to be a useful tool in both diagnosis and assessment of various treatment programs for depression.

Multiple Emotional Assessment with Adjective Checklists

Researchers have also developed a variety of techniques for gauging emotional states. One of the most popular instruments is Marvin Zuckerman and Bernard Lubin's (1965) Multiple Affect Adjective Checklist (MAACL). The MAACL assesses the extent to which subjects are experiencing three negative emotions—anxiety, depression, and anger-hostility. The authors focused on these emotions because of their involvement in emotional disorders.

The MAACL's procedure is straightforward. Subjects are asked to look over a list of 132 adjectives (*shaky, aggressive, annoyed, incensed,* and so forth) and check those which seem to describe their own feelings. For each emotion, say, anxiety, some words (such as *shaky*) have been found to be positively related (+) to that emotion. Others (such as *calm*) seem to be negatively related (−) to anxiety. The MAACL simply subtracts minus from plus scores to produce a total index for each of the three emotions. (Some researchers have criticized the MAACL's item selection procedures and statistical procedures; cf. Plutchik, 1980a.)

Another popular checklist is the Mood Adjective Checklist (MACL). The MACL is designed to measure all emotions—positive and negative. In the 1950s, Vincent and Helen Nowlis (1956) began a series of studies on the effects of such drugs as amphetamines, marijuana, and LSD on the social and emotional behavior of college students. They developed the MACL to measure students' moods after taking a drug. Originally, the MACL consisted of

200 adjectives—words like *angry, clutched up, carefree, elated,* and so forth. Students were asked to use two checks if they "definitely" felt a given mood, one check if they felt the mood "slightly," a question mark if they could not decide, and a "no" if they felt nothing. The MACL turned out to be an exceptionally useful device. One could gain a great deal of information about emotions in a fairly short time. Some researchers (Nowlis & Nowlis, 1956; Nowlis, 1970) have developed an even shorter (33-item) version of the test (see Box 7.2).

Next, researchers set out to factor-analyze the MACL to determine the number of core dimensions tapped by the scale. They were unable to agree. Some investigators concluded that the MACL included as few as 4 factors; others, that it included as many as 12 factors (McNair & Lorr, 1964; Nowlis, 1965). For example, Vincent Nowlis (1970) argued that mood included four bipolar dimensions: (a) level of activation/deactivation (from sleep to attention); (b) control/lack or loss of control (the extent to which events are in or out of control); (c) positive/negative social orientation (readiness to help and accept versus hurt, reject, or ignore others); and (d) positive/negative appraisal of how things in general are going—that is, pleasantness and unpleasantness.

Russell Green and Vincent Nowlis (1957) asked 400 University of Rochester college students to rate themselves on a 100-adjective version of the MACL. They concluded that the MACL included eight emotional factors—activation, aggression, anxiety, concentration, depression, egotism, pleasantness, and social affection.

In a sophisticated analysis, Maurice Lorr, Paul Daston, and Iola Smith (1967) asked 339 college students to indicate the moods they had felt during the past two days. The students rated 62 adjectives on a 4-point scale (ranging from "not at all," to "a little" and "quite a bit," to "extremely"). These ratings were intercorrelated and factor-analyzed. Lorr et al., too, identified eight factors—elation, activity, anger, anxiety, contemplation, hopelessness, weariness, and composure—involved in the MACL.

In summary: Is it possible to measure subjective expressions of emotion? Of course it is. This section has reviewed two typical measures that have been found to be extremely useful—self-report and adjective checklists. Which of these measures is most useful depends on your purposes. Sometimes, psychometricians are interested in assessing a single emotion. For doing so, Borg's Ratio scale is a state-of-the-art technique. Sometimes, researchers are interested in a bit more. They want to know both how emotional people are at the moment and how emotional they usually are. In such cases, a measure such as Spielberger, Gorsuch, and Lushene's State-Trait Anxiety Inventory (STAI) is called for. Finally, sometimes researchers are interested in securing a wider profile of people's emotional states. They want to know how people rate themselves on a wide variety of emotions. In such cases, a measure such as Nowlis's Mood Adjective Checklist (MACL) is especially useful.

BOX 7.2

A Short Form of the Mood Adjective Check List (MACL)

Each of the following words describes feelings or moods. Please use the list to describe your feelings at the moment you read each word. If the word definitely describes how you feel at the moment you read it, circle the double check (vv) to the right of the word. For example, if the word is *relaxed* and you are definitely feeling relaxed at the moment, circle the vv as follows:

relaxed (vv) v ? no   (This means you definitely feel relaxed at the moment.)

If the word only slightly applies to your feelings at the moment, circle the single check v as follows:

relaxed vv (v) ? no   (This means you feel slightly relaxed at the moment.)

If the word is not clear to you or you cannot decide whether or not it applies to your feelings at the moment, circle the question mark as follows:

relaxed vv v (?) no   (This means you cannot decide whether you are relaxed or not.)

If you definitely decide the word does not apply to your feelings at the moment, circle the no as follows:

relaxed vv v ? (no)   (This means you are definitely not relaxed at the moment.)

Work rapidly. Your first reaction is best. Work down the first column, then to the next. Please mark all words. This should take only a few minutes. Please begin.

angry	vv	v	?	no	kindly	vv	v	?	no
clutched up	vv	v	?	no	sad	vv	v	?	no
carefree	vv	v	?	no	skeptical	vv	v	?	no
elated	vv	v	?	no	egotistic	vv	v	?	no
concentrating	vv	v	?	no	energetic	vv	v	?	no
drowsy	vv	v	?	no	rebellious	vv	v	?	no
affectionate	vv	v	?	no	jittery	vv	v	?	no
regretful	vv	v	?	no	witty	vv	v	?	no
dubious	vv	v	?	no	pleased	vv	v	?	no
boastful	vv	v	?	no	intent	vv	v	?	no
active	vv	v	?	no	tired	vv	v	?	no
defiant	vv	v	?	no	warmhearted	vv	v	?	no
fearful	vv	v	?	no	sorry	vv	v	?	no
playful	vv	v	?	no	suspicious	vv	v	?	no
overjoyed	vv	v	?	no	self-centered	vv	v	?	no
engaged in thought	vv	v	?	no	vigorous	vv	v	?	no
sluggish	vv	v	?	no					

Nowlis (1970, p. 272). Reprinted with permission of the Annals of the New York Academy of Sciences, 65: 345–355 (1956).

However, psychologists may be reluctant at times to rely solely on people's self-reports of their emotional states. There are also times that people don't know or can't or won't admit what they are feeling. In such cases, physiological or behavioral measures can be used to gain insight into people's interior landscapes.

Psychophysiological Measures of Emotion

In the past few decades, emotions researchers have begun to be increasingly interested in the physiological aspects of emotion. Several reasons account for this interest. First, until quite recently, researchers found it difficult or impossible to access and measure physiological responses with much accuracy. As W. Grey Walter observes:

> Thirty years ago taking an EEG [a measure of cortical activity] was fun. One did not 'take' an EEG, one struggled to wrest some sort of record from a home-made rig of noisy valves, leaky batteries, fragile oscilloscopes and bulky cameras; the chance of everything working properly at the same time was small and it was all very strenuous, often exasperating, but always fun. (In Cooper, Osselton, & Shaw, 1969, p. v)

Recently, major technological advances have enhanced researchers' ability to record, display, and summarize their subjects' physiological reactions. In particular, psychophysiologists have developed sophisticated and sensitive monitoring equipment, state-of-the-art amplifiers and filters, and computerized recording and display capabilities. These have made it possible to gain access to a variety of physiological responses (see Cacioppo & Petty, 1983; Coles, Donchin, & Porges, 1986).

Second, theorists and researchers have become increasingly aware that a critical component of emotion is physiological activity. According to some theories, as we have seen, if there is no physiological reaction, there is no emotion (e.g., Schachter, 1964). Many theorists take a multimodal approach to emotion—arguing that emotion involves a complex pattern of reactions, which include physiological reactions. Researchers have recognized that they can gain a more profound understanding of the emotions if they have access to the world within the skin. In the words of James Hassett (1978), "The human senses are poorly designed to peer into the organism's inner world, to see how the human biological machine is put together. Scientific instruments extend man's limited vision" (p. 20).

Third, stress researchers have proposed links between emotion, stress, immune-system, and other physiological responses, and physical illness (discussed in chapter 13). Not surprisingly, then, many psychologists have recently become intrigued with carefully documenting the role of central and autonomic nervous system activity in the emotions. Their hope is that once they understand the links between the variables, they will be able to intervene and halt, or even reverse, disease processes.

THE BASICS OF PSYCHOPHYSIOLOGICAL MEASUREMENT

Essentially, the process of psychophysiological measurement involves monitoring minute changes in people's physiological reactions (usually at the surface of the body), electronic amplification and filtering of these signals, and displaying the signals. Therapists and researchers who are interested in the physiological aspects of emotion can use such measures to track people's physiological reactions.

Monitoring Physiological Processes

The process of psychophysiological measurement begins at the skin. First, the experimenter may carefully clean the measurement site with soap and alcohol, sometimes abrading (roughening) the skin. Then, the experimenter attaches the electrodes to the skin with an adhesive collar. Electrodes are metal conductors about the size of a nickel or a dime. They are attached to wire leads several feet long. Electrode paste or gel is often placed between the electrode and skin to ensure a good connection.

From the electrodes, electrical current runs through the leads to measuring instruments. Where does this current come from? Imagine that the human body is a reservoir of electrical energy (or potential). As people go about their lives, their CNS and ANS activity sends out a steady stream of biological electrical signals—**biopotentials.** Thus, researchers can assess, say, brain activity, facial and other muscle movements, or physiological activity throughout the body's organs by monitoring changes in electrical potentials at an appropriate site. Cognitive activity might be measured on the scalp, facial muscle movement at the brow or corner of the mouth, heart rate increases across the line of the body, and so forth. Emotion reveals itself in the body's biopotentials. Thus, the first step in psychophysiological assessment is measurement of changes in the body's electrical potentials.

Common Physiological Measures.
Where researchers place the electrodes and how they go about taking such measurements depends on the type of emotional reaction they are trying to detect. For example, emotions researchers are often primarily interested in facial muscle movements (see chapter 6). If experimenters want to measure movements of, for instance, the corrugator supercilii, they must align their electrodes along the top of an eyebrow. These electrodes are connected to an electromyograph. This measure is, therefore, called an EMG response. The EMG is difficult to measure because the facial muscles generate an extremely weak electrical signal, and so researchers have to amplify the signal. They must also carefully avoid and filter out potential

"noise." (They may have to shield all electrical equipment in the experimental rooms, line fluorescent lights with copper shielding, or buy equipment which is itself shielded. Even the electrode leads are wrapped in a web of metal shield before they are sealed in rubber or plastic.) The results, however, are worth all the trouble. Emotional states and EMG responses have been found to be tightly linked. In emotion, the neurons leading to one or another facial muscle are often active. As the facial muscles contract, they generate an electrical potential at their surface. The EMG record provides a good measure of muscle tension or "tone."

Generally, psychophysiologists have focused on a few critical indicators of emotion. Sometimes, researchers are primarily interested in measuring central nervous system (especially brain) activity. For example, as you learned in chapter 6, some researchers have contended that pleasurable emotional stimuli are processed on the left side of the brain, while painful emotional stimuli are processed on the right side of the brain. Such emotions researchers would be interested in securing a running record of neural activity. If researchers are interested in cognitive and brain activity, they place small electrodes at various locations on the subject's scalp. Neuroscientists have developed a grid system, a standardized location system, which helps researchers properly place electrodes over the brain. Brain potentials are then fed to an electroencephalograph, providing a measure of the EEG response.

Probably most psychophysiologists who are interested in emotion have been interested in measuring activity in the autonomic nervous system. As outlined in chapter 4, the ANS usually operates without a person's moment-to-moment awareness. It provides an indispensable guide to the person's emotional physiological experiences. Recall that the sympathetic division of the ANS swings into gear during stress or emergency situations—when a person is angry or afraid. The parasympathetic division is associated with energy conservation—with pleasurable relaxation. Thus, researchers have been eager to measure ANS activity—to measure such indicators of strong emotion as heart rate, respiration, perspiration, and so forth.

Researchers who are interested in assessing heart rate place electrodes across the chest and/or on the arms in an attempt to pick up neural signals to the heart. These signals are relayed to an electrocardiograph, providing a measure of the EKG response.

One of the most ancient ways to determine whether people were emotionally aroused was to see whether they were perspiring. The physician Erastratos reported using such clues in the fourth century B.C. Today, if researchers are interested in measuring the glandular activity accompanying perspiration, they attach electrodes to, say, the fingers or the palms of the hands. These electrodes detect biopotentials that originate in the eccrine (sweat) glands. Such measures are called skin potential responses, or SPRs, one type of electrical activity of the skin.

Psychophysiologists have other means at their disposal—they can do more than record biopotentials. For example, in addition to monitoring SPRs, researchers can assess sweat-gland activity by simply sending a small electrical current from one electrode to another through the surface of the skin. The skin itself serves as a variable resistor to current passing through it. As sweat-gland activity increases, resistance of the skin declines, and the amount of current that will flow through increases; this is another type of electrical activity of the skin. Originally, such changes in current were called galvanic skin responses, or GSRs. Because it can be confusing to think of decreases in resistance as a measure of increases in emotionality, researchers today generally convert skin resistance responses into their counterparts, skin conductance responses, or SCRs. In other words, as you become more emotional, your skin becomes more conductive.

What difference does it make whether researchers assess how active subjects' sweat glands are by measuring SPRs (which directly tap the eccrine gland biopotentials) or SCRs (which measure momentary changes in skin conductance)? In fact, the two measures may be closely related, especially when researchers are studying people's reactions to a specific stimulus (such as a tone signaling impending electric shock). Nonetheless, researchers have traditionally used skin conductance rather than potentials in the study of sweat-gland activity. Thus, researchers often opt for SCRs so that they can compare their results with those of previous investigators.

Applied researchers have used some of the techniques just described in an effort to detect lying. See Box 7.3.

Other Psychophysiological Measures. Still other psychophysiological techniques are available to emotions researchers. As you may know, human "core" temperature (98.6 degrees Fahrenheit) is quite stable. Peripheral temperature fluctuates markedly, however. When people are embarrassed and blush, their faces becomes hot. When they have to recite in class, some people are so frightened that they literally get cold feet. A convenient way to detect temperature change is by placing a small device, a thermistor (which monitors temperature), on the skin. The thermistor is made of a sensitive material whose resistance changes as temperature fluctuates. A dermograph, to which the thermistor is connected, sends out minute amounts of electrical current; as it passes through the thermistor, more or less current is consumed in overcoming the resistance. Thus, as temperature changes, the amount of current returning to the dermograph changes, providing an index of skin temperature.

We have discussed some of the most common psychophysiological measures of emotion. Researchers have developed an array of techniques to measure central nervous system and peripheral nervous system responses (including such things as pupillary, respiratory, and cardiovascular responses), each of which will use either one of the methods of assessment we have described or yet some other technique. Table 7.1 summarizes some of these measures.

BOX 7.3

"Lie detectors"

Over the centuries, people have been well aware that when they lie, they pay a cost. They often feel guilty, upset, or terrified that they will be caught. They may experience a variety of physiological symptoms—they blush, their hearts pound, their breath comes in rapid, deep, and jagged gasps, and their mouths become dry. Thus, it is not surprising that in ancient times, when judges were trying to figure out whether suspects were lying, they looked for these telltale signs. For example, the Bedouins of Arabia required suspects to lick a hot iron. If their tongue was burned, they were assumed to be lying. The Chinese forced suspects to chew rice powder and spit it out. If the powder was sticky with saliva, the suspects were declared innocent. If it was dry, they were presumed guilty. During the Inquisition, suspected heretics were forced to try to swallow a slice of bread and cheese. If it stuck in a suspect's throat, he or she was found guilty (Kleinmuntz & Szucko, 1984b).

In recent times, such primitive tests have been replaced by the polygraph, or lie-detector, test. John Larson (1932), a Berkeley, California police officer, devised the first modern lie-detector test. His theory was a simple one: Criminals know when they are lying. When they lie, they get upset. Therefore, one can detect lying by measuring criminals' physiological reactions to interrogation. Larson questioned suspects while they were wired to a primitive polygraph machine (see Figure 7.2). He continuously recorded suspects' blood pressure, pulse rate, and respiration.

Today, the typical lie-detector test in a criminal investigation may take three to four hours. Actually, only about 15 minutes is spent taking physiological measures. The rest of the time is spent reviewing questions, explaining the procedure, and discussing results with the clients. (See Saxe, Dougherty, & Cross, 1985 for a complete discussion of testing procedures.) A typical session would go as follows:

1. Pretest interview: The test begins with a lengthy interview. In part, these interviews allow the tester to get an impression of the suspect's personality and truthfulness. It also gives the interviewer a chance to convince the suspect that the polygraph really works. The interviewer stresses the "fact" that the test unfailingly separates the innocent from the guilty, that it cannot be beat. This conversation is intended to place truthful subjects at ease and to frighten guilty subjects—in hopes of a confession. Next, the tester reviews all the questions with the suspect. This is designed to ensure that they both share a common understanding of what is meant by each question.

2. Stimulation tests: Polygraph examiners then run what they call a "stim" test. This demonstration is designed to impress suspects with the test's infallibility. For example, suspects are told to select a card from a deck of cards. Their goal is to try to hide the identity of the card from the tester. His goal is to ferret out the truth. Usually, the tester guesses which card the suspect is holding. (Often, the cards are secretly marked so that the examiner will know the correct answer.) This demonstration, too, is designed to put innocent subjects at ease and to frighten guilty ones.

3. Testing: The logic behind the interrogator's questions and measures is simple. Investigators are to compare how emotional a suspect becomes when asked various types of questions. It is assumed that irrelevant questions ("Is your name Joe Smith?" or "Are you from Burbank?") will have almost no emotional impact. Control questions ("Did you ever steal anything before you came to college?") should be a bit more upsetting. However, the innocent and the guilty should presumably react very differently to relevant questions ("Did you steal

(continued)

BOX 7.3 (continued)

the $5,000?"). Presumably, such questions are not at all unsettling if you are innocent but terrifying if you are guilty.

Polygraphers can do their jobs best if the police have passed on some guilty knowledge about the crime, information that only a criminal could know (for example, that only $2,000, not $5,000, was actually stolen). Given this information, interrogators could devise a series of questions—"Did you steal $100? $500? $1,000? $2,000? $3,000? $5,000?" Innocent but frightened suspects might show the most fear when asked, "Did you steal $5,000?" The criminal would begin to sweat when asked, "Did you steal $2,000?" Unfortunately, polygraphers rarely possess such information.

Polygraphers can then examine the pattern of a suspect's heart rate, breathing, and electrodermal responses and make a decision as to whether the suspect is guilty or innocent, or whether it is impossible to tell.

Today, lie-detector tests have become extremely common. Tests are used (and misused) in civil and criminal court cases, in personnel selection in industry, and in periodic "honesty checks" (say, in fast food restaurants, big department stores, and the like). In 1982, 2½ million Americans were required to take such tests. In 1984, President Reagan proposed that thousands of federal employees routinely be given such tests in the interests of national security.

Applied psychologists hotly debate the usefulness of such devices (see Dawson, 1980; Kleinmuntz & Szucko, 1984a; Lykken, 1974; or Saxe et al., 1985). Serious problems, both ethical and practical, have arisen with the widespread reliance on lie-detector devices. Most people do not want to give the government, their employers, or policemen the right to pry into their private lives. Thus, they are against the indiscriminate use of lie-detector tests on ethical and political grounds.

Practical problems occur with the reliance on lie-detector tests, as well. Such tests are not completely accurate. Some polygraphers receive only a few weeks or a few months of training. Their equipment is often quite primitive. Law enforcement agencies sometimes cite impressive statistics to buttress their claims as to the validity of lie detector tests (some claim that the tests are right 90% to 98% of the time), but research tells a different story.

Lie-detector tests seem to be reasonably good at detecting the guilty. The problem is that they often conclude that the innocent are guilty, too. Of course, people may experience inner turmoil when they are lying and, of course, this turmoil would be measurable by the polygraph. Unfortunately, as David Lykken (1981) has observed, "polygraphic pens do no special dance when we are lying" (p. 10). People may experience the very same physiological reactions when they are guilty and lying or when they are innocent and merely anxious or resentful about being interrogated. In any case, such mixed reactions decrease the validity of polygraph tests. In one study, Benjamin Kleinmuntz and Julian Szucko (1984a) worked with a leading polygraph firm that was eager to demonstrate the validity of its polygraph measures. They selected polygraph charts of 50 suspects that they knew were innocent (others had later confessed to the crime) and 50 suspects that were guilty (they confessed to the theft of which they were accused). Six polygraph experts were asked to carefully examine the charts and to guess whether or not the suspects were innocent or guilty. (They were warned that only 50% of the suspects were guilty.) On the average, interpreters were fairly good at correctly classifying guilty subjects, finding 76% of them guilty. Chillingly, however, they misclassified 37% of the innocent subjects—finding them guilty as well.

(continued)

BOX 7.3 (continued)

In 1985, a team of investigators, Leonard Saxe, Denise Dougherty, and Theodore Cross (1985) reviewed more than 250 empirical studies on the validity of polygraph decisions. They, too, found that polygraph operators were far better at identifying the guilty than at dismissing the innocent. On the average, in these studies, if suspects were guilty, they were identified as guilty from 71% to 99% of the time. If they were innocent, however, they were identified as innocent 13% to 94% of the time, a wide range for possible error. If you were with a federal agency looking for potential CIA agents, you might find it worthwhile to use polygraph results to select an agent you were quite sure was loyal—even at the cost of rejecting hundreds of candidates who might be reliable but didn't test well. However, if you were on trial for your life, you would not be willing to risk so much on a polygraph test.

Some people can learn how to beat a lie detector. William Casey, former director of the CIA, used to delight in his ability to fool the lie detector. Members of organized crime sometimes put on similar demonstrations, too. In general, the more information people have about lie-detector tests and the more they practice beating them, the better they perform. As one example, Floyd Fay insisted he was innocent of murdering his friend, Fred Ery, yet a lie-detector test insisted he was guilty. Eventually, Fay was released when the real murderer was tracked down, apprehended, and convicted. Fay was innocent, after all. During his stay in prison, Fay became an expert in beating the lie detector. Once, he coached 27 inmates who were scheduled to take polygraph examinations. All the inmates admitted to Fay that they were guilty (usually of taking drugs). After about 20 minutes of instruction, 23 of the 27 inmates managed to beat the polygraph test (Lykken, 1981).

Which techniques do guilty people who want to beat the lie detector use?

Some people try not to pay too much attention to the proceedings. For example, they try to distract themselves by beginning to count backward by sevens each time the operator asks a question. If people are not paying full attention, they are less likely to react emotionally to test questions.

Some test takers take tranquilizers. Meprobamate and propanolol, for example, have been found to increase a suspect's ability to avoid detection.

Some test takers simply try to confuse the record. They make a variety of unobtrusive movements that cause the polygraph pen to jump here and there throughout the record. When asked, "Is your name Joe Smith?" they may think of terrifying things. They may take deep breaths every now and then. They may clench their teeth or other muscles every now and then. Sometimes, such behavior so distorts the record that operators are forced to classify it as "inconclusive." Researchers do not yet agree as to how effective such movements generally are in distorting the record (Lykken, 1960).

Some types of people are especially good at beating the odds. For example, psychopaths and others who are poorly socialized (as measured by the California Psychological Inventory) seem to do best at beating the lie detector (Waid & Orne, 1982). People who are a bit depressed, and thus without much affect seem to do well, too.

In 1988, Congress passed legislation severely restricting the routine use of lie-detector tests in government, by the courts, and by industry. They were concerned with both the ethics and the validity of such widespread testing. More research is obviously needed before applied psychologists discover a device that is fair, valid, and reliable.

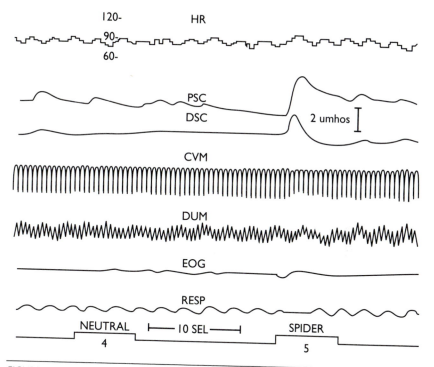

FIGURE 7.2 Sample polygraph record. Portion of a polygraph record obtained from a subject who had expressed an intense fear of spiders. HR = heart rate; PSC and DSC = two measures of skin conductance; RESP = respiration. From Hare, 1973. Also cited in Grings and Dawson, 1978, p. 30.

Table 7.1	**Some Psychophysiological Measures and Abbreviations**		
BV	Blood Volume	HR	Heart Rate
CER	Cortical Evoked Response	PP	Pulse Pressure
DBP	Diastolic Blood Pressure	PV	Pulse Volume
EEG	Electroencephalograph	REM	Rapid Eye Movements
EKG	Electrocardiogram	RR	Respiration Rate
EMG	Electromyogram	SBP	Systolic Blood Pressure
EOG	Electroculogram	SCR	Skin Conductance Response
GSR	Galvanic Skin Response	SPR	Skin Potential Response

Grings & Dawson, 1978, p. xi.

Processing Physiological Responses

The current that passes from the electrode is generally extremely faint. Before it can be recorded, the current must be amplified (sometimes millions of times). For example, EMG potentials are measured in millionths of a volt, but if they are to be recorded, they must drive equipment that requires several volts to operate, such as recorders or computerized displays.

Thus, physiological measures are fed into a polygraph (where they are amplified and filtered). As the name implies, a polygraph records several (*poly-*) physiological measures at once (such as heart rate, respiration, and electrodermal responses) on a single sheet of graph paper. The graphs are produced by a series of pens that record electrical potentials on a continuously moving roll of paper. The direction and amount of deflection of the pens is determined by the characteristics of the electrical wave form (i.e., its frequency and amplitude) received from the electrodes attached to the subject. Figure 7.2 illustrates the polygraph record from a person whose heart rate, skin conductance, respiration, and a few other responses were monitored simultaneously. (It is interesting to note, among other effects, the dramatic increase in skin conductance when a picture of a spider was shown. The subject reported a fear of spiders.)

Actually, many researchers no longer bother collecting pen and ink polygraph records. Instead, researchers are switching to computerized signal processing. A special converter transforms the psychophysiological signals into digital information, and the computer processes this data. As you might guess, the computer gives researchers enormous advantages, especially in storing the physiological data.

The next step in the signal processing circuit is filtering. The tiny electrical signals which carry information from the electrode to the polygraph or computer inevitably encounter interference, or "noise." This may be from electrical interference in the room (say, a fan or air-conditioner compressor), from the measuring instrument itself, or even from other signals within the subject. Interestingly, some of the various physiological signals we have discussed may interfere with one another during measurement. Heart beats may be reflected in the EMG record, for example. Thus, during this step, the desired signal is run through a filter, which eliminates all the conflicting signals. The purified data can then be displayed and statistically analyzed.

Recording Physiological Responses

Despite the advent of the computer age, the traditional polygraph remains the most popular equipment for displaying and recording psychophysiological data. The typical polygraph works as follows. As we have said, each type of psychophysiological response (EMG, heart rate, respiration, electrodermal response) comes in on a separate channel. The various signals proceed through preamplifiers and amplifiers, which amplify and filter them. Signals from the amplifiers activate sensitive yet powerful electromagnets. They, in turn, mechanically move pens up or down, recording subjects' reactions at a given time on a continuously flowing roll of paper. The polygraph provides a dramatic display of the ways in which the various physiological correlates of the emotions interact.

Finally, in storing, displaying, and analyzing data, computers become an indispensable accessory to the polygraph. Only a computer can handle the mass of data researchers secure when they test scores of subjects, monitoring many different physiological responses, second-by-second, over the duration of an experiment—usually hours or days. Computers tabulate and analyze the data, painstakingly measuring every movement, up and down, on the record.

STUDIES UTILIZING PSYCHOPHYSIOLOGICAL MEASUREMENT

A number of chapters in this text describe studies which have assessed emotion via sophisticated psychophysiological techniques. Here, we provide two additional examples of the kinds of psychophysiological measures that have been used.

In a series of classic studies, Walter Fenz and Seymour Epstein have explored the physiology of sport parachuting. Fenz and Epstein (1967) asked novice and experienced parachutists to describe their feelings. They also monitored their psychophysiological responses (skin conductance levels, heart rates, and respiration rates) on the day of the jump as the parachutists arrived at the airport, as they taxied along the runway, as they actually took off, as they flew to the jump site, as they prepared for the impending jump, and as the jumpers recovered after a safe landing.

Fenz and Epstein found that novice and experienced jumpers' reactions were very different. Novice jumpers reported that they were most frightened just prior to jumping. Experienced jumpers said they were most anxious just before their parachutes opened, just prior to landing. (This makes sense, since most jumpers are injured upon landing, a fact that is well learned through experience.) Their self-reports are confirmed by their physiological reactions, charted at different stages of the jump. As Figure 7.3 shows, novice jumpers were sympathetically aroused from the start. They were most aroused just before they jumped for the first time. Experienced jumpers were relatively calm throughout the early stages of the flight. They became most aroused right before the jump and right before the landing. (All three physiological measures reveal the same pattern of physiological arousal.)

Other researchers have investigated the links between frustration, anger, aggression, and physiological response. Jack Hokanson and his colleagues have conducted a series of studies on this topic. In one study, Hokanson (1961) selected 80 men who were either unusually high or unusually low in hostility to participate in an experiment. (He assessed the men's hostility using a paper-and-pencil test, which asked how aggressive/nonaggressive they generally were in their day-to-day encounters.) When the men reported for the experiment, they were told that the researchers were studying the connection between intellectual performance and physiology. Then, the men were assigned their first task. They were to count backward from 100 to 0 by

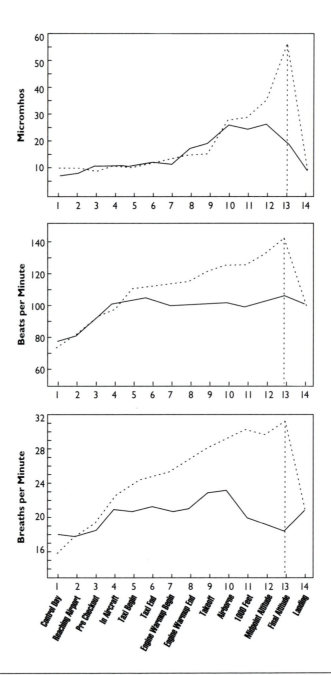

FIGURE 7.3 Physiological responses of parachutists. Responses of experienced (——) and novice (– – – –) parachutists as a function of events leading up to and following a jump: (a) skin conductance, (b) heart rate, and (c) breathing rate. Reprinted by permission of Elsevier Science Publishing Co., Inc. from Fenz and Epstein, 1967, by The American Psychosomatic Society, Inc.

threes as quickly as they could. Normally, this task is a bit frustrating in and of itself. Next, the experimenter swung into action. In the high-frustration condition, the experimenter began to repeatedly interrupt, harass, and insult the men, claiming they were counting too slowly. In the low-frustration condition, the researcher continued to smile and nod his approval at the men's performance. During this phase, the experimenter monitored all subjects' systolic blood pressures and skin conductance levels. In Table 7.2, we see how the aggressive and nonaggressive men, who were frustrated versus not frustrated, responded physiologically. As you might expect, when the men were frustrated (regardless of whether they were generally hostile or not) they became upset. The frustrated men's blood pressure and skin-conductance levels were far higher than those of the men who were treated politely. The men who were identified as hostile and aggressive seemed to suffer the most from frustration. Their blood pressures soared when they were frustrated. Low-hostility men had a much more mellow reaction to the frustrating test situation. Hokanson suggests that aggressive men may be especially predisposed to react vascularly to stress, an observation that has recently been shown to have implications for cardiovascular disease.

Behavioral Measures of Emotion

The arch-behaviorist B. F. Skinner observed that when people want to know what they or other people are feeling, they observe only behavior. They listen closely to the way people talk about their feelings, they observe their facial expressions, their tears or laughter, their gestures, and their bodily movements. In this section, we review some of the techniques psychologists have developed to measure emotional behavior.

In a previous section, we reviewed some of the self-report measures that

Table 7.2   **Frustration and Blood Pressure: Effects of Frustration Upon Systolic Blood Pressure (SBP) and Skin Conductance (SC) for High-Hostile and Low-Hostile Individuals**

	Low-Hostile Individuals	High-Hostile Individuals
Low frustration		
SBP (mm Hg)	+5.90	+ 5.00
SC (μmhos)	+1.18	+ 1.55
High frustration		
SBP (mm Hg)	+7.90	+15.00
SC (μmhos)	+1.42	+ 1.59

Adapted from Hokanson, 1961. Copyright 1961 by Duke University Press. Reprinted with permission.

have been used to assess people's inner emotional lives. When people are articulate and cooperative, researchers have the luxury of relying on self-report, paper-and-pencil questionnaires to assess their emotional experiences. (Such tests are easy, inexpensive, and efficient to administer.) Interestingly, these instruments generally ask people only about their inner experiences. Psychometricians often seem to feel that if they have the chance to question people, they should ask about the "real thing"—about people's deepest, most hidden, most secret, feelings. Unfortunately, such instruments generally neglect to ask people about their public emotional behavior.

Psychologists who have set out to develop one or another technique for assessing emotional behavior often have done so because they had to. Some were interested in studying the emotional lives of people who could not or would not express their feelings in words—infants, children, the emotionally disturbed, or the mentally disabled. Others were strictly interested in lower animals' emotional behavior. Interestingly, such measures have turned out to be extremely useful, both for learning about the original target populations' emotions and for understanding people in general.

Clinical psychologists were among the first to develop behavioral indices of emotion. They were interested in such measures for several reasons: (a) Some clinicians wanted to check clients' self-reports of their inner experiences against their actual emotional behavior. (They wanted to assure that the more subjective, "softer" verbal measures were related to the more objective, "harder" objective measures.) (b) Other clinicians worried that their clients might be unable or unwilling to reveal their feelings. Some people seek help because they have trouble communicating. They may not know what they feel. Some people are afraid to express their deepest feelings. For instance, some couples do not want their mates to discover their extramarital affairs. Some delinquents do not want anything to "leak out." Most of us would probably be reluctant to tell a therapist everything we thought or felt. For these reasons, clinicians were eager to develop techniques which would allow them to check their clients' words versus their deeds. They were eager to find some way to talk about emotional issues in a behavioral language.

Thus, clinical researchers, experimentalists, child developmentalists, animal psychologists, and others have devised an amazing array of checklists, rating scales, timers, hurdles, electric eyes, and mechanical levers to measure emotional behavior in adults, children, chimpanzees, rats, and other animals. Let us now consider a range of this research and the measures researchers have developed.

MEASURING EMOTIONAL BEHAVIORS IN ANIMALS

By necessity, animal researchers (in the laboratory) and ethologists (in the field) have been forced to rely upon behavioral measures of emotion. In the early days of psychology, if animal researchers were interested in assessing, for example, how fearful male versus female rats were in various settings, they would simply select a response or two (say, tremor, urination, and/or defecation) to serve as an indicator of fear. Then, they would carefully record each time the rat trembled, urinated, or defecated in the laboratory. They generally used electrical and mechanical instruments to count the occurrence of such behaviors. In recent years, psychologists have decided that they can learn more by studying animals' emotional behavior in more natural social contexts. Animal behavior is much richer, more varied, and more complex under these conditions. As such studies have become increasingly popular, researchers have also developed more and more sophisticated procedures for rating multiple behaviors.

Laboratory Studies

At the turn of the century, a few researchers who were studying isolated animals in laboratory settings were already trying to assess emotional responsiveness using behavioral measures. For example, Ivan Pavlov (1927), in his studies of "experimental neurosis" in dogs, was an early observer of dogs' emotional behavior. Pavlov's aim was to see what happened when a dog was required to perform a task that became more and more difficult. At first, the task was relatively easy—the dog was to salivate when a luminous circle appeared on a screen (a signal that food was coming) and not to bother making any response when an ellipse appeared. But the task soon became more difficult. The shape of the ellipse was changed by stages, until it looked more and more like a circle. Eventually, the task became impossibly difficult. The dog patiently worked on this impossible problem for three weeks. Finally, the frustrating task overwhelmed the dog. It became intensely emotional—emitting behaviors that look a great deal like anger and desperation. Gregory Kimble (1961) reports:

> At the same time the whole behavior of the animal underwent a marked change. The hitherto quiet dog began to squeal in its stand, kept wriggling about, tore off with its teeth the apparatus for mechanical stimulation of the skin, and bit through the tubes leading from the animal's room to the observer's, all behavior which had never occurred before. On being taken into the experimental room the dog now barked violently, which was also contrary to its earlier tranquility. In short, it presented symptoms of a condition which, in a human being, we would call neurosis. (Kimble, 1961, pp. 440–441)

In such settings, animals' "neuroses" can be detected in four kinds of emotional behavior: (a) They show signs of anxiety, such as whining and trembling; (b) they can no longer perform their tasks. For example, they either "jump the gun" and respond too quickly or freeze and respond too slowly on tasks they could once perform; (c) they refuse to eat in the experimental apparatus or room; and (d) they show signs of strong inhibition such as yawning, drowsiness, and sleeping unusual amounts.

Early frustration studies used similar measures to assess animals' emotionality. Laboratory rats found themselves standing on a platform several feet above the floor. They were encouraged literally to fly through the air, hurling their bodies toward either a white or a black stimulus, serving as a door in the panel in front of them (Maier & Ellen, 1952). During the training trials, the rats' task was relatively simple. If they guessed correctly and leapt toward the door with the white stimulus, the door would fall back to reveal a platform and a bit of food. If they guessed wrong, they hit a solid barrier and fell into a net. Then, the task was made impossible. Sometimes, the animals would guess correctly, leap, and secure reward. On half the trials, however, the doors were both locked in a random fashion. There was no way the rats could guess which door was correct and be rewarded on every trial.

In this frustrating situation, the animals were conflicted; some refused to jump at all. That did not give the experimenters much to observe, so they began to force the rats to jump. A tap on the base of a rat's tail did the trick—the animal would jump all right, but to which door? Typically, the conflicted animals would show a preference. They would often persist in their previously correct pattern of jumping to the white stimulus. This stereotyped response could be extremely persistent. Even when the problem was made solvable—the left side was made always correct—some of the animals persisted in jumping to the originally correct stimulus, the white door. When the animals persisted for many trials despite the fact that the problem was soluble, they were said to have an "abnormal fixation." In these studies, animals' frustration was indicated by their freezing on the platform and by "response stereotypy," or fixation. (As you will see in a later chapter, stereotyped reactions, termed "obsessions," may be observed in people suffering anxiety disorders, too.)

As researchers continued to study animals' reactions to frustration, they conceived of emotional behaviors that were easier to quantify than "fixation" or "stereotypy," and they devised instrumentation that could measure emotionality automatically. For example, in one experiment, rats were taught to press two levers in succession (call them levers 1 and 2). Initially, as soon as a rat pressed lever 1, some food pellets dropped into the box; then, the rat moved on to lever 2, pressed it, and received more pellets. Next came the frustration trials. Half the time, when the rat pressed lever 1, no reinforcement was forthcoming. Half the time, it received food pellets. (The rat never knew whether it would receive pellets or not.) Then it moved on to lever 2, where it always received a reinforcement. Soon the animals' emotionality came to be reflected in their behavior. The rats were slower to begin a trial by pressing lever 1. (Who wants to become frustrated?) After frustration, however, the rats showed a surge of energy. (Have you ever experienced the release that comes just after leaving a traffic jam? Were you tempted to "step on it"?) They pressed lever 2 faster when they had just experienced a nonreward than when they had just received a reward. Again, emotion appeared in the form of energized behavior. In this study, then, frustration could be measured by two kinds of emotional reactions—an apparent reluctance to get into the frustrating situation in the first place—slower lever pressing on lever 1—and a surge of behavior after frustration—faster lever pressing on lever 2 after nonrewarded trials (Carlson, 1968).

Some real advantages in studying emotions in single animals in a laboratory environment include the subjects' ready availability, at the experimenter's convenience. Researchers can select a simple standard stimulus. They can carefully and reliably measure a simple, precise, easily quantifiable, emotional response. The measures used have included response magnitude (such as amplitude of a reflex—how high will a scared rat jump?), response latency (how quickly will a response occur when it is available?), operant response rate or frequency (how fast will an animal run or press a lever?), and response fixation (how often will an animal repeat a response or refuse to perform altogether?).

Ethological Observations

By contrast, ethologists and psychologists who study the emotions of animals in their natural habitats may lose some of the advantages of laboratory control, but they gain a great deal in return. They can study the effects of naturally occurring, complex cues of particular interest. For example, they might study the effect of a dominant (or submissive) rat's presence on another rat's emotional reaction. Is a rat more likely to attack when angry? When frightened? Moreover, researchers who take an ethological approach can observe a variety of complex, interlocking emotional behaviors. For example, Caroline and Robert Blanchard (1984) describe the carefully scripted behavior of an intruder rat and a dominant male (alpha) rat when the intruder wanders into alpha's home territory. Notice how complex and detailed is the account of the expressive activities of these animals. Conventional, controlled laboratory studies would not permit this level of complex analysis (see Box 7.4).

Ethologists find that other species show emotional patterning as well. For example, Peter Buirski and his colleagues (Buirski, Kellerman, Plutchik, Weininger, & Buirski, 1973) studied baboons in Africa's Nairobi Park. The authors devised a special version of Robert Plutchik's (1980a) Emotions Profile Index (EPI) discussed earlier in this chapter so that they could assess animals' emotional behavior in the wild. Three researchers watched a small troop of baboons for 35 hours over a 3-week period. Each time two baboons began to groom each other, the researchers noted who groomed whom and for how long. (Baboons groom by gently combing the others' hair with their fingers and carefully plucking out insects, lice, and debris.) Finally, the trio of researchers ranked the baboons on a dominance hierarchy and rated their general emotional behavior on the baboon version of the EPI. They rated

BOX 7.4

Offensive Versus Defensive Aggression in Rats

The attack of an experienced alpha male on a stranger in his colony is very stereotyped and usually quite intense. The alpha approaches the stranger and sniffs at its perianal [anal] area. . . . If the intruder is an adult male, the alpha's sniff leads to piloerection [the animal's hair stands on end]. . . . Shortly after piloerecting, the alpha rat usually bites the intruder, and the intruder runs away. The alpha chases after it, and after one or two additional bites, the intruder stops running and turns to face its attacker. It rears up on its hind legs, using its forelimbs to push off the alpha. This distinctive "boxing" response is an active series of movements that keeps the defender's face in opposition to that of the attacker. However, rather than standing nose to nose with the boxing intruder, the attacking rat abruptly moves to a lateral orientation, with the long axis of its body perpendicular to the front of the defending rat, and with its head and posterior ends curved in somewhat toward this animal. It moves sideways toward the intruder, crowding and sometimes pushing it off balance. If the defending rat stands solid against this "lateral attack" movement, the alpha may make a quick lunge forward and around the defender's body to bite at its back.

In response to such a lunge, the defender usually pivots on its hind feet, in the same direction as the attacker is moving, continuing its frontal orientation to the attacker. If the defending rat moves quickly enough, no bite will be made.

However, after a number of instances of the lateral attack, and especially if the attacker has succeeded in biting the intruder, the stranger rat may roll backward slowly from the boxing position, to lie on its back. The attacker then takes up a position on top of the supine animal, digging with its forepaws at the intruder's sides. If the attacker can turn the other animal over, or expose some portion of its back and dorsal sides, it bites. . . . This sequence of bites, flight, chasing, boxing, lateral attack, lying on the back, and standing on top, is repeated in a rather variable sequence until the stranger rat is removed. (Blanchard & Blanchard, 1984, pp. 8–9)

Researchers have conducted sequential analyses of these behavior patterns. Flow charts make clear an internal organization for rats' offensive attacks and defensive reactions. These patterns are the same in wild and laboratory rats, demonstrating the persistence of evolutionary origins.

how "belligerent, fearful, inquisitive, irritable, defiant, depressed, dominant, playful, sociable, and submissive" the baboons were in their encounters with one another. Raters discovered that the baboons' personality/emotional profiles were surprisingly consistent. For example, when researchers examined the emotional profiles of two baboons—"Big Harry," a dominant baboon, and "Norman," his submissive compatriot, they found there was an almost perfect relationship between the baboons' dominance rank and how often they were groomed. Although Big Harry was not very sociable and rarely groomed anyone else, he received the most attention from others. The younger members of the troop were very sociable, often grooming others, but rarely received much grooming themselves. The more aggressive (and the less fearful) the animals were, the more they were groomed—in the wild, it apparently pays to be belligerent.

MEASURING EMOTIONAL BEHAVIORS IN HUMANS

Psychologists have developed an array of techniques for measuring people's emotional behavior. In fact, we discuss such behavioral measures at other points in this text: For example, you have already been introduced to some of the techniques social psychologists have used to assess emotional behavior. In chapter 6, you learned that as people think and feel, their faces and bodies silently reflect their thoughts and feelings. People's emotional experiences spark a continuous series of invisible, minute facial muscle movements. Even naïve observers are good at detecting what a person is feeling from such facial displays. However, Paul Ekman and Wallace Friesen (1975) developed the Facial Affect Scoring Technique (FAST) to help them do an even better job of reading facial expression. The FAST measures each movement of the face within each of three facial areas (brows/forehead, eyes/lids, lower face.) The FAST is an objective measure of a subject's facially expressive behavior.

You will learn a great deal more about the way people's emotions can be assessed in chapters 8–13. These chapters review what psychologists have learned about such basic emotions as depression, joy, anger, love, and fear. In this section, we examine only two types of assessment devices: those that have been developed for use with children, and those that are employed as clinical diagnostic devices. This should give you at least a flavor of the types of measures that have been developed to measure emotional behavior in humans before we go into more detail in later chapters.

Emotional Expressiveness in Children

Researchers have long been interested in finding ways to measure children's emotional expressiveness. In the early days, child developmentalists were eager to construct tests which would allow them to assess whether or not an infant was progressing at an appropriate rate. Was he as bright as he should be? Able to control his emotions? Able to signal what he wanted? The Bayley test (which was developed in 1933 and revised in 1969) is one of the oldest and most widely used techniques for assessing infant development. It includes three subscales: a mental scale, a motor scale, and the Infant Behavior Record (IBR). It is this third scale in which we are interested here. Nancy Bayley explains that the IBR "helps the clinician assess the nature of the child's social and objective orientations toward his environment as expressed in attitude, interests, emotions, energy, activity, and tendencies to approach and withdraw from stimulation" (Bayley, 1969, p. 4). Thus, the IBR gave child psychologists a standardized test for assessing infants' level of emotional development.

Using the IBR, trained observers rate infants on 30 traits—including such emotional behaviors as "fearfulness" and "excitability." They also rate the frequency, intensity, and latency of such emotional behaviors on a nine-point scale. Table 7.3 illustrates a typical item from the Infant Behavior Record. Unfortunately, researchers have found that before 18 months of age, infants'

Table 7.3   Sample Bayley IBR Record

REACTIVITY	
15. The ease with which a child is stimulated to react in general; his SENSITIVITY or EXCITABILITY; reactivity may be positive or negative in tone (Circle one)	_____Quiets _____Startles _____Quivers _____Fusses _____Cries
Rating	_____Looks alert _____Vocalizes
1 Unreactive; seems to pay little heed to what goes on around him; responds only to strong or repeated stimulation	_____Squeals _____Other (Specify)
2 Between 1 and 3	
3 Some tendency to be unreactive to the usual testing stimuli, etc.	Responds to: _____Sights
4 Between 3 and 5	_____Sounds
5 Moderately alert and responsive in reaction to test stimuli, etc.	_____Temperatures _____Touches
6 Between 5 and 7	_____Pressures
7 Quickly shows awareness of changes in test materials and situations	_____Smells _____Being jarred
8 Between 7 and 9	_____Being carried
9 Very active; every little thing seems to stir him up; he startles, reacts quickly, seems keenly sensitive to things going on around him	_____Other (Specify)

Reproduced by permission from the Bayley Scales of Infant Development. Copyright © 1969 by The Psychological Corporation. All rights reserved. (Source: Wodrich, 1984, p. 44)

IBR scores do not seem to predict their actual abilities. Once children are older, however, the Bayley does appear to be a reliable and valid standardized measure of their general abilities, their level of emotional development, and their emotional behavior (Yang, 1979). In the next chapter, we present some of the time lines which predict when infants should begin to express the various emotions.

Recently, researchers have made a number of breakthroughs in assessing emotional behavior in infants and children (see, for example, Brazelton & Yogman, 1986; Izard & Read, 1986; or Lewis & Michalson, 1983). Generally, modern-day psychologists try to gain access into infants' inner lives by observing their facial expressions (Izard & Dougherty, 1982). Carroll Izard (1979) developed two coding systems (called Affex and Max) for classifying infants' emotional expressions. In Affex (Izard & Dougherty, 1982), researchers are trained to classify the facial expressions associated with 10 fundamental emotions—interest, joy, surprise, sadness, anger, disgust, contempt, fear, shame/shyness, and guilt. They are shown photographs, artists' drawings, and videotapes, in which children are spontaneously displaying these emotions.

array of "joyous responses," so it is harder to explain why one has chosen to measure joy via response A, B, or C.

In Conclusion

In this chapter, we have discussed a variety of ways in which researchers have measured emotional experience, physiology, and behavior. Usually, researchers focus on one or another component of emotion. They measure subjects' subjective experiences, *or* their level of physiological arousal, *or* their emotional behavior. Many researchers are reconsidering that strategy. A number of theorists have pointed out that if scientists measure several aspects of emotion simultaneously, they will have a real advantage in understanding emotion. Eugene Webb and his colleagues (1966) and Ellen Berscheid (1979) argue that the only way to be certain you have correctly identified a construct (say, joy) is to measure it in several ways. Any single measure of emotion will have certain flaws. If researchers depend completely on self-report measures, they will run into trouble when subjects are unable to describe their emotions or when they lie. If researchers rely only on physiological indicators, the fact that people react in many different internal ways causes problems. Then, too, our knowledge of physiological processes is incomplete. If researchers rely strictly on overt, behavioral measures of emotion, problems arise when people insist on controlling themselves in socially appropriate ways. But although each measure may have flaws, self-report, physiological, and behavioral measures all have different flaws. Thus, if all measures together point to the same conclusion, researchers have more confidence in their conclusions. If people say they are happy, and a smile lights up their faces, and their hearts race, and they keep coming back for more, then an observer may be fairly confident that they are happy. When the various indicators are not in synchrony, however, an observer can only be less sure that he or she knows what a subject is feeling. This type of detective process is sometimes called **triangulation,** after a navigational expression for locating a point in space.

Besides giving us confidence in our inferences, Johann Stoyva and Joe Kamiya (1968) argue that often, people can better grasp the meaning of a construct by looking at it from different perspectives, using a method of **convergence.** Observations may converge at a single point. Just as we may define the construct "dreaming" by observing how self-reports ("I had a dream last night") and physiological measures (brain-wave patterns and rapid eye movements, REM, during sleep) come together, we may also converge on the meaning of emotion by approaching it from several perspectives. As we argue throughout this text, emotions are not only experiences, bodily processes, or behaviors; they are all of these, and knowledge of any one will help us better understand the other.

Summing Up

- Psychometricians use four kinds of scales to measure emotion—nominal, ordinal, interval, or ratio scales.

- Investigators have devised several techniques for securing ordinal and ratio scales of emotion. These include Likert scales and a new technique, Borg's ratio scale.

- Researchers have used two types of instruments—self-report questionnaires and adjective checklists—to measure emotional profiles.

- Self-report questionnaires are usually designed to assess relatively enduring personality characteristics or emotional predispositions. They assess how often and how intensely people feel various emotions. Adjective checklists, on the other hand, are ordinarily designed to measure current emotional states. They assess how intensely subjects are experiencing a variety of emotions at a given moment.

- An example of a self-report questionnaire is Plutchik and Kellerman's Emotions Profile Index. An example of an adjective checklist is the Multiple Affect Adjective Checklist or Nowlis's Mood Adjective Checklist.

- In the past few decades, emotions researchers have begun to grow increasingly interested in the physiological aspects of emotion. There are several reasons why this is so: Technological advances have occurred in the ability of researchers to measure physiological responses, an awareness of the importance of doing so has increased, and practical reasons for learning more about emotion, stress, the immune response, and physical illness have arisen.

- The process of psychophysiological measurement involves monitoring of minute changes in physiological reactions, electronic amplification and filtering of these signals, and the display of these signals, so that therapists and researchers can utilize this information.

- Researchers can measure emotion psychophysiologically in a number of ways, for example, by measuring EMG responses (which assess muscle tension or tone); EKG (heart rate, including blood volume and frequency of beat); EEG (brain activity); and skin potentials and conductivity (eccrine-gland activity).

- Psychophysiological measures have been used in a number of studies, including studies exploring the physiology of sport parachuting and the links between frustration, anger, aggression, and physiological responses.

- Animal researchers and ethologists have, of necessity, developed behavioral measures of emotion. Animal researchers generally select a simple standard

Sorrow

Vincent

stimulus and carefully and reliably measure a simple, precise, easily quan-tifiable, emotional response. The measures used have included response magnitude, latency, rate or frequency, and stereotypy, or fixation.

- Ethologists are more likely to study complex patterns of emotional be-havior under natural conditions.

- Behavioral methods for the study of human emotional responses include means for assessing facial expressions; infant emotionality, such as move-ments; general reactivity, or vocalizations; and clinical manifestations of emotion.

- Theorists argue that the only way to be sure that one has correctly iden-tified a construct is to measure it in several ways. Each particular measure has its flaws, but not all measures have the same flaw. This procedure has been termed convergence.

8
Sadness, Grief, and Depression

Introduction

Emotional Development of Sadness and Other Emotions
Assessing Sadness
The Sequence of Emotional Development
Emotional Milestones
Individual Differences in Emotionality
The Caretakers' Contribution

Sadness and Grief in Adulthood
Sadness
Grief

Depression
Theories of Depression
The Treatment of Depression

Summing Up

FIGURE 8.1   *Sorrow.* Vincent Van Gogh. 1882. Transfer lithograph, printed in black, composition: 15³/₈″ x 11³/₁₆″. Collection, The Museum of Modern Art, New York.

Introduction

On January 28, 1986, the family and friends of the Challenger space shuttle astronauts were assembled in the Kennedy Space Center VIP area to watch the lift-off. As the rocket rose, television cameras surveyed the amazed and delighted faces. Suddenly the rocket exploded. A confusion of emotions spread across the faces of the viewers. Some schoolchildren cheered, thinking the fiery bursts were part of the show; others were perplexed. The adults' expressions of delight turned slowly from stunned confusion to disbelief and horror. A family member or two stared at the camera, braving a sickly smile. After a few minutes, people managed to sort out their feelings. Eventually, everyone was expressing "appropriate" emotions—they looked grief-stricken or began to cry.

In this chapter, we look mainly at sadness, grief, and depression, keeping in mind, however, that in real life emotions are often messy and jumbled, which complicates the matter. Let us begin by defining these terms.

Most people feel sad, let down, and disheartened from time to time. We may define sadness as "having, expressing or showing low spirits or sorrow; unhappy; mournful, sorrowful" (Guralnik, 1982, p. 1252). **Grief** is a sharper, more painful emotion. It occurs when people lose something that they have cherished. It is defined as "intense emotional suffering caused by loss, disaster, misfortune, etc.; acute sorrow; deep sadness" (Guralnik, 1982, p. 615). Sometimes people's sadness and grief are so intense, persistent, and incapacitating that we begin to suspect that they have an emotional problem—that they are depressed. **Depression** is defined as "a state of inaccessibility to stimulation or to particular kinds of stimulation, of lowered initiative, of gloomy thoughts" (English & English, 1958, p. 144). See Box 8.1.

Emotional Development of Sadness and Other Emotions

We begin our review of the basic emotions in this and the chapters to come with a discussion of when such emotions begin to appear. Recently, psychologists have learned a great deal about when such emotions as sadness, happiness, anger, love, and fear seem to develop (Brazelton & Yogman, 1986; Lewis & Michalson, 1983; Plutchik & Kellerman, 1983). Developmental psychologists are naturally interested in the full range of emotional experience—joy *as well as* sadness, love *and* anger, contentment *and* fear. Nonetheless, psychologists know more about the development of the negative emotions—sadness, separation anxiety, fear, and anger—than the positive ones. It is doubly appropriate, then, that this chapter begin with a review of what developmentalists have discovered about emotional growth during the first four

BOX 8.1

Descriptions of Sadness, Grief, and Depression

Joel Davitz (1969), in his dictionary of emotional meanings, reports how people describe sadness, grief, and depression:

Sadness:

> There is a lump in my throat . . . a sense of loss, of deprivation. . . . I feel empty, drained, hollow. . . . There is a sense of regret. . . . I seem to be caught up and overwhelmed by the feeling . . . choked up; there is a sense of nostalgia as old memories crop up and I think of the past. . . . It's a very personal feeling. (pp. 80–81)

Grief:

> I can't smile or laugh; there is a lump in my throat; there is an inner ache you can't locate . . . a sense of regret, a sense of longing . . . of being incomplete; as if a part of me is missing. . . . I feel empty, drained, hollow, dead inside . . . choked up; there is a tight knotted feeling in my stomach . . . a sense of loss, of deprivation . . . of disbelief. I keep thinking about what happened over and over again.

> Tears come to my eyes, the sort of tears not just from my eyes, but my whole self is crying. (pp. 61–62)

Depression:

> I feel empty, drained, hollow . . . heavy, sluggish. My feelings seem dulled. It's an effort to do anything. I have no desire, no motivation, no interest; [my] wants, needs, drives are gone. It's as if everything inside has stopped. . . . Everything seems out of proportion. I feel lost. I seem to be caught up and overwhelmed by the feeling . . . vulnerable and totally off-balance. I feel insignificant. . . . Everything seems useless, absurd, meaningless. . . . There is a heavy feeling in my stomach; a sense of loss, of deprivation. There is an inner ache you can't locate. I have no appetite; I can't eat; there is a clutching, sinking feeling in the middle of my chest . . . a sense of longing, a yearning, a desire for change. . . . I'm easily irritated, ready to snap. . . . I keep searching for an explanation, for some understanding; I keep thinking, "why?" (pp. 46–47)

years of life, focusing particularly on the development of sadness, grief, and depression.

ASSESSING SADNESS

Sometimes it is difficult to intuit exactly what an infant might be feeling. Does that frown when a child is given a bottle for the first time express puzzlement or displeasure? Is that smile a gas pain or a smile of pleasure? Even when we think we know what an infant may be feeling, we hesitate. Does an infant who is "sad" feel the same way a sad adult does? It is impossible to tell. Scientists are hesitant to assume too much about a child's inner life. Parents, of course, are rarely so timid. When their week-old infant shrieks as his sister snatches his bottle from his mouth, they have no hesitancy in concluding that he is furious. When their daughter smiles and squeals when her stomach is tickled, they assume she is delighted.

Researchers who wish to study infants' emotions do as parents do—they use a multimethod approach to draw inferences about infants' feelings. They employ several measures—for example, facial expression, vocalizations, and the overall quality of behavioral activity—to assess a child's emotional state (Izard, 1982; Izard & Read, 1986). Such procedures give them some confidence that a child's "grief" is much like an adult's. Let's look at some examples.

Grim-visag'd comfortless Despair.

THOMAS GRAY

Facial Expression of Sadness

The face of sadness is a familiar one. In fact, in chapter 6, we learned that sadness is a universal emotion easily recognized by all peoples, in all times, and at all places. Carroll Izard (1977) details the look of a sad face in infants and adults:

> In the full expression of sadness the eyebrows are arched upward, and inward, sometimes forming a π-shaped arch in the lower middle forehead. The inner corners of the upper eyelids are drawn up, and the lower eyelid may appear to be pushed upward. The corners of the mouth are drawn downward, and the chin muscle pushes upward and raises the center of the lower lip. Of course, the prototype of the sadness expression and its most usual form in infancy and childhood, as well as in the adult in moments of strong grief, is the act of crying. However, the keen observer of people knows that it is necessary to look for the other signs of sadness in the adult. . . . (pp. 287–288)

Izard (1979) developed a technique (called Affex) for coding infants' and children's emotions and facial expressions. First, the experimenters show raters drawings, photographs, and videotapes of infants and young children who are experiencing a given emotion—say, happiness or sadness. The experimenters point out the sorts of changes that typically occur in infants' brows, eyes, and mouths when they are happy or sad. After this training, coders are able to make global judgments as to what emotion infants are expressing. In chapter 6, we pointed out that Paul Ekman and his colleagues (cf. Ekman & Friesen, 1975) have developed similar techniques for coding the emotions and facial expressions of children and adults.

Physiological Indicators of Sadness

In chapter 4, we discussed the fact that different emotions were associated with different autonomic nervous system reactions. In joy, anger, and fear—emotions which push people to activity—the ANS's sympathetic branch is generally dominant. People's pupils dilate, their hearts race, their breathing comes fast and shallow—they are ready for action. In sadness, when things seem hopeless and all people can do is wait it out, the ANS's parasympathetic branch is generally dominant (Stanley-Jones, 1970; Henry, 1986). Thus, sad children and adults may weep (Gellhorn, 1964); their blood pressure and heart rate decrease; muscle tone is lost, and inactivity increases. Researchers have assessed sadness in infants and young children by relying on a battery of physiological indicators—heart rate, blood pressure, and electrodermal responses (Plutchik & Kellerman, 1983; Izard, 1982).

Behavioral Indicators of Sadness

Most commonly, researchers rely on simple behavioral measures of sadness. For example, sometimes when mothers hear their infants cry, they have no idea what is wrong. They have to experiment. Is she hungry? Wet? Angry? Generally, however, mothers seem to know, somehow, what is wrong. The cry of a sad infant sounds different, somehow, from the cry of pain. In their research on infant distress, Ross Thompson and Michael Lamb (1983) developed a coding scheme which allowed them to differentiate among nine different kinds of infant crying, such as mild whimpering, fussing, angry protests, sobbing, and hyperventilated crying or screaming (see Table 8.1). They used such indicators as pitch, intensity, and rhythmicity in differentiating vocalizations.

Table 8.1   **Assessing Infant Distress Vocalizations**

---

0 *No vocalization.*
1 *Pleasure vocalization* includes squeals or shrieks of delight, cooing, or laughing.
2 *Neutral vocalization* includes babbling and other vocalizations that have neither a distressed nor a positive quality.
3 *Mild distress* includes brief whining, squeals of frustration or anguish, mild wails or sobs, and fretting and other vocalizations that have a distinctly negative quality.
4 *Calling* includes vocalizations that seem intended to signal or summon the caretaker and have a distinctly negative or distressed quality.
5 *Distress gasps* occur when the baby breathes in short, quick gasps. Often, but not always, gasping of this kind occurs as a prelude to a full-fledged cry or immediately follows a long bout of sobbing.
6 *Fussing or whimpering.*
7 *Whining.*
8 *Protest* is a hard cry that sounds as much like shouting as it does like crying and has an angry, imperative quality.
9 *Sobbing.*
10 *Screaming.*
11 *Panic cry.*
12 *Hyperventilated cry.*

Adapted from Thompson & Lamb, 1983, pp. 110-111. Reprinted by permission of the authors.

THE SEQUENCE OF EMOTIONAL DEVELOPMENT

Researchers have used the facial, physiological, and behavioral indicators of emotions that we have just described to explore how emotions develop. Theorists agree that infants possess a full complement of emotions early in life. To date, infants have been found to display anger, disgust, fear, happiness, pain, sadness, and surprise (Klinnert et al., 1983). Researchers disagree, however, about when the basic emotions first appear. Some assume they are "hardwired," emerging full blown at birth; others assume that they are like "software," taking time to develop.

For example, Berry Brazelton (1983) points out that as early as the last trimester of pregnancy, a fetus shows marked emotional preference for soft sounds over sharp noises, soft lights over bright ones, and gentle movements over lurching ones. This means that at least some preferences exist before birth.

According to some theorists, prewired neural programs set the stage for later emotional experience and expression (Ekman, Friesen, & Ellsworth, 1972; Izard, 1971). This suggests that even very young infants may possess a rich emotional life. In fact, as Dante Cicchetti and Petra Hesse (1983) conclude: ". . . it appears that virtually all emotions and emotional expressions are present at birth. Accordingly, one might ask whether it even makes sense to talk about emotional *development*" (p. 143).

The contention that from the start infants possess an array of emotions has some support. Jacob Steiner (1979), for example, photographed the facial expressions of several hundred normal infants, two anencephalic infants (infants born without a cortex), and two hydroanencephalic infants (those whose cortex has been irreparably damaged). Such infants rarely live more than a few hours. Yet, as Figure 8.2 indicates, they seemed to display a full range of emotions in the first feeble hours of life. Infants respond to sweet, sour, and bitter tastes (as well as to pleasant and aversive food-related odors) with smiles, lip pursing, and disgusted faces in the very first hours of life; observers had no trouble reading their faces. You might take a look at Figure 8.2 for confirmation of this. Since anencephalic and hydroanencephalic infants possess no higher intellectual centers, these feelings clearly must be produced in the lower, more primitive parts of the brain, at the brainstem level.

Other theorists argue that emotional experience and expression develop over time in predictable ways. For example, Lois Murphy (1983) observed that the basic emotions (as delineated by Izard, 1977) are first observable in babies at the following ages:

- *1–2 months:* Infants first display joy, anxiety, distress, interest-excitement, and sometimes anger during this period.

- *3 months on:* Infants begin to display pleasure and delight during interactions with caregivers and fear, grief, and pain at separation. A little later, they display triumph in achievement.

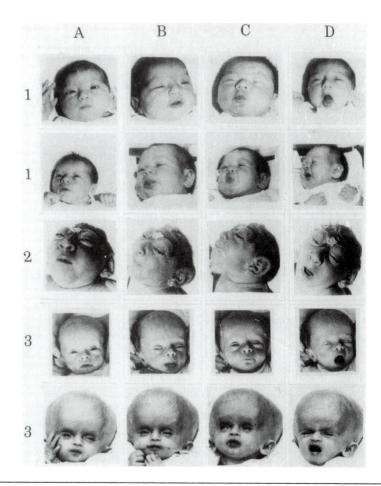

FIGURE 8.2   Normal, anencephalic, and hydroanencephalic neonates' emotional expressions. The vertical columns: A = response to distilled water; B = response to sweet water; C = to sour solution; D = to a bitter taste. The horizontal rows: I = normal, healthy neonates prior to the first breast or bottle feeding. 2 = an anencephalic neonate. 3 = two different hydro-anencephalic neonates. From Steiner, 1979, p. 269.

- *7–9 months:* Although some children show anxious reactions to strangers as early as 2 to 3 months, most children do not experience such reactions until they are 7 to 9 months old.

- *9 months on:* If the chief caretaker disappears, children will begin to display signs of depression. Such reactions continue on into the second year.

Finally, Carroll Izard (1977) contends that some emotions do not emerge until later in early childhood. These include contempt, guilt, shame, and shyness.

EMOTIONAL MILESTONES

Recently, Stanley and Nancy Thorndyke Greenspan (1985) charted the emotional milestones in the first four years of life and suggested ways parents can contribute to their children's emotional development:

Milestone 1: Self-Regulation and Interest in the World (Birth to 3 Months)

In the early weeks of life, infants confront two simultaneous challenges: (a) to feel calm and controlled, and (b) to take in the world while using all their senses. After nine months in the dark quiet of the womb, the neonate is thrust into a new world of sight, sound, taste, smell, touch, and movement. Infants possess an immature cardiorespiratory system, and so for them, there is an optimal level of stimulation. If they overdo it and try to absorb too much, too fast, they will be overwhelmed. As Brazelton (1983) notes:

> I have observed the cardiorespiratory involvement of infants with congenital cardiac defects whose circulatory balance was precarious. As they get "hooked" on and interact with an object in reach space, their breathing becomes deeper and more labored, their cardiac balance more precarious, cyanosis deepens until attention to the object is decreased momentarily, and their color returns. The return of attention to the object brings on a repetition of the same cycle of "hooked" attention, increasing autonomic imbalance, and recovery as the baby turns away briefly. From these observations it is clear that an infant's attention to an object involves behavioral, neuromotor, and autonomic systems in a predictable, alternating increase and decrease in the deployment of attention and nonattention that is designed to protect an immature and easily overloaded cardiorespiratory balance. (p. 46)

Infants must be engaged in a continuous ballet—being careful not to try to take in too much stimulation (and be overwhelmed) or to take in too little (and be bored). T. Berry Brazelton (1983) and Mary Klinnert and her colleagues (1983) point out that infants use a variety of tricks for turning up or turning down the volume. When infants are looking for action, they smile, coo and gurgle, and engage in eye-to-eye contact to initiate social exchange. When a caretaker's face appears, they hungrily search it; their eyes and face become wide, soft, and eager; they tilt their chin and crane their neck, trying to reach their caretaker. Their body tension gradually increases, but they remain still otherwise. A nurturing adult can rarely avoid being captured by such rapt attention; it is almost impossible not to respond to such signals by cuddling the baby.

On the other hand, infants are equally adept at telling the world to go away. One way infants calm themselves is by bringing their fist to their mouth and sucking on it. They may also avert their gaze or even turn their head completely away. These are clear signals that enough is enough. When startled by a loud rattle or an irritating sound, infants often jerk away and begin to cry. Their howls usually motivate those around them to spring into action. If that fails, infants often fall into an inactive sleep-like state. They close their eyes tightly, mask their expression, and hold their body tightly still. Their breathing becomes deep, jagged, and regular. Both these states help the infant turn down the volume of stimuli.

By the end of the fourth month, infants can "turn on" and "turn off" those around them (Brazelton, 1983).

Milestone 2: Falling in Love (2 to 7 Months)
Once self-control is attained, Greenspan and Greenspan (1985) suggest, infants can proceed to the next developmental task. Soon they begin to take an interest in the world. The authors note that:

> the human world is seen as the most enticing, pleasurable, and exciting of all experiences . . . you observe enraptured smiles and eager joyfulness as the baby gazes excitedly at your face, feeling your rhythmical movement, hearing your soft voice, and even, in his uncoordinated way, exploring your face. (p. 4)

We will discuss this period in some detail in chapter 11, which deals with passionate and companionate love.

Milestone 3: Developing Intentional Communication (3 to 10 Months)
In this period, children begin to smile, not just randomly or in mimicry, but in response to their parents' smiles or as they reach for a toy. When their parents coo to them, they make guttural sounds in return. Children begin to learn that their responses lead to reactions on the part of others; there is a give and take.

Milestone 4: The Emergence of an Organized Sense of Self (9 to 18 Months)
Children begin to understand the meanings of things. They may not be able to speak, but they understand functional relationships and can engage in complex patterns of behavior. A hungry child will no longer sit helplessly on a stool, crying and waiting for her mother to read her mind. The child will tug on her mother's skirt, dragging her to the refrigerator, and gesture for what she wants.

Milestone 5: Creating Emotional Ideas (18 to 36 Months)
In this period, children begin to create mental images. They can picture their mother—her look, her voice, and her smell—even when she is not there. They can imagine goblins under the bed or their father comforting them.

Milestone 6: Emotional Thinking: The Basis for Fantasy, Reality, and Self-Esteem (30 to 48 Months)
In this stage, children learn to use ideas in an emotional context. They begin to organize and manipulate their ideas into a cause-and-effect understanding

of their own emotions and the world. They can now separate fantasy from reality.

There never were in the world two opinions alike, no more than two hairs or two grains; the most universal quality is diversity.

MONTAIGNE

INDIVIDUAL DIFFERENCES IN EMOTIONALITY

People differ in every human characteristic—in size and shape of eyes, ears, noses, mouths, feet, and hands. Their internal organs—hearts, stomachs, livers—differ, too (Williams, 1956). Thus, it should come as no surprise that infants differ markedly in temperament from birth on.

For example, gender differences show themselves in emotional expression from the start. Howard Moss (1967) studied 30 infants over the first 3 months of life. Infant boys were more irritable. They smiled slightly less, vocalized less, cried and fussed more, and slept far less. At first, mothers talked to their talkative girls a little more and held the boys longer, perhaps in an effort to soothe them. By three months, however, mothers were spending less time with the irritable boys than with the more good-natured girls. Moss suggests that the mothers may have learned that it was impossible to quiet their irritable sons, whereas the girls were responsive and more likely to be quieted by maternal care. He speculates that these early gender differences may determine how attached mother and child become to each other.

A number of reasons might explain why boys are often especially irritable and difficult to soothe. Boys are more subject to inconsolable states, they have less well-organized physiological reactions, and they are more vulnerable to adverse conditions than are girls (Brazelton, 1983).

Not all investigators have found that infant boys are more irritable than infant girls, however. For example, Silvia Bell and Mary Ainsworth (1972) found that only firstborn boys were more irritable. By the end of the infants' first year, whether or not children cry and are irritable depends on how responsive their parents have been. Those children who had responsive parents have learned to signal what they want by a variety of means other than whining. Those whose parents have ignored their cries have not learned these other communication techniques and continue to fuss and cry.

Of course, regardless of gender, infants show many other individual differences in cognitive abilities and temperament. Ross Thompson and Michael Lamb (1983) outline some other typical individual differences in emotional expression among infants:

> Even the casual observer of young infants is likely to be impressed by their diversity of emotional expressiveness and affective self-regulation. Some infants, for example, are characterized by bright, animated facial and vocal expressions,

whereas others are typically more subdued. In some infants, emotional arousal reaches a climax after a prolonged and gradual build-up, whereas in others affective states begin and end more abruptly. Some infants seem capable of expressing a broad range of emotions varying in intensity, whereas others appear to have a more limited repertoire. There is also variability in the rapidity of recovery; that is, in the amount of time that must pass before an infant is 'ready for' another emotionally arousing experience. (p. 88)

Three broad analytical dimensions seem to describe these individual differences:

1. *Hedonic tone (positive or negative)*. Some infants are generally happy, while others tend to be sad, frightened, or angry a good deal of the time.
2. *Responsivity*. Infants differ in the range and intensity of their emotional expressions, in how quickly they respond, how quickly they reach a peak response, in how quickly they can change from one emotional expression to another, and in how long it takes them to settle down again.
3. *The capacity to regulate or cope with emotional arousal*. Once an emotional reaction has begun, infants differ in their ability to keep emotional arousal within tolerable limits. Such individual differences have an important impact on how children learn to deal with emotion.

A number of psychologists have been interested in how infants' temperaments relate to their personalities and temperaments in later life (Goldsmith et al., 1987). Mothers often claim that their infants and children seem to have been born with certain personality traits. "He always was stubborn," they observe. "I can remember telling him he had to stand in the corner until he apologized, and he just stood there hour after hour. Finally, I gave in. He would have died there." A few psychologists tend to dismiss such observations, suspicious that parents may see what they want to see. But many psychologists have concluded that such observations contain a grain of truth. Arnold Buss and Robert Plomin (in Goldsmith et al., 1987) define temperament as "a set of inherited personality traits that appear early in life" (p. 508). H. Hill Goldsmith and Joseph Campos (1986) identify temperament as "individual differences in the probability of experiencing and expressing the primary emotions and arousal" (p. 231). Goldsmith and Plomin (in Goldsmith et al., 1987) add that infants also possess individual differences in "the ability to recognize, decode, and feel the emotional expressions of others that are complementary to temperament. Together, temperament and these receptive differences play crucial roles in social interaction" (p. 511).

At the beginning of this section, Thompson and Lamb (1983) outlined three ways in which infants differ—they possess temperamental differences in hedonic tone, responsivity, and capacity to regulate emotional arousal. Buss and Plomin (Goldsmith et al., 1987) agree that temperament is determined by three traits: The first is **emotionality**—or the tendency to become distressed. Infants and children can vary from stoic little people who are impervious to the hardest knocks to people whose emotions are out of control—

who cry, throw temper tantrums, and refuse to be soothed. The second trait is **activity**—the infants' tempo and vigor. Some infants and children are lethargic. Others speak and move quickly, with bold and sweeping gestures. They never quit. The last trait is **sociability**—whether infants and children prefer being alone or with others. Some children can play by themselves for hours. In fact, they may be disinterested in other children or shy. Other children are intensely social. They love to receive attention from others ("Mom, look at me!") and to be involved in the give-and-take of social interaction.

Social costs and benefits are associated with each temperamental characteristic. Nonetheless, researchers Buss and Plomin (Goldsmith et al., 1987) have pointed out that difficult children seem to possess a certain temperamental profile—they are often emotional and energetic. Emotional children may be a problem because they are easily upset and are hard to soothe. Or, they may have frequent temper tantrums. Active children are troublesome because they get bored and restless, they continually test limits, and they wear out their caregivers. Thus, such difficult children are simply hard to handle.

Developmentalists have accumulated considerable evidence from longitudinal studies that infants' and children's innate temperaments seem to provide a foundation for their later personalities (Bates, in press; Rothbart, 1986). Of course, children's temperaments can be changed (Goldsmith et al., 1987). They can be taught to behave appropriately. Active infants can be taught to settle down at the dinner table, at bedtime, in school, and at church. However, on the playground, their unusual energy will probably still be evident (and a source of pride). Generally, in adulthood, people tend to select the activities that fit with their temperaments. Active people may gravitate toward fast-paced and high-energy situations. Sociable people may choose to study and work with others. Emotional people may try to avoid stressful situations. See Box 8.2.

THE CARETAKERS' CONTRIBUTION

Mothers and fathers differ in how well attuned they are to their infants' rhythms. In Figures 8.3 a and b, Brazelton (1983) illustrates two different parent-infant interactions. (In these figures, time is measured along the horizontal axis; the number of behaviors along the vertical axis.) In Figure 8.3 a, mother and infant's eye-to-eye contact is poorly coordinated. At first, the two are in synchrony. Then, the mother begins to accelerate the intensity of the encounter. She smiles, coos, touches the baby's hand, holds the baby's leg. Eventually, the baby looks away in an effort to reduce contact. The mother, however, doesn't know when to quit; she keeps trying to recapture the baby's interest. She adds facial gestures and grimaces. She continues to talk, touch, nod her head, and gesture. Finally, she begins to pat the baby. Eventually, the mother gives up and looks away.

BOX 8.2

The Consistency of Temperament

Stella Chess and Alexander Thomas (1977) provide an example of the way temperament and socialization can interact in shaping a child's personality and behavior. The New York Longitudinal Study has followed 136 children from infancy into adolescence. This is one of their case histories:

After his first term in college, Carl reported that he was depressed. He had made no friends. He was so anxious that he couldn't study. For Carl, this was a completely new experience. He had been very popular in high school, had played the piano for fun, and had done very well in school. He was bewildered at his sorry state. During an interview, he exclaimed, "This just isn't me!" (p. 220).

Out of curiosity, the interviewers retrieved Carl's early records. In infancy, Carl had been classified as an "extremely difficult child" in temperamental type. In infancy, he reacted extremely badly to new situations, becoming accustomed to them very slowly. This was true whether the "new" was a first bath, first solid food, the beginning of nursery school, or a first birthday party. Each new experience provoked loud crying and struggling to get away. His parents were very bright and nurturant and quickly learned to anticipate Carl's reactions. They knew that if they were patient and asked Carl to adapt to only one or two new things at a time, he would respond with a zestful enjoyment rather than terror. They simply had to go slowly. The parents knew that the problem wasn't their fault. They weren't bad parents. Carl was simply an emotional child. And, because they liked Carl, they interpreted their son's shrieking and turmoil as a sign of "lustiness."

Thus, things went well for Carl until he hit college. There he was confronted with too much that was too new, too soon—he confronted new students, new situations, and strange surroundings. Once Carl learned a bit about his beginnings, he quickly came up with a strategy for dealing with university life. He cut down on the number of courses he was taking and he forced himself to associate with a few other students. By the end of the academic year he was doing fine, both socially and academically. He was relieved: He now knew how to handle new situations.

In Figure 8.3 b, the mother and infant are far better coordinated. They look at each other, smile, and vocalize together. The mother seems to carefully follow the child's interest in approaching or retreating. When the baby begins to turn away, she looks down at her hands and stops her activity briefly. Seconds later, the baby looks at her. She smiles, talks, and leans forward. The baby's arms and legs cycle, and the baby coos contentedly while watching her. This ebb and flow of activity continues throughout the three-minute encounter.

As you can see from Figure 8.3 b, actually, both mother and child are in control of their interaction. The baby's needs must shape the general structure in which the interaction occurs; the mother then has the opportunity to regulate the tempo of the interaction. If she speeds up, she will reduce the baby's level of communication; if she slows down, she can expect a higher level of communication and engagement (Stern, 1974).

Sometimes, mothers are not able to shape themselves to their infants'

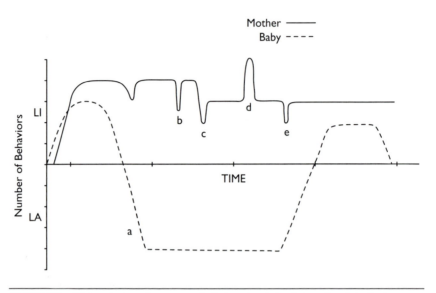

FIGURE 8.3a   Three minutes of an uncoordinated mother-infant interaction. Baby looks away in the midst of the interaction. From Brazelton, 1983, p. 46.

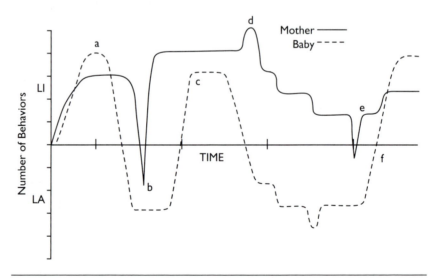

FIGURE 8.3b   Three minutes of a successful mother-infant interaction. From Brazelton, 1983, p. 47.

needs. When the infant turns its head, needing to cut down the level of stimulation that it is receiving, the young mother may panic. "The child doesn't like me. What did I do wrong?" She may intrusively force herself on the baby, looking for reassurance, but overwhelming it still further. A father, in an effort to play, may frighten the child with too much noise and movement. Or, the mother and father may give the infant too little attention. They may be bored, disinterested, or distracted. They both may be exhausted from trying to keep house and work. Generally, infants respond to such disinterest by trying to rouse their caretakers. If that proves to be impossible, they eventually withdraw completely. We might expect such parental intrusion or indifference to have a profound impact on children's strategies for dealing with emotions.

In this section, then, we have seen that infants are born with the ability to express a variety of emotions, from sadness and other negative emotions to the more positive ones. Nonetheless, in time, infants' and children's emotional repertoires develop in an orderly way. Children's caretakers seem to have a critically important impact on how children develop emotionally.

Sadness and Grief in Adulthood

In the last section, we focused on infants' and children's experiences and expressions of sadness. Let us now consider what is known about adults' reactions in the emotions of both sadness and the more intense and complex grief.

SADNESS

Antecedents and Responses

Several psychologists have interviewed adolescents and adults to determine the kinds of things that make them sad and how they generally try to cope with such feelings. In one such study, Carroll Izard (1977) interviewed 130 college students. He asked them to visualize a time when they had felt extremely "sad, discouraged, or downhearted." What had caused them to feel so sad? What did they end up doing about it? Their replies are reproduced in Box 8.3. How do most people generally deal with sadness? Izard also asked the students how they reacted when they were sad. Their replies are also shown in Box 8.3.

Izard concluded that for most people, a sense of separation is a major cause of sadness. People may feel aching sadness when they are separated from family and friends, when they feel left out, as if they do not belong, when they are unable to communicate with others, express their true feelings, or obtain sympathy. Another major cause of sadness is failure—whether imagined or real. People often feel dispirited when they have failed in a romantic affair, in social relationships, at sports, or in class. According to Izard, such sad incidents are an inevitable part of life. Thus, it is important that people learn to deal with such disheartening events effectively.

BOX 8.3

Antecedents and Consequences of Sadness

ANTECEDENTS		CONSEQUENCES	
CAUSES OF SADNESS	PERCENTAGE OF STUDENTS GIVING RESPONSE	STUDENTS' REACTIONS	PERCENTAGE OF STUDENTS GIVING RESPONSE
Thoughts		**Thoughts**	
1. About a personal problem	42.0	1. Life in general is bad	42.8
2. About failure, incompetence	19.8	2. About the cause of sadness, distress	22.9
3. Of sadness, death	16.7	3. How to overcome sadness, more pleasant things	22.5
4. About loneliness, rejection	8.7	4. About failure, incompetence	3.8
5. Other	13.2	5. About loneliness, rejection	1.5
		6. Other	6.9
Feelings		**Feelings**	
1. Distress, sadness, discouragement	33.9	1. Distress, sadness, discouragement	43.5
2. Feeling lonely, isolated, rejected	30.9	2. Mentally, physically upset	22.1
3. Physically, mentally upset	14.0	3. Loneliness, rejection	13.7
4. Feelings of failure, disappointment in self, incompetence, inadequacy	13.2	4. Felt need to be alone	5.3
5. Other	9.5	5. Anger	3.0
		6. Felt misled, used, hurt by others	2.3
		7. Felt like a failure, incompetent	2.3
		8. Other	7.6
Actions		**Actions**	
1. Something stupid, a mistake	36.1	1. Tried to get over it	29.8
2. Something to hurt others	15.9	2. Expressed sadness verbally, physically	17.5
3. Others imposed their will on subject	11.9	3. Did something specific	15.2
4. Something morally, legally wrong	7.1	4. Retreated from others	13.7
5. Passive, did nothing	7.1	5. Remained passive, did nothing	5.3
6. Retreated, withdrew	5.5	6. Thought of sadness in life	5.3
7. Other	16.7	7. Talked to someone	3.8
		8. Did something impulsive, irrational	0.7
		9. Other	8.4

Adapted from Izard (1977), pp. 302–303.

Functions of Sadness

Tomkins (1963) and Izard (1977) argue that sadness and distress have three major functions. First, sadness motivates men and women to change their lives. Many parents go to extremes to ensure that their children will never suffer as they have suffered. Many men and women tie the truth in knots to avoid hurting their mates. Yet, people must experience some sadness and distress if they are to be motivated to mature, to stretch themselves, to become better people. Sadness and loneliness push boys and girls to learn how to make friendly overtures to others. Disappointments teach us to try harder. Repeated failures teach us that not all things are possible.

Second, expressions of sadness motivate others to help. When people look sad, dejected, and downhearted, their expressions communicate to others that all is not well and that help is needed. Often, people come through and do what they can to alleviate the suffering of others.

For example, one study concerned itself with whether or not authorities took a lawbreaker's remorse into account when deciding which sort of punishment was appropriate. So, the study began with interviews of police who spotted a crime in progress as to what determined whether they merely warned a suspect or brought the suspect to the station for booking. One question asked was, "If you catch two teens racing their cars through a residential neighborhood late at night, what determines whether you arrest them or not?" The police were frank. "If it seemed like they were 'basically good kids,' you just gave them a warning and sent them home. But if they seemed like 'punks,' you took them in to the station and booked them." How did they know if someone was a "good kid"? Well, if they "were clean cut, polite, and sad or scared at being caught, you knew this was just a kid being a bit wild." "My heart just melts when some kid starts crying," one officer said. "I think of myself at the same age."

Research has shown that sadness touches most people's hearts and motivates them to help. In one study, Jeffrey Savitsky and Marguerite Sim (1974) asked students to watch a videotape of boys, first-time offenders, who had committed petty thefts or acts of vandalism. (Actually, the boys were actors.) While telling their stories, the boys' faces registered either sadness, anger, happiness, or no emotion at all. Students were then asked to judge how serious the crimes were, how likely the delinquents were to repeat the criminal activity, and how severely they should be punished for their offenses. Like the police officers we have described, students were more generous in their judgments of the sad boys than of those who seemed unrepentant (expressing either happiness or anger while telling their tale). Students recommended far less severe punishment for the sad boys than they did for the other boys. The authors speculated that the students probably felt that the sad boys had already suffered enough.

Finally, Tomkins and Izard note that sadness has one other function—it facilitates group cohesiveness. Izard points out that people are tied to their family and friends both because of the pleasures they provide and because separation is painful. He observes that the sadness we feel when our love relationships dissolve and friendships go awry is one of the great forces binding people to people.

*W*e die only once, and for such a long time!
MOLIERE

GRIEF

Sadness seems to be a relatively straightforward emotion—such expressions of unhappiness appear early in life, they involve the ANS's parasympathetic system, and they motivate both the sufferer and the observer to help set things right. What about grief? If sadness were the only emotion involved in grief, reviewing the antecedents of this emotion would be fairly straightforward. As you will see, however, grief—as well as depression—involves other emotions such as anger, which is accompanied by both parasympathetic and sympathetic activity, as well as disgust, contempt, and guilt. Thus, grief appears to be a far more complex and intense emotion than sadness.

Since death was thought too morbid an interest, it was not until the 1940s that investigators began to study bereavement and grief. Today, of course, things have changed. One journal, *Omega,* is totally devoted to publishing research on death and bereavement. Numerous books on death and dying are published each year. Elisabeth Kubler-Ross's (1969) *On Death and Dying* even hit the best-seller lists.

Stages of Grief: Shock and Numbness

In 1944, couples and families gathered in the Coconut Grove, a Boston nightclub, to celebrate. The club was jammed. In the midst of the celebration, a fire started and quickly swept through the Grove. At the first smell of fire, people panicked. They rushed to the exits but found some exit doors locked. The remaining exits were soon jammed with bodies. As frantic men and women pushed and shoved to get through the doors, many fell and were trampled underfoot. Four hundred and ninety-one people lost their lives. The Boston community sat stunned.

Psychiatrist Erich Lindemann (1944) set out to study the reactions of the bereaved survivors. He detailed the symptomatology of grief and concluded that grief is a syndrome with distinctive symptoms and a predictable course. (Recently, others have investigated the grieving process. See Solsberry & Krupnick, 1984, and Stroebe & Stroebe, 1987.) Lindemann's research showed that whether or not the loss was anticipated, the most frequent immediate reaction following death is shock, numbness, and a sense of disbelief. Because the reality of the death has not yet penetrated awareness, survivors may appear to be accepting and coping well.

An example: On December 7, 1988, an earthquake rumbled through Leninaka, Armenia. In a matter of hours, 55,000 men, women, and children were dead—buried beneath the rubble. Their families and friends stood patiently at the scene in 20-degree-below-zero weather, refusing to leave, waiting for rescue workers. Journalists asked how they were managing to cope so well when their families had been decimated. One man observed, "Before, if someone died, you were expected to cry. If you didn't, people said 'You have a heart of stone.' Now no one cries. All our hearts have turned to stone."

Stages of Grief: Despair and a Sense of Loss

Eventually, in the hours or months following a death, numbness turns to an intense feeling of loss and pain. Beverley Raphael (1983) describes the second phase of mourning this way:

> The absence of the dead person is everywhere palpable. The home and familiar environs seem full of painful reminders. Grief breaks over the bereaved in waves of distress. There is intense yearning, pining, and longing for the one who has died. The bereaved feels empty inside, as though torn apart or as if the dead person had been torn out of his body. (p. 40)

During this phase, searching behaviors—dreams in which the deceased is still alive, seeing the deceased in the street, and other misperceptions, illusions, and hallucinations—are common. When the lost person fails to return, these perceptions diminish, and despair sets in. People become sad, moody, guilty, angry, irritable, lonely, anxious, and restless. They have difficulty in concentrating. Offers of comfort and support are often rejected (Averill, 1968).

Some grieving people express their feelings in a variety of physical symptoms (Solsberry & Krupnick, 1984). They cry easily. Their stomachs are often upset. They may eat too little or too much. One moment they are agitated and restless; the next, they can barely move. They can't sleep, or they sleep all the time. They lack interest in the outside world and often give up the friends and activities they used to enjoy. They are in pain. They may begin to eat excessively or drink or take drugs. In Box 8.4, Wolfgang and Margaret Stroebe (1987) list the symptoms of grief.

Investigators find that bereavement also increases the likelihood of a host of mental and physical problems (Traupmann & Hatfield, 1981; Klerman & Clayton, 1984; Laudenslager & Reite, 1984; Stroebe & Stroebe, 1987). Among these are that bereavement:

1. increases a person's vulnerability to mental illness.
2. produces a variety of physical symptoms (including migraines, headaches, facial pain, rashes, indigestion, peptic ulcers, weight gain or loss, heart palpitations, chest pain, asthma, infections, fatigue, and so forth.)
3. aggravates existing illnesses.
4. causes physical illness.

5. predisposes a person to engage in risky behaviors (such as smoking, drinking, and drug use).
6. increases the likelihood of death.

For example, C. Murray Parkes (1964) found that of 4,486 widowers 55 years of age or older, 213 died within the first 6 months of their mate's death. This was 40% above the expected rate. After six months, the rates gradually fell back to normal. The stress of bereavement may elevate the risk of death in several ways. It may lead to depression, and the depressed may then neglect their own health (Satariano & Syme, 1981); or in extreme cases, depression may lead to drug abuse and/or suicide (Schuckit, 1977; Sendbuehler & Goldstein, 1977). The stress may also lead to dysfunctions in neuroendocrine balance and, in turn, a reduction in immunity to disease (Timiras, 1972). For example, the bereaved are at risk for coronary heart disease and cirrhosis of the liver (Jacobs & Ostfeld, 1977).

Some grief shows much of love; But much of grief shows still some want of wit.

SHAKESPEARE

Stages of Grief: Resolution

Finally, the bereaved enter the phase of resolution or reorganization. In this final phase, they can recall the deceased without being overwhelmed by sadness and are at last ready to reinvolve themselves in the world (Bowlby, 1980).

It used to be thought that the grieving process normally lasted a year or two. For example, in Lindemann's study of 101 bereaved persons, he concluded that normal bereavement followed a set pattern: After the initial shock, the bereaved felt intense sadness, withdrew, protested the loss, and then within a year or so resolved their grief.

This turns out to be not quite true. Things do get better after a year or so, but if someone really means a great deal to us, we continue to remember them and to regret their injury, suffering, or death throughout our lives. Sadness wells up when we think of what might have been. For example, in a variation on this theme, Elaine Hatfield and her colleagues (Wikler, Wasow, & Hatfield, 1981) interviewed both social workers and parents of mentally retarded children. Once, clinicians generally assumed that parents' grief would be time bound, that following the discovery of the child's condition, parents of a mentally retarded child would go through a predictable grieving process: first shock, then despair, guilt, withdrawal, acceptance, and finally adjustment (Parks, 1977). But what parents actually reported was that they experienced chronic sorrow. Again and again, on special occasions—when the child should have begun walking or talking, when younger brothers or sisters overtook the retarded child in ability, when other children his or her age were going

BOX 8.4

Grief Symptoms

SYMPTOM	DESCRIPTION
Attitudes Toward Self, the Deceased, and the Environment	
Low self-esteem	Feelings of worthlessness, inadequacy, and failure.
Self-reproach	Guilt.
Hopelessness; helplessness	Thoughts of death and suicide. Pessimism about the present and future.
Sense of unreality	Feeling of "not being there," as if one is watching events that are happening to someone else.
Suspiciousness	Doubting the motives of those who offer help or advice.
Interpersonal problems	Rejection of friendship and withdrawal from social functions.
Attitudes toward the deceased	Yearning for the deceased. Idealization. Imitation of his or her behavior. Ambivalence. Images of the deceased, often very vivid, almost hallucinatory. Firm conviction of having seen him or her. Preoccupation with the memory of the deceased and the need to talk, sometimes incessantly, about him or her.
Emotional Reactions	
Depression	
Anxiety	
Guilt	
Anger and hostility	
Inability to feel pleasure	
Loneliness	
Behavioral Reactions	
Agitation	Tenseness, restlessness, jitters.
Fatigue	
Crying	
Cognitive Impairment	
Retardation of thought and concentration	
Physiological Changes and Bodily Complaints	
Loss of appetite or overeating	
Sleep disturbances	Insomnia or oversleeping.
Energy loss	
Bodily complaints	These include headaches, back pain, cramps, nausea, vomiting, heartburn, blurred vision, tightness in throat, palpitations, tremor, hair loss, and so forth.
Duplicating physical complaints of the deceased	
Increase in drug taking	
Susceptibility to illness and disease	

Adapted from Stroebe & Stroebe (1987), p. 10.

off to the first grade, beginning to date, getting ready for their senior proms, or marrying—parents could not help but mourn for what might have been. Other observers have noted the same phenomenon (Joyce, 1984; Olshansky, 1962).

Similarly, Darrin Lehman, Camille Wortman, and Allan Williams (1987) found that men and women continue to mourn the death of those they love for many years. The researchers interviewed people who had lost a mate or a child in an automobile accident four or more years ago. They found that the bereaveds' thoughts and conversations were still filled with references to those they had lost. They were more likely to be depressed or suffering from other psychiatric symptoms than were their peers. They had difficulty functioning socially. Their marriages were shaky (if it was their child who had died), and they were plagued with financial problems. The bereaved continued to worry over the accident and wonder what might have been done to prevent it. They were unable to accept, resolve, or find any meaning in their loss.

In time, most people recover from their losses. Of course, we continue to have bittersweet memories of those we loved but lost. Eventually, however, most people form new attachments, develop new coping skills, go back to work, and begin to live again (Solsberry & Krupnick, 1984).

A few do not: Queen Victoria's Prince Albert died when they were both 42 years old. She continued to mourn his death for the next 40 years. During their marriage, Queen Victoria had been extremely dependent on Prince Albert; she could not bear even a night of separation. After his death she continued to idealize him. "To have conceived of him as anything short of perfect—perfect in virtue, in wisdom, in beauty, in all the glories and graces of man—would have been an unthinkable blasphemy" (Strachey, 1971, p. 187). She grieved and wore black throughout the remainder of her life. Her bed had attached to it, at the back and above Albert's pillow, a photograph of his head and shoulders as he lay in his coffin, surrounded by a wreath of immortelles. Victoria resented her subjects, who she thought failed to admire Albert as much as he deserved to be admired.

Who Suffers Grief the Most?

Some researchers have attempted to determine which kinds of people grieve the most and are most at risk following the death of a father or mother, husband or wife, or child (see Klerman & Clayton, 1984). Their findings are interesting. They find that children and young adults suffer the most intensely after a death in the family. (Perhaps older people, those over 60, have experienced so much suffering, illness, and death, that a new death does not touch them profoundly.) Men seem to suffer more from the loss of their mates than do women. (Perhaps this is because men generally have far fewer intimate friends than do women and are less likely to possess the social skills needed to make new close friends than are women. Thus, men lack the social support they need after a death.) For both men and women, the loss of a child is more upsetting than any other loss, even if the child is an adult. The bereaved are most at risk if they are of low socioeconomic status. (Perhaps it is hard to cope with both change and poverty.)

Therapists have long argued that the "ideal" mentally healthy person is one who is capable of both close intimacy and independence. This kind of person seems to cope best with the death of a mate, too. Men and women who were unusually dependent on their mates (like Queen Victoria) suffer especially intense grief after the loss of their mates. So do men and women who had love-hate relationships with their mates before their deaths. Couples who were ambivalent about their partners before death are plagued by wrenching and conflicting emotions—guilt and anger as well as loneliness and remorse—after the death.

Not surprisingly, people who had poor mental and physical health before their loved one's death suffer even more afterward. For example, alcoholics and drug users are more likely to become ill, be hospitalized, and commit suicide or die after their mates' deaths than are their peers.

Some deaths are sudden; others are expected. Sudden deaths—deaths due to car accidents, suicide, homicide, or war are especially shocking. Usually (more than 80% of the time), family members have at least two weeks' warning that a terminally ill person is about to die. The evidence suggests that both the kind of death and the suddenness of a death have an impact on how intensely people mourn after their partners' deaths. Not surprisingly, people have more trouble dealing with a sudden death than with one that was anticipated. If family members are warned that death is imminent, they have a chance to say all the things they want to say to the dying person, to ask for forgiveness, to try to make things right with the dying person, and to get the family affairs in order. As a consequence, family members who have some warning of an impending death seem to experience less guilt, anger, and confusion and have fewer practical problems than those who are taken by surprise. Of course, family members who have to cope with a lingering illness may confront unusual stresses and strains as well. The survivors may feel guilty that they were not up to the task of dealing with a slow, painful, and interminable illness. Or, they may simply be worn out from trying too hard for too long.

Some types of death pose special risks to the survivors. How well one can cope with the death of a family member who is killed in a war seems to depend on how much sense the death makes. If the death is seen as a heroic act in defense of one's country, it is easier to bear than if it is seen as an absurd and useless sacrifice. If one's mate committed suicide or was murdered, one's grief is likely to be far more intense than if one's mate died a natural death. Paul Theroux (1977), in *The Consul's File*, reminds us of why a murder is an assault on the family as well as on the victim:

> The least dignified thing that can happen to a man is to be murdered. If he dies in his sleep he gets a respectful obituary and perhaps a smiling portrait; it is how

we all want to be remembered. But murder is the great exposer: here is the victim in his torn underwear, face down on the floor, unpaid bills on his dresser, a meagre shopping list, some loose change, and worst of all the fact that he is alone. Investigation reveals what he did that day—it all matters—his habits are examined, his behaviour scrutinized, his trunks rifled, and a balance sheet is drawn up at the hospital giving the contents of his stomach. Dying, the last private act we perform, is made public: the murder victim has no secrets. (p. 123)

Finally, if the bereaved can rely on their families and friends to stand by and help them, they are likely to be better able to cope with death. Immediately after a death, parents are the most important source of support for young men and women. Once they begin to recover, friends become important again. For the old (whose parents are usually gone), friends are most important.

Caring for the Bereaved. In a popular book of etiquette published in England in 1929, Lady Troubridge (1979) advised readers how to behave in the face of death: "One chief rule to remember . . . is that sorrow is sacred and that it is one of the most unforgivable breaches of good behavior to intrude upon it. . . . The members of the bereaved family should be left as much alone in their grief as possible" (p. 55).

The reason the bereaved should be left to themselves, Lady Troubridge contended, was because they were in danger of breaking down and revealing unseemly emotions: "It is difficult to keep a firm hold over the emotions at such a time and it is therefore wiser to see no one if there is a chance of breaking down" (p. 57).

Today, by contrast, health-care professionals have instituted a variety of programs to help the bereaved deal with their loss (see Green, 1984, for more information on these programs). Initially, when patients are hospitalized, health-care professionals try to assure that the family and friends of the dying are informed about what is going on. Nurses visit patients each day to give them information and find out the kinds of information they want transmitted to their various relatives. The nurses then carry these progress reports to the family, displaying sympathy and making it clear that they have time to help. Thus, they can help family members deal with the grief, anger, guilt, fear, and confusion they feel when they discover their family member or friend is going to die. Most people want to know in minute detail exactly what is happening to the patient who is still alive and what caused his death afterward. The nurses also try to prepare the bereaved for the grief reactions and physical symptoms they may experience in the months to come. People generally are less anxious if they are forewarned about reactions that would otherwise seem bizarre. Nurses may help the bereaved notify the next-of-kin and make burial plans. They may also help survivors make appointments with visiting nurses, homemaker services, public welfare, or other community agencies.

Nurses may also refer survivors to specialized support groups. A variety of groups, such as "Widows to Widows," help people deal with their grief and cope with their vastly changed lives (Osterweis, 1984). The principle behind such programs is that recently bereaved persons can be helped the most by others who have been through the same things themselves and who have survived. Another widow can serve as a role model as well as help the bereaved gain perspective on their emotions (Silverman & Cooperband, 1975).

Many recently bereaved men and women need nothing more than a friend who has the patience to let the bereaved person talk about the loss. Others need reassurance that their reactions are normal—that they are not "going crazy." Friends can also provide a great deal of practical support (picking up flowers or a few groceries), especially in the first few weeks after the death.

Immediately after the death, many bereaved men and women are tempted to make a fresh start—to move to a new city that holds no memories, to take another job, to do what they've always wanted to do. Those who do make such precipitous moves often come to regret it. When people are grief stricken, their judgment is erratic. Plans that seemed a good idea at the time are often found to be wildly impractical later. Worse yet, such sudden changes may cut off men and women from the social support they desperately need.

Finally, after a long period of mourning, friends and acquaintances often sense that the bereaved hopes to be given permission to stop grieving. They long to be assured that it will not dishonor the memory of the deceased if they put the past behind them and begin to invest in new relationships and a new life. Of course, if mourning is especially severe or prolonged, the bereaved may benefit from talking to a psychologist or psychiatrist.

Depression

One of the most difficult and perplexing cases of therapists Elaine Hatfield and Richard Rapson was that of Samuel. At first glance, Samuel would seem to have everything. He was quite good-looking, Chinese and Caucasian, an all-American type. He began his education at an exclusive military school in Hong Kong, where his father was stationed, and then pursued an unusual dual career—he was a test-pilot with the U.S. Air Force while also working toward an M.D./Ph.D. in neurophysiology. In 1970, things began to fall apart. A pilot who substituted for him when he had a hangover was killed. Sam felt guilty and began to think of leaving the Air Force. At the same time, he began to have marital troubles. His wife and three sons began to insist on more time with him. Sam became irritable, short tempered, and depressed, and the couple divorced. Finally, Sam tried to kill himself. He carved his wife's name in his arms and legs and disinterestedly watched the blood flow. During therapy, he made little progress. In one session, Sam would be witty and insightful. At the next session, however, he might be deeply depressed. In that mood he despised himself, convinced that he was a loser. He felt broken and "burned out" and longed for someone to love; yet, he hated women for their "coldness and ambition." There was nothing in the world that he enjoyed doing. He simply sat in a corner and stared.

Sam had seen six other therapists. His psychiatrists had tried psycho-analysis, cognitive behavior therapy, and a variety of anti-anxiety drugs, sed-atives, antispasmodic agents, antidepressants, steroids, antipsychotic agents, monoamine oxidase inhibitors (MAOIs), as well as electric shock. Nothing helped. Hatfield and Rapson did no better. Finally, Sam left a casual message on their answering machine that he was cancelling his appointment. He was moving to London that morning. They never heard from him again.

Sam's case reads like a script for depression—low self-esteem, desperate dependence, fear, anger, inability to sleep, loss of sex drive, hopelessness, and despair. Luckily, most cases of depression can be successfully treated, as you will see in a later section. A few cases, however, escape all the best efforts.

Depression is one of mankind's oldest psychological disorders (Rosen, 1968; Zilboorg, 1939). Job's and Saul's depressions are chronicled in the Old Testament. The Greeks named depression "melancholia," or "black bile," after one of the four physiological humors they thought affected mood. In the Middle Ages, Satan was thought to cause such suffering. In the sixteenth century, Martin Luther wrote, "All heaviness of mind and melancholy comes of the Devil" (Rao, 1975).

Today, when people say someone is depressed, they may be talking about two very different things—they may be talking about either normal or psy-chotic depression. Everyone gets sad and discouraged when buffeted by fate. Such normal "depressive" episodes are of very limited duration. They are provoked by very specific events. When psychologists say someone is de-pressed, however, they mean that the person is suffering from **clinical**, or **psychotic depression**. Such depressions are severe, chronic, and often it is difficult to say exactly what is provoking them.

Clinical depression takes two very different forms. In simple **unipolar depression,** which besets two-thirds of those who have an affective (emo-tional) disorder, individuals suffer from low self-esteem, devastating depres-sion, and difficulty in performing even the simplest of tasks. The **bipolar depressions** afflict one-third of those with an affective disorder. In bipolar, or **manic-depressive disorders,** manic episodes (in which people feel all-powerful, joyous, so excited they barely eat or sleep, and frantically restless) alternate with periods of depression.

In the United States, such major affective disorders afflict 10 to 14 million Americans (Gallagher, 1986). Approximately twice as many women as men suffer from depressive disorders (Sargent, 1987). More than 15% of depressed persons commit suicide. Yet, depression remains something of a mystery to clinician and researcher alike. In this section, we discuss what we do know about this disorder. We review theories concerning its genesis and discuss that depression is the most striking example of the relationship between biological vulnerability and the psychological stresses of life. Finally, we discuss the most effective treatments for such disorders—including both drugs and psychotherapies. Generally, these treatments are quite effective. In those rare cases when people become so depressed they can no longer function (or are suicidal), they may have to be hospitalized for more intensive treatment.

THEORIES OF DEPRESSION

Theorists have looked at the cultural, psychological, and biological contributions to depression.

Cultural Contributions

Some theorists have argued that depression appears in much the same form in all periods of history and in all countries. For example, William Zung (1969) administered the Self-Rating Depression Scale (SDS) to depressed men and women in six countries—Japan, Australia, Czechoslovakia, England, Germany, and Switzerland. The SDS asks men and women to rate themselves on 20 symptoms most commonly used to characterize depressive disorders: sadness, crying spells, sleep disturbances, decreased appetite, weight loss, loss of interest in sex, rapid heart rate, constipation, fatigue, agitation, slowness, confusion, emptiness, hopelessness, indecisiveness, irritability, dissatisfaction, low self-esteem, thoughts of suicide, and diurnal (daily) variations in cycle. He found that in a variety of countries, the depressed secured high scores on the SDS and experienced the same clusters of depressive symptoms.

However, there seem to be some cultural influences in the way that depression is experienced. Anthony Marsella (1981), for example, argues that culture has an important role in shaping emotional experience. In different cultures, the depressed are assumed to think, feel, and act in different ways. For example, Andre Benoist, Michelle Roussin, Marquita Fredette, and Serge Rousseau (1965) asked French-Canadians what they meant when they said someone was depressed. Only 5% of the Canadians labeled as depression a case involving "sadness, insomnia, fatigue, and loss of interest." What they meant by depression was "a nervous breakdown." Researchers have also explored the subjective experience of depression among Japanese nationals, Japanese-Americans, and Caucasian Americans. The associations of each of these groups with the term depression, or *yuutsu*, differed greatly. Americans equated depression with inner states such as sadness, despair, and loneliness. The Japanese nationals associated it with external experiences, such as rain, clouds, and darkness (Tanaka-Matsumi & Marsella, 1976).

Depression, Marsella (1981) argues, is primarily a Western phenomenon. It is very common in England, far less common in Africa, and virtually unknown among the Anabaptist sect of Hutterites (Silverman, 1968). Debate exists, then, as to the role that cultural factors play in the genesis of depression, but no debate exists about the large role that psychological and biological factors play.

Twisted molecules lead to twisted thoughts.
FRANKLIN (1987)

Genetic Theories of Depression

It is becoming increasingly clear that certain people are genetically predisposed to depression (Kraines, 1957; Franklin, 1987). Family, twin, and adoptive studies make it clear that both simple depressive disorders and manic-depressive disorders are genetically transmitted. For example, Samuel Kraines points out that normally only 0.4% of the population ever experience a manic-depressive episode. If one parent has the disorder, however, 24% to 33% of the children will have this problem; another 17% will have a mild affective disorder. If both parents have it, as many as 67% of the children will have a manic-depressive disorder. The other 33% may have a mild affective problem. Other investigators have found that if one identical twin suffers from a manic-depressive disorder, the probability that the other will ranges between 40% and 96%. The rates are the same even when the identical twins are reared apart. For nonidentical twins, the probability that both will be depressed is 0% to 13% (see Kraines, 1957 or Gallagher, 1986).

Recently, studies by medical sociologist Janice Egeland and her colleagues at Yale, MIT, and the University of Miami (1987) provide some insights into the genetics of the affective disorders. Egeland and her colleagues studied the Old Order Amish of Lancaster County, Pennsylvania, a community of quiet-spoken, gentle pacifists. In such an ultraconservative group, people who suffer from the manifestations of manic-depressive disorders stand out. The Amish explanation for such peculiar behavior, *"Siss im blut"*—"It is in the blood"—seems to have some validity. Recent research confirms that such affective disorders are, in part, genetic. The researchers chose the Amish for the study of genetic transmission of depression for a variety of reasons. The Amish have unusually large families (seven children on the average), a tradition of marital fidelity, and little geographical mobility. They represent a closed genetic pool. All 12,000 members of the Lancaster community are descendants of only 30 pioneers who came to America during the early eighteenth century. Best of all, they keep unusually detailed handwritten genetic records.

Egeland et al. focused on one 81-member clan. A panel of four psychiatrists and one psychologist interviewed the family members. They classified 62 of them as psychiatrically healthy, 14 as having some form of bipolar (manic-depressive) disorder, and five as having a unipolar major depression. The researchers then obtained blood from each family member. Using the techniques of molecular biology, they analyzed pieces of the actual genetic material, DNA. Humans possess 23 pairs of chromosomes. The first 22 chromosomes determine whether people will have dark hair or light, brown eyes or blue, and so forth. The twenty-third pair are the sex chromosomes—they determine whether someone will be a male or a female. Women possess two X chromosomes, inheriting an X from both their mother and father. Men possess an X and a Y chromosome, receiving an X from their mother and a Y from their father. All 50,000 to 100,000 human genes are strung out along the chromosome's tiny threadlike strands. Egeland et al.'s research makes it clear that the major depressive disorders may be biologically transmitted. They found that subjects with affective disorders possessed a defect on a segment of chromosome 11. (The actual gene on which the defect is located is still to be identified.) They concluded that a gene or group of genes confers a predisposition to manic-depression. Children of individuals with this genetic anomaly have a 50% chance of inheriting it. However, even if they do, only 63% of them will show signs of the disorder, which suggests that environmental factors also play a role in bringing on the disease.

The authors have not yet uncovered the chemical underpinning of this problem. One possible candidate is the gene-encoding tyrosine hydroxylase, the enzyme that plays an important role in the metabolism of the neurotransmitter dopamine. This relates to the fact that dopamine has long been suspected to be involved in the etiology of major mental disorders, as you will see.

Scientists studying other communities have found strong evidence that several different genetic defects may contribute to the affective disorders. Miron Baron and his colleagues (1987), for example, studied five extended Jerusalem families which had a history of depressive disorders. They found 47 members who suffered from manic-depressive and related disorders. The researchers found that those who suffered from a manic-depressive illness possessed an aberrant gene on their X chromosome. To researchers, this made sense. For at least 50 years, it has been suspected that manic-depressive illness might be transmitted through the X chromosome. Several bits of data are consistent with such a hypothesis. More women than men are affected by depression. (Women possess two X chromosomes and men possess only one, so this may account for the difference.) In addition, the disorder is rarely transmitted from father to son. (The mother contributes an X, and the father contributes a Y to his son.) Both circumstances point to the X chromosome. Of course, other psychologists and psychiatrists point out that cultural reasons, as well as genetic ones, can explain why women might find their lives more depressing than do men. Susan Nolen-Hoeksema (1987) argues that, in fact, there are a variety of possible reasons for existing gender differences in depression. Let us now review this research.

Psychoanalytic Theories of Depression

Psychoanalysts have argued that early traumatic experiences, such as a separation or a loss of a parent, at a critical stage of development may make children especially vulnerable to depression. When later psychological stresses echo these early losses, the individual is overwhelmed.

In 1911, Karl Abraham (1948), a German psychoanalyst, was the first to offer a psychoanalytic theory of grief versus "melancholy" (or what we commonly call depression). He observed that when we lose someone or something, it is normal to grieve. But melancholy is grief gone haywire. It is too much for too long. In a brilliant and deceptively simple insight, Abraham pinpointed a crucial difference between the two emotions—when one has loved and lost, one grieves; but normal mourning sinks into depression when love has been laced with hatred. Depression, he thought, must be fueled by love *and* anger.

Abraham concluded that the depressed must have encountered a primal blow to their self-esteem and security during the oral-sadistic stage (a "cannibalistic" stage when children think of their parents and themselves as one) or in the anal-sadistic stage (when children are concerned with power and control). Children are narcissistic. If they are unloved, they assume that it must be because they are unlovable. They hate, and assume they are hated by, those they love. They are angry about their treatment and guilty about their anger. Later rejections again arouse these old feelings. The depressives' unconscious conflict between love and hate is paralyzing. They lose interest in the world about them. In its extreme form, this negation of life leads to suicide.

In 1917, Sigmund Freud wrote *Mourning and Melancholia.* (He suffered from depression himself and tried to raise his spirits with cocaine, which he mistakenly assumed was nonaddictive.) Freud (1959, Vol. 4) observed that grief and depression had much in common. In both were painful dejection, withdrawal of interest in the outside world, inhibition of activity, and the loss of the ability to love. But there were also some differences. In depression, one also found deflated self-esteem, self-accusation, and a delusional need for self-punishment. Melancholics love the person or career they have lost, but they are enraged, too. In the style of the child, the depressed prefer to suffer in the unconscious belief that, in the end, they will get back the person or things they have lost.

More recently, Silvano Arieti (1979; Arieti & Bemporad, 1978) has elaborated on a similar psychoanalytic view of depression. Arieti relates the disorder to a person's relationship with a "Dominant Other." Arieti argues that the severely depressed often have a strikingly similar history. In early childhood, their parents were reliable, attentive, and loving. Then, for some reason, that attention was withdrawn. Perhaps a new child appeared, the loving parent disappeared (perhaps going to war, taking a new job, or falling ill) or died. Such a child responds in one of two ways:

> One is by doing his best to live up to the expectations of the adults—by doing hard work, or by becoming a goody-goody, by attempting to placate them. Striving to regain paradise, he thus lives not for himself but for others. He believes that love is not available now, but that if he can live up to the expectations of adults,

it will be. He becomes a compliant person, a person with a strong sense of duty. When he does not succeed in obtaining what he wants, he tends to blame himself. He feels that he has not done enough. He could do more.

Later on, the child develops a type of pre-psychotic depressed personality, in which he depends entirely on others for gratification of his needs. (p. 57)

Men and women tend to put all their hopes on different kinds of "others." Women tend to be obsessively eager to please—especially to please their husbands or lovers. In return, they expect their mates to take care of them. Not surprisingly, this strategy fails. In the end, it is impossible to please everyone all the time. In the end, no one person can gratify all our needs. Women end up depressed—another reason, perhaps, why women suffer from depression twice as often as do men, who are taught to go after the things they want more directly.

Eventually, the disparity between what was sought (the love that fills all needs) and reality (that one must give a great deal to get very little) becomes painfully clear; women lose hope and become severely depressed. This theme is echoed in a passage from Marilyn French's novel *The Women's Room* (1978):

> . . . she long ago gave up the hope that she would ever find the Grail. You know . . . the love that fills all need, assuages all hurt, excites and stimulates when boredom fails, and is absolute, I mean absolute, that never fails no matter what you are or fail to be. I think we all spend our lives searching for that, and obviously we never find it. . . . So we go on searching, feeling discontent, sensing that the world or what it promised us has failed us, or even worse . . . that we have failed it. And some of us learn, late, I'm afraid, that that isn't possible. And we give up the hope. (p. 660)

Rather than their spouse, men tend to focus on a "Dominant Other" whose links to the depriving mother are less obvious—a social group, a political party, or a cause. Similarly, many men (and some women) pin their hopes on the "Dominant Goal." Arieti argues that the kind of person motivated by a Dominant Goal has unconsciously determined in early adolescence that to regain love, he or she must achieve something great in life: "to become a famous actress, to win a Nobel Prize" (p. 57). When such persons finally realize that their Dominant Goal is unattainable, that a fantasy has guided their entire life and the emptiness cannot be filled, they become depressed.

Similarly, Edward Bibring (1968), also a psychoanalyst, saw a common denominator in the depressives he treated. They were caught in a dilemma: They had inflexibly high aspirations. They wished to be: (a) worthy, loved, and appreciated; (b) strong, superior, great, and secure; or (c) good and loving. Depression set in when they realized that they were doomed to failure—when they became painfully aware of their own "inferiority." They were caught. They could not lower their standards, yet they were incapable of living up to them. No wonder they froze in the immobility of the depressive.

A lament by one depressive illustrates this process. A writer was suicidally depressed. She was trying to do far too much—nurse an invalid husband, take care of her toddler, teach, and finish a collection of short stories. When her therapist observed, "Well, all you can do is what you can do," the client sighed, "Wouldn't it be wonderful if that were true." She was unable to recognize that logically this statement must be true. She was like many depressives—attempting to maintain impossibly high standards while berating herself for failing to meet them (see Box 8.5).

Cognitive Theories of Depression

Some theorists argue that it is the depressive's view of the world that causes problems. Aaron Beck (1967) assumes that the way people think is critically important in determining how they feel and behave. He contends that depressives have problems in the way they have learned to view themselves, their world, and their futures.

Depression is often easily diagnosed. In Box 8.6, we present a diary entry by novelist Virginia Woolf (1953), who was probably a manic-depressive, written shortly before she committed suicide.

Beck (1967) developed a scale to assess how positive or negative men's and women's attitudes are. The Beck Depression Inventory is often used to diagnose depression and in conducting research on that illness. A typical depression scale might look much like the one in Table 8.2.

*D*epression is a "contagious disease."
ANONYMOUS

Depression can, of course, be diagnosed in other ways. Therapists can generally tell who is depressed and who is not by observing their own emotions. Interestingly enough, depression seems to be contagious. (See Hatfield & Rapson, 1990, for a discussion of this process.) Depressives may try to put a bright face on things, but they signal their despair via a variety of minute gestures—anguished facial micro-movements, tone of voice, and posture. Therapists may not be able to identify how they know something is wrong, but they do. For instance, they keep finding themselves nodding off, as if the depressed have sucked all of the energy out of them. Not only therapists "catch" depression. Mary Howes, Jack Hokanson, and David Lowenstein (1985) found that if college students were mildly depressed, their roommates tended to become more and more depressed as they continued to live with them.

Beck's notion that cognitive factors play a substantial role in the genesis of depression has considerable support. Depressives do see themselves as deficient and unworthy, the world as frustrating and unfulfilling, and their future as hopeless. Take the case of one depressed woman. She was trying

BOX 8.5

Anaclitic Depression

Some evidence supports Freud's first proposition—that early traumas predispose people to depression. In the 1940s, Rene Spitz (1946) began to study "anaclitic depression."

Here is a typical case history:

> ... No significant events or behavior during the first half year. She is a particularly friendly child who smiles brilliantly at the approach of the experimenter.
>
> When she was 7½ months old we noticed that her radiant smiling behavior had ceased. During the following two weeks it was impossible to approach her, as she slept heavily during the total of 12 hours we were there. After this period a change of behavior took place. . . .
>
> She lay immobile in her crib. When approached she did not lift her shoulders, barely her head, to look at the experimenter with an expression of profound suffering sometimes seen in sick animals. . . . As soon as the observer started to speak to her or to touch her she began to weep. This was not the usual crying of babies which is always accompanied by a certain amount of vocalization going into screaming. It was a soundless weeping, tears running down her face. Speaking to her in soft comforting tones only resulted in the weeping becoming more intense, intermingled with moans and sobs, shaking her whole body.
>
> In the course of a two months' observation it was found that this reaction deepened. It was more and more difficult to make contact with the child. . . . In this period she lost weight and developed a serious feeding disturbance, having great difficulties in taking any food and in keeping it down.
>
> After two months a certain measure was taken. The syndrome disappeared. (pp. 313–342)

The "certain measure" was the return of the child's mother.

Spitz studied children in a nursery and a foundling home who had been abandoned by their mothers for reasons beyond the mothers' control. He found that once children become aware of how their mother differs from all others (between six and eight months), they become vulnerable. After three months of abandonment, children are often quite depressed. If their mothers fail to return for even longer, they may die. Spitz found that the mortality rate of infants at the foundling home was inordinately high. In the course of two years, 34 of the 91 children died of diseases varying from respiratory and intestinal infections to measles.

Analysts worry that even if the children survive such early experiences, they may be forever vulnerable to depression. They speak of a "kindling" effect. Early experience provides the kindling. Later experiences provide the spark that ignites the firestorm. Evidence justifies their concern (Solsberry & Krupnick, 1984). For example, Aaron Beck (1967) of the University of Pennsylvania found that the death of a parent in childhood predisposes people to severe depressions in adulthood. A full 27% of the severely depressed (on the Beck Depression Inventory) had lost either or both parents before age 16, compared with only 15.5% of the moderately depressed and 12% of the nondepressed. Later stress merely sets things in motion.

BOX 8.6

A Page From Virginia Woolf's Diary

Lord how I suffer! What a terrific capacity I possess for feeling with intensity—now, since we came back, I'm screwed up into a ball; can't get into step; can't make things dance; feel awfully detached; see young; feel old; no, that's not quite it: wonder how a year or so perhaps is to be endured. Think, yet people do live; can't imagine what goes on behind faces. All is surface hard; myself only an organ that takes blows, one after another; the horror of the hard raddled faces in the flower show yesterday: the inane pointlessness of all this existence: hatred of my own brainlessness and indecision; the old treadmill feeling, of going on and on and on, for no reason: Lytton's death; Carrington's; a long-ing to speak to him; all that cut away, gone: . . . women: my book on professions: shall I write another novel; contempt for my lack of intellectual power; reading Wells without understanding; . . . society; buying clothes; Rodmell spoilt; all England spoilt: terror at night of things generally wrong in the universe; buying clothes; how I hate Bond Street and spending money on clothes: worst of all is this dejected barrenness. And my eyes hurt: and my hand trembles.

A saying of Leonard's comes into my head in this season of complete inanity and boredom. "Things have gone wrong somehow." (p. 171)

to keep house, raise her 18-month-old son, and conduct a full-time corporate law practice. Her husband, an advertising executive, was a very nervous man who became extremely angry anytime his daily routine was disturbed. At the slightest irritation, he would lash out verbally at his wife. When their toddler got sick while his mother was in court and could not be reached, the husband accused his wife of being an unnatural, unfeeling mother. Yet, when the bills began to pile up, he criticized her for not investing more in her career. He accused her of being a "freeloader" who couldn't pull her weight. When she was too tired to go to a movie with him, he said, without irony, "Women need less sleep than men." Surprisingly, this woman, who was so quick and feisty in court was such a pushover at home. She responded to each of his attacks by meekly accepting his criticism and berating herself for being so stupid. She continually resolved to do better next time.

Once cognitive psychologists have identified depression, the next step is to treat it. They have to replace clients' self-defeating ideas with more constructive ways of thinking. A 12-week treatment program developed by Beck combines cognitive and behavioral techniques to treat depression (Kovacs & Beck, 1985). In the initial treatment sessions, patients are asked to monitor and record their automatic, negative thoughts. (A running critique is typical: "I'm a poor father." "People must think I'm crazy." In the previously described case, the woman soon had a long litany of self-criticism: "You are a terrible mother. You should be spending more time with your child." "You are a terrible lawyer. You should be spending more time at work." "Why aren't you doing volunteer work? Selfish, selfish."

Table 8.2   **Typical Depression Inventory**

Which of the following statements best describes your feelings and behavior during the past week? Please circle the answer that seems most appropriate.

1. How is your appetite?

   1 Fine.
   2 Average.
   3 I have little interest in food.

2. How interested are you in sex?

   1 Quite interested.
   2 As interested as anyone else.
   3 I have no interest in sex.

3. How well are you sleeping these days?

   1 I am sleeping as much as I usually do.
   2 I am sleeping much more than I used to.
   3 I wake up early in the morning and have trouble getting back to sleep.

4. How optimistic/pessimistic are you about the future?

   1 I am optimistic about the future.
   2 I am uncertain about the future.
   3 I am pessimistic about the future.

5. How often do you cry?

   1 Rarely.
   2 Often.
   3 I feel like crying but am too depressed to even do that.

6. Are you thinking of killing yourself?

   1 No.
   2 Yes.

7. How would you do it? _____.

   Interviewer should rate plan:

   1 No plan.
   2 Sketchy plan.
   3 Well-conceived plan.

The higher the score, the more depressed a person is assumed to be.

The therapist can then proceed to help clients quit running old tapes and to see things a bit more realistically. For example, in the case of the woman we have just discussed, she began to realize that she had adopted a strategy of short-term appeasement by inevitably responding to each of her husband's attacks with self-criticism and attempts to appease him. Her therapist insisted that she and her husband sit down, when things were going well, and hammer out an agreement as to exactly how much time he and she would spend on household tasks, child care, and work. Then, when the inevitable disaster struck and her husband started to rant and rave, this was her signal to remind herself, "Slow down. He is just angry. You are doing exactly what the two of you agreed you should do. Hooray for you for being so calm. Shame on him for yelling at you." Essentially, she had learned to replace self-critical cognitions with self-nurturing ones. In time, when faced with her calm but unrelenting reaction, her husband learned that when he felt extremely anxious, he'd better go jogging because he was not going to get away with verbally attacking her. In time, she learned to coolly appraise a situation before responding to anyone's criticism . . . and to hire a full-time housekeeper.

Part of Beck's cognitive behavioral therapy, then, is simply teaching people how the world works. Therapists also help clients change their behavior—to prod them into planning enjoyable and productive activities and figuring out how to sweeten or avoid the tasks they hate. This challenges patients' beliefs that they are helpless and replaces them with a sense of accomplishment. Beck's cognitive therapy has been shown to be quite effective.

One's lowest ebb is nearest a true vision.
VIRGINIA WOOLF

Learned Helplessness. Martin Seligman and his colleagues argue that people are especially vulnerable to depression if they have been taught to be helpless. Early in his career, Seligman (1975) and his colleagues found that experimental animals could be taught "learned helplessness"—that they could do nothing to avoid pain, so they may as well give up and accept it. In this research, a group of dogs was restrained in harnesses and repeatedly shocked (Seligman & Maier, 1967). In this first situation, the dogs were truly helpless—they could neither avoid shock nor escape from it. Then, in a new situation, a hurdle-jumping task, the rules were changed. Now, the dogs did have control over their fate. All they had to do was learn what it took to avoid or escape shock—jump. But it was too late. Most simply stood there; they had learned to be helpless. By contrast, naïve dogs (who had not been systematically taught that "nothing worked") quickly learned how to avoid the shock.

At first, Seligman and his colleagues assumed that people learn to be depressed and passive in exactly the same way. They become depressed when they learn that their situation is uncontrollable, give up, and fall victim to learned helplessness. In the case history shown in Box 8.7, Seligman contends that "Mel" was being systematically taught to be helpless.

Seligman argued that people, like laboratory animals, begin to show motivational, cognitive, and emotional deficits when their lives are out of control;

BOX 8.7

Mel: A Case of Learned Helplessness

For the last twenty years, Mel has been a rising executive; up until a year ago, he had been in charge of production for a multimillion-dollar company involved in the space program. When the government decreased its financial support of space research, he lost his job, and was forced to take a new executive position in another city, in a company he described as "backbiting." After six miserable and lonely months he quit. For a month he sat listlessly around the house, and made no effort to find work; the slightest annoyance drove him into a rage; he was unsocial and withdrawn. Finally his wife prevailed on Mel to take some vocational guidance tests that might help him to find a satisfying job.

When the results came back, they revealed that he had a low tolerance for frustration, that he was unsociable, that he was incapable of taking on responsibility, and that routine, prescribed work best fit his personality. The vocational guidance company recommended that he become a worker on an assembly line.

This advice came as a shock to Mel and his wife, since he had twenty years of high executive achievement behind him, and was usually outgoing and persuasive, and was much brighter than most sewing-machine operators. But the tests actually reflected his present state of mind: he believed himself incompetent, he saw his career as a failure, he found every small obstacle an insurmountable barrier, he was not interested in other people, and he could barely force himself to get dressed, much less to make important career decisions. But this profile did not give a true picture of Mel's character; rather it reflected a process, probably temporary, that had been going on since he lost his job—the disorder of depression. (Seligman, 1975, pp. 75–76)

Seligman would treat someone like Mel by teaching him to set a few realistic goals, to pursue them aggressively, to experience success—and thereby to regain his confidence that he can control the events that are important to him.

that depression and learned helplessness have much in common. In both, people (a) develop a negative cognitive set; (b) perform the same stereotyped, useless, behavior again and again; (c) initiate little new activity; (d) show little aggression; (e) show loss of appetite; and (f) undergo physiological changes, such as norepinephrine depletion.

Recently, however, Seligman and his colleagues (see Abramson, Seligman, & Teasdale, 1986) have also taken into account the fact that in depression, humans differ from animals in one critical way—people think. People ask themselves why they are helpless when their world seems out of their control, and their answers have a profound effect on how they respond to stress. It matters, for example, whether people believe they are responsible for their failures (a belief in personal helplessness) or whether everyone would have fared the same (a belief in universal helplessness). It matters whether people think they are helpless in only one situation (specific helplessness) or whether they are likely to fail all life's challenges (global helplessness); also, it is important whether their failures are transient or chronic. All these factors will shape whether people's self-esteem plummets or remains high, whether they become depressed or shrug off failure, whether they try again or give up, after a devastating failure.

Early in life, people seem to develop a habitual style for explaining events (Burns & Seligman, in press). Pessimists tend to attribute sad events (such as being turned down for a date or failing an exam) to personal flaws that will plague them forever. Other, more optimistic people assume that such mistakes can be remedied. They are confident that they can think through the problem, make whatever changes are necessary, and succeed the second or third time around. Few people are totally optimistic or pessimistic, of course; most see things in shades of gray.

> *Optimism, said Candide, is a mania for maintaining that all is well when things are going badly.*
> *VOLTAIRE*

The evidence suggests that a little positive thinking is probably a good thing. At one time, psychologists took it for granted that the well-adjusted perceive the world as it is and that depressives distort reality—seeing themselves as more helpless and the world as more hopeless than it really is. Surprisingly, since that time researchers have found that it is the optimists, the well-adjusted, who engage in self-serving distortions—seeing themselves as more powerful and the world as more manageable than it really is (Alloy & Abramson, 1988). The depressed are "sadder but wiser." For example, a number of laboratory studies have systematically varied subjects' control over a game's outcome. Some games are skill games in which one has a great deal of control. Some are games of chance. Others fall somewhere in between. Nondepressed students have an "illusion of control." They assume they have more power than they really do. In most situations, depressives are more accurate and realistic. (Only in a very few situations do they underestimate their own power.)

Most individuals show self-serving biases—taking credit for their successes and explaining away their failures. Depressives seem to be far more evenhanded in assigning responsibility for events. For example, in one recent study, Alloy and Abramson (1988) studied the reactions of University of Wisconsin students to academic successes and failures. Most students' attributions for events were designed to put themselves in the best possible light. When they succeeded, they tended to take full credit. When they failed, they blamed others. Depressed students were inclined to evaluate themselves and their performances more accurately; they blamed themselves when things went awry. The authors concluded that most of us possess illusions which protect us from harsh reality. The depressed seem to have lost their capacity for distorting painful reality.

Several studies indicate that people who are in the habit of blaming themselves for their misfortunes may be especially susceptible to disease. For example, Christopher Peterson and his colleagues (1987) studied members of the Harvard graduating classes of 1942 to 1944. Initially, the men were interviewed at the end of World War II, when they were in their twenties. After that point, class members had complete physical examinations every five years. The authors found that when they were 25, optimists (men who tended to attribute bad events to external, unstable, and specific causes) and pessimists (men who attributed bad events to internal, stable, and global causes) were equally healthy mentally and physically. As time passed, however, a pessimistic explanatory style began to take its toll. Men who were optimistic in their twenties, had better health in their forties, fifties, and sixties than did the pessimists. Late in life, constitutional factors began to dominate the health picture.

The researchers were not quite sure exactly why explanatory style should affect health in middle age. Perhaps the pessimists' feelings of depression and helplessness began to take a toll on the immune system and decreased their ability to resist tumors and infections. Perhaps pessimists, who after all believe that there is little they can do to shape their lives, may have neglected their health—smoking, drinking, and failing to exercise. (Of course, it is always possible that pessimists got to be pessimistic because they are less competent, less healthy, or have had objectively more difficult lives than have others.) It is also possible that positive thinking works better in a country that extols positive thinking such as the United States, than it does in cultures that are more oriented toward realism, such as France. There, people who were too positive thinking could seem abnormal and less well adjusted (Rapson, 1988).

Seligman's learned helplessness model of depression has been a popular one. Nonetheless, it has not been without its critics (cf. Brewin, 1985).

Behavioral Models of Depression

A variety of other theorists argue that people's moods depend on how often they receive social rewards or punishments (Lewinsohn, 1986; Rehm & Plakosh, 1975; Skinner, 1953; Staats & Heiby, 1985).

For instance, Lynn Rehm and his co-workers focus on problems of self-management, that is, the way people get organized to work for long-term goals. Depressive people, he believes, eliminate the positive and accentuate the negative. They are their own severest critics. They shrug off their successes and dwell on their failures, focusing on short-term successes and failures and neglecting the long-term consequences. Rehm trains people to turn things around—to monitor, evaluate, and reward their behavior more realistically.

God gave a Loaf to every Bird
But just a Crumb to Me

EMILY DICKINSON

Peter Lewinsohn (1974 a and b) and his colleagues at the University of Oregon focus on depressives' pleasureless lives. Some depressives lack social skills. Family and friends may give them a few "rewards" for their self-pity and suffering; others are less kind. Depressives get little reward of any kind. To make matters worse, the depressed continue to be buffeted by a series of painful life events. Lewinsohn and Talkington (1979) developed the Unpleasant Events Schedule, which asks how often in the past 30 days a series of disasters has happened (accidents, school failures, mishaps, delays, sexual rejections, encounters with the police, or financial losses). As you might expect, the depressed have unusually miserable lives in terms of their perceived frequency of unpleasant events. It is not surprising that they finally give up. To turn things around, Lewinsohn teaches clients a package of skills, including daily planning, time management, relaxation, and seeking out pleasant experiences or avoiding negative ones. Considerable evidence suggests that behavioral techniques can help (Heiby, 1979).

Biochemical Theories of Depression

Emotional experiences affect the brain's chemical activity. In turn, thoughts, feelings, and behavior can be radically altered by minute chemical changes in the brain. Billions of neurons send and receive electrical messages, via neurotransmitters, the chemicals that carry these messages across the synapses. Things can go wrong at a number of points. According to William Potter (quoted in Gallagher, 1986), "something amiss in this process—faulty synthesis of a transmitter, wrong amounts dispatched, excesses not withdrawn or broken down, receptor neurons malfunctioning—is fundamental to the biology of depression" (p. 69). Researchers hypothesize that in depression, the neurochemicals norepinephrine and serotonin (and possibly dopamine) are in short supply, consequently with profound effects. Norepinephrine and serotonin dispatch messages in the brain vital to such basic functions as appetite, sleep, sex, even the desire to live.

The brain also produces 50 or so hormones. Imbalances in the neurotransmitters can also trigger a chemical imbalance in the hypothalamus, which in turn produces a pituitary imbalance. This causes the adrenal glands to pump out too much cortisol—a stress-related hormone with wide-ranging physiological effects. As you learned in chapter 4, the sympathetic and parasympathetic systems have a reciprocal relation. Anything that increases sympathetic activity should counteract parasympathetic activity and reduce distress. This is complicated, however, by the fact that grief and depression are patterns of emotions. Distress may be the predominant emotion, but others—particularly anger, disgust, contempt, and guilt—are generally involved as well.

All these emotions involve neuroendocrine patterns and both the sympathetic and parasympathetic systems.

THE TREATMENT OF DEPRESSION

Drug Therapy

Consistent with the biochemical view of depression, today, psychiatrists generally use one of three somewhat different classes of drugs to treat this disorder. Interestingly enough, the forerunners of all these drugs were discovered by accident. For example, in the early 1950s, clinicians noticed that tuberculosis patients were generally "high" for some time after being treated with the antituberculosis agent, iproniazid. This drug turned out to be useless against fighting tuberculosis but unusually effective in fighting depression. Some of the drugs used in treatment today are explained next.

The Tricyclics (TCAs). The most commonly prescribed class of agents used to combat the major depressions, especially unipolar depression, are the tricyclics, which have a range of diverse effects. Initially, psychiatrists thought that the TCAs worked by blocking the re-uptake of serotonin and norepinephrine, thus leaving more of those neurotransmitters available in the synapses (see Figures 8.4 to 8.6). Now it is known that the TCAs have a variety of complex influences. The most popular tricyclics are imipramine and amitriptyline. Clinicians start by prescribing relatively low doses of such drugs

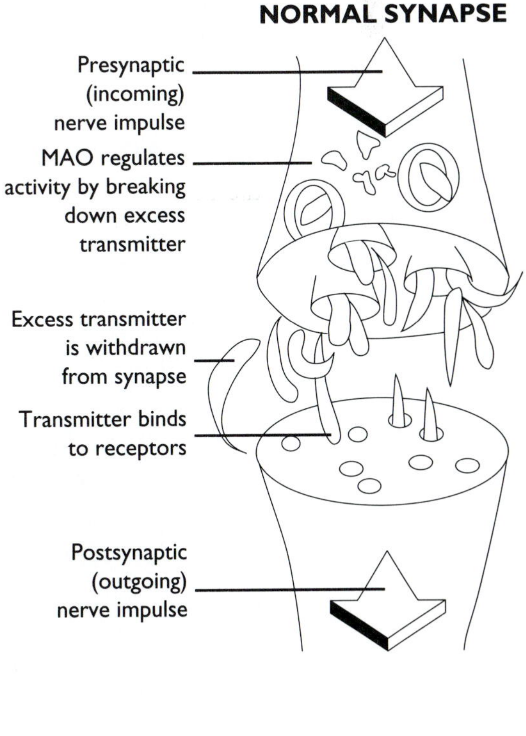

NORMAL SYNAPSE

Presynaptic (incoming) nerve impulse

MAO regulates activity by breaking down excess transmitter

Excess transmitter is withdrawn from synapse

Transmitter binds to receptors

Postsynaptic (outgoing) nerve impulse

FIGURE 8.4 A normal synapse.

EFFECT OF TRICYCLICS

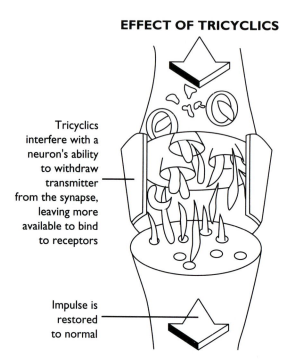

Tricyclics interfere with a neuron's ability to withdraw transmitter from the synapse, leaving more available to bind to receptors

Impulse is restored to normal

FIGURE 8.5   The effect of tricyclics.

and increasing them slowly to the point of maximum effectiveness. Patients usually begin to respond in two to four weeks and take the drugs for a few months to a year. By then, their moods should have stabilized. Unfortunately, the TCAs sometimes have side effects—including blurred vision, dryness of mouth, heart palpitations, rashes, weight gain, and fatigue (Schatzberg & Cole, 1986).

Monoamine Oxidase Inhibitors (MAOIs). Drugs such as Marplan or Desyrel are often used with patients who are both anxious and depressed. MAOIs reduce the activity of MAO, an enzyme that breaks down neurotransmitters into their metabolites (see Figure 8.6). Unfortunately, these drugs also produce undesirable side effects, such as dizziness. Patients may not eat or drink certain foods and beverages while they are taking MAOIs, including beer, wine, coffee, cheeses, pickled herring, yeast, or canned figs. If they do, they may develop severe headaches and/or elevated blood pressure, or they may lapse into a coma. (These foods increase the sympathetic nervous system's activity; they increase blood pressure and heart rate.) Normally, these effects are kept in check by MAO, which is present in the blood and other tissues of the body. When the MAOI knocks out the MAO's neutralizing effects, however, blood pressure and heart rate can soar. Thus, these foods must be avoided (see Schatzberg & Cole, 1986).

Lithium. The drug lithium seems particularly effective in the treatment of

EFFECT OF MAO INHIBITORS

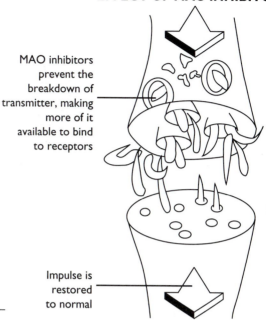

MAO inhibitors prevent the breakdown of transmitter, making more of it available to bind to receptors

Impulse is restored to normal

FIGURE 8.6 The effect of MAO Inhibitors.

recurrent bipolar depression. Exactly how lithium acts in the body is not yet known. Its effects, however, are. Lithium seems to smooth out people's mood swings—the manic highs are no longer out of control; the depressive lows are no longer so devastatingly low. The most common side effects are tremor, rashes, and weight gain (Schatzberg & Cole, 1986).

Other Therapies for Depression

Both drugs and psychotherapy are quite effective in eliminating the various forms of depression. Both seem equally effective; both succeed with 60% to 80% of depressed patients (Rosenfeld, 1985).

Recently, the National Institutes of Mental Health (NIMH) sponsored a six-year, $10-million research program with 28 therapists from Pennsylvania, Oklahoma, and Washington. They were attempting to learn which treatments psychiatrists ought to use with which kinds of patients (Leo, 1986; Mervis, 1986). The NIMH study compared the effectiveness of drug therapy with two kinds of brief therapy. In drug therapy, patients were given a standard antidepressant drug, imipramine. Other patients received 16 weeks of brief psychotherapy—either cognitive behavior therapy (Beck, 1976), discussed earlier in this chapter, or interpersonal psychotherapy, which primarily involves teaching people how to interact more appropriately with others (see Klerman & Clayton, 1984). A fourth group was given a placebo as well as support and encouragement. The results were twofold:

a) All the approaches reduced the symptoms of depression; however, symptoms were eliminated completely in 50–60% of the patients who received one of the active treatments and in only 29% of those who received the placebo plus support and encouragement.

b) The drugs seemed to work most quickly. After 12 weeks, however, the psychotherapies were equally successful. It is clear that available therapies—drug therapy, psychotherapy, or both in combination—seem to be quite effective in reducing depression.

Summing Up

- Sadness is "having or expressing low spirits or sorrow." Grief is "intense emotional suffering caused by loss, disaster, or misfortune." Depression is "a state of lowered initiative or inaccessibility to stimulation."

- In studying the development of emotions such as sadness, researchers use a multimethod approach to draw inferences about infants' feelings. They employ several measures, including facial expression, vocalizations, and the overall quality of behavioral activity.

- At birth, infants are capable of experiencing a number of emotions. Other aspects of emotional experience and expression develop over time. For example, one of the first things infants have to learn is emotional self-regulation.

- Infants show individual differences in hedonic tone, emotionality, and ability to regulate emotional arousal. The reaction of caretakers to infants contributes to these individual differences.

- In grief, the bereaved are shocked initially; because the facts have not yet sunk in, they cope well. In a few months, however, numbness turns to pain, and the bereaved are especially vulnerable to mental and physical illness. Finally, they reach some resolution of these feelings.

- Depression is one of mankind's oldest psychological disorders. It is a disorder that appears, in part, to be genetically transmitted.

- Psychoanalysts such as Abraham, Freud, Arieti, and Bibring have argued that early traumatic experiences such as a separation or a loss of a parent at a critical stage may make one vulnerable to depression. A later loss may trigger renewed depression.

- Beck proposes a cognitive model of depression. He argues that depressives have problems in the way they view themselves, their world, and their futures.

- Seligman's learned helplessness model holds that the belief that outcomes are uncontrollable leads to depression's cognitive, motivational, and emotional deficits. Recently, Seligman and his colleagues have recognized that cognitive factors are critically important in determining how people respond to uncontrollable situations.

- Behavioral theorists, such as Lewinsohn, argue that people's moods depend on how often they receive social rewards and punishments.

- Thoughts, feelings, and behavior can be radically altered by minute chemical changes in the brain. In depression, the neurochemicals norepinephrine, serotonin, and possibly dopamine are in short supply.

- In the treatment of depression, drugs and psychotherapy appear to be equally effective, but drugs have a variety of side effects.

9

Happiness and Joy

Introduction and Definitions

Happiness
The Nature of Happiness
The Experience of Happiness
How Happy Are Most People?
The Raw Materials of Happiness
The Relative Nature of Happiness: Is That All There Is?

Arranging for a Happy and Just Life
The Happy Life
Justice

Joy
The Experience of Joy and Ecstasy
The Anatomy of Joy
The Chemistry of Joy
Richard Solomon's Opponent Process Theory
Going With the Flow

Summing Up

FIGURE 9.1 *Shrovetide Revellers ("The Merry Company")*. Frans Hals. ca. 1615. 51¾" x 39". Courtesy The Metropolitan Museum of Art.

Introduction and Definitions

When people are desperate and they have no way to beg, borrow, or earn the money they need, their fantasies often turn to life's lotteries. "If only I could win the New York Lottery," ". . . break the bank at Monte Carlo," ". . . win the McDonald's Sweepstakes." But when we look at lottery winners' emotional reactions to their good fortunes, we discover that life does not always work out as hoped. Sometimes, winning does fulfill their deepest dreams. Sometimes, winners do invest their money and ensure a calm, easy life for themselves and their families. But on occasion, the dreams becomes nightmares.

Stories like that of Clayton C. Woods, an early Irish Sweepstakes winner, have been replayed throughout the years. Woods was a factory worker at the Fisher motor-body factory in Buffalo, New York. He bought a ticket on the 1931 Irish Sweepstakes and then talked four relatives—his wife, brother Kenneth, and brothers-in-law, Elmer and Clarence Batt—into chipping in to pay for the ticket. They won $886,630. (In 1931, that was an enormous amount of money. For example, Clayton was earning only $50 a week at the time.) But it wasn't long before Clayton and his relatives had to begin fighting to keep their winnings. The city of Buffalo announced that, under an old law, it planned to confiscate 100% of the winnings and use them for the poor. The IRS demanded 50% of the winnings. In short, Clayton was told that he might now owe 150% of his Sweepstakes bonanza! Letters begging for charity came in by the sackful. Investors camped outside the house. In panic, the four families fled to Canada and sought refuge in the wilderness. Eventually, the city of Buffalo relented, and the winners received their money. They were granted $647,491. The rest went for taxes.

After all this anxiety, it would be grand to report that they lived happily ever after, but they didn't. Clayton Woods's marriage could not stand the stress. It broke up. Kenneth Woods's wife suffered an emotional disorder. Elmer Batt was arrested for molesting a 15-year-old girl, was released on bail, and was found dead the next day. All attributed their troubles to the lottery (Webb, 1968).

Through the ages, social observers have contended that man is selfish and relentless in his search for happiness and joy. Moral philosophers argue that the ideal society is one which ensures the "greatest good for the greatest number." Psychologists build their theories on the assumption that people try to maximize pleasure and avoid pain. Economists assume that consumers search out the best bargains. Given the amount of effort people have expended in the pursuit of joy and happiness, it is surprising that they still haven't discovered a foolproof way to find it. You still "can't buy happiness."

Also, as yet, psychologists have devised no comprehensive theory of happiness. There exists no set of carefully interlocking experiments to illuminate its nature. Perhaps this has to do with the nature of happiness itself. Some anthropologists and neuroscientists, for example, have suggested that the brain may be incapable of experiencing sustained joy. If primitive people sat around the campfire, week after week, in a state of ecstasy, they would probably not have survived for very long. Thus, the brain may be wired so that its neurotransmitters are capable only of sparking fleeting joy. Alas, this same brain is obviously capable of sparking enduring pain and suffering. (No doubt it was to primitive man's evolutionary advantage to be motivated to fight, run, or look for solutions for as long as trouble lasted.) Thus, the cynics argue, by its nature, joy may be fleeting, suffering long. On the other hand, psychologists' lack of knowledge about joy and happiness may simply be due to the fact that until recently, they devoted little attention to these emotions. Lois Murphy (1983) has written a scathing critique of the lack of attention given to the positive emotions:

> Scientific discussions sometimes seem to be written by people whose emotional experience is stingy or narrow; in psychology books, we encounter little reference to bliss, delight, ecstasy, passion, or even enthusiasm—and even less to tenderness, love, adoration, devotion, trust, reverence, feelings of inspiration. (p. 4)

Luckily, researchers have devoted at least some attention to joyous phenomena, and their research tells us something about these emotions. Let us begin by providing definitions of happiness and joy, and then we will turn to the gentler states of happiness. We will explore how happy most people seem to be, and what makes them happy. We will find that happiness is relative and, in part, people's definitions of fairness influence their happiness. Then we will review what we know about joy. We will consider religious ecstasy, the chemistry of joy, and states of "flow."

Turning to some specific definitions, recall that in chapter 5 Robert Plutchik (1980a) argued that people are capable of experiencing eight prototype emotions—joy and ecstasy, love and acceptance, fear, anger, sadness, disgust, expectancy, and surprise. Presumably, these ancient emotional reactions came to be genetically wired in because they helped our primitive ancestors survive. According to Plutchik, these basic emotions can vary in intensity. For example, happiness/joy can vary from the more tepid happiness and contentment to passionate joy and ecstasy. Presumably, these emotions are the same in their basic natures; they differ only in intensity.

Current definitions of these emotions are generally consistent with this view. They define happiness as "a state of well-being and contentment" (Webster & Webster, 1963, p. 379).

Joy is more intense: "an emotion, usually related to present experiences, highly pleasant and characterized by many outward signs of gratification" (p. 282).

These definitions of happiness and joy will be useful here. Let us now review what we know about these emotions.

Happiness

All men are . . . endowed by their Creator with certain unalienable rights; that among these are life, liberty, and the pursuit of happiness.

THE DECLARATION OF INDEPENDENCE

Happiness is a basic emotion. It is now generally accepted that the smiling response is innate and universal. Such sensitive observers of child development as Florence Goodenough (1932), Rene Spitz and Katherine Wolf (1946), Jacob Steiner (1979) and Peter Wolff (1959) have found that infants begin to show flickering happy smiles during the first hours, or at least days, of life. Such smiles typically occur during drowsiness or light sleep. (For newborns, happiness may be the "stuff of dreams." See Emde & Koenig, 1969.) Soon, these brief smiles evolve into social smiles. In the first week of life, newborns may smile at the sound of a high-pitched voice. By the fifth week, they smile at the sight of a human face. Peter Wolff (1963) concluded that the most powerful stimulus for eliciting the smile is the normal human face.

Infants vary in how cheerful they are. Murphy (1983) points out that initially, infants' first fleeting smiles are stimulated by pleasant smells or sweet tastes. As infants' cognitive-affective abilities evolve, however, their smiles change. At about four to six months of age, depending on the children's developmental level, they begin to smile when they recognize their fathers or mothers. Such smiles are often supplemented by excited bicycling of their limbs or even entire body lurching. By preschool age, American children often signal their delight in their parents' return from work with cries of "Daddy's home!" or "Mommy's home," rushing to embrace them, and jumping up and down (pp. 12–13).

A smiling infant possesses a great advantage. Robert Emde (1980) describes with touching precision the way in which an infant's happy cooing and smiles reward its parents and the way in which the parents' delighted smiles, in turn, reward the baby's expressiveness. Happiness seems to be contagious. Smiles appear to be critical in ensuring parent/child bonding. If either parent or child is unresponsive to the other's smiles, smiling and interaction gradually decrease. If there is no reaction, why keep smiling?

THE NATURE OF HAPPINESS

Which factors seem to shape happiness in later life? Philosophers have long reflected about the stuff of happiness. Aristotle argued that happiness comes from living a well-ordered life, doing that for which one is suited—the musician is happy playing music, the weaver weaving. Both would be miserable if required to do otherwise. The Epicureans proposed that happiness comes from maximizing pleasure and minimizing pain. The economic theorist Jeremy Bentham concluded that the happiest societies are those that promote the greatest good for the greatest number.

Such definitions seem to be most appropriate in societies of abundance. When the conditions of life are more difficult, theories of happiness acquire a different emphasis. Plato insisted that in the end, happiness must depend only on living virtuously, which is all that is under human control. The Stoics took it one step further, pointing out that people are not in control of their fates. In the course of their lives they are likely to encounter sickness, poverty, heartbreak, and death. Thus, the Stoics argued, ultimate happiness can come only from indifference to pleasure or pain.

What about today? What do most people mean by happiness? What produces happiness? Several factors seem to be important. First, at the most primitive level, people will be happiest when their basic needs (for food, shelter, safety, belongingness, and esteem) are met. But happiness is more complicated than that. Happiness depends as much on what people expect as on what they have. In part, people's happiness depends on how justly they feel they have been treated.

THE EXPERIENCE OF HAPPINESS

Happiness is no laughing matter.

BISHOP WATLEY

Joel Davitz (1969) asked men and women to describe what it felt like to be happy. They did this by indicating which of 556 descriptions of emotions applied to them. The reactions shown in Table 9.1 were most common. (The percentage of people checking each statement is indicated in parentheses at the end of the sentence.)

Table 9.1   The Feelings of Happiness

There is an inner warm glow, a radiant sensation (82%).
I feel like smiling (72%).
There is a sense of well-being, a sense of harmony and peace within (66%).
There is an inner buoyancy (64%).
A warm excitement (64%).
A sense of vitality, aliveness, vibrancy, an extra spurt of energy or drive (60%).
I keep thinking how lucky I am (56%).
I feel outgoing (56%).
I want to make others happy (50%).
I feel like singing (50%), like laughing (42%).
There is a sense of accomplishment, fulfillment (40%).

In their pioneering research, Norman Bradburn and David Caplovitz (1965) and Bradburn (1969) made two surprising discoveries: First, they discovered that different people tend to think about happiness in very different ways. Some are energetic optimists. They go for pleasure, without dwelling on the costs. Others are more cautious. They care less about ecstasy than about avoiding pain. For them, happiness is the absence of trouble. An example: After landing a particularly big account, a businessman celebrated by buying his wife a $26,000 diamond ring. He expected her to whoop with joy. What she did was begin to worry. Only after she had the diamond checked to be sure it had no flaws and purchased insurance could she relax.

Bradburn and Caplovitz's second finding was that happiness is not the opposite of unhappiness. They found this in a study in which people were asked:

"During the past few weeks did you ever feel . . ."

- Pleased about having accomplished something?
- Particularly excited or interested in something? and
- So restless that you couldn't sit long in a chair?
- Bored?
- Very lonely? (p. 17)

As they expected, the authors found that happiness is positively related to the positive events in a person's life and negatively related to distressing ones. A big surprise was that these two dimensions were totally independent of each other. This finding has been confirmed by later investigators (Argyle, 1987). Some people are simply passionate about their lives—they feel the good and the bad intensely. Others are fairly low key about everything (Diener, Sandvik, & Larsen, 1985). This means that if people are happy in most areas of their lives they can be intensely upset about an event or two (such as a sick child) and still be happy overall. This same partial independence of positive and negative affects has been found in studies of marital satisfaction (Argyle & Henderson, 1984). Couples can have strong positive feelings about each other (as assessed by frequency of intercourse, for example) as well as negative ones (as assessed by frequency of fights, for example). What seems to be important in determining how happy people are is the balance in their lives—overall, how happy minus unhappy are they? So today, researchers usually calculate happiness by assessing pleasure minus pain.

HOW HAPPY ARE MOST PEOPLE?

Since the 1930s, researchers such as Norman Bradburn and David Caplovitz (1965), Gerald Gurin, Joseph Veroff, and Sheila Feld (1960), and Warner Wilson (1967) have methodically interviewed samples of Americans to determine how happy they are. Survey researchers have assessed happiness via fairly straightforward measures. For example, Alden Wessman and David Ricks (1966) asked American students:

> How elated or depressed, happy or unhappy, did you feel today?
>
> 10. Complete elation. Rapturous joy and soaring ecstasy.
> 9. Very elated and in very high spirits. Tremendous delight and buoyancy.
> 8. Elated and in high spirits.
> 7. Feeling very good and cheerful.
> 6. Feeling pretty good, 'OK'.
> 5. Feeling a bit low. Just so-so.
> 4. Spirits low and somewhat 'blue'.
> 3. Depressed and feeling very low. Definitely 'blue'.
> 2. Tremendously depressed. Feeling terrible, miserable, 'just awful'.
> 1. Utter depression and gloom. Completely down. All is black and leaden. (p. 273)

On the average, men rated their happiness at 6.0; women, 6.14. Men's and women's feelings were surprisingly stable. Their scores varied only half a point one way or another each day.

Jonathan Freedman and Philip Shaver (reported in Freedman, 1978) asked *Psychology Today* readers to assess how happy they were and to tell them a bit about the things that made them happy. Fifty-two thousand readers, ranging in age from 15 to 95, replied. You might see how you would respond to their happiness questions (see Box 9.1).

Many people tend to think of happiness as a fairly rare commodity, assuming that only the young, healthy, and wealthy delight in life and that the old, handicapped, and ill must live in misery. This pessimistic vision seems to be wrong. A variety of studies, in different countries and at very different times, have asked people about their feelings. The results are remarkably similar: Most people are surprisingly happy most of the time. For example, in Freedman and Shaver's study of *Psychology Today* readers, 60% said that they had been "moderately happy" or "very happy" over the last six months. In more carefully controlled surveys, Angus Campbell (1981) and other survey researchers find that most people consistently report themselves to be happy—about 33% being "very happy" and about 50% being "pretty happy." Only about 10% are "not too happy." Campbell observes, "There appears to be a persistent human impulse to see the world positively, to feel positively about it, to remember it positively, and to use positive language in describing it" (p. 30).

For decades, demographers throughout the world have been assessing human happiness. For example, Elizabeth and Philip Hastings (1982) report the results of surveys sampling the happiness of more than 12,000 men and women in a variety of countries. "How happy do you feel as you live now?" they ask. In Table 9.2 you can see the replies.

In the *Psychology of Happiness*, Michael Argyle (1987) systematically reviewed the evidence on happiness. When one looks at surveys that ask people

BOX 9.1

Assessing Happiness

1. *In general,* how happy have you been? (Consider your *overall state of being,* without worrying about specific parts of your life.)

_____extremely unhappy
_____very unhappy
_____moderately unhappy
_____slightly unhappy
_____neutral
_____slightly happy
_____moderately happy
_____very happy
_____extremely happy

a. Over *the past few months?* The point of this question is to get at how you are feeling now—not this one day, but over the recent period in your life.

_____extremely unhappy
_____very unhappy
_____moderately unhappy
_____slightly unhappy
_____neutral
_____slightly happy
_____moderately happy
_____very happy
_____extremely happy

b. Over *the past five years?* This may be difficult, but try to assess your average level of happiness over this period.

_____extremely unhappy
_____very unhappy
_____moderately unhappy
_____slightly unhappy
_____neutral
_____slightly happy
_____moderately happy
_____very happy
_____extremely happy

c. *During your life up to now?* This is the hardest of all, because it is difficult to combine events and feelings from years ago with those of today, but try to assess your whole life. How happy would you say it has been?

_____extremely unhappy
_____very unhappy
_____moderately unhappy
_____slightly unhappy
_____neutral
_____slightly happy
_____moderately happy
_____very happy
_____extremely happy

how happy and satisfied they are with their lives, citizens of North America, Europe, and Australia report that they are the happiest. Other investigators have been reluctant to merely take people's word for how happy they are. (They worried that perhaps some groups, such as Americans, might feel they ought to be happy, while other groups, such as the French, might feel that they ought to be realistic. If this is so, the result might be biased.) Thus, they looked at both self-reports of happiness and at a variety of social indicators—how good schools were, how good mental and general health services were, whether or not the country had free art galleries, concerts, and so forth. When one looks at such social indicators of happiness, the happiest countries seem to be Great Britain, Australia, New Zealand, and the Netherlands.

Table 9.2   **The Happiness of People in Various Countries**

COUNTRIES SURVEYED	HOW HAPPY DO YOU FEEL AS YOU LIVE NOW?					
	NO ANSWER	VERY HAPPY	FAIRLY HAPPY	NEITHER HAPPY/ UNHAPPY	FAIRLY UNHAPPY	VERY UNHAPPY
Australia	46%	44%	8%	1%	1%	–%
Brazil	40	36	21	1	1	1
Canada	39	50	8	3	–	–
France	16	51	31	2	–	–
India	14	51	25	8	2	–
Italy	10	52	31	5	1	1
Japan	12	45	40	2	1	–
Philippines	18	50	27	5	–	–
Singapore	32	58	7	3	–	–
South Korea	5	34	56	4	1	–
United Kingdom	47	44	6	2	1	–
United States	42	48	7	2	1	–
West Germany	12	49	36	1	–	2

Adapted from Hastings and Hastings, *Happiness of People in Various Countries,* 1979 (1982), pp. 538–545.

Within Europe, Belgium, Denmark, the Netherlands, and Britain are happier than France, Germany, or Italy.

Elaine and Arthur Aron (1987) contend that happiness is the normal human condition—it is the "neutral gear" of the nervous system. When people are allowed some perspective, some rest, and some time to turn inward, this background state of happiness appears. They cite an array of studies in support of this contention. For example, some researchers have found a strong positive relationship between the amount and quality of sleep students have had the night before and their euphoria and happiness the next day (Barry & Bousfield, 1935; Bousfield, 1942). Also, during meditation, people often report experiencing deep happiness.

Paradoxically, people who engage in frantic activity in search of the good life may be buying a life of tension and conflict rather than the happiness they seek. Calm, rest, and tranquility seem to be the *sine qua non* of happiness. Can anything else make a contribution?

THE RAW MATERIALS OF HAPPINESS

Nobody shall say of me that I have not known perfect happiness, but few could put their finger on the moment or say what made it.

                                        VIRGINIA WOOLF

Researchers have found that several factors seem to be important in shaping happiness.

A Talent for Happiness

In part, happiness seems to be a personality trait or "mental set." What are people with a talent for happiness like? John Robinson and Phillip L. Shaver (1969) provide some clues:

> Persons of high self-esteem or personal competence express more satisfaction with life. Satisfaction has also been found to be greater among people who are better socially adjusted, who demonstrate more trust in people, who feel less alienated, and who suffer less from anxiety, worry, and psychosomatic symptoms. (p. 35)

Both Angus Campbell (1981) and Richard Kammann (1982) argue that some people possess a "happiness set," which causes them to perceive something wonderful in the small happenings of daily life and to downplay their painful experiences. Other researchers have found that happy people process information selectively. They are more likely to pay attention to and remember (or even exaggerate) pleasant information than they are unpleasant information (Matlin & Stang, 1978; Matlin & Gawron, 1979; Dember & Penwell, 1980). Interestingly enough, we found in chapter 8 that depressed people are more accurate in their judgments of reality. They recall both good and bad events with equal, and unsettling, clarity.

Researchers find that reality plays a part in shaping happiness, too.

Happiness: a good bank account, a good cook, and a good digestion.

JEAN-JACQUES ROUSSEAU

Satisfaction of Basic Needs

To some extent, people are more likely to be happy when their basic needs are fulfilled. For example, Warner Wilson (1967) proposed that "prompt satisfaction of needs causes happiness, while the persistence of unfulfilled needs causes unhappiness" (p. 302). He suggested that three types of needs are important: (a) recurrent physiological needs such as food and shelter; (b) pleasure-seeking needs, such as stimulation and action; and (c) acquired secondary needs, such as affection, acceptance, status, achievement, and self-actualization. Today, many psychologists assume that happiness can be predicted by a simple hedonic equation: People will judge their lives to be happy if the sum of their pleasures and satisfactions is greater than the sum of their pains and dissatisfactions (Shelly, 1973).

Abraham Maslow (1954), however, argued that it is more complex than that, suggesting a hierarchy of human needs, arranged in this order of priority:

- The basic human needs: food, air, sleep, shelter, and so forth.
- The safety needs: security, stability, protection, freedom from fear, need for order, limits, and so forth.
- The belongingness needs: love, affection, and belonging.
- The esteem needs: self-esteem and esteem of others: the desire for achievement, strength, adequacy, independence and freedom. The desire for reputation, status, fame and glory, dominance, recognition, attention, dignity, and appreciation.
- Self-actualization needs: the desire to become all that one can be; individualistic, artistic, compassionate, and altruistic.

Maslow argued that people must satisfy their basic needs before higher needs can emerge. At the lowest levels of subsistence, it is all that a person can do to worry about basic concerns such as hunger, thirst, or sex. At this primitive level, people are happy if they have enough to eat and a place to live. Once these needs are fulfilled, however, they are free to move on to higher concerns. At the next levels, happiness will depend on safety, then on having someone to love, then on occupational success. Finally, once people have all that they need, they reach a stage where self-actualization becomes important. They become interested in self-fulfillment, the arts, and helping humankind. (Maslow thought the fact that people continued to want more was all to the good. Later, you will see that other theorists have taken a more pessimistic view of this fact.)

That is the theory. To what extent is it supported by the facts? In a half-century of surveys on happiness, researchers have found that one's objective circumstances do have some impact on happiness (Argyle, 1987; Diener, 1984)—but not as much as one might expect. The potpourri of factors shown in Table 9.3 seem to be most important in promoting happiness, although they differ in how significant they are for each of us.

Argyle (1987) surveys several factors—marriage, work, leisure, and health—that contribute to satisfaction; and others—anxiety, depression, and stressful life events—that contribute to psychological distress, with its devastating impact on happiness.

Table 9.3   Factors Promoting Happiness

Love	Friends and social life	Independence
Marriage	Education	Personal values
Sex	Work	Community involvement
Children	Income	House or apartment
Exercise, recreation	Recognition, success	City lived in
Health		

Close Relationships

When psychologists ask people what makes them happiest, close relations are high on their lists. For example, in one study researchers asked almost 500 men and women to take a look at a list of major positive events and to rate (on a scale ranging from 0 to 100) how much "happiness, satisfaction, or well-being" they believed each would bring to people in general (Henderson, Argyle, & Furnham, 1984). The most highly rated events are shown in Table 9.4. Note that "falling in love" leads the list.

Sociologists find that married people are happier, on the average, than those who are unmarried, widowed, or divorced. For example, Joseph Veroff, Elizabeth Douvan, and Richard Kulka (1981) found that 35% of married men and 41.5% of married women report themselves as "very happy." Only 18.5% of single men and 25.5% of single women, and 18.5% of divorced men and 15.5% of divorced women report being that happy. Surprisingly, in most studies, sociologists find that men seem to derive more happiness from marriage than do women (Vanfossen, 1981; Bernard, 1973).

People who have more friends or who spend more time with their friends also tend to be happier (Larson, 1978). Friendships are especially important for young people and the elderly.

Children's contributions to a happy life are difficult to assess. Most people think they are a source of happiness. Couples insist that their children brought them closer together (Veroff, Douvan, & Kulka, 1981) and that they provided self-fulfillment, fun, love, and companionship (Hoffman & Manis, 1982). Yet, University of Michigan surveys consistently find that couples with children feel less adequate, have more marital problems, and worry more than do childless couples. Figure 9.2 summarizes the results of a number of studies of marital satisfaction at different points in the family cycle. It is obvious that

Table 9.4 Positive Life Events	
Falling in love	78.0%
Passing an examination or gaining a qualification	75.5
Recovering from a serious illness	72.1
Going on a holiday	68.9
Making up after an argument with your husband/wife or boy/girl friend	66.0
Getting married or engaged	65.0
Birth of a child	64.6
Winning a lot of money	64.4
Getting promoted at work or getting a pay raise	59.9
Going out with or visiting friends	58.0
Getting a new job	56.1

Argyle, 1987, p. 130. Original source, Henderson, Argyle, & Furnham, 1984.

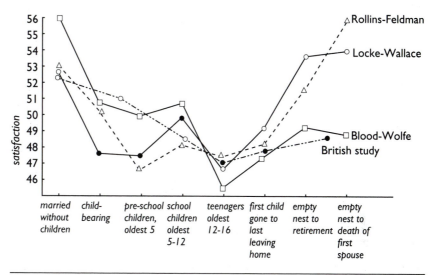

FIGURE 9.2   Marital satisfaction and the family life cycle. Argyle, 1987. Source: Walker; 1977, p. 131.

marital happiness is at an all-time low when children are in the home, especially adolescent children.

> *W*ork consists of whatever a body is **obliged** to do. . . . Play consists of whatever a body is not obliged to do.
>
> MARK TWAIN IN
> "THE ADVENTURES OF TOM SAWYER"

Work and Unemployment

In general, a happy marriage makes a far bigger contribution to overall happiness than does anything else, work included. When one is stuck in an unfulfilling job or unemployed, however, suddenly the equation changes. Job dissatisfaction and unemployment are the greatest source of unhappiness (Benin & Nienstedt, 1985). When men and women lose their jobs, their mental health may deteriorate, they lose their identities, status, and social contacts (along with their incomes) and they may become depressed, physically ill, or even suicidal (Argyle, 1987).

Most Americans believe that with a little more money they would be far happier. Yet, in the United States, economic improvement does not seem to bring increased happiness (Easterlin, 1973; Gallup, 1977). For example, Richard Easterlin (1973) found that: "In the United States, the average level of happiness in 1970 was not much different from what it had been in the late 1940s, though average income, after allowance for taxes and inflation, could buy 60% more [in 1970]" (p. 7).

Regardless of their incomes, Americans continue to insist that only 10% or 20% more money would make them happy (Strumpel, 1976). How can we explain such findings? Researchers point out that beyond the subsistence level, happiness is relative. The things that were luxuries yesterday—fruit in the winter, television sets, dishwashers—become tomorrow's necessities as soon as we become accustomed to having them. Thus, most people end up feeling that their needs outstrip their "sparse" incomes.

Leisure

Many psychologists assume that leisure is done for intrinsic rewards, for the fun of it, while work is goal directed, performed for extrinsic rewards. Leisure activities are a major source of life satisfaction; the primary forms of leisure are watching television, sports, social activities, clubs, classes, and volunteer activities.

Health

Health is closely linked with happiness. It appears to be a prerequisite to happiness, particularly for older people.

The preceding factors may contribute something to happiness, but not as much as one might expect. Aron and Aron (1987) argue that generally, there is a surprising lack of connection between any specific factors or collection of factors and happiness. For example, David Witt and colleagues (1980) reanalyzed 17 quality-of-life polls taken between 1948 and 1977 and found the entire set of objective variables surveyed by the pollsters (income, age, sex, work status, etc.) accounted for no more than 19% of the variance in happiness. Similarly, beyond the above factors, Wilson (1967) argues that happiness depends on one's expectations, which are influenced by personal values, past experience, and comparison with others.

THE RELATIVE NATURE OF HAPPINESS: IS THAT ALL THERE IS?

Those who have the most in life do not always feel the most blessed. Consider some of these examples:

Comedian Steve Martin observes that fame and a huge income have not brought him happiness. "My problem is that I don't get the same exhilaration from success as I get depression from failure" (quoted in Corliss, 1987, p. 55). Emily Dickinson (1959) put the matter more poetically: "Success is counted sweetest / By those who ne'er succeed" (p. 38).

When the very rich complain about their lives ("You just don't know how boring it is, having it all"), most Americans are tempted to sneer, "Poor things." If we had all that money, we think, we would never complain. And yet we do. Americans are surely in the top 1% in terms of possession of the world's riches. Yet, we may feel acutely deprived when we do not have enough money to go out on a Saturday night. The person whose children are starving in drought-stricken Bangladesh might be tempted to sneer, "Poor things," when hearing of our woes. See Box 9.2.

If researchers are to predict how happy people will be, then, they must know not only what people have but also what they think they deserve. For example, John Thibaut and Harold Kelley (1959) point out that social psychologists must know two things if they are to predict how satisfied people will be with their lives: First, they must know how pleasurable or painful people's lives are. Imagine that scientists asked two people, Chuck and Eileen, to rate their total life outcomes on a 20-point scale, ranging from (+10), Extremely pleasurable, to (−10), Extremely painful. Chuck might conclude that, all in all, the rewards minus costs in his life stacked up at about +7. Eileen, whose life is less pleasant, might rate her total outcomes at +4. However, to predict who was happiest, Chuck or Eileen, we would have to know something more than these ratings. (See the discussion of scales in chapter 7.) In addition, we would have to know how Chuck's and Eileen's outcomes stack up against the outcomes they expect; we would have to know what their **Comparison Levels (CLs)** are. For example, Chuck might expect a whopping +10 from life. That would be his CL. (The +7 he is actually receiving would fall far short of what he expects.) Eileen might expect a paltry +2 from life. (For her, the +4 she actually receives might seem like a windfall.)

BOX 9.2

"Is That All There Is?"

An article by I. Berkow in the *New York Times* (May 21, 1986) provides a compelling example of the fact that sometimes, not even everything is good enough.

Something's missing. Chris Evert Lloyd, in an article on her in the June issue of *Life* magazine says, regarding her life as a tennis champion and the wife of the British tennis player, John Lloyd: "We get into a rut. We play tennis, we go to a movie, we watch TV, but I keep saying, 'John, there has to be more.'"

This is no dreamy department-store clerk in cosmetics or bathroom accessories. She is Chrissie, a world-famous personage, a glittering star in the glitzy firmament of country clubs and television commercials and gossip columns and championship trophies.

And when she gets low, she can go out and buy a chocolate milkshake and not have it make much of a dent in her $3-million-a-year income. Or she can move the furniture around in her townhouse in Kingston, England, or hang new pictures in the condo in Rancho Mirage, Calif., and soon, she'll be able to rattle around the four-bedroom house she and John are building in Boca Raton, Fla.

But she believes that fame, fortune and 146 professional tennis championships, the record, are not enough.

In the background of her life one may hear the strains of the song, "Is That All There Is?" (p. B13)

How do people form their expectations as to what is reasonable to expect from life? According to Thibaut and Kelley, people's CLs are based on the outcomes they have received in the past, those their friends have received, and those they have heard about. Of course, the more salient various outcomes are to the person, the more those outcomes will "count" when he or she is deciding what is reasonable to expect from life. According to Thibaut and Kelley, how happy people will be depends on whether their outcomes are above or below their CLs. People who get more than they expect will be relatively happy. The more they get (compared with their CL), the happier they will be. People who get less than they expect will be unhappy. The less they get (compared with their CL), the unhappier they will be.

Theoretically, then, CLs are shaped by two main types of comparisons: (a) what people have received in the past, and (b) how their rewards now compare with others' rewards. Researchers have found that these two factors do have an important impact on happiness. Let us consider this research.

Poverty consists not in the decrease of one's posses-sions but in the increase of one's greed.

PLATO

Temporal Comparisons: Past Versus Present Rewards

One's comparison level does not stand still. Throughout most of recorded history, people took it for granted that as they aged, things would become progressively worse. A robust youth would be followed by poverty, squalor, and sickness, ending in an early death (at age 35, on the average). In our own era, many Americans take it for granted that "every day in every way, things are getting better and better." In one *Peanuts* cartoon, Lucy mopes, her head in her hands, "Sometimes I get discouraged." Charlie Brown tries to reassure her, "Well, Lucy, life does have its ups and downs, you know..." Lucy erupts with a volley of opposition:

> But why? Why **should** it? Why can't my life be all **"ups"**? If I want all "ups" why can't I have them? Why can't I just move from one "up" to another "up"? Why can't I just go from an "up" to an **"upper-up"**? **I don't want any "downs"! I just want "ups" and "ups" and "ups"!** (Schulz, 1967)

When people have such outsized expectations, they are bound to be disappointed. Philip Brickman and Donald Campbell (1971) warn:

> While happiness, as a state of subjective pleasure, may be the highest good, it seems to be distressingly transient. Even as we contemplate our satisfaction with a given accomplishment, the satisfaction fades, to be replaced finally by a new indifference and a new level of striving. (p. 287)

Some researchers have explored the impact that changes in people's lives have on their happiness. Usually, they find that while at first, a windfall

Reprinted by permission of UFS, Inc.

increases happiness and a catastrophe decreases it, in time, happiness drifts back to some intermediate level. For example, Philip Brickman, Dan Coates, and Ronnie Janoff-Bulman (1978) interviewed two groups of people whose fortunes had recently changed radically, for better or worse. They started with winners of the Illinois State Lottery. Of the 22 winners who were interviewed, seven won $1 million, six won $400,000, two won $300,000, four won $100,000, and three won $50,000. Next, they interviewed accident victims—11 paraplegic and 18 quadriplegics. They also surveyed 88 people whose lives had stayed relatively the same over the same time period, people who lived in the same area of the city as the lottery winners.

The men and women were interviewed 1 to 12 months after their change in fortune. They were asked a series of questions: (a) How happy were they before their windfall or before the accident? How happy were they now? How happy did they expect to be in the future? (b) Did they ask themselves, "Why me?" Did they feel that they deserved what happened?

A few months after winning the lottery, winners were no more happy with their lives than were comparison subjects (whose lives had not changed). They did not differ in how happy they thought they were before winning, how happy they were at the moment, or how happy they expected to be in the future. They reported that although the money was a big addition to their lives, it was balanced out by the fact that now their little everyday pleasures had lost some zest. The ordinary activities they had previously enjoyed, such as reading or eating a good breakfast, had become less pleasurable. Winning the lottery was apparently such an emotional high that by comparison, their ordinary pleasures had paled.

The accident victims recalled their pasts as having been a little more pleasurable than did the controls (a nostalgia effect), but their current happiness differed only slightly from that of controls. No differences were observed in how happy they expected to be in the future. This research is consistent with other research which suggests that the handicapped—the blind, retarded, and malformed—report themselves to be as happy as everyone else (Cameron, Titus, Kostin, & Kostin, 1973). Catastrophic events seem to produce some decrement in happiness, but not nearly as great a decrease as we might anticipate. A reanalysis of the Brickman et al. (1978) data found that even such extreme life events as winning a lottery or having an accident accounted for no more than 10% of the subjects' present happiness/unhappiness (Kammann, 1982).

How do lottery winners and accident victims think about the events that have befallen them? Not surprisingly, winners were far more likely to think they must have done something to deserve their fate than were accident victims. However, winners also saw chance as a more important determinant of what happened than did victims. Winners assigned 71% of their luck to chance, whereas victims (who had been paralyzed for a variety of reasons) assigned 34% of the cause to chance. Winners were less involved than victims with explaining why the outcome had happened to them. Half the lottery winner sample either did not ask, "Why me?" or could come up with no answer to the question, whereas only one of the accident victims did not ask "Why me?" and answer it.

Happiness, n. An agreeable sensation arising from contemplating the misery of another.
AMBROSE BIERCE (1911),
"THE DEVIL'S DICTIONARY"

Social Comparisons: Comparing Ourselves With Others

A growing body of literature documents the contention that happiness is relative. Brickman and Campbell (1971) point out that a second kind of comparison that has been found to influence men's and women's CLs—social comparisons. Karl Marx contended that a house could be large or small, and as long as the surrounding houses were equally large or small, everyone was content. "But let a palace arise beside the little house, and it shrinks from a little house into a hut." When people dwell on the lives of the wealthy, they may seethe with envy. When they compare themselves with the less fortunate, they may count their blessings. The person who wishes to be happy, so the theory goes, should spend a great deal of time thinking about the poor and very little time watching such shows as "Life Styles of the Rich and Famous." The *Desiderata* (Ehrmann, 1972) cautions, "If you compare yourself with others, you may become vain and bitter; for always there will be greater and lesser persons than yourself." Clever parents have long tried to use this technique to manipulate their children: "Think of all the starving children in Africa. They'd be delighted to have just one of your Brussels sprouts." And in homes all over America, this tactic regularly fails. Children mutter to themselves, "Well, send them our Brussels sprouts, then." But usually, CL theorists insist, such comparisons do work. Usually, children count their blessings and eat their Brussels sprouts. There is no doubt that, in part, happiness is influenced by the comparisons people make with others.

Arranging for a Happy and Just Life

THE HAPPY LIFE

Some authors have offered self-help advice for those who would prefer to be happier. For example, Shaver and Freedman (1976) argue:

> Because happiness is in the mind, it is easier to say what won't bring it than what will. Happiness doesn't come from therapy, religion, drugs, mysticism, or a long list of sexual conquests. Happiness has a lot to do with accepting and enjoying what one is and what one has, maintaining a balance between expectations and achievements. (p. 75)

Brickman and Campbell (1971) suggest that social planners use the knowledge social scientists have gathered about the relative nature of happiness to try to design a society in which most people are happy most of the time. They point out that optimists and pessimists might interpret Thibaut and Kelley's CL model quite differently.

If you are a pessimist, your heart might sink at the realization that happiness is relative. In time, you become accustomed to whatever you are receiving. This means that happiness is by its very nature transient. It is an ever-receding illusion. If people want to be happy, they are condemned "to live on a hedonic treadmill, to seek new levels of stimulation merely to maintain old levels of subjective pleasure, to never achieve any kind of permanent happiness or satisfaction" (p. 289).

If you are an optimist, you would look at the same facts quite differently. Once scientists understand the nature of happiness, society can commit itself to ensuring the greatest happiness for the greatest number. The authors note, "There are still wise and foolish ways to pursue happiness, both for societies and for individuals, and from a planner's point of view, there are certain distributions of goods over time, persons, and modalities that will result in greater happiness than others" (p. 289).

Some of you are optimists, others pessimists. Regardless of your philosophical bent, the authors argue that you have a role in planning the good society. The optimists are most likely to take on the task of planning the good society. Pessimists are most likely to be aware of the relativistic and elusive nature of subjective pleasure. Together, they may make some progress.

Finally, Brickman and Campbell point out that no matter what system social planners choose for allocating society's rewards and costs (for allocating prestige, money, leisure time, and so forth), in the good society, things should seem fair and equitable.

Happiness is a way-station between too little and too much.

POLLOCK (1928)

JUSTICE

Researchers such as Elaine Hatfield, G. William Walster, and Ellen Berscheid (1978) and Hatfield and her colleagues (1984) find that people will be most comfortable with their lives if they feel they are receiving just about what they deserve—not too much more, and surely no less. When people think they are receiving far more than they deserve, their delight in their rewards is mixed with unease and guilt, as well as fear that they might lose their privileged position. Of course, things are even worse when people receive far less than they deserve. Then, they become enraged for they are both deprived and unjustly treated.

Several decades of research have documented that people are concerned about both fairness and profitability in their work arrangements, casual encounters, and love relationships. Just what is seen as fair and equitable varies, of course (see Box 9.3).

Of course, people's definitions of fairness are often remarkably self-serving. One example of unashamed self-interest is this series of resolutions passed by the Assembly in New England in the 1640s, in a debate on whether they were entitled to settle on Indian-inhabited land:

1. The Earth is the Lord's and the fullness thereof. **Voted**
2. The Lord may give the Earth or any part of it to his chosen people. **Voted**
3. We are his chosen people. **Voted** (Mason, 1971, p. 242)

Nonetheless, people do care about justice, and any attempt to devise a good society, then, will have to take such facts into account. With this review of happiness behind us, let us turn to the more intense emotions, joy and ecstasy.

BOX 9.3

Differing Conceptions of Justice

Morton Deutsch (1974) observes that at different times, societies have considered very different things to be fair. In his view:

Justice has been viewed as consisting in the treatment of all people:

1. As equals.
2. So that they have an equal opportunity to compete without external favoritism or discrimination.
3. According to their ability.
4. According to their efforts.
5. According to their accomplishments.
6. According to their needs.
7. According to the supply and demand of the market place.
8. According to the requirements of the common good.
9. According to the principle of reciprocity. (p. 4)

*F*or each ecstatic instant
We must an anguish pay

EMILY DICKINSON

Joy

Whereas happiness is capable of lasting for relatively long periods of time, joy is an intense state, by its very nature a short-lived "high."

THE EXPERIENCE OF JOY AND ECSTASY

Religious writings are filled with descriptions of ecstatic states. Saints and mystics have described a variety of profound religious experiences—feeling intense ecstasy, having visions, hearing powerful voices, being struck down. Marghanita Laski (1962) wondered how common such ecstatic experiences are. Her interviews with ordinary men and women make it clear that such experiences are relatively rare. Only 11% of people report that they often have such experiences; 35% have had an ecstatic experience fewer than 25 times in their lives; 46% have had such an experience fewer than 10 times; and 5% have never had such an experience.

Laski finds that certain kinds of events are especially likely to trigger ecstatic experiences. Among these are art (21% of respondents cite this), nature (18%), sexual love (17%), religion (10%), creative work (5%), exercise (5%), beauty (4%), scientific knowledge (3%), recollection and introspection (3%), childbirth (3%), poetry (1%), and miscellaneous causes (9%).

What does ecstasy feel like? According to Laski (1962), during ecstatic experiences, some people become convinced they have gained something (they have been in touch with the creator or they have gained a sense of timelessness) or that they have lost something (they have transcended earthly things, gone beyond normal limitations). Others report quasi-physical feelings: joy so intense that it is almost painful, that "moves me with such sweetness and violence," inspiration that "flows . . . like a brook," a "bubbling up inside," the "hush of peace," "I walked on air." Especially common are feelings of intensity ("a rushing together, one swelling harmony, almost bursting," "like a great climax") or withdrawal ("a hush of peace, a soundless calm"). Arthur Koestler (1952), a Hungarian-born author and journalist, describes such a joyous experience in Box 9.4.

According to Laski, ecstatic experiences seem to be of extremely short duration. For most people (65%), they last only "an instant" or a "split second."

Oliver Sacks (1985), a neurologist, gives us some insight into ecstatic visions. He observes, "The religious literature of all ages is replete with descriptions of 'visions', in which sublime and ineffable feelings have been accompanied by the experience of radiant luminosity" (p. 158).

BOX 9.4

An Ecstatic Experience

I was sitting on a bench in the Volksgarten, one of Vienna's enchanted parks, with a pile of books beside me. On top lay a pamphlet about the latest Arab riots in Palestine, with appalling details of children put to the sword as in the days of Herod, of Jewish pioneers being killed after having been blinded and castrated. . . .

While I was reading the pamphlet, I felt myself choke and seethe with impotent anger. . . . When I had finished reading the pamphlet and had calmed down a little, I fell into one of my habitual reveries about devoting my life to the cause of the persecuted as a fighter and writer of books which would shake the conscience of the world. . . . While still in the grip of that dream, and all geared for action, I opened the next book in the pile at its marked page. . . . It was Weyl's introduction to Einstein's theory of Relativity. A phrase suddenly struck me and has remained in my memory ever since. It said that the theory of General Relativity led the human imagination "across the peaks of glaciers never before explored by any human being." This cliché had an unexpectedly strong effect. I saw Einstein's world-shaking formula—Energy equals Mass multiplied by the square of the velocity of light—hovering in a kind of rarified haze over the glaciers, and this image carried a sensation of infinite tranquility and peace. The martyred infants and castrated pioneers of the Holy Land shrank to microscopic insignificance. Beast had fed on beast in sea and jungle since the beginnings of organic life; it was a law of Nature and of history; there was nothing to get excited about. The fate of these unfortunates had to be viewed with the same serene, detached, meditative eye as that of stars bursting into novae, of sunspots erupting, of rocks decaying into swamps, and primeval forests being transformed into coal. This change in perspective was accompanied by equally pronounced physiological change. The sensation of choking with indignation was succeeded by the relaxed quietude and self-dissolving stillness of the "oceanic feeling." (pp. 128–129)

For example, take Sacks's description of the case of Hildegard of Bingen (1098–1180), a mystic, who experienced visions from earliest childhood to the close of her life. She left accounts of her ecstatic experiences in two manuscripts, *Scivas* and *Liber Divinorum Operum*. She writes:

The visions which I saw I beheld neither in sleep, nor in dreams, nor in madness, nor with my carnal eyes, nor with the ears of the flesh, nor in hidden places; but wakeful, alert, and with the eyes of the spirit and the inward ears, I perceive them in open and according to the will of God. . . .

I saw a great star most splendid and beautiful, and with it an exceeding multitude of falling stars which with the star followed southwards. . . . And suddenly they were all annihilated, so being turned into black coals . . . and cast into the abyss so that I could see them no more. (pp. 160–161)

Hildegard invested these rapturous emotional experiences with religious meaning. Her burning visions drove her to a life of holiness and mysticism.

Today, neurologists have more mundane explanations for such phenomena. Sacks points out that if a patient approached a modern neurologist with

Hildegard's symptoms, she would immediately be diagnosed as suffering from migraine headaches. Often, a sufferer is alerted that a migraine is on the way by a visual aura—a sort of visual fireworks, in which one sees colors, flashes of light—and a feeling that something strange is happening. Sacks reports, "Our literal interpretation would be that she experienced a shower of phosphenes in transit across the visual field, their passage being succeeded by a negative scotoma [a dark spot in the visual field]" (1985, p. 161). Most ecstatic visions, continues Sacks, are produced by hysterical or psychotic ecstasy or by intoxication, or they are epileptic or migrainous manifestations.

Regardless of their cause, ecstatic experiences have a profound impact on some people's lives. For example, Fyodor Dostoevsky suffered from psychomotor epilepsy. Before a seizure, many epileptics experience an aura—everyday objects look peculiar (they may have odd colors or take strange shapes or be etched against a background), peculiar smells waft through the air, things may feel eerie. This aura is sometimes accompanied by feelings of great joy, peace, or tranquility. (Unfortunately, some epileptics experience fear, anger, or sadness instead.) Paul MacLean (1986) reports, "During the aura at the beginning of the epileptic storm, the patient's mind may light up with vivid emotional feelings that, in one case or another, involve affects ranging from intense fear to ecstasy." But, like Hildegard of Bingen, Dostoevsky attributed the feelings of ecstasy to a mystical cause, and that interpretation had a powerful impact on his religious beliefs:

> There are moments, and it is only a matter of five or six seconds, when you feel the presence of the eternal harmony . . . a terrible thing is the frightful clearness with which it manifests itself and the rapture with which it fills you. If this state were to last more than five seconds, the soul could not endure it and would have to disappear. During these five seconds I live a whole human existence and for that I would give my whole life and not think that I was paying too dearly. (Quoted in Sacks, 1985, p. 162)

Such reactions are not uncommon. MacLean (1986) describes two cases treated by a Spanish neurosurgeon. In one case, a patient's epileptic attacks were characterized by "extraordinary beatitude" and "feelings completely out of this world." In the other case, a middle-aged man said that his auras "made him feel as though he knew what it was like to be in heaven" (p. 81).

THE ANATOMY OF JOY

A pioneer on the neuroanatomy of joy and pleasure was James Olds. In the 1950s, at the University of Michigan, he and his graduate assistant, Peter Milner, excited the psychological community with their discovery that the brain seemed to possess both "pleasure" and "pain centers" (Olds & Milner, 1954). Olds and Milner's discovery was a lucky accident. They were attempting to implant an electrode in the reticular formation of a laboratory rat in order to study the impact of electrical stimulation on learning. By accident, the electrode missed its mark. Its tip wound up some millimeters away, probably in the hypothalamus. The researchers found that when they electrically stimulated the rat's brain, it kept coming back for more.

Olds and Milner were intrigued by this surprising result. They quickly implanted electrodes in the septal and other regions of the brains of 15 more rats. They were interested in observing whether or not rats would work to receive electrical stimulation to their brains' pleasure centers. Things were arranged so that rats could stimulate their own brains. The rats were placed in a cage which contained a lever. Each time an animal pressed the lever, a microswitch in the stimulating circuit was flipped. This sent a tiny electrical impulse to the pleasure centers in the rat's brain. Olds and Milner found that some rats would press the lever up to 1,900 times per hour in order to receive electrical stimulation to their brains' pleasure centers. In subsequent studies, rates of many thousands of responses per hour have been obtained. Rats seemed addicted to the stimulation; they were willing to go without food, sleep, or sex; they kept coming back for more.

Olds and Milner proposed that the brain possessed pleasure, pain, and neutral centers and that it was these pleasure and pain centers that allowed animals to learn. Since Olds's classic work, neuroanatomists and neurophysiologists have learned a great deal about the neuroanatomy and neurochemistry of joy and pleasure. For example, in chapter 4, we reviewed James Henry's neuroendocrine theory of emotion. He described the role of the cortex, the limbic and neuroendocrine systems, and the brainstem in emotion. Today, we know that pleasure can be produced via electrical stimulation of many parts of the brain. Probably, the best and most reliable location is the medial forebrain bundle (MFB), which passes through the lateral hypothalamus. This pleasure center is the site of catecholaminergic and serotonergic axons (axons which transmit catecholamines and serotonin), which carry messages from the brain stem to their diencephalic and telencephalic projection areas (see chapter 4). The chemicals that spark the firing of these cells are capable of producing the experience of euphoria and of alleviating pain.

THE CHEMISTRY OF JOY

As you have seen in earlier chapters, psychologists are beginning to learn a great deal about the chemistry of joy and a potpourri of related emotions. They are also learning more about the way the various emotions, positive and negative, interact. Some evidence from this research suggests that joy and happiness may be sparked by chemicals that are general central nervous system and autonomic nervous system stimulants or depressants and drugs which selectively modify CNS and ANS function.

According to anthropologists, people in every culture and in every time have used drugs. Throughout history, artists and scholars have depicted their powerful, emotion-altering effects. In 4000 B.C., the ancient Sumerians called the poppy the "joy plant." Travelers to Hades drank from the River Lethe and became oblivious to all that had gone before. Ponce de Leon searched for a fountain of youth and instead discovered Florida. Dr. Jekyll quaffed a bubbling chemical potion and was transformed into the evil Mr. Hyde. In Aldous Huxley's *Brave New World,* captives of the future popped "soma" and were content. Today, mood-altering drugs are all around us. They are available from psychiatrists, drugstores, supermarkets, and health food stores (in the form of vitamins, herbs, and spices). What physicians refuse to prescribe, drug dealers smuggle into the country or chemists blend in illegal home laboratories. Drug peddlers sell such illegal, dangerous, but profitable drugs on the street.

Fred Leavitt (1982) provides a compendium of many of the drugs that people have used (and abused) in an effort to find a fleeting high and reviews the psychic and emotional effects they produce. Let us glance at a few that spark momentary joy, happiness, or contentment. Of course, almost all these drugs also produce a variety of not-so-appealing side effects. These range from drowsiness, to addiction, to death.

Alcohol often produces a sense of well-being, euphoria, relaxation, and drowsiness. Social inhibitions are reduced.

Amphetamines, related chemically to norepinephrine, produce a sense of well-being, elevate mood, increase mental alertness, and alleviate fatigue.

Caffeine (found in coffee, tea, and cocoa) is a powerful CNS and skeletal muscle stimulant. It enhances mental clarity and allays fatigue.

Cocaine was widely available in the United States at the turn of the century. It was sold in the form of sprays, tablets, injections, ointments, cigarettes, and soft drinks like Coca-Cola. Cocaine produces self-confidence and euphoria; it is a powerful antifatigue agent and makes one indifferent to pain. It works by stimulating the sympathetic nervous system—pupils dilate, breathing quickens, heart rate speeds up, body temperature rises, perspiration increases, and one's throat becomes dry. Lester Grinspoon and James Bakalar (1977) interviewed cocaine users as to its effects:

> "Under cocaine I feel like a king." "It gives me a hilarious, exhilarating feeling," "an illusion of supreme well-being, and a soaring overconfidence in both physical and mental ability," "like a racehorse at the gate, quivering inside." (p. 41)

Inhalants, in a vast array, include gasoline, cleaning solutions, lighter fluid, paint thinner, and various glues and cements. These chemicals alter the emotions; all contain volatile substances that depress the central nervous system. Their effects include giddiness, euphoria, a feeling of floating, slurred speech, and visual and auditory hallucinations.

One well-known gas is nitrous oxide ("laughing gas"). It was once used by physicians and dentists to relax patients. At the turn of the century, psychologist William James experimented with nitrous oxide, convinced that this mind-altering drug was enabling him to discover eternal truths. While under its influence, he felt the universe was illuminated; unfortunately, once he awoke he could not remember his brilliant insights. One night he managed to scribble down a few words before he lost consciousness. The next morning, he rushed to his notepaper, only to find that he had written: "Hogamus, Higamus. Man is polygamous. Higamus, Hogamus. Woman, monogamous." So much for brilliant insight! The nitrous oxide had produced the conviction and the joy of illumination, but not much in the way of content. Today, another inhalant, amyl nitrite, is sometimes used as an aphrodisiac (a sexual stimulant).

LSD is a sympathomimetic. Richard Lingeman (1974) offers a vivid description of the LSD experience:

> The drug's subjective effects are spectacular. . . . They are similar to those produced by other hallucinogenic drugs but on a grander scale . . . and include stimulation of the central and autonomic nervous systems, changes in mood (sometimes euphoric and megalomanic, sometimes fearful, panicky, and anxiety ridden) . . . an intensification of colors so that they seem brighter, intensification of the other senses so that inaudible sounds become magnified or food tastes better or normally unnoticed aspects of things (such as the pores in concrete) become strikingly vivid, merging of senses (synesthesia) so that sounds are seen as color patterns, a wavelike sense of time so that seconds seem like an eternity, distortions in the perception of space so that surrounding objects seem fluid and shifting, a sense of depersonalization . . . a closely related feeling of merger (dissolving) with the external world . . . a perception of ordinary things as if seen for the first time unstructured by perceptual "sets"; hallucinations of flowers, snakes, animals, other people, etc. . . . a sense of closeness to, or merger with, other persons in the room as if barriers between individuals had been dissolved, enhanced sensuousness and sexual stimulation. . . . (pp. 133–134)

Marijuana is a euphoriant. It often produces a conviction of profound insight, but it also produces difficulty in concentration, confusion, and distortions of time and space. It increases sociability, and produces hilarity as well as occasional anxiety and restlessness. Appreciation of music and colors is greatly enhanced.

Nicotine produces increased heart rate, blood pressure, and metabolic rate, whether through smoking or another form of ingestion. Its physiological effects are similar to those of sympathetic stimulation. Nevertheless, smokers claim that nicotine is calming.

Opiates, such as *morphine, opium,* or *heroin,* are derived from the poppy plant. They are powerful narcotic analgesics. Users often feel coolly detached from the environment, which helps explain opiates' popularity in harsh environments such as ghettos and battlefields. People suffering from mental or physical pain often become euphoric when pain is relieved. When heroin is administered intravenously, it produces a powerful feeling, referred to as "a rush," that is similar to the sensation of sexual orgasm.

What is the point of this review of the chemistry of joy? First, in their search for joy, excitement, and happiness, people often give up on natural sources of pleasure and turn to the "quick fix" of drugs. Second, from such natural experiments, neurophysiologists have been able to observe the sledgehammer effects that many artificial drugs have on emotional processes and to get some hints as to how natural chemical substances—the endorphins, amphetamines, and ANS sympathetic nervous system chemicals—work their subtle magic in the brain and autonomic nervous system. From such experiments, psychologists have gained some understanding of the chemicals that contribute to the subtle shadings of joy and happiness. Third, we caution readers to avoid such experiments themselves. The brain is a delicate instrument. The natural chemicals that fuel joy work subtly and in delicate combinations. To take drugs is to try to produce a precision effect with a sledgehammer. One ends up with a crude parody of the natural experience and risks dangerous and incalculable side effects.

Consider some examples: Sigmund Freud once thought of cocaine as a "cure-all." After the death of his best friend and the addiction of several friends and patients, he realized, to his dismay, that it was addictive. Since Freud's time, the evidence has been mounting that cocaine is extremely dangerous. Among the most striking of cocaine's dangers are its potentially devastating effects on the cardiovascular system, which may include heart attacks and strokes. Scientists have compiled statistics on how cocaine assaults the body. They find that cocaine's chief effects are on the nervous system and the blood vessels. Researchers have found these direct and indirect actions shown in Table 9.5.

Table 9.5   **The Effects of Cocaine**

Brain, nervous system	Stroke, seizures, tremors, delirium, and psychosis
Heart	Reduced flow of oxygenated blood to heart
	Cellular damage
	Heartbeat becomes dangerously irregular
	Heart attacks
Blood vessels	Angina
	Constriction of blood vessels
	Dangerous rise in blood pressure
Abdomen/Liver	Constriction of blood supply to intestines
	Destruction of cells
Lungs	Accumulation of fluid; drowning
Nasal passages	Damage to lining of nose
	Septum may be eaten through
	Loss of sense of smell
Reproductive system	Men may have difficulty in maintaining erection and ejaculating; women may have difficulty reaching orgasm

No wonder public health officials have cautioned men and women to "Just say no" to drugs (see Box 9.5).

Life can't be charted. Joy turns into pain. Sadness is replaced by joy.

ANONYMOUS

RICHARD SOLOMON'S OPPONENT PROCESS THEORY

Richard Solomon (1980) proposed a possible explanation for why intense joy is so fleeting. Throughout history, people have observed that pleasure and pain often seem to be curiously intertwined. For example, the Greek philosopher Plato (428–347 B.C.) (1955) observed:

> How strange would appear to be this thing that men call pleasure! And how curiously it is related to what is thought to be its opposite, pain! The two will never be found *together* in a man, and yet if you seek the one and obtain it, you are almost bound always to get the other as well, just as though they were both attached to one and the same head. . . . Wherever the one is found, the other follows up behind. So, in my case, since I had pain in my leg as a result of the

BOX 9.5

Wired

Bob Woodward (1984), in *Wired: The Short Life and Fast Times of John Belushi*, describes comedian Belushi's fascination with drugs shortly before his death from a cocaine and heroin overdose in the spring of 1982:

> One night John and his new drug enforcer Smokey Wendell went out in a limousine in New York. John was looking for drugs. He never gave an address to the driver, simply ordering, "Go straight, now turn left. . . turn right here! . . . Stop at this corner." When they got to a destination, Smokey insisted on going with him as John pounded on doors and wildly rang buzzers. He had had no luck after seven stops. After working with John for several weeks, Smokey had tried to find out what the hell was going on. . . "Why do you take drugs?" he asked.

> "Because they're there."
> "Come on," Smokey said. "I don't understand when someone like you has all this going for himself. . . . Why do you have to rely on drugs? . . . you've got to realize how it's endangering your ability to function. Like alcoholism."
> "Alcohol and drugs are different things," John said with disgust.
> "You use this, you use that," Smokey said, "and you use everything. What happens when you reach this plateau and don't get that snap, that buzz? When you get to that level and have tried every drug, at every level? What happens then?"
> John pondered for a moment and said, "I don't know. . . . I guess you'd just go crazy." (p. 198)

fetters, pleasure seems to have come to follow it up. (Plato, *Phaedo,* in Solomon, 1980, p. 691)

In more recent times, people have continued to observe that when they experience a strong emotion, joy and ecstasy or pain and terror, after the experience is over, the opposite emotion sneaks up on us, like an afterimage. Consider the report of a man's son who was struck by lightning on his way back from a golf course. He was thrown down, his golfing shorts were "torn to shreds," and his legs were burned. "When his companion sat him up, he screamed 'I'm dead, I'm dead.' His legs were numb and blue and he could not move. By the time he reached the nearest hospital [however], he was euphoric" (Taussig, 1969, p. 306).

How is it that pleasure turns to pain and pain to pleasure? Solomon (1980) proposed that under the right conditions, people can become addicted to emotionally intense experiences—to joy and ecstasy, drugs, exercise, or thrill seeking. And Solomon's **opponent-process theory** predicts that each of these addictions eventually produces its opposite. Pleasure turns to pain, pain to pleasure. The best way to understand Solomon's argument is to review what happens to the drug addict's emotions as he or she becomes addicted to drugs. According to Solomon, anytime a person experiences a strong emotion, joy or pain, a standard pattern occurs (see Figure 9.4). First, the emotional stimulus occurs. Imagine you are walking along the street, when suddenly someone blares their car horn right behind you. Immediately, your emotional reaction (panic) rises to its peak. If the car keeps honking, you may remain terrified for a second or two, but eventually you adapt to the sound and your feelings begin to return to normal. When the car proceeds down the street and disappears, however, Solomon argues that your emotions don't just return to normal (to the 0 point in Figure 9.4). Instead, they overshoot the mark, and you begin to feel feelings opposite to those you just felt. (Relief replaces terror.) You may find yourself a bit giddy with relief and happiness. Solomon argues that such opponent processes exist anytime a person experiences an emotion. Pain is replaced by pleasure; pleasure by pain.

But how much pleasure, how much pain? Solomon argues that as people try to experience more and more of various emotional highs (or are forced to endure more and more emotional lows), the balance shifts. The first time a person shoots "speed," for example, he will experience a "rush." He may experience euphoria and intense sexual pleasure throughout his body. As the drug wears off, he will feel a bit let down. But soon he is back to normal. He is not yet hooked. If, however, the person becomes a regular "speed" user, the balance of joy to pain changes. Now, when the addict shoots "speed," his thrills are markedly diminished. It is okay, but nothing special. (He has learned to tolerate the drug.) Now, it is the withdrawal period that stimulates a powerful emotional reaction. In the withdrawal period, the addict's craving for "speed" is intense. He may experience nausea, chills and shaking, and

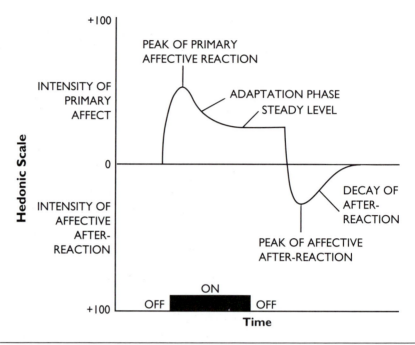

FIGURE 9.4   A standard emotional pattern. Note the five labeled distinctive features of the complex emotional reaction. From R. L. Solomon & J. D. Corbit, 1974. An opponent-process theory of motivation: I. Temporal dynamics of affect. *Psychological Review*, 81, 119–145. Copyright 1974 by the American Psychological Association. Reprinted by permission.

excruciating pain. He has become an addict. Taking the drug may provide little pleasure, but not taking the drug is impossible.

Solomon points out that the powerful emotional experiences listed earlier—joy, love, excitement seeking, and so forth—seem to follow this same pattern. At first, the primary emotional experience is what counts. But as it is repeated, its opposite comes to the fore. Two examples:

When people are first in love, they experience deep joy. As they spend more and more time together, gradually the joy of chance meetings decreases. They begin to take each other for granted. They can do nothing to bring back the passion they once felt for each other. They can hurt one another, however, if they are suddenly deprived of one another's company, if they are forced to "go cold turkey," they begin to discover the depth of their loss. They may feel suicidal and desperate.

In a second example, Seymour Epstein (1967) studied the emotional reaction of novice versus experienced parachutists (see chapter 7). When soldiers found themselves in free-fall for the first time, they were generally terrified. They often screamed in terror, their pupils dilated, their hearts pounded, their breathing was irregular, and their bodies curled forward. Once they landed safely, they often walked around, stunned, for a few minutes. Then they became greatly relieved. They were alive! They began to smile, chatter, and gesture broadly. Their post-jump elation was relatively mild and short-lived, however. The pattern of reactions for experienced jumpers was very different. They were relatively calm during free fall. (Like the addicts we described earlier, they had learned to tolerate jumping.) However, their post-jump elation was more intense and lasted longer than did the novice jumper's elation.

In sum, Solomon argues that people who seek continual joy are fighting a losing battle. If any emotion is experienced too intensely, too continuously, for too long, it begins to be replaced by its opposite. According to Solomon, addictions (and, in fact, all acquired motivations) involve three "affective" or "hedonic" phenomena. These phenomena are: (a) affective or **hedonic contrast,** (b) affective or **hedonic habituation** (tolerance), and (c) affective or **hedonic withdrawal** (abstinence) syndromes. Initially, when the stimulus (food, alcohol, a drug, and so forth) is presented, the person experiences intense pleasure. When the stimulus is removed, the person experiences a contrasting emotion. (Pleasure turns to pain.) In time, as the person becomes habituated to the positive reinforcer, it begins to produce far less pleasure than it did before. In time, one needs more, more often, to get the same thrill. One also begins to suffer more and more during withdrawal. Given this scenario, Solomon would argue that people will never be able to experience intense joy for very long; joy inevitably rebounds to its opposite.

We have focused thus far on what we know about intense and rare states of joy—ecstasy and drug-induced states. In the next section, we review what we have learned about more typical states of joy.

GOING WITH THE FLOW

One of the pioneers in emotions research is Carroll E. Izard. After reviewing all that is known about joy, Izard (1977) commented:

> Most scholars and researchers who have attempted to study joy agree that one cannot obtain it by one's own effort. It is not an experience that can be chased and caught, and it is not necessarily won by success or achievement . . . joy seems to be more of a by-product of efforts that have other aims. It seems that in most cases joy just happens, and some of the greatest moments of joy are unplanned and quite unexpected. (p. 239)

Recently, researchers have been studying some of these unplanned moments. For example, University of Chicago psychologist Mihaly Csikszentmihalyi (1975; 1990) studied "flow states." He points out that sometimes when people are engrossed in an activity—painting, working on a project, or trying to stalk an animal—they become completely lost in their task. In such states, people are not tormented by self-conscious doubts. They simply do what needs to be done. They are lost in time and space. Action follows smoothly upon action. One moment flows into the next. They couldn't care less about what people think. After the task is completed, people "wake up." Now they realize how elated they feel how refreshed they are. Now they can begin to marvel at what they have achieved. Csikszentmihalyi calls such states **flow states.**

Certain activities are especially conducive to flow, for example, sports (such as running and basketball), games (such as chess or computer games), creative activities (such as painting, mathematics, surgery, and scientific research), and spiritual experiences. In such flow activities, people report feeling euphoric and mellow; they enter an altered state of consciousness, losing all sense of themselves and their surroundings. A narrowing of consciousness and a complete absorption in the task at hand, occur. A composer of modern music observes:

> I am really quite oblivious to my surroundings after I really get going. I think that the phone could ring, and the doorbell could ring, or the house burn down, or something like that. . . . When I start working, I really do shut out the world. Once I stop, I can let it back in again. (p. 41)

According to Csikszentmihalyi, flow occurs in the zone between boredom and anxiety. If people are too skilled for the activities at hand, they become bored. When activities are too difficult, they become anxious.

Jean Hamilton and Monte Buchsbaum (quoted in Goleman, 1986) point out that people often feel most alive when they are completely immersed in a task. In their research they found that effortless and effortful attention are very different. Effortless concentration produces lowered cortical arousal. Strained concentration (working on something too easy or too difficult) requires greater activity, almost as if the brain is in the "wrong gear" for the work demanded. Researchers note that flow has much in common with other states of concentration—meditation, runner's high, and hypnosis.

Psychologists are discovering that individuals differ markedly in their abilities to become absorbed in what they do. Consider the differences between good and poor hypnotic subjects, for example. Auke Tellegen and Gilbert Atkinson (1974) observe that some people can become "lost" in a Mozart piano variation or lose themselves watching television. Such people are easily hypnotized. Ronald Pekala and Krishna Kumar (1987, quoted in Goleman, 1986) add:

> There is a group of people who readily get so absorbed in things that they become lost in them, or in their thoughts or fantasies, for that matter. . . . It is these same mental processes that seem to get intensified during hypnosis . . . when he [Dr. Ronald Pekala] simply asked them to sit quietly for a few minutes with their eyes closed, they frequently reported feelings approaching an altered state, including rapturous joy, a sense of some profound meaningfulness, vivid imagery, and an altered sense of time, all accompanying a deeply absorbed attention. (p. 23)

Such people, the authors believe, may go through much of the day lost in a pleasant, reverie-like state.

Csikszentmihalyi (1975) also studied states of "microflow." All of us perform a number of seemingly pointless activities each day; we come home tired and stare at the ceiling; we look at clouds and daydream; we swing our legs, scratch our heads, and twirl our hair. Some of us dislike these "bad habits." We can't figure our why they are so hard to shake. Csikszentmihalyi suggests an answer. Such habits are designed to promote flow—microflow experiences help keep a person alert, relaxed, creative, and feeling in control. Such behavior probably regulates the amount of stimulation available to the person—increasing novelty in a barren environment and promoting tranquility and calm in an overwhelming one.

To conclude, the material covered in this chapter has been both intriguing and disappointing. Mankind has relentlessly pursued happiness, ecstasy, and joy. Unfortunately, neither scientists nor philosophers can give seekers a road map to guarantee they will find them. In fact, if Solomon's opponent-process theory or Thibaut and Kelley's CL theory are correct, people may be unlikely ever to track down everlasting joy and happiness. Perpetual happiness, like the pot of gold at the end of the rainbow, may always seem to lie just ahead, over the next hill, only to retreat as one approaches. At this stage in the development of the psychology of emotion, we clearly need more knowledge concerning these elusive positive emotions.

Summing Up

- Survey researchers find that most people in most countries seem to be fairly happy most of the time.

- Some people seem to possess a special talent for happiness. People who have high self-esteem, who are well adjusted, who have close relationships, and who do satisfying work seem to be happy in spite of their objective circumstances.

- To some extent, people are more likely to be happy when their basic needs are fulfilled. The surprise is that the relationship between objective reality and perceived happiness is not as great as one might expect.

- Happiness is relative. It depends on how people perceive their circumstances, rather than on what those circumstances are. Two types of comparisons seem to be especially important in determining what people expect from life—temporal comparisons and social comparisons.

- Equity theorists document that people feel happiest when they think they are receiving what they deserve—no more, and certainly no less. People's judgments as to what they deserve, however, are often extremely self-serving.

- Joy has been defined as a highly pleasant emotion characterized by many outward signs of gratification. Happiness has been characterized as a state of well-being and contentment.

- In the 1950s, James Olds discovered that the brain seemed to possess both pleasure and pain centers. Today, researchers know that pleasure can be produced in many parts of the brain. The neurochemicals that spark the firing of the cells in these areas are capable of producing euphoria and alleviating pain.

- Throughout history, people have used drugs to produce joy. These drugs provide some hints as to the chemistry of joy and happiness.

- Solomon observes that people can become addicted to joy, thrills, exercise, power, and so forth. The pleasure associated with these activities follows the pattern of all addictions. They involve gradual habituation to the reinforcing stimuli and withdrawal when the reinforcement is terminated.

- Izard observed that people cannot seek joy and be certain of finding it. Often, it comes when they are deeply absorbed in some activity. Researchers have recently begun to study such flow states.

10

Anger and Aggression

Introduction

The Roots of Anger
Who Incites Anger?
What Causes Anger?

The Anatomy of Anger
The Look of Anger
The Neuroanatomy and Neurophysiology of Anger
The Visceral Determinants of Anger
Expressions of Anger

The "Hard-Wiring" of Aggression
The Sociobiological Perspective
The Psychoanalytic Approach
The Great Catharsis Debate
The Frustration-Aggression Model
Against Whom Will Aggression Be Directed?
What Form Will Aggression Take?
The Frustration-Aggression Theory Revisited

The "Programming": Social Learning Theory
Observational Learning
Reinforcement Theory

Summing Up

FIGURE 10.1 *Shikkongo Shin.* c. A.D. 733. Painted clay. Height of entire statue, 167.5 cm. Sangatsudo, Todai-jo Nara.

Introduction

In February of 1989, Iran's spiritual and political leader, the Ayatollah Khomeini, called on more than a billion Muslims to kill novelist Salman Rushdie, the author of *The Satanic Verses* (1988). According to the Ayatollah, Rushdie blasphemed Islam when he used the names of the Prophet Mohammed's wives in a dream sequence. The Ayatollah offered the Iranian who succeeded in killing Rushdie and his publishers an eternal heavenly reward. An Iranian businessman countered with a more practical offer. He would pay the successful hit man $1 million (if the killer was a foreigner) or $3 million (if the killer was an Iranian). Hundreds of thousands of Muslims marched in the streets in protest. They hurled rocks and firebombs. The police in the various countries stood their ground. Many protesters were killed. Westerners, in their turn, were stunned by the Ayatollah's death threats. They were dumbfounded that a foreign head of state would try to intervene in their affairs. First, the Western governments took action. The European Common Market members promptly withdrew their ambassadors from Iran in protest. Authors organized protests and readings of *The Satanic Verses.* Perfectly mild-mannered men and women were enraged. Calls to "nuke Iran" came from more than one person.

Was it anger that led to this mass aggressive response? In this chapter, we will review what social psychologists have learned about anger and aggression. Let us begin by seeing how psychologists have defined the first of these terms.

Anger has been defined as:

> An emotional reaction—aroused by being interfered with, injured, or threatened— that is characterized by certain distinctive facial grimaces, by marked reactions of the autonomic nervous system, and by overt or concealed symbolic activities of attack or offense. *Anger* is a passing emotional disturbance; *rage* is anger out of control. (English & English, 1958, p. 31)

Joel Davitz (1969) provides more information about the experience of anger. He asked men and women to describe what it felt like to be angry. The reactions shown in Box 10.1 were most common. (The percentage of people checking each statement is indicated in parentheses at the end of the sentence.)

Thus, anger is the emotional intent to inflict harm on another person or object, coupled with physiological sensations that seem to provide energy for aggressive acts. A great deal of research has been conducted on anger and aggression.

The Roots of Anger

Elaine Hatfield comes by her interest in anger naturally. Her mother is a very quiet, almost timid woman. Her father is calm. Both hate disturbances. When

BOX 10.1

Anger

—My blood pressure goes up (72%).

—My pulse quickens (56%).

—My heart pounds (40%).

—I feel that I'll burst or explode; as if there is too much inside to be held in (48%).

—My fists are clenched (52%).

—There is a narrowing of my senses, my attention becomes riveted on one thing (52%).

—There is an impulse to strike out, to pound, or smash, or kick, or bite; to do something that will hurt (50%).

—I want to strike out, explode, but I hold back, control myself (46%).

—I want to say something nasty, something that will hurt someone (42%).

—I keep thinking of getting even, of revenge (40%).

—I'm easily irritated, ready to snap (64%).

—My teeth are clenched (52%).

—There is a tight, knotted feeling in my stomach (38%).

—My whole body is tense (60%).

—I seem to be caught up and overwhelmed by the feeling (64%).

—My senses are perfectly focused (34%).

—I keep thinking about what happened over and over again (44%).

—My reactions seem to be exaggerated (38%).

—I'm completely wrapped up in the moment, the present, the here and now, with no thought of past or future (36%).

—I keep searching for an explanation, for some understanding; I keep thinking, "why?" (34%).

—I feel confused and mixed-up (38%).

Davitz (1969), pp. 35–36

she was about five years old, she went to her Grandma Kalahar's for a birthday party. During the course of the afternoon, a surprising event happened. Somehow, her grandmother became furious at her Aunt Rosemary and began chasing her around the large dining room, shrieking and trying to hit her with an umbrella. Her aunt ran round and round, shouting insults. Hatfield was absolutely fascinated. She had never seen anything like this. Her father picked up her and her sister, tucked them under his arm, and said, "It's time to go, girls." She peered back, trying to catch a last glimpse of the action. She is still trying.

Historically, the Hatfields are no strangers to violence. During the 1870s, the Hatfield-McCoy feud developed in a series of incidents: a trial over a razorback hog; a love affair between Johnse Hatfield and Rose Anne McCoy; the stabbing of Ellison Hatfield during an election; the vengeful shooting of the three McCoy boys who had murdered him. The feud actually went on for 20 years and even involved the governors of Kentucky and West Virginia in its last phases. Hatfields kidnapped in West Virginia were jailed in Kentucky—a states' rights mix-up that went to the U.S. Supreme Court. In the 1900s, the feud finally ended when "Devil Anse" Hatfield was baptized and the feud guns were stacked (Jones, 1948).

Since the time of the Hatfield-McCoy feud, social scientists have learned a great deal about the nature of anger. They provide information about those most likely to make us angry, what enrages us, how we react when we are furious—with aggression or with restraint—and why we act that way.

WHO INCITES ANGER?

Depending on how records are kept, most people report becoming "mildly" to "moderately" angry anywhere from several times a day to several times a week (Gates, 1926; Averill, 1982).

James Averill (1980, 1983) conducted a series of studies designed to discover what excites anger. Averill sees emotions as "social constructions," with society providing the "script." Social norms provide the rules for how stimuli are to be appraised, responses organized, and behavior monitored. People interpret their own feelings in much the same way that actors interpret a role with feeling. To test his constructivist notions, Averill conducted a series of studies. In some, Averill asked men and women to describe a recent experience of anger, preferably within the previous week, in some detail. In others, he required men and women to keep daily records of their experiences of anger and annoyance. Still other people were asked to recall incidents in which someone had gotten angry at them. Respondents were asked who was involved in the interchange, what had happened, what they thought and felt, and how they responded to the episode.

Averill's research revealed a fascinating finding. In most people's minds, anger and hatred are almost synonymous. Yet, Averill found that it is the people we love and like who are most likely to enrage us. Loved ones spark 29% of angry episodes, someone well-known and liked, 24%, and acquaintances, 25%. Only rarely does someone who is well-known and disliked (8%) or a stranger (13%) generate strong angry feelings. It appears, then, that those we love are most capable, or at least most likely, of provoking us.

WHAT CAUSES ANGER?

People are harder to infuriate than one might think. Once, at the University of Minnesota, Elaine Hatfield and her colleague, G. William Walster, tried to make college men angry as the prelude to a laboratory experiment but were singularly unsuccessful. They tried insulting and frustrating the men, but nothing worked. They then asked other colleagues to keep a record of the things that made them angry (thinking that perhaps they could reproduce the same irritations and provoke the same rage in the laboratory). For example, a University of Minnesota symphony player reported that he had sat fuming when, during one of his most complicated trumpet solos, a horn player in the next row kept sneezing on his neck.

Hatfield and Walster decided that they could reproduce that scenario. They assigned college men to work on a fast-paced test. While one man was

FIGURE 10.2 Expression of anger in a young girl.

busy calculating, a confederate of the researchers in the seat behind him kept sneezing. Each time he sneezed, he surreptitiously squeezed a spray bottle aimed at the test-taker's neck. What happened? Nothing. The test-taker patiently handed the sneezer a tissue, sympathetically murmuring, "Are you okay?" After several other failures, Hatfield and Walster finally gave up trying to produce anger on the spot and settled for asking men and women to recall times they had been angry.

Later researchers have been more successful, having found evidence that people who behave in socially unacceptable ways—who are ugly and ill-kempt (Hatfield & Sprecher, 1986b), who are phony and manipulative (Jones, 1964), who are of low character (Hatfield, Walster, & Berscheid, 1978), who are shiftless, boring, or even dare to disagree with us (Byrne, 1971)—arouse our wrath.

What causes anger in real life? Averill (1983) asked people involved in angry interchanges what had sparked the trouble. Table 10.1 reveals the replies of both the people who were angry and the targets of that anger and provides evidence that anger is an accusation.

As we see from Table 10.1, more than anything else, anger is an attribution of blame. The angry are eager to cast blame; their targets are naturally less willing to accept it. It is not that the "innocent" targets do not understand the accusations. They generally do understand why the other was angry. It is only that they deny any wrongdoing (i.e.,"I had a right to do what I did," or "It couldn't be helped").

Albert Bandura (1983) has suggested that four types of stimuli excite anger: verbal insults or threats, physical assaults, blocking the completion of some activity (thwarting), and depriving a person of reward. (Note that the first two cases involve being affected by some aversive event, whereas the other two involve the loss of some positive reinforcer.) Once anger is unleashed, what effects does it have? Let us first consider the effects anger has on the angry themselves.

The Anatomy of Anger

THE LOOK OF ANGER

It is easy to recognize the face of anger. Carroll Izard (1977) provides a careful description of the innate facial expressions associated with rage (see Figure 10.2, on the previous page). The muscles of the brow move inward and downward, creating a frown, and the eyes have a foreboding appearance, fixed in a hard stare directed toward the target. The nostrils dilate, and the wings of the nose flare out. The lips are opened and drawn back in a rectangle-like shape; the teeth are clenched. Often the face is flushed. The look is unmistakable, especially in children.

Table 10.1   **Perceptions of Angry Persons and Targets**

PERCEPTION OF INSTIGATION	ANGRY PERSON	TARGET
A voluntary and unjustified act	59%	21%
A potentially avoidable accident or event	28%	28%
A voluntary and justified act	12%	35%
An unavoidable accident or event	2%	15%

THE NEUROANATOMY AND NEUROPHYSIOLOGY OF ANGER

But what happens beneath the surface of anger? Are there clear patterns of physiological changes that occur as well? Kenneth Moyer (1986) argues that humans, rational as they are, cannot overcome their neural heritage. In the brains of all animals, specific neural systems exist which trigger anger, hostility, and aggression. Moyer (1968) posits eight kinds of aggression—predatory aggression, intermale aggression, fear-induced aggression, irritable aggression, territorial defense, maternal aggression, instrumental aggression, and sex-related aggression. The various forms of aggression have much in common; nonetheless, each type of aggression is associated with slightly different neural and endrocrine responses. Evidence for this comes from a variety of sources, including brain stimulation studies, brain pathology studies, data on neural inhibition, and evidence concerning blood chemistry. Let us take a closer look at these data.

Brain Stimulation Experiments

For medical reasons, several hundred people at various times have had electrodes implanted in their brains. Wires are attached to small sockets cemented to the skull. These patients can be invited into the laboratory, plugged in, and precise areas deep in the brain electrically stimulated. Such experiments have provided a great deal of information as to how the brain works. They provide evidence that anger may be sparked, in part, by the stimulation of various limbic system structures. Moyer (1986) observes:

> A case reported by King (1961) is particularly instructive. King's patient was a very mild-mannered woman who was a generally submissive, kindly, friendly person. An electrode was implanted in the amygdala. When this patient was stimulated with a current of 4 mA [milli-amps] there was no observable change in her behavior. When the amperage was increased to 5 mA, she became hostile and aggressive. She said such things as, "Take my blood pressure. Take it now." Then she said, "If you're going to hold me you'd better get five more men." Whereupon she stood up and started to strike the experimenter.
>
> It was possible to turn this woman's anger on and off with a simple flick of the switch because the electrode was located in a part of the neural system for hostility. She indicated having felt anger. She also reported being concerned about the fact that she was angry. She did not report pain or other discomfort. She was simply "turned-on" angry. Similar findings have been reported by other investigators (Heath, 1964; Sem-Jacobsen, 1968). (pp. 221–222)

One famous case is that of Julia (Mark & Ervin, 1970). When Julia was two, she had an attack of encephalitis which produced brain disease. By 22, she was experiencing frequent epileptic seizures and displaying severe temper tantrums. Her outbursts were followed by intense remorse. Julia seriously assaulted people at least 12 times without provocation. Finally, in desperation, surgeons implanted electrodes in the temporal lobe of her brain, thus making it possible to stimulate the brain's depths, while Julia went about business as usual. Once, when she was talking to her psychiatrist, researchers stimulated the hippocampus. Julia's EEG readings increased. She was blank for a moment and then began to furiously pound the wall with her fist. Another time, while she was singing and playing a guitar, researchers stimulated her amygdala. Again, after a buildup lasting a few seconds, she lost contact, stared ahead blankly, and was unable to answer questions. Then, during a storm of subcortical electrical activity, she swung her guitar past the head of the psychiatrist and smashed it against the wall. Of course, generally, brain stimulation made things better for Julia, not worse, as in these instances. (To remind yourself of where the various limbic system structures we have cited are located, see chapter 4, Figure 4.7.)

Brain Pathology

A number of dysfunctions in the human brain have been found to increase irritability and hostility. Brain tumors in the septal region, the temporal lobe, and the frontal lobe have been found to produce anger, verbal aggression, or even homicidal rage. If the tumors are removed, the patients regain their normal personalities. Researchers describe one such case (Sweet, Ervin, & Mark, 1969). A violent man, with a tumor of the temporal lobe, had attempted to kill his wife and daughter with a butcher knife. When brought to the hospital, he was in a full-blown rage; he snarled, showed his teeth, and attempted to hit or kick anyone who came close enough. His history revealed that over a period of six months, his personality had gradually changed. Initially, he was described as a reasonable, agreeable man. Then, he had begun to complain of blurred vision and intense headaches. Still later, the violent behavior described above became evident. The story has a happy ending. When the tumor pressing on his anterior temporal lobe was removed, his symptoms rapidly abated.

In 1966, in a similar but much less fortunate case, Charles Whitman killed his wife and mother and then went to the top of the University of Texas Tower, where he holed up with a rifle and began to spray the campus with bullets. He shot 38 people, killing 14. He kept students pinned down for more than two hours. In the end, he himself was killed by police sharpshooters. Whitman left a letter in which he recalled his "overwhelming violent impulses" and "tremendous headaches." It movingly and frighteningly described his state of mind:

> I don't understand what it is that compels me to type this letter. . . . I don't really understand myself these days. . . . I have been a victim of many unusual and irrational thoughts. These thoughts constantly recur, and it requires a tremendous mental effort to concentrate on useful and progressive tasks. . . . After my death I wish that an autopsy would be performed on me to see if there is any visible physical disorder. . . .

It was after much thought that I decided to kill my wife, Kathy, tonight after I pick her up from work. . . . I love her dearly, and she has been a fine wife to me as any man could hope to have. I cannot rationally pinpoint any specific reason for doing this. . . . At this time, though, the most prominent reason in my mind is that I truly do not consider this world worth living in, and am prepared to die, and I do not want to leave her to suffer alone in it. I intend to kill her as painlessly as possible. (Quoted in Johnson, 1972, p. 78)

His autopsy revealed a malignant brain tumor the size of a walnut in the area of the amygdala (Sweet, Ervin, & Mark, 1969).

A number of other types of brain injury produce personality changes that involve irritability and loss of impulse control. These include diffuse head injuries caused by falls or automobile accidents, some kinds of epilepsy, brain damage caused by rabies, and encephalitis lethargica (a brain inflammation).

Neural Inhibition

Thus far, we have discussed factors that might stimulate the neural systems for anger and aggression, but these systems can also be inhibited (Goldstein & Siegel, 1980). José Delgado (1963, 1975) has repeatedly shown that vicious rhesus monkeys can be tamed by the stimulation of aggression-suppressor areas. In one experiment, an aggressive "boss monkey" dominated the rest of the colony with his threatening behavior and attacks. A radio-controlled electrode was implanted in the boss's caudate nucleus. When the transmitter was activated, the nucleus was stimulated, and the animal's aggressive tendencies were blocked. The other monkeys became less frightened and less submissive in his presence.

During one phase of the experiment, the button for the transmitter was placed inside the cage near the feeding tray. One small monkey learned to stand next to the button and watch the boss monkey. Every time the boss would start to threaten, the little monkey would press the button and calm him down.

Does this example have any parallels in your experience? What "buttons" do you press (or make sure not to press) to keep your "boss" calm? Humans have suppressor areas, just as do animals. For example, Heath (1963) describes the reaction to stimulation of an epileptic patient who had had an electrode implanted in his septal area. The patient was feeling persecuted; he was enraged, agitated, and confused. Suddenly, physicians stimulated his septal area. His behavior changed almost instantly. He became euphoric. Interestingly, he was unable to explain the sudden shift in his feelings.

Blood Chemistry

Changes in the blood chemistry, including hormonal changes and a variety of pharmaceutical agents, may produce corresponding changes in anger and hostility (see Brain, 1980). Animal breeders have known for centuries that a raging bull can be converted into a gentle steer by castration, which reduces the level of testosterone in the bloodstream. Some psychologists have argued that testosterone may be equally important in humans. Harold Persky, Keith Smith, and Gopal Basu (1971) studied men who ranged in age from 17 to 66. They found that the younger men produced twice as much testosterone as did the older men. In the younger men, the production rate of testosterone also was highly related to the Buss-Durkee Hostility Inventory (which appears in this chapter). Such findings are interesting, given that violent crime in the United States is most prevalent among men between the ages of 15 to 24. Men may not be alone in showing a relationship between angry feelings and hormonal levels or changes. A few women find that they suffer during the week before menstruation when they feel irritable, hostile, and easily aroused to anger (Hopson & Rosenfeld, 1984).

Frustration and stress also influence blood chemistry and anger (Plutchik & Kellerman, 1986). Drugs may also have an influence. For example, some people who take theophyllin medications to handle asthma find that the drug makes them extremely irritable at times.

THE VISCERAL DETERMINANTS OF ANGER

Fear and anger ("flight" versus "fight") produce very similar visceral patterns. So, are there any visceral differences between these two emotions? Magda Arnold (1950) suggested that there might be. She concluded that fear is a strong arousal state of the sympathetic branch of the autonomic nervous system, whereas anger is a strong arousal state of both the sympathetic and parasympathetic branches of the autonomic nervous system (see chapter 2). Soon thereafter, research by Albert Ax provided evidence suggesting that Arnold was right (see Box 10.2).

EXPRESSIONS OF ANGER

Angry people can express their feelings in a multitude of ways—they can make a joke, sulk, demand an explanation, or stamp off in a huff. Researchers have a good idea of how angry people usually do respond. For example, in the study we described earlier, Averill (1983) asked men and women to recall the very last time they had been angry and to indicate how they had reacted. What did they wish they could have done? What did they actually do? Their answers appear in Table 10.2.

When we look at how angry people want to act, we see that they wish they could pour out their wrath; they long to say something. The desire to actually do something (i.e., "punch someone out") is less common. To a lesser extent, people want to set things right—they are inclined to calm down the situation and talk the situation over.

When we look at how angry people actually do respond, however, we see that they are fairly civilized. Usually, they respond softly—they try to calm down the situation, to talk it over. On those few occasions when they

BOX 10.2 _____

The Ax Experiments

In 1953, Albert F. Ax conducted a series of experiments to determine whether any physiological differences existed between fear and anger. He advertised for men and women to participate in a medical experiment. When volunteers arrived at his office, they were wired to a polygraph that measured heart rate, blood pressure, sweating, and muscle tension (see chapter 7, on psychophysiological methods for measuring emotion). A nurse took their blood pressure every minute. Unbeknownst to the subjects, they were about to become participants in a drama.

Sometimes, the experimenter would frighten the men and women. Suddenly, they began to feel an intermittent shock in their fingers. When they mentioned it to the experimenter, he pretended to check the wiring. Then, he pressed a concealed key that sent sparks flying. He exclaimed with alarm, "This is a dangerous high-voltage short circuit." He and the nurse dashed around in agitation, creating an atmosphere of alarm and confusion. Eventually, they "fixed the wiring" and assured the subjects that now everything was fine. As you might expect, the men and women were frightened. One woman kept pleading, "Please take the wires off. Oh! Please help me." Another said she had prayed to be spared. "Well, everyone has to go sometime," said one; "I thought this might be my time."

In another part of Ax's experiment, the men and women were angered. This time, the polygraph operator was the key figure. He was described as an emergency replacement who had previously been fired for arrogance and incompetence. When he entered the room to check the electrodes, it became clear that the decision to fire him was more than justified. He badgered the nurse, talked sarcastically to the subjects, and generally abused them. He was surly, rude, and offensive. Nearly everyone in the experiment was angry. Some of the men observed, "Say, what goes on here? I was just about to punch that character on the nose."

Ax concluded that fear and anger did differ: Fear's physiological patterns resembled those produced by an injection of adrenaline. Anger's patterns resembled those produced by a combination of adrenaline and noradrenaline. In anger, the blood "boils," the face becomes hot, the muscles tense, and the stomach churns. A feeling of power and an impulse to strike out, to attack the source of anger, prevails. Ax found that anger involved increased diastolic blood pressure, skin conductance, and muscle tension, and lowered heart rate.

We now know that Ax's equation, fear = adrenaline, anger = adrenaline + noradrenaline, is simplistic. Ax seems to have overinterpreted the small differences he found. We now know that adrenaline is an all-purpose fuel. It is the energy behind most of our emotional states. The higher the circulating levels of adrenaline, the more intense our emotional reactions—fear or anger.

(It may be however, that fear and anger differ in other ways. As you discovered in chapter 6, some scientists think that the various emotions may be linked to distinctive patterns of ANS responses and facial expressions. Whether or not that is so is yet to be determined (Ekman, Levinson, & Friesen, 1983).

lash out, they do so with their tongues—they are verbally aggressive. Rarely are they physically aggressive. In brief, how people feel like acting and how they actually do act are two different things. Generally, people coolly select the best way to express their hot feelings.

What factors determine how the angry respond? Theorists have identified

Table 10.2   **Reactions to Anger**

RESPONSE TYPE	IMPULSES FELT[a]	ACTUAL REACTIONS[a]
Nonaggressive Responses		
Engaging in calming activities	60%	60%
Talking over the incident with a neutral party; no intent to harm the offender	59%	59%
Talking over the incident with the offender without exhibiting hostility	52%	39%
Engaging in activities opposite to the instigation of anger	14%	19%
Aggressive Responses		
Indirect Aggression		
Telling a third party in order to get back at the instigator	42%	34%
Harming something important to the instigator	25%	9%
Displaced Aggression		
Against a nonhuman object	32%	28%
Against a person	24%	25%
Direct Aggression		
Verbal or symbolic aggression	82%	49%
Denial or removal of some benefit	59%	41%
Physical aggression or punishment	40%	10%

[a]Expressed as percentages of episodes in which response occurred "somewhat" or "very much."

two major factors which shape behavior. Some theorists focus on the "hard-wiring"—instinctive factors that predispose species to react aggressively or submissively. Others focus on the "programming"—factors that allow humans to learn a wide variety of techniques for getting the things they want.

The "Hard-Wiring" of Aggression

Theorists from three different traditions—the sociobiological, the psychoanalytic, and the frustration-aggression perspectives—argue that the potential to react aggressively is "wired" into individuals.

THE SOCIOBIOLOGICAL PERSPECTIVE

Sociobiologists such as Edward O. Wilson (1978) and ethologists such as Nikolas Tinbergen (1951) or the Nobel prize winner Konrad Lorenz (1965) assume that patterns of aggression are wired into all species. When appropriate stimuli are presented, aggressive patterns may be triggered.

Wilson (1978) points out that certain basic forms of instinctive response are found in almost all species—that is, (a) territorial aggression, (b) dominance aggression, (c) sexual aggression, (d) parental-disciplinary aggression, (e) weaning aggression, (f) moralistic aggression, (g) predatory aggression, and (h) antipredatory aggression. One example of predatory aggression is displayed by ants:

> One of the more dramatic spectacles of insect biology is provided by the large-headed soldiers of certain species belonging to the genus Pheidole. These individuals have mandibles shaped approximately like the blades of wire clippers, and their heads are largely filled by massive abductor muscles. When clashes occur between colonies, the soldiers rush in, attack blindly, and leave the field littered with the severed antennae, legs, and abdomens of their defeated enemies. (p. 245)

Ethologists such as Raymond Dart (1953) assumed that innate aggressive tendencies have been transferred virtually intact to humans:

> The blood-bespattered, slaughter-gutted archives of human history from the earliest Egyptian and Sumerian records to the most recent atrocities of the Second World War accord with early universal cannibalism, with animal and human sacrificial practices or their substitutes in formalized religions and with worldwide scalping, head-hunting, body-mutilating and necrophiliac practices of mankind in proclaiming this common blood lust differentiator, this mark of Cain that separates man dietetically from his anthropoidal relatives and allies him rather with the deadliest of Carnivora. (p. 255)

Today, Dart's rhetoric sounds a bit extreme. Nonetheless, most sociobiologists and ethologists assume that humans possess innate aggressive patterning. Moreover, this view accords with familiar literary conceptions of man. In the classic *Lord of the Flies* (1963), Nobel Laureate William Golding tells the tale of a planeload of schoolboys downed on an island in the Pacific. They begin as sunny, innocent, gentle youths, but as they claw for survival, they become increasingly wild, cunning, cruel, and aggressive. Golding's message is clearly that the potential for aggression is an inherited characteristic of the species.

Luckily, species also possess instinctive mechanisms which keep aggression in check. Konrad Lorenz (1965) points out that animals rarely kill members of their own species; mechanisms have evolved which inhibit intraspecies aggression. Baboons, for example, usually bare their teeth, shrieking loudly, and assume threatening postures before they fight. Generally, such threats are enough to frighten weaker baboons, and they back off. If there is a fight, baboons have a way of signaling "Uncle." When baboons are losing a fight, they often turn and present their rear end to the other baboon. The victor responds by breaking off the fight and mounting the loser (Washburn & DeVore, 1962). Other animals have evolved similar mechanisms. At the height of a struggle between two timber wolves, the loser will turn its head upward, exposing its jugular vein. This gesture automatically triggers the inhibition of the victor's aggression (Lorenz, 1965). The species which are best equipped for hunting and killing often possess the strongest inhibitory mechanisms.

The primitive human was a fairly puny species, with small teeth and brittle claws. Thus, in the sociobiological view, humans lacked the powerful instinctive mechanisms to inhibit aggression displayed by some other species. Now, with the development of modern weaponry, the capacity for destruction has far outstripped our capacity for inhibition. The evolutionary balance has been destroyed and threatens our survival.

THE PSYCHOANALYTIC APPROACH

In 1932, Albert Einstein wrote to Sigmund Freud, "What can be done to protect mankind from the curse of war?" Freud's reply was pessimistic. Human instincts, he argued, are of only two kinds: those which seek to preserve and unite (Eros) and those which seek to destroy (Thanatos). In humankind, the forces of love versus hate are in a delicate balance. Freud was convinced that as civilization evolved, cultural attitudes and the justified dread of the consequences might put an end to war. Nonetheless, humanity's destructive potential would always exist, right below the surface. Freud ended his letter to Einstein knowing that what he had said must have disappointed him (Freud, 1950).

In other writings, Freud proposed a sort of "pressure-cooker" model of anger/aggression. As instinctively generated anger builds, it seeks release in one way or another. People have a choice. They can discharge their anger in small, sizzling displays, or they can compress it until eventually there is an explosion.

Freud's model has had a profound impact on psychotherapy. Today, like Freud, most therapists assume that anger is an inevitable consequence of an intimate encounter. Unless people find some constructive way of dealing with their feelings, there will be an explosion.

Moreover, psychoanalysts warn that anger, fear, sadness, and stress can combine to overtax the immune system and make people vulnerable to a variety of diseases. For example, as Joannes Groen (1975) summarizes:

> Many doctors believe, on the basis of their clinical impressions, that emotional disturbances play an important role in the causation of functional disorders such as the cardiac arhythmias and tachycardias, Raynaud's disease, migraine and tension headaches, the hyperventilation syndrome, functional diarrhea, habitual constipation, dysmenorrhea, ejaculatio praecox, vaginismus, and impotence. A similar "psychogenic" etiology has been hypothesized for the so-called psychosomatic disorders: peptic ulcer, ulcerative colitis, essential hypertension, bronchial asthma, anorexia nervosa, and obesity. (p. 738)

Today, neurophysiologists are attempting to spell out the links among emotion, the immune system, and disease (see chapter 13). The process is by no means a simple one (Tavris, 1982). The development of our current interest in the role of emotional variables in illness can be credited to the psychoanalytic movement. In one debate, however, Freudian theory has not fared so well.

THE GREAT CATHARSIS DEBATE

In the fifth century B.C., Aristotle (1951) and Plato (1965) began tilting as to whether a link exists between what we see and what we do. Plato (*The Republic*, Book 10, Chapter 38) argued that to observe an action in the theatre is to be tempted to perform that action.

> Few, I believe, are capable of reflecting that to enter into another's feelings must have an effect on our own: The emotions of pity our sympathy has strengthened will not be easy to restrain when we are suffering ourselves. . . . Similar effects are produced by poetic representations of love and anger and all those desires and feelings of pleasure or pain which accompany our every action. It waters the growth of passions which should be allowed to wither away and sets them up in control, although the goodness and happiness of our lives depend on their being held in subjection. (pp. 338–339).

Aristotle (*The Poetics*, Section 6) took the opposite point of view:

> A tragedy, then, is the imitation of an action that is serious and also, as having magnitude, complete in itself; in language with pleasurable accessories, each kind brought in separately in the parts of the work; in a dramatic, not in a narrative form; with incidents arousing pity and fear, wherewith to accomplish its catharsis of such emotions. (p. 230)

The notion that one can purge one's emotions by expression through art has been labeled the **catharsis hypothesis**. The Freudians, of course, applauded Aristotle's position. They assumed that when people are engrossed in filmed violence, when they relive past events in therapy or shout at someone who annoys them, they are blowing off steam. According to the "pressure-cooker" theory, they should be *less* angry and aggressive than before.

In 1979, Thomas Scheff (1979) proposed an updated version of the hypothesis, arguing that catharsis is a therapeutic process for two reasons: (a) Repressed emotions such as fear and anger are discharged by laughing and crying; mood is improved and tension is reduced; and (b) in psychotherapy, ritual, and drama, people gain a sense of clarity. They can achieve "double vision," being simultaneously a participant and observer.

Freud's perspective dominated therapeutic practice in the 1960s. Couples were encouraged to imagine they were biting a piece of flesh out of someone's body, to smack each other with foam baseball bats, to give a "primal scream," and to beat on pillows in the expectation that angry feelings so powerfully expressed would spend themselves and disappear.

Does catharsis work? Not really. The evidence makes it clear that the situation is more complex than Freud had hoped (Tavris, 1982). Angry people have a dual problem—first, they have to deal with their own emotions and then deal with whatever problems they are facing. When people are enraged and feel dangerously out of control, at first it may seem to help them to cry and pound on pillows until they are exhausted. In that sense, some merit can be attached to the claim that "violent emotional expressions" may have some benefits.

But when we ask, "What next?" we see that things become more difficult. If anything, it appears that Plato, not Aristotle and Freud, has won the great debate (see Bramel, 1969; Tavris, 1982). Sometimes an expression of anger helps clear the air; but often, as Plato suggested, the direct expression of anger is self-indulgent—it begets more anger and aggression. What is probably important is not whether people express anger or withhold it in a single instance, but whether they use their anger to change the things that upset them in the first place. This is what brings about true personal peace in the long run. Let us review some of the voluminous research that leads us to these conclusions.

Catharsis and Frustration

Jack Hokanson and his Florida State University colleagues (1970) conducted a series of studies which provide an understanding of the catharsis process.

In an early study, Hokanson and Michael Burgess (1962b) set out to discover (a) the effect that frustration has on general physiological arousal, and (b) the effect that it has when one has a chance to get even.

Students were told that the authors were studying physiological responses to performance on intellectual tasks. To aid in establishing this deception, the students were first asked to take a portion of the WAIS (Wechsler Adult Intelligence Scale). Then they were to count backward from 100 to 0 by twos, as quickly as they could. (Backward counting is a common laboratory stress inducer, in this case called a "serial twos" task.) During the experiment, heart rate was monitored continuously, and blood pressure was measured every two minutes.

During this second task, a critical event happened. In the No-frustration group, the experimenter merely praised students when they reached 0. In the Frustration group, the experimenter repeatedly interrupted and harassed the subjects for counting too slowly. He made them start over three times. Finally, he insisted that the subjects' attitudes made further testing impossible. As you might expect, frustrated men and women were far more aroused than their peers. Their hearts raced and their systolic blood pressure shot up.

The next step was to see the effect that retaliation would have on arousal level. Men and women were randomly assigned to one of three different conditions: Some subjects had a chance to verbally aggress. (They were asked to fill out, in the experimenter's presence, a brief questionnaire evaluating the experimenter's capabilities as an experimenter, including the way he related to subjects.) Other subjects had a chance to physically aggress against him. (They were given 10 opportunities to shock him. Most of them depressed the shock plunger eight times.) In the No-aggression group, subjects had no chance to aggress against the experimenter, either verbally or physically. In the Fantasy-aggression group, they merely had a chance to conjure up an aggressive story if they wished.

This early study found that under the right conditions, retaliation did seem to produce some catharsis. When frustrated subjects were able to aggress either physically or verbally against the source of their frustration, their blood pressures and heart rates returned to normal with surprising rapidity. When they were not able to aggress, their blood pressures and heart rates remained high. (Additional support for the catharsis notion has been secured by Geen, Stonner, & Shope, 1975, and Kahn, 1966.)

> *A*nybody can become angry—that is easy; but to be angry with the right person, and to the right degree, and at the right time, and for the right purpose, and in the right way—that is not within everybody's power and is not easy.
>
> *ARISTOTLE*

Conditions Affecting Catharsis

However, subsequent research, much of it by social psychologists, shows that a catharsis effect can be realized only under very limited conditions:

1. People must be angry and aroused at the time they are given an opportunity to retaliate (Bramel, Taub, & Blum, 1968; Doob, 1970).
2. They must have the chance to retaliate against the person who "caused" their problem; if he or she was arbitrary, malevolent, obnoxious, and aggressive, so much the better (Konecni, 1984). Attacking a substitute does not help much (Hokanson, Burgess, & Cohen, 1963). Although many of us believe that indulging in vengeful daydreams, punching walls, or kicking the cat ventilates our feelings, research indicates that such reactions are generally useless in the long run (Berkowitz & Alioto, 1973; Goranson, 1970; Konecni, 1984; Mallick & McCandless, 1966).
3. The victim must get the retaliation deserved, no more and no less. If one goes overboard, one may feel guilty later. If one pulls one's punches, resentment may remain (Konecni, 1984; Hatfield, Walster, & Berscheid, 1978; Hatfield et al., 1984).
4. The target must be nonintimidating—so that subjects do not feel anxious afterward (Hokanson & Burgess (1962a). Of course, such conditions do not occur often, especially in combination.

But more difficulties arise for the catharsis hypothesis than simply that it has limitations. Other research warns that when people express their angry, aggressive feelings, they often get themselves so worked up that the situation may become worse than it was before. For example, Robert Arms and his colleagues report that Canadian and American football, wrestling, and hockey fans exhibit more hostility after viewing sporting events than before (Arms, Russell, & Sandelands, 1979; Goldstein & Arms, 1971). Not even a war seems to purge a people's aggressive feelings. In fact, after a war, a nation's murder rate tends to climb (Archer & Gartner, 1976). Author Fay Weldon (1987) provides a graphic description of the process by which anger begets anger:

> Bad deeds escalate: even little ones. They get tossed like a magic ball between one human being and another, back and forth, getting bigger every time: you did *this* so I'll do *that,* until the hands cannot hold it, the burden is too great: and the ball falls, and bursts, and turns out to be full of some kind of murderous corrosive acid which, once it begins to flow, cannot be stopped; a whole river of malice, burning, maiming, killing as it goes, and widows, and widowers too these days, and orphans weep every time a wrong is righted, and the people hop around the street blinded or one-legged and then the flow of malice slows to a trickle, and stops and dries up, like the chain reaction from the first atomic bombs over New Mexico. It's finished. The ball's empty. But terrible until it is. So never say a harsh word if you can say a kind one: it may be you who starts the war. (p. 126)

An array of laboratory experiments and correlational studies have come to the same conclusion—anger expressed is often anger/aggression increased. (See Ebbesen, Duncan, & Konecni, 1975; Feshbach, 1956, for a sampling of such studies.) In short, feuds such as the Hatfield and McCoy feud have their own momentum. A sassy reply leads to a slap. Justification follows justification. Soon, no one is speaking. In the old Laurel and Hardy silent comedy routines, a small irritation inevitably escalates into a pie-throwing melee, houses are razed, and city blocks collapse. It appears that sometimes, life has more in common with a Laurel and Hardy skit than we might like to believe.

Gender Differences in Catharsis

The most devastating blow to Freud's catharsis formulation was yet to come. After conducting a number of studies, Hokanson (1970) observed that men and women seemed to have quite different reactions when they were forced to deal with an impossible person. He began to suspect that people could be taught to respond to provocation in a variety of ways; if the techniques they tried worked, they would feel "cathartic-like relief." However, for men as opposed to women, the techniques that work may be quite different for cultural reasons. When men are angered, they are expected to express their anger. Usually, this works (Hokanson & Shetler, 1961; Hokanson & Burgess, 1962b). Women are supposed to react quite differently. They are expected to smile, patiently try to figure out what went wrong, and calm things down. This is "what works" (Hokanson & Edelman, 1969). In short, no universal "catharsis response" really exists.

Not surprisingly, then, Hokanson and his colleagues found that while traditionally, men benefit from expressing their angry feelings, women do not. Hokanson and Robert Edelman (1969) and Hokanson, R. R. Willers, and Elizabeth Koropsak (1968) found that men and women responded quite differently to aggression. Men showed the usual vascular arousal when shocked (their heart rates climbed and their blood pressures rose); when they retaliated, however, they showed a rapid, cathartic-like reduction in arousal level. Counteraggression was the most prevalent response made by the men. When they tried to ignore aggression or to turn things around by acting in a friendly way, catharsis, in the form of physiological arousal reduction, did not occur.

Women reacted quite differently. They, too, were upset when shocked. But, if they were friendly in return, their vascular arousal showed a cathartic-like recovery. If they tried to ignore aggression or retaliate, catharsis (in the sense of lowering of arousal) did not occur. Hokanson concluded that any response that serves to terminate, reduce, or avoid noxious stimulation from others will acquire cathartic-like properties. Perhaps it should not be surprising that the very act of performing actions that have in the past proven to be successful in reducing others' aggression is accompanied by relief, whether the act was in the form of counteraggression or friendliness.

Of course, sex roles are learned, and what is learned can be unlearned. Hokanson found that men and women could be taught new responses . . . sometimes in a matter of minutes. In one experiment (Hokanson, Willers, & Koropsak, 1968), the man or woman was seated at a console, their partner seated nearby at an identical console. The couple could communicate with each other by pressing either of two keys—"shock" or "reward." Everyone started out in a good mood. They were told that the experiment was designed to replicate real life: "If you do not like someone or what they are doing, you might try to hurt them; that is comparable to a shock response. If you like someone, you might try to do something nice for them; that is similar to a reward response." In reality, the "partner's" responses had been prearranged by the experimenters.

The partners' conversation went on for 32 rounds. The partner sent a reward 16 times, and a shock 16 times. How did the men and women respond to their enigmatic partners? The men responded angrily; they gave their partner "a taste of his own medicine." The chance to be aggressive, apparently, was a relief—to them. Their heart rates dropped and their blood pressures fell. The women responded more calmly; they provided more reward, less shock. And their generosity was a relief—to them. Their heart rates dropped and their blood pressures fell.

Suddenly, the rules changed. During the next 60 trials, the men were given a reward every time they were friendly in response to shock, and the women were given a reward every time they showed a little aggressiveness. Hokanson and his colleagues observed that two things happened as a result of this new situation: (a) The men learned the value of a generous reaction, and the women quickly learned that now aggressiveness would pay off . . . and not surprisingly, they became more aggressive than before; and (b) The traditional form of catharsis for each sex was reversed. The women showed catharsis-like reduction in heart rates and blood pressures when they responded aggressively and had a slow vascular recovery when they were friendly. The opposite was now the case for the men—catharsis now followed friendliness, not belligerence.

In a final study, Hokanson & L. Stone (1969) showed that people could learn to do almost anything, even masochistically shocking themselves if it paid off, and that such responses would reduce their arousal level.

Social psychological research, then, casts doubts on the Freudian "pressure-cooker" model of anger/aggression. It documents that people can learn a variety of techniques for dealing with angry feelings. People probably do best if they learn several ways of coping with their own feelings and with life's problems. Angry people ought to be able to explain their ideas and feelings to their partners and to try to understand their mate's point of view (Feshbach, 1956), act sweetly or angrily as the occasion demands, make practical changes so that the cause of irritation is eliminated (Straus, Gelles, and Steinmetz, 1980), or recognize when things are hopeless and abandon the relationship (Hatfield, 1984). This is discussed more in another section of this chapter, dealing with the "programming" of anger.

THE FRUSTRATION-AGGRESSION MODEL

The Origins of Aggression

In their classic monograph, *Frustration and Aggression,* John Dollard and several of his Yale colleagues (1939) proposed a sweeping hypothesis—"Frustration always leads to some form of aggression," and "Aggression is always a consequence of frustration" (p. 1).

Frustration, said Dollard and his colleagues, is anything that blocks one's attaining a goal. They defined **aggression** as fantasies, plans, or actions which are intended to hurt another (p. 9). Today, most researchers go beyond this analysis to distinguish two types of aggression—instrumental aggression and angry aggression. In **instrumental,** or **operant aggression,** people hurt others not because they want to, but because that is the only way to achieve other goals. For example, in the film *Prizzi's Honor,* a hit man and his similarly employed sweetheart systematically knifed, shot, and maimed others not because they hated them, but simply because they were honor bound to fulfill any and all contracts. In the end, of course, the newlyweds were given contracts on each other. Similarly, given this definition of instrumental aggression, most soldiers in wartime would probably say that the term accurately describes the nature of their attacks on the enemy. In short, this form of aggression is like any other operant behavior—it is performed because it is reinforced.

In **angry aggression,** by contrast, people strike out at others because they are enraged. Their aim is to hurt. Most murders are of this sort; white-hot anger sparks a violent outburst. A powerful reflexive component comes into play. Experientially, the act may seem almost out of one's control, with a force of its own. In this chapter, we are interested in the emotion of anger and, thus, angry aggression.

In a classic test of the frustration-aggression hypothesis, a team of researchers (Barker, Dembo, & Lewin, 1941) deliberately frustrated a group of preschoolers. Children were taken to a playroom, where they played happily with the tag ends of some toys that were lying about—a cup, a teapot without a lid, and an iron and board without anything to iron. Then a screen was lifted to reveal a room full of glorious toys—a doll house with lights, carpets, curtains, and full furnishings, plus a tiny island, complete with lighthouse, wharf, and a fleet of boats surrounded by sandy beaches and a lake. They could look but not touch. The frustrated children's play regressed to play typical of younger children (e.g., they whined, sulked, kicked over the ironing board, and scribbled instead of drawing). Observers rated the average regression in mental age at 17 months.

John Dollard et al. (1939) observe that frustration is especially intense when: (a) people's motivation to achieve a goal is very strong; (b) blocking is complete; and (c) frustrating experiences are repeated. Under such conditions, aggression builds and builds until it is released (see Box 10.3).

The Inhibition of Aggressive Acts

Of course, people do not strike out every time they are frustrated. Imagine that you are late for a final exam. You are very nervous, and you speed toward class. But you are stopped in a radar trap. An impossibly long delay follows, including a lecture on safe driving. We can be pretty certain that you will be angry and frustrated. But we can be equally sure that you will not tell off the police officer or run over the officer's foot with your car.

Dollard and his colleagues recognized that people's reactions to frustration are shaped by social rewards and punishments. For example, men and women will generally be more rude and aggressive if they believe that their victims are too old, too weak, or too powerless to retaliate (see Donnerstein & Donnerstein, 1972; Zimbardo, 1970.) In short, social consequences clearly have an impact on the frequency and intensity of angry aggression.

AGAINST WHOM WILL AGGRESSION BE DIRECTED?

Against whom do people wish they could aggress? Whom do they really attack? Most theorists assume that the most satisfying target for aggression is the person who caused the problem in the first place. Pinpointing the target is not always possible, however. We may not know who is responsible for

BOX 10.3

A "Sudden" Explosion of Anger

In the following quote, author Margaret Drabble (1939) vividly describes the long slow, buildup of anger that is suddenly and explosively released.

It was after midnight before the Houghtons and the Simpsons left. Having resented their presence during most of the evening, he found himself dreading their departure, knowing that he would have trouble before he was allowed to go to bed. And so he did, for Julie, once the door had closed upon them, turned upon him with an anger that had had four and a half hours to gather and thicken, and which had been not at all assuaged by her original hostilities when he had first entered. He had seen the storm signs during dinner, hung as clearly as a black cone by a bad sea: the violent way she had slopped his chicken onto his plate, the over-forceful way with which she had put that same plate down on the table before him, the way she had pulled her chair sharply to one side when he crossed behind her to get the corkscrew, the noises she made in her throat—sighings, clickings, dismissals—whenever he opened his own mouth. She had not looked at him once during the meal, nor addressed one remark to him indirectly; she had been biding her time: and now she let him have it, all of it, trembling with rage as she denounced his cruelty, his rudeness, his inadequacies as husband and father, his dullness as companion and host and guest. She went back over the whole of their past, raking up ten-year-old offences, divining in their pattern a deliberate plot of destruction, ending up, as so often, yelling at him, her face discoloured with emotion, her hair damp and oddly flying from her face in strange directions. (pp. 173–174)

our misery, we may be afraid of our tormenter, or it may not be appropriate to strike out against him or her. (It is unacceptable, for example, to hit an elderly woman in a supermarket, even if she smashes your foot with her shopping cart.)

In such circumstances, people may displace their aggression—by attacking someone or something else. In **displacement,** the man who is humiliated at his office is afraid to yell at his boss, so he yells at his wife. She, in turn, may pick on the children, who may kick the dog, who chases the cat.

Observational studies and laboratory experiments have demonstrated that frustrated individuals will displace aggression to relatively powerless minority groups. Carl Hovland and Robert Sears (1940), for example, argued that during years of economic depression, people are continually thwarted and, thus, look for trouble. During years of prosperity, when things are going well, they should be kinder. Hovland & Sears, then, proposed that there might be a negative relationship between economic prosperity and group aggression. To test their hypothesis, they chose the annual per-acre value of cotton in 14 Southern states for the years 1882–1930 as their index of economic prosperity. As a measure of aggression, they chose the number of lynchings in these same 14 states during the same period. As they expected, during the period when economic prosperity was steadily increasing, the number of lynchings steadily decreased. Of course, other factors may have played a part in producing this effect. For example, during this same period of history, other variables were operating to change people's social attitudes and behaviors. Time continued to pass and heal the wounds of the bitter Civil War. Law enforcement methods improved, and with the increasing population in the South, the opportunities for isolated and unpunished incidents such as lynchings of black men assuredly declined. This was also a period during which increased industrialization came to the South, altering old patterns of behavior sustained on the plantations. In short, Hovland and Sears's research, no matter how intriguing, is very difficult to assess.

Other, better-controlled experiments demonstrate that when men and women are frustrated, they are likely to take out their anger on a variety of minority groups—including Mexicans and Japanese (Miller & Bugelski, 1948), blacks (Cowen, Landes, & Schaet, 1959), and Jews (Campbell, 1947). One such experiment is described in Box 10.4.

How do people select their targets? According to Miller (1941), the selection depends on: (a) how frustrated individuals are; (b) how frightened they are of aggressing against their frustrator; and (c) how similar various potential targets are to their frustrator. (Evidence in support of this contention comes from Berkowitz, 1969.)

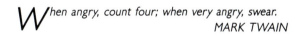

When angry, count four; when very angry, swear.
MARK TWAIN

WHAT FORM WILL AGGRESSION TAKE?

One of the most compelling scales designed to measure hostile/aggressive behaviors is the Buss-Durkee Inventory (Buss, 1961), named after its developers, Arnold Buss and Ann Durkee. Buss argues that men and women can express angry feelings in a variety of ways:

1. Resentment: jealousy and hatred of others. A feeling of anger at the world over real or fancied mistreatment.
2. Irritability: a readiness to explode at the slightest provocation. This includes quick temper, grouchiness, exasperation, and rudeness.
3. Suspicion: attribution of one's own hostility to others. This varies from merely being wary of people to being convinced that others are trying to humiliate and harm one.
4. Negativism: oppositional behavior, usually directed against authority. This involves a refusal to cooperate that may vary from passive noncompliance to open rebellion against rules or conventions.
5. Verbal aggression: negative affect expressed in both the style and content of speech. Style includes arguing, shouting, and screaming; content includes threats, curses, and being overly critical.

BOX 10.4

Frustration and Aggression

Neal Miller and Richard Bugelski (1948) conducted an ingenious experiment designed to test the hypothesis that when men and women are frustrated, they tend to take out their anger on the weak and powerless. The authors interviewed 31 young men who were working at a summer camp. Their first step was to find out how favorably or unfavorably the men usually felt about such ethnic groups as Mexicans or Japanese. Thus, they began by asking boys to indicate which of the following traits they thought were typical of either Mexicans or the Japanese. Different boys rated different groups:

friendly	selfish
smart	awkward
stingy	clean
cheerful	sly
honest	unfair
brave	cruel
polite	stupid
dangerous	patient
dirty	dependable
stubborn	good-looking
liars	peaceful

The authors calculated how positive or negative the boys' feelings were by summing up the number of positive versus negative traits the boys attributed to the ethnic groups.

The authors' next step was to frustrate the boys. They were called together and told that as part of the educational program of the camp, they were required to take a long, uninteresting battery of tests. The tests lived up to their billing. Most of the tests were so difficult that the boys were bound to fail miserably. But it became worse. Each week, the boys were allowed one special treat—they could attend "Bank Night" at a theater in town. They were allowed to go into the city to see a movie and to participate in a lottery. (The previous week one of them had won $200.) Bank Night was the highlight of the boys' week. As the boys continued to take the required tests, hour after hour, it became appallingly clear that they were going to miss the movie. Not surprisingly, the boys were irate.

Now things were ripe for the experimenters to see whether the boys' frustration would spill over into their evaluations of minority groups—such as Mexicans and Japanese. To find out, at the end of the testing session, the authors asked the boys to indicate the traits that were characteristic of whichever minority groups they had not rated earlier (the Mexicans or the Japanese.) The authors found that the frustrated boys did tend to take out their angry feelings on these minority groups. This time, the boys checked far fewer positive traits and checked far more negative traits as typical of these groups than they had before. The boys displaced their aggression toward groups of people who had done them no harm.

Not only in the "bad old days" has such racial scapegoating occurred. For example, in the case of the example with which this chapter began, some experts have suggested that the 88-year-old Ayatollah Khomeini attacked Salman Rushdie for political rather than religious reasons. The Ayatollah's policies had recently come under heavy fire. Iran was devastated from its seven-year war with Iraq, its revolution had stalled, and Iranian moderates were on the verge of gaining some power. By attacking "foreign devils," the Ayatollah may have managed to tighten his hold on the Iranian public once again.

6. Indirect aggression: both roundabout and undirected aggression. Roundabout aggression includes malicious gossip or practical jokes. Undirected aggression is expressed against no one in particular and includes temper tantrums and slamming doors.
7. Assault: physical violence against others. This includes getting into fights.

You might enjoy seeing how you would score on some items from the Buss-Durkee Inventory (see Box 10.5). Subjects are given one point for each true answer. The higher the subjects' scores, the more hostile/aggressive they are assumed to be.

THE FRUSTRATION-AGGRESSION THEORY REVISITED

Social psychologists have concluded that the assertion that frustration is a necessary and sufficient condition for aggression is at once too simple and too sweeping. Often, frustration does increase hostility and aggression; sometimes, however, it does not (see Bandura, 1973; Baron, 1977; Zillman, 1979).

Some researchers have set out to specify the conditions under which frustration ignites aggression (Berkowitz, 1978; Berkowitz & Heimer, 1988). They argue that early theorists left out an essential ingredient of their formulations—anger. A variety of aversive experiences can make people furious—insults or threats, frustration, disappointment of their hopes for reward, or physical attacks. It is annoyance, irritation, and anger that make people ready to aggress.

Leonard Berkowitz marshals an impressive array of research in support of his contention. For example, Brendan Gail Rule and Andrew Nesdale (1976) and William Gentry (1970) find that when people are insulted and angry their blood pressures rise and they become increasingly likely to try to get even with those who have provoked them.

Ethologists have pointed out that in all species, aggressive cues trigger instinctive aggression. Berkowitz and Heimer (1988) propose that in humans, aggressive cues are also a potent determinant of whether or not an angry, frustrated person will fly into a rage and act aggressively (fight) or take flight. For example, researchers find that provoked subjects retaliate more harshly when a rifle or pistol is nearby than when they are surrounded by sports equipment or no objects at all (Berkowitz & LePage, 1967): "Guns not only permit violence, they can stimulate it as well. The finger pulls the trigger, but the trigger may also be pulling the finger" (p. 22). A few experiments have failed to replicate this "weapons effect."

The previous section focused on the "hard-wiring" for aggression, the instinctive factors that predispose humans to behave aggressively or unaggressively. But if humans are anything, they are variable. They can learn to be more or less aggressive. Or, in terms of our computer analogy, they can

BOX 10.5

The Buss-Durkee Inventory

Directions: Please answer the following questions about yourself by marking either *True* or *False* on the sheet.

Resentment

T F 1. Other people always seem to get the breaks.

T F 2. Although I don't show it, I am sometimes eaten up with jealousy.

Irritability

T F 1. Sometimes people bother me just by being around.

T F 2. I often feel like a powder keg ready to explode.

Suspicion

T F 1. I tend to be on my guard with people who are somewhat more friendly than I expected.

Negativism

T F 1. When someone is bossy, I do the opposite of what he asks.

Verbal

T F 1. If somebody annoys me, I am apt to tell him what I think of him.

Indirect

T F 1. I sometimes spread gossip about people I don't like.

T F 2. When I am mad, I sometimes slam doors.

Assault

T F 1. Whoever insults me or my family is asking for a fight.

T F 2. I have known people who pushed me so far that we came to blows.

Reprinted from Buss, 1961, pp. 171-173

be "programmed" to respond in almost any way. Let us now consider some of the ways that angry men and women can be programmed to respond.

The "Programming": Social Learning Theory

OBSERVATIONAL LEARNING

Albert Bandura (1983) is skeptical of the contention that anger predisposes people to do much of anything. He contends that two processes determine how people act: (a) People learn how to act via classical conditioning, instrumental conditioning, or observational learning—learning through modeling. In his view, observational learning may be the most important of the three. (b) How people actually act depends on the rewards and punishments that exist for various types of reactions. Let us consider then, the factors that predispose people to behave angrily rather than more calmly when provoked.

Learning to Be Aggressive

People probably learn most about how it is possible to behave by studying others, remembering what they have done, and imitating their behavior when it seems appropriate. Bandura and his students (Bandura, Ross, & Ross, 1963) demonstrated the power of observational learning in a classic experiment. A Stanford nursery school child is engrossed in an art project. In another part of the room, an adult sits surrounded by Tinker Toys, a mallet, and a big, inflated Bobo doll. After playing with the Tinker Toys for a few moments, the adult rises and attacks the Bobo doll, pounding it with the mallet, kicking it, and throwing it, all the while yelling such remarks as, "Sock him in the nose," "Knock him down," and "Kick him."

After observing this amazing display, the children are deliberately frustrated. They are led to a playroom filled with appealing toys, but before they can get started, the teacher tells them that she has changed her mind; she is going to save these luscious toys for other children. Disappointed and angry, they are then taken to an adjacent room that contains a variety of toys, among them a Bobo doll and a mallet.

Normally, without the earlier experience, children rarely show any aggressive behavior toward Bobo dolls. However frustrated they may be, they play quietly. The children who have observed the aggressive adult, on the other hand, have learned something. They often pick up the mallet and smash the doll. Seeing an aggressive adult has decreased their inhibitions about behaving badly. But, more than that, they have learned a scenario for aggression. Often, the children reproduce the very acts and say the very words they have observed. In short, aggressive models both teach ways to be aggressive and lower inhibitions about doing so.

Bandura and Walters (1959) observe that in everyday life, aggressive models are found most often in one's family, one's subculture, and the mass media. We learn how to perform many routines by watching our parents. Perhaps you have listened with impatience to the traditional parental litany. (Can you fill in the blanks?):

> After all _____ [I've done for you.] I've worked my _____ [fingers to the bone] and what do I get? Well, someday, you'll find out. Someday you'll have children of your own . . . and then you'll see. But it will be _____ [too late]. I hope they make you as miserable as you've made me.

Within our families, then, we learn from thousands of such observations how intimates deal with one another. And within families, the old adage holds true: Violence breeds violence. Some social scientists have gone so far as to describe the family as the "cradle of violence" (Steinmetz & Straus, 1973). Murray Straus and his colleagues Richard Gelles and Suzanne Steinmetz

(1980) find that within the family, violence is commonplace. For example, in a study of more than 2,000 American couples, Straus et al. found that more than 25% had engaged in some form of violence during their married life (see Table 10.3). Both husbands and wives try to hurt each other, but husbands' acts are more harmful; they tend to beat their wives or use a knife or a gun. At least 1.8 million women are battered every year. Women usually limit their attacks to making accusations, hurling inanimate objects, or slapping.

Child Abuse

Children, too, are victims of verbal, sexual, and physical abuse. For example, Manhattan socialite Frances Schreuder seemed to be a well-respected member of New York society. Her children were enrolled in elite private schools, she was a patron of the arts and on the governing board of the the New York City Ballet. But she needed money, so she contracted a man to kill her wealthy father. When he failed to come through, she made an offer to someone who couldn't refuse—her 17-year-old son. During the court hearings, her son's lawyer played a tape (which had been made without Frances's knowledge) in an effort to explain how she had obtained such extraordinary power over her children. It was a record of parental abuse. During the tape, Frances verbally abuses her daughter Ariadne for four solid hours (see Box 10.6).

Recently, the public has become concerned about the rising tide of child abuse. Child developmentalists have long counseled parents that the most effective way to shape children up is to lavish praise on them when they behave properly, and either reason with them, ignore them, assign them a time out in their rooms, or withdraw their privileges, when they don't behave properly. Physical punishment is almost never effective.

Table 10.3   Percent of Couples Engaging in Violent Acts

	PERCENT IN:	
TYPE OF VIOLENCE	**1975**	**EVER**
Threw something at spouse	6.7	16.7
Pushed, grabbed, shoved spouse	13.0	23.5
Slapped spouse	7.4	17.9
Kicked, bit, or hit with fist	5.2	9.2
Hit or tried to hit with something	4.0	9.5
Beat up spouse	1.5	5.3
Threatened with a knife or gun	1.0	4.4
Used a knife or gun	0.5	3.7
Any of the above	16.0	27.8

Source: Data from M. A. Straus, R. J. Gelles, and S. K. Steinmetz, 1980, *Behind Closed Doors: Violence in the American Family.* New York: Doubleday.

BOX 10.6 _____

Child Abuse in High Society

Reporter Shana Alexander (1983), in commenting on the tape of Frances Schreuder's verbal abuse of her daughter Ariadne, writes:

> In transcription, the tape is a more than thirty-page nonstop record of a mother [Frances] goading, terrorizing, taunting, cajoling, mocking, and threatening a sniffling five-year-old [Frances' daughter Ariadne] for being unable to repeat the schoolbook definition of a sentence—that it is something which starts with a capital letter and ends with a period. One hears the child choking on her tears as the mother calls her a stupid bastard, threatens not to give her any more sleeping pills, says her grades are rotten, that she's not even trying. The mother mocks her for being a crybaby, tells her she will never have any friends, never go to "pretty parties" with "nice girls," just with "cheap, rotten Yids." The child is accused of being stupid, disobedient, a liar, and told that all of it is her own fault.
>
> Sometimes Frances' voice becomes the child. "I hate you . . . stupid!" she wails. "I'll put you in a hospital for stupid children . . . you don't come home if you're stupid. It's not like a broken neck. You live and die there. You'll never get married, never see boys, never go out and work, never see other children. You'll never see your mother again. You'll never see your house again. Or anyone else's house. They have special hospitals for children who are disturbed and cuckoo and there's something wrong. They stay there for the rest of their lives. *They are not permitted to go out—ever!*"
>
> Ariadne whimpers, is incoherent. She tries to speak. Her mother will not let her. "Whaddya *do* with such an idiot!" Frances shouts. "I hate your crying . . . it's disgusting. . . . At ten o'clock at night you *still* don't know what a sentence is! *Well, I hate your guts!*"
>
> "Mommy . . . Mommy . . . I *am* trying . . . [sniffles]"
>
> "Children like you don't go to school with other children. You have to go to nigger school, where there are only poor kids . . . little Jew kids . . ."
>
> More tears and sniffles.
>
> In utter fury: "Just tell me what a sentence is and shut up the crap! Stop crying and stop shivering! What is a sentence—you coward! You belong in a zoo with the animals and the monkeys! . . ."
>
> Becoming hysterical: "Mom . . . Mom . . . wait a second . . . Mom, don't hit me. . . . A sen . . . Mom, a senten . . . a sentence is . . . is . . . a . . . a . . . sentence is . . ."
>
> "I've asked you for four solid hours!"
>
> At last it was over. Gratefully Dr. Moench snapped off his tape recorder. Later he said frankly, "That's about as abusive a dialogue as I've ever encountered." (pp. 326–327)

Yet, a recent survey of university students revealed that during their final year of high school, more than half of them had either been threatened with or experienced actual physical punishment. Serious abuse is extremely common. In 1986, more than 2.1 million cases of child sexual and physical abuse (shaking of children or beating them) were reported. Box 10.7 describes some of the warning signs that children may be being abused. In 1986, more than 5,000 children died from such battering.

The consequences of such parental abuse extend far beyond the immediate incident. For example, often parents who abuse their children had parents who abused *them* (Straus, Gelles, & Steinmetz, 1980). (Parents who were

BOX 10.7

Child Abuse: How to Help

The signs of child abuse are often subtle. Recognizing and reporting evidence of violence can help make a difference.

What to look for:

- Unexplained bruises, welts, burns, broken bones
- Children who are consistently unkempt and hungry
- Torn, bloody underwear or genital irritation (may signify sexual abuse)

- Inappropriate dress (summer clothing in winter)
- Prolonged listlessness
- Abrupt changes in behavior
- Children who are desperate to please
- Sudden drops in school grades
- Suicide attempts

What to do:

- Most state child-welfare agencies have hot line numbers (anonymity guaranteed)
- National referral service: 1-800-4ACHILD
- In emergencies, call the police

Newsweek, Dec. 12, 1988, p. 59

abused as children are six times more likely to abuse their own children.) Violent teenagers tend to come from homes where discipline takes the form of harsh physical punishment (Bandura & Walters, 1959; Lefkowitz, Eron, Walder, & Huesmann, 1976; Straus, Gelles, & Steinmetz, 1980). At least 40% of all abuse cases involve alcohol or drugs. David Owens and Murray Straus (1975) report that individuals who experience violence as children are more likely to favor violence as a means of achieving personal and political ends as adults.

Parents are not the only models for their children. Children watch in fascination as their classmates "sass" their teachers . . . or reason things out, patiently construct a compelling argument . . . or build pipe bombs. Television and movies are powerful models. The statistics on television viewing are staggering. Most people spend about four-and-a-half to seven hours each day watching television—over 1,000 hours a year (Nielsen, 1981). The television diet contains a heavy dose of aggression. George Gerbner, Larry Gross, Nancy Signorielli, and Michael Morgan (1980) calculate that 8 out of 10 programs contain violence. Prime-time shows, such as "Miami Vice," average five violent acts per hour. Saturday morning children's programs, such as the "Roadrunner" series, average 18 violent acts per hour. By age 16, the average child (who spends more time watching television than he or she spends in the classroom) will have witnessed more than 13,000 television killings (Waters & Malamud, 1975).

What effect do heavy doses of television violence have? For a while, the verdict was unclear. The networks insisted that the violence was harmless or even cathartic. Social psychologists were more skeptical. Instances of "monkey see, monkey do" have been highly publicized:

> A woman was driving through the Roxbury section of Boston when her car ran out of gas. As she returned to the car with a 2-gallon can of gasoline, she was forced into a backyard by six young men, who beat her and ordered her to douse herself with the fuel. Then one of the men tossed a burning match on her—the woman burned to death. Just two nights prior to this incident, the film *Fuzz*, in which a similar crime is depicted, had been shown on national television. (Wrightsman & Deaux, 1981) p. 286

By now, social psychologists have conducted a great deal of research on the effects of television viewing. For example, Ross Parke and his colleagues (1977) observed a group of delinquent boys who were imprisoned in a minimum-security detention facility. In one cottage, the boys were shown aggressive movies every night for five nights. In another cottage, boys were shown neutral, nonaggressive movies those same nights. Violent movies had a definite impact on behavior. All the boys who had viewed violent films showed clear increases in verbal and physical aggression; the other boys did not. Studies of delinquent girls and of college students in a variety of countries (Leyens, Camino, Parke, & Berkowitz, 1975) have yielded similar results.

Today, the evidence seems clear. Media violence makes people callous about violence (Cline, Craft, & Courrier, 1973; Geen, 1981), increases their aggressiveness (Liebert & Baron, 1972), and shapes viewers' assumptions about the real world. Gerbner et al. (1980) surveyed adolescents and adults and found that heavy viewers (who watched television four or more hours a day) were more likely than light viewers (two or less hours a day) to exaggerate the frequency of violence in the world around them and to fear being personally assaulted. (Similar results were secured by Thomas & Drabman, 1977, and Peterson & Zill, 1981.) Heavy viewers are also more likely to tolerate aggression in others (Drabman & Thomas, 1974).

Of course, we can learn calmer ways of acting via modeling, too.

In 1900, Andrew Carnegie forecast that in the twentieth century, "To kill a man will be considered as disgusting as we in this day consider it disgusting to eat one."

(REPORTED IN MYERS, 1983, pp. 378–379)

Reducing Aggression via Modeling

Most of us want to be able to choose how we respond when we are angry. Sometimes, we want to keep our angry feelings in check while we work out things. Parents and teachers want to be able to teach children to respond gracefully to frustration. The National Hockey League wants to prod hockey players into avoiding needless violence. According to Bandura (1983), the same principles that cause people to respond angrily can be used to lead them to react in more calm, cool, and collected ways. Considerable evidence suggests that he is right.

Psychologist Gerald Patterson (1978) and Robert Johnson (1973) contend that social learning theory, which highlights the importance of observational learning and reinforcement, is a powerful guide in teaching children to respond cooperatively rather than aggressively. Consider, for example, a typical fight between five-year-olds in nursery school, depicted in one of Patterson's films. John, muttering to himself, calls Peter a "rat sticker." Peter is enraged. He hurls a rubber ball at John and knocks him down. John begins to howl in pain. Students crowd around, excited. The teacher races over. "Quit that! Peter, you apologize to John," she threatens. Peter is not about to apologize. His red, tight little face is screwed up in defiance. "My uncle can beat you up," he counters. Soon fellow students, aroused by the hubbub, are dancing around, shouting out aggressive taunts: "Oh, yeah? Well, my mother can beat up your uncle." "Dork!" another exclaims. They engage in mock violence. "Bang, bang. You're dead," they crow.

Social learning theorists point out that when we slow down the action in such encounters, it is obvious how important observational learning and reinforcement/punishment is to the action. Passive bystanders see the fight and add such action to their repertoire. They watch the teacher grant her attention (a priceless commodity to children) to the two boys locked in combat. They see aggression pay off in other ways, too. They see John's sneer of power as Peter falls. They note Peter's delight when the teacher yells at John, publicly humiliating him. They see aggression breeding aggression. Social learning theorists point out that the way to turn things around, to shape peaceful rather than aggressive behavior, is to arrange things so that children observe peaceful behavior and observe such behavior being rewarded. For example, in this setting:

1. The teacher might model alternate, nonaggressive interactions. She could show Peter and John how to cooperate on a project, how to negotiate.
2. The teacher could pay attention to the team as they work together. She could praise children and touch them affectionately when they behave appropriately.
3. The teacher could ignore minor instances of aggression, depriving the aggressive act of the reward of attention.
4. If the aggression is too blatant or too serious to ignore, she can ensure that brief aversive consequences follow. She can impose a "time out," insisting that the two boys sit alone in separate rooms for 10 minutes, deprived of toys, friends, and the excitement of the row.

Now, nursery school students observe a peaceful encounter; they add that to their repertoire. Now, they observe cooperation and negotiation leading to reward.

In this century, leaders such as Mohandas Gandhi and Martin Luther King, Jr., have been powerful models of nonviolence. Laboratory studies document that such models are critically important. Restraint is as contagious as belligerence (Donnerstein & Donnerstein, 1972; Baron, 1977).

Modeling, then, suggests ways we might behave. Whether or not we actually act that way depends on whether we expect such behavior to be rewarded, ignored, or punished.

REINFORCEMENT THEORY

In an earlier section, we distinguished between angry aggression and instrumental aggression. Let us turn now to some examples of the latter.

Increasing Aggression

When children misbehave, we spank them. When adults misbehave, we may knock them down. When nations misbehave, we bomb them. Ample evidence shows that one reason anger sparks aggression is that such behavior pays off. Averill (1983) asked men and women to think of the last time they had been angry or someone had been angry at them and to recall what the overall consequences had been.

Table 10.4 shows that by the time most people finally get worked up enough to express their angry feelings, it pays off. The angry reported that the beneficial consequences of expressing their feelings outnumbered the

Table 10.4   **Target's Perception of Long-Term Consequences of Angry Episode**

TYPE OF CHANGE	PERCENTAGE OF EPISODES IN WHICH CHANGE OCCURRED "SOMEWHAT" OR "VERY MUCH"
You realized your own faults	76%
You realized your own strengths	50%
Your relationship with the angry person was strengthened	48%
You gained respect for the angry person	44%
You did something that was good for the angry person	39%
You did something that was for your own good	38%
Your relationship with the angry person became more distant	35%
You lost respect for the angry person	29%

harmful ones by three to one. Targets rated the benefits as outnumbering the costs by two-and-a-half to one.

Children who succeed in intimidating other children naturally become even more aggressive (Patterson, Littman, & Brecker, 1967). Aggressive hockey players may be sent to the penalty box for rough play, but they do score more goals than do nonaggressive players (McCarthy & Kelly, 1978a, 1978b). In all these cases, fierceness seems to pay.

Sometimes, collective violence pays as well. In April of 1986, President Ronald Reagan and President Moammar Khadafy of Libya began to feud. Reagan called Khadafy a "mad dog" and Khadafy suggested that Reagan was "senile." Khadafy ordered terrorist attacks on Americans abroad; Reagan then sent jets to bomb Khadafy's headquarters. In the debate that ensued, the question that emerged was not whether violence pays off, but what *kind* of violence would be most effective.

The Social Learning of Gender Differences in Aggression

Evidence seems to support that in times of conflict, men and women learn to react very differently in their closest relationships (Peplau, 1983). In America, men generally have the most power. They can often afford to act with the quiet confidence that, in the end, things will go their way. Women often have to develop a variety of techniques for gaining influence.

Kelley and his colleagues (1978) studied young couples' stereotypes as to how men and women behave during conflicts and their reports (by actual young couples) as to what each one is likely to say and do. The reports were much the same. A woman was expected and reported to cry, sulk, and criticize the man for his lack of consideration and insensitivity to his effect on her. A man was expected and reported to show anger, to reject her tears, to call for a logical and less emotional approach to the problem, and to give reasons for delaying the discussion. Kelley and his colleagues conclude that men are conflict-avoidant; they find it upsetting to deal with emotional problems. Women are conflict-confronting; they are frustrated by the avoidance and ask that the problem and the feelings associated with it be confronted. Similarly, Harold Raush, William Barry, Richard Hertel, & Mary Ann Swain (1974) found that in role-play situations, husbands tried to resolve conflict and restore harmony; wives appealed to fairness and guilt or were cold and rejecting. The researchers speculated that "women, as a low power group, may learn a diplomacy of psychological pressure to influence male partners' behavior" (p. 153).

At the extremes, conflict may erupt into physical violence. Suzanne Steinmetz (1978) estimates that approximately 3.3 million American wives and more than 250,000 American husbands have been severely beaten by their mates. Obviously, in spite of their calls to reason, it is men who are most likely to engage in physical abuse. At the extremes of violence, however, homicide rates are very similar for husbands and wives.

Reducing Aggression

The United States is the most dangerous of the developed countries. Have you ever wondered what your chances are of being murdered? In 1986, the FBI released some statistics revealing that the chance of American citizens being murdered in their lifetimes is 1 in 153 (Shearer, 1986). The statistics also vary depending on sex, race, and age (see Table 10.5). Given these statistics, it is not surprising that Americans are concerned about reducing aggression.

People are very adaptable. They can learn many ways of dealing with anger. They can learn to smile, diffuse the situation, talk at length about their feelings, set limits. If all else fails, they can even learn to explode on demand (Tavris, 1982; Goldstein et al., 1981). For example, children become less aggressive when their aggressive behavior is ignored and their nonaggressive behavior is rewarded (Hamlin, Buckholdt, Bushnell, Ellis, & Ferritor, 1969). Punishment is not so effective in reducing aggression as punishment carries with it a modeling of aggression.

On the other hand, in real life, some natural checks—such as guilt, empathy, and fear of retaliation—nudge angry people to consider gentle reactions and to avoid cruel, hurtful ones. Again, the consequences are important.

Guilt. Caroline and Robert Blanchard (1982) point out that angry men and women tend to respond in ways that their families and friends deem appropriate. In Hawaii, for example, the Japanese disapprove of aggressive men and women (especially women). Thus, it is not surprising to discover that even when angered, Japanese women display little aggression. Women of Chinese, Caucasian, or Hawaiian descent come from cultures in which assertiveness is more acceptable. When angered, they feel less guilty and more free to express their feelings (see Hatfield, Schmitz, et al., 1987, for similar results).

Table 10.5   **Probability of Murder**

TOTAL UNITED STATES POPULATION	1 out of 153
Men	1 out of 100
Women	1 out of 325
TOTAL WHITE POPULATION	1 out of 240
Men	1 out of 164
Women	1 out of 450
TOTAL NONWHITE POPULATION	1 out of 47
Men	1 out of 28
Women	1 out of 117

Empathy. The attributions we make as to why people act the way they do affect our feelings about them and our reactions to them. For example, John Kremer and Laura Stephens (1983) exposed men and women to two people who treated them rudely. One person's behavior was explained: "He's really worried about a midterm." The other's was not: "Heaven knows why he acted as he did." Not surprisingly, the subjects were less insistent on retaliating against the person when they understood his motives than when they did not. Experiments by Norma and Seymour Feshbach (1981) confirm that empathy is indeed incompatible with aggression. They gave some Los Angeles elementary-school children a chance to participate in a 10-week program that trained them to recognize others' feelings, assume the perspective of other people, and share their emotions. Compared with other children in control groups, those who received this empathy training were significantly less aggressive in their school behavior.

Fear. It is hard to say what effect threatening to tear a child limb from limb if he hits his little sister one more time is supposed to have. On one hand, the enraged parent is modeling the very action he is trying to prevent. (It is hard to teach "Do as I say, not as I do.") On the other hand, the parent is making it clear that it is unprofitable to fight, that is, fighting will be punished.

Sometimes threats can be effective. For example, Blanchard and Blanchard (1984) observe that rats may behave aggressively for two very different reasons. Generally, it appears to be anger that provokes rats to attack. (Dominant rats attack intruders and lower status rats to secure the things they want.) As a rule, their frightened targets flee. Sometimes, however, it is fear that provokes rats to attack. Rats may have "their backs to the wall" and they will then fight as a form of defense.

The Blanchards observe that in humans, too, angry offensive-aggression and fearful-defensive aggression are very different processes. Angry attackers tend to attack with pinpoint aggression—with sarcasm, slaps, or punches. Fearful attackers, on the other hand, "go berserk"—they bite, they claw. An example: Imagine a young girl, the smallest girl in her class, who is followed home from school each day, taunted, and beaten up by a couple of larger children. Each day she comes home feeling sorry for herself. Finally, her mother, not knowing what else to do, says that if she comes home crying one more time she will receive a spanking. Now she is caught; she has to act. So one day after school, she is stands behind a building, in fear, watching her tormenters advancing. She is cold with terror; she can hardly breathe; she assumes she is going to be killed. As they pass by she leaps out, half insane, shrieking, clawing, and flailing away. Dumbstruck at this apparition, the other children run away. Instantly, her terror turns to elation and delight with her newfound power. This example illustrates that when sufficiently frightened, gentle individuals can be transformed into furious, aggressive counterattackers.

Interestingly, the Blanchards also have found that threats have a very different effect on powerful rats than on threatened ones. Dominant rats will soften their aggression when faced with punishment, but already frightened rats will actually become more frightened, more desperate, and more aggressive when faced with additional threats. The authors point out that the same processes operate in humans. Fear may inhibit an angry aggressor, but not so the fearful attacker:

> As fear increases, so does the extent to which the fearful attacker is unmindful of the possibility of damage done to the opponent. At the extreme of fearful attack, the attacker may be so out of control, so reflexive as opposed to calculating, that serious injury to the opponent is a distinct possibility. Reports of abused wives or children turning on their tormenters and killing them may reflect this phenomenon. (1984, p. 45)

The point is that angry aggression should be strengthened when it is effective (i.e., when it succeeds in frightening or injuring others) and inhibited when it is countered with frightening threats of retaliation. But fearful aggression should actually be magnified when it is countered by even more frightening threats; it is, after all, fear motivating the aggression in the first place.

Robert Baron (1977) has summarized the conditions under which the threat of punishment might deter actual aggression: (a) The punishment must be fair; (b) it must be strong and sure; and (c) it must immediately follow the aggressive behavior. Under such limited conditions, threats of punishment may be effective in deterring aggression. We might add that providing a clear alternative to aggression should help as well. In most situations, however, threats are counterproductive, and clear alternatives are not made available.

According to social learning theory, then, whether we act calmly or aggressively when angered depends upon the consequences we anticipate.

Summing Up

- Anger is "an emotional reaction, characterized by distinctive facial grimaces, marked reactions of the ANS, and symbolic activities of attack or offense."

- Anger and hatred are not synonymous. People become most angry at those they love and like. Anger is the attribution of blame. The angry are eager to cast blame; their targets are naturally less willing to accept it.

- Bandura contends that four types of stimuli excite anger—verbal insults or threats, physical assaults, thwarting, and depriving a person of reward.

- Brain stimulation experiments suggest that specific neural systems trigger and inhibit anger and aggression.

- In his classic study, Ax concluded that fear's physiological patterns resembled those produced by an injection of adrenaline. Anger's patterns resembled those produced by a combination of adrenaline and noradrenaline. More recent evidence suggests that the hormonal influences are more complex than Ax asserted.

- Sociobiologists and ethologists assume that patterns of aggression are wired into all species. When appropriate stimuli are presented, aggressive patterns will be automatically triggered.

- Freud believed that humankind possesses innate aggressive tendencies. He proposed a "pressure-cooker" model of anger/aggression. This catharsis hypothesis has received little experimental support, however.

- John Dollard et al. proposed the frustration-aggression model. They contended that frustration is a necessary and sufficient condition for aggression.

- Social learning theory proposes that people can learn to be aggressive or unaggressive.

- Reinforcement theory emphasizes the importance of the consequences of aggression and its reduction, including the role of guilt, empathy, and fear.

//
Passionate and Companionate Love

Introduction

What Is Love?

Passionate Love
How Do I Love Thee?—Let Me Count the Ways
The Genesis of Love
Attachment and Adult Love
The Nature of Passionate Love
Emotional Interlinkages
Behavioral Evidence That Both Pleasure and Pain May Fuel Emotion
Who Knows How to Make Love Stay?

Companionate Love
Measures and Models
Stages of Relationships: Initiation and Maintenance
Stages of Relationships: Decline and Jealousy
Stages of Relationships: The End of the Affair

Summing Up

FIGURE 11.1 *Drowning Girl.* Roy Lichtenstein. 1963. Oil and synthetic polymer paint on canvas, 67⅝" x 66¾". Collection, The Museum of Modern Art, New York. Philip Johnson Fund and gift of Mr. and Mrs. Bagley Wright.

Introduction

In 1848, Victorian writer John Ruskin determined to marry Euphema Gray. Effie was beautiful, sweet, filled with energy . . . and very young. John's possessive and controlling parents were opposed to the match (Effie's family was poor), but Ruskin insisted. When Ruskin was 22 and Effie was 12, John had written a fairy tale for her, *The King and the Golden River*. Now, seven years later, he was still passionately in love with her and determined to marry. He wrote Effie:

> You are like the bright—soft—swelling—lovely fields of a high glacier covered with fresh morning snow—which is lovely to the eye—and soft and winning on the foot—but beneath, there are winding clefts and dark places in its cold—cold ice— where men fall and rise not again. (Quoted in Quennell, 1949, pp. 56-57)

But once the couple was married and John's daydreams became a reality, he panicked. On the carriage ride to their hotel, his ardor changed to anxiety. John knew nothing about sex. He had seen statues of women, but that was all. That evening, when they were in bed and John slipped Effie's nightdress from her shoulders, he was struck dumb with horror. There was something terribly wrong with Effie! Her body was "not formed to excite passion." She disgusted him. According to historians, Effie's disgusting secret was the fact that she had large breasts and pubic hair. John had never seen a naked woman. The classical statues and sketches he had seen depicted idealized women with tiny breasts. They had no pubic hair. Thus, Effie's voluptuous body seemed deformed to him (Lutyens, 1966, p. 21).

Ruskin's passionate feelings for Effie died on their chaste wedding night. But the two silently agreed to live together in friendly companionship. In the end, the marriage failed. Eventually, the couple came to hate each other. In 1855, in the glare of publicity, the Ruskins' marriage was annulled. The course of love is rarely simple and predictable.

In this chapter, we begin by defining love. Then, we review what psychologists have learned about passionate love, a fiery but short-lived emotion, and companionate love, a gentler and deeper form of affection. Finally, we review what psychologists have learned about the initiation, maintenance, and termination of relationships. Much of the early work on love discussed here was done by Elaine Hatfield and Ellen Berscheid.

We have laughs together. I care about you. Your concerns are my concerns. We have great sex.
In WOODY ALLEN's film Manhattan,
the teenaged heroine provides this innocent and touching definition of love

What Is Love?

For most people, love is the *sine qua non* of an intimate relationship (Berscheid & Peplau, 1983). Love, however, comes in a variety of forms. When the Prince of Wales and Lady Diana Spencer became engaged, journalists asked whether they were in love. "Of course," Lady Diana said. "Whatever love means," Prince Charles added. Elaine Hatfield and G. William Walster (1978) point out that most people distinguish between two forms of love—passionate love and companionate love. **Passionate love** is sometimes labeled "puppy love," "a crush," "lovesickness," "obsessive love," "infatuation," or "being in love." They define it this way: "a state of intense longing for union with another. Reciprocated love (union with the other) is associated with fulfillment and ecstasy. Unrequited love (separation) with emptiness, anxiety, or despair. A state of profound physiological arousal" (p. 9).

By contrast, **companionate love** is sometimes called "true love" or "conjugal love." It is a far less intense emotion. Hatfield and Walster (1978) define it as "the affection we feel for those with whom our lives are deeply entwined" (p. 9).

Some researchers have proposed more elaborate typologies of the possible varieties of love. For example, Robert Sternberg (1988) has proposed a triangular model of love. He argues that love may involve three separate components—passion, intimacy, and/or the decision to love and the commitment to stay together.

Thus, Sternberg points out, one could classify love relationships—such as "infatuation," "romantic love," "companionate love," and so on—according to the amount of each of the three components they involve. Infatuation, for example, involves intense passionate arousal but little intimacy or commitment (see Figure 11.2). The most complete form of love would be consummate love, which would involve passion, intimacy and commitment.

Harold Kelley (1979) and John Alan Lee (1988) have come up with still other schemes for classifying the various forms of love. In this chapter, however, we focus on the two forms of love that are familiar to everyone—passionate love and companionate love.

Passionate Love

In *The Magic Mountain,* novelist Thomas Mann (1969) described Hans Castorp's passionate reaction to Claudia:

> In brief, our traveller was now over head and ears in love with Claudia Chauchat. . . . We have seen that the essence of his passion was something quite other than the tender and pensive mood of that oft-quoted ditty: rather it was a wild and vagrant variation upon that lovesick lute, it was mingled frost and fire, like the state of a fever patient, or the October air in these high altitudes. What he

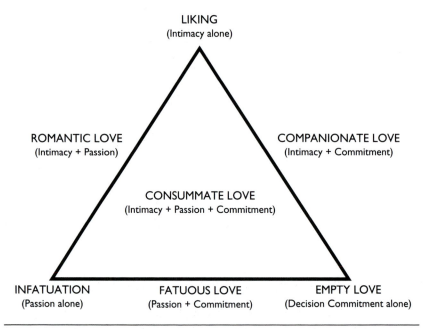

LIKING
(Intimacy alone)

ROMANTIC LOVE
(Intimacy + Passion)

COMPANIONATE LOVE
(Intimacy + Commitment)

CONSUMMATE LOVE
(Intimacy + Passion + Commitment)

INFATUATION
(Passion alone)

FATUOUS LOVE
(Passion + Commitment)

EMPTY LOVE
(Decision Commitment alone)

FIGURE 11.2 The kinds of loving: a classification. Sternberg, 1988, p. 122.

actually lacked, in fact, was an emotional bridge between two extremes. . . . For the rest, his lovesick state afforded him all the joy and all the anguish proper to it the world over. The anguish is acute, it has, like all anguish, a mortifying element; it shatters the nervous system to an extent that takes the breath away, and can wring tears from the eyes of a grown man. As for the joys, to do them justice, they were manifold, and no less piercing than the anguish, though their occasion might be trifling indeed. (pp. 229–230)

Through the centuries, researchers have been interested in passionate love. Recently, social psychologists have begun to disentangle its complexities.

HOW DO I LOVE THEE?—LET ME COUNT THE WAYS

Earlier, we defined passionate love as an "intense longing for union." Researchers generally assess passionate love via the Passionate Love Scale (PLS), which is reproduced in Box 11.1 (see Hatfield & Sprecher, 1986a). The PLS taps the following cognitive, emotional, and behavioral indicants of "longing for union."

Cognitive Components:

1. Preoccupation with the person loved.
2. Idealization of the other.
3. Desire to know and be known by the other.

BOX 11.1

The Passionate Love Scale

Think of the person you love most passionately *right now*. If you are not in love right now, think of the last person you loved passionately. If you have never been in love, think of the person you came closest to caring for in that way. Try to tell us how you felt at the time when your feelings were the most intense.

Possible answers range from:

(1)	(2)	(3)	(4)	(5)	(6)	(7)	(8)	(9)
Not at all true				Moderately true				Definitely true

1. I would feel deep despair if _____ left me.
      1 2 3 4 5 6 7 8 9
2. Sometimes I feel I can't control my thoughts; they are obsessively on _____.
      1 2 3 4 5 6 7 8 9
3. I feel happy when I am doing something to make _____ happy.
      1 2 3 4 5 6 7 8 9
4. I would rather be with _____ than anyone else.
      1 2 3 4 5 6 7 8 9
5. I'd get jealous if I thought _____ were falling in love with someone else.
      1 2 3 4 5 6 7 8 9
6. I yearn to know all about _____.
      1 2 3 4 5 6 7 8 9
7. I want _____—physically, emotionally, mentally.
      1 2 3 4 5 6 7 8 9
8. I have an endless appetite for affection from _____.
      1 2 3 4 5 6 7 8 9
9. For me, _____ is the perfect romantic partner.
      1 2 3 4 5 6 7 8 9
10. I sense my body responding when _____ touches me.
       1 2 3 4 5 6 7 8 9
11. _____ always seems to be on my mind.
       1 2 3 4 5 6 7 8 9
12. I want _____ to know me—my thoughts, my fears, and my hopes.
       1 2 3 4 5 6 7 8 9
13. I eagerly look for signs indicating _____'s desire for me.
       1 2 3 4 5 6 7 8 9
14. I possess a powerful attraction for _____.
       1 2 3 4 5 6 7 8 9
15. I get extremely depressed when things don't go right in my relationship with _____.
       1 2 3 4 5 6 7 8 9

[See Hatfield & Sprecher (1986a) for information on the reliability and validity of this scale.]

Emotional Components:

1. Attraction, especially sexual attraction, to the other.
2. Positive feelings when things go well.
3. Negative feelings when things go awry.
4. Longing for reciprocity. (Passionate lovers love and want to be loved in return.)
5. Desire for complete and permanent union.
6. Physiological arousal.

Behavioral Components:

1. Attempting to determine the other's feelings.
2. Studying the other person.
3. Assisting the other.
4. Maintaining physical closeness.

Have you ever been in love? How do your feelings compare with those of other people? Are they more intense or less intense than those of your friends? To find out, complete the PLS and add up the numbers you circled on items 1–15. Now you can compare them to the scores of some of your peers. For example, Marilyn Easton (1985) interviewed Caucasian, Filipino, and Japanese men and women. She found that on the average, men and women from a variety of ethnic groups seemed to love with equal intensity. The groups' scores on the PLS are shown in Table 11.1.

THE GENESIS OF LOVE

Leonard Rosenblum (Rosenblum, 1985; Rosenblum & Plimpton, 1981) points out that even nonhuman primates, far below humankind on the phylogenetic scale, seem to experience something very much like passionate love. In infancy, primates (such as pigtail macaque monkeys) are prewired to cling to their mothers. Separation can be deadly. If mother and child are separated, the infant is unlikely to find another caretaker. Therefore, to ensure survival, the desire for union is necessarily wired into primates.

As long as mother and child are in close proximity, all goes well. When

Table 11.1   **PLS Scores of Various Ethnic Groups**

	MEN	**WOMEN**
Caucasians (continental U.S.A)	97.50	110.25
Caucasians (Hawaii)	100.50	105.00
Filipinos	106.50	102.90
Japanese	99.00	103.95

a brief separation occurs, the child quickly becomes desperate. He howls and rushes frantically about, searching for his mother. If she returns, the infant is joyous. He clings to his mother or jumps around in excitement. If she does not return and his frantic efforts to find her fail, eventually he will abandon all hope of contact, despair, and probably die (see Figure 11.3). The experience Rosenblum describes certainly sounds much like passionate love's desire for union—and its accompanying lows and highs. This, we thought, was the groundwork for passionate attachments.

Mary Ainsworth and her colleagues (1978) and John Bowlby (1973) describe a comparable experience of attachment, separation, and loss in children. Here is Bowlby's description of the way the desire for security and the desire for freedom alternate in a small child:

> James Anderson describes watching two-year-olds whilst their mothers sit quietly on a seat in a London park. Slipping free from the mother, a two-year-old would typically move away from her in short bursts punctuated by halts. Then, after a more prolonged halt, he would return to her—usually in faster and longer bursts. Once returned, however, he would proceed again on another foray, only to return once more. It was as though he were tied to his mother by some invisible elastic that stretches so far and then brings him back to base. (pp. 44–45)

When a child's mother is around, he is generally not overly interested in her. He glances at her, sees that everything is all right, and sallies forth. Now and then he sneaks a quick glance to make sure she is still there or to

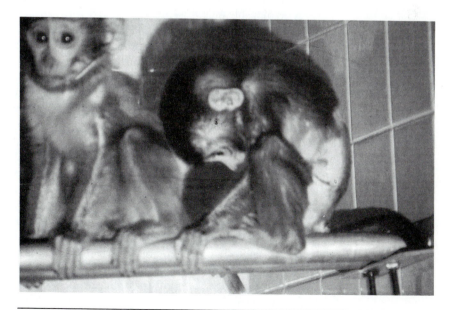

FIGURE 11.3 Pigtail macaque infants who have been separated from their mothers.

check whether she still approves of what he is doing, but then he is off again. Should his mother disappear for a moment, it is a different story. The child becomes distressed and agitated. He devotes all his energy to searching for her. New adventures lose all allure. Of course, once his mother returns, he is off again. Should she disappear permanently, agitation eventually settles into despair. Children's reactions in these situations often sound like the ecstasy/misery we label as passionate love—the longing for union with another. Theorists argue, then, that the capacity to fall passionately in love—to delight at union and to become anxious when closeness is threatened—is genetically wired into all of us. The early passionate attachment between parents and children serves as a prototype for later passionate attachments to those we love.

How early are children capable of falling passionately in love with others? Probably very early. In 1886, Sanford Bell (1902) interviewed teachers attending normal school in Indiana and interviewed and observed 800 children. All in all, he assembled 2,500 cases of children who had loved a playmate or an adult passionately. On the basis of his interviews and observations, Bell concluded that "sex-love" appeared in children as early as 3½ years of age. From three and eight years of age, children's passionate feelings could be read both in word and in deed: in hugging, kissing, lifting each other, scuffling, sitting close to each other; confessions to each other and to others; talking about each other when apart; seeking each other and excluding others; grief at being separated; giving of gifts, extending courtesies to each other that are withheld from others; making sacrifices, such as giving up desired things or foregoing pleasures; jealousies, and so forth (p. 330). Children were most likely to admit to being in love either between 4–8 or 12–15 years of age. Between ages 8 and 12, children were reluctant to admit to feeling "sex-love."

One hundred years elapsed before researchers again became interested in passionate love in children. Greenwell and Hatfield (Greenwell, 1983) developed the Childhood Love Scale (CLS), a children's version of the PLS. Each item on the PLS was translated into language so simple and concrete that a child could understand it. For example, "I want _____ to know me—my thoughts, my fears, and my hopes" became "I want _____ to know me—what I am thinking, what scares me, what I am wishing for." "I possess a powerful attraction for _____" became "When _____ is around I really want to touch him [her] and be touched."

Then, Hatfield and her colleagues (Hatfield, Schmitz, Cornelius, & Rapson, 1988) interviewed more than 200 boys and girls, ranging in age from 4–18, about their romantic feelings. Their results make it clear that Bell was right—even the youngest of children are capable of passionate love. Figure 11.4 depicts how children's passionate feelings change with time. Like Bell, Hatfield et al. found that from ages 4 to 7, children report experiencing strong passionate feelings. Boys seem to experience a "shy period" from 8 to 12 years of age, when they are less likely to report ever having experienced such feelings. Children's passionate feelings return with full intensity from about 13 to 18 years of age.

The authors admit that it is touching to interview children in love. They are often very shy. They blush and hide behind their hands. One five-year-old girl talked about a boy she loved at the preschool she had once attended. When asked the question: "If I could, when I grow up I'd like to marry _____," she began to cry. "I will never see Todd again," she said mournfully. Indeed, she may not, since her parents had no idea as to the depth of her feelings.

Subsequent research has demonstrated that anxious children and adolescents or children and adolescents under stress are particularly susceptible to falling passionately in love (see Hatfield, Brinton, & Cornelius, 1991).

Thus, the accumulating research makes it clear that children are capable of love. Such feelings may be intensified by fear or stress. Some sex researchers have contended that passion should be unusually intense at puberty. Neuroanatomists and neurophysiologists once assumed that passionate love was fueled by adolescent hormonal changes (see Gadpaille, 1975; Money, 1980). Subsequent research may tell us whether or not puberty and sexual maturity bring a new depth to passion.

ATTACHMENT AND ADULT LOVE

Psychologists have argued that childhood experiences can shape one's passionate experience in adulthood. During World War II, John Bowlby (1973 and 1980) observed the reactions of young English children who were separated from their parents. Typically, children went through three stages: The first was protest, a mixture of anger and crying, which lasted for several hours. Eventually, if the parents failed to return, despair set in; the child became quiet, listless, and noticeably sad. Finally, the child showed detachment; even if the parents returned, the child showed no interest in them.

Philip Shaver and Carin Rubenstein (1980), building on Bowlby's work, argue that lonely people are often playing out childhood scripts. They are either passionate love addicts, clingy in relationships (Bowlby calls this "anxious attachment"), or they are aloof, closed and distant (Bowlby labels this "detachment"). The authors questioned men and women about their childhood experiences and their current love experiences; they found evidence that the two were related.

Recently, Carl Hindy and J. Conrad Schwarz (1986) have made a similar proposal. The authors contend that children who receive inconsistent love and affection during childhood, especially from the opposite-sex parent, are especially "at risk" for passionate love (which they term "lovesickness"). They assume that lovesickness is reflected in three attachment phenomena: (a) anxious romantic attachment, that is, insecurity, emotional dependency,

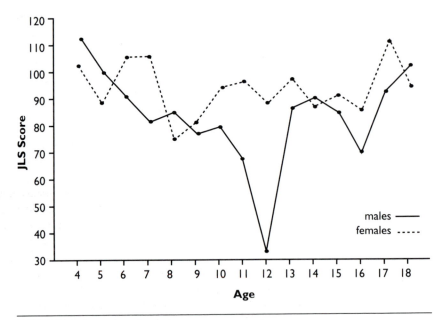

FIGURE 11.4 Age and passionate love.

and clinging in love relationships; (b) sexual jealousy; and (c) heterosexual depression, that is, mourning for a lost lover. They, too, found support for this position.

The authors interviewed 192 college seniors and recent graduates, their parents, their brothers and sisters, and their best friends in order to get a clear picture of how the subjects had been reared. They gave them a battery of tests designed to determine how good their mothers were at parenting. How stormy was the parents' marriage? Were they divorced? Then they asked subjects about their own romantic histories. How had things gone for them? Were they inclined to fall passionately in love with great frequency? To avoid entanglements? When their love affairs fell apart, how depressed were they? How jealous? They found that college students whose parents had been inconsistent in their love and nurturing were more "addicted" to love, *or* more afraid of it, than were those who had had more secure backgrounds.

Passionate love, then, begins early and can last a lifetime. What do researchers know about this powerful phenomenon?

THE NATURE OF PASSIONATE LOVE

For centuries, theorists have bitterly disagreed over the nature of love. Is love an intensely pleasurable experience, a painful one . . . or both? Early researchers took the position that passionate love was a thoroughly positive

BOX 11.2

Self-Esteem and Passionate Love

There is some evidence that when people's self-esteem has been momentarily shaken they are especially vulnerable to passionate love. In one early and classic study of the antecedents of passionate love, Hatfield (1965) invited Stanford women to participate in a "creativity" experiment. Her first step was to introduce women to a potential romantic partner. When the experimenter left the room to collect materials, women sat in the waiting room for 10–15 minutes. During that time an unusually handsome male graduate student just "happened" to drop by. The couple chatted for a while and eventually he invited the subject for a dinner date that weekend in San Francisco. He must have been appealing; all the women accepted.

The experimenter's next step was to raise or lower the women's self-esteem. When she returned she asked the women to complete the *Minnesota Multiphasic Personality Inventory,* the *California Personality Inventory,* and the *Rorschach* test. She pretended to quickly score these tests and gave women their "results." These bogus results were designed to raise or lower women's self-esteem, or

(in the control condition) to leave their self-esteem unchanged. Women were handed either an extremely flattering or an extremely disparaging analysis of their personalities, or (if they were in the control condition) told their test results were not yet available.

How drawn were the women in the various conditions to the male confederate? Hatfield found that the more women's self-esteem had been threatened, the more passionately interested they were in the prospective date.

Hatfield offered two reasons why self-esteem and passionate love might be linked. Firstly, when our self-confidence is shaken we think we *deserve* less and are, thus, grateful for any attention that is paid to us. Secondly, when our esteem is threatened, we *need* affection and reassurance more, and we are unusually appreciative when it is offered. (For additional information on the relationship between stable and momentary self-esteem and passionate and companionate love, see Jacobs, Berscheid, & Hatfield, 1971; Sprecher & Hatfield, 1982.)

experience. Such a vision is often depicted in contemporary films. For example, in Diane Kurys's *Cocktail Molotov,* 17-year-old Anne falls head-over-heels in love with Frederic after he declares his love for her. Scenes of their wild, exuberant, coltish love remind us of the delights of passion.

Theorists such as Douglas Kendrick and Robert Cialdini (1977) argued that passionate love could be explained easily by reinforcement principles. They thought that passionate feelings were fueled by positive experiences and dampened by negative ones. Donn Byrne (1971) reported a series of carefully crafted studies to demonstrate that people love/like those who reward them and hate/dislike those who punish them (see Berscheid & Hatfield, 1969, for a review of this research).

Eventually, however, social psychologists were forced to develop a far more complex concept of passionate love. Sometimes passionate love is a joyously exciting experience, sparked by exciting fantasies and rewarding encounters with the loved one. But this is only part of the story. Passionate love is like any other form of excitement. By its very nature, excitement involves a continuous interplay between elation and despair, thrills and terror. Think, for example, of the mixed and rushed feelings that novice skiers experience. Their hearts begin to pound as they wait to catch the ski lift. When they realize they have managed to get on, they are elated. On the easy ride to the top, they are still a bit unnerved; their hands shake and their knees still tremble, but they begin to relax. Moments later they look ahead and realize it is time to jump off the lift. The landing looks icy and steep. Their rush quickly turns to panic. They can't turn back. They struggle to get their feelings under control. They jump off the lift, elated and panicky; it is hard to tell which. Then they start to ski downhill, experiencing as they go a wild jumble of powerful emotions. Eventually, they arrive at the bottom of the hill, elated and relieved. Perhaps they feel like crying. Sometimes, they are so tired they are flooded with waves of depression. Usually, they get up, ready to try again. Passionate lovers experience the same rollercoaster of feelings—euphoria, happiness, vulnerability, anxiety, panic, despair. The risks of love merely add fuel to the fire.

Sometimes men and women become entangled in love affairs in which the delight is brief, but the pain, uncertainty, jealousy, misery, anxiety, and despair are abundant. Recent social psychological research makes it clear that passionate love, which thrives on excitement, is linked to a variety of strong emotions—both positive and negative.

The Cognitive Contribution

According to the folklore, people should expect passion to be a mixed blessing. For example, Dorothy Tennov (1979) interviewed more than 500 passionate lovers. Almost all lovers took it for granted that passionate love (which Tennov labels "limerence") is a bittersweet experience.

Michael Liebowitz (1983), too, provides an almost lyrical description of the mixed nature of passionate love:

> Love and romance seems [*sic*] to be one, if not the most powerful activator of our pleasure centers. . . . Both tend to be very exciting emotionally. Being with the person or even just thinking of him or her is highly stimulating. . . . Love is, by definition, the strongest positive feeling we can have. Other things—stimulant drugs, passionate causes, manic states—can induce powerful changes in our brains, but none so reliably, so enduringly, or so delightfully as that "right" other person. . . . If the relationship is not established or is uncertain, anxiety or other displeasure centers may be quite active as well, producing a situation of great emotional turmoil as the lover swings between hope and torment. (pp. 48–49)

It is clear, then, that most people assume it appropriate to use the term "passionate love" to label any "intense longing for union with another," regardless of whether that longing is reciprocated (and thus a source of fulfillment and ecstasy) or is uncertain or unrequited (and thus a source of emptiness, anxiety, or despair).

The Physiological Contribution

Since antiquity, researchers have been developing methods to detect "love-sickness." Consider this report (Mesulam & Perry, 1972):

> At the beginning of the third century, B.C., Seleucus, one of Alexander's generals and among the ablest of his successors, married a woman named Stratonice. Antiochus, his son by a previous marriage, had the misfortune to fall in love with his new stepmother. Recognizing the illicit character of his love, and the hopelessness of its consummation, Antiochus resolves not to show his feelings. Instead, he falls sick and strives his hardest to die.
>
> We may be sure that many doctors attended the young prince, but to no avail it seems, until the celebrated Greek physician Erasistratos concludes that, in the absence of bodily disease, the boy's malady must stem from some affliction of the mind, "through which the body is often strengthened or weakened by sympathy." (Appian, 2nd century, A.D.)

The physician spent day after day in the Antiochus chamber. Each time one of the court beauties (male or female) dropped by, the wily Erasistratos studied Antiochus's physiological reactions. He found that only one person produced a strong reaction in Antiochus—his stepmother, Stratonice! Each time she came to see him, "lo, those tell-tale-signs of which Sappho sings were all there in him—stammering speech, fiery flashes, darkened vision, sudden sweats, irregular palpitations of the heart, and finally, as his soul was taken by storm, helplessness, stupor, and pallor (Plutarch, 1st century, A.D.)" (reported in Mesulam & Perry [1972], p. 547). On the physician's advice, Seleucus divorced his bride, Stratonice, and his son's life was saved.

Recently, psychologists have assembled information from neuroanatomical and neurophysiological investigations, ablation experiments, pharmacological explorations, clinical investigations and behavioral research as to the social psychophysiology of passion. These authors document that the ancients' observations are, in part, correct. Their research also documents the contention that passionate love is a far more complicated phenomenon than it had at first seemed. (See Kaplan's 1979 discussion of the neuroanatomy and neurophysiology of sexual desire; Liebowitz's 1983 discussion of the chemistry of passionate love; and Hatfield & Rapson's 1987c discussion of the similarities between the two.)

The Anatomy of Love

According to psychiatrist Helen Singer Kaplan (1979), the anatomy of passionate love/sexual desire is relatively well understood. The brain's sex center consists of a network of neural centers and circuits. These are centered within the limbic system—with nuclei in the hypothalamus and in the preoptic region (see chapter 4). The limbic system is located in the limbus, or rim, of the brain. In primitive vertebrates, this system controls emotion and motivation; it ensures that animals will act so as to foster their own survival and that of their species. In man, this archaic system remains essentially unchanged. It is here that men and women's most powerful emotions are generated, their behavior most powerfully driven. In the sex centers, researchers have identified both activating and inhibitory centers.

The sexual system has extensive neural connections to other parts of the brain. For example, it has significant connections, both neural and chemical, to the brain's pleasure and the pain centers. All sexual behavior is shaped by the seeking of pleasure (i.e., seeking stimulation of the pleasure centers) and the avoidance of pain (i.e., avoiding stimulation of the pain centers).

Chemical receptor sites, located on the neurons of the pleasure centers, respond to a chemical that is produced by the brain cells. This has been tagged an *endorphin* because it resembles morphine chemically and physiologically (i.e., it causes euphoria and alleviates pain). Kaplan (1979) observes:

> It may be speculated that eating and sex and being in love, i.e., behaviors which are experienced as pleasurable, produce this sensation by stimulation of the pleasure centers, electrically, or by causing the release of endorphins, or by both mechanisms. (p. 11)

Sexual desire is also connected anatomically or chemically, or both, to the pain centers. If sexual partners or experiences are associated with too much pain, they will cease to evoke sexual desire. A chemical mediator for pain, analogous to endorphin, may exist. The brain is organized so that pain takes priority over pleasure. This, of course, makes sense from an evolutionary point of view. Kaplan (1979) acknowledges that cognitive factors have a profound impact on sexual desire. Thus, the cortex (that part of the brain that analyzes complex perceptions and stores and retrieves memories) must have extensive neural connections with the sex center.

The Chemistry of Love

Researchers are beginning to learn more about the chemistry of passionate love and a potpourri of related emotions. They are also learning more about the way that various emotions, positive and negative, interact.

Psychiatrist Michael Liebowitz (1983) has been the most willing to speculate about the chemistry of love. He argues that passionate love brings on a giddy feeling, comparable to an amphetamine "high." It is phenylethylamine (PEA), an amphetamine-related compound, that produces the mood-lifting and energizing effects of romantic love. He observes that "love addicts" and drug addicts have a great deal in common: The craving for romance is merely the craving for a particular kind of high. The fact that most romances lose some of their intensity with time may well be due to normal biological processes.

The crash that follows a breakup is much like amphetamine withdrawal. Liebowitz speculates that there may be a chemical counteractant to lovesickness: MAO (monoamine oxidase) inhibitors may inhibit the breakdown of PEA, thereby "stabilizing" the lovesick.

Liebowitz also offers some speculations about the chemistry of the emotions which criss-cross lovers' minds as they plunge from the highs to the lows of love. The highs include euphoria, excitement, relaxation, spiritual feelings, and relief. The lows include anxiety, terrifying panic attacks, the pain of separation, and the fear of punishment. His speculations are based on the assumption that nondrug and drug highs and lows operate via similar changes in brain chemistry.

In excitement, Liebowitz proposes that naturally occurring brain chemicals, similar to the stimulants (such as amphetamine and cocaine), produce the "rush" lovers feel. In relaxation, chemicals related to the narcotics (such as heroin, opium and morphine), tranquilizers (such as Librium and Valium), sedatives (such as barbiturates, Quaaludes and other "downers"), alcohol (which acts chemically much like the sedatives), and marijuana and other cannabis derivatives all produce a mellow state and wipe out anxiety, loneliness, panic attacks, and depression. In spiritual peak experiences, chemicals similar to the psychedelics (such as LSD, mescaline and psilocybin) produce a sense of beauty, meaningfulness, and timelessness.

Physiologists do not usually try to produce separation anxiety, panic attacks, or depression. Such painful feelings may arise from two sources, however: withdrawal from those chemicals that produce the highs; and other chemicals which, in and of themselves, produce anxiety, pain, or depression. Research has not yet established whether Liebowitz's speculations as to the chemistry of love are correct.

Kaplan (1979) provides some information as to the chemistry of sexual desire. In both men and women, testosterone (and perhaps LH-RF, luteinizing hormone-releasing factor) are the libido hormones. The neurotransmitter dopamine may act as a stimulant, serotonin or 5-HT (5-hydroxtryptamine) as inhibitors, to the sexual centers of the brain. Kaplan observes:

> When we are in love, libido is high. Every contact is sensuous, thoughts turn to Eros, and the sexual reflexes work rapidly and well. The presence of the beloved is an aphrodisiac; the smell, sight, sound, and touch of the lover—especially when he/she is excited—are powerful stimuli to sexual desire. In physiologic terms, this may exert a direct physical effect on the neurophysiologic system in the brain which regulates sexual desire. . . . But again, there is no sexual stimulant so powerful, even love, that it cannot be inhibited by fear and pain. (p. 14)

Kaplan ends by observing that a wide array of cognitive and physiological factors shape desire.

Finally, although passionate love and the related emotions described may be associated with specific chemical neurotransmitters (or with chemicals which increase/decrease the receptors' sensitivity), most emotions have more similarities than differences. Chemically, intense emotions do have much in common. Kaplan reminds us that, chemically, love, joy, sexual desire, excitement, anger, fear, jealousy, and hate, are all intensely arousing. They all produce an ANS sympathetic response, evidenced by the symptoms associated with all these emotions: a flushed face, sweaty palms, weak knees, butterflies in the stomach, dizziness, a pounding heart, trembling hands, and accelerated breathing. (The exact pattern of reaction varies from person to person. See Lacey, 1967.)

EMOTIONAL INTERLINKAGES

Hatfield (1971a and b) argued that the various emotions are more tightly linked than psychologists have thought. Thus far, we have talked about emotions as if they generally exist in a pure form: People are happy or sad; in love or angry. In real life, people's emotional lives are far more complex. Ingmar Bergman's film *Autumn Sonata* demonstrates this fact. Eva, a housewife, invites her mother, Charlotte, an acclaimed concert pianist, to visit her. After dinner, Charlotte is asked to play a Chopin prelude. The camera, in a tight close-up, focuses on Eva as she watches her mother perform. Eva's ambivalent feelings flicker across her face. Critic John Hartzog (1985) observes: "[Eva's] eyes and mouth reveal her awe of and respect for her mother's talent, her crushed feelings of inadequacy in the presence of her mother's superiority, her hatred of this person who cannot acknowledge her daughter's reality but swallows it up in her overwhelming personality. Eva's face communicates all of these feelings without Eva's uttering a word" (pp. 185–186). In family life, such mixed emotions are the norm. How do people make sense of such complicated arrays of feelings?

Hatfield argued that sometimes people have trouble knowing quite what they feel. For example, try this experiment. Freeze this moment in time. Now, try, with great precision, to describe what you are feeling. It is more difficult than you might have thought. When we focus on only the cognitive threads of emotion, the task is hard enough. Perhaps we feel vaguely neglected by our mate. Is "love" the appropriate label for that feeling? Or is it resentment? Indignation? Embarrassment? Anger? Sometimes, it is difficult to unravel our tangled emotions.

When we try to describe our physiological reactions, the difficulty becomes even greater. Sometimes it is easy to identify an emotion with its accompanying physiological correlates. For example, certain emotions are linked with very specific facial muscle movements. We recognize the furrowed corrugator muscle, those squinting eyes as the look of self-righteous anger. Sometimes, however, more than one emotion is linked with the same physiological correlates. Being startled, for example, produces a shower of catacholamines. But so do anger, joy, passion, and other emotions. Sometimes we don't know whether we want to laugh or cry. What about the feeling that we are about to cry: the heavy breathing, tight chest, and shaking hands? Is that hurt or anger? It is hard to tell. Perhaps we are simply getting a cold! It is equally difficult to identify emotions according to the skeletal-muscular system. For example, both joy and fury may spark the same kind of outsized, sweeping movements.

Yet another problem arises in describing our inner lives. Many emotional reactions are nonconscious. Conscious awareness is a precious commodity. George Miller (1956) has argued that people can be aware of only seven or so things at a time. Thus, much cognitive and emotional processing must be run off automatically in other parts of the brain. For example, if a given perceptual-behavioral sequence is replayed again and again, it will soon become automatic. We offer an opinion, our mother cries or grows angry, we become angry or frightened in return; we apologize and comfort her; the relationship returns to normal. The same sequence occurs again and again. Soon the complex actions and reactions begin to happen automatically. We lose consciousness of our own feelings. Instead, as soon as we begin to speak, incipient anxiety, well below the level of consciousness, begins to stir. Without even thinking of it, our hand reaches out and pats our mother's shoulder. Our precious consciousness can be devoted entirely to the conversation; other parts of the brain can reel out the appropriate emotional coordination sequences.

Often, if we try, we can replay such sequences and retrieve our feelings; at the very least we can focus attention on our feelings, and "catch" them the next time the inevitable sequence happens. Usually, however, such self-conscious regulation is unnecessary. Consciousness is too valuable to be wasted on the routine. If we are not even conscious, then, of the many potential emotions that flicker across our minds, it certainly makes it difficult to know exactly what emotions are interacting at a given time.

Of course, in real life time does not stand still. Emotions are labile. People can move from elation, through terror, to the shoals of despair, and back again within seconds. Passionate love often involves such complicated interplay. Joy and pain often criss-cross consciousness.

These observations led Hatfield to argue that psychologists must study not only pure emotions but must devote some attention to analyzing how emotions interact. Logically, emotions should be able to interact in several major ways. First, when one is experiencing several emotions, one may sometimes identifiably feel the ebb and flow of separate emotions. One experiences a series of distinct emotions, or emotional blends. In 1945, for example, Christabel Bielenberg, the English wife of a prominent German lawyer, entered a grim office along Berlin's Prinz Alberechstrasse. The Nazis planned to interrogate her in the expectation that she and her husband would be found guilty of plotting to kill Hitler. She later observed: "Oh, I was terrified when I got there—I was so weak at the knees I could hardly get up the steps." As she waited, however, a secretary leaned forward and struck a prisoner across the face, irritated that the prisoner expected to read his "confession" before signing it. Mrs. Bielenberg now remembers: ". . . I realized that you can't have two very strong emotions at the same time. I was so angry it just wasn't possible to go on being frightened" (p. 31). That surge of anger, which carried over into the nine-hour interrogation, convinced the Gestapo that she must either be innocent or possess extremely powerful political connections. At any rate, she was allowed to go free, and her husband was released from Ravensbruck prison (Caudwell, 1989, p. 31).

Secondly, it is possible for contradictory emotions to cancel each other out. In addition, Hatfield proposed that one will generally experience the effects of **emotional spillover** (sometimes called **cross-magnification**): A given emotional experience is intensified by emotions which briefly precede, coexist with, or follow the target emotion. Once, for example, one of your authors was literally dancing with joy because her first article had been accepted by the *Journal of Personality and Social Psychology*. Just then her cat, hurtling across the room, ran beneath her feet, and she barely kept from falling. In milliseconds, her joy had turned into fury, and she found herself poised to smack the cat; an act she normally would never have considered. Somehow, her extravagant happiness had turned into equally extravagant anger. The two emotional states had somehow "summed." Once aware of the concept of emotional spillover, however, we begin to notice examples of it everywhere. We find ourselves responding rudely to a friend, then remind ourselves to settle down, remembering that we are simply overwrought from having to rush around all day. We dissolve in a fit of giggling after we trip on the stairs and barely save ourselves from hurtling down the steps. What is so funny about that?

Hatfield argued that, in life, such emotional spillover effects can have powerful consequences. Most intense emotional experiences involve blends of emotions. Perhaps this is not a coincidence. Perhaps emotions (especially positive ones) have a better chance to rise to fever pitch when several emotions are activated.

According to Hatfield, considerable evidence testifies to the existence of such cross-magnification processes. We now turn to evidence that, under the right conditions, either pleasure or pain (or a combination of both) can fuel passion.

BEHAVIORAL EVIDENCE THAT BOTH PLEASURE AND PAIN MAY FUEL EMOTION

Passionate love is such a risky business. Success sparks delight, failure invites despair. We get some indication of the strength of our passion by the intensity of our delight or despair. Of course, trying to calibrate our emotions is difficult. Sometimes it is hard to determine the degree to which your lover is responsible for your delight versus the degree to which it springs from the glorious day and your own readiness for romance. It may be difficult to tell how much of your misery arises from your lover's coolness, how much from loneliness, and how much from fear of going your own way. Or is it simply that you're feeling low today? In any case, an abundance of evidence supports the contention that, under the right conditions, a variety of intensely positive or intensely negative emotions, or neutral but energizing experiences, can add to the passion of passion.

Passion and the Positive Emotions

Elaine Hatfield and G. William Walster's (1978) definition of love states that "reciprocated love (union with the other) is associated with fulfillment and ecstasy" (p. 2). No one has doubted that love is such a delightful experience in its own right that the joys of love generally spill over and add sparkle to everything else in life. What has been of interest to psychologists is the converse of this proposition: that the adrenalin associated with a wide variety of highs can spill over and make passion itself more intense—a sort of "better loving through chemistry" phenomenon.

A number of carefully crafted studies make it clear that a variety of positive emotions—listening to a comedy routine (White, Fishbein, & Butstein, 1981), sexual fantasizing (Stephan et al., 1971), erotic excitement (Istvan & Griffitt, 1978), or general excitement (Zuckerman, 1979)—can intensify passion.

In one investigation, for example, Joseph Istvan, William Griffitt, and Gerdi Weidner (1983) aroused men by showing them pictures of men and women engaged in sexual activities. Other men were shown nonarousing, neutral fare. The researchers then asked the men to evaluate the appeal of both beautiful and unappealing women. When the woman was pretty, the aroused men rated her as more attractive than they normally would have. When the woman was unattractive, however, the aroused men rated her as *less* attractive than they normally would have. It seems the men's sexual arousal spilled over and intensified whatever they would have normally felt for the woman, for good or ill. Similar experiments have shown that sexually aroused women find handsome men more appealing, and homely men less appealing, than usual.

> *A*nd anyway, who could recount, without convincing herself of madness, the true degrees of love? Those endless discussions on that endless theme, the trembling, the waiting, the anguish when he left the room for a moment . . . the terror that each time he left my sight he would die?
>
> MARGARET DRABBLE

Passion and the Negative Emotions

In defining passionate love, Hatfield and Walster also observe: "Unrequited love (separation) is associated with emptiness, anxiety, or despair" (p. 2). Many psychologists have noted that the failure to acquire or sustain love is an extraordinarily painful experience. Theorists such as John Bowlby (1973), Anne Peplau and Daniel Perlman (1982), or Robert Weiss (1972) describe the panic, despair, and eventual detachment that both children and adults feel at the loss of someone they love.

By now, psychologists have also amassed considerable evidence for the proposition that people are especially vulnerable to love when their lives are turbulent. Passion can be intensified by the spillover of feeling from one realm to another. A variety of negative experiences have been found to deepen desire. For example, Donald Dutton and Arthur Aron (1974), in a duo of studies, discovered a close link between fear and sexual attraction. In one experiment, the researchers invited men and women to participate in a learning experiment. When the men showed up, each found that his "partner" was a strikingly beautiful woman. He also discovered that, by signing up for the experiment, he had gotten into more than he had bargained for. The experimenter was studying the effects of electric shock on learning. Sometimes the experimenter quickly went on to reassure the men that they had been assigned to a control group and would be receiving only a barely perceptible "tingle" of a shock. In other conditions, the experimenter tried to terrify the men. He warned them that they'd be getting some fairly painful electric shocks.

Before the supposed experiment was to begin, the experimenter approached each man privately and asked how he felt about the beautiful woman who "happened" to be his partner. He asked the men to tell him, in confidence, how attracted they were to her (for example, "How much would you like to ask her out for a date?" or "How much would you like to kiss her?"). The investigators predicted that fear would facilitate attraction. It did. The terrified men found the women much sexier than did the calm and cool men.

In another study, the investigators compared the reactions of young men crossing two bridges in North Vancouver, Canada. The first, the Capilano Canyon suspension bridge, tilts, sways, and wobbles for 450 feet over a 230-foot drop to rocks and shallow rapids. The other bridge, a bit farther upstream, is a solid, safe structure. As each young man crossed the bridge, an attractive college woman approached him, explained that she was doing a class project, and asked him to fill out a questionnaire for her. When the man had finished, she offered to explain her project in greater detail, and wrote her telephone number on a small piece of paper so that the man could call her for more information. Which men called? Nine of the 33 men on the suspension bridge called her, but only two of the men on the solid bridge.

This study can, of course, be interpreted several ways. Perhaps the men who called after making it across the precarious Capilano bridge really were interested in the woman's project rather than sex. Perhaps it was not fear but relief at having survived the heights, paired with the lovely lady, that stimulated desire. It is always possible to find alternative explanations for any single study.

Emotional spillover made simple by renowned psychiatrist Dr. Lucy Van Pelt. Reprinted by permission of UFS, Inc.

But by now a great deal of experimental and correlational evidence provides support for the more intriguing contention that, under the right conditions, a variety of awkward and painful experiences can deepen passion—anxiety and fear (Aron, 1970; Brehm, Gotz, Goethals, McCrimmon & Ward, 1978; Dienstbier, 1978; Dutton & Aron, 1974; Hoon, Wincze, & Hoon, 1977; Riordan & Tedeschi, 1983), embarrassment (Byrne, Przybyla, & Infantino, 1981), the discomfort of seeing others involved in conflict (Dutton, 1979), jealousy (Clanton & Smith, 1987), loneliness (Peplau & Perlman, 1982), anger (Barclay, 1969), anger at parental attempts to break up an affair (Driscoll, Davis, & Lipetz, 1972), grisly stories of a mob mutilating and killing a missionary while his family watched (White et al., 1981), or even grief.

Passion and Emotionally Neutral Arousal

Recent laboratory research indicates that passion can even be stirred by excitation transfer from such emotionally neutral but physically arousing experiences as riding an exercise bicycle (Cantor, Zillman, & Bryant, 1975) or jogging (White, Fishbein, & Rutstein, 1981). The latter researchers conducted a series of elegant studies to demonstrate that passion can be intensified by any intense experience. In one experiment, some men (those in the high-arousal group) were required to engage in strenuous physical exercise (they ran in place for 2 minutes). Other men (those in the low-arousal group) ran in place only 15 seconds. In and of itself, the exercise did not affect the men's moods. A variety of self-report questions and heart-rate measures established that these two groups did, however, vary greatly in arousal.

The men then watched a videotaped interview with a woman they expected to meet soon. Half the time the woman was attractive; half the time, unattractive. After the interview, the men gave their first impression of the woman, estimating her attractiveness and sexiness. They also indicated how attracted they felt to her; how much they wanted to kiss and date her.

The authors proposed that exertion-induced arousal would intensify men's reactions to the woman, for good or for ill. Aroused subjects would be more attracted to the attractive confederate and more repulsed by the unattractive confederate than would subjects with lower levels of arousal. The authors found exactly that. If the woman was beautiful, the men who were aroused via exertion judged her to be unusually appealing. If the woman was unattractive, the men who were aroused via exertion judged her to be unusually unappealing. The effect of arousal, then, was to intensify a person's initial "intrinsic" attractivenness. Arousal enhanced the appeal of the pretty woman as much as it impaired the appeal of the unattractive one. (See Zillman, 1984, for a review of this research on excitation transfer.)

The evidence suggests that various states of arousal—whether emotional or simply physically intense—can spill over and influence one another. Adrenalin makes the heart grow fonder. Delight is one stimulant of passionate love, yet anxiety and fear, or simply high arousal, can often play a part.

WHO KNOWS HOW TO MAKE LOVE STAY?

Passionate love is a fleeting phenomenon (Berscheid, 1983; Hatfield & Walster, 1978). Marriage and family texts warn that romantic love is temporary. It is bound to settle down once couples begin to live together. Eric Klinger (1977) observed that highs "are always transitory. People experience deliriously happy moments that quickly fade and all attempts to hang on to them are doomed to fail" (p. 116).

Theodor Reik (1972) warned that the best a couple intensely in love can hope for after several years of living together is a warm "afterglow." Passionate love does seem to erode with time. In a series of studies, Hatfield and her colleagues (see Traupmann & Hatfield, 1981) interviewed dating couples, newlyweds, and older women. The older women had been married from 1 to 59 years. The average length of their marriages was 33 years. (Unfortunately for our purposes, the older women's husbands were not interviewed.)

The authors predicted that passionate love would decline precipitously with time, but that companionate love would not. They took it for granted that men and women could remain friends for a lifetime. The data led them to a slightly different conclusion, however. Over time, passionate love did seem to plummet (see Figure 11.5). Couples started out loving their partners intensely. Both steady daters and newlyweds expressed "a great deal of passionate love" for their mates. But after many years of marriage, women reported that they and their husbands now felt only "some" passionate love for one another. From the first, however, couples' level of companionate love was extremely high. (Again, see Figure 11.5.) Both steady daters and newlyweds express "a great deal" to "a tremendous amount" of companionate

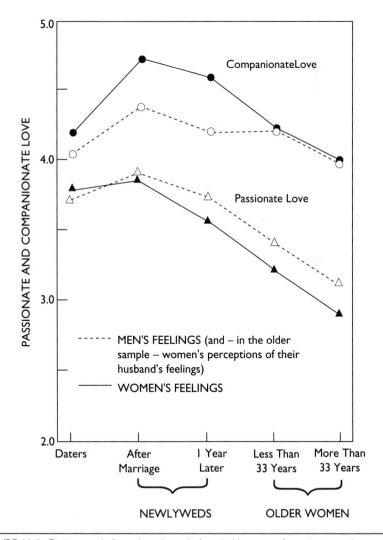

FIGURE 11.6 Dating couples', newlywed couples', and older women's passionate and companionate love for their partners.

love for their partners. Although couples' companionate feelings do seem to erode a bit with time, men and women still felt a great deal of love for each other even after 33 years of marriage. Typically, older women reported feeling "a great deal" of companionate love for their mates.

Other researchers have found that children present a special challenge to marriages. With the birth of the first child, marriages tend to decline in happiness and satisfaction; when children enter grade school or leave home for good, marital happiness shows an upturn (see Brehm, 1985). Ellen Berscheid (1983) observes:

> To many, the prospect of an "afterglow" seems distinctly pallid and uninteresting compared with the flame of the fire itself, but, much as one wishes to hold on to the intensely positive emotions, to retain the euphoric state, there is little that is known about the underlying dynamics of emotion and of its antecedents . . . that suggests this is possible. The afterglow of comfort, contentment, and affection that Reik describes as the best outcome possible under the circumstances is congruent with what is known about the role of arousal in emotion. (p. 158)

Companionate Love

If passion cannot last, then, let us turn to a form of love that can—companionate love.

MEASURES AND MODELS

Companionate love (sometimes called "true" or "conjugal" love) is a far less intense emotion. It combines feelings of deep attachment and friendly affection. Such a warm, caring, intimate relationship was depicted in the film *On Golden Pond*. At the beginning of this chapter, Hatfield and Walster (1978) defined companionate love as "the affection we feel for those with whom our lives are deeply entwined" (p. 9). According to Robert Sternberg (1988), companionate love, intimacy, and commitment go hand in hand.

Psychologists have used a variety of scales to measure companionate love. For example, in the study we just described, after describing what they meant by companionate love, Hatfield and her colleagues measured couples' companionate love for each other with a single-item measure:

How much companionate love do you feel for _____?

- ■ None at all
- ■ Very little
- ■ Some
- ■ A great deal
- ■ A tremendous amount

Other social psychologists have developed measures which include several items tapping companionate love. For example, Zick Rubin (1970) has studied both romantic love (which seems to include elements of both passionate and companionate love) and liking (which seems to include elements of both companionate love and liking). Rubin sifted through a jumble of lovers', novelists', and scientists' descriptions of love and friendship. He concluded that romantic love includes such elements as idealization of the other, tenderness, responsibility, the longing to serve and be served by the loved one, intimacy, the desire to share emotions and experiences, sexual attraction, the exclusive and absorptive nature of the relationship, and finally, a relative lack of concern with social norms and constraints. Liking includes such elements as appreciation of the other person, respect, and a feeling that the two friends have a great deal in common. Rubin has developed excellent scales to measure both love and liking.

Just for fun, you might want to try a few items from Rubin's scales (see Box 11.3). His scales originally contained 13 items each. On the answer sheet that follows the scales, indicate how you feel about your date, lover, or mate. Choose the number from 1 ("Not at all true; disagree completely") through 9 ("Definitely true; agree completely") that best represents your feelings about your partner.

Although the Rubin scales include some items which tap companionate love, they are not really "pure" measures of companionate love since the scales include other items that tap romantic (passionate) love or liking as well.

As we mentioned earlier, Robert Sternberg (1988) proposed a triangular model of love. He argued that companionate love results from a combination of the decision/commitment and intimacy components of love.

The Triangular Model: Decision/Commitment

This component of love requires both a short-term decision and a long-term commitment. In the short run, men and women must make a decision as to whether or not they love the other. But this is not enough. In the long run, what is more important is whether couples feel committed to that love.

The Triangular Model: Intimacy

Many theorists have tended to equate companionate love with intimacy. But what do theorists mean by intimacy? The word *intimacy* is derived from the Latin *intimus*, meaning "inner" or "inmost." To be **intimate** means to be close to another. Hatfield (1984) defines intimacy as "a process in which people attempt to get close to another; to explore similarities (and differences) in the way they think, feel, and behave" (p. 207).

Intimate relationships have three main characteristics:

1. Cognitive characteristics: Intimates are willing to reveal themselves to one another. They disclose information about themselves and listen to their partners' confidences. In deeply intimate relationships, friends and lovers feel free to reveal most facets of themselves. As a result, intimates

BOX 11.3

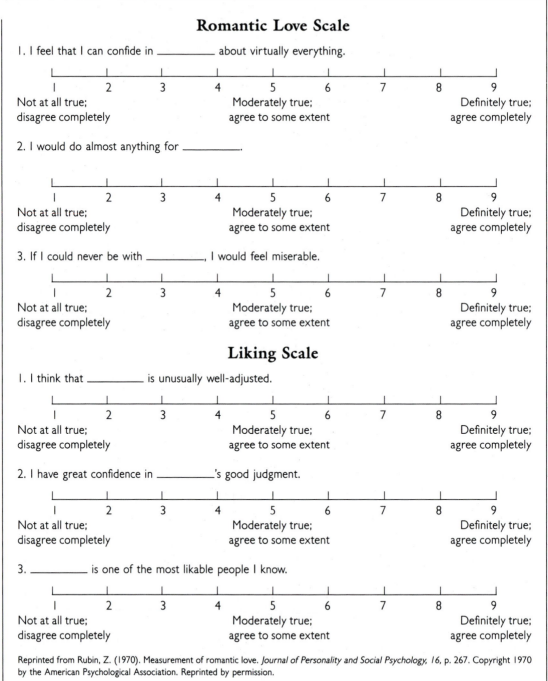

Romantic Love Scale

1. I feel that I can confide in _____ about virtually everything.

1	2	3	4	5	6	7	8	9

Not at all true;   Moderately true;   Definitely true;
disagree completely   agree to some extent   agree completely

2. I would do almost anything for _____.

1	2	3	4	5	6	7	8	9

Not at all true;   Moderately true;   Definitely true;
disagree completely   agree to some extent   agree completely

3. If I could never be with _____, I would feel miserable.

1	2	3	4	5	6	7	8	9

Not at all true;   Moderately true;   Definitely true;
disagree completely   agree to some extent   agree completely

Liking Scale

1. I think that _____ is unusually well-adjusted.

1	2	3	4	5	6	7	8	9

Not at all true;   Moderately true;   Definitely true;
disagree completely   agree to some extent   agree completely

2. I have great confidence in _____'s good judgment.

1	2	3	4	5	6	7	8	9

Not at all true;   Moderately true;   Definitely true;
disagree completely   agree to some extent   agree completely

3. _____ is one of the most likable people I know.

1	2	3	4	5	6	7	8	9

Not at all true;   Moderately true;   Definitely true;
disagree completely   agree to some extent   agree completely

Reprinted from Rubin, Z. (1970). Measurement of romantic love. *Journal of Personality and Social Psychology, 16*, p. 267. Copyright 1970 by the American Psychological Association. Reprinted by permission.

share profound information about each other's histories, values, strengths, weaknesses, idiosyncracies, hopes, and fears (Altman & Taylor, 1973; Huesmann & Levinger, 1976; Jourard, 1964).

2. Emotional characteristics: Intimates care deeply about each other. People generally feel more intense love for intimates than for anyone else. Yet, because intimates care so much about one another, they have the power to hurt each other as well. The dark side of love is jealousy, loneliness, depression, and anger. It is this powerful interplay of conflicting emotions that gives vibrancy to the most intimate of relationships (see Berscheid, 1979 and 1983; Hatfield & Walster, 1978). Basic to all intimate relationships is trust. People are not going to expose their deepest feelings to another unless they know it is safe to do so. If intimates use their secret knowledge to hurt their mates whenever they are angry at them, their mates will quickly learn to keep their secrets to themselves. A betrayal is often irreparable.

> *There is no disguise which can for long conceal love where it exists or simulate it where it does not.*
> *LA ROCHEFOUCAULD*

3. Behavioral characteristics: Intimates are comfortable in close physical proximity. They gaze at one another (Argyle, 1967), stand close to one another (Allgeier & Byrne, 1973), lean on each other (Galton, 1884; Hatfield, Roberts, & Schmidt, 1980), and perhaps touch.

STAGES OF RELATIONSHIPS: INITIATION AND MAINTENANCE

Psychologists have observed that relationships develop and change over time. George Levinger (1983) enumerates five potential phases in personal relationships. (These are stages that *can* occur. A given relationship may or may not include all stages.)

1. Acquaintance.
2. Buildup of an ongoing relationship. Couples assess the pleasures and problems of connecting with each other.
3. Commitment to a long-term relationship. Couples continue to consolidate their relationship in a relatively durable midstage.
4. Deterioration or decline of the interconnections.
5. Ending of the relationship through death or separation.

Ellen Berscheid (1983) points out that in each stage of a relationship, intimates are confronted with very different emotional challenges:

The initiation of an adult heterosexual relationship, for example, is often associated with the emotions of joy, romantic love, and ambivalence; the development and maintenance of a close relationship is not infrequently characterized by anger, hatred, and contempt, as well as satisfaction, contentment, and happiness; and the dissolution of a close relationship is often the occasion for grief, melancholy, and depression. (p. 118)

Love relationships seem to spark extremely powerful human emotions—love, jealously, loneliness, and grief. In the 1970s and 1980s, social psychologists devoted a great deal of energy to exploring companionate love and intimacy. (See, for example, the reviews of Berscheid & Hatfield, 1978; Brehm, 1985; Hatfield & Walster, 1978; or Kelley et al., 1983.) They have explored the factors which shape the development, maintenance, disorder, and repair or dissolution of personal relationships. Unfortunately, we can present only a sprinkling of this voluminous research. Let us begin with a discussion of some of the factors which contribute to companionate love and to the development and maintenance of relationships. We will close with a discussion of couples' reactions to the end of such affairs. Students who are interested in learning more about the factors that shape couples' success or failure at deepening their relationships as they move from one stage to another, might consult Steve Duck and Robin Gilmour (1981a, 1981b, and 1981c) and Duck (1982, 1984), who have published an encyclopedic review of this research.

*W*e cannot tell the precise moment when friendship is formed. As in filling a vessel drop by drop, there is at last a drop which makes it run over; so in a serview of kindnesses there is at last one which makes the heart run over.

JAMES BOSWELL

Companionate Love and Reinforcement Theory

Many theorists cite the principle of **reinforcement** to explain why people are attracted to some people and repelled by others (Byrne & Murnen, 1988; Thibaut & Kelley, 1959; Berscheid & Hatfield, 1969). They contend that people come to like and love those who reward them and dislike those who punish them. Baron and Byrne's (1981) argument goes as follows:

1. Most stimuli can be identified as either rewarding or punishing.
2. Rewarding stimuli arouse positive feelings; punishing stimuli arouse negative feelings. These feelings, or affective responses, fall along a continuum from extremely positive to extremely negative.
3. The evaluation of any given stimulus as good or bad, enjoyable or unenjoyable, depends on whether it arouses positive or negative feelings. How positively or negatively people evaluate one another depends on the strength of the aroused affect. They continue:

To take an obvious example, if a stranger were to walk up to you on the street and give you a swift kick in the shins, negative feelings would be aroused. If asked to evaluate the person, you would no doubt say that you did not like the individual. Because you also *learned* to associate negative feelings with the person, you would also indicate dislike for him in the future, but that is not all you learned in the situation. It may be less obvious, but your negative feelings aroused by the kick would also be likely to extend to any innocent bystander who happened to be there . . . to the street where the kicking took place, and to anything else that was associated with the unpleasant interaction. And the reverse would be true: positive feelings—and hence liking—would be evoked by a passing stranger who presented you with a gift such as a free sample. (p. 212)

In this view, the human mind functions like a calculator. The mind tallies up how emotionally pleasurable versus painful a lifetime of intimate encounters with Person X have proved to be, sums, and returns an emotional reaction. A very handy tally, indeed. Byrne (1971) even proposed a formula, a law of attraction, to predict how people will evaluate others.

$$Y = m\left[\frac{\Sigma\text{PR}}{(\Sigma\text{PR} + \Sigma\text{NR})}\right] + k$$

To simplify Byrne's formula, the Y stands for attraction. On the other side of the equation, the symbol PR stands for positive reinforcement (reward) and NR stands for negative reinforcement (which Byrne equates with punishment). Therefore, attraction increases as reward increases and punishment decreases.

At first glance, one's reaction to this law of attraction might be: "So what? We figured that out long ago!" Reinforcement research, however, leads to some conclusions that are not so obvious. Researchers have found that people also come to like and love people who are merely associated with pleasure and to dislike those who are merely associated with pain. For example, when surfers are sitting around on the beach, relaxing after riding a big wave, they may feel a rush of affection for friends who just happen to be around. Conversely, when college students have a splitting headache, are rushing to finish an overdue term paper, and are frustrated because their apartment is furnished chiefly with dirty dishes and cat hair, they may well feel a little angry at the unfortunate person who just happens to drop by.

Social psychologists have amassed considerable evidence for their contention that we all practice love, or guilt, by association. In one experiment, Abraham Maslow and Norbett Mintz (1956) invited men and women to look at photographs of other men and women. Half the subjects met in a pleasant room with soft lighting, elegant draperies, beautiful paintings and sculpture, and plush, comfortable chairs. The others met in an ugly, shabbily furnished room, with dirty, torn shades. The room was harshly lit by a bright overhead bulb; the walls were stark and colorless; the tin ashtrays were full to over-flowing; the room was neither swept nor dusted.

The researchers predicted that when men and women met in the attractive room, they would feel at ease, and their warm feelings would generalize to anything they were asked to judge. When they were in the ugly room, they would feel angry and depressed, and once again their negative mood would generalize. The authors were right. Men and women who met in the beautiful room were far more positive about the photographs than were men and women in the ugly room.

In short: We like people who reward us and dislike those who punish us. We also like (or dislike) people who are merely associated with reward (or punishment). In *The Attraction Paradigm*, Byrne (1971) provides an encyclopedic review of evidence in support of these propositions. Byrne and Murnen (1988) observe: "There is thus a convincing body of results indicating a parallel between what is found in the laboratory and what is found in actual relationships" (p. 295).

What rewards seem most critical in love relationships? Byrne and Murnen (1988) argue that if couples are going to maintain a loving relationship, they have to be careful to keep communicating positive feelings to each other. In new relationships, this is easy. Couples indicate their positive responses to each other by initiating physical closeness, making eye contact, expressing sexual interest, uttering kind words, holding hands, giving presents, and generally expressing their love and liking. The authors observe: "Very often, a given act—a thoughtful phone call informing a partner you will be late, a sexual interaction, or a birthday gift—is more important for the message of love it sends than for its intrinsic value" (p. 301).

Unfortunately, as people settle into a relationship, these gentle niceties begin to occur less frequently; harsh evaluations begin to creep into the relationship. For some reason, married couples begin to treat each other worse than they would treat total strangers. Some couples stop catching each other's eyes; they stop touching. The authors observe: "We also seem to feel free in a close, loving relationship to criticize, nag, and complain. . . . Compounding the problem is the fact that negative words and deeds from someone we like is unexpected and more upsetting than such responses from someone we dislike" (p. 302).

Gary Birchler, Robert Weiss, and John Vincent (1975) and John Gottman and his colleagues (1976) compared married couples who were relatively happy versus couples who were distressed. They found that happy couples generally have positive exchanges. They smile, nod, and make eye contact. They speak to each other in soft, tender, happy voices. They lean forward to catch each other's words. Distressed couples have evolved corrosive patterns of interacting. They try to influence one another not with honeyed words but by complaints and punishment. They sneer, cry, and frown at each other. Their voices are tense, cold, impatient, and whining. They make rude gestures, point, jab, shrug their shoulders in disgust; or they simply don't pay any attention to one another. When one partner begins to utilize such tactics, the other tends to respond in a similar fashion, leading to an escalation of reciprocal aversiveness.

Byrne and his colleagues contend that companionate love and liking are the most important rewards/costs involved in a relationship. What other things seem to be important? Hatfield and her colleagues (1984) interviewed over 1,000 dating couples, 100 newlyweds, and 400 elderly women as to the rewards (or lack thereof) that they found to be most critical in their relationships. Their answers, some of which are shown in Box 11.4, were surprisingly similar:

The Equity Theory of Companionate Love
Couples are concerned with the rewards and punishments they encounter in their relationships, but they care about more—they care about how fairly they are treated. Intimates generally believe that if their partners love them they will wish to treat them fairly.

Researchers find that if men and women receive either far more or far less than they are entitled to in a relationship, and for too long a time, it begins to cause serious trouble. Let us begin by reviewing equity theory (see Hatfield & Walster, 1978; Hatfield et al., 1984) and then discuss some research findings.

Equity theory is a simple theory consisting of four propositions:

Proposition I: Individuals will try to maximize their outcomes (where outcomes equal rewards minus punishments).
Proposition II: Groups can maximize collective reward by evolving accepted systems for equity, and will attempt to induce members to accept and adhere to these systems. Groups will generally reward members who treat others equitably and punish those who treat others inequitably.
Proposition III: When individuals find themselves participating in inequitable relationships, they will become distressed. The more inequitable the relationship, the more distress they will feel.
Proposition IV: Individuals who discover that they are in inequitable relationships will attempt to eliminate their distress by restoring equity. The greater the inequity that exists, the more distress they will feel, and the harder they will try to restore equity. (Hatfield et al., 1984, pp. 1–2)

Essentially, then, the equity argument runs as follows: People are motivated by self-interest. But people in society soon learn that they can probably do best if they play according to society's rules . . . or at least appear to be doing so. Thus, equity theory argues that humans feel most content when they are getting exactly what they think they deserve out of life—no more and certainly no less. Anytime individuals exploit others or allow themselves to be exploited they experience distress. There is surely no mystery as to why people who are not getting all they deserve from a relationship should

BOX 11.4

Rewards in Love Relationships

Personal Rewards

This included such rewards as "social grace" (having a partner who is sociable, friendly, and relaxed in social settings), "intellect" (having a partner who is intelligent and informed), and "appearance" (having a physically attractive partner).

Emotional Rewards

1. Liking and loving
   Being liked by your partner
   Being loved by your partner.

2. Understanding and concern
   Having your personal concerns and emotional needs understood and responded to.

3. Acceptance
   Because of your partner's acceptance and encouragement, being free to try out different roles occasionally—for example, being a baby sometimes, a mother, a colleague or a friend, an aggressive as well as a passive lover, and so on.

4. Appreciation
   Being appreciated for contributions to the relationship; not being taken for granted by your partner.

5. Physical affection
   Receiving open affection—touching, hugging, kissing.

6. Sex
   Experiencing a sexually fulfilling and pleasurable relationship with your partner.
   Having a partner who is faithful to your agreements about extramarital relations.

7. Security
   Being secure in your partner's commitment to you and to the future of your relationship together.

8. Plans and goals for the future
   Planning for and dreaming about your future together.

Day-to-Day Rewards

1. Day-to-day operations
   Having a smoothly operating household because of the way you two have organized your household responsibilities.

2. Finances
   Gaining income and other financial resources through your "joint account."

3. Sociability
   Having a pleasant living-together situation because your partner is easy to live with on a daily basis.
   Having a good companion who suggests fun things to do and who also goes along with your ideas for what you might do together.
   Knowing your partner is interested in hearing about your day and what is on your mind, and in turn will share concerns and events with you.
   Having a partner who is compatible with your friends and relatives; who is able to fit in.

4. Decision making
   Having a partner who takes a fair share of the responsibility for making and carrying out decisions that affect both of you.

5. Remembering special occasions
   Having a partner who is thoughtful about sentimental things; who remembers, for example, birthdays, and other special occasions.

Opportunities Gained and Lost

"Opportunities gained" include the things that one gets from being married—for example, the chance to become a parent, the chance to be included in "married couple" social events, and having someone to count on in old age.

"Opportunities foregone" include the things that one has to give up in order to be in a relationship—other possible mates, a career, travel, and so forth.

feel angry and resentful. They are, after all, being cheated. Less obvious is why their overbenefited mates should feel uneasy. But, a moment's reflection makes it clear why they might be. When men and women know they are taking advantage of the person they should love the most, they may feel guilty and ashamed, wonder what can be wrong with their mates, or worry that they may eventually lose their privileged position.

How do couples who are caught up in inequitable relationships handle such feelings of distress? Couples have been found to reduce distress via three techniques.

The first of these is restoration of actual equity. One way a person can restore equity to an unjust relationship is by voluntarily setting things right . . . or prodding the partner to do so. A great deal of evidence shows that couples do often make considerable effort to balance things out. The husband who has been crabby for a while because of stress at work may take his wife on a trip when things let up.

A second technique for reducing distress is restoration of psychological equity. Unfortunately, when couples find themselves in an inequitable relationship, they can reduce distress by distorting reality and convincing themselves (and perhaps others as well) that things are perfectly fair left as they are.

A variety of studies document the imaginative techniques that men and women use to justify injustice. Studies have demonstrated, for example, that people rationalize the harm they have inflicted on another by denying that they are responsible for the victim's suffering, by insisting that the victim deserved to suffer, or by minimizing the degree to which the victim actually did suffer from their actions (see Brock & Buss, 1962; Glass, 1964; Sykes & Matza, 1957). There is even some sparse experimental evidence that, under the right circumstances, victims will justify their own exploitation (see Austin & Hatfield, 1974; Leventhal & Bergman, 1969).

One of the first experiments to demonstrate that people routinely justify the harm they do was conducted by Keith Davis and Edward Jones (1960). They recruited college students to take part in an experiment on "first-impression" formation. The students' main task was presumably to form a first impression of a man in an adjoining room. First, the experimenter interviewed the man while the students listened. The interviewee was actually a confederate who attempted to answer all questions in a friendly way; he seemed slightly nervous and quite involved in creating a favorable, yet honest, impression of himself. When the interview was over, the experimenter asked students to rate the confederate. (This gave the experimenter some idea of how they felt about the soon-to-be victim.)

At this point, the experimenter explained to the students that he was also interested in how people respond to extremely flattering or negative evaluations of themselves. He then showed students two prepared evaluations. The first was complimentary; it contained such statements as:

You sound like one of the most interesting persons that I have met since I came to Chapel Hill. I would really like to get to know you much better. (p. 404)

The other evaluation was harsh. It said:

As I understand it, my job is to tell you in all honesty what my first impression of you is. So here goes: I hope that what I say won't cause any hard feelings, but I'll have to say right away that my overall impression was not too favorable. To put it simply, I wouldn't go out of my way to get to know you. . . . Your general interests and so on just strike me as those of a pretty shallow person. To be more specific: Frankly, I just wouldn't know how much I could trust you as a friend after hearing your answers to those moral questions. (p. 405)

The experimenter then asked the students to read one of these evaluations to the other person so that they could observe how he reacted to flattery or insult. (In fact, all students were asked to claim that the harsh evaluation was their own.) After the students had delivered the insulting evaluation, the experimenter asked the students to rate the other's likeability, warmth, conceit, intelligence, and adjustment. The authors found that students generally salved their consciences by convincing themselves that their fellow student deserved a cruel evaluation. After they had delivered the negative evaluation, students tended to denigrate the other student's likeability, warmth, lack of conceit, intelligence, and adjustment. Researchers have found, then, that people often justify the harm that they do.

A third way that couples can restore equity to an inequitable relationship is by leaving the relationship. One member of a couple may emotionally abandon the partner, or neglect him or her for the children, friends, or extramarital affairs, or they may simply leave.

Researchers have devised some simple techniques to measure how equitable a relationship is. Technically, an equitable relationship is said to exist if the profits of both partners in the relationship are roughly proportional to their investments; that is, where:

$$\frac{(O_A - I_A)}{(|I_A|)^{k_A}} = \frac{(O_B - I_B)}{(|I_B|)^{k_B}}$$

In this formula, I indicates what Persons A and B are investing or putting into their relationship; O indicates what they are getting out of it. This formula, then, says that in a fair relationship, those men and women who put the most into a relationship should be getting the most out of it. Relationships are patently unfair if Person A does all the giving and Person B does all the taking.

Researchers such as Jane Traupmann and her colleagues (1983) have measured how equitable couples perceive their relationships to be by asking men and women:

Considering what you put into your (dating relationship) (marriage), compared to what you get out of it . . . and what your partner puts in compared to what (s)he gets out of it, how does your (dating relationship) (marriage) "stack up"?

+3: I am getting a much better deal than my partner.
+2: I am getting a somewhat better deal.
+1: I am getting a slightly better deal.
  0: We are both getting an equally good, or bad, deal.
−1: My partner is getting a slightly better deal.
−2: My partner is getting a somewhat better deal.
−3: My partner is getting a much better deal than I am. (p. 1)

On the basis of their answers, men and women can be classified as overbenefited (receiving more than they deserve), equitably treated, or underbenefited (receiving less than they deserve).

In a number of studies, equity considerations have been found to be extremely important in determining who gets into relationships in the first place, how the relationships go, and how likely they are to end. Specifically, researchers arrive at three conclusions.

First, dating couples who feel that their relationships are equitable are most likely to move on to even more intimate relationships. For example, in one study 537 college men and women who were dating were interviewed (Hatfield et al., 1978). It was found that equitable couples were most in love and most likely to become sexually involved with one another. Couples in inequitable relationships tended to stop before becoming sexually involved. The researchers also asked the couples who were sexually intimate why they had engaged in sexual relations. Couples in equitable relationships were most likely to say that they had had intercourse because they both wanted to. Those who felt extremely overbenefitted or extremely underbenefitted were less likely to indicate that sex had been a mutual decision. It is not surprising then, that couples in equitable relationships have more satisfying sexual lives (Traupmann, et al., 1981). Other studies document that it is equitable couples who expect their relations to evolve into more permanent ones.

A second conclusion is that equitable relationships are comfortable relationships. Researchers have interviewed dating couples, newlyweds, couples married for various lengths of time, and the long married. All the studies arrive at a consistent finding: Equitable relations are the most compatible relations. Inequity is distressing for couples at all ages and at all stages of a relationship. In general, men and women seem to feel uncomfortable receiving either far more or far less than they think they deserve. It appears that one never gets used to injustice.

Third, in committed relationships, equitable relations are especially stable. Couples who feel equitably treated in their relationships are more secure about their marriages than are either overbenefited or underbenefitted men and women. A second indication of the stability of a relationship is the willingness of a spouse to become sexually involved with someone outside of marriage. Hatfield, Traupmann, and Walster (1979) found that in equitable relationships, both partners are motivated to be faithful. Inequitable relationships are more fragile; the underbenefited, who feel they are not getting what they deserve in their marriages, are more likely to explore love affairs. The underbenefited tend to have more extramarital affairs sooner in the relationship.

Recently, Margaret S. Clark and her colleagues (Clark, 1984; Clark, Quellette, Powell, & Milberg, 1987; Clark & Reis, 1988; Hatfield et al., 1984) have begun to study the difference between "communal" versus "exchange" relationships. In **communal relationships** (love relationships and friendships), people feel a special responsibility for the needs and welfare of their partners and take it for granted that their partners will share their feelings; they see too obvious a concern with giving and getting as unfriendly and inappropriate. In **exchange relationships** (casual or business relationships), acquaintances are less concerned with one another's emotions and needs, keep more careful records, and are concerned that people repay one another fairly quickly.

Gender Differences in Willingness to Sacrifice in Relationships

Equity researchers who have studied couples' implicit marriage contracts—their understanding as to what sort of give-and-take is fair, have attempted to determine how fair men and women perceive their respective contracts to be.

Researchers generally find that regardless of whether couples are dating, newly wed, or long married, both men and women agree that the men are getting the "best deal." Both agree that, in general, men contribute less to a marriage than women do and get more out of it (Hatfield et al., 1984).

Jesse Bernard (1973) provides additional support for the notion that women sacrifice more for love than men do. In her review of the voluminous literature contrasting "his marriage versus her marriage," Bernard observes a strange paradox: Women are more eager to marry than are men; yet women are the losers in marriage. She notes, for example, that "being married is about twice as advantageous to men as to women in terms of continued survival" (p. 27). As compared with single men, married men's mental health is far better, their happiness is greater, their earning power is greater, after middle age their health is better, and they live longer. The opposite is true for married as compared with single women. For example, all symptoms of psychological distress appear more frequently than expected among married women: nervous breakdowns, nervousness, inertia, insomnia, trembling or perspiring hands, nightmares, fainting, headaches, dizziness, and heart palpitations. They appear much less frequently than expected among unmarried women. These data, then, suggest that, like it or not, women sacrifice the most for love.

*I didn't know that anybody could hurt so much and
live. I suppose it's jealousy. I didn't know it was like
this. I thought jealousy was an idea. It isn't. It's a pain.
But I don't feel as they do in Broadway melodrama. I
don't want to kill anybody. I just want to die.*

FLOYD DELL *in*
"Love in Greenwich Village" (1926, p. 231)

STAGES OF RELATIONSHIPS: DECLINE AND JEALOUSY

Thus far, we have focused on factors within a relationship that strengthen or weaken it. Of course, things outside the relationship can also be important. For example, a couple will have a harder time if one of them is having an affair, if they must live in different parts of the world for months at a time, if they must deal with aging parents or difficult children, or if their work lives are miserable. In this section, let us consider a single emotion, jealousy, that occurs when a relationship seems besieged by outside threats.

What is Jealousy?

Simone de Beauvoir (1967), in *The Woman Destroyed,* writes about a jealous wife's shattered world. When she discovers that her husband, Maurice, is having an affair, she experiences a torrent of emotions. She wants to hurt and punish him; she disdains him; and she loves him more than ever. She minutely compares the amounts of time Maurice spends with her and Noellie, his lover. She calls Maurice's office to check on him and camps outside Noellie's apartment in the hope of seeing them together, believing she can gauge the intensity of Maurice's love for Noellie by his gaze, by how they walk together. She both avoids information and seeks it desperately.

> I am afraid of sleeping, on the nights that Maurice spends with Noellie. That empty bed next to mine, these flat, cold sheets. . . . I take sleeping pills, but in vain, for I dream. Often in my dreams I faint with distress. I no longer know anything. The whole of my past life has collapsed behind me, as the land does in those earthquakes where the ground consumes and destroys itself—is swallowed up behind you as you flee. There is no going back. (pp. 193–195)

De Beauvoir's chronicle details the chaotic jumble of emotions that jealousy creates. What do social scientists know about these painful feelings? In our classes, when we ask "What would you most like to know about jealousy?" students' answers are surprisingly similar. They ask: "What is jealousy?" and, whatever it is, "How can you get rid of it?" A scattering of anthropologists, sociologists, and psychologists—as well as a tidal wave of novelists—have addressed these two questions.

What is jealousy? Since Aristotle's time, theorists have insisted that jealousy is properly equated with "love/hate," "a perverse kind of pleasure," "shock," "uncertainty," "confusion," "suspicion," "fear of loss," "hurt pride," "rivalry," "sorrow," "shame," "humiliation," "anger," "despair," "depression," or "a desire for vengeance." Today, we might wonder whether this is a description of jealousy or of the emotions that accompany it. Most early theorists, however, agreed that jealousy possessed two basic components: (a) a feeling of bruised pride and (b) a feeling that one's "property rights" have been violated.

There is more self-love than love in jealousy.
LA ROCHEFOUCAULD

According to such notables as Otto Fenichel (1955), Sigmund Freud (1922), and anthropologist Margaret Mead (1931), jealousy is really little more than wounded pride. For example, Margaret Mead contends that the more shaky one's self-esteem, the more vulnerable one is to the pangs of jealousy. When men and women have low self-esteem, they wonder, "Why would anyone stay with *me?*" Mead observes, "Jealousy is not a barometer by which the depth of love can be read. It merely records the degree of the lover's insecurity. . . . It is a negative miserable state of feeling having its origin in a sense of insecurity and inferiority" (p. 92).

According to others, jealousy is really little more than a fear of losing one's property. For example, in 1936, sociologist Kingsley Davis provided a fascinating sociological analysis of jealousy: "In every case it [jealousy] is apparently a fear . . . or rage reaction to a threatened appropriation of one's own, or what is desired as one's own property."

Today, psychologists have confirmed that men and women are most likely to feel jealous when they are insecure about their romantic relationships, when they are dependent on those relationships, and when these relationships are threatened. The more serious the threat, the more jealous they are likely to feel (see Clanton & Smith, 1987; Brehm, 1985).

Ellen Berscheid and Jack Fei (1977) point out that the more people depend on a relationship to make them happy, the more susceptible to jealousy they will be. Bram Buunk (1982) secured evidence in support of this contention. He found that subjects who described themselves as emotionally dependent on their relationships (e.g., "I can't imagine what my life would be without my partner"; "It would be difficult for me to find any other person with whom I would be as happy as with my present partner") were most likely to say that they would feel jealous if their partners became interested in someone else.

People may be dependent on their current relationships for several kinds of rewards—emotional closeness, sexual intimacy, or for the thousand-and-one practical benefits that come from dating and marriage. The more serious the threat to the relationship, the more jealous men and women will be. People are more jealous of rivals who are physically attractive, intelligent, and personable than of rivals who are fairly ordinary.

The Experience of Jealousy

Research has demonstrated that jealousy is a complex emotional experience. Thomas Ankles (1939) asked university graduates:

> What are the emotions and feelings involved in jealous behavior? (Cross out those which do not apply.)

(1) Anger	**(8)** Narcissism or self-love
(2) Fear	**(9)** Antagonism
(3) Ridicule	**(10)** Pleasure
(4) Joy	**(11)** Stupidity
(5) Cruelty	**(12)** Respect
(6) Hate	**(13)** Elation
(7) Self-feeling	**(14)** Shame

To Ankles's surprise, he found that at least a few of his respondents insisted that jealousy was associated with all of the preceding emotions. Joel Davitz (1969) interviewed 50 people and secured 50 different descriptions of jealousy. In a more recent study, psychologists (Pines & Aronson, 1983) found once again that subjects experienced both positive feelings when they were jealous (such as "excitement," "love," "feeling alive") as well as negative reactions ("emotional distress," "physical distress," "social embarrassment"). People also felt a broad range of emotions when someone was jealous of them. The targets of jealousy were associated with feeling good, anxious, happy, pitiful, angry, confused, superior, victimized, and passionate. These authors, too, found that one subject or another endorsed each of the 27 different feelings listed on the questionnaire as the way he or she felt when they were the targets of jealousy. Thus, jealousy can indeed involve a large and varied range of emotional reactions. Nonetheless, jealousy produces more pain than joy. It is not surprising, then, that people are often eager to control such feelings.

Can Jealousy Be Controlled?

The answer to this question usually depends on whom you ask. The traditionalists believe that marriage should be permanent and exclusive. Thus, they have a certain interest in believing that jealousy is a natural emotion, "bred in the bone." They generally begin their spirited defense of jealousy by pointing out that even animals are jealous, citing the jealous courtship battles of stags, antelopes, seals, kangaroos, and so on (see Bohm, 1967).

The "new humanists" see things differently. Radical reformers such as Marguerite and Willard Beecher (1971) or Nena and George O'Neill (1972) argue that our personal lives would be more satisfying and our professional lives more creative if we felt free to love all humankind—or at least a larger subset of it. Thus, they prefer to believe that society has the power to arouse or to temper jealousy as it chooses.

In most societies, men are allowed to have more than one partner. For example, Clellan Ford and Frank Beach (1951) report that in 84% of the 185 societies they studied, men were allowed to have more than one wife. Only 1% of the societies permitted women to have more than one husband. Most societies also look more tolerantly on premarital and extramarital sex than does our own. Alfred Kinsey (1953) reports that most societies permit men to have extramarital relations if they are reasonably circumspect about it—if they are careful not to neglect their families, outrage their relatives, or cause a scandal. Extramarital activity is much less frequently permitted for women. Nonetheless, women are allowed to engage in such activities with certain people or on certain special occasions (at weddings, during planting season, and so forth). For example, Ford and Beach report that when Chuckchi men (in Siberia) travel to distant communities, they often engage in sexual liaisons with their hosts' mates. The visitors reciprocate in kind when their hosts visit their communities.

The new humanists point out that, traditionally, American society has strongly fostered marital permanence, exclusivity—and jealousy. Yet, in spite of the fact that their culture tells men and women they should be jealous of their mates, many Americans say they are not. For example, Kinsey and his associates (Kinsey, 1953) found that if a husband learned about his wife's extramarital relations, his discovery reportedly caused "serious difficulty" only 42% of the time; 42% of the time, it caused "no difficulty at all." With a little effort, they argue, we can train ourselves to be far less jealous. People are far more jealous of one another when they are newlyweds than at any other time. The longer couples are married, the less jealous they are.

Recent research suggests that the truth probably lies somewhere between these two extremes. Almost everyone experiences jealousy at some time or other. Nonetheless, society can shape who and what inspires jealousy, and how intensely jealousy is felt and expressed.

For example, recently Clanton and Smith (1987) reviewed the existing clinical research on jealousy (see Gottschalk in Bohm, 1967; Reik, 1949; Corzine, 1974) and found that the following differences seem to exist in the way American men and women respond when they are jealous:

> Men are more apt to *deny* jealous feelings; women are more apt to *acknowledge* them. Men are more likely than women to express jealous feelings through rage and even violence, but such outbursts are often followed by despondency. Jealous men are more apt to focus on the outside *sexual* activity of the partner and they often demand a recital of the intimate details; jealous women are more likely to focus on the *emotional* involvement between her partner and the third party. Men are more likely to *externalize* the cause of the jealousy, more likely to blame the partner, or the third party, or "circumstances." Women often *internalize* the cause of jealousy; they blame themselves. Similarly, a jealous man is more likely

to display *competitive* behavior toward the third party while a jealous woman is more likely to display *possessive* behavior. She clings to her partner rather than confronting the third party.

In general, we may say that male and female experiences and expressions of jealousy reflect male and female role expectations. (p. 11)

California psychologist Jeff Bryson (1977) found that most people respond to jealousy in one of two ways: (a) Some try to protect their own egos—for example, they berate or beat their partners, trying to get even; (b) some try to improve their floundering relationship—to make themselves more attractive, talk things out, and so forth. He concluded that men and women seem to respond quite differently to jealous provocation. In general, jealous men concentrate on shoring up their sagging self-esteem. Jealous women are more likely to do something to strengthen the relationship. Bryson speculates that perhaps these male/female differences are due to the fact that most societies are patriarchal. It is acceptable for men to initiate relationships. Thus, when threatened, they can easily go elsewhere. Women may not have the same freedom, and thus devote their energies to keeping the relationship from floundering.

STAGES OF RELATIONSHIPS: THE END OF THE AFFAIR

People cannot always predict how they will feel when their relationships end—be it in separation, divorce, or death. When one man's teenage son was killed in Vietnam, instead of feeling devastated, he felt nothing at all. Conversely, one couple was engaged in a bitter divorce and custody battle; they counted the days until they would be free. Unexpectedly, the husband died in an airplane crash. To her surprise, the widow found that her "liberation" had turned to ashes. Too late, she realized how much she loved her husband. She was inconsolable.

How can we explain such paradoxical outcomes? Why are people's feelings toward their intimates sometimes so different when they are available versus once they are gone? Berscheid (1983) provides some answers: She defines a "close" relationship as one in which "the causal interconnections between participants' chains of events are strong, frequent, and diverse" (p. 118). She contends that intimates may or may not experience affect—positive or negative, intense or mild—while they are caught up in a close relationship. Nonetheless, intimates are "emotionally invested" in such close relationships, whether or not they are aware of it. When such relationships end, the couples' lives will be severely disrupted. The more emotionally invested couples are, the more emotional their partings will be.

The argument continues: In a marriage, the couple's plans, behaviors, or organized action sequences ("intrachain and interchain sequences") may be more or less linked. For example, imagine that every Sunday John and Susan entertain their respective parents. John and Susan could be totally independent. (Their intrachain sequences would be independent). He might take his parents to a Korean restaurant; she would entertain hers at home. Or, John and Susan's lives could be tightly meshed. (Their intrachain sequences would be almost completely interdependent.) If they were a compatible couple, their connections would be facilitative. When they shop, she might read through the grocery list and tick off items; he might run from aisle to aisle, tossing groceries in the cart as he goes.

If they were a strife-torn couple, their connections would be disruptive. As she tried to read through the list, he might sigh in irritation, shifting from foot to foot in boredom. Then, pushed beyond endurance by her need for an extra bottle of Worcestershire sauce, he might begin to berate her for her extravagance. This cheery conversation might soon degenerate into claims and counterclaims against, say, their respective families.

Berscheid argues that when couples lose their mates, they lose, in part, the ability to run off their well-oiled action sequences. She keeps losing her place in the grocery list. She can't find anything on the shelves. It was John who knew where everything was. She has no one with whom to share "that look" when their parents begin to argue about Oliver North's role in the Iran-Contra affair. There are no hidden understandings.

Berscheid's propositions have some fascinating implications. For example, as long as they were together, both the independent couple and the dependent facilitative couple (whose intrachain and interchain sequences were flawlessly meshed) may have felt exactly the same emotions for one another—a sort of tepid affection. Both couples may simply have taken one another for granted. One would be wrong to predict that both couples would respond similarly to the loss of their mates, however. The independent couple's relationship may have been emotionally dead for some time. Their mate's actual death may produce surprisingly little emotion, surprisingly little change in their lives. The couple whose life was tightly linked, however, had a relationship that was very much alive. Under its tranquil surface was an emotional time bomb, ticking. Once they are separated, the world explodes. Almost every act reminds them of their loss; almost every act is difficult now that they are alone.

How the couple joined in hostility will feel about each other once they are separated is harder to predict. On one hand, such couples often discover that separation is simply a relief. To them, separation means the severing of painful and destructive ties. On the other hand, some conflict-ridden couples discover that they have lost more than they expected. It is easy to focus on the things that don't work well in a relationship; it is harder to remember all the things that do—the literally thousands of interconnected action sequences that may run off without a pause. Couples who lose their sense of perspective may discover after a spouse's death how much their mates really meant to them.

In sum, for most people, love relationships are capable of engendering extraordinarily powerful emotions. When they are passionately in love, normally sedate men and women often engage is extreme behavior to be near their beloved. King Edward VIII startled a nation when he announced he was giving up the throne of England to be with his beloved Wallace Simpson, a twice-married American divorcée. We have all probably observed in amazement normally reserved, controlled people, literally or figuratively pounding on their beloved's door, begging for forgiveness.

In this chapter, we reviewed some of the factors that make the delights of passionate love so electrifying and its accompanying fear of abandonment so terrifying. Next, we considered a more practical, hardier emotion—companionate love. We considered a variety of factors that influence the initiation, maintenance, and dissolution of relationships. We found that relationships are more likely to be maintained if they are loving, intimate, rewarding, and perceived as equitable. Finally, we found that people don't always realize how dependent they are on those they love and take for granted. When relationships are dissolved, couples are often surprised at the depth of their suffering.

Summing Up

- Passionate love is defined as a state of intense longing for union with another. Reciprocated love is associated with fulfillment and ecstasy, unrequited love with emptiness, anxiety, or despair. Passionate love involves a state of profound physiological arousal.

- The Passionate Love Scale is designed to measure cognitive, physiological, and behavioral indicants of "longing for union."

- Primates, far below humans on the phylogenetic scale, seem to experience passionate love. Children seem able to love passionately by three to four years of age.

- Liebowitz argues that passionate love brings on a giddy feeling, comparable to an amphetamine high. It is PEA, an amphetamine-related compound, that produces the mood-lifting and energizing effects of romantic love. The crash that follows a breakup is much like amphetamine withdrawal.

- Chemically, intense emotions have much in common. Love, joy, sexual desire and excitement, as well as anger, fear, jealousy, and hate, produce a sympathetic response in the nervous system.

- Emotions are often interlinked. Sometimes cross-magnification or emotional spillover occurs. Under the right conditions, positive experiences, negative experiences, or even emotionally neutral arousal can fuel passion.

- Companionate love is defined as the affection we feel for those with whom our lives are deeply entwined.

- People like those who reward them (or who are merely associated with reward) and dislike those who punish them (or who are merely associated with punishment).

- Couples in equitable relationships are more likely to stay in relationships, are more content in their relationships, and are less likely to be tempted to explore other relationships than are couples in less equitable relationships.

- Traditional theorists tended to associate jealousy with bruised pride and a feeling that one's property rights had been violated.

- Men and women have been found to differ in how they experience and react to jealousy.

- Couples' feelings before a separation do not always predict how upset they will be when a relationship ends. The more tightly interlinked couples' intrachain sequences are, the more distressed they will be when their relationships are terminated by separation or death.

12

Fear and Anxiety

Introduction

Definitions

Anxiety Disorders
Whatever Happened to Good Old Neuroses?
Phobic Disorder
Generalized Anxiety Disorder
Panic Disorder
Obsessive-Compulsive Disorder
Post-Traumatic Stress Disorder (PTSD)
Some Words of Reassurance

Approaches to Fear and Anxiety
Psychodynamic Approaches to Fear and Anxiety
Physiological Approaches to Fear and Anxiety
Behavioral Approaches to Fear and Anxiety
Cognitive-Learning Approaches to Fear and Anxiety

Measuring Anxiety and Fear
Self-Report Measures
Psychophysiological Measures
Behavioral Measures

Other Perspectives on Fear
Cross-Cultural Aspects of Fear
Fear of Success
Controlling Fear

Summing Up

FIGURE 12.1 *The Scream.* Edvard Munch. 1895. Lithograph, 32 x 25 cm. Oslo, Oslo Community Art Collection. Munch Museum.

Introduction

United Flight 811 roared into the night sky on the flight to New Zealand from Honolulu. Passengers and crew chatted casually during the uneventful takeoff and gradual ascent to cruising altitude. For the passengers, the trip was to bring them to families, friends, tour groups, and business affairs in New Zealand and elsewhere. For the crew, it was a routine run across the South Pacific. Suddenly, for everyone, this everyday flight turned into a nightmare of noise, terror, pain, and death. About 17 minutes after takeoff, passengers throughout the plane heard an explosion. The cabin instantly decompressed. Deafening, hurricane-like winds suddenly swept through the passenger area, sucking out passengers, equipment, baggage and pieces of the plane through a gaping hole that appeared in the wall of the business class cabin. Close to the hole, the force of the wind threw chief purser Laura Brentlinger and two other flight attendants into a heap on the floor.

> Brentlinger grabbed for the spiral staircase next to her. "We were literally holding on for our lives," she said. "I was clutching anything I could get hold of." (*Honolulu Advertiser,* March 3, 1989, p. A1)

A flight engineer struggled down the staircase to assess the damage. Apparently, a cargo door had blown out, taking part of the fuselage with it. The engine closest to the door had stopped. Within minutes, a fire started in another engine, forcing shutdown. "Dear God, please get us down," screamed Brentlinger to the flight engineer. The cabin was a "dark, eerie, cold wasteland." Several of the terrified passengers sitting strapped to their seats near the hole found themselves staring out into the night sky for the remainder of the flight as it turned back to Honolulu. There was nothing to do but wait and hope. The plane finally reached the airport and landed safely with the remaining passengers seriously shaken but alive.

*E**ven the bravest are frightened by sudden terrors.*
TACITUS

Definitions

Everyone knows what the chill of fear and anxiety feels like—from the delicious shiver of fear we experience when we listen raptly to a ghost story, to the pounding heart when we narrowly escape an accident on the highway, to the nameless anxiety we feel when we think of eating in a restaurant, alone, on a Saturday night, all eyes upon us. Two overriding reasons explain why fear and anxiety are a part of everyone's life: Humans are endowed with an innate capacity to develop fear—in fact, we may be better at it than some other species; and the environment, both by accident and by design, is filled with sources of fear.

What is fear? Arthur Reber (1985) defines **fear** as "an emotional state in the presence or anticipation of a dangerous or noxious stimulus. Fear is usually characterized by an internal, subjective experience of extreme agitation, a desire to flee or to attack and by a variety of sympathetic reactions" (p. 271).

What is anxiety? According to Horace and Ava English (1958), anxiety and fear seem to have a great deal in common. **Anxiety** is defined as "a fusion of fear with the anticipation of future evil ... a continuous fear of low intensity ... a feeling of threat, especially of a fearsome threat, without the person's being able to say what he thinks threatens" (pp. 34–35).

Rollo May (1980) points out that fear and anxiety are part of the human condition: "The distinctive quality of human anxiety arises from the fact that man is a valuing animal, who interprets his life and world in terms of symbols and meanings. It is the threat to these values—specifically, to some value that the individual holds essential to his existence as a self—that causes anxiety" (p. 241). In short, because everyone holds deeply felt values and because there are always challenges to such values, anxiety is inevitable. This is a somewhat cognitive and philosophically existential perspective on fear, but it is consistent with other perspectives that we will review.

The definitions of fear and anxiety leave us a bit confused. Are these two terms really different labels for the same emotion, or are fear and anxiety different emotions? Some theorists have argued that fear and anxiety are somewhat distinctive. (We take a different view.) For example, Reber (1985) suggests that "fear is a reaction to present danger, anxiety to an anticipated or imagined one" (p. 271). Other researchers have pointed out that fear and anxiety may differ in yet other ways. Sigmund Freud (1949a, 1949b) argued that fear (which he called *objective anxiety*) and anxiety (which he termed *neurotic anxiety*) also differ in how easy it is to pinpoint the cause of the experience. A frightened person is afraid of something specific. The anxious person feels ill at ease, but he or she does not quite know why; anxiety is more pervasive and diffuse. (See Fisher, 1969 or Mandler, 1984 for a further discussion of this point.) Irving Sarnoff and Philip Zimbardo (1961) conducted an experiment to demonstrate that fear and anxiety may have different causes and different consequences, as discussed in Box 12.1.

Most theorists and researchers, however, assume that fear and anxiety are really one and the same thing. They argue that it is unnecessary and confusing to try to distinguish between the two. They point out that the state of fear/anxiety possesses a number of common experiential, behavioral, and physiological components. Among these: (a) It is an emotional state with a distinctive quality; (b) it is unpleasant; (c) it is directed toward the future in the sense of impending threat; (d) there are subjective bodily discomforts—

BOX 12.1 _____

Fear Versus Anxiety

Like Freud, Sarnoff and Zimbardo (1961) assume that neurotic anxiety and fear are very different emotions. Fear is aroused when people are threatened with real, objective dangers. Fearful people, they continue, are generally eager to socialize. They expect others to reassure them that things are not as bad as they seem or to help them to deal with their problems. Anxiety is very different. Presumably, neurotics become anxious when they begin to become dimly aware of their own infantile, forbidden, repressed desires. Anxious people, the authors continue, are ashamed of their neurotic feelings and thus will be reluctant to share their concerns with others. They are afraid of being ridiculed or censured. Thus, they try to avoid the company of other people.

To test their hypotheses, the authors set out to produce fear or anxiety in college students: Students were invited to participate in an experiment on "people's physiological responses to sensory stimuli." The experimenter explained that he wanted to see how the various sense organs respond to various kinds of stimulation. He said there had been a good deal of controversy about the relative sensitivity of the fingertips (or lips) and upper surface of the hand (or palate). The experiment was designed to help scientists draw a detailed map of the "cutaneous sensitivity of the human hand (mouth)." Students were then randomly assigned to one of four conditions—the high- or low-fear conditions or the high- or low-anxiety conditions.

Students in the high-fear condition were then led to believe that they would soon receive a series of extremely painful electric shocks. A sign which read "Danger/High Voltage" was posted on the wall. A laboratory assistant, dressed in a white coat, proceeded to attach electrodes to the students' arms and fingers; long wires dangled ominously from the electrodes. The students' arms were then strapped to a cotton-padded board. From where students were sitting, they could see a massive-looking "electric stimulator." It was lined with banks of dials. It buzzed now and then menacingly. Finally, students were told that they would soon receive a series of extremely painful electric shocks.

In the low-fear condition, everything that could be done to make students feel relaxed was done. Students were reassured that they would merely be exposed to a mild stimulus (they would barely feel it) for a few seconds.

In the high-anxiety condition, the authors attempted to stimulate students' "oral libido." According to psychodynamic theory, many people possess an infantile desire to return to childhood, to obtain pleasure by sucking on their mother's breast. Presumably, such desires are completely repressed. Should they begin to become conscious, people would experience intense anxiety. The authors tried to arouse such neurotic anxiety in the following way. The assistant, again dressed in a white laboratory coat, attached electrodes to a corner of the subjects' mouths. Subjects were told that they would be required to suck on their thumbs and on an array of other objects for two minutes while their physiological reactions were recorded via these electrodes. On the table in front of the subjects were a variety of baby bottles, oversized nipples, pacifiers, breast shields (nipples women wear over their breasts while nursing), and lollipops.

In the low-anxiety condition, everything that could be done to put subjects at ease was done. Subjects where reassured that they would merely be asked to blow on a series of objects. They were shown whistles, balloons, kazoos, and pipes.

The authors' first step was to assess whether subjects in the high-fear and high-anxiety conditions were more upset than those in the low-arousal conditions. Ideally, they would have simply ascertained how anxious or fearful subjects in the various conditions were. They worried that subjects might

(continued)

BOX 12.1 *(continued)*

be reluctant to reveal their feelings, however, so they simply showed the men a picture of someone in the same experiment and asked how upset *he* seemed to be about participating in the experiment. The authors found that subjects judged him to be far more "upset," "concerned," and "ill at ease" in the high-arousal than in the low-arousal conditions.

The authors also predicted the high-fear and high-anxiety subjects would differ in their eagerness to affiliate with other students. Thus, subjects were told that they would have to wait about 10 minutes while the experiment was set up. Would they prefer to wait alone or with some other students who were participating in the same experiment? As predicted, the authors found that high-fear students preferred to while away their time in the company of other students. High-anxiety students preferred to wait by themselves.

Desire for Social Affiliation

	NUMBER OF STUDENTS CHOOSING TO BE	
	Together	Alone
Fear		
Low	12	3
High	19	1
Anxiety		
Low	11	4
High	10	12

Of course, this experiment has not been without its critics. Some have pointed out that the authors never asked subjects whether they were feeling anxious or afraid. They simply found that high-anxious and high-fear subjects were more upset, concerned, and ill at ease than low-arousal subjects. Perhaps high-anxious subjects were really more embarrassed. Perhaps these students were wondering whether the experimenter was playing a crude joke on them (sucking nipples, after all!). In addition, it does not seem neurotic or irrational to worry that people who heard that you spent the experimental hour sucking on nipples, breast shields, and the like might ridicule you. Students had every reason to expect to be ribbed if they confided their plight to others.

including tightness in the chest and throat, difficulty in breathing, and muscle weakness, especially in the legs; and (e) there are manifest bodily disturbances in both voluntary activities, such as running and screaming, and involuntary activities, such as dryness of the mouth, sweating, and abdominal pain (Lewis, 1980).

Is fear/anxiety something that is fairly persistent from day to day, or is it transient, appearing and disappearing as people find themselves in more or less frightening circumstances? One answer to this question is "both" (Spielberger, 1966). Psychologists distinguish between state anxiety/fear (one's level of anxiety/fear at any given moment) and trait anxiety/fear (one's usual, overall level of anxiety/fear).

In this chapter, then, we face a choice. Should we try to separate what is known about fear versus anxiety and present information concerning these two emotions in separate sections of the chapter ... or should we simply review what theorists have learned about a single emotional state—anxiety/fear? We choose the latter strategy. It is true, as we have seen, that some theorists carefully distinguish between two types of feelings, but most do not. Most theorists and researchers use the terms fear and anxiety interchangeably. In fact, no compelling evidence exists that the two are very different. Most of the theoretical work we review applies to both anxiety and fear. Thus, in this chapter, we will begin by reviewing the various forms severe anxiety can take. Then, we review what various theorists—such as psychodynamic theorists, behaviorists, and cognitive behaviorists—have had to say about the development of normal and extreme fear and anxiety. Next, we describe the most popular measure of anxiety and fear—the State-Trait Anxiety Inventory. Finally, we review what theorists have learned about the control of anxiety/fear.

Let us begin by reviewing what psychotherapists have had to say about the development of anxiety, especially neurotic anxiety.

Anxiety Disorders

WHATEVER HAPPENED TO GOOD OLD NEUROSES?

In everyday language, the terms neurotic and anxious are often used synonymously. The word *neurosis* was introduced in England in the 1700s by William Cullen in referring to defects in the nervous system that underlie disorders of mood. However, as we learned in chapter 2, it was in the 1900s that Freud gave the term new meaning by relating neuroses to psychological conflicts and to his complex theories of the human psyche. Freudian conceptions of neurosis, to which we will return, have special significance in modern, distressing times; neurosis refers either to the experience of anxiety or to the counterproductive behaviors that may accompany it.

When the American Psychiatric Association updated the *DSM-II,* a guide which assists psychiatrists and psychologists in diagnosing and treating emotional problems, they decided to eliminate the term *neurosis* from the language of health professionals. It was considered to be too broad and indefinite in meaning to be of much use. The *DSM-III-Revised* (1987) replaces the single generic concept of *neurosis* with precise definitions of the various anxiety disorders (and the disorders in which anxiety plays a substantial part) in the hope of improving diagnosis and treatment of these problems. Let us look at some of the anxiety disorders *DSM-III-R* describes.

When anxiety is pathological, "it will usually be detrimental to thought and action, will be accompanied by other features of mental disorder (especially depression), and will affect perception, memory, judgment and other cognitive abilities" (Lewis, 1980, p. 15). Neurobiologist Antony Kidman (in press) adds, "A person suffering from anxiety experiences an unpleasant emotional state characterized by tension, nervousness, heart palpitations, tremor, nausea, dizziness, inability to think clearly and on some occasions inability to even speak; other symptoms may include backache, headache and diarrhoea."

Of course, everyone has fears. Few of us have them frequently enough, or in sufficient intensity, to be labeled as disordered. Nonetheless, we begin our discussion by reviewing the anxiety disorders delineated in *DSM-III-R*. These are:

1. Phobic disorder
2. Generalized anxiety disorder
3. Panic disorder
4. Obsessive-compulsive disorder
5. Post-traumatic stress disorder

We are interested in such disorders for two reasons. First, anxiety seems to be on a continuum. We can gain some insight into everyday fears by understanding the origins and nature of severe anxiety. Second, the anxiety disorders are actually fairly prevalent. Common estimates are that 4% of the American population—about 10 million people—experience a full-blown anxiety disorder at some time in their lives (Kidman, 1988). Thus, let us now consider the various anxiety disorders.

The one permanent emotion of the inferior man is fear—fear of the unknown, the complex, the inexplicable. What he wants beyond everything else is safety.
H. L. MENCKEN

PHOBIC DISORDER

When people are persistently and unrealistically afraid of some *thing*, they are said to be phobic, but they are not necessarily disordered. Among college students, the most common phobias are associated with public speaking (standing up before a class) and test-taking—especially taking final examinations. Many people are also uncomfortable around spiders, cockroaches, and other furry-legged insects. Some common phobias are listed in Table 12.1. Perhaps you can find one or two things that especially bother you.

Table 12.1   **Some Phobias**

PHOBIA	FEAR OF
acrophobia	heights
autophobia	oneself
claustrophobia	confinement
gammophobia	marriage
herpetophobia	snakes
hypergiaphobia	responsibility
ideophobia	ideas
nyctophobia	darkness
social phobia	public appearances
xenophobia	the unknown

To classify as a **phobic disorder,** a fear must also possess one of two essential features—it must either cause severe distress or markedly interfere with one's life. For example, although the phobic students described above may be so worried about their exams that they find it difficult to concentrate, they would still be classified as normal, since they are only mildly distressed and since their fear is not really very disruptive. On the other hand, people who become intensely anxious each time they think of leaving the house and who end up trapped in their own homes would be diagnosed as agoraphobic. The difference between a phobia and a phobic disorder is both one of quantity (how distressed the phobic person is) and one of quality (how far the person is willing to go to attempt to control distress).

Sometimes the origin of a phobic disorder is fairly apparent. Such cases lend credence to the view that phobias are acquired through principles of learning, for instance, through classical association between events (see chapter 14). Consider a young boy who survives a harrowing experience in a small plane piloted by his father. They are caught at night in a thunderstorm, with all the accoutrements—blinding rain, lightning, deafening thunder, air pockets that repeatedly drop the aircraft several hundred feet in a split second, and ominous sounds from the engine for added attraction. Some years later, he goes through periods of severe anxiety on flights to and from his home in Hawaii, despite the fact that the skies are clear at 30,000 feet, and that the overseas Boeing 747s are large and relatively quiet, and possess many of the comforts of home. The origin of the later fear seems quite obvious.

Other phobias—such as scopophobia (the fear of being stared at) or autophobia (the fear of oneself)—are not so readily understood. The origins of these irrational fears are obscure. Perhaps for this reason, psychologists developed complex psychodynamic and biological theories in an attempt to make sense of these puzzling reactions. We discuss these explanations later in the chapter.

GENERALIZED ANXIETY DISORDER

Generalized Anxiety Disorder is the most common form of anxiety disorder. Some people are almost always anxious. They experience "free-floating anxiety"—a vague dread that something terrible is about to happen; their minds race, ever vigilant. They are jittery and tense and find it impossible to relax. According to the *DSM-III-R*, to be diagnosed as suffering a generalized anxiety disorder, people must possess several of the following behavioral, physiological, or cognitive symptoms:

- *Motor tension:* This includes such symptoms as trembling, twitching or feeling shaky, muscular tension, aches or soreness, restlessness, and the tendency to tire easily.

- *Autonomic hyperactivity:* This includes such symptoms as shortness of breath, an accelerated heart rate, sweating or cold, clammy hands, dry mouth, dizziness, nausea, diarrhea, flushes, frequent urination, or difficulty in swallowing.

- *Vigilance and scanning:* This includes such symptoms as having trouble concentrating, having one's mind go blank because of anxiety, feeling keyed up, on edge, irritable, having an exaggerated startle response, and having trouble falling asleep.

PANIC DISORDER

Every now and then, a few people, for no particular reason, panic. Suddenly, intense dread, terror, and apprehension begin to sweep over them. They think they may go mad, die, or lose control of themselves. Physically, symptoms of panic appear—their hearts begin to pound, their muscles become tight and strained, their shirts become wet with perspiration, they begin to tremble so violently that a coffee cup clatters on its saucer. Such panic attacks last for a matter of minutes. Then they gradually subside, leaving the person shaken.

In this entry from her diary, Virginia Woolf (1953) describes just such a panic attack:

> Wednesday, August 17th. Now I think I have corrected the C. R. [*The Common Reader*] till I can correct no longer. And I have a few minutes holiday before I need take the proofs in to L. Shall I then describe how I fainted again? That is, the galloping hooves got wild in my head last Thursday night as I sat on the terrace with L. How cool it is after the heat! I said. We were watching the downs draw back into fine darkness after they had burnt like solid emerald all day. Now that was being softly finely veiled. And the white owl was crossing to fetch mice from the marsh. Then my heart leapt: and stopped: and leapt again: and I tasted that queer bitterness at the back of my throat; and the pulse leapt into my head and beat and beat, more savagely, more quickly. I am going to faint, I said, and slipped off my chair and lay on the grass. Oh no, I was not unconscious. I was alive: but possessed with this struggling team in my head: galloping, pounding.

I thought, something will burst in my brain if this goes on. Slowly it muffled itself up and staggered, with what infinite difficulty and alarm, now truly fainting and seeing the garden painfully lengthened and distorted, back, back, back—how long it seemed—could I drag myself?—to the house: and gained my room and fell on my bed. Then pain, as of childbirth; and then that too slowly faded; and I lay presiding, like a flickering light, like a most solicitous mother, over the shattered splintered fragments of my body. A very acute and unpleasant experience. (p. 185)

Panic episodes often occur without an identifiable reason. Not surprisingly, they themselves may come to be a source of additional anxiety due to their unpredictability.

OBSESSIVE-COMPULSIVE DISORDER

Therapists sometimes treat people such as the young woman described below. She was obsessed with cleanliness and order. She spent a great deal of time compulsively trying to scrub away any trace of bacteria from her kitchen. She lined up the cups, knives and forks, and dishes with military precision. She meticulously spaced the coat hangers in her closet one inch apart. Each day, as she walked to work, she was very careful to scan the pavement so that she didn't accidentally step on a shard of glass. (The next time you go for a walk, notice how many shimmering spots of light you see on the ground. Each could be a "sliver of glass.") "What if I tracked the glass home!" she exclaimed. "Someday, an infant might come to visit, crawl around on the carpet, accidentally pick up and swallow that small sliver of glass, and die!" Her "cleanliness" made her life miserable.

This woman had an obsessive-compulsive anxiety disorder. **Obsessions** are persistent and recurrent thoughts, images, or impulses. The obsessive attempts to ignore or suppress these taboo thoughts or to neutralize them by thinking of something else or performing some ritual action. **Compulsions** are ritualistic activities designed to prevent some dreaded event. Many obsessions and compulsions are common: Most people ask themselves, "Did I turn off the coffee pot?" Most people insist on having coffee and toast for breakfast, even when traveling in foreign countries where rice and a piece of fish are traditional. But again, an obsessive/compulsive disorder requires thoughts and activities that are persistent, serious, and disruptive. What are the most common obsessions? The most common worry is about dirt and contamination (Akhtar, Wig, Verma, Pershod, & Verma, 1975). (Obsessive-compulsives may worry that their hands are dirty; they may scrub them so often that they become red and chapped.) Second are aggressive fantasies. (Parents may have a repeated fantasy about killing the child they love most.) Others worry about orderliness. (They notice that all the pictures need to be straightened, that the wallpaper is dirty.) Others are troubled by sexual ideas or impulses. Next most common are religious obsessions, such as those had by a Catholic woman who worried that her sexual fantasies might be a sin. She was assured by a priest that since they occurred during marital sex, they were permitted. However, she went to yet another priest and another for reassurance. "Perhaps the priests didn't really know," she exclaimed. "Perhaps they drank and didn't realize what they were saying."

Obsessions and compulsions generally occur in tandem. In one study, 70% of patients who reported one difficulty reported experiencing the other as well (Welner, Reish, Robbins, Fishman, & van Doren, 1976). Therefore, they are considered to be a single form of anxiety disorder. In their severe forms, obsessions and compulsions can be debilitating. They preclude creative thinking and interfere with taking sensible action.

Why are obsessions and compulsions considered anxiety disorders when they may or may not be accompanied by distress? Theorists generally assume that the origin of obsessional thoughts or actions is the attempt to control anxiety—to keep one's mind so full of other thoughts and one's hands so busy with compulsive activities that one has no time to dwell on worries and fears. As Woody Allen observes in his movie *Manhattan:*

> People in Manhattan . . . are constantly creating these real, unnecessary neurotic problems for themselves, because it keeps them from dealing with more unsolvable, terrifying problems about the universe.

Existential psychotherapists such as Irvin Yalom (1980) argue that people often busy themselves with the trivial details of life because they are terrified of confronting concerns that are rooted in human existence—death (the fact that "one day we will cease to be"); freedom (recognizing that "the individual is entirely responsible for . . . his or her own world, life design, choices, and actions . . . beneath us there is no ground—nothing, a void, an abyss"); existential isolation (recognizing that "no matter how close each of us becomes to another, there remains a final, unbridgeable gap; each of us enters existence alone and must depart from it alone"); and meaninglessness ("What meaning does life have? . . .") (pp. 8–9).

POST-TRAUMATIC STRESS DISORDER (PTSD)

People who have been exposed to severely traumatic events—such as combat, rape, being held hostage, or a variety of natural disasters—sometimes show a consistent pattern of behavioral, physiological, and cognitive reactions. Unfortunately, psychologists and physicians did not recognize until fairly recently that survivors may suffer from this anxiety syndrome.

When Vietnam veterans began returning home, mental health professionals were forced to recognize the existence of PTSD. For example, in 1988, the Research Triangle Institute reported to Congress that 15%, or about 470,000 of the 3.14 million men who served in Vietnam and about 7,000 of the women (mostly nurses) who served there, were suffering from PTSD. The closer to combat the veteran had been, the higher the incidence of the disorder.

In World Wars I and II soldiers suffered briefly from shell shock and battle fatigue. But their problems were often short-lived. Why were Vietnam veterans hit so hard? We do not yet know, but we can make some guesses. The Vietnam war was fought primarily by very young men. The typical Vietnam fighting man was 19 years old; the average World War II soldier was 26. Modern combat involved powerful and destructive weaponry. One 18-year-old veteran observed that he would never again be as powerful as he had been in Vietnam. With a flick of his finger, he could signal bombers to wipe out a village. Fighting was intense; there was never a "time-out." Death could occur at any time—one never knew whether that elderly stooped man or that cute five-year-old was a friend or an enemy about to toss a grenade into the jeep. Drugs and alcohol abuse were more common. Then, too, veterans did not come home to a warm welcome. There were few postwar parades and celebrations. (On the contrary, more than one veteran reported that old "friends" called him a "murderer" on his return home.) Protesters condemned the war. Perhaps this treatment contributed to the veterans' problems. On discharge, many men flew directly from a Vietnamese battlefield to a way-station in the Pacific, or even back home, all in a single day. There was no opportunity for "decompression." On their return, many had trouble finding jobs. All these facts may have contributed to the Vietnam veterans' vulnerability to PTSD (Wilson, 1980).

Whatever the reasons, many veterans returned from combat plagued with a pattern of difficulties, including recurring attacks of anxiety and panic, nightmares and other sleep disturbances, painful flashbacks to combat experiences, difficulty in concentration, anger, guilt, depression, and tendencies toward substance abuse. Some veterans began to show PTSD symptoms only years after their return, in a delayed reaction to the traumatic events of the war (Blank, 1982). Here is one soldier's description of the flashbacks he has been forced to grapple with since his return from Vietnam:

> Two movie projectors run in my head. The dominant one rolls out the sights and sounds and smells of the present in powerful color. The other projects cracked images from the past in faint black and white. Recently I was sitting in a restaurant, listening to a friend's story, when the projectors changed dominance.
>
> . . . As Robert spoke, I could hear the put-put of his Navy patrol boat in the ominous silence of the Mekong. I could hear rifle fire and smell the acrid gunpowder. I could see the stubs of defoliated palm trees silhouetted against an exploding sky.
>
> . . . I glanced away, my eye catching my own image in the mirror behind Robert. The brocade decor of the restaurant dissolved. Instead, I saw myself standing once again in the specimen room of a hospital outside Ho Chi Minh City, formerly Saigon. It was 1983. The smell of formaldehyde tinged the air. In the dim light I could make out glass crocks lining each wall, floor to ceiling, wall to wall, row upon gray row.
>
> Each crock cradled a full-term baby. One infant had four arms, another a bowl in place of her cranium, a third a face on his abdomen, a fourth his navel

protruding from his forehead. All the babies had been born in the early 1980s to women from provinces heavily sprayed with Agent Orange.

A Vietnamese doctor opened the wooden shutters with their silver liquid mirrors that shimmered, row upon row. I shrank back. In each mirror I could see that I remained my normal self.

... Psychologists have given names—"Vietnam syndrome," "flashback," "post-traumatic stress syndrome"—to the experience of that second movie projector's dominating conscious reality. (Borton, 1988, p. 16)

In laboratory tests, some veterans were found to show exaggerated physiological reactions to combat-related stimuli—including accelerated heart rates and heightened electrodermal responses (Malloy, Fairbank, & Keane, 1983). The results of PTSD are sometimes tragic—broken homes, hospitalization for substance abuse, and homicide and suicide, to list a few (Wilson, 1980).

It is, of course, unfortunate that it took mental health professionals so long to recognize that the PTSD syndrome is a unique and particularly serious disorder. Many veterans would surely have been helped by earlier treatment. Now that the existence of PTSD has been recognized, researchers are beginning to learn more about the nature of this anxiety disorder (Chemtob, Roitblat, Hamada, Carlson, & Twentyman, 1988). Such knowledge makes it easier to treat both Vietnam veterans and survivors of other traumatic events—those who have been through natural disasters such as hurricanes, tornadoes, earthquakes, or traumatic personal events such as a rape or mugging.

SOME WORDS OF REASSURANCE

Most human fears differ from the severe anxiety disorders reviewed. Normal fears are less severe, persistent, and have a different quality than do the anxiety disorders.

Fear is one of the most common of human emotions. It can be activated by an infinite variety of events. Generally, fear is an enormously adaptive mechanism. Although sometimes, in Franklin Roosevelt's words, "The only thing we have to fear is fear itself," it is equally important to recognize that, in general, people should also fear the absence of fear. Fear is a powerful motivator; it is a source of constructive energy (prodding students to study harder at final exam time). Journalist E. W. Howe once observed that "a good scare is worth more to a man than good advice." It helps people avoid real dangers. (One reason why teenagers drive so recklessly is that it is hard for young people to believe they could be killed. Death, like old age, happens to other people.)

Most people, most of the time, do a fairly good job of managing their fears. Most seem able to walk a fine line—they are well aware of their feelings and are guided by them, but they manage to resist being overwhelmed by fear. People can limit the intensity of their feelings in a variety of ways. Some try not to think too much about the things that frighten them. Others avoid people and places that are overwhelming. In short, fear is a natural and useful human emotion. What people need is more understanding of the origins and nature of fear, not necessarily more control over this ubiquitous state of behavior, physiology, and cognition. A truly fearless person would be in deep trouble.

Approaches to Fear and Anxiety

Over the past 50 years or so, psychologists have speculated about the origins of fear and anxiety. Some have speculated that people possess an innate tendency to be fearful. John B. Watson (1930) contended that at birth, along with rage and love, infants possess the emotional response of fear (which could be evoked by such events as loud noises or falling). Similarly, Jeffrey Gray (1971) suggests that certain stimuli (such as darkness or high places) generate fear, owing to their significance in the evolutionary history of the species. Intense stimuli (such as noises) and novel or unexpected stimuli (or the absence of expected stimuli) are also innate sources of fear in this view. However, both these theorists also recognized the importance of social factors in the development of fear reactions. Today, most theorists regard fear as largely acquired. They have developed sophisticated models of fear development—whether they emphasize cognitive, physiological, or behavioral aspects of the fear response. Let us now consider some of the theories that have been developed to explain how people develop fears and anxieties—whether normal or extreme.

PSYCHODYNAMIC APPROACHES TO FEAR AND ANXIETY

Those who take a psychodynamic view of fear and anxiety focus primarily on the experiential and motivational properties of the emotion. Sigmund Freud was, of course, the first psychoanalyst to deal with emotion (see chapter 2), but when we try to discover what he had to say about anxiety, we find that our task is not an easy one. His views continually evolved. Charles Rycroft (1968) reports, "Freud had three theories of anxiety. The first was that it was a manifestation of repressed LIBIDO, the second was that it represented a repetition of the experience of birth . . . while the third, which can be regarded as the definitive psychoanalytic theory of anxiety, is that there are two forms: *primary anxiety* and *signal anxiety,* both of which are responses of the EGO to increases of instinctual or emotional TENSION" (p. 8).

According to Freud (1920), usually the ego is able to shield a person against threatening material. **Primary anxiety** occurs when that shield fails and threatening information comes cascading in. Such anxiety is a conscious and an extraordinarily painful experience. Early on, Freud thought that the trauma of birth itself may well be the prototypical experience of fear upon which other forms of anxiety are based. However, by 1926 he had concluded that the birth trauma was only one of many anxiety-producing traumas that infants experience. In infancy, the ego is immature and is unable to fully protect the infant.

During the seventh to the twelfth month of life, the infant's ego develops enough so that it can begin to plan and make decisions. It can begin to bend its (id) desires and needs to the demands of the real world. At this stage, anxiety takes on new meaning. It now provides a warning signal that the child is being overwhelmed—by the demands of the id, by external stimuli, or by the super-ego (the child's conscience). For the infant, primary anxiety is terrifying. **Signal anxiety** is a far more mild emotion. It merely warns the child that the ego must take action to ward off danger.

In Freud's view, anxieties can differ in their source as well as their intensity. According to Freud, anxiety can arise from three kinds of conflict—conflict between the ego and the world (which leads to reality or objective anxiety), between the ego and the superego (which leads to moral anxiety), and between the ego and the id (which leads to neurotic anxiety). **Objective anxiety** is realistic; it is evoked by the ego's assessment of realistic dangers. (One example would be a person's fear that if he speeds through an icy intersection, he might skid out of control.) **Moral anxiety,** or guilt, on the other hand, is evoked when the superego's harsh codes are violated (the guilt students feel when they think of cheating on an exam, for example.) **Neurotic anxiety** occurs when people begin to become uneasily aware of their repressed id impulses (their instinctual tendencies). Anxiety serves as a warning signal, alerting the ego to the fact that repressed, unconscious wishes are about to break into consciousness; if they were to do so, people would experience overwhelming anxiety or panic. Generally, childhood is the time when neurotic anxiety is instilled. Children learn that some of their instinctive sexual and aggressive desires are taboo, and that some nameless, dread punishment will follow if they try to express them.

The neurotic anxiety which results from people's internal conflicts may take a variety of forms. Interestingly, Freudian notions concerning neurotic conflict and anxiety are, even today, reflected in *DSM-III-R*'s classification system (which psychiatrists use in diagnosing and treating patients). That is, neurotic anxiety may be expressed in generalized or "free-floating" anxiety (in which a person is unsettled by vague and pervasive anxiety) or in phobias, in which a person is terrified of a specific stimulus. Freud assumed that the stimulus identified as dangerous is symbolic and relates to a childhood experience in which the expression of an impulse was punished. Finally, neurotic anxiety may be expressed in panic reactions, where fear arises suddenly and intensely. Here, too, Freud would assume that anxiety is based in a childhood experience in which an id impulse was severely punished.

As we discussed in chapter 2 (see Table 2.3), in Freud's view people use a variety of *ego defense mechanisms* in order to deal with anxiety. Defense mechanisms operate at the unconscious level. They protect the ego from the conscious experience of neurotic anxiety. Generally, the defensive process works fairly well. People feel secure enough to go about the business of living. Such mechanisms are adaptive. Sometimes, however, neurotics rely too much on one or another defense mechanism to protect themselves. Their protective stance toward the world gets in the way of living. For instance, in **reaction formation,** people try to prove that they are what they are not. When carried too far, simple hypocrisy begins to look like neurosis. If a reformer's campaign against pornography leads him to attack *National Geographic,* he is likely to be labeled "sick." Jules Masserman (1961) provides an excerpt from a letter he received from an antivivisectionist. The writer betrays the unconscious hostility and sadism which lie beneath his "humanity":

> I read [a magazine article] . . . on your work on alcoholism. . . . I am surprised that anyone who is as well educated as you must be to hold the position that you do would stoop to such a depth as to torture helpless little cats in the pursuit of a cure for alcoholics. . . . A drunkard does not want to be cured—a drunkard is just a weakminded idiot who belongs in the gutter and should be left there. Instead of torturing helpless little cats why not torture the drunks or better still exert your would-be noble effort toward getting a bill passed to *exterminate* the drunk. . . . My greatest wish is that you have brought home to you a torture that will be a thousand fold greater than what you have, and are doing to the little animals. . . . If you are an example of what a noted psychiatrist should be I'm glad I am just an ordinary human being without letters after my name. I'd rather be just myself with a clear conscience, *knowing I have not hurt any living creature,* and can sleep without seeing frightened terrified dying cats—because I know they must die after you have finished with them. No punishment is too great for you and I hope I live to read about your mangled body and long suffering before you finally die—and I'll laugh long and loud. (p. 38)

Compulsive people may experience little anxiety as long as they are allowed to carry out their rituals. Nonetheless, their friends may well accuse them of being neurotic. The "perfect" husband—who feels compelled to clean the kitchen immediately after dinner, even if it means forgoing the chance to relax, make love, or talk with his children before they go to bed—would seem a bit odd. Freudians use the term *neurosis* to describe either the anxiety that people experience when they catch a glimmering of their own primitive impulses or the extreme actions they take in an effort to ward off that anxiety.

In 1926, Freud also proposed that anxiety (or what is now termed *separation anxiety*) has a profound impact on later love relationships. He argued that "only a few of the manifestations of anxiety in children are comprehensible to us. . . . They occur, for instance, when a child is alone or in the dark, or when it finds itself with an unknown person instead of the one to whom it is used—such as its mother. These three instances can be reduced to a single condition—namely, that of missing someone who is loved and longed for. But here, we have a key, I think, to an understanding of anxiety" (pp. 136–137).

Later, John Bowlby (1969) spelled out how this process works. By the time most infants are about six months old, they have formed a tight bond with their mothers. When separated, they respond with protest and other signs of fear. Normally, this separation anxiety is adaptive. In a wide variety of species, powerful social attachments serve clear functions. Because "birds of a feather flock together," they feed and mate together as well, their chances of survival increase, and they are in a position to protect one another. Thus, separation anxiety discourages breaking ties with other members of one's species and has functional value intrinsic to the process of attachment.

When mother and child are separated for too long, however, things begin to go wrong. Children experience a predictable sequence of emotions—their initial protests are followed by despair, and eventually, detachment. At first, in the protest stage, abandoned children's primary feelings are of fear. This fear motivates them to search for the mothers they need. Anxiously attached infants, who experience too much separation too often, may well carry their fears into later relationships. Bowlby (1969) suggests that "loss of mother-figure, either by itself or in combination with other variables yet to be clearly identified, is capable of generating responses and processes that are of the greatest interest to psychopathology. . . . These responses and processes . . . are the very same as are known to be active in older individuals who are still disturbed by separations that they suffered in early life" (p. xiii).

If the infant's protests fail to bring the mother, the child begins to despair, that is, to grieve and mourn the loss. If the suffering continues, children will eventually learn to blunt their profound despair. They will learn how to defend themselves against such feelings of the loss. They become detached—utilizing such defense mechanisms as denial, displacement of anger, or isolation of feeling. Later theorists, such as Mary Ainsworth (1982), argue that a child's fears relating to separation depend on factors other than simply attachment, including wariness, affiliation, and exploration.

PHYSIOLOGICAL APPROACHES TO FEAR AND ANXIETY

Pale as his shirt, his knees knocking each other.
                                                    SHAKESPEARE

When men and women are frightened, they show a distinctive pattern of physiological response. As an example, Tom Wolfe's (1987) *Bonfire of the Vanities* begins with Sherman, a young, socially aspiring stockbroker, and Maria, his mistress, driving home from the airport. They take a wrong turn and suddenly, horrifyingly, find themselves lost in the slums of the South Bronx. They panic. Frantically, they twist and turn down side streets, trying to spot an entrance to the expressway. Without warning, they confront a roadblock—the street is piled high with tires. Sherman gets out of the car to move the tires. Then, Maria screams a warning. Two young men, predatory men, walk menacingly toward Sherman. In a panic, Sherman races to his Mercedes, leaps in, starts and lurches onto the highway ... out of danger. But once on the highway, after the danger has passed, Sherman experiences the familiar physiological symptoms of fear—his eyes sting with perspiration, his hands shake uncontrollably; he can feel his heart pounding in his throat. His shirt is soaking wet. His lungs struggle for oxygen. "His heart was racing along with hollow thuds, as if it had broken loose inside his rib cage." In the midst of all this inner turmoil, Sherman reassures himself. "Just take it easy." "We're okay now, we're okay" (p. 88).

In chapter 4, we discussed the anatomy, chemistry, and functional nature of the autonomic nervous system. Many researchers have attempted to develop neurological and biochemical models of fear.

The Physiological Fear Response

Walter Cannon (1929) proposed that fearful animals have two options—they can flee or fight in their own defense. Consider the following scenario, reported by Robert and Caroline Blanchard (in press).

A small, sunny field opens in the midst of a forest. A group of wild *Rattus norvegicus* rats live underground in interlocking burrows at the edge of the wood. Normally, they are in their burrows. If they must cross the open field, they do so cautiously, keeping a sharp eye out before scampering across. Should a cat or any predator enter the open field, the mood of the community immediately changes. Their immediate response is flight. Terrified, the rats race for their burrows. Once there, they freeze: They remain hidden inside until all sounds of danger pass. Then, very cautiously, they try to assess whether it is safe to come out. They poke a nose out of their holes, then dart back to safety; then a head, a paw, and finally their whole body. As time passes with no further evidence of danger, they reenter the danger zone to explore it. They make brief, cautious forays followed by rapid retreat. If the danger signals are absent, the forays grow longer. They are alert; at the first sign of trouble, they pop back inside their holes. It may take hours or days for things to return to normal. It is easy to see why rats are so cautious; one misstep and they are dead.

On rare occasions, a rat cannot flee. It is cornered. In such cases, the rat's only recourse is to freeze. If the threat continues, the frightened rat will make a defensive threat. If the predator continues to close in, the rat will finally resort to an explosive jump attack. The rat will hurl itself against the predator, biting at the attacker's eye-snout area; if it survives, it will then flee.

One can easily distinguish dominant rats when they are attacking an intruder from rats that are fighting as a last resort. Their patterns of response are quite different. For example, when dominant rats attack, they aim their bites at the intruders' backs. Terrified rats go all out—they screech and hurl themselves at the predator, generally aiming for the facial area.

Regardless of whether a frightened animal, rat, or man fights or flees, Walter Cannon observed, the biological requirements are the same. People must become physiologically aroused so that they have the energy to engage in swift and sustained effort. They need extra oxygen and nutrients to supply the muscles (including the heart itself) and a means of eliminating waste materials from the cells. Essentially, fearful people can be expected to show elevated heart rate and blood pressure, increased breathing rate, lowered surface (dermal) blood flow, increased muscular blood flow, lower levels of alpha activity and higher levels of beta activity in the brain, higher catecholamine (especially epinephrine) levels, higher urinary and plasma corticosteroid hormone levels, suppressed digestive reactions, and a variety of additional responses indicative of heightened arousal, vigilance, and readiness for action (Lader, 1980). When people feel anxious, for example, just before getting up on stage to give a speech, they are in part experiencing these symptoms: a pounding heart, palms that are cold but sweaty, a funny feeling in the stomach, and a mouth so dry they can hardly swallow. Considerable evidence supports the hypothesis that fear produces profound psychophysiological changes.

Heart Rate and Skin Conductance

Researchers have long studied laboratory-induced fear. Commonly, while subjects sit and anticipate receiving an electric shock, their heart rate and/ or skin conductance (a function of eccrine gland activity) is measured. Researchers such as Lyle Miller and Barry Shmavonian (1965) find that both responses increase during the waiting period. Similarly, Edward Katkin (1966) found that subjects who were especially emotional to begin with (as measured by the Affect Adjective Checklist) were especially slow in returning to their resting skin conductance levels following electric shock. Such evidence is consistent with the common view that people who are generally anxious will be especially sensitive to momentary fear stimuli.

Paul Obrist (1976) points out that frightened people can attempt to cope with their feelings via two techniques—by active versus passive coping. In **active coping**, people are in control of events. They can do something to try to avoid danger (for example, they may be able to press a button to avoid electric shock). In such cases, fear sparks a large increase in sympathetic nervous system activity; heart rate may or may not increase. Interestingly, fear may so overwhelm the system that heart rate shows little relationship to the energy demanded by the coping task. In **passive coping**, on the other hand, individuals have little power to ward off danger (sometimes all they can do is sit there). In such cases, despite the imminent danger, heart rate may show little increase. The parasympathetic nervous system controls heart rate, which is tightly synchronized to the amount of bodily activity a given task requires. Such a linkage is termed somatic coupling. That is, if little or nothing can be done, heart rate may not change appreciably, despite the imminent danger. (However, if the task at hand involves any movement, then heart rate will increase accordingly, in line with its basic role in supplying the tissues with blood.) Obrist's work makes it clear that the relationship between fear and heart rate is complex. It is truly a psycho-physiological relationship; whether or not people believe they have control over a situation determines cardiac functioning.

Skin Temperature

The temperature of the skin changes as the peripheral blood vessels dilate or constrict. In anxiety-arousing situations, as sympathetic neural activity increases, the peripheral arterioles constrict. In some people, skin temperature of the hands may drop as much as 20 to 30 degrees Fahrenheit (to levels in the 60- to 70-degree range). What biological advantage could such a drop possibly have? One advantage is that in emergencies demanding fight or flight a large supply of blood can be shunted to critically important deep muscles and organs. Not incidentally, this same mechanism accounts in part for the fact that when people are frightened, their blood pressure increases. These effects have been known for some time. For example, Bela Mittleman and Harold Wolff (1939) observed that subjects' self-reports of emotions, including anxiety, embarrassment, and depression, were associated with decreases in finger temperature. (Such results serve to remind us that fear has much in common with several other emotions—all rely on similar physiological mechanisms.) More recently, Carmen Diaz and John Carlson (1984) found that when subjects anticipated electric shock, they displayed dramatic decreases in skin temperature. Similarly, when college women reported for the first session of an experiment billed as having to do with the measurement of "physiological responses," their finger temperatures fell to as low as 70 degrees in some cases (Carlson, 1977). One of the most dramatic effects occurred as the women simply sat quietly and relaxed, as baseline measures were taken. As they relaxed, their finger temperature climbed back to normal. Presumably, as the women became accustomed to the situation, including the ominous wires leading to the equipment, and as they became confident that the investigators were not "evil scientists" bent on causing pain, a shift from sympathetic to parasympathetic dominance occurred. As the subjects relaxed, they could literally "warm up" to the experimenters.

Muscle Tension

Another sign of anxiety is tenseness of the muscles. In chapter 6, in our review of facial expression, we found that fear and anxiety are revealed in the facial muscles. Accordingly, studies of anxiety often use an electromyograph to measure movements in these muscles so small they cannot be felt or detected by the naked eye. While Gary Schwartz, Paul Ekman, and others

FIGURE 12.2 Man wincing.

have tried to link emotions with particular facial muscle patterns (see Schwartz, Fair, Greenberg, Freedman, & Klerman, 1974), most researchers have been content to study the link between emotion and more fairly global measures of facial activity. For example, many researchers have studied the relationship between stressful emotions and activity of the frontalis (forehead) muscle. This muscle is easy to measure and one that is known to reflect facial activity generally (Basmajian, 1983). Although this method does not allow researchers to know which specific pattern of muscle movements is involved, they can at least say that there is tension in the forehead area and other areas of the face (such as the jaw). For instance, in the study by Diaz and Carlson (1984) cited above, it was found that during the period immediately preceding anticipated electric shock, subjects showed marked increases in frontalis muscle tension. (Figure 12.2 depicts such an expression.)

Endocrine Activity

When people are frightened, they show a number of ANS changes. Thus far, the fear reactions we have described can be detected by recording what is going on at the surface of the body. Researchers have taken another approach—they have assessed frightened animals' glandular reactions by taking blood or urine samples.

 One of the earliest physiologists to posit a link between fear (and a number of other emotions) and sympathetic activity was Walter Cannon (1914). Later, Albert Ax (1953) concluded that fear and anger showed a bit more differentiation than Cannon had thought—fear was associated with epinephrine, while angry outbursts were linked to a combination of epinephrine plus norepinephrine. As you learned in chapter 4, today we know that the catecholamines, epinephrine and norepinephrine, are produced in the medulla portion of the adrenal during periods of emergency, owing to the demands of the sympathetic nervous system.

Since Cannon and Ax's time, a number of studies have documented that during times of stress, people's catecholamine levels soar. In one study, students' epinephrine levels were found to increase markedly during final examination time; norepinephrine levels sometimes increased as well (Bogdonoff, Estes, Harlan, Trout, & Kirschner, 1960). Ax might conclude from such findings that students were more frightened than angry about having to take final exams.

Lennart Levi (1972) tracked the feelings of viewers of Stanley Kubrick's unsettling film *Paths of Glory*. This is a story of young World War I recruits who are forced to fight in a terrifying, hopeless campaign. He found that as subjects became more and more frightened, their epinephrine levels, but not their norepinephrine levels, showed corresponding increases. In one intriguing study, urinary assays revealed that although epinephrine and norepinephrine levels of military pilots rose during their flights, their passengers' epinephrine levels rose while their norepinephrine levels did not (Von Euler & Lundberg, 1954). Obviously, the relationship between anxiety and adrenal output is not a simple one. One possibility is that when people (such as passengers on aircraft) are not in control of events, fear and anxiety are accompanied by epinephrine secretion alone. When one has some control (as does a pilot), however, fear and anxiety may be accompanied by both catecholamines (Frankenhauser, 1978).

Walter Hess (1954) has attempted to unravel the mystery of how fear (and other emotions that involve high arousal and a great deal of activity) is related to endocrine functioning. In Hess's view, neuroendocrine balance is maintained by an opposing system of ergotropic (arousing) and trophotropic (quieting) mechanisms. The former is an activating mechanism, which fosters CNS and ANS arousal, as is required in emergency situations. The latter is a relaxation mechanism, serving to lower CNS arousal and foster an ANS parasympathetic reaction. Bernard Brodie and Parkhurst Shore (1957) have proposed that the catecholamines are the neural messengers for the ergotropic system, thus accounting for their increase during states of fear, and that the indolamines (such as serotonin) are the modulators for the activities of the trophotropic system, such as quiet relaxation or sleep. The accumulating research on the opposing neurotransmitters appears to generally support this position (Whybrow, 1984).

Another physiological measure of anxiety is obtained by assays of plasma and urinary corticosteroid hormones produced by the cortex of the adrenals during sustained emergencies. Elevated cortisol levels have been observed in a variety of circumstances, including oral examinations (Bloch & Brakenridge, 1972); anticipated surgery (Knight et al., 1979); and simulated aircraft emergencies and artillery shell barrages during military exercises—but, interestingly, not during simulated forest fires or radioactive fallout (Berkun, Bialek, Kern, & Yagi, 1962). In an array of studies, Frankenhauser (1978) has related cortisol levels to behavior in the workplace, in the home, and in school settings. In her view, distress generally leads to the production of cortisol mainly in situations in which an active response is required.

In sum, then, we see that the frightened person is ready for action. The ANS provides the energy people need to aggressively deal with their fears or to avoid a fearful situation entirely. Fear produces profound psychophysiological changes in heart rate and skin conductance, in skin temperature, in muscle tension and in endocrine activity. Let us now explore what psychologists have learned about fearful behavior.

BEHAVIORAL APPROACHES TO FEAR AND ANXIETY

Two-Process Approaches

The learning theorist, O. Hobart Mowrer (1947), took a two-process approach to explaining fear reactions. He proposed that different principles explain how people acquire fears versus how they learn to deal with them. Today, most learning theorists follow Mowrer's lead in acknowledging the importance of both **classical (Pavlovian) conditioning** and **instrumental (operant) conditioning** in the development and maintenance of fear responding. Let us review Mowrer's ideas.

According to Mowrer, most fear reactions are initially acquired (at the autonomic level) through an association process called sign learning (an early term for classical conditioning). In an initial contact with an unpleasant event, some part of the unconditioned fear or pain reaction becomes conditioned to other events that are happening simultaneously because the two are so closely linked in time. For example, a child who is startled by a barking dog may well acquire a learned fear reaction to the sight of the animal (through classical conditioning). In Mowrer's view, this fear reaction is largely visceral; it consists of the emergency responses we have previously discussed as part of the sympathetic arousal mechanism—including cardiovascular, respiratory, digestive, and endocrine responses. These visceral responses are a source of tension, or drive, in Mowrer's view; they motivate frightened people to try to reduce their fear and anxiety.

Mowrer goes on to outline a second process by which people learn to deal with their fears and anxieties; they learn to avoid or escape fearful situations. He calls this solution learning. (Today, it would be called instrumental learning.) Essentially, the frightened child learns to do whatever works to reduce fear, which can include a variety of reactions—from quite specific, fine-grained movements (such as telephoning the dogcatcher) to relatively general, gross activities (such as hiding from the dog). In learning theory terms, running away from actual harm is termed **escape,** whereas staying away from potential harm is termed **avoidance.** In either case, theoretically, the instrumental activity is reinforced through the successful removal or termination of conditioned fear stimuli—the sight of the dog, the sound of its barking, and the like—and the resulting reduction in fear drive or tension. In the past 40 years, researchers have assembled considerable evidence for Mowrer's two-process theory.

The impact of Mowrer's original formulations concerning fear conditioning was enormous. His theory virtually shaped the thinking and research of learning psychologists on this subject for decades. The tremendous acceptance of Mowrer's approach at the time is probably owed to several features: (a) The theory makes common sense—that is, nearly everyone can think of things they learned to fear via association. It makes sense that people learn to avoid people, places, and events that make them anxious. (b) The theory utilized learning principles that were in vogue from the time of Mowrer's original formulations on into the 1950s. (c) The theory had (and still has) immediate applications in clinical settings. Mowrer's views provided a model to help clinicians understand the basis of neurotic fears. Better yet, the theory suggested how such fears might be treated behaviorally—through extinction, adaptation, and counterconditioning. It also suggested practical ways the average person might deal with everyday fears and anxiety.

In the 1960s, challenges to the Mowrer formulation began to appear. For example, researchers were unable to document a link between animals' ANS reactions and the learning and maintenance of avoidance and escape behavior. Some frightened animals' ANS reactions were quick and intense, but for some reason they failed to learn to avoid or escape pain. Other animals' ANS reactions were minimal, but they quickly learned to avoid or escape punishment. (Rescorla & Solomon, 1967). Researchers also found that rats could learn to avoid certain stimuli (such as, poisoned food) in a single trial, even though the taste of the food and the effects of the poison were separated by hours (Revusky & Garcia, 1970). These findings challenged the notion that a gradual and temporally contiguous Pavlovian pairing process was involved in fear conditioning. Also contrary to a traditional Pavlovian view that any stimulus may serve as a conditioned stimulus for fear, researchers found that some stimuli are far more effective than others in generating fear. Stanley Rachman (1977) suggests that people may be prepared through evolution to become more fearful of some stimuli than others and that the phylogenetic background of a species must be taken into account if one is to understand its fear and avoidance behavior. For instance, pigeons are more likely to be able to use auditory stimuli than visual stimuli as cues for learning to avoid shock (Lolordo & Furrow, 1976). Similarly, people are much more likely to become fearful of, say, spiders or high places than, say, rocks or chairs.

These and other difficulties with the two-process theory as originally proposed, have led to considerable research and to the development of alternative models of fear across the past 20 years. Some theorists argue that researchers gain little by talking about fear. They believe that avoidance and escape behavior can be explained by a single process—operant conditioning (Herrnstein, 1969). They argue that organisms simply learn to do whatever it takes to reduce or eliminate negative reinforcers (noxious events) from their lives.

Stanley Rachman (1977) takes issue with Mowrer's contention that Pavlovian conditioning alone is responsible for the development of fear. Rachman proposes three pathways to fear:

1. One way people can learn to be afraid is by Pavlovian classical conditioning. This is, of course, the path emphasized by Mowrer.
2. A second way people can learn to be afraid is by modeling. If we see other people blanching, crying in fear, and running in terror, we, too, are likely to become frightened (Venn & Short, 1973).
3. Finally, simply receiving information about certain objects or events can strike terror in our hearts. If people warn us about thunderstorms, stray dogs, or people who are different from ourselves, we may come to fear them. There is evidence that mere information can produce fear, as measured by electrodermal (GSR) activity (Grings & Dawson, 1978).

*F*ear is stronger than love.

FULLER

Psychodynamic Behavior Theory

In the 1940s and 1950s a group of Yale scientists set out on an ambitious project. They thought they could translate the insights of Freud's psychodynamic theory into the precise language of learning theory. Thus, they thought, psychology would have the best of both worlds. For example, Neal Miller and his Yale colleagues (Miller, 1959) attempted to demonstrate that they could teach even rats to behave neurotically. Their analysis of the kind of situation that produces neurosis, and its accompanying irrational behavior went this way: Often animals, from rats to men, are motivated both to approach and to avoid something. In dating, for instance, teenagers are often faced with a painful decision "Should I call that witty, good-looking girl in my class for a date ... or shouldn't I? She could say 'yes,' but on the other hand, she might tell me to get lost." In later life, men and women deal with the same fundamental conflict, as they face the much more difficult decision, "Should I marry ... or not?"

Miller was able to create a parallel of such choices in a laboratory experiment. One group of hungry rats was trained to run down a straight alley. At the end of the runway was their reward, food. Once they were well trained, the experimenters measured how strongly the rats would pull against springs attached to their harnesses, as a function of their distance from the goal box containing the food. He found that the closer the rats got to the food, the harder they pulled.

A second group of rats was given a very different kind of training in the same alley. Instead of receiving food in the goal box, they received a strong electric shock. Once the rats had received several shocks, they were fitted with the same kind of harness-and-spring hookups, but this time their pull in the opposite direction was measured. Again, researchers found that the closer rats were to the shock, the harder they pulled to get away. The next step was to see what would happen if a third group of hungry rats was first trained to find food in the goal box and then were given a series of shocks when they entered the goal box. What happens when rats confront an approach-avoidance decision? How do they react when either food or shock awaits at the end of the runway? (In human terms, what happens when we know that the outcome of a telephone call could be either a date or rejection?)

Miller argued that with a limited set of postulates one could predict how rats and humans would react in approach-avoidance situations. Among these postulates:

1. The tendency to approach or avoid a goal is stronger the nearer the goal. This is called a "goal-gradient" hypothesis of approach or avoidance.
2. The strength of avoidance increases more rapidly than the strength of approach the nearer the goal (i.e., the gradient of avoidance is steeper than the gradient of approach). By varying the amount of hunger or the strength of the electric shock, it is always possible to raise or lower either gradient. However, the avoidance gradient always seems to be the steeper of the two.
3. When two incompatible responses conflict, the one with the stronger tendency will occur.

So far, so good. But what happens when the hungry rats reach that point in the runway where the approach and the avoidance gradients are equally powerful? (Many difficult decisions seem to involve exactly such a dilemma.) When rats reach the point where the gradients intersect, they stop. Each time they take a tentative step toward the food, the avoidance gradient rises, their fear rises, and they run back to the point of intersection. Each time the rats try to back out of the situation, the avoidance gradient falls, and the animals are drawn again into the conflict by their hunger. Sometimes, a conflicted rat will simply sit down on the runway. Then, as it grows hungrier, it will inch toward the goal.

Students may recognize the rat's dilemma. They pick up the telephone to call a prospective date, but as they start to dial, they become more and more frightened. As the phone begins to ring, they hang up—shaking and with a knot in their stomach. They chastise themselves for their timidity and try again. Like the rat, the "hungrier" they become for a date, the more they will inch toward actually making the telephone call. If it is critical to have a date for Friday night (friends will hoot with laughter if you report you've struck out again), you will be more likely to brave the phone call. On the other hand, if the dangers associated with the goal increase (someone alerts you that your date-to-be may be seeing someone else), you may back off. It is now easier not even to pick up the phone.

We see, then, that psychodynamic observations as to the genesis of neurotic anxiety and fear seem to make a great deal of sense when translated into learning terms. When people are faced with an insurmountable problem, they sometimes engage in behavior that may look odd but is, in fact, an attempt to deal with a no-win situation. As their desires become more intense, they become increasingly willing to risk pain to achieve their goals.

Fear always springs from ignorance.

EMERSON

COGNITIVE-LEARNING APPROACHES TO FEAR AND ANXIETY

Recently, many researchers such as Donald Meichenbaum (1977) and Aaron Beck (Beck, Emery, & Greenburg, 1985) have speculated that people's cognitions, specifically their expectations, might play a critical role in the development of fear and fear avoidance. For example, in his book on anxiety and phobias (Beck et al., 1985), Beck argues that if people make an erroneous assessment of how dangerous a particular situation is, they will experience inappropriate feelings of anxiety. Such erroneous assessments are usually caused by one or more of the following erroneous expectations:

1. Overestimating the chance of a dangerous event ("People are likely to push me onto the subway tracks if I stand too close to the edge").
2. Overestimating the severity of the feared event. ("If I flunk this course, my life will be ruined").
3. Underestimating your coping resources (what you can do to help yourself).
4. Underestimating others' willingness to assist you.

Cognitive behaviorists argue that people fear those things they expect to lead to pain or harm. They avoid things when they *expect* such avoidance to prevent unpleasantness (Reiss, 1980).

Albert Bandura (1977) has proposed one of the most popular cognitive theories of human behavior. He acknowledges that people become fearful when they expect fearful consequences. However, contrary to traditional two-process learning theory, in Bandura's model, fear is not the powerful force that motivates forms of emotional expression, nor is fear reduction critical in reinforcing avoidance behavior. Instead, fear and all emotional behaviors (including avoidance) simply coexist. It is, rather, expectancies that are critical in shaping all emotional behavior. Fear can, however, serve as an index of the extent to which people believe they have the ability to avoid unpleasant outcomes.

In Bandura's view, people can learn their repertoires of defensive behaviors in three ways:

1. By past experience. People expect that the things that helped them avoid aversive outcomes in the past may well work again.
2. By vicarious experience. People observe how others overcome unpleasant events and model their behavior.
3. By the use of other information, such as verbal instructions. Others may give good advice as to which strategies for avoiding pain work and which do not.

As a consequence of their experiences, Bandura proposes that people develop more or less confidence in their own self-efficacy, more or less confidence that they have the ability to deal with specific impending dangers. As a consequence, anxiety will be manageable. By contrast, Bandura also notes that if people are extremely anxious in a given situation, this is a tip-off to themselves that they may not have the ability to deal with the dangers. By way of example, suppose that a group of drama students has agreed to audition for a university production. As the day of the auditions approaches, the students will vary greatly in confidence and fear. Those who have acted on stage all their lives, have seen other actors receive standing ovations and flowers, or have received their teachers' encouragement ("You can do it") will have strong feelings of self-efficacy. On the other hand, other students will probably have little confidence and great fear if they have to audition first, if they have given a speech only once in their lifetime, and especially if on that occasion the audience yawned, coughed, or booed. Bandura would suggest that in such situations, one's lack of self-efficacy would affect performance.

Of course, previous experience may lead people to be more confident than they should be. For example, take the three-year-old boy who playfully challenges his father to a boxing match. As the child pummels his father to the ground, Dad musters fake cries of "Don't hit me!" and "I give up!" The boy is, of course, delighted. However, if Dad has been too convincing in his act, the three-year-old may find himself being punched out in nursery school as he tries to repeat his once-in-a-lifetime performance.

Cognitive-learning theories seem to make a great deal of sense. They explain some phenomena that troubled earlier learning theorists. Nonetheless, cognitive theories of fear and avoidance have their critics as well (see Delprato & McGlynn, 1984). These criticisms, however, go beyond the scope of this discussion.

Measuring Anxiety and Fear

By the 1960s, researchers had already developed well over 100 measures of fear and anxiety. Theorists were eager to develop measures that distinguished between trait and state anxiety (Spielberger et al., 1970), that assessed the behavioral, physiological, or phenomenonological manifestations of anxiety (Lewis, 1980), or that tapped anxiety in the very special situations in which they were interested (assessing social anxiety, test anxiety, and so forth). Thus, researchers have constructed a number of excellent self-report questionnaires, physiological assays, and behavioral measures to assess a variety of anxieties and fears. Let us examine a few of these measures.

SELF-REPORT MEASURES

Personality theorists were the first to try to develop self-report measures of anxiety. They attempted to measure persistent anxiety using paper-and-pencil tests. For example, the Taylor Manifest Anxiety Scale (MAS) was designed to assess chronic anxiety (Taylor, 1953). Anxiety items such as "I work under a great deal of tension" and "I am a high-strung person" were selected. People were asked to respond to the items with a "true" or "false." The first version of the MAS correlated quite well with other anxiety measures. In later versions, the MAS was pared from 50 to 20 items (Bendig, 1956). To give you some idea of what anxiety tests look like, a few items from this briefer test are reproduced in Table 12.2. It, too, proved to be both reliable and valid.

Today, probably the most popular measure of fear and anxiety is Spielberger, Gorsuch, and Lushene's (1970) State-Trait Anxiety Inventory (STAI). The STAI attempts to distinguish between state anxiety, how people happen

---

Table 12.2   **Items From the Bendig Version of the Taylor Manifest Anxiety Scale**

---

1. I believe I am no more nervous than most others.
2. I work under a great deal of tension.
3. I frequently find myself worrying about something.
4. I am usually calm and not easily upset.
5. I have periods of such great restlessness that I cannot sit long in a chair.
6. I find it hard to keep my mind on a task or job.
7. I am a high-strung person.

Hoyt & Magoon (1954).

to feel at the moment, and trait anxiety, how they usually feel (see chapter 7). In this test, subjects are asked to look at statements such as "I am tense," "I am jittery," or "I feel 'high-strung' " and to indicate how they feel right now, at this moment. Possible answers range from zero equals not at all to 3 equals very much so. The trait anxiety scale consists of 16 items. They look like this: "I feel like crying," "I feel that difficulties are piling up so that I cannot overcome them," and "I lack self-confidence." On this part of the scale, men and women are asked to indicate how they generally feel. Possible answers range from 1 equals almost never to 4 equals almost always. Statistical analyses of the STAI's structure have established that it does, in fact, measure these two very different dimensions of anxiety (Spielberger, Vagg, Barker, Dorham, & Westberry, 1980).

PSYCHOPHYSIOLOGICAL MEASURES

In his presidential address to the Society for Psychophysiological Research, Peter Lang (1979) proposed that people's thoughts ("imaginal activity"), psychophysiological reactions ("visceral and somato-motor activity"), and behavior are tightly linked, a position that we have maintained throughout this text. Psychologists have long known that when people think about performing an activity, their muscles may play out their thoughts. The more vivid peoples' images, the stronger their muscle movements have been found to be (Shaw, 1940). For example, subjects who imagine being attacked by a leopard show greater heart rate and respiration increases and skin resistance decreases than do subjects who imagine strolling near a flock of grazing sheep. Lang has attempted to spell out exactly how this process works in an ingenious series of experiments. First, he asked subjects to actively imagine a frightening scene. In some conditions, he read them a script focusing on a fearful *stimulus*.

> You are alone taking a steam bath and and temperature of the sauna starts to become unbearable. Thick clouds of white mist swirl around you, while droplets of the condensed steam accumulate on the walls, mingling in small riverlets of moisture which stream down the wooden walls and onto the floor. The heavy fog blankets the room with an almost impenetrable whiteness. The large wooden door is tightly closed, swollen from all the steam and jammed shut. The wooden walls of the small room surround you, closing you in with the oppressive steam.

Sometimes, the script instead focused upon the person's frightened *response:*

> You are alone taking a steam bath and the temperature of the sauna becomes unbearable. *You sweat great buckets* of perspiration, which roll down your skin and mingle with the condensed moisture from the swirling clouds of steam. The heavy fog hampers your breathing and *you take deep rapid gulps* of the seeming liquid air. *You tense all the muscles of your forehead, squinting to exclude* the burning steam from your eyes, as they dart *left and right to glimpse* the exit, as *you pull with all your strength* on the door, which is jammed shut. (Lang, 1979, p. 504)

Lang reasoned that subjects who focus on a stimulus should react differently than subjects who focus on their own response to the stimulus. In the first scenario, when subjects are focusing on the fear stimulus, they might be playing out the scene in any number of ways—they might be imagining the *heat,* listening to the *steam,* or looking at the *sauna.* Probably different subjects would show muscle movements at different sites. When the subjects are asked to focus on their own responses, however, the experimenter knows exactly where to look for a response. When they are visualizing "*tensing* their foreheads," "*squinting,*" "*looking* left and right," and so forth, the experimenter has only to assess the appropriate muscle sites to see whether there is a response.

To see whether subjects responded as he thought they would, Lang measured subjects' physiological reactions—heart rate, skin conductance, eye movement, EMG recordings from the head and neck, and respiration—continuously during the entire test session. Lang found that imagery and physiological response were linked exactly as he had expected. When the fear scenario described a frightened person's physiological responses, subjects' heart rates and respiration increased, and they showed a small increase in muscle tension. No differences were detected in a variety of control conditions.

Throughout his career, Lang has conducted a number of studies in an attempt to spell out the links between thought and psychophysiological response. For example, Lang wanted to compare people who are very poor at imagining emotional scenes with those who are good at visualizing such scenes. Interestingly enough, a few people seem to have no language at all for describing their own emotions. They are said to be suffering from **alexithymyia.** Lang wanted to contrast the responses of people who are poor to average at visualizing emotional scenes with those who are very good at vivid visualization (or who have been trained to be very good at visualization). What Lang thought was important, however, was not the ability to visualize emotional stimuli, but to visualize one's own emotional reactions, because it is this kind of visualization that should generate an intense psychophysiological response. To facilitate such comparisons, Lang assigned some subjects to a control condition (where they received no training of any kind) and other subjects to one of two very different training programs—one training subjects to focus on emotional stimuli or one training them to focus on their own emotional responses.

1. In the stimulus training program, Lang tried to teach subjects to vividly imagine the emotional setting. Subjects were reinforced each time they gave a report which emphasized the color, form, and pictorial vividness of the scene. The experimenter ignored them if they began to describe their own emotional behavior. Not surprisingly, Lang found that subjects soon "came to report rich tapestries of sense impression during imagery" (p. 503).

2. In the response training program, Lang asked subjects to listen to a script describing an emotional scene and to try to imagine the scene. Then, he asked subjects to report their thoughts. If subjects merely recounted a description of the stimulus situation, the experimenter was silent. But anytime subjects went on to describe their own emotional reactions—saying such things as "My muscles were tense," "I felt myself running," "My heart was racing," "I was gasping for breath," and so forth—the experimenter brightened up and praised them. Not surprisingly, Lang found that such training worked. Response subjects soon learned to give vivid reports of their own emotional behavior.

In subsequent experiments, Lang found that both control subjects and those who had been taught to focus on emotional stimuli showed fairly muted psychophysiological reactions to emotional scenes. Those who had been taught how to visualize themselves responding to such emotional situations, however, showed far bigger changes in heart rate, respiration, and sweating.

Lang points out that the discovery that fear and anxiety are so closely linked to psychophysiological response and behavior has some clinical implications for the treatment of fear and anxiety. If one wishes to reduce fear and anxiety, the steps are clear. First, the therapist must find out exactly which sorts of stimuli provoke fearful imagery (and thus inappropriate physiological and behavioral responses). Then, the patient must be confronted with the provoking stimulus situation and a plan of action drawn up. The patient must rehearse new behaviors. These behaviors are designed to prod the patient into overcoming the fear and behaving normally . . . and to stop behaving in a fearful and anxious way. The therapist can try to encourage normal behavior by rewarding the patient when he or she makes a small step in overcoming fear as well as by trying to facilitate the extinction of fear.

BEHAVIORAL MEASURES

Among the first psychologists to try to measure fear with some objectivity were animal researchers (see May, 1948). In one classic experiment, Judson Brown, Harry Kalish, and I. E. Farber (1951) showed that if two frightening events occur simultaneously, animals will have an unusually strong fear response. Researchers paired a stimulus (a buzzer plus a light) with electric shock and then presented the stimulus when rats were startled by a loud noise (a shot from a toy pistol). Rats showed an unusually large startle reaction. Judson Brown and his colleagues argued that the fear stimulus (buzzer and light) added to the animals' drive or tension levels and made them jump higher when they were startled by the pistol shot. In this case, fear was measured in terms of the strength of the startle response. (An analogy at the human level might be the tendency to become "jumpy" while watching a horror movie on the late show. A door that suddenly bangs in the wind during the movie could evoke a large response.)

Clinicians designed many of the behavioral measures of fear; they wanted to replace therapists' subjective reports with more objective indices of anxiety. For instance, William Zung (1971) used the following strategy to assess anxiety: He compiled a list of the symptoms psychiatrists usually use in diagnosing anxiety and then asked psychiatrists to rate the severity of each of these symptoms (see Table 12.3). As you can see from the table, psychiatrists assumed that a slightly anxious person might have trouble with insomnia; only when anxiety had gotten completely out of hand would a person be likely to experience "mental disintegration." Interestingly, Zung found that clients' self-reports of felt anxiety were generally in accord with psychiatrists' more objective ratings on the Zung anxiety scale. This gives us some confidence that people know what they are talking about when they claim to be anxious. Such findings, of course, also argue for the validity of the scale.

Those who have worked with children, and have been unable to rely on verbal reports, have also been eager to utilize more objective behavioral rating scales. For instance, Sandra Scarr and Philip Salapatek (1970) were interested in exploring how frightened children (from infancy to two years of age) were of six types of fear stimuli—a mechanical dog, a jack-in-the-box, masks, strangers, noise, and heights. Fear was assessed by such behavioral indicants as "sober, cautious, stops ongoing activity" and, more severely, "fretting, crying, and fleeing to mother." The authors concluded that while fear of heights increases steadily from infancy to about 1½ years of age, fear of the other stimuli increases until the child is 7 to 10 months of age and then levels off at that high level.

We have reviewed only a few of the ways researchers have systematically assessed fear and anxiety in subjects' behavior. Potentially, of course, a scientific Sherlock Holmes could sniff out the presence of fear in any number of ways. In *Nonreactive Measures in the Social Sciences*, Eugene Webb and his colleagues (1981) review a number of extraordinarily creative techniques

---

Table 12.3   **Severity of Anxiety Symptoms**

1. Mental disintegration	11. Urinary frequency
2. Tremors	12. Sweating
3. Body aches and pains	13. Fatigue
4. Anxiousness	14. Dysphea
5. Apprehension	15. Nightmares
6. Nausea and vomiting	16. Restlessness
7. Fear	17. Dizziness
8. Panic	18. Faintness
9. Palpitation	19. Face flushing
10. Parasthesias	20. Insomnia

Zung (1971), p. 378

researchers have used to assess emotion. Of special interest to us, of course, is the variety of related ways researchers have found to assess fear. How frightened children were during a ghost-story-telling session was measured by noting the shrinking diameter of a circle of seated children. Bullfighters' beards are known to be longer on the day of a fight than on any other day. No one knows whether the *toreros'* beards grow faster because of biochemical changes in anxiety or whether the bullfighters simply stand farther away from the razor blade when it trembles in hand. In any case, fear and beard length are correlated (Conrad, 1958). Applied psychologists assessed how big a toll a series of air crashes took on the nerves of Chicago airport passengers by comparing the sales of alcoholic drinks (Hillebrandt, 1962) and flight insurance policies before and after the disasters.

In his description of mob boss Frank Costello's expressive hands, during Costello's forced appearance before Senator Estes Kefauver's organized-crime hearings, Gould (1951) suggested that anxiety could be read in every gesture:

> As he [Costello] sparred with Rudolph Halley, the committee's counsel, the movement of his fingers told their own emotional story. When the questions got rough, Costello crumpled a handkerchief in his hands. Or he rubbed his palms together. Or he interlaced his fingers. Or he grasped a half filled glass of water. Or he beat a silent tattoo on the table top. Or he rolled a little ball of paper between his thumb and index finger. Or he stroked the side piece of his glasses lying on the table. His was video's first ballet of the hands. (p. 1)

Evidence confirms that Gould was right. Researchers have assumed that anxiety is reflected in such nervous behavior as "leg jiggling" and have used it to study patrons' emotions in coffee shops, bars, and movie theaters (Kretsinger, 1952; Sechrest & Flores, 1971). For example, Sechrest (1965) found that conversations between men and women are more frequently punctuated by quick, jerky, nervous gestures than are conversations between two men. All these studies testify to the fact that fear and anxiety can be gauged by any number of unobtrusive behavioral measures.

Other Perspectives on Fear

CROSS-CULTURAL ASPECTS OF FEAR

Charles Darwin believed that cultural universals could be found in emotional experience and expression; the emotions had evolved, after all, because they increased animals' chances of survival. Anthropologists such as Otto Klineberg (1940) and Margaret Mead (1975), however, challenged his contention. They maintained that cultural differences in emotion were all important. The current prevailing view recognizes the wisdom of both approaches—certain fundamental emotions, such as fear, do indeed appear to be universal. Cultural differences, however, show themselves in the specific forms of expression that are considered to be appropriate.

One group that has explored the meaning and prevalence of fear or anxiety across cultures is Spielberger's (Spielberger & Diaz-Guerrero, 1976). In cross-cultural research, of course, one must start by translating the personality measure into the appropriate languages. The State-Trait Anxiety Inventory (STAI), has been translated into such languages as Spanish, Japanese, Malay, Swedish, Turkish, and many others (Spielberger & Sharma, 1976). These scales correlate well with other measures of anxiety in other societies. Among Hindi subjects, for example, the STAI has shown moderately high correlations with other anxiety tests, including the Taylor MAS. In a variety of studies, the authors have documented the usefulness of the STAI in assessing anxiety levels of Spanish psychiatric patients; in contrasting anxiety levels of Mexican and American high-school students; and of relating anxiety to academic performance in Puerto Ricans. Thus, Spielberger and his co-workers have succeeded in developing cross-cultural measures for anxiety which have a wide range of potential applications. In addition, the general pattern of results from his studies and those of others suggests that verbal expressions of anxiety, as measured by the STAI, may indeed be, in part, universal.

On the other hand, the evidence also makes clear the considerable distinctiveness in the face of fear in different cultures. Ekman and Friesen (1969) note that the display rules for the expression of emotions differ greatly from Japan to the United States to New Guinea, despite underlying commonalities of facial muscle movements. Evidence supports the proverbial inscrutability of the Oriental. The authors found that although Japanese and Americans seem to feel the same emotions and to display them with similar intensity when they think no one is present, the two cultures seem to have very different rules for public display. In public, the Japanese mute fear and anxiety; Americans often do not. It is interesting to note that some authors, such as J. P. Leff (1973), have proposed that a link may exist between a society's level of language development and the subtlety with which it expresses emotion.

Even within the bounds of Southeast Asia, people in different cultural groups may worry about very different things (Tan, 1980). For example, Malaysian people often worry about the functioning of their sexual organs and the adequacy of their sexual performance. In some Chinese groups, frigophobia (fear of the cold) is unusually common. Tan thinks that cultural myths and folklore may predispose people to express their neuroses by focusing on one anxiety versus another. Cultures support certain belief systems and may thereby reinforce certain forms of anxious expression.

In short, although fear sometimes speaks a universal language, in different societies, people do experience and express fear in somewhat different ways. Society even shapes the form anxiety takes when it is ostensibly out of control. In Indonesian societies, people may run amok, running through the village destroying crockery and everything else that is breakable in their path. In a tightly controlled religious school, nervous students may be seen as out of control when they giggle. Belief systems, modeling, cultural learning, and culture-specific stimuli, and other factors, all contribute to the forms anxiety and the other emotions take.

FEAR OF SUCCESS

In America, there may appear to be gender differences in how frightened men and women are of success versus failure. Most people are frightened of failure, which is not surprising. Failure connotes loss—loss of pride, loss of social esteem, financial loss, and so forth. But who fears success? In 1968, Matina Horner performed a series of experiments for her dissertation that were to become as controversial as they were interesting. Horner asked men and women college students to write stories about several hypothetical situations. For women, the situation was: "At the end of first-term finals, Anne finds herself at the top of her medical-school class." For men, "John" was found to be in this situation. The stories the students told were then rated for a number of themes. It was found that when women wrote stories about Anne's success, they often referred to the loneliness, guilt, and unpopularity that Anne would encounter if she continued to star in medical school. The men, on the other hand (as well as women who had been asked to write a story about John), emphasized the positive results of success. Two typical scenarios capture these differences:

Female:

Anne is an acne faced bookworm. She runs to the bulletin board and finds she's at the top ... A chorus of groans is the rest of the class's reply ... She studies 12 hours a day, and lives at home to save money. She rents her books. "Well it certainly paid off. All the Friday and Saturday nights with my books, who needs dates, fun—I'll be the best woman doctor alive." And yet, a twinge of sadness comes thru—she wonders what she really has. (Horner, 1968, p. 107)

Male:

John is very pleased with himself and he realizes that all his efforts have been rewarded, he has finally made the top of his class. John has worked very hard, and his long hours of study have paid off.... He realizes he can give [his girl-friend] all the things she desires after he becomes established. He will go on in med school making good grades and be successful in the long run. (Horner, 1968, pp. 108–109)

Feminists, social psychologists, and students alike found such differences intriguing; related experiments followed in quick succession (Tresemer, 1977). In the process, the picture changed. David Tresemer found that not only women feared success; in his study, men were as frightened of success and of its requirements (cited in Tresemer, 1977). Other studies suggested that women's fear of success may be a peculiarly 1960s phenomenon. It appears that women feared success not because they were projecting their own fears onto Anne, but because they and everyone else correctly perceived that in the late 1960s, aspiring women were likely to have trouble competing in a "man's world." For instance, both men and women had positive associations to John's successes and more negative ones to Anne's. Other researchers argued that Horner had really demonstrated that women fear gender-inappropriate behavior, not that they fear success (Cherry & Deaux, 1978). For example, women might have felt far more comfortable about an Anne who was judged "Mother of the Year."

Nonetheless, Horner highlighted a reality. Even in America, which is probably as success oriented as any culture, some women and men have learned to fear success. Children who have critical and controlling parents are more likely to fear success than are children whose parents are more permissive and positive in their evaluations (Canavan-Gumpert, Garner, & Gumpert, 1978). Perhaps such children worry, and rightly so, that they will never "measure up." Once people begin to doubt their own abilities and fear success, a sort of self-fulfilling prophesy may occur. If individuals who fear success do succeed on a task, they may begin to doubt themselves and become so nervous that they perform more poorly the next time around, thereby ensuring their own failure. Normally, of course, success would breed confidence and more success.

Fear not.

OLD TESTAMENT

CONTROLLING FEAR

We have spent an entire chapter discussing fear—discovering that humans are predisposed to be fearful of a few things and that they learn to fear still other dangers in the social and physical world. People also possess the ability to be quick studies; they can quickly learn to fear many things that other animals could never be bothered about (social snubs, atomic warfare, the meaninglessness of life, etc.). After all this discussion, you may react by wondering whether there is any hope that people can have the best of both worlds—to be fully aware of their feelings, including their fears, so that they can use such information in managing their lives, yet be able to conquer and subdue fears that are paralyzing? Of course there is. We belong to a species that is capable of dealing with several widely varying ideas at the same time. We are able, at our best, not to see things in rigid blacks and whites but in more complicated shades of gray. The same capacity that allows us to learn to fear in the first place allows us to learn to manage those fears . . . or even unlearn them.

In chapter 14, we will spend a great deal of time reviewing techniques people can use to manage their emotions. But for now, to close this chapter on fear on the upbeat, it will help us to review a few of the techniques psychologists have studied that people may use to deal with their fears.

Cognitive Methods for Dealing With Fear and Anxiety

Psychologists have developed a number of cognitive techniques for helping patients deal with anxiety. Early on, as we have seen, Freud recognized that one way people keep anxiety within bounds is by the use of defense mechanisms (such as repression, denial, projection, and so forth) which push anxiety below the surface. He argued that people often use such techniques unconsciously and automatically. In addition, people can also make a conscious effort to keep their feelings out of sight and out of mind. They can force themselves to stop thinking about things that upset them. ("Stop it," we sometimes say to ourselves, giving our heads a little shake as if to toss away unpleasant thoughts.) In chapter 14, we will also examine a number of cognitive behavior modification techniques that can be used to consciously control anxiety. These methods include self-instruction, imagery, modeling, problem solving, and a variety of other means which people can use to gain rational control over their fears.

Physiological Methods for Dealing With Fear and Anxiety

People also try to regulate their fears through drugs, either those dispensed through prescriptions, including tranquilizers and barbiturates, and nonprescription remedies, such as alcohol, cocaine, heroin, or marijuana. In fact, anxiety may be effectively diminished by drugs for two reasons: First, in part, drugs are yet another form of avoidance and escape. People speak of taking drugs to "escape" from their problems. Second, in part, drugs alter people's physiological states. Unfortunately, drug dependence has a number of unfortunate consequences, which we discussed in an earlier chapter. We will consider some of the fear-alleviating substances and their effects in chapter 14.

Behavioral Methods for Dealing With Fear and Anxiety

Finally, let us consider a variety of the behavioral methods psychologists have studied for dealing with fear and anxiety.

Avoidance and Escape. People often caution, "You can't run away from your problems." In fact, however, generally the sensible person will do just that. A variety of folk statements testifies to the wisdom of avoiding trouble: "Keep your nose clean"; "Don't stir the pot"; "He who fights and runs away, lives to fight another day." As Mowrer (1947) and many others have argued, fear can be reduced or eliminated altogether by avoidance and escape. For Richard Lazarus (1977), fear and avoidance are natural allies: "To some extent, the person selects the environment to which he/she must respond; shapes his/her commerce with it; plans, chooses, avoids . . . escapes. . . . In regulating one's emotional life, a person is also thereby affecting the bodily reactions that are an integral part of any emotional state" (p. 77). Lazarus terms such activities, **coping processes.** To cope is often to avoid and escape. People alter their fears, in part, by taking control of their lives.

Avoidance and escape are probably the most natural and effective means for the self-regulation of fear. Of course, people can carry a good thing too far. Some people are too timid. They are unwilling to endure any stress or to take any risks to make their lives better. They agree with everyone's ideas, work extraordinarily hard for extraordinarily little money, avoid walking under ladders, manage not to get sunburned, or avoid staying out late at night. Their lives become very narrow. (A woman once cautioned her daughter not to go to the corner drugstore at night because she might be "eaten by mad dogs." Indeed, one can avoid mad dogs and other dangers by choosing to be imprisoned, but for most people, it is not worth it.) Worse yet, such timidity ensures that people will never adapt to new situations and, in the view of behavioral theory, that their fears will never be extinguished. You may seemingly manage your fear of public speaking by never giving a speech, but you may end up fearing public speaking all your life. For such overly timid people, the secret is to venture out in slow steps, adapting to the new, and becoming a bit braver step by step. Otherwise, they run the risk that over time they may simply become more and more frightened about less and less.

People can carry things too far in a second way: The techniques they choose to avoid fear may themselves be maladaptive. For example, as we have seen, some neurotics learn to keep fear in check by keeping their minds and hands busy; they perform a bizarre series of rituals each day. They may wash their hands 200 times each day; or precisely measure out their food, eating only minute amounts, and the like.

"Flooding" and Desensitization. Clinicians can treat such fears using a number of behavioral methods. Let us consider two of them—flooding techniques and systematic desensitization.

In some cases, psychologists will try to extinguish fear by **flooding techniques**—they suggest that clients repeatedly expose themselves to the feared stimulus. For example, comedian Wally Cox was once painfully shy. He decided to confront his worst fears. He practiced making a fool of himself in public, such as by ordering Chinese food in a Mexican restaurant or asking where Times Square was while pointing to the sign. In time, he got used to being the "class clown." Similarly, one way to overcome a fear of public speaking may be to take a course in the Speech department that requires a number of presentations before an audience. Psychologist Alfred Adler (1929) describes his attempts as a five-year-old to overcome his fears:

> I remember that the path to the school led over a cemetery. I was frightened every time and was exceedingly put out at beholding the other children pass the cemetery without paying the least attention to it, while every step I took was

accompanied by a feeling of fear and horror. Apart from the extreme discomfort occasioned by this fear I was also annoyed at the idea of being less courageous than the others. One day I made up my mind to put an end to this fear of death. Again, I *decided upon a treatment of hardening.* I stayed at some distance behind the others, placed my schoolbag on the ground near the wall of the cemetery and ran across it a dozen times, until I felt that I had mastered the fear. (pp. 179–180)

As unpleasant as such experiences sound, flooding methods have been found to be quite effective in overcoming clinical fears. Two theorists coined the term *implosion therapy* to refer to the "internal explosion" that seemingly takes place upon exposure to a full-blown fear stimulus (Stampfl & Levis, 1967).

Other psychologists utilize **systematic desensitization** techniques. When clients are frightened, they are taught how to relax, rather than to express fear, as they are systematically exposed to more and more frightening material. The assumption is that, in time, the once fearful stimulus will produce relaxation rather than tension—a process termed **counterconditioning.** How does it work? Try this. First take a deep breath; try to relax your mind and muscles as best you can. Relax your toes, place your legs in a comfortable position, move your shoulders about, swivel your neck about until you are thoroughly at ease. Say "relax" to yourself as you exhale a few times. Feel better? If so, now think about the upcoming exam in this class on emotion. Relax. Imagine yourself coming to the testing room, sitting down, opening the test, and beginning to write down some answers. Still feel all right? If not, you had better back up, try to relax again, and then come back to thoughts of the exam. This is a greatly oversimplified form of the actual process of systematic desensitization, but it contains most of the essentials. Most importantly, when competent therapists carefully guide their patients, the method works (see Wolpe, 1973).

Biofeedback. Psychologists may teach clients other techniques for the self-control of fear. Notable among the more recent ones is **biofeedback-assisted relaxation training.** The most common biofeedback method is muscle-tension control. The process works this way: Electrodes are placed on, say, the patient's forehead muscle (the frontalis). The natural bioelectrical activity of this muscle is fed into the biofeedback instrument, amplified, and sent back to the patient in the form of feedback, say, a tone whose pitch varies with the muscle tension. Clients thus possess a continual record of whether their tension level, at least in the targeted muscle, is rising or falling. The patient's task is simple; he or she is to relax the forehead muscle. The feedback tells them whether they have succeeded or failed. The idea is, of course, that if patients are to relax their facial muscles, they must relax overall, and that should contribute to a general lowering of arousal, such as exists in anxiety (Stoyva & Budzynski, 1974).

Some investigators have argued, however, that more general muscle relaxation through biofeedback may be a more effective method than simple facial relaxation (e.g., Carlson, Basilio, & Heaukulani, 1983). Recently, relaxation training of several muscle groups simultaneously through biofeedback has been shown to reduce both autonomic and self-report indicators of anxiety, suggesting a more promising approach to anxiety control (Shirley, Burish, & Rowe, 1982; Carlson, Muraoka, Uchino, & Uchigakiuchi, 1989).

Theoretically, anxiety and relaxation are incompatible. Investigators such as LeBoeuf (1974) have demonstrated that chronically anxious clients who are given muscle biofeedback training do show improvement in their condition. Interestingly, in LeBoeuf's study, the technique seemed to work best with those people who habitually expressed their anxiety by tensing up their muscles. If the subjects expressed tension autonomically (say, in terms of digestive upset), the muscle relaxation technique was not effective. This suggests that biofeedback training may be most beneficial within the part of the physiology it is designed to measure and affect.

Of course, people do not always want to control their fears. Sometimes, people enjoy scaring themselves. Children enjoy shivery thrills as they tell ghost stories or sneak a cigarette in the bathroom. Adults enjoy horror films, roller coasters, race cars, and skiing partly for the thrills they provide (Zuckerman, 1979).

Psychologists sometimes provoke their clients' anxiety as well as teach them how to dampen it. Psychoanalytically trained therapists, in an attempt to give their clients insight, may take them on a guided tour of their fearful memories and thoughts. The ultimate goal is, of course, to defuse the power of their long-buried fears. Behaviorally oriented therapists, as we have seen, may try to help clients adapt to frightening stimuli by arranging for them to step out into the world in small steps or allow frightening stimuli to implode in a client's flood of emotion. Sometimes, then, people can gain self-understanding and perhaps reach their fullest potential by experiencing and working through their fears, rather than simply suppressing and controlling them.

Summing Up

- Fear/anxiety possesses a number of distinctive components: It is an emotional state, with a distinctive experienced quality; it is unpleasant; it is directed toward the future; it involves bodily discomfort and bodily disturbance. Theorists have distinguished between trait and state anxiety.

- In popular language, the terms *neurosis* and *anxiety* are often used interchangeably. Recently, however, the American Psychiatric Association replaced the generic concept of neurosis with precise definitions of the various anxiety disorders—the phobias, generalized anxiety disorders, panic disorders, obsessive-compulsive disorders, and post-traumatic stress disorder.

- People possess an innate tendency to be fearful. Gray suggests that intense stimuli, novel stimuli, and stimuli associated with danger in a species' evolutionary history are innately feared.

- Mowrer took a two-process approach to explaining fear reactions. He used different principles to explain how people acquire fears versus how they learn to deal with them. Fear reactions are acquired through Pavlovian conditioning. Avoidance and escape reactions are learned through instrumental learning processes. This view has had its critics; today, theorists emphasize the importance of cognition and single-process theories.

- In another behavioral approach, Miller studied approach-avoidance conflicts in animals and humans.

- Physiological researchers have found that fear is reflected in such psychophysiological measures as heart rate, skin conductance, skin temperature, and muscle tension. Fear is also associated with elevated levels of the catecholamines, epinephrine and norepinephrine, and the adrenocorticotrophic hormones, in particular, cortisol.

- Cognitive-learning approaches to fear have been developed for both animal and human behavior. In Bandura's view, people can learn defensive behaviors in three ways—by experience, by observation, and by receiving related information.

- In the psychodynamic view, Freud distinguished between primary anxiety, moral anxiety, and neurotic anxiety. He proposed that people develop ego defense mechanisms to minimize anxiety.

- Bowlby proposed that when mother and child are separated, the child experiences separation anxiety. Children experience a predictable sequence of emotions—protest, despair, and detachment.

- Measures of fear include behavioral observation, self-report measures, and physiological measures.

- Certain fundamental emotions, such as fear, appear to be universal; there are, however, cultural differences in the specific forms of expression that are considered to be socially appropriate.

- Fear of success may develop as a function of certain cultural rearing patterns, different for males and females from childhood.

- Cognitive, physiological, and behavioral techniques exist for controlling fear.

13

Emotions, Stress, and Physical Health

Introduction

Emotional Stress
Early Contributions to the Study of Stress
Sources of Stress

Emotional Responses to Stress
Physiological Responses
Behavioral Responses
Cognitive Responses to Stress

The Diseases of Emotional Stress
Ulcers
Cardiovascular Disease
Disease and Immunity

Coping With Emotional Stress
What It Means "To Cope"
Coping Resources

Pain and Pain Management
How Is Pain Transmitted to the Brain?
Brain Mechanisms for Pain
Pain and Cognition
Methods of Pain Control

Summing Up

FIGURE 13.1 *Les Baigneuses.* Pablo Picasso. 1919. Oil on canvas, 27 by 22 cm. *Editions de la Réunion des Musées Nationaux,* Paris.

Introduction

In the summer of 1973, Americans sat glued to their television sets. During the previous presidental campaign, five men had been caught trying to bur- glarize the headquarters of the Democratic National Committee, located in the Watergate (which contained suites of rooms). Each day, there were new revelations. It was becoming clear that President Nixon, the Attorney General, and several of the President's aides were involved in either the break-in itself or at least the subsequent cover-up. When things got too hot, the President tried to stall the investigation by firing the special prosecutor assigned to in- vestigate the scandal, but that only added fuel to the fire. Then, Senate hearings revealed that the President had secretly taped all his conversations in the Oval Office. The Senate could find out without a doubt "when he knew and what he knew" about the break-in. Nixon insisted that presidential executive privilege meant he did not have to release the tapes, but the Supreme Court disagreed. And the tapes made it clear that Nixon knew about his aides' attempted cover- up. Congress began to prepare to impeach him. In August, 1974, Nixon re- signed, the only president ever to do so. He retreated to San Clemente, Cal- ifornia. Several top aides were sent to jail.

How did Nixon react to the intense stress? Earlier, he had described how he typically reacted to pressure—with physical symptoms: "his muscles tense up, his breathing comes faster, his nerves tingle, his stomach churns, his nights sleepless" (Nixon, 1962, p. xv). A month after he left office, Nixon developed a life-threatening problem in his left leg. The disease was phlebitis, an inflam- mation of a vein and the formation of large blood clots. If the clots break loose and move to the heart, the patient dies. Nixon had a clot 18 inches long in his leg. He was also continually in a great deal of pain, for the clots kept his blood from circulating. His leg had become so swollen that he couldn't put on his pants. A small clot broke loose from his leg and lodged in his lung. He had surgery on his leg twice and was left in critical condition. Doctors warned that he could die at any moment. His wife, Pat, and his family rallied around him. President Ford made a special trip to visit him in the hospital. Nixon thought that this support helped him to pull through his illness. Today he is fully re- covered (adapted from Watson, in press).

What effect do intense emotional experiences have on physical health? How are people's emotions, stress, physical disease, and pain related? In this chapter, we begin to find out. In earlier chapters, we discussed the impact that emotions—such as anxiety, depression, and anger—have on mental health. In this chapter, we will focus on the impact that emotions have on stress reactions, pain, and physical health. Increasingly, René Descartes' dualistic view of man, which sharply distinguished mind and body, has been elbowed aside by re- searchers in the related areas of behavioral medicine and health psychology.

They now know that psychological and physical factors interact in complex ways to shape physical health. An explosion of knowledge has occurred in this area, making an understanding of this research critical to a full understanding of the psychology of emotion.

Much of the research we review here is surprisingly recent. Psychologists and scientists from a variety of disciplines who are interested in the impact of individual and social factors on physical health have allied under the banner of **behavioral medicine.** Behavioral medicine takes a multidisciplinary approach to the assessment, prevention, and treatment of physical disease, emphasizing behavioral science knowledge and techniques (Schwartz & Weiss, 1978). Within this field, psychologists who are interested in the impact of psychological factors on physical health are called health psychologists. In fact, the American Psychological Association now has a division devoted to such interests (Division 38, Health Psychology). The newness of such organizations is evidenced by the fact that the first meeting of the now historic Yale Conference on Behavioral Medicine was held in 1977. One of the prime areas of interest to these researchers is the emotions, emotional stress, and the role that related psychological factors play in health (cf. Carlson & Siefert, 1991).

Emotional Stress

Situations that generate strong emotions—anger, fear, depression and perhaps even joy—produce stress. What do psychologists mean by **stress?** Researchers use the concept in two very different ways. Sometimes, when researchers use the term *stress,* they are thinking of it as a cause, that is, as a stressor. Sometimes, they are focusing on stress as a response or a complex of reactions.

EARLY CONTRIBUTIONS TO THE STUDY OF STRESS

The recognition that psychological stress may increase a person's vulnerability to disease is not new. In the 1700s, physicist Robert Hooke coined the term *stress* in explaining how physical bodies were pushed out of shape by external forces. In the 1800s, the eminent physiologist Claude Bernard recognized parallel effects in the impact of physiological stress on the body. But it was in this century that Hans Selye, the "father of stress," tried to spell out the links between stress, physiological responses, and physical illness.

In his early research, Selye exposed rats to a wide variety of prolonged stressors. He found that all stressors seemed to produce essentially the same pattern of physiological responses. In time, rats developed such problems as enlarged adrenal cortexes, shrunken thymus and lymph glands, and ulcerated stomachs and duodenums. Selye concluded that stress "is the state manifested by the specific syndrome which consists of all the nonspecifically induced changes within a biologic system" (Selye, 1956, p. 54).

Such discoveries led Selye (1956) to propose a model linking emotion, stress, the "general adaptation syndrome," and illness. In this model, when animals encounter stress, they mobilize for action. It matters little whether the stressful event is a saber-tooth tiger, the threat of a corporate raid, running a 26-mile marathon, or winning a lottery. All these events put stress on the organism; all demand action. And, according to Selye, the body comes through in the same way each time. Regardless of the cause of the threat, animals respond with the same nonspecific pattern of reactions. This mobilization effort is controlled in part by the adrenal glands, which pump out adrenaline, in turn stimulating sympathetic nervous system activity (see chapter 4).

In fact, the general adaptation syndrome has three stages: In the first stage, the **alarm stage,** animals mobilize to meet the threat. In the second, the **resistance stage,** the animal tries to cope with the threat—generally through fight or flight. If the animal fails in dealing with the threat, however, eventually it will run out of steam, and the third stage, **exhaustion,** will occur. (We review these stages in greater detail in a later section.) Over time, repeated stress takes its toll, contributing to wear and tear on the animal's system and leaving it vulnerable to disease. In fact, repeated emotional stress has been implicated in such disorders as essential hypertension (high blood pressure), cardiovascular disease, arthritis, and immune-related deficiencies, among many others.

Selye's early formulation influences research even today. His model, of course, has not been without its critics. John Mason (1975) sums it up in this way: "There are still some workers who accept Selye's views of stress, some who use modifications of them, some who regard them yet as unproven working hypotheses, and some who simply reject or ignore them" (p. 10). He offers several criticisms of the Seyle model (Mason, 1971, 1974). For example: (a) Psychological appraisals of events are critically important in determining people's physiological responses. People who endure cold, hunger, and exhaustion as part of a test of manhood respond far differently to such stressors than do people who are forced to endure them in emergency situations. (b) Different stressors can produce somewhat different patterns of endocrinological responses. For example, if people are frightened as they try to give a speech in front of a hostile audience, their epinephrine levels rise. When these same people exercise, their norepinephrine levels shoot up.

It is also the case that different kinds of stressors may trigger different CNS and behavioral reactions. For instance, Marc Gellman, Neil Schneiderman, Jeffrey Wallach, and William LeBlanc (1981) found that stimulation of the medial hypothalamus produces increases in heart rate, blood pressure, and overt aggression. Stimulation of the anterior and posterior hypothalamus produces decreases in heart rate and blood pressure and behavioral immobility. In short, it now appears that stressors may produce either specific or nonspecific stress responses, depending upon a variety of factors. Therefore, we define stress as both the specific and nonspecific reactions to stimulus events that are perceived as endangering one's well-being.

SOURCES OF STRESS

In daily life, people encounter a variety of emotionally stressful stimuli. Physical stressors include such things as changes in the weather, natural disasters (earthquakes, floods, droughts), accidents (rock slides or avalanches), or equipment failures (cars that will not start, vending machines that swallow quarters, computers that crash). Social stressors include such things as irrational bosses, acquaintances who ask for help and then resent the assistance, or a smugly superior classmate. Finally come the intensely personal stressors. These include such searing experiences as the death of a loved one, the loss of a job, the impact of early memories such as rape or child abuse, wartime memories, and the like. When one lacks the social skills required for coping with such stressors, their effects may be especially devastating. We discuss later some of the social skills that protect people from such troubles (see Box 13.1).

Major Stressors

Psychiatrists Thomas Holmes and Richard Rahe (1967) developed the Social Readjustment Rating Scale, or SRRS (to measure the amount of stress individuals are subject to, see Table 13.1 for a view of this scale). Holmes and Rahe's logic was straightforward: Major life events, from marriage to death, are stressful because they force people to make significant changes in their lives. For example, when a spouse dies, everything changes—one has lost a lover, a best friend, a financial ally, someone to go to the movies with, and so forth. Other events, say, getting a traffic ticket, are far less serious; they involve only a minor "hassle." Table 13.1 lists a variety of potentially stressful events. They range from most stressful—"death of a spouse" and "divorce"—to least stressful—"vacation," "Christmas," and "minor violations of the law." Each event is assigned a number of points, which indicate the amount of change, on the average, such events make in people's lives. These points are termed life change units (LCUs).

The Schedule of Recent Experiences (SRE) asks people to look through the SRRS and check off every event that has occurred within the past year. To calculate a final score, researchers simply total up the LCU units associated with those events. People vary, of course, in how much their lives have changed over the past year. A score of 300 is considered to indicate high stress. Presumably, the higher the score, the more vulnerable people will be to careless accidents and illness.

In predicting the impact SRE scores will have on physical health, Holmes and Rahe make four assumptions:

1. People regard some events (such as the death of a spouse) to be far more stressful than other events (such as having trouble with the boss).

BOX 13.1 _____

Death by Stress

It has long been suspected that too much stress may lead to accidents, illness, or even death. Oliver Sacks (1983) provides one case study of such a stress-death connection. Rolando P. was suffering from Parkinson's disease; he was hospitalized.

Rolando P's mother was exceptionally understanding and deeply devoted: thus it was she who would always defend him in his earliest years. . . . Despite progressive age and arthritis she would visit Rolando every Sunday without fail. . . . By the summer of 1972, however, Mrs. P. had become so disabled by arthritis that she was no longer able to come to the hospital. The cessation of her visits was followed by a severe emotional crisis in her son—two months of grief, pining, depression and rage, and during this period he lost twenty pounds. Mercifully, however, his loss was mitigated by a physiotherapist we had on the staff, a woman who combined the skills of her craft with an exceptionally warm and loving nature. . . . Under this benign and healing influence, Rolando's wound began to heal over—he became calmer and better-humoured, gained weight and slept well.

Unfortunately, at the start of February, his beloved physiotherapist was dismissed from her job. . . . Rolando's first reaction was one of stunned shock, associated with denial and unbelief: . . . his conscious reactions were different—they were exceedingly "sensible," exceedingly "rational." "These things happen," he would say with a nod. "They are very unfortunate, but they can't be helped. . . . No use crying over spilt milk, you know. . . . One has to *carry on* —life goes on regardless . . ." but at a deeper level . . . he had sustained a wound from which he would not recover.

By the middle of February, Rolando was showing severe mental breakdown, compounded of grief, depression, terror, and rage. . . .

Towards the end of February his state changed again, and he moved into a settled and almost inaccessible corpse-like apathy; he became profoundly Parkinsonian once again, but beneath the physiological Parkinsonian mask one could see a worse mask, of hopelessness and despair; he lost his appetite and ceased to eat; he ceased to express any hopes or regrets; he lay awake at nights, with wide-open, dull eyes. It was evident that he was dying, and had lost his will to live. (pp. 116–117)

As Sacks predicted, Rolando died soon after.

2. Both positive and negative events are stressful. Marriage, Christmas, or the birth of a child all are unsettling. (Selye, 1974, made a parallel assumption. He concluded that both positive stress and negative stress provoke very similar responses at some levels.)

3. Stressors have different "values" of seriousness—divorce has a higher value than, say, one's son or daughter leaving home.

4. Stressors are additive. (Being fired twice in one year and the death of a spouse both have the same social readjustment value.)

Some evidence exists that stress, as measured by the scale, can be injurious to your health. Holmes and Rahe (1967) found that as men's and women's SRE scores began to push above 300, 70% of them began to break down and show signs of physical illness. Only 50% of those who scored between 150

Table 13.1   **Holmes-Rahe Social Readjustment Rating Scale**

RANK	LIFE EVENT	MEAN VALUE
1	Death of spouse	100
2	Divorce	73
3	Marital separation	65
4	Jail term	63
5	Death of close family member	63
6	Personal injury or illness	53
7	Marriage	50
8	Fired at work	47
9	Marital reconciliation	45
10	Retirement	45
11	Change in health of family member	44
12	Pregnancy	40
13	Sex difficulties	39
14	Gain of a new family member	39
15	Business readjustment	39
16	Change in financial state	38
17	Death of close friend	37
18	Change to different line of work	36
19	Change in number of arguments with spouse	35
20	Mortgage over $10,000	31
21	Foreclosure of mortgage or loan	30
22	Change in responsibilities at work	29
23	Son or daughter leaving home	29
24	Trouble with in-laws	29
25	Outstanding personal achievement	28
26	Wife begin or stop work	26
27	Begin or end school	26
28	Change in living conditions	25
29	Revision of personal habits	24
30	Trouble with boss	23
31	Change in work hours or conditions	20
32	Change in residence	20
33	Change in schools	20
34	Change in recreation	19
35	Change in church activities	19
36	Change in social activities	18
37	Mortgage or loan less than $10,000	17
38	Change in sleeping habits	16
39	Change in number of family get-togethers	15
40	Change in eating habits	15
41	Vacation	13
42	Christmas	12
43	Minor violations of the law	11

From Holmes & Rahe (1967), p. 216.

and 300 showed such signs. (Similar results were secured by Holmes & Masuda, 1973.) Stressful life events are also associated with depression and suicide (Paykel, 1974). You might wish to calculate your own SRE score to see whether or not stress seems to be associated with your tendency to get colds, spill coffee on your clothes, feel blue, and so forth.

Some researchers have leveled a number of criticisms at the Holmes and Rahe life events scale: (a) The SRE assumes that everybody responds to stressful emotional events in much the same way and that all are equally vulnerable to disease. Yet, people vary enormously in the amount of stress they can handle before they buckle. One person can handle a series of disasters with aplomb. Another person becomes so hassled trying to change lanes on the freeway that she is forced to head for home with a migraine. How well people deal with stress depends on cultural factors, temperament, constitutional factors, and the like. (b) Other critics complain that in the SRE, positive and negative emotional stressors are jumbled together. Yet the two surely have very different effects on health (Lefcourt, Miller, Ware, & Shenk, 1981). In fact, as we noted earlier, even the various negative stressors themselves have different physiological effects (Gellman et al., 1981). (c) Sometimes an absence of change (boredom or the inability to improve things at work) may be upsetting. (d) Worst of all, critics point out that the relationship between stressful life events and disease is actually fairly low (Rabkin & Streuning, 1976).

Because of these difficulties, researchers have tried to develop other life event scales. For example, Irwin Sarason, James Johnson, and Judith Siegel (1978) constructed the Life Experiences Survey. These authors listed 57 life events ("marriage," "death of a spouse," "gaining a new family member") that people might have experienced either recently (in the last 0 to 6 months) or in the recent past (7 months to a year ago.) This time, however, people were asked to indicate whether that change had been negative or positive. Possible alternatives ranged from:

- −3 Extremely negative
- −2 Moderately negative
- −1 Somewhat negative
-   0 No input
- +1 Slightly positive
- +2 Moderately positive
- +3 Extremely positive

On this scale, subjects receive three different scores: how many positive changes they have experienced in the past six months or a year, how many negative changes they have endured, and how many total changes (positive and negative) they have experienced in the same period. The authors proposed that the negative changes would be most tightly linked to emotional stress and to stress-related illnesses.

Some evidence suggests that this scale does a bit better in predicting health. In one study, researchers found that people's scores on the Life Experiences Survey's negative change items predicted how likely they were to fall ill six months after taking the test (Johnson & Sarason, 1979).

Life's Little "Hassles"

Of course, it is not only the big dramatic events that shape our lives. Often, it is the little day-to-day pleasures that sustain us . . . and the irritating little hassles that discourage us, giving us a headache or worse. For this reason, Richard Lazarus and his colleagues set out to develop two scales—the Uplifts Scale and the Hassles Scale.

Allen Kanner, James Coyne, Catherine Schaefer, and Richard Lazarus (1981) define daily uplifts as positive emotional experiences—the joy of love, relief at hearing good news, the pleasure of a night's rest, and so forth. Recall that Hans Selye and Holmes and Rahe assumed that any change—positive or negative—was a change for the worse; presumably, any major change causes stress and puts people at risk. By contrast, Kanner and his colleagues argued that life's little delights might actually buffer people against stress. They speculated that daily uplifts could play an important role in coping—for example, serving as "breathers" from repeated stressful encounters, "sustainers" of coping activity, and "restorers" which help people replenish the resources they have depleted as they try to recover from loss.

Kanner and his colleagues (1981) also developed a scale to measure life's "daily hassles." In the words of the authors:

> *Hassles* are the irritating, frustrating, and distressing demands that to some degree characterize everyday transactions with the environment. They include annoying practical problems such as losing things or traffic jams and fortuitous occurrences such as inclement weather, as well as arguments, disappointments, and financial and family concerns. (p. 3)

The Hassles Scale consists of 117 possible annoyances. Some items from this scale are reproduced in Box 13.2. No dispute has arisen about the role that psychologists thought hassles would have; the more hassles, the more the person should be at risk.

What sorts of things hassle you the most? The ten things that bother most people are indicated in Table 13.2.

Kanner and his colleagues (1981) set out to find out exactly what impact daily uplifts and hassles would have on people's mental and physical health. The authors asked 100 middle-aged men and women to fill out the SRRS Life Events Scale (which we described earlier), the Uplifts and Hassles Scales, and measures of mental and physical health once a month for 10 consecutive months. They used the Bradburn Morale Scale as their index of psychological

BOX 13.2

The Hassles Scale

Directions: Hassles are irritants that can range from minor annoyances to fairly major pressures, problems, or difficulties. They can occur few or many times.

Listed in the center of the following pages are a number of ways in which a person can feel hassled. First, circle the hassles that have happened to you *in the past month.* Then look at the numbers on the right of the item you circled. Indicate by circling a 1, 2, or 3 how SEVERE each of the *circled* hassles has been for you in the past month. If a hassle did not occur in the last month do NOT circle it.

SEVERITY
1. Somewhat severe
2. Moderately severe
3. Extremely severe

1. Misplacing or losing things	1	2	3
2. Inconsiderate smokers	1	2	3
3. Concerns about owing money	1	2	3
4. Too many responsibilities	1	2	3
5. Problems getting along with fellow workers	1	2	3
6. Laid off or out of work	1	2	3
7. Having to wait	1	2	3
8. Inability to express yourself	1	2	3
9. Too many meetings	1	2	3

Kanner, et al. (1989), pp. 24-30

The authors scored the Hassles Scale in two different ways: First, they calculated a measure of how frequently subjects were hassled. They gave subjects one point for each hassle checked. Possible scores ranged from 0–117. Second, they calculated a measure of how intense subjects' hassles were. They simply added up subjects' intensity scores (1, 2, or 3) and divided that total by the total number of hassles subjects had checked. Possible scores ranged from 0 to 3. In both cases, the higher the score, the more hassles subjects were experiencing.

well-being. The Bradburn asks people to assess both how positively and how negatively they are feeling emotionally. They used the Hopkins Symptom Checklist to assess subjects' psychological symptoms.

As they had expected, the authors found that Uplift scores were related to positive emotions; Hassle scores to negative ones. No clear evidence was found as to whether or not Uplifts protected men and women against mental and physical disease. It may be that daily Uplifts have two contradictory effects. In part, positive life events may brighten people's lives and protect them against illness. At the same time, these positive life events may cause

Table 13.2   **The Ten Most Frequent Hassles**

	PERCENTAGE OF TIMES CHECKED
1. Concern about weight	52.4
2. Health of a family member	48.1
3. Rising prices of common goods	43.7
4. Home maintenance	42.8
5. Too many things to do	38.6
6. Misplacing or losing things	38.1
7. Yard work or outside home maintenance	38.1
8. Property, investment, or taxes	37.6
9. Crime	37.1
10. Physical appearance	35.9

problems. (Christmas may mean chaos and trouble as well as the pleasure of a celebration.) The "Uplifts," then, may be a mixed blessing.

The effects of negative life changes and daily hassles are clearer—they cause problems. The authors found that it is not the major life traumas, but the little daily hassles that are the biggest threat to mental and physical health in the long run. In fact, Shelley Taylor (1986) concludes, "It may ultimately emerge that it is the wear and tear of daily life that more reliably predicts illness and psychological well-being than more major but rare life events" (p. 168).

In a later study, researchers asked subjects to complete both the measures they used in the preceding study as well as the Health Status Questionnaire (DeLongis, Coyne, Dakof, Folkman, & Lazarus, 1982). This questionnaire asks people to indicate whether or not they are suffering from a number of specific somatic symptoms (chest pain, back trouble, headaches, and stomach pain), from chronic conditions (such as hypertension), and from problems in working, eating, dressing, and being able to move around. Respondents are also asked whether their energy level is high or low. (Do they have trouble sleeping? Are they worn out at the end of the day?) The authors found results similar to those we have previously reported. It seems that it is often not the major life catastrophes that cause the most serious health problems. Rather, the small, daily emotional hassles seem to grind people down and cause mental and physical health problems.

Emotional Responses to Stress

Now that we have reviewed some of the things that precipitate stress, we are ready for a closer look at the emotional consequences of stress.

PHYSIOLOGICAL RESPONSES

Two major areas of knowledge contribute to our understanding of how people respond physiologically to stress. First, we have reviewed the anatomy, physiology, and functions of the autonomic nervous system in chapters 2 and 4. You might find it helpful to review that material for the current discussion. Second, Hans Selye's discussion of the three stages of response which characterize the general adaptation syndrome provides information as to how people can be expected to respond physiologically to emotional stress.

Selye (1956) proposed that stress aroused the **general adaptation syndrome (GAS),** a complex pattern of bodily responses designed to serve an adaptive function for the organism. The GAS consists of three phases—alarm, resistance, and, eventually, exhaustion.

The first reaction to stress is an alarm reaction. As seen in Figure 13.2, the sympathetic adrenal-medullary system (see chapter 4), swings into action. The person begins to mobilize for an emergency. It matters little whether the emergency is psychological or physical; the person's response is the same. From that portion of the adrenal glands called the adrenal medulla, an outpouring of the hormonal neurotransmitters, epinephrine and norepinephrine,

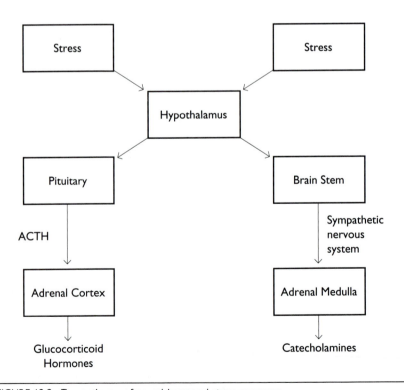

FIGURE 13.2 Two pathways of neural-hormonal stress responses.

begins. At the same time, the sympathetic portion of the ANS swings into action. Heart rate shoots up, breathing quickens, blood sugar levels rise, peripheral blood vessels constrict (subsequently redirecting blood to the brain and deep muscles), digestion is suppressed, and a variety of other effects occur. During the evolution of the species, such alarm mechanisms were essential if our ancestors were to fight or take flight so that they could survive another day. The alarm reaction is relatively short-lived. It generally lasts only a few minutes, depending on how long the stressor persists. At most, it lasts a few hours. Once the stress ends, the other part of the ANS—the parasympathetic nervous system—takes over, and the body begins to rebuild its resources.

Not all stresses end there, however. If the stress continues, people enter a second stage, the resistance stage. Now they begin to deal with the problem in a more specific way. In this stage, people's bodies begin to use a system designed to cope with long-term stress—the so-called hypothalamico-pituitary-adrenocortical system—and to return to normal other systems that are not immediately involved in dealing with the threat (again, see Figure 13.2). Some aspects of the alarm reaction begin to diminish. The person is maximally prepared to resist the stressor, but there is a price to pay.

During the resistance stage, in response to the hypothalamus, in the midst of the brain the anterior portion of the pituitary gland begins to secrete a hormone, ACTH (adrenocorticotrophic hormone). ACTH acts upon the cortex (outer portion) of the adrenal glands, which begin to pour out the glucocorticoid hormones—hydrocorticosone, corticosterone, and cortisol. These hormones have a variety of functions: They help the ANS maintain its sensitivity to epinephrine and norepinephrine. They stimulate the conversion of fats and proteins to sugar, and they promote the storage of glycogen in the liver, which increases the body's supply of energy. Unfortunately, the glucocorticoid hormones have several effects which sometimes work to disadvantage despite their immediate adaptive function: First, cortisol and other adrenal hormones act to reduce swelling, inhibit the formation of antibodies, produce a decrease in white-cell production, lower the effectiveness of lymphoid tissue, and retard the growth of new tissue around a wound. Sometimes, such responses are useful. For example, when people are forced to continue to fight even though their muscles and joints have been injured, the absence of restrictive swelling will promote their movement. Sometimes, however, such responses are counterproductive. For example, when people are trying to stave off infections, the reduction of antibodies and white cells may be serious.

These hormones may cause other problems as well. In the resistance stage, resources are shunted to essential activities and away from nonessential ones. Normally, such a procedure makes a great deal of sense. When fleeing from a tiger, it is not adaptive to pause to pick an appealing berry or to stop for sex. Thus, during the resistance stage, people may lose their appetites and their sexual interest. (Testosterone and sperm production may fall, and menstruation may cease.) In short, people may succeed in holding their own against one kind of threat only to end up thin, sick, and with sexual problems. The generally adaptive GAS may be maladaptive in specific cases.

Finally, if stress continues too long, people may reach a third and final exhaustion stage. The pituitary gland and adrenals have reached their limits and lost their ability to function. As their products decline, aspects of the alarm reaction reappear and then decline as well. The body can no longer adapt. Continued, unrelieved chronic stress may lead to death.

To summarize, when we think of stress in neural-hormonal terms, we realize that two very different systems may be active: The so-called sympathoadredomedullary system (in which the adrenal medulla releases epinephrine and norepinephrine) is especially important when the organism is fighting, fleeing, or engaged in active coping. Cardiovascular, respiratory, glandular, and other responses act together to give the organism the energy to actively cope with the problem (Abrahams, Hilton, & Zbrozyna, 1960).

The other system, the hypothalamico-pituitary-adrenocortical system, comes into play when an organism has to face chronic stress or has no way to cope with a stressor. For example, when an assistant is forced to suffer silently every day while his boss rants, this system may be called into action. In the brain, the hypothalamus stimulates the pituitary gland to secrete ACTH into the bloodstream, in turn stimulating the adrenal cortex to release the steroid hormones. The organism shows heightened attention and sympathetic activation. Heart rate decreases and movement is inhibited (Von Holst, 1972).

One study, by David Anderson and Julij Tosheff (1973), demonstrates these two processes as a function of two experimental conditions. Dogs were first restrained for a period of time before they were given the opportunity to avoid electric shock. During the period of restraint, their heart rates decreased, and their blood pressures increased. Once they were allowed to react, however, their heart rates increased, and their blood pressure levels held steady. Not surprisingly, situations of the first type—when stress is severe but nothing can be done about it, when the only response is to watch and wait—are most likely to provoke stress-related illnesses (Henry & Stephens, 1977).

BEHAVIORAL RESPONSES

More overt, obvious reactions to stress are also common. Actress Bette Midler described her attempts to cope with a movie, *Jinxed*, that was difficult to make, a critical laughingstock, and a box-office catastrophe:

> "I think I had a nervous breakdown" ... Bette was on the skids. "I would just wake up crying," she explains. "I would go to sleep crying. I would get on the phone. I'd cry. I'd read. I'd cry. I'd watch TV, I'd cry. I just couldn't stop crying." How did it end? "I started to party. And I drank so much that I didn't really notice it any more." (Anonymous, 1987, p. 194)

When people find themselves in stressful situations, they must find some way to deal with their problems; they must act. Exactly how a person copes depends, of course, on a variety of factors—how serious the situation is, whether it was anticipated, how long it has persisted, and whether the person can do anything about it.

Raquel Cohen & Frederick Ahearn (1980) found that after a major disaster (such as a tornado or an accident), survivors go through a predictable series of stages. First comes shock, or psychic numbness. Then, survivors seem to go on "automatic pilot." They sift through the rubble and pick up a photograph; they stuff a broken teacup in their pocket. Soon, however, they develop plans and begin to take more effective action. They contact their insurance companies. They go to the bank and try to borrow money to rebuild. They bury their dead. Often, at this point, survivors feel a sense of great accomplishment. Rarely, however, does such elation last. In the next stage, they experience a letdown and begin to mourn their losses. Finally, they start to recover.

Such emotional transitions are not uncommon. For example, in 1987, when the stock market plummeted, brokers reported that at first, an air of excited gaiety accompanied the crash. Brokers worked feverishly to try to turn things around. Later, when their losses sank in, some investors began to react violently. (One investor shot his broker.) Others, defeated, were barely able to get out of bed.

When stress is severe and prolonged, sufferers begin to display a variety of maladaptive behaviors. People begin to act in rigid, stereotyped ways. They simply go through the motions with little thought or feeling. Under stress, people lose their competitive instincts (Henry & Stephens, 1977), and task peformance goes downhill (Weiss & Glazer, 1975). Some people become antisocial or even aggressive. Others begin to self-destruct (even commit suicide). People smoke too much, drink too much, overeat, or lose their appetites (Ritter, Pelzer, & Ritter, 1978). Let us consider some of these typical reactions in more detail.

Overeating

Some people begin to overeat when they are stressed emotionally (Antelman, Rowland, & Fisher, 1976), and there may be a biological basis for this kind of reaction. First, fear and eating stimulate incompatible bodily processes. (In the early days of low-altitude, bumpy air travel, airlines tried giving passengers free meals in hopes that this would reduce their anxiety.) Whereas fear involves the sympathetic system, digestion stimulates the parasympathetic system. The one may tend to cancel out the other. As Selye suggests, "a well-filled stomach and intestine shift a great deal of blood to the abdomen, resulting in a relative decrease in brain circulation which tranquilizes by decreasing mental alertness" (1978, p. 176). However, there is a limit. Although munching a candy bar may alleviate mild stress, it will do nothing to mitigate severe stress. Nonetheless, the habit of overeating may persist, even though it serves no useful function. A second possibility is that because the hypothalamus is involved in both stress reactions (see Figure 13.2) and eating behavior (Almli, 1978), perhaps those who overeat when under stress are exhibiting the dual functions of this brain structure.

Aggression

As we discussed in the earlier chapter on anger, both frustration and pain may breed aggression. Hence, it is not surprising that under stress, people are more snappish and hostile than they would normally be. It is a truism that the woman who gets yelled at by her boss comes home and yells at her family. Other people turn their angry feelings inward. They heap blame on themselves, do penance, or even commit suicide if their painful feelings overwhelm them. In a study of Vietnam veterans suffering from post-traumatic stress syndrome (see chapter 12), John Wilson (1980) found that the veterans' suicide rates were 23% to 33% higher than the national average.

COGNITIVE RESPONSES TO STRESS

One of the oldest "laws" in psychology is the **Yerkes-Dodson principle** (named after Robert Yerkes & John Dodson, 1908). These theorists proposed a curvilinear relationship between motivation (arousal) and performance. If people are completely unmotivated, they are not likely to do well. As they become increasingly motivated, they will perform better and better . . . up to a point. Eventually, however, people reach their limits. After that, it does not help to increase motivation. In fact, the more people's motivation increases, the worse they do. (Think of World Series players who "choke" or "clutch.") How much arousal is too much depends on the task. If a task is extremely simple (such as "pass the salt"), people can perform well even at extremely high levels of motivation. If a task is intricate, complex, or difficult, however (like installing a computer chip), people may begin to fall apart at the first sign of too much stress. Stress researchers have often used the Yerkes-Dodson principle in attempting to predict how stress will affect cognitive functioning and performance (e.g., Malmo, 1975).

Recently George Mandler (1982, 1984) has proposed a cognitive model for understanding stress. His views have been helpful for interpreting the effects of stress on conscious thought. He states that "in the short-term case, stress is associated with high levels of autonomic arousal and, usually, with a negative evaluation of the arousing conditions" (1984, pp. 229–230). Under some conditions, however, stress can sharpen attention to critical events in the environment and improve performance. People under stress, for example, may pay less attention than usual to trivial events and focus on relevant ones. Nevertheless, "the most important effect of stresses on thought processes is that they interfere with the smooth operation of these conscious cogitations and cognitions" (Mandler, 1984, p. 252). The key to the cognitive effect of stress is intensity. Mild stressors may actually improve performance, whereas intense stressors disrupt it.

Why does intense stress often interfere with people's ability to process information? One reason for this, as J. A. Easterbrook (1959) proposed in his cue utilization model, is that the more emotional people are, the fewer cues they are able to utilize. Similarly, Mandler contends that beyond some optimal level, intense stress restricts the range of attention; relevant cues may be missed.

In addition, stress determines where conscious attention will be directed. The degree of disruption depends upon the degree of importance the individual assigns to his or her behavior. If a task is all important, say, avoiding danger itself, stress may well improve performance. If a task is judged to be peripheral, performance will suffer. People's imaginations close down; "thought becomes stereotyped and habitual" (1984, p. 262). If an old solution works, fine; if not, people may have great difficulty learning to think and solve problems in new ways.

Mandler also proposes that stress may affect memory. The critical events that dominated consciousness during stress may be seared into memory, but almost everything else that happened will be lost. Little evidence has yet been gathered in support of this contention, however.

Researchers have documented that stress causes problems in self-esteem, in perception, in planning, and in creative thinking. Stress leads to anxiety and/or depression. Irving Janis (1982) points out that stress may reduce people's ability to envision alternative solutions to problems and that it may produce rigid, stereotyped thought patterns. In one study of 4,000 children, for example, researchers calculated a "stress index," which assessed how many family and physical problems a child had to deal with. They found that the higher a child's stress level, the worse he or she performed on visual discrimination tasks and standard IQ tests (Brown & Rosenbaum, 1983).

To summarize, in the current view of stress, a wide variety of physiological, behavioral, and cognitive effects have been related to exposure to stressors. In general, theorists speculate that the more intense or chronic the exposure, the more widespread and potentially destructive are the effects of stress. In the extreme, it is believed that bodily imbalance or deterioration may be the basis for a host of physical problems—the diseases of stress.

The Diseases of Emotional Stress

The notion that stress can be related to a variety of physical illnesses is a very ancient one. Interestingly, in A.D. 100, Rufus of Ephesus contended that the stress of malarial fever could cure some disorders, including melancholia (depression), asthma, convulsions, and epilepsy (cited in Selye, 1978). More commonly, however, commentators have taken the opposite view: that stress can be injurious to health. Stress has been linked to asthma, arthritis, cancer, diabetes, heart disease, and a wide range of other so-called "psychosomatic disorders." Some researchers believe that stress may underlie 50% to 80% of the disorders for which people consult doctors; these diseases may have no organic basis (Pelletier, 1977).

Clearly, we can touch on the role of stress in the etiology of only a very few diseases. We will focus on one historically important disease category (ulcers); one of current major concern (the cardiovascular disorders); and one in which future breakthroughs seem imminent and exciting (immunity to disease).

ULCERS

As we observed earlier, some of the most important research linking stress to disease was conducted in the laboratory of Hans Selye. In *The Stress of Life*, Selye (1978) describes his early research on the effects of injections of sex hormones and a variety of other stressors on animals. The three major classes of physiological response to the injections were: (a) enlargement of the adrenal cortex (recall the role of this organ in the general adaptation syndrome discussed earlier); (b) shrinking of lymphatic structures involved in immunulogic defenses; and (c) deep, bleeding ulcers in the portion of the digestive system just below the stomach, termed the duodenum. Selye also suggested a link among emotional stress, the production of peptic digestive hormones, and peptic ulcers.

Today, it is widely accepted that stress is implicated in the development of some types of ulcers. In a classic study, Stuart Wolf and Harold Wolff (1947) studied an ulcer patient, Tom, who had been fitted with a gastric fistula (an opening in the stomach which allowed acid to drain from the stomach). This allowed the researchers to record Tom's emotions and to observe how they affected the appearance of the gastric mucosa and acid secretion. When Tom was angry, his stomach acids began to flow, and the mucosa reddened and became irritated. On the other hand, when Tom was depressed and withdrawn, the mucosa became pale, and acid secretion diminished. At the time, these findings provided exciting confirmation that strong emotions may well irritate the lining of the stomach. Since then, evidence has continued to accumulate. For example, more recently it was demonstrated that air-traffic controllers, who have one of the most stressful of occupations, are far more prone to peptic ulcers than are control subjects (Cobb and Rose, 1973).

Nonetheless, in spite of the fact that researchers have been studying these phenomena for almost 50 years, all the answers are still not in. In the first place, despite considerable theoretical speculation, it is still not clear what the mechanisms are by which emotional stressors cause physiological damage in the gastrointestinal system (Wolf, Almy, Bachrach, Spiro, Sturdevant, &

Weiner, 1979). In addition, stress may have a different effect on stress ulcers versus peptic ulcers. Our knowledge of one kind of ulcer may not contribute to our knowledge of the other. Researchers sum up what is known this way: Traumatic, painful, and catastrophic events, such as burns or surgery, clearly induce so-called "stress ulcers"; these are generally the kinds of ulcers seen in animal studies as well. But stress ulcers differ in a number of respects from peptic ulcers of the duodenum or stomach. "In fact, the typical stress ulcer offers only limited support to the concept that peptic ulcer has a significant behavioral component" (Elliott & Eisdorfer, 1982, p. 263). A related observation is that the incidence of peptic ulcer disease appears to be declining in this country, but no one has yet suggested that stressful events are taking a similar course.

This history of research on ulcers is illustrative of the difficulties researchers face in trying to ferret out the role of stress in physical disease. A multitude of factors can potentially be involved in laying the groundwork for stress-related disease.

CARDIOVASCULAR DISEASE

In ancient Egypt and Greece, people believed that the heart was the center of emotional activity. Even today, this idea survives. We warn emotional friends that the "heart is ruling the head." The martyred parent wails, "I'm having a heart attack," when their headstrong children threaten to go their own ways. In a powerful film some years ago, we learned that *The Heart Is a Lonely Hunter* in people who are deaf and mute and who face enormous difficulties in communicating emotionally with others.

By the seventeenth and eighteenth centuries, however, scientists had begun to learn rudiments of how the cardiovascular system functioned. William Harvey described in detail how the heart causes blood to circulate. Stephen Hales found a way to measure blood pressure. It also became increasingly clear that heart rate and blood pressure were correlates of stress. In the 1890s, Cesare Lombroso (cited in Hassett, 1978) argued that blood pressure measurement could assist criminologists in detecting when criminals were lying.

Today, we have a much better understanding of the role that the ANS, the heart, and the blood vessels play in preparing people to cope with emotional stress. The circulatory system's main function, of course, is to pump the blood, which carries oxygen and nutrients to the muscles and organs. In times of stress, blood flow to critical areas in the body increases. This happens in two ways. Heart rate (and thus cardiac output) may increase. In addition, the diameter of the peripheral blood vessels, arterioles, decreases. This ensures that less blood will now flow to peripheral tissues, especially the skin, and that more will flow to where it is needed—the deep muscles and internal organs. (Interestingly, the fact that the skin now contains less blood also helps ensure that if animals are wounded, external bleeding will be reduced—an adaptive feature if you are fighting for your life or running away in fear.)

The sympathetic portion of the ANS directly innervates the peripheral arterioles. The smooth muscles in their walls contract, and the blood vessels narrow. Each person possesses approximately five quarts of blood. Since the blood is forced to rush through the tightly constricted vessels, blood pressure, not surprisingly, rises precipitously. There are, however, some limits on how high blood pressure can soar. Baroreceptors, located in the aortic arch and the carotid sinus (the carotid arteries are the large arteries in the neck that shunt blood to the brain), send signals to the medulla in the brain when pressure becomes too high. The brain, in turn, signals a decrease in heart rate and dilation of the arteries, thus lowering pressure to safe levels.

If animals are preparing to fight or flee, the changes we have described are adaptive. If stress is acute or chronic, however, these same cardiovascular changes may not be so beneficial; they may instead lay the groundwork for disease. Researchers have investigated the link between stress and three major types of cardiovascular diseases: (a) atherosclerosis and its consequences; (b) essential hypertension, or high blood pressure; and (c) arrhythmia of the heartbeat and sudden cardiac death. We will look briefly at the first two categories.

Atherosclerosis

In atherosclerosis, or "hardening of the arteries," the major arteries are blocked by the accumulation of plaques of lipids (cholesterol). If the arteries leading to the heart become sufficiently clogged, the person may experience angina (pain) and/or a myocardial infarction (heart attack). Stress is known to play a role in atherosclerosis. In stress, the sympathoadrenomedullary system facilitates the release of epinephrine and norepinephrine via the process depicted in Figure 13.2. Through a complex sequence of events, especially when there is emotional stress and little physical activity, these hormones increase the tendency for deposition of a particularly dangerous form of lipids on the walls of blood vessels (McCabe & Schneiderman, 1985).

Meyer Friedman and Ray Rosenman (1959) characterize a "Type A" person as one who is very competitive, compulsive, achievement-oriented, and mentally active. This individual is always under pressure, driven by a sense of urgency. Friedman and Rosenman propose that such people will be especially predisposed to atherosclerosis. Research shows that Type A people are much more likely to have a heart attack than are their opposites (Type B people). In fact, Type A men are more susceptible to all types of cardiovascular disease (Haynes & Feinleib, 1980). More recently, some research has suggested that it is level of hostility that makes Type A men especially vulnerable to heart problems (e.g., Thoresen, Telch, & Eagleston, 1981). Other researchers have suggested that this may be because of fundamental differences in the makeup of the parasympathetic division of the ANS in hostile versus nonhostile people, that is, because of a constitutional weakness in the hostile individual which prevents rapid recovery from stressors (Williams, 1989).

One author emphasizes societal pressures "related to the role of men in our society that push them to develop the coronary-prone behavior pattern, and this makes a major contribution to men's higher risk of coronary heart disease" (Waldron, 1976, p. 8). Some speculate that as women begin to fill high-level management positions and the demands on them increase, traditional male-female differences in heart disease and mortality may begin to disappear.

Several kinds of emotional stressors have been found to have a role in precipitating cardiovascular diseases. Case histories linking stress and heart attacks abound. For example, Doris Kearns (a political scientist) reports that President Lyndon Johnson's last years were filled with disappointment. When he retired, he abandoned a lifetime of power and influence. His critics continued to attack his Vietnam policy. When discussing President Nixon's plans to cut off funds for the "Great Society," Johnson compared his programs to a starving woman. "And when she dies," said Johnson, who had had a heart attack in 1955, "I too will die" (Engel, 1977, p. 114). Nixon was inaugurated for a second term on January 20, 1973. The next day he announced plans to completely dismantle Johnson's Great Society. The following day, on January 22, Lyndon Johnson died of a heart attack.

Sometimes the link between disappointment and death is a coincidence. Sometimes, however, severe disappointments may play some role. When people's prestiges decline, when they change jobs or are fired, when their living arrangements change, or when their mates die, the risk of heart attack increases (Kavanagh & Shepart, 1973; Syme, 1984). The loss of a marital partner is especially threatening. Widowhood is tightly linked to increased morbidity and mortality rates (Traupmann & Hatfield, 1981). Widows have an unusually large number of complaints about their health—especially in the first year following bereavement. Surviving spouses are at increased risk for death from a variety of diseases (see Berkman & Syme, 1979). For example, Murray Parkes (1964) found that 213 of 4,486 widowers, 55 years of age and older, died within the first six months of their bereavement. Myocardial infarctions are a leading cause of such deaths, at a rate 40% above the expected level for that age group (Parkes, Benjamin, & Fitzgerald, 1969). After six months, rates gradually fall back to normal. In a recent review of the literature, Selby Jacobs and Adrian Ostfeld (1977) agree that the bereaved are at risk for coronary heart disease and cirrhosis. Initially, men are harder hit than are women by a spouse's death. Men remain at risk for only six months, however, while women stay at risk two years. The degree of hazard for widowed persons is aggravated by preexisting health problems.

The stress of bereavement may elevate the risk of death in several ways. It may lead to depression, and the depressed spouse may then neglect his or her own health (McGlone & Kick, 1978). Stress of bereavement may lead to dysfunctions in neuroendocrine balance and, in turn, to a reduction in immunity to disease (Timiras, 1972). Suzanne Haynes and her colleagues (1978) found that, among older men and women, even marital disagreement could increase a mate's risk for coronary heart disease.

Essential Hypertension

Essential hypertension is high blood pressure without an identifiable organic cause. It is also a silent killer, making it particularly dangerous. People do not feel it when their blood pressure rises—but they do ultimately feel the consequences. Hypertension causes the bodily organs—especially the heart, blood vessels, and kidneys—to deteriorate. As many as 95% of people with the disorder die of its results.

Generally, people whose systolic/diastolic blood pressure is 140/90 or above are considered to have high blood pressure. Traditionally, doctors have measured blood pressure by how high in millimeters mercury rises in the traditional blood pressure instrument, the sphygmomanometer. Today, blood pressure cuffs and equipment can be found in almost every drugstore. Blood pressure is translated into digital terms. The higher number, systolic pressure, is that achieved when the heart contracts. The lower number, diastolic pressure, is that maintained when the heart is midway between contractions. People with essential hypertension may show high pressure on one or both measures.

Blood pressure is a positive function of both cardiac output (the volume of blood moved in the beating of the heart) and resistance of the peripheral blood vessels (described above). The smaller the diameter of the arterioles, the greater the resistance. Systolic pressure generally parallels cardiac output; diastolic pressure generally parallels peripheral resistance. Both measures appear to be a function of the amount of psychological "excitement" and the amount of physical effort. In some stressful situations, the peripheral blood vessels constrict (experienced as "getting cold feet" or "shivering in fright"). When people physically exert themselves, heart rate increases and, hence, so does blood pressure.

Not surprisingly, given what is known about the cardiovascular system, physicians generally assume that emotional stress will increase one's vulnerability to heart disease. However, the best evidence for such a link comes from studies in which the stress was relatively brief, blood pressure elevations were relatively slight, and blood pressure returned to normal fairly quickly. For example, the blood pressure of medical students has been found to rise before an exam (Frankenhauser, 1978); the blood pressure of laboratory rats increases after a startling noise (Farris, Yeakel, & Medkoff, 1945) or multimodal stimulation (Perhach, Ferguson, & McKinney, 1976).

The evidence that chronic stress can produce sustained increases in blood pressure is not so clear. Sometimes rats or monkeys who are in stress-avoidance experiments show permanent blood pressure increases (e.g., Herd, Morse, Kelleher, & Jones, 1969). Rats can, in fact, be trained to increase their already high blood pressure if that helps them to avoid shock. (Benson, Herd, Morse, & Kelleher, 1969). Intriguing data linking stress and hypertension has also come from a series of studies which demonstrated that mice, forced to live in overcrowded conditions, developed not only chronic hypertension but a variety of other cardiovascular disorders (Henry, Stephens, & Santisteban, 1975).

A potpourri of other evidence interlocks in implicating environmental stressors as a cause of hypertension. For example, people in wartime—on the battlefield or under siege—suffer from essential hypertension (Graham, 1945). People who report they have been forced to endure too many of life's "little hassles" (as measured by the Hassles Scale reproduced in Box 13.2) for too long are candidates for hypertension, too (Weiner, 1977). Conversely, the fact that relaxation training (see chapter 14) tends to lower blood pressure implicates relief from chronic stress as a way to control hypertension (Benson, 1975).

Finally, chronic stress may interact with a host of other factors in producing hypertension. Other factors which seem to be important are the existence of a genetic predisposition to hypertension (Friedman & Iwai, 1976), nutrition (especially the amount of sodium in the diet) (Dahl, Heine, & Tassinari, 1965), and the existence of renal infections (Lipman & Shapiro, 1967).

It is part of the cure to wish to be cured.

SENECA

DISEASE AND IMMUNITY

The role of stress in immunity is a relatively new research area. This speciality has the tongue-twisting title of psychoneuroimmunology. It explores the contribution of psychological and neurological factors in immune-system functioning. Until relatively recent times, the medical community assumed that psychological factors had little impact on immunity to disease. The evidence is altering that notion.

It is now clear that emotional stressors can alter a person's vulnerability to infectious diseases and influence chances of recovering from them. It appears that in short or low-level doses, some stressors (such as regular, moderate aerobic exercise) may actually enhance immunity to disease (Haskell, 1985). However, prolonged or severe stress may have a negative impact on the body's immune system. Stress has been found to play a role in respiratory infections (Jacobs, Spelken, Norman, & Anderson, 1970), influenza (Imboden, Canter, & Cluff, 1961), mononucleosis (Greenfield, Roessler, & Crosley, 1959), and strep infections (Meyer & Haggerty, 1962). More recently, psychosocial stress and cancer have been linked. Some researchers, for example, reported that men and women who say they were not close to their parents in childhood are especially prone to developing lung cancer later (Horne & Picard, 1979). Children's relationships with their fathers may be especially important (Thomas, Duzynski, & Shaffer, 1979). Similarly, recent, depressing losses and feelings of helplessness have been correlated with cancer (LeShan, 1966; Schmale & Iker, 1971). Horne and Picard (1979) identified a recent loss, lack of job stability, and absence of future planning to be the foremost predictors of a later diagnosis of cancer.

Such theorizing is exciting, but researchers have not yet pinned down how such processes operate, if in fact they do. Anecdotal evidence that emotional stress and cancer may be linked abounds. Empirical data, however, are sparse. Nonetheless, some progress is being made on understanding the role that psychosocial stress plays in the suppression of immunity to disease. As pointed out by Priscilla Campbell and John Cohen (1985), a wide range of factors alter lymphocyte (including "T-cell") functioning, which is involved in immunity to disease. It has been shown, for example, that mourning a loved one may depress lymphocyte function (Bartrop, Luckhurst, Lazarus, Kiloh, & Penny, 1977). People who indicate on a questionnaire that their life has changed a great deal recently and who are unable to cope show reduced immunity to disease (Greene, Betts, Ochitill, Iker, & Douglas, 1978). In animals, Robert Ader and his colleagues, among others, have shown that immune responses can be learned, indicating the important role of brain processes in immunity (Ader, 1991). The mechanisms for these effects probably involve both nervous system and hormonal processes about which we have much to learn. Such research, nonetheless, suggests the extremely important role that emotions can play in susceptibility to disease. We will be examining other studies relating disease resistance to stress and coping with stress throughout this chapter.

The diseases of the mind are more destructive than those of the body.

CICERO

Coping With Emotional Stress

WHAT IT MEANS "TO COPE"

Richard Lazarus, whose model we reviewed in chapter 3, points out that people face two problems when they are trying to cope with stressful situations: First, they have to deal with the problem itself—to eliminate the stressor or blunt its consequences. They may fight, flee, or engage in a host of other such activities. Second, people have to deal with their own emotional reactions to the stressor, to calm themselves down so that they can cope effectively. Or, if nothing can be done, they must reconcile themselves to the inevitable (Folkman & Lazarus, 1980). A commuter, for example, who encounters irritating traffic tie-ups on the way to work each day, might engage in "problem-focused coping." This person might move closer to work or alter his or her work schedule in order to avoid problems. He/she might also engage in emotion-focused coping or palliation. If selling the house or going to work earlier are not viable options, the person might install a good stereo system in the car and listen to relaxing music or to tapes designed to teach relaxation skills. Such techniques might calm down the commuter.

Lazarus and Folkman (1984) define coping as "constantly changing cognitive and behavior efforts to manage specific external and/or internal demands" (p. 141). Coping is, in short, a process that occurs in given situations (i.e., stressful ones); it involves activity—both overt and cognitive. This means that a person's coping activities will change as the interpretation of the situation and the situation itself changes.

Other theorists have had a great deal to say about the coping techniques Lazarus describes. Psychodynamic and recent cognitive psychologists have been concerned with how people perceive and interpret (appraise) the world, how they think through problems, and how they utilize defense mechanisms (Vaillant, 1977). Learning theorists emphasize survival. They have much to say about how animals learn to avoid threatening events entirely or escape from them once they occur (Miller, 1980).

The views of Lazarus and his colleagues are similar to those of George Mandler. Mandler (1984) argues that coping is essentially the "mastery of stress." The sense of mastery "reduces the deleterious effects of stress and alleviates the subjective sense of emotional disturbance . . . under two conditions." In the first condition, any action "directly related" to the stressor may remove the threat itself. In the second condition, "a situation may be reinterpreted in such a way that the events are not perceived as interrupting any more" (p. 258). Interestingly, Mandler suggests that people may reinterpret both the cognitive and the physiological concomitants of stress (that is, autonomic arousal). In the latter case, the person interprets the arousal (which may still exist) differently and thus has a different reaction to it. For example, a child might rethink his feelings as he retells his experiences on the roller coaster. This time around, he feels exhilaration and joy rather than terror.

In short, people can cope with stress in a variety of ways. How they choose to cope and how successful they will be depends on some of the factors we next discuss.

*Early to bed and early to rise,
Makes a man healthy, wealthy, and wise.*

BENJAMIN FRANKLIN

COPING RESOURCES

In the Lazarus model, a person's first step in coping with stress is primary appraisal, an assessment of the problem. The next step involves secondary appraisal, in which people assess their resources for coping with the stress.

Personality Factors

Researchers have observed that people's personalities may have a profound effect both on whether or not they experience emotional stress in the first place and on how effectively they deal with the stress they do experience. For example, some people are introverts, who thrive when they are by themselves and things are quiet and orderly. They are easily overwhelmed by too many people and too much noise and confusion. Other people are extraverted sensation seekers. They thrive on people, excitement, and the hubbub of daily life. Obviously, different kinds of situations will be stressful to introverts versus extraverts.

People's personalities also determine how effectively they cope with the stress they do experience. For example, people who have high self-esteem (Leventhal & Nerenz, 1982), a lively intelligence (Krasnoff, 1959), a sense of purpose in life (Visotsky, Hamburg, Goss, & Lebovitz, 1961), and a sense of humor (Moody, 1978; Cousins, 1979) are likely to deal relatively well with stress.

In Box 13.3 we describe the work of Suzanne Kobasa (1979), who has studied the personality variable of hardiness. She argues that some people, the hardy, are unusually resilient in perceiving and dealing with stress.

We see, then, that personality factors influence people's primary appraisals—how stressful they judge various events to be. Lazarus and Folkman (1984) list a number of resources that people may take into account in the process of secondary appraisal—when they calculate whether or not they can cope with a potentially stressful situation. The authors have found the following resources to be important: health and energy, a positive attitude, problem-solving skills, social skills, social support, and material resources. Let us consider some of these resources.

> *A merry heart doeth good like a medicine: but a broken spirit drieth the bones.*
> *PROVERBS 17:22 (KING JAMES VERSION)*

Health and Energy

Generally people have more ability to deal effectively with problems when they are feeling well than when they are feeling ill. Nonetheless, if they have to, people may cope surprisingly well even when they are sick or exhausted (Bulman & Wortman, 1977).

BOX 13.3

Hardiness

Suzanne Kobasa, Salvatore Maddi, and Mark Puccetti (1982) studied 137 middle- and upper-level business executives from a large utilities firm. They were trying to find out what made some executives invulnerable to the stresses and strains of executive life. The authors' first step was to find a group of men who had been exposed to severe stress. Then they could attempt to discover what distinguished men who easily survived the onslaught from those who become ill in the face of stress. They did this in the following way: They asked a large sample of executives to complete the Schedule of Life Events. Executives who had experienced many changes in the past three years (such as those who had gotten married, moved to a new city, or received a raise) were classified as the "high-stress group." Those who had been exposed to few life changes were classified as "low stress." Then the executives completed the Seriousness of Illness Survey, a self-report checklist, which asked which of 126 mental and physical symptoms or diseases they were experiencing. Physicians rated the prognosis, duration, degree of discomfort, degree of disability, and threat to life of each of the illnesses, so the researchers knew exactly how serious the executives' health problems were. In addition, the researchers scanned the executives' medical records whenever they could. On the basis of these records, men were placed in one of two groups—those who had recently experienced only minor illnesses (such as colds, sore throats, and the like) versus those who had serious health problems (cancer, heart attacks, and so forth). The authors' next question was a straightforward one: What distinguished the executives who thrived in high-stress conditions from those who quickly became ill? The authors concluded that the healthy but highly stressed executives possessed a personality style that the authors labeled *hardiness.*

Hardy people seemed to possess three general characteristics: (a) an ability to feel deeply committed to the activities of their lives, (b) the belief that they could control or influence events, and (c) the anticipation of change as an exciting challenge to further development.

A sense of commitment versus alienation from self and work: Hardy people possess a sense of purpose. They are committed to their own ideals, to their families and friends, to their jobs, and to American social institutions. Their alienated counterparts are apathetic and detached from life; they find life to be boring, meaningless, and threatening. (Typical of items measuring commitment versus alienation were: "The attempt to know yourself is a waste of effort," "Life is empty and has no meaning for me," or "I wonder why I work at all." A high score on these items indicates a sense of alienation.)

A sense of control versus a feeling of powerlessness: Hardy people feel in control of their lives. They assume that what they imagine, say, and do will have an impact on their lives. Other people feel powerless in the face of overwhelming forces, believing that life is best when it involves no change. They are passive in their interactions with the world. (Typical of items which measure the belief that people can control their own lives were: "People's misfortunes result from the mistakes they make" and "Capable people who fail to become leaders have not taken advantage of their opportunities.")

Viewing change as a challenge versus a threat: Hardy people are curious. They value a life filled with interesting experiences. They view change as the norm rather than as a catastrophe. Change is a chance to learn something about themselves and the world. Other people try to avoid change at all costs. They see the slightest change as a threat. What they care about is security. (Typical of items that measure the extent to which executives valued challenge versus safety, stability, and predictability were:

(continued)

BOX 13.3 *(continued)*

"From each according to his ability; to each according to his needs" and "To achieve freedom from want is a large enough goal for anyone." A high score on these items indicated a dislike of challenge.)

The authors found that hardy people—as a result of their sense of commitment, control, and enthusiasm for challenge—appraise potentially stressful life events more optimistically than do their peers. Therefore, they may take more direct action to find out about impending events, to incorporate change into their life plans, and to learn from their experiences. Consequently, hardy individuals automatically seem to transform potentially stressful events into positive opportunities. They avoid stress and the illness that stressful events can cause by redefining the situation. Hardiness seems to enrich life as well as facilitate survival in the face of stress.

Other researchers have documented that executives who start out with hardy personalities and who are subsequently exposed to stress will have fewer symptoms of illness during the next two years (Kobasa, Maddi, & Kahn, 1982). Hardiness becomes a more and more important determinant of health as the stresses continue to mount.

Positive Beliefs

In the past few years, "new age" philosophies, a sort of a blend of spirituality, superstition, and faith healing, have become extremely faddish. Magazines with names like *New Age; Body Mind, Spirit;* and *Brain/Mind Bulletin* make extravagant claims as to the "power of positive thinking." "Expect a miracle!" they advise. They insist that with clear thinking aided by channeling, crystals, numerology, Tibetan bells, exotic herbal teas, solar energizers, occult books and tape recordings, or the laying on of hands, people can be almost anything they want to be (Fredrick, 1987). Such "mind control" may be marginally helpful if all people need is a little optimism to help them deal more bravely with life. Such philosopies are dangerous if they lead people to spend their energies developing the "right" attitudes and neglect getting the psychiatric and medical help, the education, and the jobs that have a far greater impact on human destiny.

In dismissing the hype, however, we need not go too far. People's attitudes and beliefs do have some effect on how well they can cope with stress. Norman Cousins, best known as the long-time editor of *Saturday Review,* contended that a positive attitude and a large dose of humor were responsible for his surprising recovery from a connective tissue disease and cardiovascular problems (1979, 1983). Conversely, both anecdotal reports (Cannon, 1942) and experimental ones (Richter, 1957) confirm the fact that extreme stress may produce sudden death. It is not unusual for African tribesmen to report that a voodoo curse has doomed them. Even though Western scientists reassure them that such curses can have no effect and hospital teams do their best to save them, these men waste away and die. Evidently, people may be literally frightened to death (Lachman, 1983). The notion that belief systems may have an impact, directly or indirectly, on people's physical health is a popular one; how this process works remains to be determined.

Other researchers have attempted to show a relationship between beliefs about self-efficacy and locus of control, physiological control, and health (Carlson, 1982). A belief in self-efficacy means that people believe they have the ability (efficacy) to deal successfully with the environment (Bandura, 1977). A belief in an internal versus external locus of control means that people believe they have control over the resources they need in the environment (Rotter, 1966). Beliefs about efficacy and control have been tied to physiological self-control (Carlson, 1977) and to a variety of health-related behaviors. For example, Bonnie Strickland (1978) points out that people who differ in perceived locus of control differ in patterns of coping—including how likely they are to seek health information and to try to protect themselves against disease.

Problem-Solving Skills

People must also make a quick calculation of their problem-solving abilities when deciding how they ought to cope with problems. "Problem-solving skills include the ability to search for information, analyze situations for the purpose of identifying the problem in order to generate alternative courses of action, weigh alternative courses of action, weigh alternatives with respect to desired or anticipated outcomes, and select and implement an appropriate plan of action" (Lazarus & Folkman, 1984, p. 162). In turn, people's assessments of their abilities will depend on their intellectual abilities, self-control, and past experience (Rosenbaum, 1980).

Social Skills

Traditionally, IQ tests such as the Wechsler have assessed language and mathematical ability. Recently, psychometricians have begun to recognize the additional importance of social skills in people's successfully dealing with their environments. (For example, we all know brilliant people who are so arrogant, irritating, or insensitive that their intelligence seems to do them little good. Others end up muttering, "I'll be darned if I'll cooperate with that idiot.") "*Social skills* refer to the ability to communicate and behave with others in ways that are socially appropriate and effective" (Lazarus & Folkman, 1984, p. 163). Social skills allow people to shape social situations, cooperate with others, and solve problems. To say that someone has social skills may be to refer either to a general trait or to specific behaviors (McFall, 1982). In any case, people's assessments of their social competence cannot help but influence how comfortable they are in social settings and how adeptly they deal with social difficulties—thus affecting real or perceived stress.

Social Support

In recent years, people have begun to recognize how much of a "safety net" other people provide (Cohen, 1980). Newly divorced men and women joke,

"I'm building up my support system," as they go about the process of making new friends and rebuilding their lives. New employees speak of "networking." People can receive all sorts of support from others—emotional, informational, and practical. If you are ill with the flu, a friend can drop by to cheer you up, bring you some orange juice and a hot meal, and telephone your office to say you won't be able to come in to work. People who have no one to help may find themselves walking shakily to the store on icy sidewalks or trying to negotiate with the drugstore's delivery service when they have a fever of 102 degrees. When social support networks are weak, even mild stressors begin to take a toll; severe stressors may prove impossible to deal with (Nerem, Levesque, & Cornhill, 1980). In old age, as family members and friends die, colleagues forget to call, and social support systems are lost, the elderly become more vulnerable to disease (Holahan & Moos, 1981), and mortality rates increase (Berkman & Syme, 1979). On the other hand, after a divorce or death of a spouse, after unemployment or retirement, or following an illness, if people make new friends, join volunteer groups, or go back to work part-time, thus bulwarking their social support networks, their problems begin to disappear (Pilisuk, 1982).

Material Resources

Money may not be able to buy happiness, but it may make it possible to avoid a host of stressors. Recently, a bright graduate student at the University of Hawaii reviewed his problem. If he could deliver some graphics he had drawn, he'd get paid. But he couldn't deliver them because his car was uninsured. (It is illegal to drive in the state without insurance.) He couldn't get insurance because he was too poor to buy the tires he needed to pass the safety inspection. And on through the cycle. Without money, everything becomes difficult.

Although the oft-cited positive relationship between socioeconomic level and longevity may be complicated by a variety of factors, it is nonetheless well documented (Antanovsky, 1979). Money may be used to buy a house in the safest neighborhood, near the best schools, and allow one to avoid the stress of overcrowded conditions, crime, and helplessness (Selye, 1978). Money can be used to buy houskeeping and gardening services (saving time and energy and avoiding frustration for dual-career families), to secure the best medical treatment, to hire legal assistance, and to modify the physical environment in an infinite variety of stress-reducing ways. It is not surprising that socioeconomic status and health are related.

Pain and Pain Management

Pain is usually considered a sensation or an experience, not an emotion per se. However, its integral role as a cause or result of emotion and its links to physical disorders demands that we consider the role of pain in a chapter on physical health and emotion. People's emotional experiences can often be painful. When people recall a bittersweet love affair, or cringe as they recall the time they made a fool of themselves, or mourn the loss of a child, they experience pain. Conversely, intense physical pain can spark an array of emotions—sadness, remorse, fear, and anger. Let us now review what we know about the links among emotion, pain, and pain management.

Pain has both a psychological and an organic basis. The two may or may not go hand in hand. Sometimes, people will suffer intense pain, even though there is nothing wrong organically. At other times, people will feel fine, even though they have sustained considerable physical damage.

Claudia Wallis (1984) estimates that approximately one-third of the people in the United States experience chronic or recurring pain. The rest of us can empathize with their suffering. We all have experienced short-lived pain at one time or other. We stub our toe, catch our fingers in car doors, cut our fingers slicing potatoes in the kitchen, get splitting headaches when our sisters get into our things, and suffer when the dentist hits a nerve or even when the doctor assures us, "This won't hurt a bit." Given the universality of pain and the inordinate amounts of time, energy, and financial resources committed to its amelioration, we might expect that a pain-free life would be an ideal one.

This is not the case. Pain provides invaluable information; it motivates us to take care of ourselves. Consider the plight of people who are congenitally insensitive to pain. In childhood, their parents are forced to watch them every minute. Such children are fearless and reckless. They casually jump off high walls, get into skirmishes with other children, skin their arms and legs sliding into home plate, and so forth. Since nothing hurts them, nothing stops them. If their parents weren't ever vigilant, these children would surely be killed. By adulthood, such people end up with atypical scars and deformed limbs. In the end, pain-free people do die younger than the average person (Manfredi, Bini, Cruccu, Accornero, Beradelli, & Medolago, 1981). In one case, Richard Sternbach (1968) reports that a young girl who was congenitally insensitive to pain seriously damaged the tip of her tongue through chewing on it. Another time, she leaned on a radiator and severely burned herself. We all know the early warning signs of a heart attack. What might happen if you could not feel pain on your left side? Pain alerts us that we should find some way to avoid or escape from threatening situations. Without such pain, our lives would be touched with far more suffering.

HOW IS PAIN TRANSMITTED TO THE BRAIN?

While the experience of pain is as old as humankind, scientists still know relatively little about it. They have, however, made some advances in understanding the physiology of pain in recent years. It is now evident that there is no single "pain center." The perception of pain may well depend on both central and peripheral structures. Some of the most critical events in pain perception occur before pain messages ever get to the brain.

The eye possesses light receptors, and the ear has receptors for sound. But there seem to be no specific receptors anywhere for pain. Damage to bodily tissues, say, at the skin or in a surface muscle, releases several strong chemicals, including prostaglandins which, in turn, stimulate general nerve endings in the area.

Two kinds of peripheral nerves carry pain signals to the brain. One kind conducts relatively quickly, owing to a covering, or myelin sheath. In general, the myelinated nerves appear to carry "pricking" pain signals—those with fast onset and equally fast offset. The other kind of peripheral nerve is uncovered, or nonmyelinated, and carries the slower "burning" or "dull" kinds of pain. Both kinds of peripheral nerves lead to the spinal cord and eventually to the thalamus of the brain.

In 1965, Ronald Melzack and Patrick Wall (also, Melzack, 1973, 1980) proposed an influential theory, called the **gate control theory of pain**. These researchers argued that nature has devised two very different systems for telegraphing pain messages to the brain. System 1 is designed to alert the brain that the person has suffered or is about to suffer some external injury (say, a child is about to burn her hand on the hot stove). It is important for the brain to be alerted to the impending threat as quickly as possible so that it can send an immediate message to the body to respond (for the child's hand to pull back quickly from the stove). Thus, in System 1, for dealing with external injury, pain messages are telegraphed along the most sensitive and fastest nerve fibers—the largest nerves. Once the brain receives the message, it can close down the pain "gates." The child is free to carry on her activities without being distracted by her painful injuries. (She is able to find her mother and get her hand bandaged.) Doctors who staff battalion hospitals or who work in emergency rooms can testify to the existence of this gating mechanism. Immediately after injury, soldiers and accident victims may feel no pain. Bergland (1985) observes:

> You have probably experienced the protection of the gate-closing mechanism: when the human thumb touches a hot stove or is slammed by a misdirected hammer, the initial pain pulls the hand back by reflex action. Then for a few minutes the gates are closed and the intensity of the pain is greatly diminished. It is later in the day, or in the night, when the gates are open again that the full intensity of the pain is appreciated by the brain. (pp. 77–78)

System 2 works completely differently. It is designed to alert the brain that something is wrong inside the body. (The brain must be alerted that the person has a headache or stomach pain, for example.) In such cases, speed is not of the essence. The message can be carried along the delicate nerve fibers, which fire at a slower rate. Once the signals reach the brain, the brain can begin to deal with what may be a long-term problem (the person may be sick for weeks). Thus, the brain's first step is to open the pain gates. This allows the brain to monitor mild stimuli, that would normally not be perceived, for long periods of time. The person's continuing pain also motivates him or her to rest and repair themselves. Most of the chronic pains that people experience—arthritis, back pain, stomach cramps, and angina, occur because the gates are open.

This, then, is an overview of Melzack and Wall's "gating theory." Let us now consider in a bit more detail what the theory has to say about the *transmission* of pain to the brain. The spinal cord acts as a "gating mechanism," by which pain transmission is modulated before its signals reach the brain. In the theory, both small neural fibers (which carry pain information) and large fibers (which carry primarily touch and pressure information) converge on pain transmission cells in the spinal cord. In addition, cells of a dense area in the nucleus of the spinal cord, called the substantia gelatinosa, control a "gate" for the signals of the large and small fibers to the pain transmission cells. If activity in the large fibers is high relative to activity in the small fibers—that is, if there is substantial pressure or touch stimulation relative to pain stimulation—the substantia gelatinosa cells inhibit the transmission of pain information. In the absence of competing stimulation from the large fibers, pain information is relatively free to pass through the gate to the transmission cells and on to the brain. (It is important to note that the transmission cells are also influenced by neural activity descending from the brain, a point that takes on special significance in later discussion of pain-control mechanisms, cf. Larbig, 1991.)

The evidence for the gate-control model of pain is mixed. In theory, the small, pain fibers adapt to repeated stimulation and fire less frequently, whereas the large pressure and touch fibers do not adapt in this way. In favor of the model is the observation that intermittent rubbing of a sore area, tingly ointments, scratching of an itch, or vibrations from an electric massager, may all relieve pain. Presumably, the small fibers have been overstimulated. They have habituated. They no longer fire at the same rate, thus the pain disappears. Other supportive evidence includes the observation that stimulation of large fibers directly reduces pain (Wall & Sweet, 1967). The theory also makes it clear why acupuncture (intermittent stimulation at the skin) and electrical stimulation at these same points may be effective in pain-control therapy (Raquena, 1986).

On the other hand, not all the evidence supports the gate-control theory. For example, the effects of acupuncture appear to persist long after the stimulation. Why should this be so? Moreover, when the large nerve fibers are damaged, people may experience relatively little pain. Again, this causes problems for the theory. The fact that the large nerve/small nerve ratio has altered suggests, in fact, that pain should be unusually intense (Nathan, 1976). These and other questions have made researchers wonder whether the spinal cord *is* the key to pain control (Nathan & Rudge, 1974). It has led many researchers to other, more central mechanisms for understanding of the neurophysiology and biochemistry of pain.

*T*he history of a soldier's wound beguiles the pain of it.

                                            LAURENCE STERNE

BRAIN MECHANISMS FOR PAIN

One of the primary areas of the brain that has been identified with the experience of pain is the thalamus. Different portions of the thalamus appear to be involved in the experience of touch, temperature, chronic pain, and certain motivational and emotional aspects of pain (Winters, 1985). In addition, neuronal connections between the thalamus and the frontal lobes may be involved in the experience of pain. When these pathways are accidentally damaged or cut surgically, people can still perceive pain, but they may lose a sense of its emotional significance. They are in pain, but they just don't care.

Much of the recent interest in pain has focused on the role of neurotransmitters in pain transmission, with a particular concern for analgesic (pain-reducing) effects which would help in the development of pain-management techniques. (You may recall the discussion of the role of neurotransmitters in emotion in chapter 4.) It is known, for instance, that electrical stimulation of the brain stem produces analgesia in animals that may persist for hours and be as effective as the opiate morphine, a well-known analgesia (Mayer & Liebeskind, 1974). It is thought that the mechanism for this effect are cells that activate inhibitory neurons through the neurotransmitter serotonin. At a subsequent stage, it is believed that an endorphin inhibits transmission from the neurons carrying pain signals to the brain. (The term *endorphin*, short for *endogenous morphine*, refers to an amino acid chain, the effects of which are like those of morphine, but which are produced by the brain itself rather than administered, like morphine.) In short, through neural effects that descend from the brain through the spinal cord, pain may be inhibited.

The evidence for this mechanism is fairly extensive (e.g., Basbaum, Marley, & O'Keefe, 1976; Behbahani & Fields, 1979). It includes the fact that when naloxone—a substance that blocks or reduces the effects of endorphins by preventing binding at receptor sites—is administered, the effects of morphine are reduced, and pain returns. It has been found that naloxone also blocks the effects of electrical stimulation in the brain stem that otherwise would inhibit pain, in short, mimicking the effects of blocking endorphins (Akil, Mayer, & Liebeskind, 1976). Other evidence to support the view that descending information from the brain blocks pain transmission in the spinal cord comes from the observation that both electrical stimulation of the brain stem and morphine are relatively quickly tolerated, that is, they lose their effects unless larger amounts are administered. Moreover, when one of these analgesics loses its effectiveness, so does the other. This suggests the substitutability of one for the other owing to common mechanisms of effect. (Recall at this point that the gate-control theory of Melzack and Wall also provides a mechanism for the influence of descending information upon the gating process.)

It now appears that many neurons in the brain contain receptors for opiates and that the brain produces its own opiates in a form much more powerful than morphine—called *enkaphalins* (that is, "in the head"). It is therefore possible that the brain generates these pain-relieving substances during chronic pain and that morphine is simply a substance that produces some of the same effects.

These brain mechanisms for pain inhibition fit with a number of anecdotal reports and with some research findings about the perplexing nature of pain. For instance, although pain is usually adaptive, in some stressful circumstances it is not. In these situations, people must simply do what they have to do, pain or no pain, if they are to survive. Surprisingly, in such emergency situations, pain sometimes disappears or is muted. Accordingly, it has been found that only 25% of men wounded in war requested relief of pain through medications, whereas 80% of civilians with similar wounds made the request (Beecher, 1956). Also, the pain of wounds are most felt in field hospitals *after* a battle.

It is known that beta-endorphin is stored in the pituitary gland and circulates when the body is in pain. Recall from an earlier discussion that ACTH, the hormone which maintains autonomic reactions during stress, is also released by the pituitary. Interestingly, ACTH is chemically related to beta-endorphin. During times of stress, a built-in mechanism is most likely in place for the relief of any pain that may occur.

As an illustration, imagine a man who is out for a morning jog. While jogging, he falls and seriously twists his foot. An ominous "popping" sound is heard. Owing to a similar experience a few years earlier, he is aware that he has probably broken a bone and, moreover, that he probably has as much as one to two hours virtually without pain to get himself back to his car and to a hospital before the pain will start. Fortunately, his timing is about right— his foot is x-rayed and in a cast before he feels a thing. This suggests that during the exercise, both ACTH and endogenous opiates are released by the brain; these protect the man from pain immediately after the injury. This mechanism is highly adaptive. If the pain had started immediately, he would have been immobilized at a great distance from help. Assuming this analysis is correct, what would you predict as a probable pain scenario if you somehow broke your foot while doing something that was not strenuous—say, getting up from a chair after watching television?

PAIN AND COGNITION

If the central nervous system helps determine whether or not pain will be felt, it suggests that such central events as learned thoughts and beliefs ought to be able to influence pain. Considerable evidence supports this possibility.

Throughout the ages, dramatic accounts have been written of religious mystics who have tried to subdue their bodies. In the Middle Ages, Catholic zealots trekked from town to town in Europe, rhythmically whipping their backs with leather whips, until rivulets of blood flowed down their backs. (Today, their counterparts parade in Spain on feast days.) Fire walkers in India or California stroll on glowing coals. Indian fakirs thrust long pins through their arms, and the like. Clearly, some mechanisms for the central control of the pain experience must be involved to protect such mystics from crying out, fainting, or showing other signs of pain while injuring themselves.

More commonplace examples of "mind over matter" can be found. For example, cultures differ greatly in how they think people should react to pain. Physicians have reported that while some cultural groups tend to exaggerate their suffering, others deny they are feeling much of anything at all, even in medical settings that call for objective reports. The Irish tend to think one ought to be stoic in the face of pain. In public, they accept pain impassively. When no one is around, however, they may cry or groan, suggesting that they have been suffering more than they have admitted. In other cultures, people think it is appropriate to be more expressive. For example, Jewish and Italian patients tend to express fully any pain they may be experiencing. The presence of friends and family may actually intensify their expressions of suffering (Zbrowski, 1969; Sternbach & Tursky, 1965). Similarly, researchers have found that whether or not men in a pain program freely express their discomfort depends on social as well as physical factors. Men express more pain if they think a supportive spouse is watching. They express far less pain if they think their partner will not be sympathetic (Block, 1980). Of course, in such studies, it is hard to be sure that social factors are actually influencing the experience of pain, rather than simply increasing or decreasing patients' willingness to acknowledge their feelings. If cognitive factors can indeed influence the experience of pain, it would have implications for pain management.

METHODS OF PAIN CONTROL

Most people who attempt to control their own pain utilize a combination of techniques. Some techniques are fairly simple. (Parents try to divert a sobbing toddler's attention to a toy. The embarrassed athlete who has skinned her knee may simply act as if she feels no pain.) Other techniques are as advanced as the space-age technology of the pharmaceutical industry. Let us now look at some popular methods of pain control. To simplify our task, we examine the various techniques one by one, although in fact, many of these methods are used in concert. Our tripartite model for the study of emotion will serve us well here.

Physiological Methods

Physicians often use surgical, electrical, or chemical means—most popular by far—to deal with pain. Surgery generally requires the removal of brain tissue or the severing of neurons, especially those transmitting pain signals from the spinal cord. The thalamus has a critical role in the experience of pain. Thus, surgery which removes portions of the thalamus or which severs the neurons that lead to or from the thalamus may dramatically reduce pain. Unfortunately, after surgery the brain often develops new collateral neural pathways, and the pain returns.

As we noted in our discussion of the gate-control theory, pain can sometimes be muted by electrical stimulation, particularly stimulation in the region of the brain stem. One device that pain patients may use is the transcutaneous stimulator (or TENS unit). The TENS unit may be worn on the belt. It delivers intermittent bursts of stimulation to the spinal cord and brain. Such mild shocks have been found to be especially useful in reducing muscle pain. Modern-day acupuncture may also rely on a similar process. The needles are sometimes used to transmit a small electrical charge to the skin, which helps to diminish pain (Xia, Rosenfield, & Huang, 1991).

The most common physiological methods for pain control, however, are chemical. Aspirin is a common pain-control drug. Do you know how it works? Earlier, we described the substance prostaglandins, which is released in the tissues when there is injury or inflammation. Aspirin has anti-inflammatory properties; it inhibits the formation of prostaglandins. Hence, aspirin is often effective in relieving minor pain, especially when (as in arthritis) swelling of tissues is involved.

When pain is more severe, narcotic analgesics may be prescribed. These include morphine, codeine, or various synthetic relatives—such as heroin or demerol. When we recall our discussion of the role of endorphins in natural pain relief, the function of these various drugs becomes apparent—basically, they serve to block neural transmission, especially from the spinal cord.

During surgery, anesthesiologists often utilize general anesthetics. These include barbiturates (such as nembutal), which act on the synapses to reduce neural transmission and, ultimately, produce unconsciousness. General anesthesia involves some risks, however. In addition, sometimes patients must be conscious so that they can help direct the surgeon. In such cases, local anesthetics may be used. These include procaine and novocaine, which alter ion flow in the neurons and thereby inhibit neural impulse generation.

Cognitive and Behavioral Methods of Pain Control

Normally, people are sympathetic when someone comes to them in pain. Parents can kiss a child's finger to make it better. Roommates bring home "chicken soup" (in all its forms) and a magazine for a friend with a cold. We listen with infinite patience to our great uncle's recital of how much he suffered when his blood sample was taken. When people must endure persistent or chronic pain, however, a different strategy may be called for. Professionals may decide to begin to persuade patients to focus less on pain and more on trying to lead a near normal life despite their pain.

Wilbert Evans Fordyce (1977) and the staff of the hospital's Clinical Pain Service at the University of Washington take exactly such a tack. Fordyce argues that chronic pain is not a stimulus but a response. It can be learned, and it can be unlearned. In normal circumstances, when pain threatens, people tend to focus on it, limit their activity, and wait for recovery. When pain is chronic, however, Fordyce believes that people must adopt a less natural strategy. They must learn to be active despite, or because of, their pain. This model underlies Fordyce's innovative and effective pain program.

Like most pain-treatment programs, Fordyce takes a multimodal approach to pain management, emphasizing several different techniques. The first step is to try to wean patients from the drugs on which they have usually become dependent. One problem with pain killers is that patients tend to wait until they are in pain before they take them; then, it is too late. Patients spend some time in intense pain, desperately waiting for the drugs to take effect. Finally they feel their rewarding effects. This "on-demand" routine has some unfortunate behavioral consequences. Patients generally think they need more medication than they really do. (They keep taking pills until the first pill takes effect. They think they need more pills; what they may really need is fewer pills but sooner. Also, the pills may actually reward the patient for having been in pain.) In his pain clinic, Fordyce uses a different procedure: Patients are given a "pain cocktail," a tasty drink containing the patient's medication, at regular times each day, rather than in response to expressions of pain. During the early days and weeks of the program, the drug content of the cocktail is systematically reduced. Eventually, few pain-killing drugs need be included in the cocktail.

Meanwhile, the patients are taught several pain-management techniques: They may be taught to be less expressive of their pain—for example, not to cry, moan, or to recount their pain experiences unless it is absolutely necessary. The staff is instructed to ignore patients when they dwell on their pain but to pay careful attention to them, rewarding them when they talk about other things. Early in treatment, patients may well resent the staff's apparent lack of concern. Later, they simply learn that the pain program is one place where they do not express pain. It simply does not pay off.

Patients are also taught that when pain threatens, they should not sit or lie down until it passes. Instead, they should encourage themselves to engage in pleasurable or profitable activities. The object of this part of the treatment is mainly to alter the quality of the chronic pain patient's life. Fordyce argues that if patients must endure persistent pain, they may as well have as rewarding a life as possible despite the pain. Moreover, for some patients, rewarding activities may be learned in response to pain. Pain then becomes an occasion for *doing* rather than for lying down and suffering. Such pain programs have been quite effective. In a few months, Fordyce's pain patients generally reduce their dependence on pain-killing drugs and resume at least semiactive lives.

Multimodal pain-treatment programs employ a potpourri of other techniques. Some programs combine individual and group therapy, relaxation training and exercise, with vocational counseling and rehabilitation (Sternbach, 1974; Swanson, Floreen, & Swenson, 1976). In studies of patients in such pain-treatment programs, a common finding is that although patients' reported pain does not seem to diminish greatly, they can learn to get by with fewer drugs and their activity levels do increase dramatically. The impact of pain is reduced, and the patient's life is enhanced.

Pain-reduction clinics often teach relaxation techniques. A number of studies have shown relaxation training to be very effective in pain reduction—in fact, more effective than cognitive methods or hypnosis (McAmmond, Davidson, & Kovitz, 1971; Blanchard & Ahles, 1979). Some clinics teach patients biofeedback techniques, which enable them to relax the tension in specific muscle groups or in their muscles generally. Biofeedback for muscle relaxation is especially effective in dealing with specific muscle pain and muscle-tension headaches (e.g., Budzynski, Stoyva, Adler, & Mullaney, 1973) or in simply teaching people to generally handle stressors (Shirley, Burish, & Rowe, 1982; Diaz & Carlson, 1984). Alternatively, some therapists rely heavily on temperature biofeedback training (especially for hand warming) in their treatment of the pain in migraine headaches (Ford, 1982).

Other techniques for pain management include forms of cognitive therapy. Patients are taught to use pleasant imagery to counter the pain experience (Horan & Dellinger, 1974). In the latter study, imagery was found to be more effective than simple distraction in muting pain. Interestingly, in a medical context, the mere knowledge that pain is imminent may alleviate the subsequent pain (Johnson & Rice, 1974), presumably because forewarning allows patients time to develop a strategy for coping with the pain. Perhaps patients may even be able to increase their endorphin production in anticipation of pain.

Finally, another form of cognitive therapy, hypnosis, may be used to alter some patients' consciousnesses and thus dampen pain. Some obstetricians have used hypnosis to alleviate pain in a large percentage of their deliveries, including those requiring Caesarian deliveries (Hilgard & Hilgard, 1974). Some critics, however, point out that generally, less than a third of all individuals are susceptible to hypnosis.

In this chapter, we have explored the interlinkages among emotional stress, pain, and physical health. Researchers are divided about whether positive emotions are stressful; they can agree, however, that negative emotional experiences generate stress. They also agree that emotional stress may provoke accidents, illnesses, and even death. Theories such as Hans Selye's help us understand why emotional stress sparks a series of physiological responses that can lead, eventually, to illness and death. Finally, we described a variety of techniques people can utilize to cope with their emotions, with stress, and with pain in order to maintain mental and physical health.

Summing Up

- Health psychologists are interested in the impact of psychological factors on physical health.

- For more than a century, researchers have recognized that psychological stress may increase people's vulnerability to disease. Hans Selye, the "father of stress," tried to spell out the links between stress, physiological response, and physical illness. Selye believed that all stressors produce the same nonspecific changes. Theorists today realize that different stressors can produce different physiological reactions.

- In daily life, people may encounter physical stressors, social stressors, and personal stressors. Holmes and Rahe's Schedule of Recent Experiences (SRE) assesses how much people's lives have changed in the past 12 months. The Hassles Scale by Lazarus and his colleagues assesses the number of mildly irritating events that occur each day. Both scales are related to physical health.

- Selye (1956) proposed that stress aroused the general adaptation syndrome. The GAS consists of three phases—alarm, resistance, and eventually, exhaustion.

- After a major disaster, survivors go through a predictable series of stages. First comes shock. Then, survivors seem to go on "automatic pilot." Soon, however, they begin to take more effective action. At this point, they feel a sense of accomplishment. Rarely, however, does such elation last. Eventually, they experience a letdown.

- When stress is severe, behavior becomes less adaptive—thinking becomes rigid and stereotyped, and people perform poorly on tasks, act aggressively, and engage in self-destructive behavior—they smoke too much, drink too much, overeat, or lose their appetites. Some commit suicide.

- Mandler points out that stress often causes problems in cognitive processing. It produces selective attention, cue restriction, memory deficits, and problem-solving difficulties.

- The diseases of stress, traditionally referred to as psychosomatic disorders, include a wide range of physiological problems—from asthma to cancer and heart disease. Some researchers believe that as many as 80% of all physician visits owe to diseases that have no organic bases.

- Stress is implicated in some types of ulcers and in such cardiovascular disorders as atherosclerosis (hardening of the arteries) and essential hypertension. Type A people, who are competitive, achievement oriented, and especially those who are hostile are vulnerable to atherosclerosis. Stress may also lead to hypertension (a silent killer) and failure of the immune system.

- Lazarus points out that in order to cope with stress, people must gain control of their own fears and feelings *and* deal with external problems. The appraisal by individuals of their own resources shapes how they will try to deal with stress. Coping resources include health and energy, beliefs, problem-solving skills, social skills, and social support.

- Pain is a source of valuable information. At times, however, it can be maladaptive. For tens of millions of Americans who experience chronic or persistent pain, its control consumes enormous emotional and financial resources.

- Pain is transmitted to the brain from peripheral nerve endings that transmit information via neurons in the spinal cord. The gate-control theory of pain argues that pain may be modulated within the spinal cord. Within the brain, the thalamus and its interconnections to other structures influence the amount of pain a person feels. The brain also produces its own opiates—the endorphins.

- A variety of methods for pain management exists. One can use such physiological techniques as drugs, surgery, or electrical stimulators. Behavioral methods of pain control include relaxation training, biofeedback, vocational counseling and rehabilitation, and the strategic employment of reinforcement. Cognitive therapies emphasize imagery, attention redirection, and consciousness alteration (especially in hypnosis).

14

Dealing With Emotions

Introduction: Sense or Sensibility?

Some Recollections and a Model for Emotional Control

The Cognitive Control of Emotion
Cognitive Therapies
Some Risks of Cognitive Therapies

The Physiological Control of Emotion
Biofeedback
Psychopharmacological "Therapies"

The Behavioral Control of Emotion
Behavioral Therapies for Emotional Control
Relaxation and Meditation
Exercise

Should You Try to Control Your Emotions?
Reasons for Sense *and* Sensibility
Emotions May "Transform" Us
Conclusion

Summing Up

FIGURE 14.1   *Guernica*. Pablo Picasso. Oil on canvas, 11' 5½" x 25' 5¼". On extended loan to the Museum of Modern Art, New York.

Introduction: Sense or Sensibility?

People can deal with their emotions in a variety of ways. Jane Austen, in *Sense and Sensibility*, contrasts the attitudes of two sisters who deal with the loss of love very differently. Marianne, an advocate of sensibility, loves drama and passionate displays of feeling. Her tough-minded sister, Elinor, insists that good sense and control must prevail.

> Marianne would have thought herself very inexcusable had she been able to sleep at all the first night after parting from Willoughby. She would have been ashamed to look her family in the face the next morning, had she not risen from her bed in more need of repose than when she lay down in it. . . . She was awake the whole night, and she wept the greatest part of it. She got up with a headache, was unable to talk, and unwilling to take any nourishment; giving pain every moment at her mother and sisters, and forbidding all attempt at consolation from either. Her sensibility was potent enough!
>
> . . . The evening passed off in the equal indulgence of feeling. She played out every favourite song that she had been used to play to Willoughby, every air in which their voices had been oftenest joined, and sat at the instrument gazing on every line of music that he had written out for her, till her heart was so heavy that no further sadness could be gained; and this nourishment of grief was every day applied.
>
> . . . Such violence of affliction could not be supported forever; it sunk within a few days into a calmer melancholy. (p. 110)

When Elinor's hopes are similarly dashed, her strategy is quite different:

> Elinor's feelings . . . required some trouble and time to subdue. But as it was her determination to subdue it, and to prevent herself from appearing to suffer more than what all her family suffered on his going away, she did not adopt the method so judiciously employed by Marianne, on a similar occasion, to augment and fix her sorrow, by seeking silence, solitude and idleness. Their means were as different as their objects, and equally suited to the advancement of each.
>
> Elinor sat down to her drawing table as soon as he was out of the house, busily employed herself the whole day, neither sought nor avoided the mention of his name, appeared to interest herself almost as ever in the general concerns of the family, and if, by this conduct, she did not lessen her own grief, it was at least prevented from unnecessary increase, and her mother and sisters were spared much solicitude on her account. (pp. 128–129)

In this chapter, we look at the possibilities that exist for dealing with emotions with "sense" *and* "sensibility." Our aim is not to persuade people to rely on one technique versus another in dealing with emotions, but to look at the advantages and disadvantages of a variety of techniques for controlling, enjoying, and experiencing emotions.

Some Recollections and a Model for Emotional Control

We have now come full circle; we are ready to to look back at some of the concepts we have touched on at various places throughout our discussions and see what they have to tell us about emotional management.

French philosopher René Descartes was one of the first to formally theorize about emotion. Recall that Descartes made a sharp distinction between mind and body. Reason was enshrined; bodily manifestations of the emotions were seen as animal-like and primitive—a useless and dangerous collection of impulses. Luckily, mankind possessed reason, so people could control the bestial side of their nature. In Descartes' view, man not only *could* control emotions, he *should* exercise this control, and thereby distinguish himself from the rest of the animal kingdom.

For example, from the Victorian era through today, the fictional detective Sherlock Holmes has been admired for his rational approach to life. In this quotation, we see that even in love, Holmes could not be seduced into feeling.

> To Sherlock Holmes she is always *the* woman.... It was not that he felt any emotion akin to love for Irene Adler. All emotions, and that one particularly, were abhorrent to his cold, precise but admirably balanced mind. He was, I take it, the most perfect reasoning and observing machine that the world has seen; but as a lover, he would have placed himself in a false position. He never spoke of the softer passions, save with a gibe and a sneer. They were admirable things for the observer—excellent for drawing the veil from men's motives and actions. But for the trained reasoner to admit such intrusions into his own delicate and finely adjusted temperament was to introduce a distracting factor which might throw a doubt upon all his mental results. Grit in a sensitive instrument, or a crack in one of his own high-power lenses, would not be more disturbing than a strong emotion in a nature such as his. And yet there was ... one woman to him.... (Doyle, 1974, p. 161)

Even today, people often echo Descartes' sentiments. We hear such expressions as "I was really mad, but I managed to control myself," "I know you are suffering, but try to get a hold on yourself," and "She loved him so much that she could hardly restrain herself." Self-help books, cassette tapes, and popular magazines are filled with advice on how to control mood (see Box 14.1).

Readers can also recollect what more recent theorists have had to say about emotion and emotional control. For example, Richard Lazarus (1977) emphasized the coping process in his model of emotion. He observed that people can try to deal with emotional situations in two ways—they can try to calm themselves, or they can try to eliminate the problem itself. His model reminds us that people may choose to deal with emotion by using different means at different times, and in different situations.

In her novel *Female Friends,* Fay Weldon (1974) provides a compendium of the way women deal with terror and resentment:

BOX 14.1

Mood Control

In an issue of *Self* magazine (November, 1981), several writers suggest techniques for "how to think your way through emotional slosh," "how to control your moods," "four mood-wrenching traps to avoid," what to do when moods "bite into job success" or "climb into your bed," and the like. In successive articles, readers are given tips on the relationship between moods and diet, emotions and body chemistry, sexual synchrony, stress, boredom, and a host of causes and cures of emotional distress.

The message is clear—control your moods and become a happier, healthier, more successful, sexier person.

Suggestions for means to control one's emotions vary, but one list (based on the work of Daniel Goleman) suggests a breakdown depending upon whether a person experiences emotions primarily physically (a "body symptom" type), mentally (a "mind" type), or both. (See Figure 14.2, below.) Which type are you?

MOOD CHANGERS

In picking your relaxer, fit the activity you choose to your mood-symptom responses. Be sure to choose only activities you'll really enjoy. If your mood changer isn't fun, you'll find it worsens your tension instead of relieving it.

BODY RELAXERS	MIND RELAXERS	MIND/BODY RELAXERS
• If you are a Body symptom type, these sorts of physical activities are for you: Dancing Jogging Bike riding Calesthenics Aerobics Swimming laps Jumping rope A vigorous walk Heavy garden work Housecleaning Deep-muscle relaxation Hatha yoga A hot bath or sauna A massage	• If you are a Mind type, try mental activities like: Doing crossword puzzles Reading a book or magazine Seeing a movie Playing chess or *Scrabble* Meditating Sewing or crocheting Cooking gourmet meals Talking to a close friend Keeping a diary Undertaking an absorbing, creative project, like painting, pottery or making a Japanese rock garden	• If you are a Mind/Body type, you'll benefit from competitive sports such as: Tennis Racquetball Volleyball Or try any combination of activities from the lists for the Mind and Body types

FIGURE 14.2 Mood changers. Bennett, 1981, p. 70.

Marjorie, Grace and me. How do we recover from the spasms of terror and resentment which assail us, in our marriages and in our lives? . . . When we cry and sob and slam doors and know we have been cheated, and are betrayed, are exploited and misunderstood, and that our lives are ruined, and we are helpless. When we walk alone in the night planning murder, suicide, adultery, revenge—and go home to bed and rise red-eyed in the morning, to continue as before.

. . . Marjorie recovers her spirits by getting ill. She frightens herself with palpitations, slipped discs, stomach cramp. Snaps out of anxiety and depression and into hypochondria. . . . Life continues.

Grace takes direct action. She throws out the offending lover, has hysterics, attempts to strangle, breaks up her home, makes obscene phone calls, issues another writ, calms down. . . . Life continues.

> I, Chloe, move in another tradition. . . . Mine is the mainstream, I suspect, of female action and reaction—in which neglected wives apply for jobs as home helps, divorcees go out cleaning, rejected mothers start playgroups, unhappy daughters leave home and take jobs abroad as au pairs.
>
> Rub and scrub distress away, hands in soap suds, scooping out the sink-waste, wiping infants' noses, the neck bowed beneath the yoke of unnecessary domestic drudgery, pain in the back already starting, unwilling joints seizing up with arthritis. Life continues. (pp. 143–144)

Finally, readers might recollect that throughout this text, we have used a tripartite definition of emotion. We have defined emotion as a predisposition to respond experientially, physiologically, and behaviorally to certain events. This broad definition allowed us to synthesize what theorists from a variety of perspectives have speculated and learned about emotion. A tripartite view of emotion also implies that people should be able to learn a trio of techniques—experiential (cognitive), physiological, and behavioral—for controlling emotion. In fact, since, theoretically, each of the three aspects of emotion can be dealt with in three ways, conceivably people could go about altering their emotional reactions in nine distinctively different ways. They could cope with their physiological reactions via certain behaviors, with their cognitions via certain physiological measures, with their emotional behaviors via other cognitive strategies, and so forth. (See if you can think of examples of all nine categories.)

In this chapter, we discuss some of the most effective ways people can cope with their emotions. Some of the techniques we consider require the assistance of a psychotherapist or support group; some can be used by people on their own. We also consider a few popular techniques for dealing with emotion (namely, the use of alcohol and drugs) that people persist in using despite their dangerous side effects.

One caveat: Any brief review of the vast research literature on emotional control is bound to oversimplify, distort, and neglect some critically important research. Obviously, when people do try to deal with their emotions in the day-to-day world, things are far more complex than our model may imply. For example, although we review techniques one by one, people rarely use any single technique in isolation. Usually, when problems become serious enough, people try to deal with their feelings by employing every technique at their disposal. However, the model at least gives us a starting point for sorting things out.

Of course, the question also arises as to whether people *should* try to keep a tight rein on their feelings. In Western societies, people have a predilection for trying to control everything; they often carry the desire for control of their emotions too far. Then, too, there is a question as to how much people really *can* disguise or manage their feelings. They are often less effective at hiding and controlling their emotional intentions than they think they are.

Nonetheless, these reservations aside, let us review what psychologists now know about emotional control. Imagine that you are upset at the way your life has been going. You are eager to calm things down so that you can begin to figure out how to solve your problems, or at least learn to live with them. What is the best way to deal with your emotions?

The Cognitive Control of Emotion

One of the three major ways people try to deal with their feelings is to focus on controlling their emotional experiences, modifying their thoughts, beliefs, attitudes, ways of looking at their problems, and all the myriad of cognitions that accompany emotional states. The overwrought may try to calm themselves down enough so that they can instigate effective action. They may puzzle through alternative actions and reasons for their feelings. Or, if the situation is hopeless, they may concentrate on reconciling themselves to the irreconcilable. Cognitive approaches are becoming extremely popular.

American pop psychology would have us believe that "thinking makes it so." True devotees of positive thinking vastly exaggerate the possibilities of feeling what you want to feel, of being what you want to be. Bestsellers include such self-help books as *The Maximum Mind, When Bad Things Happen to Good People, Pulling Your Own Strings, Out On A Limb,* or *Reclaimed Power* that emphasize the power of positive thinking, believing, or visualization in securing an emotionally controlled—and therefore "better"—life. Realistic constraints are waved away with a dismissive gesture. The cover of *Rapid Relief from Emotional Distress* promises:

> If you're depressed, lonely, guilty, anxious, or otherwise emotionally ill, you don't have to be. The first step is to realize that you *do* have power over the way you feel. The second step is to master the simple, no-nonsense, five-minute strategies. . . .
> Rapid Cognitive Therapy has been tested and proven effective. It is based on the ACT Formula: Accept your current reality. Choose to create what you want in your life. Take action to create it. (Emery & Campbell, 1986)

In some measure, then, the American tradition of believing in "mind over matter" and American optimism have combined to provide the soil which has nourished cognitive psychology. Clinicians have developed several cognitively based therapies which teach people to use cognitive techniques to shape emotion and behavior. Let us now review some of these techniques. They may not be as all-powerful as the New Age mythology or new cognitive-control advocates contend, but they are effective in varying degrees.

COGNITIVE THERAPIES

Since the early 1900s, intellectuals have been aware of psychodynamic principles, defense mechanisms, and the fact that people employ a variety of unconscious strategies to shield themselves from pain and anxiety. More recently, cognitive theorists have begun to explore the conscious cognitive techniques people can use to mask or alter their feelings. Several cognitive therapy programs are especially popular. These include Albert Ellis's (1962) Rational-Emotive Therapy (RET), Donald Meichenbaum's (1977, 1985) Stress Inoculation Training, and Aaron Beck's (1976) cognitive therapy. Let us now consider these three forms of cognitive therapy as applied to the emotions in some detail.

Rational-Emotive Therapy (RET)

Albert Ellis (1962) contends that it is mankind's facility with language, the very thing that makes people most human, that most often gets them into emotional trouble. Ellis's argument runs like this:

People are biologically "wired" so that they often draw the wrong conclusions from their own experiences. People naturally think irrationally. (For example, children must often do precisely what their parents say, "or else." There is no reason why a 50-year-old son should be terrified of his aging mother's disapproval. But he often is. His biology has led him to overgeneralize.) Then, too, Ellis suggests, society, religion, schools, and the media preach a great deal of utter nonsense. To make things worse, people keep repeating these irrational ideas to themselves. Ellis adds that "man is not only a highly suggestible but an unusually *auto*suggestible animal. And probably the main reason, I would insist, why he *continues* to believe most of the arrant nonsense with which he is indoctrinated during his childhood is not merely the influence of human laws of mental inertia ... but because he very actively and energetically keeps verbally reindoctrinating himself with his early-acquired hogwash" (pp. 19–20). People carry on running conversations with themselves, assuring themselves, for instance, that certain things are terrible, when at their worst they are merely inconvenient or annoying.

Ellis lists eight irrational but commonly held ideas that make people miserable:

1. *I must be loved and approved by virtually everyone.* In fact, Ellis argues, although it is convenient to be liked, in no way can people guarantee that others will like them. It is simply illogical to expect to be liked by everyone.

2. *I am a worthwhile person only if I am thoroughly competent, adequate, and successful.* The most important goal in a person's life should be to be happy and to fulfill his or her own nature. A focus on external approval sidetracks people and causes them to compete with others.

3. *Certain people are bad, wicked, or villainous and should be severely punished for their villainy.* People's biosocial makeup (heredity and training) make people fallible; it is only realistic to expect them to sometimes make mistakes. People can try to become better than they are; they will never become perfect.

4. *If things don't go the way I want them to, it will be a catastrophe.* In fact, the world is not always rational, fair, or kind; it is simply as it is. People's impossible expectations make them unnecessarily miserable and make it difficult for them to take effective action.

5. *People have no real ability to shape their own emotional experiences—whether they are happy or sad depends on what other people do and what happens in the world.* People are free to choose whether to allow other people to upset them.

6. *If something is dangerous or frightening, people should be terribly concerned about it and should keep dwelling on the possibility of its happening.* Once you have taken all reasonable precautions, worrying buys you nothing.

7. *It is easier to avoid life's responsibilities and difficulties than to face them.* Ellis is certainly not a believer in passive accommodation. He argues that though it might seem easier to avoid trouble in the short run, in the long run, one does better by facing one's problems.

8. *People need someone to take care of them.* For Ellis, the costs of dependency are too high. One gives up one's freedom to gain security and ends up without even security.

Ellis points out that all four fundamental life operations—sensing, thinking, emoting, and moving—are interlinked. If people sense something (e.g., see a stick), they tend at the same time to think about it (to recall what other people, or they themselves, have said about sticks), to have some feelings about it (like or dislike), and to do something about it (pick it up or throw it away). While we may have little feeling about sticks, the four fundamental life operations have a great deal to suggest with respect to our relations with other people and emotional events. Thinking, language, attitudes, and beliefs are critically important in determining how people perceive events, how they respond to them emotionally, and how they try to deal with them. Emotional disturbances persist if irrational thinking persists.

Ellis quotes Epictetus to make his point: "Men are disturbed not by things, but by the views which they take of them" (1962, p. 54). By contrast, people who think rationally are happier, more emotionally stable, and more effective than those who do not.

Change is possible. Rational-emotive therapy is designed to teach people to perceive, think, and act rationally. The therapist is an active, directive teacher who first demonstrates to clients the nature of their irrational cognitions and explains how such incorrect ideas cause emotional disturbance. The therapist then tries to teach clients to replace their illogical ideas (to *un*think, *un*say, and *un*do) with more logical and rational views of the world. In this process, the therapist uses encouragement, persuasion, reason, instruction, confrontation, homework assignments, and any other instructional device that may work to alter a client's cognitions. In Ellis's words:

> The effective therapist should continually keep unmasking his patient's past, and, especially, his present illogical thinking or self-defeating verbalizations by (a)

bringing them forcefully to his attention or consciousness; (b) showing him how they are causing and maintaining his disturbance and unhappiness; (c) demonstrating exactly what the illogical links in his internalized sentences are; and (d) teaching him how to re-think, challenge, contradict, and reverbalize these (and other similar) sentences so that his internalized thoughts become more logical and efficient. (Ellis, 1962, pp. 58–59)

Few people ever consult an orthodox rational-emotive therapist. Nonetheless, many of Ellis's suggestions can be tried on a day-by-day basis. Try this yourself. Think of an emotional reaction that you have that you would like to tone down. Perhaps you become so frightened during exams that your mind goes blank. You'd like to calm down. What do you think about when you're in a state of panic? "Oh Lord. What if the professor asks something from the book I couldn't get at the library? I'll die!" "The professor will think I'm a fool. I won't be able to look her in the eye. She'll think I'm an idiot." "My parents will kill me." To follow Ellis's model, tell yourself to "quit it." Are you thinking logically or are you catastrophizing? In this case, the latter. Try to make a more honest assessment of the status quo. You have studied reasonably hard and will probably pass. Even if you do poorly on the exam, it will *not* be the end of the world. You can study even harder next time. If your parents get upset, that is their problem, not yours. You did study, after all. If your father shouts at you, it may be unpleasant, but you will survive. The chances are that someday you will graduate anyway. By thinking logically, students can reduce their anxiety about exams to a more manageable level and perhaps ensure that they can at least reveal what they do know on the exam. We might call this procedure "self-RET" (self-rational-emotive therapy).

Ellis's approach has been harshly criticized. Some critics contend that his theory is neither a theory nor a model, but merely a set of "loosely related and poorly elucidated propositions" (Mahoney, 1977). Others complain that Ellis strives for "a total alteration in the client's philosophy of life," whereas alternative cognitive therapies respect the client's personality, values, and little quirks, and try merely to "alter dysfunctional beliefs or attitudes" (Garfield & Bergin, 1986, p. 445). Research has not yet shown whether RET or the other cognitive approaches are relatively more effective. Finally, still other critics complain that RET errs in overemphasizing logical, left-brain control—and undervaluing right-brain processes. They contend that RET is extreme, teaching people to intellectualize and rationalize at the expense of honest emotional experience. Nevertheless, the method is effective for some people.

Meichenbaum's Stress-Inoculation Training

Donald Meichenbaum's (1977) approach to cognitive therapy—termed *cognitive-behavior modification*—emphasizes the client's thinking, or "inner dialogue," and its relationship to a person's emotional and other activities. Meichenbaum (1977) suggests that "how one responds to stress in large part is influenced by how one appraises the stressor, or to what he attributes the arousal he feels, and how he assesses his ability to cope" (p. 202).

These processes of appraisal, attribution, and assessment are a function of the person's self-statements: "[O]ne function of internal dialogue in changing affect, thought, and behavior is to *influence the client's attentional and appraisal processes*" (Meichenbaum, 1977, pp. 206–207). For example, through cognitive therapy, subjects can change their labeling of emotional arousal:

> Sweaty palms, increased heart and respiratory rates, muscular tension, now became "allies," cues to use the coping techniques for which they had been trained.... This shift in cognitions in itself may mediate a shift in autonomic functioning. The present theory postulates that it is not the physiological arousal *per se* that is debilitating but rather what the client says to himself about that arousal that determines his eventual reaction. (1977, pp. 207–208)

Meichenbaum tries to "inoculate" students against stress. The immunization procedure consists of three graded phases—the educational phase, the rehearsal phase, and the application phase. In the first, educational, phase, clients are given a logical framework which enables them to (a) interpret their emotional response to stress and (b) to develop a general plan for dealing with problems. For example, they might be told that their first response to stress may well be panic, but that it is only a first response. A sensible person can proceed to deal with problems by using an orderly sequence of responses: preparation, confrontation, coping, and, eventually, self-reinforcement for coping.

In the rehearsal phase, clients are taught a variety of coping strategies. They practice taking direct action—learning how to reshape difficult situations or escape from them. They are taught cognitive coping techniques. For example, they are told to become alert when they start making negative self-statements (e.g., "You moron, what are you doing?") and to use such statements as a cue for making positive self-statements that can ease coping (for example, "Relax, you're in control; take a slow, deep breath"; "When fear comes, just pause"; "You can develop a plan to deal with the problem, you'll see"; or "It worked; you did it.").

In the third, critical, application training phase, clients are exposed to stressors in the clinic. They are expected to deal with them by utilizing the techniques they have just practiced. If they fail, the therapist can model appropriate coping strategies. Luckily, the techniques clients practice in the clinic do seem to generalize to real-life situations. "It was quite common for clients in the stress-inoculation group to report spontaneously that they had successfully applied their new coping skills in other stressful situations, including final exams and dental visits.... The change in attitude seemed to encourage clients to initiate confrontations with real-life problems" (Meichenbaum, 1977, p. 159).

Beck's Cognitive Therapy

Cognitive therapy is based on the simple premise that people's thoughts and self-statements are important in molding their behavior. If we analyze the cognitions of people with emotional problems and discover how they perceive and interpret the world, their feelings and behavior now make a great deal of sense. Aaron Beck (1976) observes: "The role of anticipations in influencing feelings and action is far more dominant than is generally recognized" (pp. 40–41). In addition, a given culture or family may teach children rules—which they internalize—which simply do not work. Such nonfunctional rules may produce emotional disorders. Beck (1976) notes: "When rules are discordant with reality or are applied excessively or arbitrarily, they are likely to produce psychological or interpersonal problems" (p. 52).

The premise that the meanings people assign to events determines how they will respond emotionally "forms the core of the cognitive model of emotions and emotional disorders" (Beck, 1976, p. 52). Among these disorders:

1. Beck maintains that depression is initiated by the experience of real or perceived loss. In especially severe cases, the depressed assume that their problems are their own fault but that they can do nothing to change things. In such cases, the depressed sometimes become so desperate they commit suicide (see chapter 8).
2. Anxiety is initiated by real or perceived threats to control (or by actual loss of control). The anxious may become paralyzed by fear—alert to the smallest danger, obsessively worrying about what might be. They overgeneralize—terrorized by a host of mythical dragons. Their bodies may remain in a permanent state of "physiological readiness" to the detriment of their health, or they may simply fail to function (see chapter 12).
3. Cognitive distortions produce both the sorts of hysterical reactions Freud discussed (such as when a neurotic person becomes paralyzed) and psychosomatic disorders. For example, the person who continually catastrophizes may put an unbearable strain on the body. Eventually, the cognitions may produce a problem with no organic basis (in the case of hysteria) or even a real physical breakdown (in the case of the stress-related disorders; see chapter 13).

Beck's (1976) cognitive therapy aims at "correcting faulty conceptions and self-signals" that underlie psychological distress (p. 214). Therapists go through a series of steps in cognitive therapy. The first step is to persuade clients that the therapist is trustworthy and credible. This takes a bit of time; they have to get to know each other. Then the therapist can point out that "a perception of reality is not the same as reality itself.... [The client's] interpretations of his sensory input are dependent on inherently fallible cognitive processes" (pp. 233–234). As therapists get to know their clients, they learn just what sorts of self-defeating ideas the clients have. This is easier than it seems, since certain standard self-defeating ideas are associated with various emotional problems. For example, the depressed tend to blame themselves for things that go wrong and to see themselves, others, and the world in bleak ways. Clients are encouraged to adopt a new, more realistic view of reality. Then they can begin to deal with their problems in more practical ways. In short, Beck, like most other cognitive therapists, believes that cognitive reorganization is the first step in effecting behavior change.

SOME RISKS OF COGNITIVE THERAPIES

The philosophy of the cognitive theorists of today harkens back to Descartes' mind-body dualism of the 1600s. Whereas Ellis emphasizes the causal impact of "illogical ideas" in generating unpleasant emotions, Meichenbaum focuses more upon the gradual development of cognitive (as well as behavioral) methods for dealing with stressors. Beck, in his turn, focuses especially on self-defeating ideas and their role in depression. Together, the cognitive therapists, in the Cartesian tradition, propose that what one thinks or believes has a profound impact on what one feels and does.

An overreliance on a cognitive approach presents some dangers: Some theorists exaggerate the role of human conscious experience and the power of reason in changing things. A few disciples of cognitive theory seem to possess an almost magical belief that, somehow, thoughts can automatically become reality. Moreover, some critics of the cognitive approach argue that an overemphasis on reason and logic can lead people to be insensitive to the yeasty fermentation of a rich emotional life. Such a philosophy, critics contend, leads people to overvalue reason and ignore the fact that people are necessarily emotional beings—expressing their emotions in a variety of ways (see Box 14.2).

While cognitive techniques such as those developed by Ellis, Meichenbaum, or Beck are useful, people often wish to supplement them with other methods.

The Physiological Control of Emotion

In this section, we outline some physiological techniques for reducing painful emotions to manageable proportions by focusing on two popular techniques: the use of biofeedback techniques and the use of psychoactive drugs. In biofeedback, clients are given a visual or auditory "print-out" of their physiological state. They learn how to keep their level of ANS activity within normal bounds. When people take over-the-counter drugs, prescription drugs, or "street drugs," they are attempting primarily to control CNS processes and certain ANS responses, and thereby gain control over their emotions. (Of course, surgical and electrical methods for altering brain activity

BOX 14.2 _____

The Costs of Denying Emotion

The following example illustrates both the prevalence of the belief that it is the rational man (like Mr. Spock of the television series "Star Trek," who has no emotions) who is most to be trusted, and the disastrous consequences of such a view. In the 1980s, Bud McFarlane was President Reagan's National Security advisor. He was the essence of the rational man, who kept a stiff upper lip under difficult circumstances. President Reagan reportedly instructed McFarlane to go to Iran, meet with leaders there, and work out a deal to exchange arms for hostages. The trip was a disaster. When rumors of the trip spread, a scandal erupted, and McFarlane attempted suicide. Newspapers reported:

> At the White House the morning after Mr. McFarlane's attempted suicide, none of his former colleagues brought it up at the staff meeting.
> "We were embarrassed by it," said one Presidential aide. "Washington is a town that does not know how to deal with emotion."
> Another former official agreed. "This city doesn't know what to do with a howl of pain," he said. "That message doesn't come through on people's beepers." (Dowd, 1987, p. 9)

also exist. Since the average person rarely relies on such techniques, however, we do not discuss them here.)

BIOFEEDBACK

In the 1960s, revolutionary advances took place in electronics. For the first time, researchers could begin to apply well-known principles of physiology and learning to teach people how to relax, control stress reactions, and manage stress-related diseases. These new biofeedback methods were instantly heralded as a panacea for a variety of stress-related and other physical ills. Now, after more than two decades of research, certain biofeedback principles and technology have found a solid place in the armamentaria of health psychology and behavioral medicine, while a few of the more extravagant claims for its effectiveness have been debunked. We can speak from experience about the benefits and difficulties of using biofeedback techniques to treat various disorders.

The Rationale of Biofeedback

Biofeedback refers to monitoring of a biological response plus providing information regarding the reaction (feedback) to the person who is monitored in order to change the response. Biofeedback includes several steps. First, electrodes are affixed to the surface of the skin. They pick up those minute changes in, say, heart rate, facial muscle tension, or skin conductance that accompany emotion. Second, these tiny reactions are then electronically magnified (sometimes more than a million times) by the biofeedback instrument.

Third, the amplified signals are displayed so that clients can observe the moment-to-moment changes in their bodily activity. Such displays take a variety of forms: A light may change from a cool blue to a fiery red as surface body temperature rises. A sound may increase in pitch as the heartbeat races. A number may appear on a television screen as skin conductance decreases. In a laboratory, people may be told to "listen to your facial muscles and notice how the pitch of the tone goes down as you relax." People are thus given instantaneous feedback about their biological processes, much as we have more natural and direct feedback, say, from our stomachs when we have a cramp or from our joints to tell us the positions of our arms or legs.

Educators have long understood that if students are to learn a skill, they must have feedback as to how they are doing. In one sense, feedback is information. It enables people to fine-tune their reactions so that they can more and more closely approximate an ideal standard. Feedback may also provide reinforcement. It tells people they have successfully modified their behavior—one must be motivated to make use of feedback. In either case, whether feedback provides information or reinforcement, or both, it is hard to imagine how people could learn anything—from word processing, to catching a flyball, to flying an airplane—without continuous or regular feedback.

By the 1970s, researchers had discovered that with biofeedback, people are capable of learning to control physiological responses that researchers once thought no one could control—including brain-wave activity (Lubar & Bahler, 1976) and such autonomic responses as heart rate (Lang & Twentyman, 1974), blood pressure (Fey & Lindholm, 1975), hand temperature (Mullinix, Norton, Hack, & Fishman, 1978), and muscle tension in places (such as the forehead) where people are usually not even aware of whether they are tense or relaxed (Carlson, 1977). (Interestingly, the very term *autonomic response* means "automatic"—*not* susceptible to conscious control. The fact of control through biofeedback challenges our traditional conceptions of the nature of the autonomic and central nervous systems outlined in chapter 4.)

How can biofeedback help a person deal with emotion? In chapter 13, we found that intense or chronic stress produces sustained ANS sympathetic activity, which may eventually lead to physical illness and exhaustion. How might biofeedback short-circuit this process? In one scenario, theorists have proposed that people can learn to use stress as a cue. When people find themselves becoming emotionally aroused, they can learn to relax and thereby neutralize their ANS sympathetic activity, thus preserving their health. If the heart, the blood vessels, and certain muscles are involved in an emotional response, then learning to quiet the heart, dilate the blood vessels, and relax the muscles should counter the stress reaction; relaxation and stress responses are antagonistic reactions. (Although the principles appear different, the outcome has much in common with the counterconditioning process we outlined in our discussion of anxiety management in chapter 12.)

The Uses of Biofeedback

Despite the clear rationale for its use, today the evidence as to the effectiveness of biofeedback is oddly mixed. On one hand is the fact that practitioners use such techniques clinically to successfully treat a wide array of stress-related disorders (White & Tursky, 1982). A large and enthusiastic group, including clinical psychologists, medical doctors, nurses, physical therapists, social workers, and others, testify to the effectiveness of biofeedback methods and publish their clinical findings. (More than 2,000 health specialists are members nationally of the Association for Applied Psychophysiology and Biofeedback.) On the other hand, in carefully controlled laboratory experiments, attempts to determine how effective biofeedback techniques are in altering specific physiological responses have not always yielded clear-cut results (e.g., Carlson et al., 1983). Nevertheless, let us consider one recent study that did demonstrate the effectiveness of biofeedback methods in modifying physiological responses.

Health psychologists often teach patients to control emotions such as anxiety by using biofeedback techniques to relax facial and other muscles. For example, patients can try to keep anxiety in check by learning to relax their *frontalis* (forehead) muscles, which, in turn, appears to lower the tension of other facial muscles as well. Given what you know about the link between emotion and the facial musculature, this procedure would seem to make sense. In a recent study, John Carlson and a co-worker, Carmen Diaz, attempted to assess the effectiveness of a trio of biofeedback and relaxation techniques in teaching undergraduates to control their fear when they thought they would have to endure electric shock (Diaz & Carlson, 1984). The first group of subjects was given relaxation training of the facial muscles using electromyographic (EMG) biofeedback—in this case, a tone correlated with tension in the forehead muscles. A second group of subjects was given more general EMG biofeedback relaxation training, using muscles of the facial area, neck, and forearm. The third group was given the general EMG biofeedback training plus a tape to use at home on which were additional relaxation instructions. The fourth group (control) was not given relaxation training. Finally, all the subjects were brought to the laboratory for an "anxiety test" session in which they were told that a they would receive a warning signal that might be followed by a painful electric shock. Which group did best in keeping anxiety under control when face-to-face with danger? The authors found that the first three groups had learned something—as assessed by facial muscle tension. All the groups trained in biofeedback relaxation techniques were physiologically far calmer than were the control subjects. In some ways, however, the third group, who had learned biofeedback techniques in the laboratory and practiced relaxation at home, learned the most. These subjects' skin-conductance levels were the lowest of those in any group. (You will recall that skin conductance often provides a measure of sympathetic arousal.) This study, then, did not demonstrate that there is something magical about bio-feedback techniques. Subjects who had learned biofeedback techniques and took a relaxation tape home did better than those who only learned biofeed-back techniques. This study does demonstrate, however, that people can prof-itably utilize a variety of techniques—traditional relaxation procedures and biofeedback methods—in concert to control stress (see also Shirley, Burish, & Rowe, 1982).

One physiological technique people can use, then, for controlling emo-tions is biofeedback. Even more popular, however, are psychopharmacological techniques for controlling emotions. These include such things as antide-pressants and anti-anxiety drugs and such attempts at self-medication as al-cohol and "street" drugs.

PSYCHOPHARMACOLOGICAL "THERAPIES"

We begin by examining three major kinds of psychoactive drugs that are used to deal with emotional disorders: the antidepressants (some of which were discussed in chapter 8), lithium, and the antianxiety drugs.

Antidepressants

When people are merely sad, mildly depressed, or are briefly depressed for reasons that are obvious, antidepressants are not recommended. If these people feel they need therapy, psychotherapy is the treatment of choice. (If psycho-therapy can be completely effective, in and of itself, in helping people reshape their lives, there is no need to resort to drugs which have unpleasant side effects.) Even when patients are suffering from moderate to severe depression, some studies have shown that psychotherapy is as effective as drug therapy (Murphy, Simons, Wetzel, & Lustman, 1984). However, when depression is unusually severe, persistent, and of unclear cause, antidepressant drug therapy (or drug therapy supplemented with psychotherapy) is indicated. Psychiatrists may prescribe two types of antidepressants: the tricyclic compounds and the monoamine oxidase inhibitors (MAOIs). Some of the more common names for these drugs are shown in Table 14.1.

Both the tricyclics and the MAOIs are prescription drugs. Both come in tablet form, and both have been found useful in dealing with depression. About 70% of depressed patients can benefit from antidepressant drugs (Mor-ris & Beck, 1974). The tricyclics have been shown to alleviate sadness, hope-lessness, helplessness, worthlessness, guilt, loss of appetite, and diminished libido. In a given patient, the drugs may alleviate only one or two symptoms. People's reactions to drugs are quite variable. When the more popular tricyclic agents are not effective, the MAO inhibitors may be prescribed. Both the tricyclics and the MAOIs have been shown to be effective in dealing with depression, with no consistent advantage to either (Blain & Prien, 1983; Klein, Gittleman, Quitkin, & Rifkin, 1980).

Table 14.1	**Common Names for Antidepressants**

GENERIC NAME	BRAND NAME
Tricyclics	
Amitriptyline	Amitid, Amitril, Elavil
Desipramine	Norpramin, Pertofrane
Doxepin	Adapin, Sinequan
Imipramine	Antipress, Tofranil
Nortriptyline	Aventyl, Pamelor
Protriptyline	Vivactil
Fluoxetine	Prozac
MAO Inhibitors	
Isocarboxazid	Marplan
Phenelzine	Nardil
Tranylcypromine	Parnate

Price & Lynne (1986), p. 589

In 1987, a new antidepressant called Prozac entered the market. It soon became America's most widely prescribed antidepressant. Prozac works on the same principle as the tricyclics, with one difference. Both the tricyclics and MAOIs work by bolstering the action of serotonin and norepinephrine, those neurotransmitters that carry through the nervous system the impulses associated with pleasure and excitement, respectively. The tricyclics work by blocking reabsorption of these messengers by the nerve cells; the MAOIs work by interfering with enzymes that break down these messengers. Prozac works on the same principle as the tricyclics, but focuses exclusively on serotonin rather than on both serotonin and norepinephrine. (It keeps serotonin in the system by blocking its reabsorption.) However, very recent controversy has surfaced indicating the possibility of increased suicidal tendencies among some Prozac users.

The antidepressants as a group have some disadvantages. Typically, they must be taken for two or more weeks before their effects are felt. During this time, seriously depressed people may despair and even commit suicide. (In such cases, although clinicians tend to use it as a last resort, electroconvulsive shock therapy, which has more immediate effects, may be prescribed; see chapter 8.) A second problem with antidepressants is that they have serious side effects. Tricyclic antidepressants can make some patients irritable; other side effects include heart palpitations, rashes, weight gain, and fatigue (Schatzberg & Cole, 1986). Since many people tend to disapprove of drug use, prescription or not, such side effects may help to account for the fact that depressives show relatively high levels of noncompliance—failure to take their prescriptions. About a fifth of all depressed patients refuse drugs, and half those who initially agree later drop out because of their attitudes toward drugs, or because of specific side effects, or both (Blackwell, 1982). On occasion, patients experience acute manic episodes or schizophrenic symptoms after taking antidepressants if they have suffered from such problems previously (Flaherty, 1979).

Lithium

Manic episodes and manic-depression—now known as bipolar affective disorder—may be effectively treated with lithium, one of the "great successes" of psychiatry. Lithium is usually prescribed to control manic episodes. It is generally effective in 70% to 80% of such cases (Baldessarini, 1977). Lithium is also prescribed for depressed patients who do not respond to the tricyclics or the MAOIs. In one study, lithium elevated depressives' moods for up to eight days (Henninger, Charney, & Sternberg, 1983). In Table 14.2, we see that lithium also seems to have dramatic effects on how likely mania or depression is to recur. As one might expect, placebos are quite ineffective in preventing a return of symptoms.

Again, like other drugs, lithium has unfortunate side effects. The most common minor side effects are tremor, rashes, and weight gain. If not carefully administered, it may become a toxin, producing serious complications.

Anti-Anxiety Drugs

Sometimes people suffer from intense anxiety. They can feel their hearts pound, they gasp for breath, their stomachs churn, and the like. Under such conditions, psychiatrists or physicians may try to dampen their symptoms with prescription drugs. The most frequently used anti-anxiety drugs are the major tranquilizers, the minor tranquilizers, barbiturates, beta blockers, and the antidepressants (see Table 14.3).

Table 14.2   **Rate of Recurrence of Mania or Depression in Bipolar Manic-Depressives With Lithium Versus Placebo**

TREATMENT	PERCENTAGE OF RELAPSE*	
	Manic Patients	**Depressive Patients**
Lithium	29.2	36.5
Placebo	70.8	63.5
"Protection Ratio" (Placebo: Lithium)	2.4	1.7

*Data are mean percent of patients relapsing in the manic or depressive phases of bipolar affective illnesses during treatment with lithium or placebo. Lithium appears to produce a protective effect against both types of relapse. It is interesting to note that manic patients were most likely to have a relapse regardless of the treatment.
Source: Baldessarini (1977), p. 63

Table 14.3   **Anti-Anxiety Drugs**

COMPOUND	GENERIC NAME	TRADE NAME	SIDE EFFECTS
Major Tranquilizers			
	Chlorpromazine	Largactil	Drowsiness. Possible
	Haloperidol	Serenace	neurological problems.
	Thioradazine	Melleril	
Minor Tranquilizers			
Benzodiazepines	Chlordiazepoxidase	Librium	Drowsiness. Some people
	Diazepam	Valium	become addicted with
	Nitrazepam	Mogadon	long-term usage.
Barbiturates	Amobarbital	Amytal	Drowsiness. An overdose
	Sodium amobarbital	Sodium amytal	can produce very serious
	Sodium secobarbital	Seconal	complications.
Beta-blockers	Metoprolol	Lopressor	Slower pulse rate. Can
	Propranolol	Inderal	cause wheezing in asthma sufferers.
Tricyclic antidepressants	Imipramine	Tofranil	Constipation, dry mouth, drowsiness, others.

The major tranquilizers are generally used to treat severe emotional disorders. Occasionally, they are prescribed for anxiety and tension. The drugs do have side effects: People feel drowsy, and a few may feel shaky as well.

Almost 15% of Americans have taken a minor tranquilizer in times of intense stress. They do reduce anxiety. Unfortunately, they also have both short-term side effects (drowsiness) and long-term side effects: Taking too many tranquilizers for too long can produce staggering movements, slurred speech, and double-vision. People can also become dependent on them.

Barbiturates induce relaxation by day and sleep at night. Their use is restricted, however, because of their toxicity following overdose.

Beta blockers relieve two of the most common symptoms of anxiety—palpitations and shakiness. (They are so named for their neurotransmitter action, which results in a slower heart rate.) They do have some undesirable side effects. Because they suppress adrenaline production, they may cause faintness and wheezing, particularly in asthma suffers.

A recent development in psychopharmacology has been the development of antidepressants, especially the tricyclics, which are effective in treating panic attacks. We see then, that a variety of prescription drugs can be used to treat anxiety.

Alcohol and Marijuana

Some people deal with their emotional problems by drinking. For example, film star Rock Hudson generally tried to calm himself down by repressing or denying his emotions. When his emotions did break through, he would drink, in a desperate effort to hide his painful feelings. See Box 14.3.

At first, it may seem odd to include two popular "street drugs," alcohol and marijuana, in a list of pharmaceutical agents used for emotion control. For that reason, we loosely labeled this section "Psychopharmacological 'Therapies.'" Yet it is easy to see that such drugs are often used as a form of self-medication. In fact, alcohol is used far more frequently than all of the drugs we have discussed to this point.

Alcohol has been used for celebrations and to promote relaxation throughout history. Even in ancient times, over 8,000 years ago, records indicate that people drank mead, brewed from honey. Today, people refer to having a "drink after work" and use the phrase "to relax" in almost the same breath. Alcohol is classified as a depressant, but in fact it appears to have biphasic effects: At low doses, it depresses central nervous functioning in those areas of the brain that normally suppress emotion and behavior; it removes inhibitions. As the inhibitions against expressing emotions crumble, drinkers generally become happier, but may become unusually sentimental, maudlin, or furious as well. Alcohol also may enhance feelings of relaxation and serve as a release from the cares of the day. These effects are more pronounced

BOX 14.3 _____

Emotional Problems and Drinking

Rock was developing a mental discipline that would allow him to control his thoughts and feelings. He did not call it "positive thinking," he never showed any interest in psychology or religion, but he had an extraordinary ability to wipe from his mind any matter that disturbed him. He could will a problem out of his thoughts so that it no longer existed. George Nader says, "That was how he handled problems—he tuned them out. He had a marvelous way of deciding that something simply had not happened." If a friend gave Rock unpleasant news, a veil would drop over his face. He would fall silent, or change the subject, or go on talking as if he had heard nothing. (p. 119)

The years Rock spent with Jack were a happy period, years of good times and stability and very little friction. Jack says he and Rock never argued or had a disagreement. "If some

thing bothered him, he wouldn't talk about it, he would get silent, but his silence was more devastating than anyone's anger because you could feel it all through the house." Joy would ask Jack, "What's wrong. Did you do something?"

"No, did you?" Jack said.

"Maybe it's something at the studio," Joy said, and they would sit down in the kitchen and try to figure it out. (p. 152)

Jack found it startling and "a little scary" that Rock could shut it off so fast. "I got a feeling of great loneliness in him. He had learned to protect himself too well; he never shared his life with anybody." (Hudson & Davidson, 1986, p. 218)

When repression failed, Rock resorted to alcohol.

when blood alcohol is rising than when it is falling. Thus, people are tempted to keep on drinking once they begin. Soon they reach the point (.01% to .10% blood alcohol) at which alcohol begins to cause depression, sedation, and impairment of cognitive functioning and motor activity (see Figure 14.3).

While people who drink only a little now and then may derive some pleasure and relaxation from alcohol, alcoholics drink far too much. Johns Hopkins University Hospital in Baltimore, Maryland, uses test questions such as these to decide when a person is an alcoholic:

SYMPTOMS OF ALCOHOLISM
Are You An Alcoholic?

To answer this question ask yourself the following questions and answer them as honestly as you can.

	Yes	No
1. Do you lose time from work due to drinking?	☐	☐
2. Is drinking making your home life unhappy?	☐	☐
3. Do you drink because you are shy with other people?	☐	☐
4. Is drinking affecting your reputation?	☐	☐
5. Have you ever felt remorse after drinking?	☐	☐
6. Have you ever gotten into financial difficulties as a result of drinking?	☐	☐
7. Do you turn to lower companions and an inferior environment when drinking?	☐	☐
8. Does your drinking make you careless of your family's welfare?	☐	☐
9. Has your ambition decreased since drinking?	☐	☐
10. Do you crave a drink at a definite time daily?	☐	☐
11. Do you want a drink the next morning?	☐	☐
12. Does drinking cause you to have difficulty sleeping?	☐	☐
13. Has your efficiency decreased since drinking?	☐	☐
14. Is drinking jeopardizing your job or business?	☐	☐
15. Do you drink to escape from worries or trouble?	☐	☐
16. Do you drink alone?	☐	☐
17. Have you ever had a complete loss of memory as a result of drinking?	☐	☐
18. Has your physician ever treated you for drinking?	☐	☐
19. Do you drink to build up your self-confidence?	☐	☐
20. Have you ever been to a hospital or institution on account of drinking?	☐	☐

If you have answered YES to any one of the questions, there is a definite warning that **You may be alcoholic.**

If you have answered YES to any two, the chances are that you ARE AN ALCOHOLIC.

If you answered YES to three or more, you are definitely an alcoholic.

(The above Test Questions are used by Johns Hopkins University Hospital, Baltimore, MD. in deciding whether or not a patient is alcoholic. By permission of Johns Hopkins University.)

Alcohol Levels in the Blood

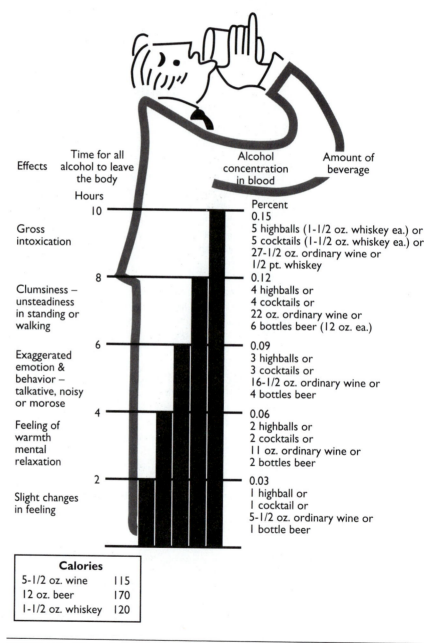

Effects	Time for all alcohol to leave the body		Alcohol concentration in blood	Amount of beverage
	Hours		Percent	
Gross intoxication	10		0.15	5 highballs (1-1/2 oz. whiskey ea.) or 5 cocktails (1-1/2 oz. whiskey ea.) or 27-1/2 oz. ordinary wine or 1/2 pt. whiskey
Clumsiness — unsteadiness in standing or walking	8		0.12	4 highballs or 4 cocktails or 22 oz. ordinary wine or 6 bottles beer (12 oz. ea.)
Exaggerated emotion & behavior — talkative, noisy or morose	6		0.09	3 highballs or 3 cocktails or 16-1/2 oz. ordinary wine or 4 bottles beer
Feeling of warmth mental relaxation	4		0.06	2 highballs or 2 cocktails or 11 oz. ordinary wine or 2 bottles beer
Slight changes in feeling	2		0.03	1 highball or 1 cocktail or 5-1/2 oz. ordinary wine or 1 bottle beer

Calories	
5-1/2 oz. wine	115
12 oz. beer	170
1-1/2 oz. whiskey	120

FIGURE 14.3 Effects of alcohol consumption on emotion and behavior. Reprinted with permission of Time: The Weekly News Magazine. Copyright Time, Inc., 1974.

When people begin to drink heavily, the costs—to themselves, to their families, and to society—skyrocket. One alcoholic described his feelings this way:

> It was as if I started out in a hole—a little lower than everyone else. I lacked self-respect, love, the ability to do much of anything right. So I drank. But each drink I took was like taking a step deeper. Pretty soon I was so far down—I was lacking in love, so needy, I had done so many unforgivable things to so many people—I looked up and saw the hole was now so deep and the sides so slippery, that I knew I could never climb out.

Some approaches to the control of the problems of alcohol are extreme. Carry Nation's was fanatical (see Box 14.4). Nonetheless, alcoholics and their families do face some serious problems, and serious measures are often necessary. An alcoholic's life expectancy is shortened by 10 to 12 years (DeLuca, 1980). It has been estimated that 55% of automobile accidents and 50% of all homicides involve alcohol abuse (Kinney & Leaton, 1982). Alcoholic mothers are likely to give birth to children suffering from a variety of birth defects. In 1985–1986, 37% of high school seniors reported a drinking bout of 5 or more drinks within two weeks of the survey (*The New York Times,* Dec. 24, 1987, p. Y7). Society spends at least $13 billion per year attempting to deal with alcohol-related diseases (Mayer, 1983). In short, alcohol is an extraordinarily common but expensive technique for emotional control.

Recently, authors such as Claudia Black (1982) in *It Will Never Happen to Me!* and Robin Norwood (1985) in *Women Who Love Too Much*, and groups such as Al-Anon (which helps alcoholics' families) have begun to observe the personality changes that occur in alcoholics' families—in their husbands, wives, and children—as they try futilely to accommodate themselves to the relentless demands of alcoholics. Meanwhile, the alcoholics inevitably deny that anything is wrong with them.

According to Norwood (1985) (who bases her conclusions on her clinical experience, the folklore of Alcoholics Anonymous and Al-Anon, and a bit of research) children of alcoholics—especially women—tend to develop some typical characteristics for dealing with those they love:

1. Typically, you come from a dysfunctional home in which your emotional needs were not met.
2. Having received little real nurturing yourself, you try to fill this unmet need vicariously by becoming a care-giver, especially to men who appear in some way needy.
3. Because you were never able to change your parent(s) into the warm, loving caretaker(s) you longed for, you respond deeply to the familiar type of emotionally unavailable man whom you can again try to change, through your love.
4. Terrified of abandonment, you will do anything to keep a relationship from dissolving.

BOX 14.4

Carry Nation's Proscriptions

Carry Nation (1905) was a Christian evangelist— part dedicated social reformer and part eccentric. She traveled from town to town, and when she spotted a tavern, she hurled rocks at its mirrors and windows, smashed its liquor bottles, and attempted to close it down. Her relentless efforts led, in part, to Prohibition. In her autobiography, she reprints a statement by the Council of the British Medical Temperance Association, the American Medical Temperance Association, and the Society of Medical Abstainers in Germany, detailing the evils of drink:

> In view of the terrible evils which have resulted from the consumption of alcohol . . . we, members of the medical profession, feel it to be our duty, as being in some sense the guardians of the public health, to speak plainly about the nature of alcohol, and of the injury to the individual and the danger to the community which arise from the prevalent use of intoxicating liquors as beverages.
>
> We think that it ought to be known that:

1. Experiments have demonstrated that even a small quantity of alcoholic liquor, either immediately or after a short time, prevents mental action, and interferes with the functions of the cells and tissues of the body, impairing self-control by producing other markedly injurious effects. Hence alcohol must be regarded as a poison, and ought not to be classed among foods.

2. Observation establishes the fact that a moderate use of alcoholic liquors, continued over a number of years, produces a gradual deterioration of the tissues of the body, and hastens the changes which old age brings, thus increasing the average liability to disease (especially to infectious disease), and shortening the duration of life.

3. Total abstainers, other conditions being similar, can perform more work, possess greater powers of endurance, have on the average less sickness, and recover more quickly than non-abstainers, especially from infectious diseases, while altogether escape diseases specially caused by alcohol.

4. All the bodily functions of a man, as of every other animal, are best performed in the absence of alcohol, and any supposed experience to the contrary is founded on delusion, a result of the action of alcohol on the nerve centers.

5. Further, alcohol tends to produce in the offspring of drinkers an unstable nervous system, lowering them mentally, morally and physically. Thus deterioration of the race threatens us, and this is likely to be greatly accelerated by the alarming increase of drinking among women, who have hitherto been little addicted to this vice. Since the mothers of the coming generation are thus involved the importance and danger of this increase cannot be exaggerated.

> Seeing, then, that the common use of alcoholic beverages is always and everywhere followed, sooner or later, by moral, physical and social results of most serious and threatening character, and that it is the cause, direct or indirect, of a very large proportion of the poverty, suffering, vice, crime, lunacy, disease and death, not only in the case of those who take such beverages, but in the case of others who are unavoidably associated with them, we feel warranted, nay, compelled to urge the general adoption of total abstinence from all intoxicating liquors as beverages, as the surest, simplest, and quickest method of removing the evils which necessarily result from their use. Such a course is not only universally safe, but it is also natural.
>
> We believe that such an era of health, happiness and prosperity would be inaugurated thereby that many of the social problems of the present age would be solved. (pp. 186–187)

5. Almost nothing is too much trouble, takes too much time, or is too expensive if it will "help" the man you are involved with.
6. Accustomed to lack of love in personal relationships, you are willing to wait, hope, and try harder to please.
7. You are willing to take far more than 50 percent of the responsibility, guilt, and blame in any relationship.
8. Your self-esteem is critically low, and deep inside you do not believe you deserve to be happy. Rather, you believe you must earn the right to enjoy life.
9. You have a desperate need to control your men and your relationships, having experienced little security in childhood. You mask your efforts to control people and situations as "being helpful".
10. In a relationship, you are much more in touch with your dream of how it could be than with the reality of your situation.
11. You are addicted to men and to emotional pain.
12. You may be predisposed emotionally and often biochemically to becoming addicted to drugs, alcohol, and/or certain foods, particularly sugary ones.
13. Being drawn to people with problems that need fixing, or by being enmeshed in situations that are chaotic, uncertain, and emotionally painful, you avoid focusing on your responsibility to yourself.
14. You may have a tendency toward episodes of depression, which you try to forestall through the excitement provided by an unstable relationship.
15. You are not attracted to men who are kind, stable, reliable, and interested in you. You find such "nice" men boring. (pp. 10–11)

Alcohol is likely to cause problems, then, for not only the alcoholic, but his or her family and co-dependents, friends, co-workers, and society as well.

One "street drug" that has been commonly used in the United States since the 1960s for mood alteration is marijuana. It is usually smoked but may be chewed or used as an ingredient in foods; for example, the *Alice B. Toklas Cookbook* (1960) lists "a bunch of *canobis satova* or *canibus sativa*" [*sic*] as one ingredient to include in brownies (p. 274). Subjectively, marijuana's short-term effects (which are due to its major ingredient, THC, or tetrahydrocannabinol) include a sense of well-being, relaxation, release from daily cares and concerns, and sedation.

In a study cited by the National Commission on Marijuana and Drug Abuse (1973), marijuana users appeared more sociable, flexible, and empathic, and nonusers more responsible, self-controlled, and conformist, in their scores on the California Psychological Inventory. Users themselves report that marijuana increases their sociability and makes them more comfortable in social situations. The report by the 1973 Commission concluded that "if anything, marijuana generally seems to inhibit [violent and aggressive] behavior" (p. 91). Researchers have drawn a similar conclusion from laboratory research. For example, Rodney Myerscough and Stuart Taylor (1985) gave students a low, medium, or high dose of THC, and then provoked the students. They found that those students who had a low dose of marijuana responded more aggressively than those who had been given a moderate or a strong dose. Such findings suggest some reasons for the relative popularity of the drug. (Not all researchers would agree with this conclusion. They point out that the English word *assassin* derives from the Arabic *hashshashin,* or hashish-eater. The original assassins were hardly peaceable folk, especially after eating hashish, a drug made, like marijuana, from the hemp plant. A few modern-day researchers speculate that some people, in some circumstances, may become more aggressive when they use marijuana or hashish. Exactly what those conditions might be must be determined by research, however.)

Among the physiological effects of marijuana are changes in cardiovascular functioning (e.g., increased heart rate and reddening of the eyes) and decreased salivation. Its effects as an intoxicant may include impairment of vision and motor abilities. Thus, marijuana may impair motor performance (such as driving a car or operating a locomotive). Marijuana is a mild hallucinogen. If people take a great deal of it or use the more potent THC-derivative hashish, they may experience distortions of time, space, or perception. Some users report thought fragmentation, memory impairment, hallucinations and, paradoxically, intense anxiety (see Peterson, 1984, for a review of existing research).

When researchers compare the advantages of alcohol and marijuana as techniques for altering mood, they find that marijuana *may* have some physiological advantages. Chronic alcoholics seem to suffer a host of disorders. As far as we know, marijuana users do not. However, frequent and heavy users of marijuana do seem to show cardiovascular changes (Price & Lynn, 1986) and cellular and other changes in the lungs (Jones, 1980). The evidence on whether marijuana use also produces chromosomal damage remains controversial.

In any case, the continuing legal sanctions in the United States for cultivation, use, and sale of marijuana (and its related paraphernalia in some states) makes it illegal and dangerous to use—an additional source of anxiety. This and its other disadvantages suggest clear drawbacks in using marijuana as a means for emotional control, just as with the other drugs we have described.

The Behavioral Control of Emotion

People can try to control their emotions in yet another way—by controlling their emotional behavior. Pop artist Andy Warhol tried to control his fears by avoiding intimate relationships and keeping himself so busy he didn't care.

> Maybe it's time to do away with the oft-repeated point about Warhol's lack of feeling. "If you want to know all about Andy Warhol," said Andy, "just look at the surface of my paintings and films and me, and there I am. There's nothing behind it." There may be nothing behind the surfaces, but there's a lot contained

in the surfaces themselves. In these pictures there's a powerful tension between the feeling implicit in the images and Andy Warhol's attempt to keep his emotions under control. "I still care about people but it would be so much easier not to care," he said. "It's too hard to care. . . . I don't want to get involved in other people's lives. . . . I don't want to get too close. . . . I don't like to touch things . . . that's why my work is so distant from myself."

Viva, one of the "superstars" Warhol created in his movies, recalled that if she tried to touch him "he would actually shrink away. Shrink. I mean shrink backwards and whine. . . . We were all always touching Andy just to watch him turn red and shrink. Like the proverbial shrinking violet." Warhol . . . made another, more social point: "During the '60s, I think, people forgot what emotions were supposed to be. And I don't think they've ever remembered. I think that once you see emotions from a certain angle, you can never think of them as real again. That's what more or less has happened to me."

. . . "I want to be a machine," said Warhol. (Kroll, 1987, pp. 65–66)

In a sense, of course, everything a person does—from thinking to running a marathon—is behavior. Some psychologists, such as George Reynolds (1968), have distinguished between private and public activities. Private behaviors are those that occur within our own skins and are not so easily observable (such as thinking or feeling); public behaviors are those that can be easily observed by others (such as talking or gesturing). In this chapter, however, we distinguish between the things people think or feel and the things that they say or do. The latter is what psychologists generally mean by *behavior*. Thus, for clarity, in our present categorization scheme, we will restrict the term *behavioral* to the more overt things people may do to control their emotions.

BEHAVIORAL THERAPIES FOR EMOTIONAL CONTROL

Some clinical psychologists and others in the helping professions call themselves behavior therapists. Their approaches borrow conceptually from the traditions of learning theory, as it evolved in the first half of this century. These therapies can be roughly grouped according to the learning principles they emphasize—Pavlovian (or classical) conditioning and operant (or instrumental) conditioning. (A third category of learning, observational learning, or *modeling,* is recognized by cognitive psychologists, some of whose views were outlined earlier in this chapter.) Behavioral therapies may influence cognitive states and physiological responses directly or indirectly, but they emphasize overt behavioral change. In this section, we examine some methods of emotional control that rely on Pavlovian and operant learning principles.

Therapies Emphasizing Pavlovian Principles

In a variation of the story of Peter and the rabbit, Mary Cover Jones (an associate of the arch-behaviorist John Watson) reported more than 60 years ago the case history of Peter, a child who was afraid of animals and a great deal more. When observed, Peter exhibited signs of fear at an assortment of cues including fur rugs, a laboratory rat, cotton, a rabbit, and feathers. Jones and Watson tried to help Peter overcome his fears:

> We determined then to use another type of procedure—that of *direct uncondi-tioning*. We did not have control over his meals, but we secured permission to give him his mid-afternoon lunch consisting of crackers and a glass of milk. We seated him at a small table in a high chair. The lunch was served in a room about 40 feet long. Just as he began to eat his lunch, the rabbit was displayed in a wire cage of wide mesh. We displayed it on the first day *just far enough away not to disturb his eating*. This point was then marked. The next day the rabbit was brought closer and closer until disturbance was first barely noticed. This place was marked. The third and succeeding days the same routine was maintained. Finally, the rabbit could be placed upon the table—then in Peter's lap. Next tolerance changed to positive reaction. Finally he would eat with one hand and play with the rabbit with the other. . . . [Moreover] *fear responses to cotton, the fur coat, and feathers were entirely gone*. (Watson, 1930, p. 174)

Systematic Desensitization. Today, the techniques used by these early behaviorists have been refined both conceptually and procedurally. They are referred to as **systematic desensitization** (Wolpe, 1982). The principal meth-ods in this process are training in relaxation and gradual exposure to stimuli that more and more closely resemble those that evoke fear or anxiety. For instance, if you are one of the many thousands of people who are afraid of flying in an airplane, the process might look like this:

First, a therapist would make a determination of the hierarchy of events that arouse fear in you—which are most feared, which are more moderate, which do not bother you at all. Next, the therapist would provide brief training in relaxation: You would be seated in a comfortable chair with your eyes closed. Then you would be asked to relax the muscle groups, one after the other (e.g., facial muscles, arms, chest, etc., right down to your toes) until you report feeling very much at ease. Next, from your hierarchy, a scene related to your fear would be introduced that is very mildly anxiety-arousing—for instance, you might be asked to imagine that you are planning a trip and that you make a call to your travel agent. If you feel comfortable thinking about this, you proceed to the next step. You are asked to imagine that you are on your way to the airport the day of the trip. If at this point you begin to feel slightly anxious, you alert the therapist who tells you to stop imagining the scene and return to the relaxation exercises. In short, gradually (usually across weeks of therapy sessions), the imagined scenes bring you closer and closer to being on an airplane, taking off, enjoying a movie at 35,000 feet, and, finally, going through the experience of landing—all with the careful attempt to prevent the occurrence of anxiety.

As a supplement to the imaginal processes in the clinic, your therapist might then encourage actual exposure to some of the feared events—a process called *in vivo* (real-life) desensitization. You might take a trip to the airport, have lunch there, respond to the announcement of a flight, walk to the gate, and even enter the plane and sit down for a few minutes (with the cooperation of the airlines, who are often pleased to help because they may gain another customer).

In another example of *in vivo* training, one clinician regularly has his snake-fearing clients handle a large (and, of course, friendly) boa constrictor at the end of therapy, in part simply to thoroughly convince them that the treatment works. It does.

These procedures are said to countercondition the old fearful responses to new relaxation responses. Presumably, one cannot experience both fear and relaxation at the same time. Here, clinicians assume that since Pavlovian conditioning produced the problem, it is poetic justice that the same techniques be used to condition new and more adaptive responses. Systematic desensitization is especially effective in the case of phobias, since there the stimulus is easy to identify (see chapter 12).

Implosion Therapy. Classical conditioning principles have also been used to control fear responses via a technique called **implosion therapy.** In such therapy, fearful people are exposed from the start to the very thing they fear most (Levis, 1980: Stampfl & Levis, 1967). For example, in one method, called *flooding,* clients are asked to immerse themselves into an imagined encounter with the source of fear. A man phobic about snakes might be asked to imagine that he has fallen into a snake pit, with no hope of escape. He must try to visualize all of the following events: The snakes are everywhere—on the floor, the walls, hanging from the ceiling. They crawl toward you. They slither up your body, bite you, and get in your mouth and nose, and so forth. (Imagine the worst!) The woman who fears flying might be asked to visualize being on a plane in a terrible storm: Lightning strikes the rolling and pitching craft, fire breaks out, the plane begins to fall, there is screaming, and so on. The terrifying scene is rehearsed over and over—not just in the clinic, but at home, at work, in the car, at a friend's house—until gradually the scene loses its power. It no longer has the effect it once had. In short, theoretically, through repeated forced exposure to the most feared stimulus, extinction takes place, and fear reactions diminish (see Box 14.5).

Which method, systematic desensitization or implosion therapy, is the more effective? Clearly, systematic desensitization sounds like the more tolerable, even enjoyable, process; implosion therapy sounds potentially terrifying. (It is hard for many people to imagine that it would not increase their fear, rather than reducing it. Indeed, implosion therapy is not for the novice or "weekend" therapist. It is a potentially very powerful treatment technique that requires close, professional clinical supervision by a well-trained and qualified therapist with experience in the area of anxiety disorders.) In fact,

BOX 14.5

Flooding

People can learn to control their fears by directly confronting the feared stimulus itself. Watergate conspirator G. Gordon Liddy describes dramatically his own conquest of fear in his 1980 autobiography, *Will*. When he was 14, Liddy writes, he decided to overcome his fear of thunderstorms. His method provides a gripping example of a kind of *in vivo* implosion therapy:

> On a Saturday afternoon in September, the western sky blackened and the wind rose. Severe thunderstorms had been predicted over a wide front. Thunder began far away. Soon I could see the glow of lightning in the distance. . . .
>
> I left the house quietly by the back door and went around the back of the detached garage into the wooded area to avoid notice by my parents as they glanced apprehensively through the big picture windows at the approaching lightning. Our house sat on the crest of a hill and had been struck by bolts in the past; they feared a fire. I brought with me a four-foot safety belt I'd fashioned by raiding a clothesline rope and fixing a D-ring on one end and a metal snap-link on the other.
>
> The tree I had chosen was a pin oak about seventy-five feet tall. The rain came as I started to climb. It slanted in on the west wind, making the trunk slippery and hard to shinny to the first branches just beyond reach of a jump from the ground.
>
> After ten minutes of climbing, I gained the highest point that would hold my weight—some sixty feet up—and I lashed myself to the trunk with the belt. By now the storm was very close; there was almost no interval between flash and thunder. The wind was shifting as the storm hit, whipping the trunk, slender at that height, in all directions.
>
> My eyes were closed—against the stinging rain, I told myself, knowing it was a lie. I didn't want to see the great blue flashes of lightning. It was bad enough that through the wind I

could feel the air shuddering as thunder shook the universe, and worse still that the flashes were so bright they penetrated my closed eyelids. I was probably up too high. . . . my weight could be too much for the trunk at this point; it might break off and hurl me to my death below. That was acceptable. Anything was better than what I was anticipating: death by electrocution.

> Open your eyes. Open your eyes. I commanded myself, OPEN YOUR EYES!
>
> I did. It was chaos. The earth danced as the tree trunk swayed and snapped back in the wind. Water streamed into my eyes and I had to fight to hold them open, not daring to let go of the tree long enough to wipe them.
>
> There was a short, enormous tearing sound that overwhelmed the screaming of the wind, and the world turned strobe blue. KEEP YOUR EYES OPEN! The instantaneous thunderclap wasn't a rumble; it was an explosion of such short duration and intensity it sounded like a twelve-gauge shotgun blast six inches from my ear. Moments later I found I had been holding my breath. I let it out with an unintelligible shout of pure joy. I was still alive! I had looked it in the face and lived!
>
> With a reckless abandon I released one hand and shook my fist at the wildly pitching sky. "Kill me!" I shouted, "Go ahead and try! I don't care! I DON'T CARE," and I started to laugh uncontrollably as I rode the whirlwind. (pp. 30–31)

Liddy's attempt to discipline his emotions may have worked too well. He became so good at numbing himself that on one occasion, to demonstrate his self-control, he held one hand over a candle-flame, impassive, while his flesh burned. Perhaps it was this emotional "insensitivity training" which led him to volunteer to become a "hit man" for the Nixon administration (which rejected the flamboyant offer) and ultimately involved him in the Watergate break-in, for which he was imprisoned.

however, the evidence indicates that both methods work very well. For instance, one group of researchers used systematic desensitization to reduce an 11-year-old child's fears of heights, blood, and taking tests (Van Hasselt, Hersen, Bellack, Rosenbloom, & Lamparski, 1979). As can be seen in Figure 14.4, desensitization procedures were effective in reducing all of the child's complaints. A follow-up study demonstrated that the fears were reduced even several months later. Similarly, Isaac Marks (1977) reports that flooding and implosion therapy are effective in reducing phobic disorders. Recent applications of flooding to post-traumatic stress disorder (see chapter 12) demonstrate its effectiveness across a range of anxiety disorders (Keane, Fairbank, Caddell, & Zimering, 1989).

Aversion Therapies. You might be surprised to learn that sometimes therapists use Pavlovian conditioning principles to create fear and anxiety in order to help clients control illegal or dangerous activities—for example, drinking, exposing oneself, or molesting children. Such therapy is termed **aversion therapy.** Perhaps you recall seeing such methods used in Stanley Kubrick's film *A Clockwork Orange,* based on the novel by Anthony Burgess. (Filmgoers were sharply divided as to whether the kind of aversion therapy shown in the film should actually be used to turn a sociopath into a milquetoast.) In aversion therapies, a client (for example, a pedophile) is given training in which an unpleasant stimulus (say, electric shock) is linked to a second stimulus (say, looking at pictures of nude children), in an effort to reduce the appeal of the unwanted stimulus. In effect, the therapist tries to induce a phobic reaction.

Aversion therapies are used most often in the treatment of alcoholism. When most people think of toasting a friend with a glass of champagne, they envision bubbly excitement, a warm glow, and so on. But how might they feel if each time they took a sip they became violently ill? Presumably, they would quickly decide to celebrate instead with sparkling cider or, better, cake and ice cream.

Cannon and his co-workers conducted a series of studies to find out which aversive stimuli—electric shock or emetics (chemicals that cause nausea and vomiting)—worked best in conditioning alcoholics to dislike the taste of alcohol. It was found that nothing succeeds like emetics. For example, Cannon and Baker (1981) paired an emetic and electric shock with alcoholic and nonalcoholic flavors. Only the emetic seemed to be effective in producing aversion to alcohol. The electric shock was useless. It appears, then, that only certain kinds of stimuli may be useful in producing aversions, perhaps as a function of the type of aversion desired. Do such laboratory-manufactured aversions last? In one study, patients were still totally abstaining from liquor nearly a year after treatment (Cannon, Baker, & Wehl, 1981).

Can you think of other uses for aversion therapy? Can you imagine

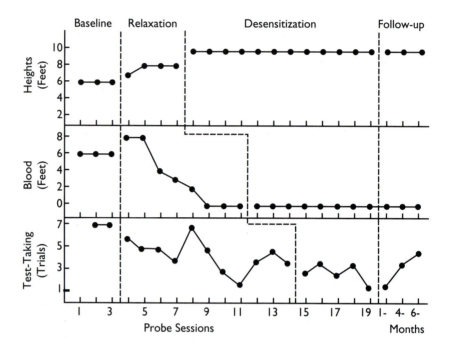

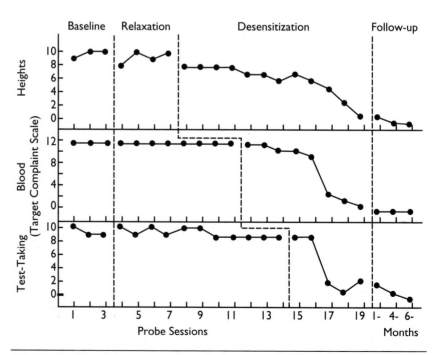

FIGURE 14.4 Tripartite assessment of the effects of systematic desensitization in a multiphobic child: an experimental analysis. From Van Hasselt et al., 1979, p. 53.

activities so offensive you would want to forcibly eliminate them from people's repertoires forever?

Methods That Emphasize Operant Behavior

Early on, learning theorists, who wished to apply behavior-modification principles to real-life situations, had to concoct some simple ways to reward clients for good behavior and punish them for bad. They devised the "token economy" system. In this method, the therapist targets behaviors that he wants to increase (via positive reinforcement) or eliminate (via extinction procedures). If a behavior is encouraged, a token (say, a poker chip or a point) is given as a reinforcer. These chips or points can be collected and exchanged later for more significant reinforcers. In a mental hospital, for example, patients can earn points for "proper" behavior and exchange them for such privileges as the opportunity to watch television on the ward (Ayllon & Azrin, 1968). In a recent study, Smith and Fowler (1984) demonstrated the effectiveness of tokens which could be exchanged for such activities as kite-flying, frisbee-throwing, and softball. Kindergartners who exhibited "oppositional and disruptive behaviors," such as running, shouting, fighting, or throwing materials, were reinforced with tokens by both teachers and their classmates. Both groups were effective in reducing the percentage of disruptive emotional behaviors by reinforcing opposite activities and withholding tokens for acting out.

Child psychologists often use these principles to reduce children's aggressive behavior. But what role might parents have in the development of aggression? Gerald Patterson (1978) suggests that

> The parents of aggressive children do not necessarily have "psychiatric problems," nor are they "stupid" or "bad" people. Many of them have already reared several children very effectively. Parents of the aggressive child do have one thing in common, though; they do not provide consistent consequences for hitting or noncompliance. They will occasionally punish hitting, teasing, or noncompliant behavior, but more often than not the behaviors are reinforced. Some parents have been told that their child is retarded, brain-damaged, or emotionally disturbed, with the implications that the limits and structure would be "bad" for the child. Some children have been cared for by baby sitters or grandparents who have provided no consequences for such behaviors. Some parents have simply been so busy with the world outside the family that they have not taken the time to track the child's behavior and provide consequences. . . .
>
> Again, it should be stressed that these children are not born bad. They do not have something wrong with them. They have been trained to be high rate hitters by members of their own family. Parents from all walks of life can accidentally slip into the pattern which will produce this kind of training. Most importantly, the family can retrain such a child to reduce his rates of hitting. (pp. 126–127)

Patterson (1978) has designed a model behavior-modification program to teach children to react civilly instead of aggressively. First, parents are taught to carefully observe and record instances of aggressive behavior. ("Rachel threw a rock at Jason." "Tim bit Kevin.") Then they can begin to modify such behavior. Parents can begin to systematically reward children by giving attention and tokens when they behave appropriately, and withholding them when they don't. For example, imagine a child who has cleverly learned to whine, beg, shriek, and bite to get what he wants. His terrified parents have tried to buy his good behavior by giving in to him—rather like people who feed pigeons so that the birds will go away, and soon find themselves surrounded by an entire flock. Patterson has shown that if parents systematically ignore children when they behave badly (whining, yelling, or hitting) and give them full attention when they speak in a pleasant, quiet way, and do not hit others, the children's aggressive behavior can be reduced 60% on the average. Parents can also *mildly* punish some aggressive acts. They can give the offender a brief *time-out*—that is, confine the child to a bedroom or study where there is nothing for him or her to do. Such procedures help children to learn more socially appropriate ways of behaving.

People can also use a self-modification program to keep their own fears, anxieties, and other emotional responses in check. David Watson and Roland Tharp (1989) suggest a series of steps to increase self-control. You might be able to use some of these techniques yourself.

> Successful self-modification always contains certain essential elements: self-knowledge, planning, information gathering, and modification of plans in the light of new information. There is definite sequence in deliberate self-modification. Most self-change programs involve these steps:
>
> 1. Select a goal and specify the behaviors you need to change in order to reach the goal. These behaviors are called *target behaviors.*
> 2. Make observations about the target behaviors. You may keep a kind of diary describing those behaviors or count how often you engage in them. Try to discover the events that stimulate your acts and the things that reward them.
> 3. Work out a plan for change, applying basic psychological knowledge. Your plan might call for changing a pattern of thought that leads to unwanted behavior. You might gradually replace an unwanted behavior with a desirable one. You might reward yourself for a desired action. . . .
> 4. Readjust your plans as you learn more about yourself. As you practice analyzing your behavior, you will be able to make more sophisticated and effective plans for change.
> 5. Take steps to ensure that you will maintain the goals you make. (pp. 13–14)

Let us try to apply Watson and Tharp's model to a common student problem: shyness. Philip Zimbardo (1977) observes that to be shy means to be timid, cautious, and easily frightened. Shy people shrink from self-assertion, are overly careful about what they say or do, and feel uncomfortable in the presence of others. Zimbardo gave the Stanford Shyness Survey to more than 5,000 people. The survey asks:

Do you presently consider yourself to be a shy person?
          ____yes   ____no.

If you answered "no," was there ever a period in your life when you considered yourself to be a shy person?
          ____yes   ____no. (1977, p. 24)

Zimbardo found that shyness seems to be universal. More than 80% reported that they had been shy at some point in their lives. Of these, over 40% considered themselves to still be shy. Suppose that, like most students, you are painfully shy when it comes to dating. You blanch when you think of dialing the telephone, cringe at the thought of being left standing at a discotheque, feel terrible when you imagine having to say "no" (or "yes") to someone's sexual initiatives. Not surprisingly, your social life is nil.

An intervention program would work this way: First, you must target the exact behaviors that are difficult for you. For instance, perhaps you have trouble simply saying "hi" to others, much less asking someone out. You decide to work on meeting potential dates and enlarging your circle of friends (perhaps they can introduce you to someone). The next step is to get some base-rate data: Count how often you asked someone out during the past week. If the answer is "never," that should be recorded as a zero. If you did make some attempts, record what was going on just before you approached potential dates. (For example, "Rene dropped a book; I picked it up, we chatted, and I asked her out.") Also record the consequences of your bid. Did Rene say anything? Did she look at you kind of funny? The next step is to develop a plan of action. Figure out a way to approach potential dates and friends. Maybe there is a "familiar stranger" whom you often see in the cafeteria. Plan what you will say the next time you meet—something like, "I see you here a lot; do you have a class nearby?" You might plan to follow that up with one or two other remarks; you don't want to end up running out of things to say and having to make a fast exit to save embarrassment. Try saying hello to one or two other potential friends. That is enough to start with.

You might limit yourself to greetings and conversation at the start; there's no point in escalating until you feel comfortable with friendly conversation. Try to notice which things evoke positive responses—smiles, pleasant replies, and so forth. Do or say more of those things. Eventually, it will be time to make more ambitious plans: Try to arrange to meet someone for lunch in the cafeteria in a day or two. If you succeed, you will have successfully arranged a first "date." Even though this date may be far from what you have in mind, you are still making progress and learning social skills. By making a series of successive approximations, you can continue to raise the criterion on your own behavior, little by little, until you have taken the plunge—you've asked someone out to a football game or dance. (Zimbardo's 1977 book *Shyness* provides good practical advice to the painfully afflicted.)

Often it is helpful to involve other people in your own self-modification program. Suppose that you are in the habit of complaining. Nothing is ever good enough. Not surprisingly, you are often very depressed. Recall Fordyce's pain-management procedures (chapter 13). In his clinic, the staff was instructed to socialize with patients, acting fully interested in what they had to say *except* when they complained about their pain. Then they were to strictly ignore them. Patients soon began to ignore their own aches and pains and to get on with the business of living. Using this model, you may want to try to enlist the help of your family and friends in helping you to "shape up" your emotions. Until now, you may well have assumed that the more complaining your friends would tolerate, the better friends they were. In reality, the fact that some friends willingly listen with infinite patience to your most trivial emotional complaints may be part of the problem. By listening so attentively, by crooning "Oh, how sad," by trying hard to come up with practical solutions that you rejected firmly as "not quite right," they may actually have succeeded not in eliminating your depression, but in reinforcing your disagreeable behavior and intensifying your moods. You might try this strategy: Make a contract with your friends and family that if you complain about your life even once in conversation, they are to ignore you . . . maybe even walk away. When you talk about other topics (possibly even about how things were actually "not too bad" today), your friends should brighten up and give you full attention. Such experiments are worth a try. And if they work, you'll be saved the time and money involved in seeing a therapist weekly.

In fact, family therapist Carolyn Attneave (Speck & Attneave, 1973) has used just such procedures combined with therapy. For example, she once worked with an American Indian boy who was so depressed he was literally unable to get out of bed in the morning to go to school. Attneave's idea was ingenious. She assembled more than 50 Iroquois tribe members in a large hall, and asked everyone to figure out what they could do to ensure that this boy got up in the morning, bathed, dressed, ate breakfast, attended class, studied, and so forth. Actually, the project sounded like a lot of fun to the audience. One man volunteered to see that the teenager was shaken awake each morning. Another agreed to walk him to school. Tribe members ignored his depression and literally prodded, poked, dragged, and cajoled this boy into attending school. He finally gave in and became a cheerful student.

Other Behavioral Methods

Sometimes people are not quite sure how they learned to handle their emotions. They learned to stay calm in emotionally arousing settings because they had to. Michael Crichton (1988) was a physician before he became a novelist. In *Travels* he describes the evolution of a young physician's feelings as he dissects a human face:

> The eyes were inflated, staring at me as I cut. We had dissected the muscles around the eyes, so I couldn't close them. I just had to go through with it, and try to do it correctly.

> Somewhere inside me, there was a kind of click, a shutting off, a refusal to acknowledge, in ordinary human terms, what I was doing. After that click, I was all right. . . . I later learned that this shutting-off click was essential to becoming a doctor. You could not function if you were overwhelmed by what was happening. In fact, I was all too easily overwhelmed. I tended to faint . . . I learned that the best doctors found a middle position where they were neither overwhelmed by their feelings nor estranged from them. That was the most difficult position of all, and the precise balance—neither too detached nor too caring—was something few learned. (p. 11)

Presumably, principles of reward and punishment determine how aware of their feelings people can afford to be.

RELAXATION AND MEDITATION

Increasingly, researchers have begun to recognize the importance of behavioral relaxation techniques in reducing stress. People may be trained by a psychotherapist, a meditation instructor, or a Zen master; they may be self-taught or have devoured some of the pop psychology literature. In any case, the methods they will use to relax, if effective, will rely on behavioral principles. Moreover, all relaxation procedures are designed in some respects to reduce the anxiety that accompanies stress.

Herbert Benson, whose popular book *The Relaxation Response* (1975) motivated millions to try to relax, argues that the benefits of relaxation may include decreased oxygen consumption, respiration rate, heart rate, blood pressure, and muscle tension. In turn, such physiological effects counter the harmful effects of the repeated occurrence of the fight-or-flight response—in particular, heart attacks and strokes.

Benson recommends a four-part program for relaxation:

(1) a quiet environment;

(2) a mental device, such as a word or a phrase [such as the word, "one"] which should be chanted over and over;

(3) the adoption of a passive attitude, which is perhaps the most important of the elements; and

(4) a comfortable position. (1975, p. 27)

Benson suggests that if this procedure is practiced for 20 minutes, once or twice a day, it should "markedly enhance your well-being." If you would like to practice Benson's technique yourself, you might follow the procedures outlined in Box 14.6.

In many respects, Benson's program is essentially a modern-day version of ancient Eastern meditative techniques (which also have been found to produce deep relaxation). In the 1960s and 1970s, Westerners became increasingly aware of traditional Eastern religions and meditative practices. India has embraced Yogic tradition for thousands of years. Brahmanism, Hinduism, Buddhism, and other Eastern philosophies and religions incorporate

BOX 14.6

Benson's Relaxation Response Method

(1) Sit quietly in a comfortable position.

(2) Close your eyes.

(3) Deeply relax all your muscles, beginning at your feet and progressing up to your face. Keep them relaxed.

(4) Breathe through your nose. Become aware of your breathing. As you breathe out, say the word, "ONE," silently to yourself. For example, breathe IN . . . OUT, "ONE"; IN . . . OUT, "ONE"; etc. Breathe easily and naturally.

(5) Continue for 10 to 20 minutes. You may open your eyes to check the time, but do not use an alarm. When you finish, sit quietly for several minutes, at first with your eyes closed and later with your eyes opened. Do not stand up for a few minutes.

(6) Do not worry about whether you are successful in achieving a deep level of relaxation. Maintain a passive attitude and permit relaxation to occur at its own pace. When distracting thoughts occur, try to ignore them by not dwelling upon them and return to repeating "ONE." With practice, the response should come with little effort. Practice the technique once or twice daily, but not within two hours after any meal, since the digestive processes seem to interfere with the elicitation of the Relaxation Response.

Benson (1975), pp. 162-163

many of its ideas. Essentially, Yoga meditation emphasizes concentration on a single point, such as a thought or an object. The purpose of this is to block the distractions of day-to-day life and to achieve a passive attitude. In the 1960s, an updated version of Yoga meditation—transcendental meditation, or TM—was introduced to the Western world. In TM, students begin by sitting quietly, relaxed, with closed eyes; they rhythmically chant a "mantra" (a spoken sound, typically in ancient Sanskrit) for 20 minutes, twice a day. Sometimes, meditators discover that their minds keep darting here and there with a flood of thoughts; the mantra is submerged. When this happens, people are simply told to return to the mantra or some other focus of concentration, without forcing it or becoming tense in the process. The ultimate goal is to empty consciousness of its myriad thoughts, ideas, fantasies, and the like. The parallel between Benson's methods and those of TM are apparent. In fact, if you want to try meditation, you may simply use the steps Benson prescribes and add your own mantra, repeated over and over (see Shapiro, 1980).

EXERCISE

Finally, an increasingly popular way to begin or end a stressful day is by exercising. Exercise is yet another behavioral method for emotional control.

Actually, the Greeks were the first to note the benefits of a sound mind in a sound body. Joyce Feld (1986) observes:

> In the past ten years exercise has become one of this country's national pastimes. Most people believe that exercise is beneficial for them, and participants claim it makes them feel better. Distance runners report experiencing "runner's high," a feeling of extreme well-being. . . . Certainly an affinity for fitness is not new; the ancient Greeks long ago upheld the ideal of "a sound body and a sound mind." (p. 1)

One depressed man found an answer for his problem when he discovered biking. At first, he simply pedalled near his house. Then he began to ride to work each morning. Finally, he became obsessed with biking. He spent almost every spare second on his bike. On weekends he pedalled from morning to night. Biking had become a euphoric experience for him. Once, on a trip to the jagged Bernese Oberland area of Switzerland, he found himself on the B-310 highway, a ribbon of concrete that cuts through the mountains. After reaching the summit of one mountain and passing through a tunnel, he began the long downhill glide to Grindelwald. The bike went faster and faster. Then the rain began. Drops began to pelt down. The highway turned to glass. He pulled on his brakes and found that they were gone; he was "aquaplaning." Rather than fearful, he was euphoric. He began to pedal faster and faster, finally hitting perhaps 50–60 mph. He knew somehow that at that moment he was invulnerable. Had there been a red light at the end of the stretch, he could not have stopped. He knew he would have been killed by oncoming traffic. But, luckily the light was not red. "How could it have been otherwise?" he asked. "It had been a perfect day."

From such accounts, sports psychologists and the American public have come to believe that jogging, squash, swimming, walking, tennis, golf, and a myriad of other sports can lessen anxiety and depression. Surprisingly, however, little sound evidence exists to support this widely held belief. Let us review a few of the generally positive studies that exist.

In one study, researchers contacted a group of women undergraduates who were "slightly" or more depressed, according to the Beck Depression Inventory (McCann & Holmes, 1984). The women were then assigned to one of three conditions: Some were taught aerobic exercises, some received relaxation training, and others (those in the control group) were given no training at all. Women who exercised showed the most improvement. Their mood was elevated, again as measured by the Depression Inventory, and so was their aerobic capacity; those in the other conditions showed little change.

Why should mood be elevated by exercise? Some researchers have proposed a biochemical explanation for the link. For example, researchers suggest that endorphin levels (a natural brain opiate) rise during exercise. In one study, non-athletic women were enrolled in a two-month conditioning program. Medical personnel assayed their plasma endorphin levels after the women had engaged in strenuous exercise on a bicycle ergometer shortly after they enrolled in the program, and again two months later. They found that women's beta-endorphins did increase during exercise—they showed small increases early in training and more pronounced effects after conditioning. Nonetheless, the increases were fairly small. Whether such small biochemical changes can account for the link between euphoria and exercise is still not known (Carr et al., 1981).

To further complicate matters, in a recent study, experienced runners were given the Profile of Mood States (POMS) scale both before and after running one hour. Then, the researchers gave half the subjects an injection of naloxone, a substance that is known to reverse the neurochemical effects of endorphins. The other subjects, the control subjects, were given a placebo injection of saline. Finally, the POMS scale was administered again. The runners' mood improved significantly after running; their scores on the anger-hostility, depression-dejection, and tension-anxiety scales made it clear that mood was linked to exercise. No evidence could be found, however, that the production of endorphins had anything to do with this phenomenon. It did not matter whether subjects received naloxone or the placebo. The subjects still maintained their "runner's high" (Markoff, Ryan, & Young, 1982).

Therefore, although it appears that exercise does have effects on emotional experience, we do not know exactly how in physiological terms this process works. Like many other intriguing questions in the psychology of emotion, it is young researchers who will have to provide answers to these questions from their own discoveries.

Fear not.
Suffer in silence.
Quit crying.
Be cool.

TRADITIONAL MAXIMS

Should You Try to Control Your Emotions?

We have now reviewed a myriad of cognitive, physiological, and behavioral methods people can use to keep their feelings reined in. However, at the start of this chapter, we raised an issue that we must return to here: Is it wise to focus so single-mindedly on emotional control? On the contrary, we would argue that, in many instances, perhaps the best way to deal with emotions is to fully experience them; to be quite aware of what we are feeling and why; to decide how much of our inner life we are willing to share with others; and to take the time to explore in depth how we want to handle our feelings and the events that provoke them.

Some people have such a firm grip on their feelings that they are unaware of feeling anything at all. Consider this example: Elaine Hatfield and her colleague Richard Rapson once saw a couple in marital counseling. They were charming, intelligent, and sweet. They had lived together, apparently blissfully, for 12 years. She was now 39 and thought it was time to marry and have children. He didn't want to marry, but didn't know why. As we talked to them about this potentially emotional-laden topic, the counselors found it easy to understand her. The three spoke "the same language." But it was extraordinarily difficult for them to understand him. He seemed to lack even a language for expressing feelings. He hadn't the faintest idea why he didn't want to get married. Did he feel pinned down? Frightened at the responsibility? Bored with her? Irritated? He couldn't say. He seemed unable to quite grasp what we wanted from him. It was as if we three were speaking French, while he understood only Romanian. In the course of therapy, he learned to be more aware of his thoughts and emotions; only then could he begin to talk about his hopes for the relationship.

> *Out of the marriage of reason with emotion there issues clarity with passion. Reason without emotion would be impotent, emotion without reason would be blind. The combination of emotion and reason guarantees man's high degree of freedom.*
>
> SILVAN TOMKINS

REASONS FOR SENSE *AND* SENSIBILITY

Such cases of marital difficulty are sharp reminders that an emotional vocabulary, and emotional awareness, serve some critically important functions.

Information

Most people get a great deal of information by checking out their feelings. "Would you like Mexican food tonight?" your spouse asks. Semi-consciously, you might find out by visualizing a forkful of chicken enchilada. If you feel a stir of hunger, you say, "Sounds good." If not: "*Bor*ing." People who have little or no access to their interior landscapes are seriously handicapped in figuring out what they like and don't like. Clients who have no habit of feeling their preferences are reduced to such absurd practices as observing their behavior as if from a distance when deciding what they want to do: "Let's see, do I like Suzy? Well, I don't know. I guess I like Suzy. I've dated Suzy more than anyone else. But really, I guess either Suzy or Fran are okay. What do you think?"

By exploring their inner lives and reactions to the outside world, people gain information about not only themselves, but about other people's personalities, characters, and emotions. For example, one of Elaine Hatfield's colleagues is a big bear of a man. Their encounters are always exciting. Yet, she noticed that each time she engaged him in conversation, she felt a flash of anxiety. "What's going on?" she wondered. Then she noticed how ill at ease he also was in these and virtually all other social situations—fidgeting, looking furtively away, squirming. She was picking up his anxiety by a kind of contagion. That information enabled her to try to put him at ease as they talked. We can learn a great deal about other people—whether they are depressed (we begin to get sleepy and sluggish), anxious (we panic), passively aggressive (we know we should like them, but our hearts sink at their approach; they bring out the worst in us), and so forth. If we are trying to figure out other people, intellect plus emotion allow us to do far better detective work than does the operation of naked intellect alone. Theodor Reik (1948) describes this process:

> The torch that psychoanalysis puts into the hands of the investigator lights up the darkest corners and throws a beam down the deepest shafts. The "instincts," which indicate, point out, hint at and allude, warn and convey, are sometimes more intelligent than our conscious "intelligence." . . . The psychoanalyst has to learn how one mind speaks to another beyond words and in silence. He must learn to listen "with the third ear." The task of the analyst is to observe and record in his memory thousands of little signs and to remain aware of their delicate effects upon him. . . . The student often analyzes the material without considering that it is so much richer, subtler, finer than what can be caught in the net of conscious observation. The small fish that escapes through the mesh is often the most precious. (pp. viii, 144–145)

Dealing With Others

There is a second reason why people must learn to become comfortable with emotion: People cannot live wholly alone or within a tight little emotionally controlled group like themselves. They must enter the larger world and deal with a variety of people—people who are tight and constrained, people who scream and threaten to "get them," people who weep and confess how badly they have behaved. When people have learned to deal with their own emotions only by keeping a tight lid on them, they often have difficulty dealing with more expressive people.

One place where this problem shows up most poignantly is in intimate encounters. Abundant anecdotal evidence shows that men and women differ in how comfortable they are in dealing with emotionally "hot" topics. (See Box 14.7.)

Recently Shere Hite (1987), in *Women and Love*, interviewed 4,500 women about the men in their lives. This sample was admittedly haphazard. Hite found that the vast majority of the women who responded to her questions were disillusioned with men and marriage. They complained that men did not talk or listen, would not do enough of the emotional work in the relationship, and expected to be the stars in the relationship, while the women were treated as satellites, revolving around them. Worse yet, they reported,

BOX 14.7 _____

The "Right" Way to Deal With Anger

May Sarton (1982), in her novel *Anger* highlights some failures to communicate emotionally. At first, Anna and her mother discuss Ned's inability to engage in intimate conversation:

> "Well," Ernesta said in her practical voice, "that is no news. All men wince at a woman's tears. It's in the genes." And she added, "My husband simply cleared out and left the house when I cried. They take it as an assault, and unfair weapon, and act accordingly."
>
> "Why is it unfair to be upset? Why is it feeling, almost *any* feeling, if expressed is an assault? That's what I can't understand. Ned won't even talk about it quietly after we have a fight. He says things like 'We have had one scene already!'" (pp. 114–115)

Anna tries, but fails, to explain her feelings to Ned:

> "I think you were conditioned never to allow yourself anger. Was it considered a crime in your mother's house?"
> "Yes, it was."

> "Why?"
> "We were brought up to believe that the surfaces must be kept pleasant."
> "And if they were, then everything was presumed to be all right? So your brother tried to commit suicide and you bury your feelings so deep you can't behave like a human being!"
> "It's a matter of ethos, Anna, can't you see?"
> "Oh yes, I see all right," Anna said bitterly. "But you married someone with quite a different ethos."
> "Unbuttoned ego, my mother calls it."
> "I think it's much healthier to let anger out than to bury it so deep you don't even know it is there."
> "It may be better for oneself but it's hard on other people."
> "Oh Ned, do you think it's easy on me when you freeze up against me? Can't you see that that is just as punishing as you feel I am when I attack you? And it's worse, maybe, because you refuse to have it out. You refuse to talk. And every time you do that and bury your own anger, we get further apart." (p. 89)

men showed little interest in changing. As a result, the women said, they were distancing themselves—pouring their energy into affairs, children, or work. Some were filing for divorce. (Of course, if men had been interviewed, some of them would surely have been equally bitter.)

There is some evidence that men and women do tend to deal with emotional issues somewhat differently (Brehm, 1985). In America, men generally have the most power. They can often afford to act with the quiet confidence that in the end things will go their way. Women often have to develop a wide variety of techniques for gaining influence (Snodgrass, 1985). Harold Kelley and his colleagues (1978) argue that men are conflict-avoidant. They find it upsetting to deal with emotional problems. Women are conflict-confronting. They are frustrated by the avoidance and ask that the problem and the feelings associated with it be confronted. A woman in Hite's study expresses such a frustration: "I would like for us to be able to say what is on our minds. . . . My clue that something is bothering him is when he grinds his teeth when he sleeps" (Hite, 1987, p. 6).

Men and women possess somewhat different strengths in trying to sort out the threads in an emotionally tangled situation. Typically, women are more comfortable with emotional conversation and expression than are men. They appear to be especially adept at sending and receiving nonverbal messages (Hall, 1978). Perhaps this is because they are trained to be more socially sensitive, perhaps because they spend more time dealing with the intense passions of children, or perhaps because love relationships are more important to them. Women are better able to paint a clearer picture of their emotional ideas and feelings and listen patiently to others (Miller, Berg, & Archer, 1983). They may also be better at dealing with people in distress. Men tend to condemn people who are upset, ignore their feelings, or try to distract them in some way. Women are more likely to acknowledge people's feelings and try to deal with their emotional problems (Burleson, 1982).

However, men have other special talents for dealing with emotion. In an extensive study of communication in marriage, researchers have found that husbands are most eager to restore harmony and resolve conflict. They show more concern for their wives' feelings; reassure them more, seek forgiveness more, and attempt to compromise more than do women. Wives tend to either appeal to fairness or guilt or else be cold and rejecting. The researchers observed that "women, as a low-power group, may learn a diplomacy of psychological pressure to influence male partners' behavior" (Raush, Barry, Hertel, & Swain, 1974, p. 153). Husbands may be calmer and more problem-oriented when discussing conflict-ridden topics (Gottman, 1979).

At the extremes, conflict may erupt into physical violence. Steinmetz (1978) estimates that approximately 3,300,000 American wives and 250,000 American husbands have been severely beaten by their mates. Obviously, it is men who are most likely to engage in physical abuse. At the extremes of violence, however, men and women are equally violent; their homicide rates are very similar.

It is evident that couples would fare better if both men and women became more comfortable about talking through and dealing with emotional problems. It is probably the androgynous man and woman of the future who is likely to do best in emotional encounters—people who possess the strengths of both men and women. In Box 14.8, a program for training men and women to communicate about their feelings is described.

EMOTIONS MAY "TRANSFORM" US

There is another reason that people need to be alive to their emotions: Ironically, it is those very people who know full well what they feel, and who have learned to be comfortable dealing with their own and others' emotions, who have the potential to reveal or manage their feelings in the most appropriate way. There are many reasons why this is so. If people are fully aware of their feelings, they can recognize their own warning signs, and do something to calm themselves down before erupting. The unaware can only store

BOX 14.8

Teaching Couples to Communicate About Their Emotions

Today, the things men and women say they value most in their close relationships are intimacy, companionship, and communication (Berscheid & Peplau, 1983). Not surprisingly, then, couples often enter therapy when something goes wrong in those areas. The most common complaints in therapy are along these lines: "We just can't communicate"; "Talking to her is like talking to a brick wall"; "I can't get an answer out of him; he simply clams up at the first sign of trouble"; "She's irrational—the minute I try to talk to her, she starts to cry"; and "I'm terrified of trying to discuss these problems."

When partners try to get closer to their mates, and begin trying to share their feelings, they are often stopped in their tracks. The other partner often becomes extremely frightened. What makes individuals afraid to risk intimacy? They have a variety of answers: If they love someone, they risk loss, hurt and abandonment; they fear that their partner will find out "who they really are"; they feel that making choices means forsaking other choices; they believe their mates will use anything they learn against them; they fear someone will smother them and they will hate it—or worse, love it; and so forth. Couples have a great deal of trouble figuring out how to combine the need for independence with the need for intimate connection (Wolfman, 1985; Hatfield, 1984).

Therapists, recognizing such fears in relationships, have developed training programs to teach people the skills they need to begin to communicate more intimately and effectively with friends and lovers (see Hatfield, 1984). These include:

1. Encouraging people to accept themselves as they are. Unless people believe that they are entitled to be what they are—to have the ideas they have, feel the emotions they feel, and possess their own set of quirky behaviors—they will be afraid to reveal themselves, for fear that their partners will try to change them.

2. Encouraging people to recognize their intimates for what they are . . . and let them be.

It is difficult to gain entry into someone's inner life when you are trying to change them.

3. Encouraging people to express themselves. This is harder than one might think. People's intimate relations are usually their most important relationships. When passions are so intense, consequences so momentous, people are often frightened and hesitant to speak the truth. To be intimate, people have to push toward a more honest, graceful, complete, and patient communication; to understand that a person's ideas and feelings are necessarily complex, with many nuances, shadings, and inconsistencies; and to understand that in love relationships, there is time to clear things up.

4. Teaching people to deal with their intimate's reactions. To say that people should communicate their ideas and feelings, and must communicate if they are to have an intimate affair, does not mean their partners are going to like it. Intimates can expect that when they try to express their deepest feelings, it will hurt. Their friends may tell them frankly how deeply they have hurt them, and that will make them feel extremely guilty. Or they may react with intense anger. Intimates have to learn to stop responding in an automatic fashion to such emotional outbursts—to quit backing up, apologizing for what they have said, measuring their words. They have to learn to stay calm, remind themselves that they are entitled to say what they think, feel what they feel, listen to their partners think and feel, and keep on trying. Only then is there a chance of an intimate encounter.

From our description of this training process, it is probably evident that an eclectic therapist may use a great many of the techniques we have described in teaching men and women to deal with their fears and anxieties.

anger until they explode. If people feel comfortable dealing with emotion, they can be generous and still set limits. When people possess the ability to say "no" they can gracefully sidestep situations that are irritating, provoking, and emotionally charged.

Carl Jung (see chapter 3) argued that the decision to express or repress feelings confronts us with a fundamental paradox: If we act out all our feelings, we will be punished—by our families, friends, and society. Yet if we deny and repress our feelings, they will emerge in one way or another—perhaps in neurotic conflicts or psychophysiological problems. James Hillman (1970), a commentator on Carl Jung, expresses a resolution for this dilemma:

> The great conundrum of affect is the double bind: "Thou shalt not repress," [and] "Thou shalt not act out." . . .
>
> This leaves but one choice: living affects in, keeping them, holding onto them with all the intensity they bring with them, in order to gain their secret, their image, their fantasy, their purpose in my life. If held and watched and felt, the affect will ultimately reveal its image. . . . By living-in the affect, by concentrating upon it, by fantasying the terror, the hatred, the lust right through to the end—neither repressing nor acting out—by dreaming the dream along in the phrase of Jung, one does answer [the novelist Joseph] Conrad's question "how to be" with Conrad's own answer: "Immerse yourself in the destructive element." For then, experience shows that the [feeling] will, with grace, transform itself into emotion; through the vigil one has kept with it, there has been added consciousness to what was hitherto blind. By having lived close to it, one has joined with it. . . . Thus can affect transform us, rather than we it; it transforms our life and our awareness into emotional and symbolic experience. What hitherto was a symptom in our case history, to be dealt with or explained, now, with grace, is psychologically integrated, part of experience, and built into our soul-history. (p.133)

CONCLUSION

In this chapter, we have observed that in different circumstances, people may choose to deal with their emotions in a variety of ways. At times it is critically important to be able to control feelings, especially their overt expression and their physiological aspects. Perhaps there are even times when it is best not to know what you feel. In this chapter, we have reviewed a variety of cognitive, physiological, and behavioral techniques that allow people to control their emotional thoughts, their feelings, and their emotional behaviors.

Sometimes, however, people want to fully experience their feelings. Generally people want to fully experience the cognitive aspect of their emotions; to attempt to understand the cause and consequences of their feelings. There is more often less virtue in fully experiencing the potentially debilitating physiological aspect of emotion or expressing the potentially antisocial behavioral aspects of emotion. Yet, sometimes it is simply a pleasure to be able to relax, feel wildly elated or silly, or even—in retrospect—to have plumbed the depths of anxiety, anger, or despair. To be an emotional person means to be part of the rich intensity that is life; to be without feeling is to be dead to the possibilities of experience. More eloquently, William James, the philosopher-psychologist who helped introduce us to the topic of emotion early in this text, will now leave us with closing thoughts:

> [As with love] . . . so with fear, with indignation, jealousy, ambition, worship. If they are there, life changes.

Summing Up

- People choose to deal with their emotions in a variety of ways—some try to suppress them (those with "sense") while others enjoy giving their emotions full rein (those with "sensibility"). Psychologists have explored the possibilities for dealing with emotions employing both sense and sensibility.

- The tripartite model implies that people should be able to learn a variety of experiential, physiological, and behavioral techniques for dealing with emotions.

- One way people can try to deal with their feelings is by trying to control their emotional experiences—trying to alter their thinking, attitudes, or beliefs. Three clinical techniques are especially popular: Albert Ellis's rational-emotive therapy, which emphasizes rational thinking; Donald Meichenbaum's stress-inoculation training, which attempts to inoculate clients against stress in a three-phase process (education, rehearsal, and application); and Aaron Beck's cognitive therapy, which tries to alter clients' faulty notions about themselves, others, and the world.

- Cognitive methods of emotion control have been criticized for exaggerating the importance of intellectualization, denial, and repression and thereby diminishing the richness of emotional experience.

- People may also use physiological methods, such as biofeedback or drugs, to reduce painful emotions to manageable proportions. In biofeedback, clients are given a reproduction of the physiological state and taught to keep their ANS levels within normal bounds. Although biofeedback techniques are popular in the clinic and appear to help reduce sympathetic arousal, the evidence regarding their effectiveness for specific disorders is mixed.

- When people take prescription or over-the-counter drugs, they often are attempting to control CNS processes and thereby gain control over their emotions. Prescription drugs include the antidepressants, lithium, and anti-anxiety drugs, such as tranquilizers. Unfortunately, drugs may lead to increased drug tolerance, dependence, unpleasant side effects, or all these.

- Alcohol is used and misused far more often than all other drugs taken for anxiety and stress reduction. Alcoholism takes a toll on alcoholics, their families, and society. Marijuana is less popular. It alters mood and increases sociability. Heavy users may experience some disturbing effects, and also must endure societal proscriptions against the drug.

- Finally, learning theorists have proposed a number of behavioral methods for dealing with emotions. Pavlovian methods include systematic desensitization, in which clients are trained to relax while being gradually exposed to stimuli that more and more closely resemble those that evoke fear; implosion therapy, in which people are encouraged to imagine the very things they fear; and aversion therapies, which use Pavlovian conditioning principles to evoke unpleasant sensations (such as nausea) in their clients to help them control illegal or dangerous propensities.

- Other clinicians emphasize operant behavior. They reinforce desirable behaviors (such as cooperation) and ignore or punish undesirable behavior (such as aggression). People can also use self-modification techniques to keep their own emotions in check; they may also elicit family and friends to help in their personal modification programs.

- Researchers have begun to recognize the importance of relaxation and meditation in reducing stress. Both are learned in a quiet environment, use self-instruction or imagery, and may include breathing exercises to achieve a deep state of wakeful relaxation. The meditator may additionally focus his awareness on a mantra or mental image.

- Finally, an increasingly popular way to control emotion is exercise. Some sports psychologists believe that physical exertion can produce euphoria and lessen anxiety; however, only sparse evidence supports this widely held belief, and the physiological mechanisms are not yet understood.

- It may be that the best way to deal with emotions is to fully experience them; to be quite aware of what one is feeling and why; to decide how much of one's inner life he or she is willing to share with others; and to decide how one wants to handle the feelings and the events that provoke them.

- There are at least four broad reasons why "sense" should be combined with "sensibility": (a) We get a great deal of knowledge—of ourselves and others—from checking out our feelings; (b) We must deal with the larger world, including a variety of people who experience and express emotions in a variety of ways; (c) Emotional flexibility is especially important in intimate situations; (d) Emotions have the potential to "transform" us.

- If we know full well what we feel, and if we learn to be comfortable with our own and others' emotions, we may have the greatest potential to manage and experience our feelings in the most enriching ways.

References

Abraham, K. (1948). Notes on the psycho-analytical investigation and treatment of manic-depressive insanity and allied conditions, (1911). *Selected papers of Karl Abraham: Selected papers on psycho-analysis, The international psychoanalytical library, Third impression, 13,* (pp. 137–163). (D. Bryan & A. Strachey, Trans.). London: The Hogarth Press.

Abrahams, V. C., Hilton, S. M., & Zbrozyna, A. (1960). Active muscle vasodilation produced by stimulation of the brain stem: Its significance in the defense reaction. *Journal of Physiology (London), 154,* 491–513.

Abramson, L. Y., Seligman, M. E. P., & Teasdale, J. E. (1986). Learned helplessness in humans: Critique and reformulation. In J. C. Coyne (Ed.), *Essential papers on depression* (pp. 259–301). New York: New York University Press.

Ader, R. (1991). Behavior in autoimmune mice. In J. G. Carlson & R. Seifert (Eds.), *Self-regulation and health: An international perspective* pp. 163–181. New York: Plenum Press.

Adler, A. (1929). *The practice and theory of individual psychology.* New York: Harcourt, Brace & World.

Ainsworth, M. D. S., Blehar, M. C., Waters, E., & Walls, S. (1978). *Patterns of attachment: Assessed in the strange situation and at home.* Hillsdale, NJ: Erlbaum.

Ainsworth, M. D. S. (1982). Attachment: Retrospect and prospect. In C. M. Parks and J. Stevenson-Hinde (Eds.), *The place of attachment in human behavior* (pp. 3–30). London: Tavistock.

Akhtar, S., Wig, N. H., Verma, V. K., Pershod, D., & Verma, S. K. (1975). A phenomenological analysis of symptoms in obsessive-compulsive neurosis. *British Journal of Psychiatry, 127,* 342–348.

Akil, H., Mayer, B., & Liebeskind, J. C. (1976). Antagonism of stimulation-analgesia by Naloxone, a narcotic antagonist. *Science, 191,* 961–962.

Alexander, S. (1983). *Nutcracker.* New York: Dell.

Allerhand, A. M. (1967). *Remembrance of feelings past: A study of phenomenological genetics.* Unpublished doctoral dissertation, Columbia University, New York.

Allgeier, A. R., & Byrne, D. (1973). Attraction toward the opposite sex as a determinant of physical proximity. *Journal of Social Psychology, 90,* 213–219.

Alloy, L. B., & Abramson, L. Y. (1988). Depressive realism: Four theoretical perspectives. In L. B. Alloy (Ed.), *Cognitive processes in depression* (pp. 223–265). New York: Guilford.

Allport, G. W. (1961). *Pattern and growth in personality.* New York: Holt, Rinehart and Winston.

Almli, C. R. (1978). The ontogeny of feeding and drinking behavior. Effects of early brain damage. *Neuroscience and Behavioral Reviews, 2,* 281–300.

Altman, I., & Taylor, D. A. (1973). *Social penetration: The development of interpersonal relationships.* New York: Holt, Rinehart and Winston.

American Psychiatric Association. (1987). *Diagnostic and statistical manual of mental disorders* (3rd rev. ed.). Washington, DC: American Psychiatric Association.

Anderson, D. E., & Tosheff, J. G. (1973). Cardiac output and total peripheral resistance changes during pre-avoidance periods in the dog. *Journal of Applied Physiology, 34,* 650–654.

Angier, N. (Reported by C. Garcia and E. Taylor.) (January 28, 1985). Sexes: Finding trouble in paradise. *Time*. p. 76.

Ankles, T. M. (1939). *A study of jealousy as differentiated from envy*. Boston: Bruce Humphries.

Anonymous (1987, December). Winning Bette. *Vanity Fair*, p. 194.

Anson, R. S. (1984). *Exile: The unquiet oblivion of Richard M. Nixon*. New York: Simon and Schuster.

Antanovsky, A. (1979). *Health, stress, and coping*. San Francisco: Jossey-Bass.

Antelman, S. M., Rowland, N. E., & Fisher, A. E. (1976). Stimulation bound ingestive behavior: A view from the tail. *Physiology and Behavior, 17,* 743–748.

Archer, D., & Gartner, R. (1976). Violent acts and violent times: A comparative approach to postwar homicide rates. *American Sociological Review, 41,* 937–963.

Argyle, M. (1967). *The psychology of interpersonal behavior*. Baltimore, MD: Penguin.

Argyle, M. (1987). *The psychology of happiness*. London: Methuen.

Argyle, M., & Henderson, M. (1984). *The anatomy of relationships*. London: Heinemann.

Arieti, S. (1979). Roots of depression: the power of the dominant other. *Psychology Today, 12 (11),* 54–93.

Arieti, S., & Bemporad, J. (1978). *Severe and mild depression*. New York: Basic Books.

Aristotle. (1951). The poetics. *Aristotle's theory of poetry and fine art* (4th ed.). (pp. 1–111). (S. H. Butcher, Trans.). New York: Dover Press.

Arms, R. L., Russell, G. W., & Sandelands, M. L. (1979). Effects on the hostility of spectators of viewing aggressive sports. *Social Psychology Quarterly, 42,* 275–279.

Arnold, M. (1950). An excitatory theory of emotion. In M. L. Reymert (Ed.). *Feelings and emotions: The Mooseheart symposium* (pp. 11–33). New York: McGraw-Hill.

Aron, A. (1970). Relationship variables in human heterosexual attraction. Unpublished doctoral dissertation, University of Toronto, Toronto, Canada. *International Dissertation Abstracts, 32,* Issue 6, Part A, p. 3419.

Aron, E. N., & Aron, A. (1987). The influence of inner state on self-reported long term happiness. *Journal of Humanistic Psychology, 27,* 248–270.

Austen, J. (1969). *Sense and sensibility*. Boston: Penguin English Library.

Austin, W., & Hatfield, E. (1974). Reactions to confirmations and disconfirmations of expectancies of equity and inequity. *Journal of Personality and Social Psychology, 30,* 208–216.

Averill, J. R. (1968). Grief: Its nature and significance. *Psychological Bulletin, 70,* 721–748.

Averill, J. R. (1980). A constructionivist view of emotion. In R. Plutchik & H. Kellerman (Eds.), *Emotion: Theory, research, and experience. Vol. 1: Theories of emotion* (pp. 305–339). New York: Academic Press.

Averill, J. R. (1982). *Anger and aggression: an essay on emotion*. New York: Springer-Verlag.

Averill, J. R. (1983). Studies on anger and aggression: Implications for theories of emotions? *American Psychologist, 38,* 1145–1160.

Ax, A. F. (1953). The physiological differentiation between fear and anger in humans. *Psychosomatic Medicine, 15,* 433–442.

Ayllon, T., & Azrin, N. (1968). *The token economy: A motivational system for therapy and rehabilitation*. New York: Appleton-Century-Crofts.

Azrin, N. H., Hutchinson, R. R., & Hake, D. F. (1966). Extinction-induced aggression. *Journal of the Experimental Analysis of Behavior, 9,* 191–204.

Babinski, M. J. (1914). Contribution à l'etude des troubles mentaux dans l'hemiplegie organique cerebrale (anosognosie). *Revue Neurologique, 27,* 845–848.

Baldessarini, R. J. (1977). *Chemotherapy in psychiatry.* Cambridge, MA: Harvard University Press.

Bandura, A. (1970). The social learning perspective: Mechanisms of aggression. In H. Toch (Ed.), *Psychology of crime and criminal justice* (pp. 198–236). New York: Holt, Rinehart and Winston.

Bandura, A. (1973). *Aggression: A social learning analysis.* Englewood Cliffs, NJ: Prentice-Hall.

Bandura, A. (1977). Self-efficacy: Toward a unifying theory of behavioral change. *Psychological Review, 84,* 191–215.

Bandura, A. (1983). Psychological mechanisms of aggression. In R. Geen & E. Donnerstein (Eds.), *Aggression: Theoretical and empirical reviews* (Vol. 1) (pp. 1–40). New York: Academic Press.

Bandura, A., Ross, D. & Ross, S. (1963). Imitation of film-mediated aggressive models. *Journal of Abnormal and Social Psychology, 66,* 3–11.

Bandura, A., & Walters, R. H. (1959). *Adolescent aggression.* New York: Ronald Press.

Barclay, A. M. (1969). The effect of hostility on physiological and fantasy responses. *Journal of Personality, 37,* 651–667.

Bard, P., & Rioch, D. McK. (1937). A study of four cats deprived of neocortex and additional portions of the forebrain. *Bulletin of Johns Hopkins Hospital, 60,* 73–147.

Barker, R., Dembo, T., & Lewin, K. (1941). Frustration and regression: An experiment with young children. *University of Iowa Studies: Studies in Child Welfare, 18 (Whole No.386).* Iowa City, IA: University of Iowa Press, 1–314.

Baron, M., Risch, N., Hamburger, R., Mandel, B., Kushner, S., Newman, M., Durmmer, D., & Belmaker, R. H. (1987, March 19). Genetic linkage between X-chromosome markers and bipolar affective illness. *Nature, 326,* 289–292.

Baron, R. A. (1977). *Human aggression.* New York: Plenum Press.

Baron, R. A., & Byrne, D. (1981). *Social psychology: Understanding human interaction* (3rd ed.), Boston: Allyn and Bacon.

Barry, H., Jr., & Bousfield, W. A. (1935). A quantitative determination of euphoria and its relation to sleep. *Journal of Abnormal and Social Psychology, 29,* 385–839.

Bartrop, R. W., Luckhurst, E., Lazarus, L., Kiloh, L. G., & Penny, R. (1977). Depressed lymphocyte function after bereavement. *Lancet, 1,* 834–836.

Basbaum, A. I., Marley, N., & O'Keefe, J. (1976). Spinal cord pathways involved in the production of analgesia by brain stimulation. In J. J. Bonica & D. Albe-Fessard (Eds.), *Advances in pain research and therapy: Proceedings of the First World Congress on pain. Vol. 1,* (pp. 511–515). New York: Raven Press.

Basmajian, J. (1983). *Biofeedback: Principles and practice for clinicians.* New York: Williams and Wilkins.

Bates, J. E. (in press). Temperament in infancy. In J. D. Osofsky (Ed.), *Handbook of infant development* (2nd ed.). New York: Wiley.

Bateson, G. (1972). *Steps to an ecology of mind.* New York: Ballantine.

Bavelas, J. B., Black, A., Lemmery, C. R., & Mullett, J. (1987). Motor mimicry as primitive empathy. In N. Eisenberg & J. Strayer, *Empathy and its development* (pp. 317–338). New York: Cambridge University Press.

Bayley, N. (1969). *Manual for the Bayley scales of infant development.* New York: Psychological Corporation.

Beaumont, W. (1833). Experiments and observations on the gastric juice and the physiology of digestion. Plattsburgh, NY: F. P. Allen.

Beck, A. T. (1967). *Depression: Clinical, experimental, and theoretical aspects.* New York: Hoeber.

Beck, A. T. (1976). *Cognitive therapy in the emotional disorders.* New York: International Universities Press.

Beck, A. T., Emery, G., & Greenburg, R. L., (1985). *Anxiety disorders and phobias: A cognitive perspective.* New York: Basic Books.

Beecher, H. K. (1956). Relationships of significance of wound to the pain experienced. *Journal of the American Medical Association, 161,* 1609–1613.

Beecher, M., & Beecher, W. (1971). *The mark of Cain: An anatomy of jealousy.* New York: Harper & Row.

Behbahani, M. M., & Fields, H. L. (1979). Evidence that an excitatory connection between the periaqueductal gray and nucleus raphe magnus mediates stimulation-produced analgesia. *Brain Research, 170,* 85–93.

Bell, S. (1902). A preliminary study of the emotion of love between the sexes. *American Journal of Psychology, 13,* 325–354.

Bell, S. M., & Ainsworth, M. D. S. (1972). Infant crying and maternal responsiveness. *Child Development, 43,* 1171–1190.

Bem, D. J. (1972). Self-perception theory. In L. Berkowitz (Ed.), *Advances in experimental social psychology, 6,* 1–62. New York: Academic Press.

Bendig, A. W. (1956). The development of the short form of the Manifest Anxiety Scale. *Journal of Consulting Psychology, 20,* 384.

Benin, M. H., & Nienstedt, B. C. (1985). Happiness in single- and dual-earner families: The effects of marital happiness, job satisfaction, and life cycle. *Journal of Marriage and the Family, 47,* 975–984.

Bennett, T. L. (1981, November). How to slip into a terrific evening after a bad day. *Self,* 68–70.

Benoist, A., Roussin, M., Fredette, M., & Rousseau, S. (1965). Depression among French Canadians in Montreal. *Transcultural Psychiatric Research Review, 2,* 52–54.

Benson, H. (1975). *The relaxation response.* New York: Morrow.

Benson, H., Herd, J. A., Morse, W. H., & Kelleher, R. T. (1969). Behavioral induction of arterial hypertension and its reversal. *American Journal of Physiology, 217,* 30–34.

Bergland, R. (1985). *The fabric of mind.* New York: Viking Penguin.

Bergman, I. (1987). *The magic lantern.* London: Hamish Hamilton, Ltd.

Berkman, L., & Syme, S. L. (1979). Social networks, host resistance, and mortality: A nine-year follow-up of Alameda County residents. *American Journal of Epidemiology, 109,* 186–204.

Berkow, I. (1986, May 21). Is that all there is? *The New York Times,* p. B13.

Berkowitz, L. (1969). The frustration-aggression hypothesis revisited. In L. Berkowitz (Ed.), *Roots of aggression: A reexamination of the frustration-aggression hypothesis* (pp. 29–34). New York: Atherton Press.

Berkowitz, L. (1978). Whatever happened to the frustration-aggression hypothesis? *American Behavioral Scientist, 21,* 691–708.

Berkowitz, L., & Alioto, J. T. (1973). The meaning of an observed event as a determinant of its aggressive consequences. *Journal of Personality and Social Psychology, 28,* 206–217.

Berkowitz, L., & Heimer, K. (1988). Aversive events and negative priming in the formation of feelings. *Aggressive Behavior, 14,* 3–11.

Berkowitz, L., & LePage, A. (1967). Weapons as aggression-eliciting stimuli. *Journal of Personality and Social Psychology, 7,* 202–207.

Berkun, M. M., Bialek, H. M., Kern, R. P., & Yagi, K. (1962). Experimental studies of psychological stress in man. *Psychological Monographs, 76* (Whole No. 534).

Bernard, J. (1973). *The future of marriage.* New York: Bantam.

Bernstein, I. S., & Gordon, T. P. (1974). The function of aggression in primate societies. *American Scientist, 62,* 304–311.

Berscheid, E. (1979, June). *Affect in close relationships.* Unpublished manuscript, University of Minnesota.

Berscheid, E. (1983). Emotion. In H. H. Kelley, E. Berscheid, A. Christensen, J. H. Harvey, T. L. Huston, G. Levinger, E. McClintock, L. A. Peplau, & D. R. Peterson (Eds.), *Close relationships* (pp. 110–168). New York: Freeman.

Berscheid, E., & Fei, J. (1977). Romantic love and sexual jealousy. In G. Clanton & L. G. Smith (Eds.), *Jealousy* (pp. 101–114). Englewood Cliffs, NJ: Prentice-Hall.

Berscheid, E., & Hatfield, E. (1969). *Interpersonal attraction.* Reading, MA: Addison-Wesley.

Berscheid, E., & Hatfield, E. (1978). *Interpersonal attraction* (2nd ed.). Reading, MA: Addison-Wesley.

Berscheid, E., & Peplau, L. A. (1983). The emerging science of relationships. In H. H. Kelley, E. Berscheid, A. Christensen, J. H. Harvey, T. L. Huston, G. Levinger, E. McClintock, L. A. Peplau, & D. R. Peterson (Eds.), *Close relationships* (pp. 1–19). New York: W. H. Freeman.

Bibring, E. (1968). The mechanism of depression. In W. Gaylin (Ed.), *The meaning of despair* (pp. 154–181). New York: Science House.

Bierce, A. (1911). *The Devil's dictionary.* New York: Dover Publications.

Birchler, G. R., Weiss, R. L., & Vincent, J. P. (1975). Multimethod analysis of social reinforcement exchange between maritally distressed and nondistressed spouse and stranger dyads. *Journal of Personality and Social Psychology, 31,* 349–360.

Birdwhistell, R. L. (1963). The kinesic level in the investigation of the emotions. In P. H. Knapp (Ed.), *Expression of the emotions in man* (pp. 123–139). New York: International Universities Press.

Black, C. (1982). *It will never happen to me.* Denver, CO: M. A. C. Press.

Blackwell, B. (1982). Anti-depressant drugs: Side effects and compliance. *Journal of Clinical Psychiatry, 43,* 14–18.

Blain, J. D., & Prien, R. F. (1983). The role of anti-depressants in the treatment of affective disorders. *American Journal of Psychotherapy, 37,* 502–520.

Blanchard, D., & Ahles, T. A. (1979). Behavioral treatment of psychophysiological disorders. *Behavior Modification, 3,* 518–549.

Blanchard, D. C., & Blanchard, R. J. (1982). Violence in Hawaii: A preliminary analysis. In A. Goldstein & M. Segal (Eds.), *Global perspectives on aggression* (pp. 159–192). New York: Pergamon Press.

Blanchard, D. C., & Blanchard, R. J. (1984). Affect and aggression: An animal model applied to human behavior. *Advances in the Study of Aggression* (Vol. 1) (pp. 1–63). Orlando, FL: Academic Press.

Blanchard, D. C., & Blanchard, R. J. (in press). Ethoexperimental approaches to the biology of emotion.

Blanchard, E. B., & Epstein, L. H. (1978). *A biofeedback primer.* Reading, MA: Addison-Wesley.

Blaney, P. H. (1986). Affect and memory: A review. *Psychological Bulletin, 99,* 229–246.

Blank, A. A., Jr. (1982). Stresses of war: The example of Vietnam. In L. Goldberger & S. Breznitz (Eds.), *Handbook of stress.* New York: Free Press/Macmillan.

Bloch, S., & Brakenridge, C. J. (1972). Psychological performance and medical factors in medical students under examination stress. *Journal of Psychosomatic Research, 16,* 25–33.

Block, A. (1980). An investigation of the response of the spouse to chronic pain behavior. *Pain, 9,* 243–252.

Block, J. (1957). Studies in the phenomenology of emotions. *Journal of Abnormal and Social Psychology, 54,* 358–363.

Bogdonoff, M. D., Estes, E. H., Harlan, W. R., Trout, D. L, & Kirschner, N. (1960). Metabolic and cardiovascular changes during a state of acute central nervous system arousal. *Journal of Clinical and Endocrinological Metabolism, 20,* 1333–1340.

Bohm, E. (1967). Jealousy. In A. Ellis & A. Abarbanel (Eds.), *Encyclopedia of sexual behavior* (pp. 56–64). New York: Hawthorne Books.

Borg, G. (1982). A category scale with ratio properties for intermodal and interindividual comparisons. In H.-G. Geissler & P. Petzold (Eds.), *Psychophysical judgment and the process of perception.* (pp. 25–34). Oxford, England: North-Holland Publishing Co.

Borton, L. (1988, January 28). Hers. *The New York Times,* p. Y16.

Bourne, P. G. (1970). *Men, stress, and Vietnam.* Boston, MA: Little-Brown.

Bousfield, W. A. (1942). Certain subjective correlates of sleep quality and the relation to the euphoric attitude. *Journal of Applied Psychology, 21,* 487–498.

Bower, G. H. (1981, February). Mood and memory. *American Psychologist, 36 (2),* 129–148.

Bower, G. H., & Cohen, P. R. (1982). Emotional influences in memory and thinking: Data and theory. In M. S. Clark & S. T. Fiske (Eds.), *Affect and cognition* (pp. 291–331). Hillsdale, NJ: LEA.

Bower, G. H., Monteiro, K. P., & Gilligan, S. G. (1978). Emotional mood as a context for learning and recall. *Journal of Verbal Learning and Verbal Behavior, 17,* 573–585.

Bowlby, J. (1969). *Attachment and loss: Vol 1. Attachment.* New York: Basic Books.

Bowlby, J. (1973). Affectional bonds: Their nature and origin. In R. Weiss (Ed.), *Loneliness: The experience of emotional and social isolation* (pp. 38–52). Cambridge, MA: MIT Press.

Bowlby, J. (1980). *Loss: Sadness and depression. Vol. 3.* New York: Basic Books.

Bradburn, N. M. (1969). *The structure of psychological well-being.* Chicago: Aldine.

Bradburn, N. M., & Caplovitz, D. (1965). *Reports on happiness.* Chicago: Aldine.

Brady, J. V., Porter, R. W., Conrad, D. G., & Mason, J. W. (1958). Avoidance behavior and the development of gastroduodenal ulcers. *Journal of the Experimental Analysis of Behavior, 1,* 69–72.

Brain, P. F. (1980). Diverse action of hormones on aggression in animals and man. In L. Valzelli & I. Morgese (Eds.), *Aggression and violence: A psychobiological and clinical approach* (pp. 99–149). Milan, Italy: Edizioni/Saint Vincent.

Bramel, D. (1969). Interpersonal attraction, hostility, and perception. In J. Mills (Ed.), *Experimental social psychology* (pp. 3–120). New York: Macmillan.

Bramel, D., Taub, B., & Blum, B. (1968). An observer's reaction to the suffering of his enemy. *Journal of Personality and Social Psychology, 8,* 384–392.

Brazelton, T. B. (1983). Precursors for the development of emotions in early infancy. In R. Plutchik & H. Kellerman (Eds.), *Emotion: Theory, research and experience* (Vol. 2), pp. 35–56. New York: Academic Press.

Brazelton, T. B., & Yogman, M. W. (1986). *Affective development in infancy.* Norwood, NJ: Ablex Publishing Co.

Brehm, J. W., Gatz, M., Goethals, G., McCrimmon, J., & Ward, L. (1978). Psychological arousal and interpersonal attraction. *JSAS Catalogue of Selected Documents in Psychology, 8, (63)* (ms. No. 1724).

Brehm, S. S. (1985). *Intimate relationships.* New York: Random House.

Brewin, C. (1985). Depression and causal attributions: What is their relation? *Psychological Bulletin, 98,* 297–309.

Brickman, P., & Campbell, D. T. (1971). Hedonic relativism and planning the good society. In M. H. Appley (Ed.), *Adaptation-level theory: A symposium* (pp. 287–304). New York: Academic Press.

Brickman, P., Coates, D., & Janoff-Bulman, R. (1978). Lottery winners and accident victims: Is happiness relative? *Journal of Personality and Social Psychology, 36,* 917–927.

Brock, T. C., & Buss, A. H. (1962). Dissonance, aggression, and evaluation of pain. *Journal of Abnormal and Social Psychology, 65,* 197–202.

Brod, J., Fencl, V., Hejl, Z., & Jirka, J. (1959). Circulatory changes underlying blood pressure elevation during acute emotional stress (mental arithmetic) in normotensive and hypertensive subjects. *Clinical Science, 18,* 269–279.

Brodie, B. B., & Shore, P. A. (1957). A concept for the role of serotonin and norepinephrine as chemical mediators in the brain. *Annals of the New York Academy of Science, 66,* 631–662.

Brody, N. (1987). *Personality and Social Psychology Bulletin, 13, Whole (3),* 291–429.

Brown, B., & Rosenbaum, L. (1983). *Stress effects on I.Q.* Paper presented at the meeting of the American Association for the Advancement of Science. Detroit, MI.

Brown, J. S., Kalish, H. I., & Farber, I. E. (1951). Conditioned fear as revealed by magnitude of startle response to an auditory stimulus. *Journal of Experimental Psychology, 41,* 317–328.

Bryden, M. P., & Ley, R. G. (1983). Right-hemispheric involvement in the perception and expression of emotion in normal humans. In K. M. Heilman & P. Satz (Eds.), *Neuropsychology of human emotion* (pp. 6–44). New York: Guilford Press.

Bryson, J. B. (August, 1977). Situational determinants of the expression of jealousy. In H. Sigall (Chair), *Sexual jealousy.* Symposium presented at the meeting of the American Psychological Association, San Francisco, CA.

Buck, R. (1980). Nonverbal behavior and the theory of emotion: The facial feedback hypothesis. *Journal of Personality and Social Psychology, 38,* 811–824.

Buck, R. (1986). The psychology of emotion. In J. E. LeDoux & W. Hirst (Eds.), *Mind and brain: Dialogues in cognitive neuroscience* (pp. 275–299). Cambridge, England: Cambridge University Press.

Buck, R., & Duffy, R. J. (1980). Nonverbal communication of affect in brain damaged patients. *Cortex, 16,* 351–362.

Budzynski, T., Stoyva, J., Adler, C., & Mullaney, D. (1973). EMG biofeedback and tension headache: A controlled outcome study. *Psychosomatic Medicine, 35,* 484–496.

Buirski, P., Kellerman, H., Plutchik, R., Weininger, R., & Buirski, N. (1973). A field study of emotions, dominance and social behavior in a group of baboons (Papio anubis). *Primates, 14,* 67–78.

Bulman, R. J., & Wortman, C. B. (1977). Attributions of blame and coping in the "real world": Severe accident victims react to their lot. *Journal of Personality and Social Psychology, 35,* 351–363.

Burleson, B. R. (1982). The development of comforting communication skills in childhood and adolescence. *Child Development, 53,* 1578–1588.

Burns, M. O., & Seligman, M. E. P. (in press). Explanatory style across the lifespan: Evidence for stability over 52 years.

Buss, A. H. (1961). *The psychology of aggression.* New York: John Wiley and Sons.

Buss, A. H. (1971). Aggression pays. In J. L. Singer (Ed.), *The control of aggression and violence: Cognitive and physiological factors* (pp. 7–18). New York: Academic Press.

Buunk, B. (1982). Anticipated sexual jealousy: Its relationship to self-esteem, dependency, and reciprocity. *Personality and Social Psychology Bulletin, 8,* 310–316.

Byrne, D. (1971). *The attraction paradigm.* New York: Academic Press.

Byrne, D., & Murnen, S. K. (1988). Maintaining loving relationships. In R. J. Sternberg & Michael L. Barnes (Eds.), *The psychology of love.* New Haven, CT: Yale University Press.

Byrne, D., Przybyla, D. P. J., & Infantino, A. (1981, April). The influence of social threat on subsequent romantic attraction. Paper presented at the meetings of the Eastern Psychological Association, New York.

Cacioppo, J. T., Martzke, J. S., Petty, R. E., & Tassinary, L. G. (1988). Specific forms of facial EMG response index emotions during an interview: From Darwin to the continuous flow hypothesis of affect-laden information processing. *Journal of Personality and Social Psychology, 54,* 592–603.

Cacioppo, J. T., & Petty, R. E. (1979a). Attitudes and cognitive response: An electrophysiological approach. *Journal of Personality and Social Psychology, 37,* 2181–2199.

Cacioppo, J. T., & Petty, R. E. (1979b). Neuromuscular circuits in affect-laden information processing. *Pavlovian Journal of Biological Science, 14,* 177–185.

Cacioppo, J. T., & Petty, R. E. (1983). *Social psychophysiology: A sourcebook.* New York: The Guilford Press.

Cacioppo, J. T., Petty, R. E., Losch, M. E., & Kim, H. S. (1986). Electromyographic activity over facial muscle regions can differentiate the valence intensity of affective reaction. *Journal of Personality and Social Psychology, 50,* 260–268.

Cacioppo, J. T., Petty, R. E., Tassinary, L. G. (in press). Social psychophysiology: A new look. To appear in L. Berkowitz (Ed.), *Advances in Experimental social psychology.*

Cameron, P., Titus, D. G., Kostin, J., & Kostin, M. (1973). The life satisfaction of nonnormal persons. *Journal of Counseling and Clinical Psychology, 41,* 207–214.

Campbell, A. A. (1947). Factors associated with attitudes toward Jews. In T. M. Newcomb & E. L. Hartley (Eds.), *Readings in social psychology* (pp. 518–527). New York: Holt.

Campbell, A. (1981). *The sense of well-being in America: Recent patterns and trends.* New York: McGraw-Hill.

Campbell, J. (Ed.). (1971). *The portable Jung.* New York: Penguin Books (Viking Press).

Campbell, P. A., & Cohen, J. J. (1985). Effects of stress on the immune response. In T. M. Field, P. M. McCabe, & N. Schneiderman (Eds.), *Stress and coping* (pp. 135–145). Hillsdale, NJ: Erlbaum Associates.

Campos, J. J., & Sternberg, C. R. (1981). Perception, appraisal and emotion: The onset of social referencing. In M. Lamb & L. Sherrod (Eds.), *Infant social cognition* (pp. 273–314). Hillsdale, NJ: Erlbaum Associates.

Canavan-Gumpert, D., Garner, K., & Gumpert, P. (1978). *The success-fearing personality.* Lexington, MA: D. C. Heath.

Candland, D. K. (1977). The persistent problems of emotion. In D. K. Candland, J. P. Fell, E. Keen, A. I. Leshner, R. Plutchik, & R. M. Tarpy (Eds.), *Emotion* (pp. 1–84). Monterey, CA: Brooks/Cole.

Candland, D. K., Fell, J. P., Keen, E., Leshner, A. I., Plutchik, R., & Tarpy, R. M. (Eds.). (1977). *Emotion.* Monterey, CA: Brooks/Cole.

Cannon, W. B. (1914). The emergency function of the adrenal medulla in pain and the major emotions. *American Journal of Physiology, 33,* 356–372.

Cannon, W. B. (1929). *Bodily changes in pain, hunger, fear and rage, on account of recent researches into the function of emotional excitement* (2nd ed.). New York: Appleton.

Cannon, W. B. (1942). "Voodoo" death. *American Anthropologist, 44,* 169–181.

Cannon, D. S., & Baker, T. B. (1981). Emetic and electric shock alcoholic aversion therapy: Assessment of conditioning. *Journal of Consulting and Clinical Psychology, 49,* 20–33.

Cannon, D. S., Baker, T. B., & Wehl, C. K. (1981). Emetic and electric shock alcoholic aversion therapy: Six and twelve-month follow-up. *Journal of Consulting and Clinical Psychology, 49,* 360–368.

Cantor, J., Zillman, D., & Bryant, J. (1975). Enhancement of experienced sexual arousal in response to erotic stimuli through misattribution of unrelated residual excitation. *Journal of Personality and Social Psychology, 32,* 69–75.

Capitol Times. (March 11, 1975). Leave love alone, Prox urges profs. p. 4.

Capote, T. (1958). *Breakfast at Tiffany's.* New York: Random House.

Carlson, J. G. (1968). Effects of within-chain response delay upon post-delay operant performance. *Psychonomic Science, 11,* 308–310.

Carlson, J. G. (1977). Locus of control and frontal electromyographic response training. *Biofeedback and Self-Regulation, 2,* 259–271.

Carlson, J. G. (1982). Some concepts of perceived control and their relationship to bodily self-control. *Biofeedback and Self-Regulation, 7,* 341–375.

Carlson, J. G., Basilio, C. A., & Heaukulani, J. D. (1983). Transfer of EMG training: Another look at the generalization issue. *Psychophysiology, 20,* 530–536.

Carlson, J. G., Muraoka, M., Uchino, B., & Uchigakiuchi, P. (1989). *A model for multi-site EMG relaxation training*. Annual meeting of the Association for Applied Psychophysiology, San Diego.

Carlson, J. G., & Seifert, R. (Eds.), (1991). *Self-regulation and health: An international perspective*. New York: Plenum Press.

Carlson, N. R. (1986). *Physiology of behavior* (3rd ed.). Boston: Allyn and Bacon.

Carr, D. B., Bullen, B. A., Shrinar, G. S., Arnold, M. A., Rosenblatt, M., Beitings, I. Z., Martin, J. B., & McArthur, J. W. (1981). Physical conditioning facilitates the exercise-induced secretion of beta-endorphin and beta-lipotropin in women. *New England Journal of Medicine, 305,* 560–563.

Cattell, R. B. (1946). *The description and measurement of personality*. New York: Harcourt Brace Jovanovich.

Cattell, R. B. (1957). *Personality and motivation: Structure and measurement*. New York: Harcourt Brace Jovanovich.

Caudwell, S. (1989, February, 19). A stranger in a strange land. *The New York Times,* pp. 1–31.

Chaikin, T., & Telander, R. (1988, October 24). The nightmare of steroids. *Sports Illustrated,* pp. 84–102.

Chemtob, C. M., Roitblat, H. L., Hamada, R. S., Carlson, J. G., & Twentyman, C. (1988). A cognitive action theory of post-traumatic stress disorder. *Journal of Anxiety Disorders, 2,* 253–275.

Cherry, F., & Deaux, K. (1978). Fear of success versus fear of gender inappropriate behavior. *Sex Roles, 4,* 97–101.

Chess, S., & Thomas, A. (1977). Temperamental individuality from childhood to adolescence. *Journal of the American Academy of Child Psychiatry, 16,* 218–226.

Chivalisz, K., Diener, E., & Gallagher, D. (1988). Autonomic arousal feedback and emotional experience: evidence from the spinal cord injured. *Journal of Personality and Social Psychology, 54, (5),* 820–829.

Cicchetti, D., & Hesse, P. (1983). Affect and intellect: Piaget's contributions to the study of infant emotional development. In R. Plutchik & H. Kellerman (Eds.), *Emotion: Theory, research and experience*. Vol. 2 (pp. 115–170). New York: Academic Press.

Clancy, J., & Noyes, R., Jr. (1976). Anxiety neurosis: A disease for the medical model. *Psychosomatics, 17,* 90–93.

Clanton, G., & Smith, L. G. (Eds.), (1987). *Jealousy*. Lanham, MD: University Press of America.

Clark, M. S. (1982). A role for arousal in the link between feeling states, judgments, and behavior. In M. S. Clark & S. T. Fiske (Eds.), *Affect and cognition* (pp. 263–290). Hillsdale, NJ: Erlbaum.

Clark, M. S. (1984). Record keeping in two types of relationships. *Journal of Personality and Social Psychology, 47,* 549–557.

Clark, M. S., & Fiske, S. (Eds.). (1982). *Affect and cognition*. Hillsdale, NJ: Erlbaum.

Clark, M. S., Ouellette, R., Powell, M. C., & Milberg, S. (1987). Recipient's mood, relationship type, and helping. *Journal of Personality and Social Psychology, 53,* 94–103.

Clark, M. S., & Reis, H. T. (1988). Interpersonal processes in close relationships. *Annual Review of Psychology, 39,* 609–672.

Cline, V., Craft, R., & Courrier, S. (1973). Desensitization of children to television violence. *Journal of Personality and Social Psychology, 27,* 360–365.

Cobb, S., & Rose, R. M. (1973). Hypertension, peptic ulcer, and diabetes in air-traffic controllers. *Journal of the American Medical Association, 224,* 489–492.

Cohen, N., Ader, R., Green, N., & Bovbjerg, D. (1979). Conditioned suppression of a thymus independent antibody response. *Psychosomatic Medicine, 41,* 487–491.

Cohen, R. E., & Ahearn, F. L., Jr. (1980). *Handbook for mental health care of disaster victims.* Baltimore, MD: Johns Hopkins University Press.

Cohen, S. (1980). Aftereffects of stress on human performance and social behavior: A review of research and theory. *Psychological Bulletin, 88,* 82–108.

Coles, M. G. H., Donchin, E., & Porges, S. W. (1986). *Psychophysiology: Systems, processes, and applications.* New York: The Guilford Press.

Conrad, B. (1958). *The death of Manolete.* Cambridge, MA: Houghton Mifflin.

Conrad, J. (1947). Heart of darkness. In M. D. Zabel (Ed.), *The portable Conrad* (pp. 490–603). New York: The Viking Press.

Cooper, R., Osselton, J. W., & Shaw, J. C. (1969). *EEG technology* (3rd ed). London, England: Butterworth & Co.

Corliss, R. (1987, August 24). Show business: "Sensational Steve." *Time,* p. 55.

Corzine, W. L. (1974). The phenomenon of jealousy: A theoretical and empirical analysis. Unpublished Ph.D. dissertation. United States International University, San Diego, CA.

Cousins, N. (1979). *The anatomy of an illness as perceived by a patient: Reflections on healing and rejuvenation.* New York: Norton.

Cousins, N. (1983). *The healing heart.* New York: Norton.

Cowen, D., Landes, H., & Schaet, D. E. (1959). The effects of mild frustration on the expression of prejudiced attitudes. *Journal of Abnormal and Social Psychology, 58,* 33–38.

Cox, D. J. (1983). Menstrual symptoms in college students: A controlled study. *Journal of Behavioral Medicine, 6,* 335–338.

Crichton, M. (1988). *Travels.* New York: Knopf.

Critchley, M. (1969). Disorders of higher nervous activity: Introductory remarks. In P. J. Vinken & G. W. Bruyn (Eds.), *Handbook of clinical neurology: Vol. 3: Disorders of higher nervous activity* (p. 1–10). Amsterdam: North-Holland Publishing Co.

Csikszentmihalyi, M. (1975). *Beyond boredom and anxiety.* San Francisco, CA: Jossey-Bass.

Csikszentmihalyi, M. (1990). *Flow: The psychology of optimum experience.* New York: Harper & Row.

Dahl, L. K., Heine, M., & Tassinari, L. J. (1965). Effects of chronic salt ingestion. Further demonstration that genetic factors influence the development of hypertension: Evidence from experimental hypertension due to cortisone and to adrenal regeneration. *Journal of Experimental Medicine, 122,* 533–545.

Dalton, K. (1977). *The premenstrual syndrome and progesterone therapy* (pp. 140–149). Chicago: Year Book Medical Publishers, Inc.

Dart, R. A. (1953). The predatory transition from ape to man. *International Anthropological and Linguistic Review, 1 (4),* 201–213.

Darwin, C. (1859/1964). *On the origin of species by means of natural selection; The preservation of favoured races in the struggle for life.* Cambridge, MA: Harvard University Press.

Darwin, C. (1872/1965). *The expression of the emotions in man and animals.* Chicago, IL: University of Chicago Press.

Davis, K. (1936). Jealousy and sexual property. *Social Forces, 14,* 395–405.

Davis, K. E., & Jones, E. E. (1960). Changes in interpersonal perception as a means of reducing cognitive dissonance. *Journal of Abnormal and Social Psychology, 61,* 402–410.

Davitz, J. R. (1969). *The language of emotion.* New York: Academic Press.

Dawson, M. E. (1980). Physiological detection of deception: Measurement of responses to questions and answers during counter measure maneuvers. *Psychophysiology, 17,* 8–17.

de Beauvoir, S. (1967). *The woman destroyed.* (P. O'Brien, Trans.). New York: Putnam.

DeKosky, S., Heilman, K. M., Bowers, D., & Valenstein, E. (1980). Recognition and discrimination of emotional faces and pictures. *Brain and Language, 9,* 206–214.

deLaszlo, V. S. (Ed.). (1959). *The basic writings of C. G. Jung.* New York: Modern Library (Random House).

Delgado, J. M. R. (1963). Cerebral heterostimulation in a monkey colony. *Science, 141,* 161–163.

Delgado, J. M. R. (1975). Inhibitory systems and emotions. In L. Levi (Ed.), *Emotions: Their parameters and measurement* (pp. 183–204). New York: Raven.

Dell, F. (1926). *Love in Greenwich Village.* New York: George H. Doran.

DeLongis, A., Coyne, J. C., Dakof, G., Folkman, S., & Lazarus, R. S. (1982). Relationship of daily hassles, uplifts, and major life events to health status. *Health Psychology, 1,* 119–136.

Delprato, D. J., & McGlynn, F. D. (1984). Behavioral theories of anxiety disorders. In S. M. Turner (Ed.), *Behavioral theories and treatment of anxiety.* New York: Plenum Press.

DeLuca, J. R. (Ed.). (1980, January). *Fourth special report to the U.S. Congress on alcohol and health.* Washington, DC: U.S. Department of Health, Education, and Welfare.

Dember, W. N., & Penwell, L. (1980). Happiness, depression, and the Pollyanna principle. *Bulletin of the Psychonomic Society, 15,* 321–323.

Descartes, R. (1694/1967). The passions of the soul. *The philosophical work of Descartes, Vols. 1 and 2* (pp. 329–427). (E. S. Haldane & G. R. T. Ross, Trans.). Cambridge, England: Cambridge University Press.

Deutsch, M. (1974). Awakening the sense of injustice. In M. Lerner & M. Ross (Eds.), *The quest for justice: Myth, reality, ideal* (pp. 19–41). Toronto/Montreal, Canada: Holt, Rinehart and Winston of Canada.

Diamond, S. J., & Farrington, L. (1977). Emotional response to films shown to the right or left hemisphere of the brain measured by heart rate. *Acta Psychologica, 41,* 255–260.

Diaz, C., & Carlson, J. G. (1984). Single- and successive-site EMG training in responding to anticipated pain. *Journal of Behavioral Medicine, 7,* 231–246.

Dickinson, E. (1959). In R. N. Linscott (Ed.), *Selected poems and letters of Emily Dickinson.* Garden City: Doubleday Anchor.

Diener, E. (1984). Subjective well-being. *Psychological Bulletin, 95,* 542–575.

Diener, E., Sandvik, E., & Larsen, R. J. (1985). Age and sex effects for emotional intensity. *Developmental Psychology, 21,* 542–546.

Dienstbier, R. A. (1978). Emotion-attribution theory: Establishing roots and exploring future perspectives. In H. E. Howe & R. A. Dienstbier (Eds.), *Nebraska Symposium on Motivation, 26* (pp. 237–306). Lincoln: University of Nebraska Press.

Dollard, J., Doob, L. W., Miller, N. E., Mowrer, O. H., Sears, R. R., Ford, C. S.,

Hovland, C. I., & Sollenberger, R. T. (1939). *Frustration and aggression.* New Haven, CT: Yale University Press.

Donnerstein, E., & Donnerstein, M. (1972). White rewarding behavior as a function of the potential for black retaliation. *Journal of Personality and Social Psychology, 24,* 327–333.

Doob, A. N. (1970). Catharsis and aggression: The effect of hurting one's enemy. *Journal of Experimental Research in Personality, 4,* 291–296.

Dostoevsky, F. (1950). Notes from the underground. *White nights and other stories* (pp. 79–80). (C. Garnett, Trans.). New York: Macmillan.

Douglas, K. (1988). *The ragman's son.* New York: Simon & Schuster.

Dowd, M. (1987, March 2). McFarlane suicide attempt: 'What drove me to despair.' *The New York Times,* p. 136.

Doyle, A. C. (1974). *Sherlock Holmes: His most famous mysteries.* New York: Grosset & Dunlap.

Drabble, M. (1972). *The needle's eye.* New York: Knopf.

Drabble, M. (1969). *The waterfall.* New York: Knopf.

Drabman, R. S., & Thomas, M. H. (1974). Does media violence increase children's tolerance of real-life aggression? *Developmental Psychology, 10,* 418–421.

Driscoll, R., Davis, K. E., & Lipetz, M. E. (1972). Parental interference and romantic love: The Romeo and Juliet effect. *Journal of Personality and Social Psychology, 24,* 1–10.

Duck, S. (Ed.) (1982). *Personal relationships: 4: Dissolving personal relationships.* New York: Academic Press.

Duck, S. (Ed.) (1984). *Personal relationships: 5: Repairing personal relationships.* New York: Academic Press.

Duck, S., & Gilmour, R. (Eds.) (1981a). *Personal relationships: 1: Studying personal relationships.* New York: Academic Press.

Duck, S. & Gilmour, R. (Eds.) (1981b). *Personal relationships: 2: Developing personal relationships.* New York: Academic Press.

Duck, S., & Gilmour, R. (Eds.) (1981c). *Personal relationships: 3: Personal relationships in disorder.* New York: Academic Press

Duffy, E. (1957). The psychological significance of the concept of "arousal" or "activation." *The Psychological Review, 64,* 265–275.

Duffy, E. (1962). *Activation and behavior.* New York: Wiley.

Duke, M., & Nowicki, S. (1986). *Abnormal psychology.* New York: Holt, Rinehart and Winston.

Dutton, D. (1979). The arousal-attraction link in the absence of negative reinforcement. *Canadian Psychological Association,* Toronto, Canada.

Dutton, D., & Aron, A. (1974). Some evidence for heightened sexual attraction under conditions of high anxiety. *Journal of Personality and Social Psychology, 30,* 510–517.

Dworetzky, J. P. (1985). *Psychology.* St. Paul, MN: West Publishing Co.

Easterbrook, J. A. (1959). The effect of emotion on cue-utilization and the organization of behavior. *Psychological Review, 66,* 183–201.

Easterlin, R. (1973). Does money buy happiness? *The Public Interest, 30 (Winter),* 3–10.

Easton, M. (1985). Love and intimacy in a multi-ethnic setting. Unpublished doctoral dissertation. University of Hawaii, Honolulu, HI.

Ebbesen, E. G., Duncan, B., & Konecni, V. J. (1975). Effects of content of verbal aggression on future verbal aggression: A field experiment. *Journal of Experimental Social Psychology, 11*, 192–204.

Egeland, J. A., Gerhard, D. S., Pauls, D. L., Sussex, J. N., Kidd, K. K., Allen, C. R., Hostetter, A. M., & Housman, D. E. (1987, February 26). Bipolar affective disorders linked to DNA markers on chromosome 11. *Nature, 325*, 783–787.

Ehrmann, M. (1972). *Desiderata.* Los Angeles: Brook House.

Eibl-Eibesfeldt, I. (1973). The expressive behavior of the deaf- and blind-born. In M. von Cranach & I. Vine (Eds.), *Social communication and movement* (pp. 163–194). New York: Academic Press.

Eimas, P. D. (1985). The perception of speech in early infancy. *Scientific American, 252*, 46–52.

Ekman, P. (1971). Universals and cultural differences in facial expressions of emotion. In J. K. Cole (Ed.) *Nebraska Symposium on Motivation, 19* (pp. 207–282). Lincoln: University of Nebraska Press.

Ekman, P. (1973). Cross-cultural studies of facial expression. In P. Ekman (Ed.), *Darwin and facial expression: A century of research in review* (pp. 169–222). New York: Academic Press.

Ekman, P. (1980). *The face of man: Expression of universal emotions in a New Guinea village.* New York: Garland STPM Press.

Ekman, P. (Ed.). (1982). *Emotion in the human face.* London: Cambridge University Press.

Ekman, P. (1984). Expression and the nature of emotion. In K. R. Scherer & P. Ekman (Eds.), *Approaches to emotion* (pp. 319–343). Hillsdale, NJ: Erlbaum.

Ekman, P. (1985). *Telling lies.* New York: Berkley Books.

Ekman, P., & Friesen, W. V. (1967). Head and body cues in judgment of emotion: A reformulation. *Perceptual and Motor Skills, 24*, 711–724.

Ekman, P., & Friesen, W. (1969). The repertoire of nonverbal behavior: Categories, origins, usage, and coding. *Semiotica, 1*, 49–98.

Ekman, P., & Friesen, W. V. (1971). Constants across cultures in the face and emotion. *Journal of Personality and Social Psychology, 17*, 124–129.

Ekman, P., & Friesen, W. V. (1975). *Unmasking the face.* Englewood Cliffs, NJ: Prentice-Hall.

Ekman, P., & Friesen, W. V. (1986). A new pan-cultural facial expression of emotion. *Motivation and Emotion, 10*, 159–168.

Ekman, P., Friesen, W. V., & Ancoli, S. (1980). Facial signs of emotional experience. *Journal of Personality and Social Psychology, 39*, 1125–1134.

Ekman, P., Friesen, W. V., & Ellsworth, P. (1972). What are the similarities and differences in facial behavior across cultures? In P. Ekman (Ed.), *Emotion in the human face* (pp. 128–143). Cambridge, England: Cambridge University Press.

Ekman, P., Friesen, W. V., & O'Sullivan, M. (1988). Smiles when lying. *Journal of Personality and Social Psychology, 54*, 414–420.

Ekman, P., Levenson, R. W. & Friesen, W. V. (1983, Sept. 16). Autonomic nervous system activity distinguishes among emotions. *Science, 221*, 1208–1210.

Ekman, P., & Scherer, K. (1984). Questions about emotion: An introduction. In K. Scherer & P. Ekman (Eds.), *Approaches to emotion.* Hillsdale, NJ: Erlbaum.

Elliott, G. R., & Eisdorfer, C. (Eds.). (1982). *Stress and human health: Analysis and implications of research.* New York: Springer.

Ellis, A. (1962). *Reason and emotion in psychotherapy.* Secaucus, NJ: Lyle Stuart.

Emde, R. N. (1980). Emotional availability: A reciprocal reward system for infants and parents with implications for prevention of psycho-social disorders. In P. M. Taylor (Ed.), *Parent-infant relationships* (pp. 87–115). New York: Grune and Stratton.

Emde, R. N., & Koenig, K. L. (1969). Neonatal smiling and rapid eye-movement states. *Journal of the American Academy of Child Psychiatry, 8,* 57–67.

Emerson, R. W. (1970). In C. D. Mead (Ed.), *"The American scholar" today: Emerson's essays and some critical views.* New York: Dodd, Mead, and Co.

Emery, G., & Campbell, J. (1986). *Rapid relief from emotional distress.* New York: Ballantine Books.

Engel, G. (1977, November). Emotional stress and sudden death. *Psychology Today,* pp. 114–154.

English, H. B., & English, A. C. (1958). *A comprehensive dictionary of psychological and psychoanalytical terms.* New York: David McKay.

Epstein, S. M. (1967). Toward a unified theory of anxiety. In B. A. Maher (Ed.), *Progress in experimental personality research* (Vol. 4). New York: Academic Press.

Exline, R. V. (1982). Gaze behavior in infants and children: A tool for the study of emotions? In C. Izard (Ed.), *Measuring emotions in infants and children* (pp. 164–177). Cambridge, England: Cambridge University Press.

Farris, E. J., Yeakel, E. H., & Medkoff, H. (1945). Development of hypertension in emotional gray Norway rats after air-blasting. *American Journal of Physiology, 144,* 331–333.

Fehr, F. S., & Stern, J. A. (1970). Peripheral physiological variables and emotion: The James-Lange theory revisited. *Psychological Bulletin, 74* (6), 411–424.

Feld, J. L. (1986). *Psychophysiological reactivity to psychological stressors as a function of cardiovascular fitness and exercise.* Unpublished doctoral dissertation. University of Hawaii, Honolulu, HI.

Fenichel, O. (1955). *The psychoanalytic theory of neurosis.* London: Routledge & Kegan Paul.

Fenz, W. D., & Epstein, S. (1967). Gradients of physiological arousal in parachutists as a function of an approaching jump. *Psychosomatic Medicine, 29,* 33–51.

Feshbach, N. D., & Feshbach, S. (1981). Empathy training and the regulation of aggression: Potentialities and stimulations. Paper presented at the Western Psychological Association meetings, Los Angeles, CA.

Feshbach, S. (1956). The catharsis hypothesis and some consequences of interaction with aggression and neutral play objects. *Journal of Personality, 24,* 449–462.

Fey, S. G., & Lindholm, E. (1975). Systolic blood pressure and heart rate changes during three sessions involving biofeedback or no feedback. *Psychophysiology, 12,* 513–519.

Fischer, K. W., Shaver, P. R., & Carochan, P. (1990). How emotions develop and how they organize development. *Cognition and Emotion, 4,* 81–127.

Fisher, W. F. (1969). Towards a phenomenology of anxiety. In B. P. Rourke (Ed.), *Explorations in the psychology of stress and anxiety.* Don Mills, Ontario: Longmans Canada Ltd.

Flaherty, J. A. (1979). Psychiatric complications of medical drugs. *Journal of Family Practice, 9,* 243–254.

Folkman, S., & Lazarus, R. S. (1980). An analysis of coping in a middle-aged community sample. *Journal of Health and Social Behavior, 21,* 219–239.

Ford, C. S., & Beach, F. A. (1951). *Patterns of sexual behavior.* New York: Harper & Row.

Ford, M. (1982). Biofeedback treatment for headaches, Raynaud's disease, essential hypertension, and irritable bowel syndrome: A review of the long-term follow-up literature. *Biofeedback and Self-Regulation, 7,* 521–536.

Fordyce, W. E. (1977). *Behavioral methods for chronic pain and illness.* St. Louis: C. V. Mosby.

Frankenhauser, M. (1978). Psychoendocrine approaches to the study of emotion. In H. Howe (Ed.), *Nebraska Symposium on Motivation, Vol. 26* (pp. 123–161). Lincoln: University of Nebraska Press.

Frankenhauser, M., Lundberg, U., & Forsman, L. (1980). Note on arousing Type A persons by depriving them of work. *Journal of Psychosomatic Research, 24,* 45–47.

Franklin, J. (1987). *Molecules of the mind: The brave new science of molecular psychology.* New York: Atheneum.

Freedman, J. L. (1978). *Happy people.* New York: Harcourt, Brace, Jovanovich.

French, M. (1978). *The women's room.* New York: Jove.

Freud, A. (1966). *The ego and the mechanisms of defense* (rev. ed.). New York: International Universities Press.

Freud, S. (1900/1953). *The interpretation of dreams.* In J. Strachey (Ed.), *The standard edition of the complete psychological works of Sigmund Freud* (Vols. 4 and 5). London: Hogarth Press.

Freud, S. (1905). Fragment of an analysis of a case of hysteria. *Sigmund Freud: Collected Papers, Vol. 3, No. 9* (A. & J. Strachey, Trans.) New York: Basic Books.

Freud, S. (1920). Beyond the pleasure principle. In J. Strachey (Ed.), *The standard edition of the complete psychological works of Sigmund Freud* (Vol. 18.) (pp. 7–64). London: Hogarth Press.

Freud, S. (1922). Certain neurotic mechanisms in jealousy, paranoia and homosexuality. In *Collected papers* (Vol. 2). New York: Basic Books.

Freud, S. (1921/1946). Instincts and their vicissitudes. In *Collected Papers* (Vol. 4). London: Hogarth Press.

Freud, S. (1949a). *Inhibitions, symptoms, and anxiety.* London: Hogarth. (Original work published 1936)

Freud, S. (1949b). *New introductory lectures on psychoanalysis.* London: Hogarth. (Original work published 1933)

Freud, S. (1950). Why war? In J. Strachey (Ed.), *The standard edition of the complete psychological works of Sigmund Freud* (Vol. 22) (pp. 273–287. London: Hogarth Press.

Freud, S. (1959). Fragment of an analysis of a case of hysteria. *Sigmund Freud: Collected Papers,* Vol. 3. No. 9 (pp. 13–146). (A. & J. Strachey, Trans.). New York: Basic Books.

Freud, S. (1959). In E. Jones (Ed.), *Sigmund Freud: Collected papers. Vol. 4. The international psycho-analytical library, No. 10,* (J. Riviere, Trans.). New York: Basic Books.

Freud, S. (1970). Instincts and their vicissitudes and the unconscious. In W. A. Russell

(Ed.), *Milestones in motivation* (pp. 324–343). New York: Appleton-Century-Crofts.

Fridlund, A. J., & Izard, C. E. (1983). Electromyographic studies of facial expressions of emotions and patterns of emotion. In J. T. Cacioppo & R. E. Petty (Eds.), *Social psychophysiology: A sourcebook* (pp. 243–286). New York: Guilford Press.

Friedman, M., & Rosenman, R. H. (1959). Association of specific overt behavior pattern with blood and cardiovascular findings: Blood cholesterol level, blood clotting time, incidents of arcus senilis and clinical coronary artery disease. *Journal of the American Medical Association, 169,* 1286–1296.

Friedman, R., & Iwai, J. (1976). Genetic predisposition and stress-induced hypertension. *Science, 193,* 161–162.

Friedrich, O. (1987, December 7). New Age harmonies. *Time,* 62–72.

Friesen, W. V. (1972). Cultural differences in facial expression in a social situation: An experimental test of the concept of display rules. Unpublished doctoral dissertation. University of California, San Francisco.

Gadpaille, W. (1975) *The cycles of sex.* New York: Scribner.

Gallagher, W. (1986, May). The dark affliction of mind and body. *Discover,* 66–76.

Gallup, G. (1977). Human needs and satisfaction: A global survey. *Public Opinion Quarterly, 40,* 459–467.

Galton, F. (1884). Measurement of character. *Fortnightly Review, 36,* 179–185.

Garfield, S. L., & Bergin, A. E. (1986). *Handbook of psychotherapy and behavior change* (3rd ed.). New York: Wiley.

Gates, G. S. (1926). An observational study of anger. *Journal of Experimental Psychology, 9,* 325–331.

Geen, R. G. (1981). Evaluation apprehension and social facilitation: A reply to Sanders. *Journal of Experimental Social Psychology, 17,* 252–256.

Geen, R. G., Stonner, D., & Shope, G. L. (1975). The facilitation of aggression by aggression: Evidence against the catharsis hypothesis. *Journal of Personality and Social Psychology, 31,* 721–726.

Gellhorn, E. (1964). Motion and emotion: The role of proprioception in the physiology and pathology of emotions. *Psychological Review, 71,* 457–572.

Gellman, M., Schneiderman, N., Wallach, J., & LeBlanc, W. (1981). Cardiovascular responses elicited by hypothalamic stimulation in rabbits reveal a medio-lateral organization. *Journal of the Autonomic Nervous System, 4,* 301–317.

Gentry, N. D. (1970). Effects of frustration, attack, and prior aggressive training on overt aggression and vascular processes. *Journal of Personality and Social Psychology, 16,* 718–725.

Gerbner, G., Gross, L., Signorielli, N., & Morgan, M. (1980). Television violence, victimization, and power. *American Behavioral Scientist, 23,* 705–716.

Gershorn, M. D., Dreyfus, D. F., & Rothman, T. P. (1979). The mammalian enteric nervous system: A third autonomic division. In S. Kalsner (Ed.), *Trends in autonomic pharmacology* (Vol. 1), pp. 59–102.

Glass, D. C. (1964). Changes in liking as a means of reducing cognitive discrepancies between self-esteem and aggression. *Journal of Personality, 32,* 520–549.

Golding, W. (1963). *Lord of the Flies.* New York: Coward-McCann.

Goldsmith, H. H., Buss, A. H., Plomin, R., Rothbart, M. K., Thomas, A., Chess, S., Hinde, R., & McCall, R. (1987). Roundtable: What is temperament? Four approaches. *Child Development, 58,* 55–529.

Goldsmith, H. H., & Campos, J. J. (1986). Fundamental issues in the study of early temperament: The Denver Twin Temperament study. In M. E. Lamb & A. Brown (Eds.), *Advances in developmental psychology* (pp. 231–283). Hillsdale, NJ: Erlbaum.

Goldstein, A. P., Garr, E. G., Davidson, W. S., III, & Wehr, P. (1981). *In response to aggression: Methods of control and prosocial alternatives.* Elmsford, NY: Pergamon Press.

Goldstein, J. H., & Arms, R. L. (1971). Effects of observing athletic contests on hostility. *Sociometry, 34,* 83–90.

Goldstein, J. M., & Siegel, J. (1980). Suppression of attack behavior in cats by stimulation of neutral tegmental area and nucleus accumhens. *Brain Research, 183,* 181–192.

Goldstein, K. (1948). *Language and language disturbances.* New York: Grune and Stratton.

Goleman, D. (1986, March 4). Concentration is likened to euphoric states of mind. *The New York Times,* page C1–22.

Goodenough, F. L. (1932). Expressions of the emotions in a blind-deaf child. *Journal of Abnormal and Social Psychology, 27,* 328–333.

Goranson, R. E. (1970). Media violence and aggression behavior. A review of experimental research. In L. Berkowitz (Ed.), *Advances in experimental social psychology* (Vol. 5, pp. 1–31). New York: Academic Press.

Gottman, J., Notarius, C., Gonso, J., & Markman, H. (1976). *A couple's guide to communication.* Champaign, IL: Research Press.

Gottman, J. M. (1979). *Marital interaction.* New York: Academic Press.

Gould, J. (1951, March 4). Costello TV's first headless star; only his hands entertain audience. *The New York Times, 100* (34), p. 1.

Graham, J. D. P. (1945). High blood-pressure after battle. *Lancet, 248,* 239–240.

Gray, J. A. (1971). *The psychology of fear and stress.* London: Weidenfeld & Nicolson.

Green, M. (1984). Roles of health professionals and institutions. In M. Osterweis, F. Solomon, & M. Green (Eds.), *Bereavement: Reactions, consequences, and care* (pp. 215–238). Washington, DC: National Academy Press.

Green, R. F., & Nowlis, V. (1957). A factor analytic study of the domain of mood; Independent validation of the factors. Technical Report No. 4, Research Project No. NR 171–342. Rochester, NY: University of Rochester.

Greene, W. A., Jr., Betts, R. F., Ochitill, H. N., Iker, H. P., & Douglas, R. G. (1978). Psychosocial factors and immunity: Preliminary report. *Psychosomatic Medicine, 40,* 87.

Greenfield, N. S., Roessler, R., & Crosley, A. P., Jr. (1959). Ego strength and length of recovery from infectious mononucleosis. *Journal of Nervous and Mental Disorders, 128,* 125–128.

Greenspan, S., & Greenspan, N. T. (1985). *First feelings.* New York: Viking.

Greenwell, M. E. (1983). Development of the juvenile love scale. Unpublished master's thesis. University of Hawaii, Honolulu, HI.

Grings, W. W., & Dawson, M. E. (1978). *Emotions and bodily responses: A psychophysiological approach.* New York: Academic Press.

Grinspoon, L., & Bakalar, J. (1977, March). A kick from cocaine. *Psychology Today, 10,* 41–42.

Groen, J. J. (1975). The measurement of emotion and arousal in the clinical physiological laboratory and in medical practice. In L. Levi (Ed.), *Emotions: Their parameters and measurement* (pp. 727–746). New York: Raven Press.

Guralnik, D. B. (1982). *Webster's New World Dictionary* (2nd ed.). New York: Simon & Schuster.

Gurin, G., Veroff, J., & Feld, S. (1960). *Americans view their mental health.* New York: Basic Books.

Guyton, A. C. (1981). *A textbook of medical physiology* (6th ed.). Philadelphia: Saunders.

Haggard, E. A., & Isaacs, K. S. (1966). Micromomentary facial expressions as indicators of ego mechanisms in psychotherapy. In C. A. Gottschalk & A. Averback (Eds.), *Methods of research in psychotherapy* (pp. 154–165). New York: Appleton-Century-Crofts.

Hall, C. S., & Lindzey, G. (1970). *Theories of personality.* New York: Wiley.

Hall, C. S., & Nordby, V. J. (1973). *A primer of Jungian psychology.* New York: Mentor.

Hall, J. A. (1978). Gender effects in decoding nonverbal cues. *Psychological Bulletin, 85,* 845–857.

Hamlin, R. L., Buckholdt, D., Bushell, D., Ellis, D., & Ferritor, D. (1969, January). Changing the game from "get the teacher" to "learn". *Trans-action, 6* (3), 20–31.

Hanson, J. D., Larson, M. E., & Snowdon, C. T. (1976). The effects of control over high intensity noise on plasma cortisol levels in rhesus monkeys. *Behavioral Biology, 16,* 333–340.

Harre, R. (1986). *The social construction of emotions.* Oxford, England: Basil Blackwell Ltd.

Hartzog, J. (1985). Autmn sonata. In F. N. Magill (Ed.), *Magill's Survey of Cinema. Foreign Language Films* (Vol . 1) (pp. 184–189). Englewood Cliffs, NJ: Salem Press.

Haskell, W. L. (1985). Exercise programs for health promotion. In J. C. Rosen & L. J. Solomon (Eds.), *Prevention in health psychology* (pp. 111–129). Hanover, NH: University Press of New England.

Hassett, J. (1978). *A primer of psychophysiology.* San Francisco: W. H. Freeman.

Hastings, E. H., & Hastings, P. K. (Eds.). (1982). *Index to international public opinion, 1980–1981.* Westport, CT: Greenwood Press.

Hastorf, A. H., Osgood, D. E., & Ono, H. (1966). The semantics of facial expression and the prediction of the meanings of stereoscopically fused facial expressions. *Scandinavian Journal of Psychology, 7,* 179–188.

Hatfield, E. (1971a). Passionate love. In B. I. Murstein (Ed.), *Theories of attraction and love* (pp. 85–99). New York: Springer.

Hatfield, E. (1971b). Studies testing a theory of positive affect. Proposal for National Science Foundation Grant 30822X.

Hatfield, E. (1965). The effect of self-esteem on romantic liking. *Journal of Experimental Social Psychology, 1,* 184–197.

Hatfield, E. (1984). The dangers of intimacy. In V. Derlaga (Ed.), *Communication, intimacy, and close relationships* (pp. 207–220). New York: Academic Press.

Hatfield, E., Brinton, C., & Cornelius, J. (1991). Passionate love and anxiety in young adolescents. *Motivation and Emotion, 13,* 271–289.

Hatfield, E., & Rapson, R. L. (1987a). Passionate love/sexual desire: Can the same paradigm explain both? *Archives of Sexual Behavior, 16,* 259–278.

Hatfield, E., & Rapson, R. L. (1987b). Gender differences in love and intimacy: The fantasy vs. the reality. In W. Ricketts, H. Gochros (Eds.), *Intimate relationships: Some social work perspectives on love* (pp. 15–26). New York: Hayworth Press.

Hatfield, E., & Rapson, R. (1990). Emotions: A trinity. In E. A. Bleckman (Ed.), *Emotions and the family: For better or worse* (pp. 11–33) Hillsdale, NJ: Erlbaum.

Hatfield, E., Roberts, D., & Schmidt, L. (1980). The impact of sex and physical attractiveness on an initial social encounter. *Recherches de psychologie sociale, 2,* 27–40.

Hatfield, E., Schmitz, E., Cornelius, J., and Rapson, R. L. (1988). Passionate love: How early does it begin? *Journal of Psychology and Human Sexuality, 1,* 35–52.

Hatfield, E., Schmitz, E., Parpart, L., & Weaver, H. B. (1987). Ethnic and gender differences in emotional experience and expression. Unpublished manuscript. University of Hawaii, Honolulu, HI.

Hatfield, E., & Sprecher, S. (1986a). Measuring passionate love in intimate relations. *Journal of Adolescence, 9,* 383–410.

Hatfield, E., & Sprecher, S. (1986b). *Mirror, mirror: The importance of looks in everyday life.* Albany, NY: SUNY Press.

Hatfield, E., Traupmann, J., Sprecher, S., Utne, M. & Hay, J. (1984). Equity and intimate relations: Recent research. In W. Ickes (Ed.), *Compatible and incompatible relationships (pp. 1–27).* New York: Springer-Verlag.

Hatfield, E., Traupmann, J., & Walster, G. W. (1979). Equity and extramarital sex. In M. Cook & G. Wilson (Eds.), *Love and attraction: An international conference* (pp. 323–334). Oxford, England: Pergamon Press.

Hatfield, E., & Walster, G. W. (1978). *A new look at love.* Lanham, MD: University Press of America.

Hatfield, E., Walster, G. W., & Berscheid, E. (1978). *Equity: Theory and research.* Boston: Allyn & Bacon.

Hatfield, E., Walster, G. W., & Traupmann, J. (1978). Equity and premarital sex. *Journal of Personality and Social Psychology, 37,* 82–92.

Haynes, S. G., & Feinleib, M. (1980). Type A behavior and the incidence of coronary heart disease in the Framingham heart study. In H. Denolin (Ed.), *Advances in cardiology (Vol. 29), Psychological problems before and after myocardial infarctions.* Basel, Switzerland: Karger.

Haynes, S. G., Feinleib, M., Levine, S., Scotch, N. & Kannel, W. B. (1978). The relationship of psychosocial factors to coronary heart disease in the Framingham Study. II: Prevalence of coronary heart disease. *American Journal of Epidemiology, 107,* 385–402.

Heath, R. G. (1963). Electrical self-stimulation of the brain in man. *American Journal of Psychiatry, 120,* 571–577.

Heath, R. G. (1964). Developments toward new physiologic treatments in psychiatry. *Journal of Neuropsychiatry, 5,* 318–331.

Heiby, E. M. (1979). Conditions which occasion depression: A review of three behavioral models. *Psychological Reports, 45,* 683–714.

Heider, F. (1980). *The psychology of interpersonal relations.* New York: Wiley.

Heilman, K. M., Scholes, R., & Watson, R. T. (1975). Auditory affective agnosia: Disturbed comprehension of affective speech. *Journal of Neurology, Neurosurgery, and Psychiatry, 38,* 69–72.

Heilman, K. M., Watson, R. T., & Bowers, D. (1983). Affective disorders associated with hemispheric disease. In K. M. Heilman & P. Satz (Eds.), *Neuropsychology of Human Emotion* (pp. 45–64). New York: Guilford Press.

Henderson, M., Argyle, M., & Furnham, A. (1984). The assessment of positive events. Cited in Argyle, M. (1987). *The psychology of happiness.* London: Methuen.

Henninger, G. R., Charney, D. S., & Sternberg, D. E. (1983). Lithium carbonate augmentation of anti-depressant treatment. *Archives of General Psychiatry, 40,* 1335–1442.

Henry, J. P. (1982). The relation of social to biological processes in disease. *Social Science and Medicine, 16,* 369–380.

Henry, J. P. (1986). Neuroendocrine patterns of emotional response. In R. Plutchik & H. Kellerman (Eds.), *Emotion: Theory, research, and experience* (Vol. 3) (pp. 37–60). New York: Academic Press.

Henry, J. P. (in press). Emotions and psychosocial hypertension. *Receuil de Médecine Veterinaire D'Alfort.*

Henry, J. P., & Meehan, J. P. (1981). *Psychosocial stimuli, physiological specificity and cardiovascular disease.* New York: Raven Press.

Henry, J. P., & Stephens, P. M. (1977). *Stress, health, and the social environment. A sociobiologic approach to medicine.* New York: Springer-Verlag.

Henry, J. P., Stephens, P. M., & Santisteban, G. A. (1975). A model of psychosocial hypertension showing reversibility and progression of cardiovascular complications. *Circulation Research, 36,* 156–164.

Herd, J. A., Morse, W. H., Kelleher, R. T., & Jones, L. G. (1969). Arterial hypertension in the squirrel monkey during behavioral experiments. *American Journal of Physiology, 217,* 24–29.

Herrnstein, R. J. (1969). Method and theory in the study of avoidance. *Psychological Review, 76,* 49–69.

Herrnstein, R. J., & Morse, W. H. (1957). Some effects of response-independent positive reinforcement on maintained operant behavior. *Journal of Comparative and Physiological Psychology, 50,* 461–467.

Hess, W. R. (1935). Hypothalamus und die Zantren des autonomen Nervensystems: Physiologie. *Archiv fur Psychiatrie und Nervenkrankheiten, 104,* 548–557.

Hess, W. R. (1954). *Diencephalon: Autonomic and extrapyramidal functions.* New York: Grune-Stratton.

Hilgard, E. R., & Hilgard, J. R. (1974, Spring-Summer). Hypnosis in the control of pain. *The Stanford Magazine,* 58–62.

Hillebrandt, R. H. (1962). Panel design and time-series analysis. Unpublished master's thesis. Northwestern University, Chicago, IL.

Hillman, J. (1970). C. G. Jung's contributions to "feelings and emotions": Synopsis and implications. In M. B. Arnold (Ed.), *Feelings and emotions: The Loyola Symposium* (pp. 125–134). New York: Academic Press.

Hilton, S. M. (1966). Hypothalamic regulation of the cardiovascular system. *British Medical Bullentin, 22,* 243–248.

Hindy, C. G., & Schwarz, J. C. (1986) "Lovesickness" in dating relationships: An attachment perspective. Unpublished manuscript. University of North Florida, Jacksonville, FL.

Hirschman, R. (1975). Cross-modal effects of anticipatory bogus heart rate feedback in a negative emotional context. *Journal of Personality and Social Psychology, 31,* 13–19.

Hite, S. (1987). *Women and love.* New York: Knopf.

Hoffman, L. W. & Manis, J. D., (1982). The value of children in the United States. In F. I. Nye (Ed.), *Family relationships.* Beverly Hills: Sage.

Hohmann, G. W. (1966). Some effects of spinal cord lesions on experienced emotional feelings. *Psychophysiology, 3,* 143–156.

Hokanson, J. E. (1961). Vascular and psychogalvanic effects of experimentally aroused anger. *Journal of Personality, 29,* 30–39.

Hokanson, J. E. (1970). Psychophysiological evaluation of the catharsis hypothesis. In E. I. Megaree & J. E. Hokanson (Eds.), *The dynamics of aggression* (pp. 74–86). New York: Harper & Row.

Hokanson, J. E., & Burgess, M. (1962a). The effects of status, type of frustration and aggression on vascular processes. *Journal of Abnormal and Social Psychology, 65,* 232–237.

Hokanson, J. E., & Burgess, M. (1962b). The effects of three types of aggression on vascular processes. *Journal of Abnormal and Social Psychology, 64,* 446–449.

Hokanson, J. E., Burgess, M., & Cohen, M. F. (1963). Effects of displaced aggression on systolic blood pressure. *Journal of Abnormal and Social Psychology, 67,* 214–218.

Hokanson, J. E., & Edelman, R. (1969). Arousal reduction via self-punitive behavior. *Journal of Personality and Social Psychology, 12,* 72–79.

Hokanson, J. E., & Shetler, S. (1961). The effect of overt aggression on physiological arousal. *Journal of Abnormal and Social Psychology, 63,* 446–448.

Hokanson, J. E., & Stone, L. (1969). Intensity of self-punishment as a factor in intropunitive behavior. Unpublished manuscript. Florida State University, Tallahassee, FL.

Hokanson, J. E., Willers, K. R., & Koropsak, E. (1968). The modification of autonomic responses during aggressive interchange. *Journal of Personality, 36,* 386–404.

Holahan, C. J. & Moos, R. H. (1981). Social support and psychological distress: A longitudinal analysis. *Journal of Abnormal Psychology, 90,* 365–370.

Holmes, T. H., & Masuda, M. (1973). Life change and illness susceptibility. In B. S. Dohrenwend & B. P. Dohrenwend (Eds.), *Stressful life events: Their nature and effects* (pp. 45–72). New York: Wiley.

Holmes, T. H., & Rahe, R. H. (1967). The social readjustment rating scale. *Journal of Psychosomatic Research, 11,* 213–218.

Honolulu Advertiser (March 3, 1989) p. A1.

Hoon, P. W., Wincze, J. P., & Hoon, E. F. (1977). A test of reciprocal inhibition: Are anxiety and sexual arousal in women mutually inhibitory? *Journal of Abnormal Psychology, 86* (1), 65–74.

Hopson, J., & Rosenfeld, A. (1984). PMS: Puzzling monthly symptoms. *Psychology Today, 18,* 30–35.

Horan, J. J., & Dellinger J. K. (1974). "In vivo" emotive imagery: A preliminary test. *Perceptual and Motor Skills, 39,* 359–362.

Horne, R. L., & Picard, R. S. (1979). Psychosocial risk factors for lung cancer. *Psychosomatic Medicine, 41,* 503–514.

Horner, M. S. (1968). Sex differences in achievement motivation and performance in competitive and noncompetitive situations. *Dissertation Abstracts International, 30,* 407b.

Horvath, F. S. (1977). The effects of selected variables on the interpretation of polygraph records. *Journal of Applied Psychology, 62,* 127–136.

Hothersall, D. (1985). *Psychology.* Columbus, OH: Bell and Howell.

Hovland, C., & Sears, R. (1940). Minor studies of aggression: VI: Correlations of lynchings with economic indices. *Journal of Psychology, 9,* 301–310.

Howes, M. J., Hokanson, J. E., & Lowenstein, D. A. (1985). Induction of depressive affect after prolonged exposure to a mildly depressed individual. *Journal of Personality and Social Psychology, 49,* 1110–1113.

Hoyt, D. P., & Magoon, T. M. (1954). A valid study of the Taylor Manifest Anxiety Scale. *Journal of Clinical Psychology, 10,* 357–361.

Hsee, C. K., Hatfield, E., & Chemtob, C. (in press). Clinicians' assessments of clients' emotional states: Conscious judgments versus emotional contagion.

Hsee, C. K., Hatfield, E., Carlson, J. G., & Chemtob, C. (1990). The effect of power on susceptibility to emotional contagion. *Cognition and Emotion, 4,* 327–340.

Hudson, R., & Davidson, S. (1986). *Rock Hudson.* New York: William Morrow.

Huesmann, L. R., & Levinger, G. (1976). Incremental exchange theory: A formal model for progression in dyadic social interaction. In L. Berkowitz & E. Hatfield (Eds.), *Advances in Experimental Social Psychology. Equity theory: Toward a general theory of social interaction.* New York: Academic Press, 9, 192–230.

Hyde, J. S. (1986). Understanding human sexuality. (3rd ed.) (p. 98). New York: McGraw-Hill.

Imboden, J. B., Canter, A., & Cluff, L. E. (1961). Convalescence from influenza: A study of the psychological and clinical determinants. *Archives of Internal Medicine, 108,* 393–399.

Istvan, J., & Griffitt, W. (1978). Emotional arousal and sexual attraction. Unpublished manuscript, Kansas State University, Manhattan, KS.

Istvan, S., Griffitt, W., & Weider, G. (1983). Sexual arousal and the polarization of perceived sexual attractiveness. *Basic and Applied Social Psychology, 4,* 307–318.

Izard, C. E. (1971). *The face of emotion.* New York: Appleton-Century-Crofts.

Izard, C. (1972). *Patterns of emotions.* New York: Plenum Press.

Izard, C. E. (1977). *Human emotions.* New York: Plenum Press.

Izard, C. E. (1979). *The Maximally Discriminative Facial Movement Coding System (Max).* Newark: Instructional Resources Center, University of Delaware.

Izard, C. E. (1982). *Measuring emotions in infants and children.* London, England: Cambridge University Press.

Izard, C. E., & Dougherty, L. M. (1982). Two complementary systems for measuring facial expressions in infants and children. In C. E. Izard (Ed.), *Measuring emotions in infants and children* (pp. 97–126). Cambridge, England: Cambridge University Press.

Izard, C. E., & Read, P. B. (1986). *Measuring emotions in infants and children* (Vol. 2). London, England: Cambridge University Press.

Jacobs, L., Berscheid, E., & Hatfield, E. (1971). Self-esteem and attraction. *Journal of Personality and Social Psychology, 17,* 84–91.

Jacobs, M. H., Spelken, A. Z., Norman, M. M., & Anderson, L. S. (1970). Life stress and respiratory illness. *Psychosomatic Medicine, 32,* 233–242.

Jacobs, S., & Ostfeld, A. (1977). An epidemiological review of the mortality of bereavement. *Psychosomatic Medicine, 39,* 344–357.

James, W. (1890). *Principles of psychology* (Vols. 1 and 2). New York: Dover Publications.

James, W. (1890/1922). *Principles of psychology* Vols. 1 and 2. New York: Dover Publications.

James, W. (1890/1984). What is an emotion? In C. Calhoun and R. C. Solomon (Eds.), *What is an emotion?* (pp. 125–142). New York: Oxford University Press.

James, W. (1892/1961). In G. Allport (Ed.), *Psychology: The briefer course.* New York: Harper & Row.

Janis, I. L. (1982). Decision making under stress. In L. Goldberger & S. Breznitz (Eds.), *Handbook of stress* (pp. 69–87). New York: Free Press.

Johnson, A. J. (1986a). *He: Understanding masculine psychology.* New York: Harper & Row.

Johnson, A. J. (1986b). *She: Understanding feminine psychology.* New York: Harper & Row.

Johnson, J. E., & Rice V. H. (1974). Sensory and distress components of pain: Implications for the study of clinical pain. *Nursing Research, 23*, 203–209.

Johnson, J. E. & Sarason, I. G. (1979). Recent developments in research on life stress. In V. Hamilton & D. Warburton (Eds.), *Human stress and cognition: An information processing approach.* London: Wiley.

Johnson, R. (1973). Emotional development: Aggression. A film in the Developmental Psychology Series, F-E115. New York: McGraw-Hill.

Johnson, R. N. (1972). *Aggression in man and animals.* Philadelphia: Saunders.

Jones, B., & Mishkin, M. (1972). Limbic lesions and the problem of stimulus-reinforcement associations. *Experimental Neurology, 36,* 362–377.

Jones, E. E. (1964). *Ingratiation.* New York: Appleton-Century-Crofts.

Jones, E. E., Kanouse, D. E., Kelley, H. H., Nisbett, R. E., Valines, S., & Weiner, B. (Eds.). (1971). *Attribution: Perceiving the causes of behavior.* Morristown, NJ: General Learning Press.

Jones, R. T. (1980). Human effects: An overview. In R. C. Peterson (Ed.). *Marihuana research findings: 1980.* (NIDA Research Monograph No. 31). Washington, D. C.: U. S. Government Printing Office.

Jones, V. C. (1948). *The Hatfields and the McCoys.* Chapel Hill, NC: The University of North Carolina Press.

Jourard, S. M. (1964). *The transparent self.* Princeton, NJ: Van Nostrand.

Joyce, C. (1984, November). A time for grieving. *Psychology Today,* 18, No. 11. 42–46.

Jung, C. G. (1938). *Psychological Types.* (H. G. Baynes, Trans.). New York: Harcourt, Brace and Co.

Jung, C. G. (1953). Two essays on analytical psychology. In H. Read, M. Fordham, and G. Adler (Eds.), *Collected works, Vol. 7.* (pp. 243–292). Princeton, NJ: Princeton University Press.

Jung, C. J. (1954a) Spirit of psychology. *Spirit and nature. Papers from the Eranos Yearbooks,* Vol. 1, Series xxx. Bollingen, NY: Pantheon Books.

Jung, C. J. (1954b). The development of personality. In H. Read, M. Fordham, and G. Adler (Eds.), *Collected works, Vol. 17* (pp. 165–186). Princeton, NJ: Princeton University Press.

Jung, C. G. (1959). The archetypes and the collective unconscious. In H. Read, M. Fordham, and G. Adler (Eds.). *Collected works, Vol. 9, Part I* (pp. 1–86). (R. F. C. Hull, Trans.). New York: Pantheon Books.

Jung, C. G. (1961). *Memories, dreams, reflections.* A. Jaffe (Ed.). New York: Pantheon.

Jung, C. G., & von Franz, M.-L., Henderson, J. L., Jacobi, J., & Jaffe, A. (1964). *Man and his symbols.* Garden City, NY: Doubleday and Co.

Jung, C. G. (1968). *Analytical psychology: Its theory and practice. The Tavistock lectures.* New York: Pantheon.

Jung, C. G. (1973). Experimental researches. In H. Read, M. Fordham, G. Adler, and W. McGuire. (Eds.). *Collected works, Vol. 2.* (pp. 439–465.) (L. Stein, Trans.). Princeton, NJ: Princeton University Press.

Kadish, W. (1983). Personality traits and the norepinephrine to epinephrine ratio. Unpublished master's thesis. Yale University, New Haven, CT.

Kahn, M. (1966). The physiology of catharsis. *Journal of Personality and Social Psychology, 3,* 278–286.

Kammann, R. (1982, August). Personal circumstances and life events as poor predictors of happiness. Paper presented at the meetings of the American Psychological Association. Washington, DC.

Kanner, A. D., Coyne, J. C., Schaefer, C., & Lazarus, R. S. (1981). Comparison of two modes of stress measurement: Daily hassles and uplifts versus major life events. *Journal of Behavioral Medicine, 4,* 1–39.

Kaplan, H. S. (1979). *Disorders of sexual desire.* New York: Simon & Schuster.

Katkin, E. S. (1966). The relationship between a measure of transitory anxiety and spontaneous autonomic activity. *Journal of Abnormal Psychology, 71,* 142–146.

Kavanagh, T., & Shephard, R. J. (1973). The immediate antecedents of myocardial infarction in active men. *Canadian Medical Association Journal, 109,* 19–22.

Kazantzakis, N. (1952). *Zorba the Greek.* (C. Wildman, Trans.). New York: Simon & Schuster.

Keane, T. M., Fairbank, J. A., Caddell, J. M., & Zimering, R. T. (1989). Implosive (flooding) therapy reduces symptoms of PTSD in Vietnam combat veterans. *Behavior Therapy, 20,* 245–260.

Keillor, G. (1986). *Lake Wobegon days.* New York: Penguin.

Kellerman, H., & Plutchik, R. (1968). Emotion-trait interrelations and the measurement of personality. *Psychological Reports, 23,* 1107–1114.

Kelley, H. H. (1967). Attribution theory in social psychology. *Nebraska Symposium on Motivation, 14,* 192–241.

Kelley, H. H. (1979). *Personal relationships: Their structures and processes.* Hillsdale, NJ: Erlbaum.

Kelley, H. H., Berscheid, E., Christensen, A., Harvey, J. H., Huston, T. L., Levinger, G., McClintock, E., Peplau, L. A., & Peterson, D. R. (Eds.) (1983). *Close relationships.* New York: W. H. Freeman.

Kelley, H. H., Cunningham, J. D., Grisham, J. A., Lefebvre, L. M., Sink, C. R., & Yablon, G. (1978). Sex differences in comments made during conflict within close heterosexual pairs. *Sex Roles, 4,* 473–491.

Kemper, T. D. (1987). How many emotions are there? Wedding the social and the autonomic components. *American Journal of Sociology, 93,* 263–289.

Kendrick, D. T., & Cialdini, R. B. (1977). Romantic attraction: Misattribution vs. reinforcement explanations. *Journal of Personality and Social Psychology, 35,* 381–391.

Kidman, A. (in press). Neurochemical and cognitive aspects of anxiety disorders. *Progress in Neurobiology.*

Kimble, G. S. (1961). *Hilgard and Marquis' conditioning and learning.* New York: Appleton-Century-Crofts.

King, H. E. (1961). Psychological effects of excitation in the limbic system. In D. E. Sheer (Ed.), *Electrical stimulation of the brain* (pp. 477–486). Austin, TX: University of Texas Press.

Kinney, J., & Leaton, G. (1982). *Loosening the grip: A handbook of alcohol information.* St. Louis, MO: C. V. Mosby.

Kinsbourne, M. (1981, May). The brain: Sad hemisphere, happy hemisphere. *Psychology Today,* p. 92.

Kinsey, A. C. (1953). *Sexual behavior in the human female.* Philadelphia: Saunders.

Klaus, M. H. (1970). Mothers separated from their newborn infants. *Pediatric Clinics of North America, 17,* 1015–1037.

Klaus, M. H., & Kennel, J. H. (1982). *Parent-infant bonding.* St. Louis, MO: C. V. Mosby.

Kleck, R. E., Vaughan, R. C., Cartwright-Smith, J., Vaughan, K. B., Colby, C. Z., & Lanzetta, J. T. (1976). Effects of being observed on expressive subjective and physiological responses to painful stimuli. *Journal of Personality and Social Psychology, 34,* 1211–1218.

Klein, D. F., Gittleman, R., Quitkin, F., & Rifkin, A. (1980). *Diagnosis and drug treatment of psychiatric disorders: Adults and children.* Baltimore, MD: Williams & Wilkins.

Kleinmuntz, B., & Szucko, J. J. (1984a). A field study of the fallibility of polygraphic lie detection. *Nature, 308,* 449–450.

Kleinmuntz, B., & Szucko, J. J. (1984b). Lie detection in ancient and modern times: A call for contemporary scientific study. *American Psychologist, 39,* 766–776.

Klerman, G. L., & Clayton, P. (1984). Epidemiological perspectives on the health consequences of bereavement. In M. Osterweis, F. Solomon, & M. Green (Eds.), *Bereavement: Reactions, consequences, and care* (pp.15–46). Washington, DC: National Academy Press.

Klineberg, O. (1940). *Social psychology.* New York: Holt.

Kling, A. S. (1986). The anatomy of aggression and affiliation. In R. Plutchik & H. Kellerman (Eds.), *Emotion: Theory, research, and experience. Vol. 3: Biological foundations of emotion* (pp. 237–264). New York: Academic Press.

Klinger, E. (1977). *Meaning and void: Inner experience and the incentives in people's lives.* Minneapolis: University of Minnesota Press.

Klinnert, M. D. (1981, April). *Infants' use of mothers' facial expressions for regulating their own behavior.* Paper presented at a meeting of the Society for Research in Child Development, Boston, MA.

Klinnert, M. D., Campos, J. J., Sorce, J. F., Emde, R. N., & Svejda, M. (1983). Emotions as behavior regulators: Social referencing in infancy. In R. Plutchik & H. Kellerman (Eds.), *Emotion: Theory, research, and experience* (Vol. 2) (pp. 57–86). New York: Academic Press.

Knight, R., Atkins, A., Eagle, C., Evans, N., Finkelstein, J., Fukushima, D., Katz, J., & Weiner, H. (1979). Psychological stress, ego defenses, and cortisol production in children hospitalized for elective surgery. *Psychosomatic medicine, 41,* 40–49.

Kobasa, S. C. (1979). Stressful life events and health: An inquiry into hardiness. *Journal of Personality and Social Psychology, 37,* 1–11.

Kobasa, S. C., Maddi, S. R., & Kahn, S. (1982). Hardiness and health. *Journal of Personality and Social Psychology, 42,* 168–177.

Kobasa, S. C., Maddi, S. R., & Puccetti, M. C. (1982). Personality and exercise as buffers in the stress-illness relationship. *Journal of Behavioral Medicine, 5,* 391–404.

Koestler, A. (1952). *Arrow in the blue.* New York: Macmillan.

Konecni, V. J. (1984). Methodological issues in human aggression research. In R. M. Kaplan, V. J. Konecni, & R. W. Novaco (Eds.), *Aggression in children and youth* (pp. 1–43). The Hague: Martinus Nijhoff Publishers.

Kovacs, M., & Beck, A. T. (1985). Maladaptive cognitive structures in depression. In J. C. Coyne (Ed.), *Essential papers on depression.* New York: New York University Press.

Kraines, S. H. (1957). *Mental depressions and their treatment.* New York: Macmillan.

Krasnoff, A. (1959). Psychological variables and human cancer: A cross-validation study. *Psychosomatic Medicine, 21,* 291–295.

Kremer, J. F., & Stephens, L. (1983). Attribution and arousal as mediators of mitigations effect on retaliation. *Journal of Personality and Social Psychology, 45,* 335–343.

Kretsinger, E. A. (1952). An experimental study of restiveness in preschool educational television audiences. *Speech Monographs, 26,* 72–77.

Kroll, J. (1987, March 9). The arts. *Newsweek.*

Kubler-Ross, E. (1969). *On death and dying.* New York: Macmillan.

Lacey, J. I. (1967). Somatic response patterning and stress: Some revisions of activation theory. In M. H. Appley & R. Trumbull (Eds.), *Psychological stress: Issues in research* (pp. 14–42). New York: Appleton-Century Crofts.

Lacey, J. I., & Lacey, B. C. (1970). Some autonomic-central nervous system interrelationships. In P. Black (Ed.), *Physiological correlates of emotion* (pp. 205–227). New York: Academic Press.

Lachman, S. J. (1983). A physiological interpretation of voodoo illness and voodoo death. *Omega, 13,* 345–360.

Lader, M. (1980). Psychophysiological studies in anxiety. In G. D. Burrow & B. Davies (Eds.), *Handbook of studies on anxiety* (pp. 59–88). Amsterdam: Elsevier/North-Holand Biomedical Press.

Laird, J. D. (1984). The real role of facial response in the experience of emotion: A reply to Tourangeau and Ellsworth, and others. *Journal of Personality and Social Psychology, 47,* 909–917.

Laird, J. D., Wagener, J. J., Halal, M., & Szegda, M. (1982). Remembering what you feel: Effects of emotion and memory. *Journal of Personality and Social Psychology, 42,* 646–675.

Lang, P. J. (1979). A bio-informational theory of emotional imagery. *Psychophysiology, 16,* 495–512.

Lang, P. J., Melamed, B., & Hart, J. (1970). A psychophysiological analysis of fear modification using automated desensitization procedure. *Journal of Abnormal Psychology, 76,* 220–234.

Lang, P. J., Rice, D. G., & Sternbach, R. A. (1972). The psychophysiology of emotion. In N. S. Greenfield & R. A. Sternbach (Eds.), *Handbook of psychophysiology.* New York: Holt, Rinehart and Winston.

Lang, P. J., & Twentyman, C. T. (1974). Learning to control heart-rate: Binary vs. analogue feedback. *Psychophysiology, 11*, 616–629.

Lange, C. (1885/1922). The emotions. In E. Dunlap (Ed.), *The emotions.* (I. A. Istar Haupt, Trans.). Baltimore, MD: Williams and Wilkens.

Lange, C. G., & James, W. (1922). *The emotions* (Vol. 1). Baltimore, MD: Williams and Wilkens.

Langley, J. N. (1921). *The autonomic nervous system.* Cambridge: Heffer.

Lanzetta, J. T., Cartwright-Smith, J., & Kleck, R. E. (1976). Effects of nonverbal dissimulation on emotional experience and autonomic arousal. *Journal of Personality and Social Psychology, 33*, 354–370.

Lanzetta, J. T., & McHugo, G. J. (1986, October). The history and current status of the facial feedback hypothesis. Paper presented at the twenty-sixth annual meeting of the Society for Psychophysiological Research, Montreal, Quebec, Canada.

Larbig, W. (1991). Gate control theory of pain perception. In J.G. Carlson & R. Seifert (Eds.). *International perspectives on self-regulation and health.* New York: Plenum Press.

Larson, J. A. (1932). *Lying and its detection.* Chicago: University of Chicago Press.

Larson, R. (1978). Thirty years of research on the subjective well-being of older Americans. *Journal of Gerontology, 33*, 109–125.

Laski, M. (1962). *Ecstasy: A study of some secular and religious experiences.* Bloomington, IN: Indiana University Press.

Laudenslager, M. L., & Reite, M. L. (1984). Losses and separations. Immunological consequences and health implications. In P. Shauer (Ed.), *Review of Personality and Social Psychology. Emotions, Relations and Health, 5* (pp. 285–312). London: Sage Publications.

Lazarus, R. S. (1968). Emotions and adaptation: Conceptual and empirical relations. In W. J. Arnold (Ed.), *Nebraska symposium on motivation, 16* (pp. 175–270). Lincoln: University of Nebraska Press.

Lazarus, R. S. (1977). A cognitive analysis of biofeedback control. In G. E. Schwartz & J. Beatty (Eds.), *Biofeedback: Theory and research* (pp. 69–71). New York: Academic Press.

Lazarus, R. S. (1984). Thoughts on the relations between emotion and cognition. In K. Scherer & P. Ekman (Eds.), *Approaches to emotion* (pp. 247–257). Hillsdale, NJ: Erlbaum.

Lazarus, R. S., & Folkman, S. (1984). Coping and adaptation. In W. G. Gentry (Ed.), *The handbook of behavioral medicine* (pp. 282–325). New York: Guilford Press.

Lazarus, R. S., Kanner, A. D., & Folkman, S. (1980). Emotions: A cognitive phenomenological analysis. In R. Plutchik & H. Kellerman (Eds.), *Emotion: Theory, research and experience* (Vol. 1) (pp. 189–218). New York: Academic Press.

Leavitt, F. (1982). *Drugs and behavior.* New York: John Neley and Sons.

LeBoeuf, A. (1974). The importance of individual differences in the treatment of chronic anxiety by EMG biofeedback techniques. Paper presented at the annual meetings of the Biofeedback Society of America, Colorado Springs, CO.

Le Carré, J. (1980). *Smiley's people.* New York: Knopf.

LeDoux, J. E. (1986). The neurobiology of emotion. In J. E. LeDoux & W. Hirst (Eds.), *Mind and brain: Dialogues in cognitive neuroscience* (pp. 301–354). Cambridge, England: Cambridge University Press.

LeDoux, J. E., Sakaguchi, A., & Reis, D. J. (1983). Subcortical efferent projections of the medial geniculate nucleus mediate emotional responses conditioned to acoustic stimuli. *Journal of Neuroscience, 4,* 683–698.

LeDoux, J. E., Wilson, D. H., & Gazzaniga, M. S. (1977). A divided mind: Observations on the conscious properties of the separated hemispheres. *Annals of Neurology, 2,* 417–421.

Lee, J. A. (1988). Love-styles. In R. J. Sternberg & M. L. Barnes (Eds.), *The psychology of love.* New Haven: Yale University Press.

Leeper, R. W. (1948). A motivational theory of emotion to replace "emotion as disorganized response". *Psychological Review, 55,* 5–21.

Lefcourt, H. M., Miller, R. S., Ware, E. E., & Sherk, D. (1981). Locus of control as a modifier of the relationship between stressors and moods. *Journal of Personality and Social Psychology, 41,* 357–369.

Leff, J. P. (1973). Culture and the differentiation of emotional states. *British Journal of Psychiatry, 123,* 299–306.

Lefkowitz, M. M., Eron, L. D., Walder, L. O., & Huesmann, L. R. (1976). *Growing up to be violent.* New York: Pergamon.

Lehman, D. R., Wortman, C. B., & Williams, A. F. (1987). Long term effects of losing a spouse or child in a motor vehicle crash. *Journal of Personality and Social Psychology, 52,* 218–231.

Lehmann-Haupt, C. (1988, August 4). Books of the times: How an actor found success, and himself. *The New York Times,* p. 2.

Leo, J. (1986, May 26). Behavior: Talk is as good as a pill. NIMH study shows psychotherapy lifts depression. *Time,* p. 43.

LeShan, L. (1966). An emotional life history pattern associated with neoplastic disease. *Annual New York Academy of Sciences, 125,* 780–793.

Leventhal, G. S., & Bergman, J. T. (1969). Self-depriving behavior as a response to unprofitable inequity. *Journal of Experimental Social Psychology, 5,* 153–171.

Leventhal, H., & Nerenz, D. R. (1982). A model for stress research and some implications for the control of stress disorders. In D. Meichenbaum & M. Jaremko (Eds.) *Stress prevention and management: A cognitive behavioral approach.* New York: Plenum Press.

Levi, L. (1972). Psychological and physiological reactions to and psychomotor performance during prolonged and complex stressor exposure. *Acta Medicus Scandanavia, Supplement, 528,* 119–142.

Levinger, G. (1983). Development and change. In H. H. Kelley, E. Berscheid, A. Christensen, J. H. Harvey, T. L. Huston, G. Levinger, E. McClintock, L. A. Peplau, & D. R. Peterson (Eds.), *Close relationships* (pp. 315–359). New York: W. H. Freeman.

Levis, D. J. (1980). Implementing the technique of implosive therapy. In A. Goldstein & E. B. Foa (Eds.), *Handbook of behavioral interventions: A clinical guide.* New York: Wiley.

Lewinsohn, P. (1974a). A behavioral approach to depression. In R. J. Friedman & M. M. Katz (Eds.), *The psychology of depression: Contemporary theory and research* (pp. 157–185). Washington, DC: V. H. Winston & Sons.

Lewinsohn, P. (1974b). Clinical and theoretical aspects of depression. In K. Calhoun, H. Adams, & K. Mitchell (Eds.), *Innovative treatment methods in psychopathology* (pp. 63–120). New York: Wiley .

Lewinsohn, P. M. (1986). A behavioral approach to depression. In J. C. Coyne (Ed.),

Essential papers on depression (pp. 150–180). New York: New York University Press.

Lewinsohn, P. M., & Talkington, J. (1979). Studies on the measurement of unpleasant events and relations with depression. *Applied Psychological Measurement, 3,* 83–101.

Lewis, A. (1980). Problems presented by the ambiguous word 'anxiety' as used in psychopathology. In G. D. Burrows & B. Davies (Eds.), *Handbook of studies on anxiety.* Amsterdam: Elsevier/North-Holland Biomedical Press.

Lewis, M., & Michalson, L. (1983). *Children's emotions and moods: Developmental theory and measurement.* New York: Plenum Press.

Ley, R. G., & Bryden, M. P. (1979). Hemispheric differences in processing emotions and faces. *Brain and Language, 7,* 127–138.

Ley, R. G., & Bryden, M. P. (1982). A dissociation of right and left hemispheric effects for recognizing emotional tone and verbal content. *Brain and Cognition, 1,* 3–9.

Leyens, J. P., Camino, L., Parke, R. D., & Berkowitz, L. (1975). Effects of movie violence on aggression in a field setting as a function of group dominance and cohesion. *Journal of Personality and Social Psychology, 32,* 346–360.

Liddy, G. G. (1980). *Will: The autobiography of G. Gordon Liddy.* New York: St. Martin's Press.

Liebert, R. M., & Baron, R. A. (1972). Some immediate effects of televised violence on children. *Developmental Psychology, 6,* 469–475.

Liebowitz, M. R. (1983). *The chemistry of love.* Boston: Little, Brown.

Likert, R. (1932). A technique for the measurement of attitudes. *Archives of Psychology, 140,* 44–53.

Lindemann, E. (1944). Symptomatology and management of acute grief. *American Journal of Psychiatry, 101,* 141–149.

Lindsley, D. B. (1957). Psychophysiology and motivation. In M. R. Jones (Ed.), *Nebraska symposium on motivation* (pp. 44–105). Lincoln: University of Nebraska Press.

Lindzey, G., Hall, C. S., & Thompson, R. F. (1978). *Psychology,* New York: Worth Publishers.

Lingeman, R. (1974). *Drugs from A to Z: A dictionary.* New York: McGraw-Hill.

Lipman, R. L., & Shapiro, A. (1967). Effects of a behavioral stimulus on the blood pressure of rats with experimental pyelonephritis. *Psychosomatic Medicine, 29,* 612–618.

Littman, R. A., & Manning, H. M. (1954). A methodological study of cigarette brand discrimination. *Journal of Applied Psychology, 38,* 185–190.

Lolordo, V. M., & Furrow, D. R. (1976). Control by the auditory or the visual element of a compound discriminative stimulus: Effects of feedback. *Journal of the Experimental Analysis of Behavior, 25,* 251–256.

Lorenz, K. (1965). *Evolution and the modification of behavior.* Chicago: University of Chicago Press.

Lorr, M., Daston, P., & Smith, I. R. (1967). An analysis of mood states. *Educational and Psychological Measurement, 27,* 89–96.

Lubar, J. F., & Bahler, W. W. (1976). Behavioral management of epilectic seizures following EEG biofeedback training of the sensorimotor rythm. *Biofeedback and Self-Regulation, 1,* 77–104.

Lutwak, L., Whedon, G. D., Lachance, P. A., Reid, J. M., & Lipscomb, H. S. (1969). Mineral electrolyte and nitrogen balance studies of Gemini VII fourteen day orbital space flight. *Journal of Clinical Endocrinology and Metabolism, 29,* 1140–1156.

Lutyens, M. (1966). *Young Mrs. Ruskin in Venice.* New York: Vantage Press.

Lykken, D. T. (1960). The validity of the guilty knowledge technique: The effects of faking. *Journal of Applied Psychology, 44,* 258–262.

Lykken, D. T. (1974). Psychology and the lie detector industry. *American Psychologist, 29,* 725–739.

Lykken, D. T. (1981). The lie detector and the law. *Criminal Defense, 8,* 19–27.

MacLean, P. D. (1949). Psychosomatic disease and the "visceral brain": Recent developments bearing on the Papez theory of emotion. *Psychosomatic Medicine, 11,* 338–353.

MacLean, P. D. (1975). Sensory and perceptive factors in emotional function of the triune brain. In R. G. Grenell & S. Gabay (Eds.), *Biological foundations of psychiatry* Vol. 1 (pp. 177–198). New York: Raven Press.

MacLean, P. D. (1986). Ictal symptoms relating to the nature of affects and their cerebral substrate. In R. Plutchik & H. Kellerman (Eds.), *Emotion, theory, research, and experien*ce. Vol. 3. Biological foundations of emotion (pp. 61–90). New York: Academic Press.

Mahoney, J. J. (1977). A critical analysis of rational-emotive theory and therapy. *Counseling Psychologist, 7*(1), 43–46.

Maier, N. R. F., & Ellen, P. (1952). Studies of abnormal behavior in the rat. XXIII. The prophylactic effects of guidance in reducing rigid behavior. *Journal of Abnormal and Social Psychology, 47,* 109–116.

Mallick, S. K., & McCandless, B. R. (1966). A study of catharsis of aggression. *Journal of Personality and Social Psychology, 4,* 591–596.

Malloy, P. F., Fairbank, J. A., & Keane, P. M. (1983). Validation of a multi method assessment of post traumatic stress disorders in Vietnam veterans. *Journal of Consulting and Clinical Psychology, 51,* 488–494.

Malmo, R. B. (1975). *On emotions, needs, and our archaic brain.* New York: Holt, Rinehart and Winston.

Mandler, G. (1975a). *Mind and emotion.* New York: Wiley.

Mandler, G. (1975b). The search for emotion. In L. Levi (Ed.), *Emotions: Their parameters and measurement.* New York: Raven Press.

Mandler, G. (1982). Stress and thought processes. In L. Goldberger & S. Breznitz (Eds.), *Handbook of stress.* New York: Free Press/Macmillan.

Mandler, G. (1984). *Mind and body: Psychology of emotion and stress.* New York: Norton.

Manfredi, M., Bini, G., Cruccu, G., Accornero, N., Beradelli, A., & Medolago, L. (1981). Congenital absence of pain. *Archives of Neurology, 38,* 507–511.

Mann, T. (1969). *The magic mountain.* New York: Vintage.

Mark, V. H., & Ervin, F. R. (1970). *Violence and the brain.* New York: Harper.

Markoff, R. A., Ryan, P.R., & Young, T. (1982). Endorphins and mood changes in long-distance running. *Medicine and Science in Sports and Exercise, 14,* 11–15.

Marks, I. M. (1977). Phobias and obsessions. In J. Maser & M. Seligman (Eds.), *Experimental psychopathology* (pp. 174–213). New York: John Wiley & Sons.

Marsella, A. J. (1981). Depressive experience and disorder across cultures. In H. C.

Triandis & J. G. Draguns (Eds.), *Handbook of cross cultural psychology: Psychopathology.* (Vol. 6) (pp. 237–289). London: Allyn and Bacon.

Marshall, G., & Zimbardo, P. (1979). The affective consequences of inadequately explained physiological arousal. *Journal of Personality and Social Psychology, 37,* 970–988.

Maslach, C. (1979). Negative emotional biasing of unexplained arousal. *Journal of Personality and Social Psychology, 37,* 953–969.

Maslow, A. H. (1954). *Motivation and personality.* New York: Harper & Row.

Maslow, A. H., & Mintz, N. L. (1956). Effects of esthetic surroundings: I. Initial effects of three esthetic conditions upon perceiving 'energy' and 'well-being' in faces. *Journal of Psychology, 41,* 247–254.

Mason, J. W. (1971). A re-evaluation of the concept of "non-specificity" in stress theory. *Journal of Psychiatric Research, 8,* 323–333.

Mason, J. W. (1974). Specificity in the organization of neuroendocrine response profiles. In P. Seamon & G. Brown (Eds.), *Frontiers in neurology and neuroscience research* (pp. 68–80). Toronto: University of Toronto.

Mason, J. W. (1975). A historical view of the stress field. Part I. *Journal of Human Stress, 1,* 6–12.

Masserman, J. (1946). *Principles of dynamic psychiatry.* Philadelphia: Saunders.

Masserman, J. H. (1961). *Principles of dynamic psychiatry* (2nd ed.). New York: Saunders.

Matlin, M. W., & Gawron, V. J. (1979). Individual differences in Pollyannaism. *Journal of Personality Assessment, 43,* 411–412.

Matlin, M. W., & Stang, D. J. (1978). *The Pollyanna principle: Selectivity in language, memory and thought.* Cambridge, MA: Schenkman.

Maugham, W. Somerset. (1953). *Of human bondage.* New York: Pocket Books.

May, M. A. (1948). Experimentally acquired drives. *Journal of Experimental Psychology, 38,* 66–77.

May, R. (1980). Value conflicts and anxiety. In I. L. Kutash, B. Schlesinger, & Associates (Eds.), *Handbook on stress and anxiety.* San Francisco: Jossey-Bass.

Mayer, D. J., & Liebeskind, J. C. (1974). Pain reduction by focal electrical stimulation of the brain: An anatomical and behavioral analysis. *Brain Research, 68,* 73–93.

Mayer, W. (1983). Alcohol abuse and alcoholism: The psychologist's role in prevention, research, and treatment. *American Psychologist, 38,* 1116–1121.

McAmmond, D. M., Davidson, P. O., & Kovitz, D. M. (1971). A comparison of the effects of hypnosis and relaxation training on stress reactions in a dental situation. *American Journal of Clinical Hypnosis, 13,* 233–242.

McCabe, P. M., & Schneiderman, N. (1985). Psychophysiologic reactions to stress. In J. T. Tapp & N. Schneiderman (Eds.), *Behavioral medicine: The biopsychosocial approach* (pp. 99–131). Hillsdale, NJ: Erlbaum.

McCann, L., & Holmes, D. S. (1984). Influence of aerobic exercise on depression. *Journal of Personality and Social Psychology, 46,* 1142–1147.

McCarthy, J. F., & Kelly, B. R. (1978a). Aggressive behavior and its effect on performance over time in ice hockey athletes: An archival study. *International Journal of Sport Psychology, 9,* 90–96.

McCarthy, J. F., & Kelly, B. R. (1978b). Aggression, performance variables, and anger self-report in ice hockey players. *Journal of Psychology, 99,* 97–101.

McCauley, E. A., & Ehrhardt, A. A. (1976). Female sexual response: Hormonal and behavioral interactions. *Primary Care, 3*, 455–476.

McDougall, W. (1908). *An introduction to social psychology.* London: Methuen.

McFall, R. M. (1982). A review amd reformulation of the concept of social skills. *Behaviorial Assessment, 4*, 1–33.

McGlone, F. B., & Kick, E. (1978). Health habits in relation to aging. *Journal of the American Geriatrics Society, 26*, 481–488.

McGraw, K. O. (1987). *Developmental Psychology.* New York: Harcourt, Brace, Jovanovich.

McHugo, G. J. (1983). *Facial EMG and self-reported emotion.* Paper presented at the 23rd annual meeting of the Society for Psychophysiological Research, Asilomar, CA.

McNair, D. M., & Lorr, M. (1964). An analysis of mood in neurotics. *Journal of Abnormal and Social Psychology, 69*, 620–627.

McNally, R. (1987). Preparedness and phobias. *Psychological Bulletin, 101*, 283–303.

Mead, M. (1931). Jealousy: Primitive and civilized. In S. Schmalhausen & V. F. Calverton (Eds.), *Woman's coming of age* (pp. 35–48). New York: Liveright.

Mead, M. (1975). Review of Darwin and facial expression. *Journal of Communication, 25*, 209–213.

Meichenbaum, D. (1977). *Cognitive-behavior modification: An integrative approach.* New York: Plenum.

Meichenbaum, D. (1985). *Stress inoculation training.* Elmsford, NY: Pergamon.

Melzack, R. (1973). *The puzzle of pain.* New York: Basic Books.

Melzack, R. (1980). Psychological aspects of pain. In J. J. Bonica (Ed.), *Pain* (pp. 143–154). New York: Raven.

Melzack, R., & Wall, P. D. (1965). Pain mechanisms: A new theory. *Science, 150*, 971–979.

Mervis, J. (1986, July). NIMH data points way to effective treatment. *The APA Monitor, 17*, 1–13.

Mesulam, M-M., & Perry, J. (1972). The diagnosis of love-sickness: Experimental psychophysiology without the polygraph. *Psychophysiology, 9*, 546–551.

Meyer, R. J., & Haggerty, R. (1962). Streptococcal infections in families: Factors altering individual susceptibility. *Pediatrics, 29*, 539–549.

Miczek, K. A. (1973). Effects of scopolamine, amphetamine, and benzopliazepines on conditioned suppression. *Pharmacology, Biochemistry, and Behavior, 1*, 401–411.

Millenson, J. R. (1967). *Principles of behavioral analysis.* New York: Macmillan.

Millenson, J. R., & Leslie, J. C. (1974). The conditioned emotional response (CER) as a baseline for the study of anti-anxiety drugs. *Neuropharmacology, 13*, 1–9.

Millenson, J. R., & Leslie, J. C. (1979). *Principles of behavioral analysis* (2nd ed.). New York: Macmillan.

Miller, G. A. (1956). The magical number seven, plus or minus two: Some limits on our capacity for processing information. *Psychological Review, 63*, 81–97.

Miller, L., Berg, J. H., & Archer, R. L. (1983). Openers: Individuals who elicit intimate self-disclosure. *Journal of Personality and Social Psychology, 44*, 1234–1244.

Miller, L. H., & Shmavonian, B. M. (1965). Replicability of two GSR indices as a function of stress and cognitive activity. *Journal of Personality and Social Psychology, 2*, 753–756.

Miller, N. E. (1941). The frustration-aggression hypothesis. *Psychological Review, 48,* 337–342.

Miller, N. E. (1959). Liberalization of basic S-R concepts: Extensions to conflict behavior, motivation, and social learning. In S. Koch (Ed.), *Psychology: A study of a science* (Vol. 2) (pp. 196–292). New York: McGraw-Hill.

Miller, N. E. (1980). A perspective on the effects of stress and coping on disease and health. In S. Levine & H. Ursin (Eds.), *Coping and health* (pp. 323–353). (NATO Conference Series III: Human Factors) New York: Plenum.

Miller, N. E., & Bugelski, R. (1948). Minor studies in aggression: The influence of frustration imposed by the in-group on attitudes expressed toward out-groups. *Journal of Psychology, 25,* 437–442.

Mittleman, B., & Wolff, H. G. (1939). Affective states and skin temperature: Experimental study of subjects with "cold hands" and Raynaud's syndrome. *Psychosomatic Medicine, 1,* 271–292.

Money, J. (1980). *Love and love sickness.* Baltimore, MD: Johns Hopkins University Press.

Monte, C. F. (1987). *Beneath the mask.* New York: Holt, Rinehart and Winston.

Moody, R. A. (1978). *Laugh after laugh: The healing power of humor.* Jacksonville, FL: Headwaters Press.

Moore, S. (1960). *The Stanislavski system.* New York: Viking.

Morris, J. B., & Beck, A. T. (1974). The Efficacy of antipsychotic drugs. *Archives of General Psychiatry, 30,* 667–671.

Morrow, L., Vrtunski, P. B., Kim, Y., & Boller, F. (1981). Arousal responses to emotional stimuli and laterality of lesion. *Neuropsychologia, 19,* 65–72.

Moscovitch, M., & Olds, J. (1982). Asymmetries in emotional facial expressions and their possible relation to hemispheric specialization. *Neuropsychologia, 20,* 71–81.

Moss, H. (1967). Sex, age, and state as determinants of mother-infant interaction. *Merrill-Palmer Quarterly of Behavior and Development, 13,* 19–36.

Mowrer, O. H. (1947). On the dual nature of learning—a re-interpretation of "conditioning" and "problem-solving." *Harvard Educational Review, 17,* 102–148.

Mowrer, O. H. (1960). *Learning theory and behavior.* New York: Wiley.

Moyer, K. E. (1968). Kinds of aggression and their physiological basis. *Communications in Behavioral Biology, 2,* 64–87.

Moyer, K. E. (1986). Biological bases of aggressive behavior. In R. Plutchik & H. Kellerman (Eds.), *Emotion: Theory, research and experience* (Vol. 3) (pp. 219–236). New York: Academic Press.

Mullinix, J. M., Norton, B. J., Hack, S., & Fishman, M. A. (1978). Skin temperature feedback and migraine. *Headache, 17,* 242–244.

Murphy, G. E., Simons, A. D., Wetzel, G. D., & Lustman, P. J. (1984). Cognitive therapy and pharmacotherapy. *Archives of General Psychiatry, 41,* 33–41.

Murphy, L. B. (1983). Issues in the development of emotion in infancy. In R. Plutchik & H. Kellerman (Eds.), *Emotion: Theory, research, and experience* (Vol. 2) (pp. 1–34). New York: Academic Press.

Myerscough, R., & Taylor, S. (1985). The effects of marijuana on human physical aggression. *Journal of Personality and Social Psychology, 49,* 1541–1546.

Nathan, P. W. (1976). The gate-control theory of pain: A critical review. *Brain, 99,* 123.

Nathan, P. W., & Rudge, P. (1974). Testing the gate-control theory of pain in man. *Journal of Neurology, Neurosurgery, and Psychiatry, 37*, 1366–1372.

Nation, C. A. (1905). *The use and need of the life of Carry A. Nation.* Topeka, KS: F. M. Steves & Sons.

National Commission on Marijuana and Drug Abuse. (1973). *Drug use in America: Problem in perspective. Report of the National Commission on marijuana and drug abuse.* Washington, DC: U.S. Government Printing Office.

Nerem, R. M., Levesque, M. J., & Cornhill, J. F. (1980). Social environment as a factor in diet-induced arteriosclerosis. *Science, 208*, 1475–1476.

New York Times (1986, April 25). FBI says crime reports in the U. S. rose 4% in 1985. P. 84.

New York Times (December 24, 1987), p. Y7.

Nielsen Television 81. (1981). Chicago: A. C. Nielsen.

Nixon, R. M. (1962). *Six crises.* Garden City, N.Y.: Doubleday.

Nolen-Hoeksema, S. (1987). Sex differences in unipolar depression: Evidence and theory. *Psychological Bulletin, 101*, 259–282.

Norwood, R. (1985). *Women who love too much.* Los Angeles: Jeremy P. Archer.

Nowlis, V. (1965). Research with the Mood Adjective Checklist. In S. S. Tomkins & C. Izard (Eds.), *Affect, cognition, personality* (pp. 352–389). New York: Springer.

Nowlis, V. (1970). Mood: Behavior and experience. In M. Arnold (Ed.), *Feelings and emotions* (pp. 261–277). New York: Academic Press.

Nowlis, V., & Nowlis, H. H. (1956). The description and analysis of mood. *Annals of the New York Academy of Sciences, 65*, 345–355.

Obrist, P. A. (1976). The cardiovascular-behavioral interaction—as it appears today. *Psychophysiology, 13*, 95–107.

Olds, J. (1977). *Drives and reinforcements.* New York: Raven.

Olds, J., & Milner, P. (1954). Positive reinforcement produced by electrical stimulation of septal area and other regions of rat brain. *Journal of Comparative and Physiological Psychology, 47*, 419–427.

Olshansky, S. (1962, April). Chronic sorrow: A response to having a mentally defective child. *Social Casework,* pp. 190–193.

O'Neill, N., & O'Neill, G. (1972). *Open marriage: A new lifestyle for couples.* New York: M. Evans.

Ornstein, R., & Thompson, R. F. (1984). *The amazing brain.* New York: Houghton Mifflin.

Osterweis, M. (1984). Bereavement intervention programs. In M. Osterweis, F. Solomon, & M. Green (Eds.), *Bereavement: Reactions, consequences, and care* (pp. 239–282). Washington, DC: National Academy Press.

O'Toole, R., & Dubin, R. (1968). Baby feeding and body sway: An experiment in George Herbert Mead's "taking the role of the other." *Journal of Personality and Social Psychology, 10*, 59–65.

Owens, D. J., & Straus, M. A. (1975). The social structure of violence in childhood and approval of violence as an adult. *Aggressive Behavior, 1*, 193–211.

Papalia, D. E., & Olds, S. W. (1985). *Psychology* (p. 333). New York: McGraw-Hill.

Papez, J. W. (1937). A proposed mechanism of emotion. *Archives of Neurology and Psychiatry, 38*, 725–743.

Parke, R. D., Berkowitz, L., Leyens, J. P., West, S. G., & Sebastian, R. S. (1977).

Some effects of violent and nonviolent movies on the behavior of juvenile delinquents. In L. Berkowitz (Ed.), *Advances in experimental social psychology* (Vol. 10) (pp. 135–172). New York: Academic Press.

Parkes, C. M. (1964). The effects of bereavement on physical and mental health: A study of the records of widows. *British Medical Journal, 2,* 274–279.

Parkes, C. M., Benjamin, B., & Fitzgerald, R. G. (1969). Broken heart: A statistical study of increased mortality among widowers. *British Medical Journal, 1,* 740–743.

Parks, R. (1977). Parental reactions to the birth of a handicapped child. *Health Social Work, 2,* 52–66.

Patel, C., Marmot, M. G., & Terry, D. (1981). Controlled trial of biofeedback-aided behavioral methods in reducing mild hypertension. *British Medical Journal, 282,* 2005–2008.

Patterson, G. R. (1978). *Families: Applications of social learning to family life.* Champaign, IL: Research Press.

Patterson, G. R., Littman, R. A., & Brecker, W. (1967). Aggression behavior in children: A step toward a theory of aggression. *Monographs of the Society for Research in Child Development, 32,* (5, Serial No. 113).

Pavlov, I. P. (1927). *Conditioned reflexes.* (G. V. Anrep, Trans.). London: Oxford University Press.

Paykel, E. S. (1973). Life stress and psychiatric disorder: Application of the clinical approach. In B. S. Dohrenwend & D. P. Dorenwend (Eds.), *Stressful life events: Their nature and effects* (pp. 135–149). New York: Wiley.

Pekala, R. J., & Kumar, V. K. (1987). Predicting hypnotic susceptibility *via* a self-report instrument: A replication. *American Journal of Clinical Hypnosis, 30,* 57–65.

Pelletier, K. R. (1977). *Mind as healer, mind as slayer: A holistic approach to preventing stress disorders.* New York: Delta.

Pennebaker, J. W. (1982). *The psychology of physical symptoms.* New York: Springer-Verlag.

Peplau, L. A. (1983). Roles and gender. In H. H. Kelley, E. Berscheid, A. Christensen, J. H. Harvey, T. L. Huston, G. Levinger, E. McClintock, L. A. Peplau, & D. R. Peterson (Eds.), *Close relationships* (pp. 220–260). New York: W. H. Freeman.

Peplau, L. A., & Perlman, D. (1982). *Loneliness.* New York: Wiley-Interscience.

Perhach, J. L., Ferguson, H. C., & McKinney, G. R. (1976). Evaluation of antihypertensive agents in the stress-induced hypertensive rat. *Life Science, 16,* 1731–1736.

Persky, H., Smith, K. D., & Basu, G. K. (1971). Relation of psychologic measures of aggression and hostility to testosterone production in man. *Psychosomatic Medicine, 33,* 265–277.

Peterson, C., Seligman, M. E. P., & Vaillant, G. E. (1987). Explanatory style and illness: Personality and physical health. *Journal of Personality, 55,* 237–265.

Peterson, J. L., & Zill, N. (1981). Television viewing in the United States and children's intellectual, social, and emotional development. *Television and Children, 2* (2), 21–28.

Peterson, R. C. (1984). Marijuana overview. In M. D. Glantz (Ed.). *Correlates and consequences of marijuana use.* DHHS Publication No. ADM 84–1276. Washington, DC: U. S. Government Printing Office.

Pilisuk, M. (1982). Delivery of social support: The social inoculation. *American Journal of Orthopsychiatry, 52,* 20–36.

Pines, A., & Aronson, E. (1983). Antecedents, correlates, and consequences of sexual jealousy. *Journal of Personality, 51,* 108–136.

Platman, S. R., Plutchik, R., & Weinstein, B. (1971). Psychiatric, physiological, behavioral and self-report measures in relation to a suicide attempt. *Journal of Psychiatric Research, 8,* 127–137.

Plato. (1955). *Phaedo.* (R. S. Bluck, Trans.). Indianapolis, IN: Bobbs-Merrill.

Plato. (1965). *The republic.* (F. M. Cornford, Trans.). New York: Oxford University Press.

Plutchik, R. (1962). *The emotions: Facts, theories, and a new model.* New York: Random House.

Plutchik, R. (1965). What is an emotion? *Journal of Psychology, 61,* 295–303.

Plutchik, R. (1970). Emotions, evolution and adaptive processes. In M. Arnold (Ed.), *Feelings and emotions.* New York: Academic Press.

Plutchik, R. (1980a). *Emotion: A psychoevolutionary synthesis.* New York: Harper & Row.

Plutchik, R. (1980b). A general psychoevolutionary theory of emotion. In R. Plutchik & H. Kellerman (Eds.), *Emotion: Theory, research and experience,* Vol. 1 (pp. 3–33). New York: Academic Press.

Plutchik, R. (1984). A general psychoevolutionary theory. In K. Scherer & P. Ekman (Eds.), *Approaches to emotion* (pp. 197–219). Hillsdale, NJ: Erlbaum.

Plutchik, R., & Kellerman, H. (1974). *Emotions Profile Index manual.* Los Angeles: Western Psychological Services.

Plutchik, R., & Kellerman, H. (Eds.) (1983). *Emotion: Theory, research, and experience. Vol. 2: Emotions in early development.* New York: Academic Press.

Plutchik, R. & Kellerman, H. (Eds.) (1986). *Emotion: Theory, research, and experience. Vol. 3: Biological foundations of emotion.* New York: Academic Press.

Poe, E. A. (1971). In W. T. Bandy (Ed.), *Seven tales.* New York: Schocken Books.

Poletti, C. E., Kliot, M., & Boytin, M. (1984). Metabolic influence of the hippocampus on hypothalamus, preoptic and basal forebrain is exerted through amygdalofugal pathways. *Neurosciences Letters, 45,* 211–216.

Pollock, C. (1928). *Mr. Moneypenny.* New York: Brentanos.

Price, R. H., & Lynn, S. J. (1986). *Abnormal psychology.* Chicago, IL: The Dorsey Press.

Proust, M. (1928). In C. K. S. Moncrieff (Ed.), *Swann's way,.* New York: Modern Library College Edition.

Quennell, P. (1949). *John Ruskin: The portrait of a prophet* (pp. 56–57). London: Collins.

Rabkin, J. G., & Streuning, E. L. (1976). Life events, stress, and illness. *Science, 194,* 1013–1020.

Rachman, S. (1977). The conditioning theory of fear-acquisition. A critical examination. *Behaviour Research and Therapy, 15,* 375–387.

Rao, A. (1975). India. In J. Howells (Ed.), *World history of psychiatry.* New York: Brunner/Mazel.

Raphael, B. (1983). *The anatomy of bereavement.* New York: Basic Books.

Rapson, R. (1980). *Denials of doubt: An interpretation of American history.* Lanham, MD: University Press of America.

Rapson, R. (1988). American yearnings: Love, money, and endless possibility. Lanham, MD: University Press of America.

Raquena, Y. (1986). Acupuncture's challenge to Western medicine. *Advances, 3,* 46–55.

Raush, H. L., Barry, W. A., Hertel, R. K., & Swain, M. A. (1974). *Communication, conflict and marriage.* San Francisco: Jossey-Bass.

Reber, A. S. (1985). *The penguin dictionary of psychology.* New York: Penguin.

Rehm, L., & Plakosh, P. (1975). Preference for immediate reinforcement in depression. *Journal of Behavior Therapy and Experimental Psychiatry, 6,* 101–103.

Reik, T. (1948). *Listening with the third ear.* New York: Farrar, Straus, & Giroux.

Reik, T. (1949). *Of love and lust.* New York: Farrar, Straus & Co.

Reik, T. (1972). *A psychologist looks at love.* New York: Holt, Rinehart and Winston.

Reiss, S. (1980). Pavlovian conditioning and human fear: An expectancy model. *Behavior Therapy, 11,* 380–396.

Rescorla, R. A. (1988). Pavlovian conditioning. It's not what you think it is. *American Psychologist, 43,* 151–160.

Rescorla, R. A., & Solomon, R. L. (1967). Two-process learning theory: Relationships between Pavlovian conditioning and instrumental learning. *Psychological Review, 74,* 151–182.

Reston, J. (March 14, 1975). Proxmire on love. *The New York Times,* p. 13.

Reston, J. S. (1986). *Understanding Human Sexuality.* (3rd Ed.), New York: McGraw-Hill. p. 98.

Revusky, S. H., & Garcia, J. (1970). Learning associations over long delays. In G. H. Bower (Ed.), *The psychology of learning and motivation.* (Vol. 4) (pp. 1–84). New York: Academic Press.

Reynolds, G. S. (1968). *A primer of operant conditioning.* Glenview, IL: Scott-Foresman.

Richter, C. P. (1957). On the phenomenon of sudden death in animals and man. *Psychosomatic Medicine, 19,* 191–198.

Riordan, C. A., & Tedeschi, J. T. (1983). Attraction in aversive environments: Some evidence for classical conditioning and negative reinforcement. *Journal of Personality and Social Psychology, 44,* 683–692.

Ritter, S., Pelzer, N. L., & Ritter R. C. (1978). Absence of glucoprivic feeding after stress suggests impairment of noradrenergic neuron function. *Brain Research, 149,* 399–411.

Robins, N., & Aronson, S. M. L. (1985). *Savage grace.* New York: William Morrow.

Robinson, J. P., & Shaver, P. R. (1969). *Measures of social psychological attitudes.* Ann Arbor, MI: The University of Michigan ISR.

Rolls, E. T. (1976). The neurophysiological basis of brain-stimulation reward. In A. Wauguier & E. T. Rolls (Eds.), *Brain-stimulation reward* (pp. 65–87). Amsterdam: North Holland Publishing Co.

Rosen, G. (1968). *Madness in society: Chapters in the historical sociology of mental illness.* New York: Harper & Row.

Rosenbaum, M. (1980). A schedule for assessing self-control behaviors: Preliminary findings. *Behavior Therapy, 11,* 109–112.

Rosenblatt, P. C. (1967). Marital residence and the functions of romantic love. *Ethnology, 6,* 471–480.

Rosenblum, L. A. (Sept. 18, 1985). Discussant: Passionate love and the nonhuman primate. Paper presented at the International Academy of Sex Research meetings, Seattle, WA.

Rosenblum, L. A., & Plimpton, L. A. (1981). The infant's effort to cope with separation. In M. Lewis & L. Rosenblum (Eds.), *The uncommon child* (pp. 225–257). New York: Plenum Press.

Rosenfeld, A. H. (1985, June). Depression: Dispelling despair. *Psychology Today*, 29–34.

Rossi, A. S., & Rossi, P. E. (1980). Body time and social time: Mood patterns by menstrual cycle phase and day of the week. In J. E. Parsons (Ed.), *The psychobiology of sex differences and sex roles* (pp. 269–304). New York: McGraw-Hill.

Rothbart, M. K. (1986). Longitudinal home observation of infant temperament. *Developmental Psychology, 22,* 356–365.

Rotter, J. B. (1966). Generalized expectancies for internal versus external control of reinforcement. *Psychological Monographs: General and Applied, 80* (Whole No. 609).

Rubin, Z. (1970). Measurement of romantic love. *Journal of Personality and Social Psychology, 16,* 265–273.

Rule, B. G., & Nesdale, A. R. (1976). Emotional arousal and aggressive behavior. *Psychological Bulletin, 83,* 851–863.

Rushdie, S. (1988). *The Satanic Verses.* New York: Viking.

Russell, J. A., & Mehrabian, A. (1977). Evidence for a three-factor theory of emotions. *Journal of Research in Personality, 11,* 273–294.

Russell, W. A. (1970). *Milestones in motivation. Contributions to the psychology of drive and purpose.* New York: Appleton-Century-Crofts.

Rycroft, C. (1968). *A critical dictionary of psychoanalysis.* London: Penguin.

Sackheim, H. A., & Gur, R. C. (1978). Lateral asymmetry in intensity of emotional expression. *Neuropsychologia, 16,* 473–482.

Sackheim, H. A., Weinnman, A. L., Gur, R. C., Greenberg, M., Hungerbuhler, J. P., & Geshwind, N. (1982). Pathological laughing and crying: Functional brain asymmetry in the experience of positive and negative emotions. *Archives of Neurology, 39,* 210–218.

Sacks, O. (1983). *Awakenings.* New York: E. P. Dutton.

Sacks, O. (1984). *A leg to stand on.* New York: Harper & Row.

Sacks, O. (1985). *The man who mistook his wife for a hat.* New York: Harper & Row.

Sarason, I. G., Johnson, J. H., & Siegel, J. M. (1978). Assessing the impact of life changes: Development of the Life Experiences Survey. *Journal of Consulting and Clinical Psychology, 46,* 932–946.

Sarnoff, I., & Zimbardo, P. (1961). Anxiety, fear, and social affiliation. *Journal of Abnormal and Social Psychology, 62,* 356–363.

Sarton, M. (1982). *Anger.* New York: Norton.

Satariano, W. A., & Syme, S. L. (1981). Life changes and disease in elderly populations: Coping with change. In J. L. McGaugh & S. B. Kiesler (Eds.), *Aging: Biology and behavior* (pp. 311–327). New York: Academic Press.

Savitsky, J. C., & Sim, M. E. (1974). Trading emotions. Equity theory of reward and punishment. *Journal of Communication, 24,* 140–146.

Saxe, L., Dougherty, D., & Cross, T. (1985). The validity of polygraph testing: Scientific analysis and public controversy. *American Psychologist, 40,* 355–366.

Scarr, S., & Salapatek, P. (1970). Patterns of fear development during infancy. *Merrill-Palmer Quarterly of Behavior and Development, 16,* 3–90.

Schachter, S. (1964). The interaction of cognitive and physiological determinants of emotional state. In L. Berkowitz (Ed.), *Advances in experimental social psychology* (Vol. 1) (pp. 49–80). New York: Academic Press.

Schachter, S. (1966). The interaction of cognitive and physiological determinants of emotional state. In C. D. Spielberger (Ed.), *Anxiety and behavior* (pp. 193–224). New York: Academic Press.

Schachter, S. (1971). *Emotion, obesity, and crime.* New York: Academic Press.

Schachter, S. (1975). Cognition and peripheralist-centralist controversies in motivation and emotion. In M. S. Gazzaniga & C. Blakemore (Eds.), *Handbook of psychobiology* (pp. 529–564). New York: Academic Press.

Schachter, S., & Singer, J. (1962). Cognitive, social, and physiological determinants of emotional state. *Psychological Review, 69,* 379–399.

Schachter, S., & Wheeler, L. (1962). Epinephrine, chlorpromazine, and amusement. *Journal of Abnormal Social Psychology, 65,* 121–128.

Schaefer, E. S., & Plutchik, R. (1966). Interrelationships of emotions, traits, and diagnostic constructs. *Psychological Reports, 18,* 399–410.

Schatzberg, A. F., & Cole, J. O. (1986). *Manual of clinical psychopharmacology.* Washington, DC: American Psychiatric Press.

Scheff, T. J. (1979). *Catharsis in healing, ritual, and drama.* Los Angeles: University of California Press.

Scheflen, A. E. (1964). The significance of posture in communication systems. *Psychiatry, 27,* 316–331.

Scherer, K. R. (1982). The assessment of vocal expression in infants and children. In C. E. Izard (Ed.), *Measuring emotions in infants and children* (pp. 127–163). Cambridge, England: Cambridge University Press.

Schlosberg, H. (1941). A scale for the judgment of facial expressions. *Journal of Experimental Psychology, 29,* 497–510.

Schlosberg, H. (1954). Three dimensions of emotion. *Psychological Review, 61,* 81–88.

Schmale, A. H., & Iker, H. P. (1971). Hopelessness as a predictor of cervical cancer. *Social Science and Medicine, 5,* 95–100.

Schmeck, H. M. (1983, September 9). Study says smile may indeed be an umbrella. *The New York Times,* pp. 1–16.

Schuckit, M. A. (1977). Geriatric alcoholism and drug abuse. *The Gerontologist, 17,* 168–174.

Schuckit, M. A., Daly, V., Herrman, G., & Hineman, S. (1975). Premenstrual symptoms and depression in a university population. *Diseases of the Nervous System, 36,* 516–517.

Schultz, D. (1976). *Theories of personality.* Monterey, CA: Brooks/Cole.

Schulz, C. H. (1967). *Peanuts.* United Media. [Also appearing in Myers, C. G. *Social Psychology.* 3rd Ed. McGraw Hill: p. 383.]

Schwartz, G. E., Fair, P. L., Greenberg, P. S., Freedman, M., & Klerman, J. L. (1974). Facial electromyography in the assessment of emotions. *Psychophysiology, 11,* 237.

Schwartz, G. E., & Weiss, S. M. (1978). Yale conference on behavioral medicine: A proposed definition and statement of goals. *Behavioral Medicine, 1,* 3–12.

Sechrest, L. (1965). Situational sampling and contrived situations in the assessment of behavior. Unpublished manuscript, Northwestern University, Evanston, IL.

Sechrest, L., & Flores, L., Jr. (1971). The occurrence of a nervous mannerism in two cultures. *Asian Studies, 9* (1), 55–63.

Seligman, M. E. P. (1970). On the generality of the laws of learning. *Psychological Review, 77,* 406–419.

Seligman, M. E. P. (1971). Phobias and preparedness. *Behavior Therapy, 2,* 307–320.

Seligman, M. E. P. (1975). *Helplessness: On depression, development, and death.* San Francisco: W. H. Freeman.

Seligman, M. E., & Maier, S. F. (1967). Failure to escape traumatic shock. *Journal of Experimental Psychology, 74,* 1–9.

Selye, H. (1956). *The stress of life.* New York: McGraw-Hill.

Selye, H. (1974). *Stress without distress.* Philadelphia: Lippincott.

Selye, H. (1978). *The stress of life* (rev. ed.). New York: McGraw-Hill.

Sem-Jacobsen, C. W. (1968). *Depth-electrographic stimulation of the human brain and behavior.* Springfield, IL: Thomas.

Sendbuehler, J. M., & Goldstein, S. (1977). Attempted suicide among the aged. *Journal of the American Geriatric Society, 25,* 245–253.

Shapiro, D. H. (1980). *Meditation.* Hawthorne, NY: Aldine.

Shaver, P., & Freedman, J. (1976, August). Your pursuit of happiness. *Psychology Today, 10,* 26–75.

Shaver, P., & Rubenstein, C. (1980). Childhood attachment experience in adult loneliness. In L. Weiner (Ed.), *Review of Personality and Social Psychology* (Vol. 1) (pp. 42–73). Beverly Hills, CA: Sage.

Shaw, W. A. (1940). The relation of muscular action potentials to imaginal weight lifting. *Archives of Psychology, 247,* 50.

Shearer, L. (1986, September 28). Murder is closer than you think. *Parade Magazine,* p. 20. [Summary of the F.B.I.'s. Appendix 5: Probability of Lifetime Murder Victimization, 1984. *Crime in the United States.*]

Shelly, M. W. (1973). *Sources of satisfaction.* Lawrence, KS: University of Kansas Press.

Sherif, C. W. (1980). A social psychological perspective on the menstrual cycle. In J. E. Parsons (Ed.), *The psychobiology of sex differences and sex roles* (pp. 245–268). New York: McGraw-Hill.

Shirley, M. C., Burish, T. G., & Rowe, C. (1982). Effectiveness of multiple-site EMG biofeedback in the reduction of arousal. *Biofeedback and Self-Regulation, 7,* 167–184.

Silverman, C. (1968). *The epidemiology of depression.* Baltimore: Johns Hopkins Press.

Silverman, P. R., & Cooperband, A. (1975). On widowhood: Mutual help and the elderly widow. *Journal of Geriatric Psychiatry, 8,* 9–27.

Skinner, B. F. (1938). *Behavior of organisms.* New York: Appleton-Century-Crofts.

Skinner, B. F. (1953). *Science and human behavior.* New York: Macmillan.

Skinner, B. F. (1962). *Walden two.* New York: Macmillan.

Skinner, B. F. (1990). The place of feeling in the analysis of behavior. In E. A. Blechman & M. J. McEnroe. (Eds.) *Emotions in the family: For better or worse.* Hillsdale, NJ: Erlbaum.

Smith, A. (1966). *The theory of moral sentiments.* New York: Augustus M. Kelley. (Original work published 1759)

Smith, L. K. C., & Fowler, S. A. (1984). Positive peer pressure: The effects of peer monitoring on children's disruptive behavior. *Journal of Applied Behavior Analysis, 17,* 213–227.

Snodgrass, S. E. (1985). Women's intuition: The effect of subordinate role on interpersonal sensitivity. *Journal of Personality and Social Psychology, 49,* 146–155.

Solomon, R. L. (1980). The opponent-process theory of acquired motivation: The costs of pleasure and the benefits of pain. *American Psychologist, 35,* 691–712.

Solomon, R. L., & Corbit, J. D. (1974). An opponent process theory of motivation. I. The temporal dynamics of affect. *Psychological Review, 81,* 119–145.

Solsberry, V., & Krupnick, J. (1984). Adults' reactions to bereavement. In M. Osterweis, F. Solomon, & M. Green (Eds.), *Bereavement: Reactions, consequences, and care* (pp. 47–68). Washington, DC: National Academy Press.

Speck, R. V., & Attneave, C. L. (1973). *Family networks.* New York: Pantheon.

Spielberger, C. D. (1966). Theory and research on anxiety. In C. D. Spielberger (Ed.), *Anxiety and behavior* (pp. 3–20). New York: Academic Press.

Spielberger, C. D., & Diaz-Guerrero, R. (Eds.) (1976). *Cross-cultural anxiety* (Vol. 1). Washington, DC: Hemisphere.

Spielberger, C. D., Gorsuch, R. L., & Lushene, R. E. (1983). *Manual for the State-Trait Inventory (STAI).* Palo Alto, CA: Consulting Psychologist Press.

Spielberger, C. D., & Sharma, S. (1976). Cross-cultural measurement of anxiety. In C. D. Spielberger & R. Diaz-Guerrero (Eds.), *Cross-cultural anxiety* (Vol. 1) (pp. 13–25). Washington, DC: Hemisphere.

Spielberger, C. D., Vagg, P. R., Barker, L. R., Donham, G. W., & Westberry, L. G. (1980). The factor structure of the State-Trait Inventory. In I. G. Sarason & C. D. Spielberger (Eds.), *Stress and anxiety* (Vol. 7). New York: Hemisphere/Wiley.

Spitz, R. A. (1946). The psychoanalytic study of the child. *Anaclitic depression: An inquiry into the genesis of psychiatric condition in early childhood, II* (pp. 313–342). New York: International Universities Press.

Spitz, R., & Wolf, K. (1946). The smiling response: A contribution to the ontogenesis of social relations. *Genetic Psychology Monographs, 34,* 57–125.

Sprecher, S., & Hatfield, E. (1982). Self-esteem and romantic attraction: Four experiments. *Recherches de Psychologie Sociale, 4,* 61–81.

Springer, S. P., & Deutsch, G. (1981). *Left brain, right brain* (rev. ed.). New York: W. H. Freeman.

Staats, A. W., & Heiby, E. M. (1985). Paradigmatic behaviorism's theory of depression: Unified, explanatory, and heuristic. *Theoretical issues in behavior therapy* (pp. 279–330). New York: Academic Press.

Stampfl, T. G., & Levis, D. J. (1967). Essentials of implosive therapy: A learning theory-based psychodynamic behavioral therapy. *Journal of Abnormal Psychology, 72,* 496–503.

Stanley-Jones, D. (1970). The biological origin of love and hate. In M. B. Arnold (Ed.), *Feelings and emotions* (pp. 25–37). New York: Academic Press.

Steiner, J. E. (1979). Human facial expressions in response to taste and smell stimulation. *Advances in Child Development and Behavior, 13,* 257–295.

Steinmetz, S. K. (1978). Violence between family members. *Marriage and Family Review, 1* (3), 1–16.

Steinmetz, S. K., & Straus, M. A. (1973). The family as cradle of violence. *Society, 10,* 50–56.

Stephan, W., Berscheid, E., & Hatfield, E. (1971). Sexual arousal and heterosexual perception. *Journal of Personality and Social Psychology, 20,* 93–101.

Stern, D. (1974). The goal and structure of mother-infant play. *Journal of the American Academy of Child Psychiatry, 13,* 402–421.

Sternbach, R. A., (1968). *Pain: A psychophysiological analysis.* New York: Academic Press.

Sternbach, R. A. (1974). *Pain patients: Traits and treatment.* New York: Academic Press.

Sternbach, R. A. & Tursky, B. (1965). Ethnic differences among housewives in psychophysical and skin potential responses to electric shock. *Psychophysiology, 1,* 241–246.

Sternberg, R. J. (1988). Triangulating love. In R. J. Sternberg & M. L. Barnes (Eds.), *The psychology of love* (pp. 119–138). New Haven, CT: Yale University Press.

Stewart, L. H. (1987). A brief report: Affect and archetype. *Journal of Analytical Psychology, 32,* 35–46.

Stock, G., Schlor, K. H., Heidt, H., & Buss, J. (1978). Psychomotor behavior and cardiovascular patterns during stimulation of the amygdala. *Pfluegers Archives, 376,* 177–184.

Stoyva, J., & Budzynski, T. (1974). Cultivated low arousal—an anti-stress response? In L. V. DiCara (Ed.), *Recent advances in limbic and autonomic nervous system research.* New York: Plenum Press.

Stoyva, J., & Kamiya, J. (1968). Electrophysiological studies of dreaming as a prototype of a new strategy in the study of consciousness. *Psychological Review, 75,* 192–205.

Strachey, L. (1971). *Queen Victoria.* Harmondsworth, England: Penguin Books. (Originally published 1921)

Strack, F., Martin, L. L., & Stepper, S. (1988). Inhibiting and facilitating conditions of facial expressions: A non-obtrusive test of the facial feedback hypothesis. *Journal of Personality and Social Psychology, 54,* 768–777.

Straus, M. A., Gelles, R. J., & Steinmetz, S. K. (1980). *Behind closed doors: Violence in the American family.* New York: Anchor/Doubleday.

Strickland, B. R. (1978). Internal-external expectancies and health-related behaviors. *Journal of Consulting and Clinical Psychology, 46,* 1192–1211.

Stroebe, W., & Stroebe, M. S. (1987). *Bereavement and health: The psychological and physical consequences of partner loss.* New York: Cambridge University Press.

Strumpel, B. (1976). Economic life-styles, values, and subjective welfare. In B. Strumpel (Ed.), *Economic means for human needs.* Ann Arbor, MI: Institute for Social Research, University of Michigan.

Swanson, D. W., Floreen, A. C., & Swenson, W. M. (1976). Program for managing chronic pain. II. Short-term results. *Mayo Clinic Proceedings, 51,* 409–411.

Sweet, W. H., Ervin, F. R., & Mark, V. H. (1969). The relationship of violent behavior to focal cerebral disease. In S. Garattini & E. B. Sigg (Eds.), *Aggressive behavior* (pp. 336–352). New York: Wiley.

Swenson, L. C. (1980). *Theories of learning: Traditional perspectives/contemporary developments.* Bealmont, CA: Wadsworth.

Sykes, G. M., & Matza, D. (1957). Techniques of neutralization: A theory of delinquency. *American Sociological Review, 22,* 664–670.

Syme, S. L. (1984). Sociocultural factors and disease etiology. In W. D. Gentry (Ed.), *Handbook of behavioral medicine* (pp. 13–37). New York: The Guilford Press.

Tacitus, Caius Cornelius (1969). *Tacitus* (J. Jackson, Trans.). Cambridge, MA: Harvard University Press.

Tan, E. S. (1980). Transcultural aspects of anxiety. In G. D. Burrow & B. Davies (Eds.), *Handbook of studies on anxiety* (pp. 133–144). Amsterdam: Elsevier/North-Holland Biomedical Press.

Tanaka-Matsumi, J., & Marsella, A. J. (1976). Cross-cultural variations in the phenomenological experience of depression: Word association. *Journal of Cross Cultural Psychology, 7,* 379–396.

Taussig, H. B. (1969). "Death" from lightning and the possibility of living again. *American Scientist, 57,* 306–316.

Tavris, C. (1982). *Anger: The misunderstoood emotion.* New York: Simon & Schuster.

Taylor, J. (1953). A personality scale of manifest anxiety. *Journal of Abnormal and Social Psychology, 48,* 285–290.

Taylor, S. E. (1986). *Health psychology.* New York: Random House.

Tellegen, A., & Atkinson, G. (1974). Openness to absorbing and self-altering experiences ("absorption"), a trait related to hypnotic susceptibility. *Journal of Abnormal Psychology, 83,* 268–277.

Tennov, D. (1979). *Love and limerence.* New York: Stein and Day.

Theroux, P. (1977). *The consul's file.* New York: Penguin.

Thibaut, J. W., & Kelley, H. H. (1959). *The social psychology of groups.* New York: Wiley.

Thomas, C. B., Duzynski, K. R., & Shaffer, J. W. (1979). Family attitudes reported in youth as potential predictors of cancer. *Psychosomatic Medicine, 21,* 287–302.

Thomas, M. H., & Drabman, R. S. (1977). Toleration of real-life aggression as a function of exposure to televised violence and age of subject. *Merrill-Palmer Quarterly, 21,* 227–232.

Thompson, R. A., & Lamb, M. E. (1983). Individual differences in dimensions of socioemotional development in infancy. In R. Plutchik & H. Kellerman (Eds.), *Emotion: Theory, research and experience* (Vol. 2) (pp. 87–114). New York: Academic Press.

Thoresen, C. E., Telch, M. J., & Eagleston, J. R. (1981). Altering Type A behavior. *Psychosomatics, 8,* 472–482.

Timiras, P. S. (1972). *Developmental physiology and aging.* New York: Macmillan.

Tinbergen, N. (1951). *The study of instinct.* Oxford, England: Clarendon Press.

Toklas, A. B. (1960). *The Alice B. Toklas cookbook.* New York: Doubleday Anchor.

Tomkins, S. S. (1962). *Affect, imagery, consciousness. Vol. 1. The positive affects.* New York: Springer.

Tomkins, S. S. (1963). *Affect, imagery, consciousness. Vol. 2. The negative affects.* New York: Springer.

Tomkins, S. S. (1980). Affect as amplification: Some modifications in theory. In R. Plutchik & H. Kellerman (Eds.), *Emotion: Theory, research, and experience* (Vol. 1) (pp. 141–164). New York: Academic Press.

Tomkins, S. S. (1981). The quest for primary motives. Biography and autobiography of an idea. *Journal of Personality and Social Psychology, 41,* 306–329.

Tomkins, S. S. (1984a). Affect as amplification: Some modifications in theory. In R.

Plutchik and H. Kellerman (Eds.), *Emotion: Theory, research, and experience* (Vol. 1) (p. 141–164). New York: Academic Press.

Tomkins, S. S. (1984b). Affect theory. In K. Scherer & P. Edman (Eds.) *Approaches to emotion* (pp. 163–195). Hillsdale, NJ: Erlbaum.

Torgerson, S. (1979). The nature and origin of common phobic fears. *British Journal of Psychiatry, 134,* 343–351.

Traupmann, J., & Hatfield, E. (1981). Love and its effect on mental and physical health. In R. Fogel, E. Hatfield, S. Kiesler, & E. Shanas (Eds.), *Aging: Stability and change in the family* (pp. 253–274). New York: Academic Press.

Traupmann, J., Hatfield, E., & Wexler, P. (1983). Equity and sexual satisfaction in dating couples. *British Journal of Social Psychology, 22,* 33–40.

Traupmann, J., Peterson, R., Utne, M., & Hatfield, E. (1981). Measuring equity in intimate relations. *Applied Psychological Measurement, 5,* 467–480.

Tresemer, D. W. (1977). *Fear of success.* New York: Plenum Press.

Troubridge, L. (1979). *A book of etiquette.* Kingswood: Cedar Books. (Originally published 1929)

Vaillant, G. E. (1977). *Adaptation to life.* Boston: Little, Brown.

Valins, S. (1966). Cognitive effects of false heart rate feedback. *Journal of Personality and Social Psychology, 4,* 400–408.

Vanfossen, B. E. (1981). Sex differences in the mental health effects of spouse support and equity. *Journal of Health and Social Behavior, 22,* 130–143.

Van Hasselt, V. B., Hersen, M., Bellack, A. S., Rosenbloom, N., & Lamparski, D. (1979). Tripartite assessment of the effects of systematic desensitization in a multiphobic child: An experimental analysis. *Journal of Behavior Therapy and Experimental Psychiatry, 10,* 57–66.

Vaughan, K. B., & Lanzetta, J. T. (1980). Vicarious instigation and conditioning of facial expresssive and autonomic responses to a model's expressive display of pain. *Journal of Personality and Social Psychology, 38,* 909–923.

Venn, J. R., & Short, J. G. (1973). Vicarious classical conditioning of emotional responses in nursery school children. *Journal of Personality and Social Psychology, 28,* 249–255.

Veroff, J., Douvan, E., & Kulka, R. A. (1981). *The inner American.* New York: Basic Books.

Vickers, H. (1985). *Cecil Beaton.* New York: Donald Fine/Primus.

Visotsky, H. M., Hamburg, D. A., Goss, M. E., & Lebovitz, B. Z. (1961). Coping behavior under extreme stress. *Archives of General Psychiatry, 5,* 423–448.

Von Euler, U. S., & Lundberg, U. (1954). Effect of flying on the epinephrine excretion in Air Force personnel. *Journal of Applied Physiology, 10,* 347–354.

Von Holst, D. (1972). Renal failure as a cause of death in *Tupaia belangeri* (tree shrews) exposed to persistent social stress. *Journal of Comparative Physiology, 78,* 236–273.

Waid, W. M., & Orne, M. T. (1982). The physiological detection of deception. *American Scientist, 70,* 402–409.

Waldron, I. (1976, July/August). Why do women live longer than men? *Social Science and Medicine, 10,* 349–362.

Walker, C. (1977). Some variations in marital satisfaction. In R. Chester & J. Peel (Eds.), *Equalities and inequalities in family life* (pp. 127–139). London: Academic Press.

Wall, P. D., & Sweet, W. H. (1967). Temporary abolition of pain in men. *Science,* *155,* 108–109.

Wallis, C. (1984, June 11). Unlocking pain's secrets. *Time,* 58–66.

Ward, I. L. & Weisz, J. (1980). Maternal stress alters plasma testosterone in fetal males. *Science, 207,* 328–329.

Washburn, S., & DeVore, I. (1962). The social life of baboons. In C. H. Southwick (Ed.), *Primate social behavior.* Princeton, NJ: Van Nostrand.

Waters, H. F., & Malamud, P. (1975, March 10). Drop that gun, Captain Video. *Newsweek,* pp. 81–82.

Watson, D., & Tellegen, A. (1985). Toward a consensual structure of mood. *Psychological Bulletin, 98,* 219–235.

Watson, D. L. (in press). *Psychology for life: A practical introduction.* Pacific Grove, CA: Brooks-Cole.

Watson, D. L., & Tharp, R. G. (1989). *Self-directed behavior: Self-modification for personal adjustment* (4th ed.). Monterey, CA: Brooks-Cole.

Watson, J. B. (1919). *Psychology from the standpoint of a behaviorist.* Philadelphia: Lippincott.

Watson, J. B. (1924/1930). *Behaviorism.* Chicago: The University of Chicago Press.

Watson, J. B. (1928). *Psychological care of infant and child.* New York: Norton.

Weaver, V. (1977). Descriptive anatomical and quantitative variation in human facial musculature and the analysis of bilateral asymmetry. Ph.D. dissertation, University of Colorado. Ann Arbor, MI: UMI Dissertation Information Service.

Webb, A. (1968). *The clean sweep: The story of the Irish hospitals sweepstake.* London, England: George Harrap and Co.

Webb, E. J., Campbell, D. T., Schwartz, R. D., & Sechrest, L. (1966). *Unobtrusive measures: nonreactive research in the social sciences.* Chicago: Rand McNally.

Webb, E. J., Campbell, D. T., Schwartz, R. D., Sechrest, L., & Grove, J. B. (1981). *Nonreactive measures in the social sciences.* Boston: Houghton Mifflin.

Webster, G., & Webster, C. (1963). *Webster's seventh new collegiate dictionary.* Springfield, MS: G. and C. Merriam Co.

Weill, K. (Music), Brecht, B. (Lyrics) & Mark Blitzstein (Translator). *Die Drei-Groschen Oper (The three-penny opera).* New York: Columbia Masterworks.

Weiner, H. M. (1977). *Psychobiology and human disease.* New York: Elsevier.

Weiss, J. M. (1972). Psychological factors in stress and disease. *Scientific American, 226, No. 6,* 104–113.

Weiss, J. M., & Glazer, H. I. (1975). Effects of acute exposure on subsequent avoidance-escape behavior. *Psychosomatic Medicine, 37,* 499–521.

Weiss, R. S. (1972) *Loneliness: The experience of emotional and social isolation.* Cambridge, MA: MIT Press.

Weldon, F. (1974). *Female friends.* New York: St. Martin's Press.

Weldon, F. (1987). *The Shrapnel academy.* New York: Viking.

Welner, A., Reish, T., Robbins, I., Fishman, R., & van Doren, T. (1976). Obsessive-compulse neurosis. *Comprehensive Psychiatry, 17,* 527–539.

Wenger, M. A. (1948). Studies of autonomic balance in Army Air Forces personnel. *Comparative Psychology Monographs, 19* (4, Serial No. 101).

Wenger, M. A. (1950). Emotion as a visceral action: An extension of Lange's theory. In M. L. Raymert (Ed.), *Feelings and Emotions* (pp. 3–10). New York: McGraw-Hill.

Wessman, A. E., & Ricks, D. F. (1966). *Mood and personality*. New York: Holt, Rinehart and Winston.

White, G. L., Fishbein, S., & Rutstein, J. (1981). Passionate love and the misattribution of arousal. *Journal of Personality and Social Psychology, 41,* 56–62.

White, L., & Tursky B. (Eds.). (1982). *Clinical biofeedback: Efficacy and mechanisms*. New York: The Guilford Press.

Whybrow, P. (1984). Contributions from neuroendocrinology. In K. R. Scherer & P. Ekman (Eds.), *Approaches to emotion* (pp. 59–72). Hillsdale, NJ: Erlbaum.

Wikler, L., Wasow, M., & Hatfield, E. (1981). Chronic sorrow revisited: Parent vs. professional depiction of the adjustment of parents of mentally retarded children. *American Journal of Orthopsychiatry, 51,* 63–70.

Williams, R. B., Jr. (1989). *The trusting heart: Great news about Type A behavior*. New York: Random House.

Williams, R. J. (1956). *Biochemical individuality*. New York: Wiley.

Wilson, E. O. (1978). *Sociobiology: The new systhesis*. Cambridge, MA: Harvard University Press.

Wilson, J. P. (1980). Conflict, stress, and growth: The effects of war on the psychosocial development of Vietnam veterans. In C. R. Figley & S. Leventman (Eds.), *Strangers at home: Vietnam veterans since the war* (pp. 123–165). New York: Praeger.

Wilson, T. D. (1985). Strangers to ourselves: The origins and accuracy of beliefs about one's own mental status. In J. N. Harvey & G. Weary (Eds.), *Attribution: Basic issues and applications* (pp. 9–36). New York: Academic Press.

Wilson, W. (1967). Correlates of avowed happiness. *Psychological Bulletin 67,* 294–306.

Winters, R. (1985). Behavioral approaches to pain. In N. Schneiderman & J. T. Tapp (Eds.), *Behavioral medicine: The biopsychosocial approach* (pp. 565–587). Hillsdale, NJ: Erlbaum.

Witt, D. D., Lowe, G. D., Peek, C. W., & Curry, E. W. (1980). The changing association between age and happiness: Emerging trend or methodological artifact? *Social Forces, 58,* 1302–1307.

Wodrich, D. L. (1984). *Children's psychological testing: A guide for nonpsychologists*. Baltimore: Paul H. Brookes.

Wolf, S., Almy, T. P., Bachrach, W. H., Spiro, H. M., Sturdevant, R. A. L., & Weiner, H. (1979). The role of stress in peptic ulcer disease. *Journal of Human Stress, 5,* 27–37.

Wolf, S., & Wolff, H. G. (1947). *Human gastric function*. New York: Oxford University Press.

Wolfe, T. (1987). *The bonfire of the vanities*. New York: Farrar, Straus, and Giroux.

Wolff, P. H. (1959). Observations on newborn infants. *Psychosomatic Medicine, 21,* 110–118.

Wolff, P. H. (1963). Observations on the early development of smiling. In B. M. Foss (Ed.), *Determinants of infant behavior. II* (pp. 113–134). New York: Wiley.

Wolff, W. (1933). The experimental study of forms of expression. *Character and Personality, 2,* 168–173.

Wolfman, I. (1985, September). The closer you get, the faster I run. *Ms,* 34–112.

Wolpe, J. (1973/1982). *The practice of behavior therapy* (3rd ed.). New York: Pergamon.

Woodward, B. (1984). *Wired: The short life and fast times of John Belushi*. New York: Simon & Schuster.

Woodworth, R. S. (1938). *Experimental psychology*. New York: Henry Holt.

Woolf, V. (1953). *A writer's diary*. New York: Harcourt, Brace, and World.

Wrightsman, L. S., & Deaux, K. (1981). *Social psychology in the 80s* (3rd ed.). Monterey, CA: Brooks/Cole.

Wundt, W. M. (1897/1969). *Outlines of psychology*. (C. H. Judd, Trans.). New York: G. E. Stechert.

Xia, L. Y., Rosenfeld, J. P., & Huang, K. H. (1991). Evidence for role of cortex in acupuncture analgesia. In J.G. Carlson & R. Seifeert (Eds.), *International perspectives on self-regulation and health* (pp. 267–280). New York: Plenum Press.

Yalom, I. D. (1980). *Existential psychotherapy*. New York: Basic Books.

Yang, R. K. (1979). Early infant assessment: An overview. In J. D. Osofsky (Ed.), *Handbook of infant development* (pp. 165–184). New York: Wiley.

Yeager, C., & Janos, L. (1985) *Yeager*. New York: Bantam.

Yerkes, R. M., & Dodson, J. B. (1908). The relation of strength of stimulus to rapidity of habit formation. *Journal of Comparative Neurology and Psychology, 18,* 459–482.

Zajonc, R. (Fall 1990). The face as window and machine for the emotions. *LSA magazine*. Ann Arbor, MI: University of Michigan, 17–22.

Zajonc, R. B. (1980). Feeling and thinking: Preferences need no inferences. *American Psychologist, 35,* 151–175.

Zajonc, R. B., Murphy, S. T., & Inglehart, M. (1989). Feeling and facial efference: Implications of the vascular theory of emotion. *Psychological Review, 96,* 396–416.

Zajonc, R. B., Pietromonaco, P., & Bargh, J. (1982). Independence and interaction of affect and cognition. In M. S. Clark & S. T. Fiske (Eds.), *Affect and cognition* (pp. 211–227). Hillsdale, NJ: LEA Publications.

Zbrowski, M. (1969). *People in pain*. San Francisco: Jossey-Bass.

Zeisset, R. M. (1968). Desensitization and relaxation in the modification of psychiatric patients' interview behavior. *Journal of Abnormal Psychology, 73,* 18–24.

Zilboorg, G. (1939). *A history of medical psychology*. New York: Norton.

Zillman, D. (1979). *Hostility and aggression*. Hillsdale, NJ: Erlbaum.

Zillman, D. (1984). *Connections between sex and aggression*. Hillsdale, NJ: Erlbaum.

Zimbardo, P. G. (1970). The human choice: Individuation, reason, and order versus deindividuation, impulse, and chaos. In W. J. Arnold & D. Levine (Eds.), *Nebraska symposium on motivation, 1969* (pp. 237–307). Lincoln: University of Nebraska Press.

Zimbardo, P. G. (1977). *Shyness: What it is, what to do about it*. Reading, MA: Addison-Wesley.

Zuckerman, M., (1979). *Sensation seeking: beyond the optimal level of arousal*. Hillsdale, NJ: Erlbaum.

Zuckerman, M., DePaulo, B. M., & Rosenthal, R. (1981). Verbal and nonverbal communication of deception. *Advances in Experimental Social Psychology, 14,* 1–59.

Zuckerman, M. & Lubin, B. (1965). *Manual for the Multiple Affect Adjective Check List*. San Diego: Educational and Industrial Testing Service.

Zung, W. (1969). A cross-cultural survey of symptoms in depression. *American Journal of Psychiatry, 126,* 116–121.

Zung, W. W. K. (1971). A rating instrument for anxiety disorders. *Psychosomatics, 12,* 371–379.

Index

Page numbers in italics refer to figures.
Page numbers followed by "t" refer to
tables.

Abnormal emotional behavior, Millen-
son's approach to, 176. *See also*
Anxiety disorders; Depression
Abraham, Karl, 292
Abramson, L. Y., 300-301
Acetylcholine (ACh), 108
ACh. *See* Acetylcholine (ACh)
ACTH. *See* Adrenocorticotropin
(ACTH)
Acting, and facial expression, 202
Active coping, 449
Activity, as component of tempera-
ment, 274
Adaptation, 53-54, 172-174
Ader, Robert, 498
Adjective checklists, 234, 235-238
Adler, Alfred, 72, 469-470
Adrenal glands, 108, 134, 302, 486,
487, 488
Adrenaline, 108, 355
Adrenocorticotropin (ACTH), 128,
134, 136, 140, 142, 487, 488
Affect. *See* Emotion
Afferent nerves, 105
Affex coding system, 256-257, 266
Aggression. *See also* Anger
angry aggression, 365
behavior modification of, 549-550
catharsis hypothesis of, 359-364
child abuse, 372-375
definition of, 364
displacement of, 366-367, 368
empathy and, 380

family violence, 372, 372t, 378,
560
fear and, 380-381
forms of, 367, 369
frustration-aggression model, 364-
365, 369-370
gender differences in, 378
guilt and, 379
increase of, 377-378, 377t
inhibition of, 365
instrumental aggression, 364
modeling and reduction of, 375-
377
observational learning and, 370-
372
operant aggression, 364
origins of, 364-365
psychoanalytic approach to, 358-
359
reduction of, 375-377, 379-381
reinforcement theory and, 377-
381, 377t
research on, 254
social learning theory and, 370-
381
sociobiological prespective on,
356-358
stress and, 490
"sudden" explosion of, 366
targets of, 365-367
television violence, 374-375
types of, 351
Ahearn, Frederick, 489
Ainsworth, Mary, 272, 391, 447
Alarm stage of stress, 478, 486-487
Alcohol, 333, 535-541, *538*
Alexander, Shana, 373
Alexithymia, 461

Allen, Woody, 386, 441
Allerhand, Melvin, 51
Alloy, L. B., 300-301
Allport, Gordon, 205
Amphetamines, 333
Amygdala, 44, 119, 121, 122, 124,
132-133
Anaclitic depression, 295
Analytical psychology, 65-72
Anderson, David, 488
Anesthetics, 511
Anger. *See also* Aggression
blood chemistry and, 353-354
brain pathology and, 352-353
brain stimulation experiments and,
351-352
causes of, 349-350, 350t
dealing with, 559
definition of, 346
descriptions of, 346, 347
expressions of, 354-356, 356t
facial expression of, *348*, 350
Millenson's approach to, 165t,
167-168
neural inhibition and, 353
neuroanatomy and neurophysiology of, 351-354
neuroendocrine bases of, 128, *129*,
132-134, 135
people inciting anger, 348-349
physiological patterns of, 44, 354,
355
roots of, 346-350, 350t
Watson on, 55
Angry aggression, 365
Anima, 70-71
Animus, 70-71
Ankles, Thomas, 423

ANS. *See* Autonomic nervous system (ANS)
Anti-anxiety drugs, 534–535, 535t
Antidepressants, 303–305, *303–305*, 532–534, 533t, 535t
Antithesis, principle of, 49, 50–51, *52*
Anxiety
    behavioral explanations for, 453–457
    behavioral measures for, 462–464, 463t
    behavioral therapies for, 468–471
    cognitive therapies for, 468
    cognitive-learning explanations for, 457–459
    control of, 466–471
    cross-cultural aspects of, 464–466
    definition of, 433
    fear compared with, 433–436
    measurement of, 233–234, 257–258, 459–464
    Millenson's approach to, 165t, 166–167
    moral anxiety, 445
    neurotic anxiety, 445
    objective anxiety, 445
    physiological explanations for, 447–453
    physiological methods for dealing with, 468
    primary anxiety, 444–445
    psychodynamic behavior theory of, 455–457
    psychodynamic explanations for, 444–447
    psychophysiological measures for, 460–462
    self-report measures for, 459–460, 459t
    signal anxiety, 445
    two-process approaches to, 453–455
Anxiety disorders
    generalized anxiety disorder (GAD), 439
    neuroses and, 436–437
    obsessive-compulsive disorder, 440–441
    panic disorder, 439–440
    phobic disorder, 437–438, 438t
    post-traumatic stress disorder (PTSD), 441–443
Aphasia, 196, 197
Appraisals, cognitive, 80–81
Apraxia, 197
Archetypes, 69–72, 78, 141–144
Argyle, Michael, 315–317, 319
Arieti, Silvano, 292–293
Aristotle, 312, 359, 360, 421

Arms, Robert, 362
Arnold, Magda, 354
Aron, Arthur, 317, 322, 404
Aron, Elaine, 317, 322
Aspirin, 511
Assessment. *See* Measurement of emotion
Atherosclerosis, 494–496
Atkinson, Gilbert, 340
Attachment, 143–144, 391–394, 446–447
Attitudes, Jung on, 72
Attneave, Carolyn, 552
Attribution theory, 79–80
Austen, Jane, 518
Autonomic nervous system (ANS)
    anger and, 354
    facial expression and, 206–212, *209, 210*
    fear and, 354, 451–453
    generalized effects on emotion, 110–112
    LeDoux's approach to, 109–113
    measurement of, 240
    reactions produced by intense emotions, 400
    research on, 110–113
    specific effects on emotion, 112–113
    stress and, 487, 493–494
    structure of, 106, *107*, 108–109
Averill, James, 348–349, 350, 354, 377
Aversion therapies, 547, 549
Avoidance, 175–176, 454, 468–469
Ax, Albert F., 44, 112, 207, 208, 354, 355, 452
Azrin, Nathan, 168

Babinski, M. J., 195
Baekeland, Antony, 28–29
Bakalar, James, 333
Baker, T. B., 547
Bandura, Albert, 350, 370–371, 375–376, 457–458
Barbiturates, 511, 534–535, 535t
Bard, Philip, 42, 115
Baron, Miron, 291
Baron, Robert, 381, 412–413
Barry, William, 378
Basu, Gopal, 354
Bateson, Gregory, 8
Battering. *See* Family violence
Bavelas, Janet Bevin, 205, 206
Bayley Scales of Infant Development, 255–256, 256t
Beach, Frank, 424
Beaton, Cecil, 198
Beaumont, William, 207–208

Beck, Aaron, 294, 295, 298, 457, 523, 527–528
Beck Depression Inventory, 294, 555
Beecher, Marguerite, 423
Beecher, Willard, 423
Behavioral analysis
    abnormal emotional behavior, 176
    adaptation and habituation, 172–174
    anger and, 165t, 167–168
    anxiety and, 165t, 166–167
    avoidance, 175–176
    elation and, 165t, 168–169
    emotion control, 171–176
    emotional coordinate system, 169–171
    emotions as public events, 161–163
    emotions as reflex patterns, 163–164
    emotions as widespread changes in behavior, 164–165, 165t
    masking, 174–175
    model of emotion, 165–171
    physical illness, 177
Behavioral approaches
    to depression, 301–302
    to emotion, 55–58, 155, 156, 156t
    to fear and anxiety, 453–457
Behavioral measurement
    of emotion, 249–259
    of fear and anxiety, 462–464, 463t
    of sadness, 267
Behavioral medicine, 477
Behavioral responses to stress, 488–489
Behavioral therapies
    aversion therapies, 547, 549
    exercise, 554–556
    for fear and anxiety, 468–471
    implosion therapy, 545–547
    meditation, 553–554
    operant behavior used in, 549–552
    for pain control, 511–513
    Pavlovian principles used in, 543–549
    relaxation, 470–471, 513, 531, 553–554
    self-modification programs, 550–552
    systematic desensitization, 544–545, *548*
Bell, Sanford, 392
Bell, Silvia, 272
Belushi, John, 336
Bem, Daryl, 80, 200
Benign-positive, appraisal as, 80
Benoist, Andre, 289
Benson, Herbert, 138, 553, 554
Bentham, Jeremy, 313

Bereavement. *See* Grief
Bergland, R., 506
Bergman, Ingmar, 109–110, 400
Berkow, I., 323
Berkowitz, Leonard, 369
Berman, Edgar, 143
Bernard, Claude, 477
Bernard, Jesse, 420
Berscheid, Ellen, 96, 228, 230, 232, 259, 328, 408, 411–412, 422, 425–426
Beta blockers, 534–535, 535t
Bibring, Edward, 293
Bielenberg, Christabel, 401–402
Biochemical approaches
    to depression, 302–303
    to emotion, 41–48
Biofeedback, 470–471, 513, 519–532
Biofeedback-assisted relaxation training, 470–471
Biopotentials, 239
Bipolar depression, 288, 534, 534t
Bipolar quality, of emotions, 153–154
Birchler, Gary, 414
Birdwhistell, Ray, 184
Black, Claudia, 539
Blanchard, Caroline, 253, 379, 380–381, 448
Blanchard, Robert, 253, 379, 380–381, 448
Blaney, Paul, 95–96
Block, Jack, 153
Blood chemistry, and anger, 353–354
Blushing, 190
Boller, François, 197
Borg, Gunnar, 231–232
Borg scale, 231–232, 236
Bourne, Peter, 140
Bower, Gordon, 91–96
Bowlby, John, 30, 391, 393, 404, 447
Bradburn, Norman, 314
Bradburn Morale Scale, 483–484
Brady, Joseph, 177
Brain. *See also* Central nervous system (CNS); and specific structures of brain
    anger and, 351–353
    Bower's approach to, 91
    in conscious emotional experience, 124–126
    feedback and, 113–114
    LeDoux's approach to, 105–106, 113–114, 115–126
    measurement of brain activity, 240
    pain mechanisms in, 508–509
    pain transmission in, 505–508
    Papez loop in, 115–118, *118*
    and perception of control, 130–131

physiology of stimulus evaluation, 121–123
    pleasure centers of, 332, 398
    sex center of, 397–398, 399
    stimulus evaluation and reward, 123–124
    structures and functions of, 42, *43*, 44–48, *45–47*, 115–121, *116–118*, *120*
    Zajonc's approach to, 91
Brain hemispheres, 78, 124–125, 145, 192–197, 240
Brain pathology, and anger, 352–353
Brainstem, 45, *45*
Brazelton, T. Berry, 268, 270, 274
Brickman, Philip, 324, 325, 326, 327
Broca's aphasia, 196, 197
Broca's area, 124, 192, 196
Brod, J., 111
Brodie, Bernard, 452
Brown, Judson, 462
Bryden, Philip, 193–194
Bryson, Jeff, 425
Buchsbaum, Monte, 340
Buck, Ross, 197, 211
Bugelski, Richard, 368
Buirski, Peter, 253
Burgess, Michael, 360
Buss, Arnold, 273, 274, 367
Buss, J., 133
Buss-Durkee Hostility Inventory, 354, 367, 369, 370
Buunk, Bram, 422
Byrne, D., 395, 412–413, 414, 415

Cacioppo, John, 212–221
Caffeine, 333
Campbell, Angus, 315, 318
Campbell, Donald, 324, 326, 327
Campbell, Priscilla, 498
Campos, Joseph, 79, 273
Cancer, 498
Candland, Douglas, 96, 97
Cannon, D. S., 547
Cannon, W. B., 111
Cannon, Walter, 36, 41–42, 44, 47–48, 58, 108, 110, 115, 131, 174, 208, 448, 449, 451–452
Cannon-Bard theory of emotion, 42
Caplovitz, David, 314
Capote, Truman, 135
Cardiovascular disease, 493–497
Caretakers
    and behavior modification of aggression in children, 549–550
    children's attachment to, 391–394
    importance in children's emotional development, 274–277, *276*
    mother-infant bonding, 143–144

passionate love and, 390–393, *391*
Carlson, John, 450, 451, 531
Carlson, Neil, 195
Casey, William, 244
Catecholamines, 138, 332
Catharsis hypothesis of aggression, 359–364
Cattell, Raymond, 152
Central nervous system (CNS). *See also* Brain
    in conscious emotional experience, 124–126
    feedback and, 113–114
    Henry's approach to, 127–128, *127*
    LeDoux's approach to, 113–114, 115–126
    Papez loop in, 115–118, *118*
    physiology of stimulus evaluation, 121–123
    stimulus evaluation and reward, 123–124
    structures and functions of, 103, *104*, 115–121, *116–118, 120*
    traditional views of, 115–118
Cerebellum, 45–46, *45*
Cerebrum, 47, *47*
Chaikin, Tommy, 133
Chess, Stella, 275
Child abuse, 372–375
Childhood Love Scale (CLS), 392
Children
    aggression and, 371, 378
    attachment and, 391–394, 446–447
    caretakers and, 274–277, *276*
    child abuse, 372–375
    depression in, 295
    ego development in, 444–445
    emotional milestones of, 270–272
    frustration and, 365
    happiness and, 312, 320–321, *321*
    impact on marriages, 408
    individual differences of emotionality in, 272–274
    measurement of emotion in, 255–257, 256t, 266, 267
    mother-infant bonding, 143–144
    passionate love and, 391–393, *394*
    reduction of aggression in, 376, 549–550
    sadness in, 266, 267
    sequence of emotional development in, 268–269, *269*
Chivalisz, Kathleen, 114–115
Cialdini, Robert, 395
Cicchetti, Dante, 268
Cingulate gyrus, 44, 117, 119–120, 121
Clancy, John, 257–258

Clanton, G., 424–425
Clark, Margaret S., 94, 420
Classical conditioning, 453
Clinical depression, 288
CLS. *See* Childhood Love Scale (CLS)
Cluster, 217
Coates, Dan, 325
Cocaine, 333, 335, 336
Cognition
    emotion and, 79–97
    Jung on, 73
    pain and, 510
    Zajonc on, 88–89
Cognitive appraisals, 80–81
Cognitive-behavior modification, 524–525
Cognitive-learning approaches to fear and anxiety, 457–459
Cognitive theories of depression, 294, 296–298
Cognitive therapies, 468, 511–513, 522–528
Cohen, John, 498
Cohen, P. R., 91–94
Cohen, Raquel, 489
Collective unconscious, 67–68, 71–72
Communal relationships, 420
Companionate love
    decline stage and jealousy in, 421–425
    definition of, 387
    end of, 425–427
    equity theory of, 415, 417–420
    gender differences in willingness to sacrifice in, 420
    initiation and maintenance stages of, 411–420
    measures and models of, 408–411
    rewards of, 414–415, 416
    stages of relationships, 411–427
    triangular model of, 409, 411
Comparison levels of happiness, 323–326
Complexes, 67
Compulsions, 440–441
Conditioned response, 164
Conditioned stimulus (CS), 163
Conditioned suppression, 166
Conditioning. *See* Operant conditioning; Pavlovian conditioning
Conjugal love. *See* Companionate love
Conrad, Joseph, 35
Consciousness
    current views on, 77–78
    Jung on, 66
    LeDoux on, 124–126
Continous emotional feedback loop, 96, *97*
Control

depression and, 136–137
    perception of, 129–132
Control of emotion. *See* Emotional control
Control responses, 217
Convergence, 259
Coping, 81–83, 449, 469, 498–504, 519
Corbit, John, 153
Corpus callosum, 192
Corticosterone, 140–141, 487
Cortisol, 128, 134–135, 136, 140, 453, 487
Costello, Frank, 464
Counterconditioning, 470
Cousins, Norman, 502
Cox, Daniel, 143
Cox, Wally, 469
Coyne, James, 483
Crichton, Michael, 552–553
"Crooked" expressions, and lying, 190–191
Cross, Theodore, 244
Cross-magnification, 402
CS. *See* Conditioned stimulus (CS)
Csikszentmihalyi, Mihaly, 339–340, 341
Cullen, William, 436
Cultural differences
    aggression, 379
    depression, 289–290
    facial expression, 184–188, 186t, 187t, *188*
    fear, 464–466
    love, 390, 390t
    sexual behavior, 424

Da Vinci, Leonardo, 182
Dalton, Katharina, 142
Dart, Raymond, 357
Darwin, Charles, 4, 18, 48–51, 58, 150, 184, 199, 464
Darwin, John, 212
Daston, Paul, 236
Davis, Keith, 417
Davis, Kingsley, 422
Davitz, Joel, 265, 313, 346, 347, 423
Dawson, Michael, 113
De Beauvoir, Simone, 421
Death. *See* Grief
Defense mechanisms, 32–34, 33t, 445–446, 447
Defense response, 111
DeKosky, Steven, 196
Delgado, Jose, 41, 353
Demerol, 511
DePaulo, Bella, 192
Depression
    anaclitic depression, 295
    behavioral models of, 301–302

biochemical theories of, 302–303
bipolar depression, 288, 534, 534t
clinical depression, 288
cognitive theories of, 294, 296–298
cognitive therapy for, 527–528
cultural contributions to, 289–290
definition of, 264
description of, 265, 287–288
drug therapy for, 303–305, *303–305*, 532–534, 533t, 534t
fear compared with, 136–137
genetic theories of, 290–291
learned helplessness, 298–301
measurement of, 294, 297
neuroendocrine bases of, 128, *129*, 135–138
psychoanalytic theories of, 291–294, 295
theories of, 289–303
treatment of, 296–298, 303–306
unipolar depression, 288
Dermograph, 241
Descartes, René, 19, 102, 476, 519, 528
Desensitization, 470, 544–545, *548*
Destruction responses, 152
Deutsch, Morton, 328
Diagnostic and Statistical Manual No. III: Revised (DSM III-R), 160, 257, 436–437, 445
Diagnostic concepts, 158, 160
Diamond, Stuart, 194
Diaz, Carmen, 450, 451, 531
Dickinson, Emily, 322
Diener, Ed, 114–115
Direct action, 83
Direct action of the excited nervous system, principle of, 49, 51
Diseases. *See* Physical illnesses
Displacement, 366–367, 368
Display rules, 184
Dodson, John, 490
Dollard, John, 167, 364–365
Domestic violence. *See* Family violence
Dopamine, 302, 399
Dostoevsky, Fyodor, 331
Dougherty, Denise, 244
Douglas, Kirk, 202
Douvan, Elizabeth, 320
Drabble, Margaret, 366
Drug therapy. *See also* Treatment
    anti-anxiety drugs, 534–535, 535t
    for depression, 303–305, *303–305*, 532–534, 533t, 534t
    for emotional control, 532–535, 533t, 534t, 535t
    lithium, 534, 534t
    for pain, 511, 512
Drugs, illegal, 332–336, 399

DSM III-R (Diagnostic and Statistical Manual No. III: Revised), 160, 257, 436-437, 445
Duck, Steve, 412
Duffy, Elizabeth, 36
Duffy, Robert, 197
Durkee, Ann, 367
Dutton, Donald, 404

Easterbrook, J. A., 491
Easterlin, Richard, 321
Easton, Marilyn, 390
Eating. *See* Overeating
Ecstasy, 329-331
Edelman, Robert, 363
EEG. *See* Electroencephalograph (EEG)
Efferent nerves, 105
Egeland, Janice, 290-291
Ego, 34, 66, 444-445
Einstein, Albert, 358
EKG. *See* Electrocardiograph (EKG)
Ekman, Paul, 13, 21, 44, 110, 112, 185-192, 194, 202, 203-204, 206, 208-210, 255, 266, 450, 465
Elation. *See* Joy
Electrocardiograph (EKG), 240
Electroencephalograph (EEG), 240
Electromyographic (EMG) biofeedback, 531
Electromyographic (EMG) recordings, 213-220, *216, 218*, 239-240, 245-246
Ellis, Albert, 523-525, 528
Ellsworth, Phoebe, 21, 187
Emde, Robert, 312
Emergency model of emotion, 111
EMG recordings. *See* Electromyographic (EMG) recordings
Emotion. *See also* Facial expression; Measurement of emotion; Personality; Temperament; and specific emotions
    behavioral analysis (Millenson), 161-177
    behavioral approaches to, 55-58
    biochemical approaches to, 41-48
    caretakers' contribution and, 274-277, *276*
    classification as good or bad, 15-17
    cognitive approaches to, 79-97
    communication about, 558-561
    control of, 19-20, 171-176
    definitions of, 4-7, 56-57, 79, 521
    evolutionary approaches to, 48-54, *52*, 57
    experiential approaches to, 29-36, 29t, 30t

    expression of, 194-195, 196-197
    expressive approaches to, 29t, 48-58
    Freud's approach to, 34-36
    gender differences in, 272
    importance of, 17-18
    individual differences in emotionality, 272-274
    information from, 557-558
    interlinkages among, 400-402
    issues in, 12-21
    James and, 36-38
    Jung's approach to, 64-78
    language of, 155-156, 156t
    Lazarus's approach to, 81
    learning and, 18-19, 57
    length of, 14-15
    measurement of, 76-77
    milestones of, 270-272
    neuroendocrine theory (Henry), 126-145
    neurological approaches to, 41-48
    neurophysiological theory (LeDoux), 103-126
    number and organization of, 12-13, *14, 15*, 36, 152, 153-158, 165-171
    perception of, 193-194, 196
    physiological approaches to, 29t, 36-48
    psychoevolutionary synthesis (Plutchik), 151-160
    psychophysiology of, 36-41
    as public events, 161-163
    rationale for awareness of, 556-563
    rationale for study of, 7-10
    as reflex patterns, 163-164
    research on, 10-12, 37
    sequence of emotional development, 268-269, *269*
    sequence of events in, 38-41, *39, 96, 155, 155t*
    theory of, 10-12
    transformative quality of, 560, 562
    as widespread changes in behavior, 164-165, 165t
Emotion solid, 154-155, *154*
Emotional contagion, 204-206
Emotional control
    alcohol and, 535-541, *538*
    anti-anxiety drugs and, 534-535, 535t
    antidepressants and, 532-534, 533t
    and awareness of emotions, 556-563
    behavioral approaches to, 542-556
    biofeedback and, 529-532
    cognitive therapies and, 522-528

    and costs of denial of emotion, 529
    exercise and, 554-556
    lithium and, 534, 534t
    meditation and, 553-554
    Millenson on, 171-176
    physiological approach to, 528-542
    psychopharmacological approaches to, 532-542
    reflections on, 519-522
    relaxation and, 553-554
Emotional mixtures, 156-158
Emotional spillover, 402
Emotional stress. *See* Stress
Emotionality, as component of temperament, 273-274
Emotions Profile Index (EPI), 160, 234-235, 253
Empathy, 380
Employment. *See* Work
Endocrine activity, and fear, 451-453
Endorphins, 136-137, 140, 398, 508, 509, 555-556
English, Ava, 311, 433
English, Horace, 311, 433
Enkaphalins, 509
Enteric nervous system, 110
EPI. *See* Emotions Profile Index (EPI)
Epictetus, 524
Epicureans, 312-313
Epinephrine, 108, 113, 128, 133, 134, 135, 137, 138, 452, 486, 488
Epstein, Seymour, 247, 338-339
Equilibrium, 73
Equity theory of companionate love, 415, 417-420
Ery, Fred, 244
Escape, 454, 468-469
Essential hypertension, 496-497
Ethology, 253-254, 356-357, 369
Evolutionary approaches to emotion, 48-54, *52*, 57
Evolutionary biology, 44
Exchange relationships, 420
Exhaustion stage of stress, 478, 488
Experiential approaches to emotion, 29-36, 29t, 30t
Expressive approaches to emotion, 29t, 48-58
Exteroceptors, 105, 122
Extinction, 172-174
Extraverts, 72
Eyes, and lying, 190

Facial Affect Scoring Technique (FAST), 187, 255
Facial EMG responses, 213
Facial expression
    acting and, 202
    of anger, *348,* 350

arrangement of facial patterns, 203–204
autonomic nervous system and, 206–212, *209, 210*
brain hemispheres and, 192–197
cultural masks, 184–188, 186t, 187t, *188*
emotional contagion and, 204–206
emotional experience and, 197–212, *205, 209, 210*
facial feedback, 198–206
fear and anxiety and, 450–451
historical interest in, 182, 184
lying and, 188–192
measurement of, 213–221, *214, 216, 218*, 255
motor mimicry and, 204–206, *205*
research on, 201–206
of sadness, 266
social psychophysiology of, 212–221, *214, 216, 218*
studies with neurological patients, 195–197
theoretical conclusions on, 219–221
universal and cultural bases of, 182–192
Facial feedback, 198–206
Facial muscles, 182, *183*, 184
Family violence, 372, 372t, 378, 560
Farber, I. E., 462
Farrington, Linda, 194
FAST. *See* Facial Affect Scoring Technique (FAST)
Fay, Floyd, 244
Fear
aggression and, 380–381
anxiety compared with, 433–436
anxiety disorders compared with, 443–444
behavioral explanation for, 453–457
behavioral measures for, 462–464, 463t
behavioral therapies for, 468–471
cognitive therapies for, 468
cognitive-learning approaches to, 457–459
control of, 466–471
cross-cultural aspects of, 464–466
definition of, 433
depression compared with, 136–137
endocrine activity and, 451–453
fear of success, 466–467
heart rate and, 449–450
Henry on, 144
Jung on, 144
measurement of, 459–464

muscle tension and, 450–451
neuroendrocrine bases of, 128, *129,* 134–135
Pavlovian conditioning of, 163–164
phobic disorder, 144, 437–438, 438t
physiological approaches to, 44, 354, 355, 447–453
physiological methods for dealing with, 468
psychodynamic approaches to, 444–447
psychodynamic behavior theory of, 455–457
psychophysiological measures for, 460–462
self-report measures for, 459–460, 459t
skin conductance and, 449–450
skin temperature and, 450
two-process approaches to, 453–455
Watson on, 55–56
Fear of success, 466–467
Feedback
continuous emotional feedback loop, 96, *97*
facial feedback, 198–206
neurophysiological approaches to, 113–115
Feelings. *See also* Emotion
definition of, 15
Jung on, 73–77
LeDoux on, 124–126
Skinner on, 57
Zajonc on, 90–91
Fei, Jack, 422
Feld, Joyce, 555
Fencl, V., 111
Fenichel, Otto, 422
Fenz, Walter, 247
Feshbach, Norma, 380
Feshbach, Seymour, 380
Field, Sheila, 314
Flooding techniques, 469–470, 545, 546
Flow states, 339–341
Folkman, S., 499, 500
Ford, Clellan, 424
Fordyce, Wilbert Evans, 512
Forgas, Joseph, 94
Forsman, Lennart, 137
Frankenhauser, Marianne, 137, 453
Franklin, Jon, 115
Fredette, Marquita, 289
Freedman, Jonathan, 315, 327
Freud, Anna, 33
Freud, Sigmund
on aggression, 358, 359, 360

on anxiety, 444–446
on cocaine, 335
critique of, 55
on depression, 292, 295
on fear and anxiety, 433
on jealousy, 422
Jung and, 65
on lying and facial expression, 189
on neurosis, 436
personality of, 72
"pressure cooker" model of emotional expression, 211, 358
psychodynamic theory of, 29, 30, 31–36, 33t, 53, 58, 64, 66, 67, 68, 69, 74
Friedman, Meyer, 494
Friesen, Wallace V., 21, 44, 112, 185–188, 194, 202, 203–204, 208–209, 255, 465
Frustration
catharsis and, 360–361
definition of, 364
frustration-aggression model, 364–365, 369–370
Frustration-aggression model, 364–365, 369–370
Functional language, of emotions, 155, 156, 156t
Functions, 72–77

GAD. *See* Generalized anxiety disorder (GAD)
Galen, 36, 103
Gallagher, Dennis, 114–115
Galvanic skin response (GSR), 77, 241
Gandhi, Mohandas, 377
Ganglia, 106
GAS. *SEE* General adaptation syndrome (GAS)
Gate control theory of pain, 506–507
Gates, Georgiana, 167
Gelles, Richard, 371–372
Gellman, Marc, 478
Gender differences
in aggression, 378
in cardiovascular disease, 495
in catharsis, 362–364
in communication about emotion, 558–560
in depression, 293
in emotionality, 272
in fear of success, 466–467
in jealousy, 424–425
in sexual behavior, 424
in willingness to sacrifice in relationships, 420
General adaptation syndrome (GAS), 478, 486–488

Generalized anxiety disorder (GAD), 439
Genetic theories of depression, 290-291
Gentry, William, 369
Gerbner, George, 374, 375
Gillhorn, Ernst, 200
Gilmour, Robin, 412
Golding, William, 357
Goldsmith, H. Hill, 273
Goleman, Daniel, 520
Gonadotrophic hormone, 133
Goodenough, Florence, 51, 53, 312
Gorsuch, Richard, 14, 236, 459
Gottman, John, 414
Gould, J., 464
Gray, Jeffrey, 444
Green, Russell, 236
Greenspan, Nancy Thorndyke, 270, 271
Greenspan, Stanley, 270, 271
Greenwell, M. E., 392
Grief
    care for the bereaved, 286-287
    characteristics of those suffering grief the most, 284-286
    definition of, 264
    description of, 265
    risk of death and, 495-496
    stages of, 280-282, 284
    symptoms of, 283
Griffitt, William, 403
Grings, William, 113
Grinspoon, Lester, 333
Groen, Jannes, 358
Gross, Larry, 374
GSR. See Galvanic skin response (GSR)
Guilt, 379
Gur, Ruben, 194-195
Gurin, Gerald, 314

Habituation, 172-174
Haggard, Ernest, 220
Hales, Stephen, 493
Hall, Calvin, 77
Hamilton, Jean, 340
Happiness. See also Joy
    assessment of, 314-317, 317t
    of children, 312
    close relationships and, 320-321, 320t, 321
    comparison levels of, 323-326
    definition of, 311
    experience of, 313-314, 313t
    factors in, 317-322, 319t, 320t, 321
    health and, 322
    justice and, 328

leisure and, 322
nature of, 310-313
relativity of, 322-326
satisfaction of basic needs and, 318-319, 319t
self-help advice for, 327
social comparisons of, 326
talent for, 318
temporal comparisons of, 324-326
in various countries, 315-317, 317t
work and unemployment and, 321-322
Hardiness, 500, 501-502
Hartzog, John, 400
Harvey, William, 493
Hassett, James, 238
Hassles, 483-485, 485t
Hassles Scale, 483
Hastings, Elizabeth, 315
Hastings, Philip, 315
Hatfield, Elaine, 184, 228, 230, 232, 282, 287-288, 328, 346-347, 349, 387, 392-393, 395, 400, 401, 402, 403, 406, 409, 415, 420, 557-558
Hatfield-McCoy feud, 347, 362
Health, and happiness, 322. See also Physical illnesses
Health Status Questionnaire, 485
Heart rate, and fear, 449-450
Heath, R. G., 353
Hedonic contrast, 339
Hedonic habituation, 339
Hedonic withdrawal, 339
Heider, Fritz, 80
Heidt, H., 133
Heilman, Kenneth, 196, 197
Heimer, K., 369
Hejl, Z., 111
Helplessness. See Learned helplessness
Henry, James P., 119, 120, 126-145, 211, 332
Heroin, 334, 511
Herrnstein, R. J., 169
Hertel, Richard, 378
Hess, Walter, 111, 452
Hesse, Petra, 268
Hildegard of Bingen, 330-331
Hillman, James, 75-76, 562
Hindy, Carl, 393-394
Hippocampal-pituitary-adrenocortical reaction, 137
Hippocampus, 44, 117, 118, 119, 120, 121, 122-123, 136, 137
Hippocrates, 103
Hohmann, George W., 39-40, 40, 87, 114
Hokanson, Jack, 247, 249, 294, 360, 362-364
Holmes, Thomas, 479, 480, 481, 483

Hooke, Robert, 21, 477
Hopkins Symptom Checklist, 484
Horne, R. L., 498
Horner, Matina, 466
Hostility. See Aggression; Anger
Hovland, Carl, 366-367
Howe, E. W., 443
Howes, Mary, 294
Hudson, Rock, 535-536
Humphrey, Hubert, 143
Huxley, Aldous, 333
Hydrocorticosone, 487
Hypertension, essential, 496-497
Hypnosis, 513
Hypothalamus, 44, 115, 117, 118, 119, 121, 130-131, 133, 134, 302, 397, 487, 490

IBR. See Infant Behavior Record (IBR)
Id, 34, 445
Illnesses. See Physical illnesses
Immunity, 497-498
Implosion therapy, 545-547
Individual response stereotypy, 109
Individuation, 66
Infant Behavior Record (IBR), 255-256, 256t
Infants. See Children
Inferior parietal lobule (IPL), 125-126
Inhalants, 333-334
Instincts, 34, 68-69
Instrumental aggression, 364
Instrumental conditioning, 453
Intensity, of emotions, 154
Interoceptors, 105
Interval scaling, 229, 232
Intimacy, 409, 411. See also Love
Intrapsychic palliation, 82
Introverts, 72
IPL. See Inferior parietal lobule (IPL)
Irrelevant, appraisal as, 80
Isaacs, Kenneth, 220
Istvan, Joseph, 403
Izard, Carroll, 16, 53, 185, 200, 256, 257, 266, 269, 277-278, 279-280, 339, 350

Jacobs, Selby, 495
James, William, 30, 36-38, 41, 42, 44, 47-48, 55, 58, 96, 115, 161, 199, 207, 208, 563
James-Lange theory of emotion, 38-41, 42, 84
Janis, Irving, 491
Janoff-Bulman, Ronnie, 325
Jealousy, 421-425
Jirka, J., 111
Jobs. See Work
Johnson, James, 482

Johnson, Lyndon, 495
Johnson, Robert, 376
Jones, Edward, 417
Jones, Mary Cover, 543–544
Joy. *See also* Happiness
    anatomy of, 331–332
    chemistry of, 332–336
    definition of, 311
    experience of, 329–331
    flow states and, 339–341
    Millenson's approach to, 165t,
        168–169
    neuroendocrine bases of, 128, *130,*
        140–141
    opponent process theory of, 336–
        339, *338*
Judgments
    snap judgments, 93
    social judgments, 93–94
Jung, Carl Gustav
    analytical psychology of, 20, 30,
        64–72
    archetypes and, 69–72, 78, 141
    on communication about emotion,
        562
    critique of, 77–78
    implications of work of, 74–76
    measurement of emotion, 76–77
    personality theory of, 65–72, 97
    psychological types of, 72–77
Justice, 328

Kalish, Harry, 462
Kamiya, Joe, 259
Kammann, Richard, 318
Kanner, Allen, 483
Kaplan, Helen Singer, 397, 398, 399
Katkin, Edward, 449
Kearns, Doris, 495
Keillor, Garrison, 173
Kellerman, Henry, 234
Kelley, Harold, 323–324, 327, 378,
    387, 559
Kendrick, Douglas, 395
Khadafy, Moammar, 378
Khomeini, Ayatollah, 346, 368
Kidman, Antony, 437
Kim, Hai Sook, 219
Kim, Youngjai, 197
Kimble, Gregory, 251
King, Martin Luther, Jr., 377
Kinsbourne, Marcel, 195–196
Kinsey, Alfred, 424
Kleck, Robert, 202
Kleinmuntz, Benjamin, 243
Klineberg, Otto, 184, 464
Klinnert, Mary, 185, 270
Kobasa, Suzanne, 500, 501–502
Koestler, Arthur, 329, 330

Koropsak, Elizabeth, 363
Kraines, Samuel, 290
Kubler-Ross, Elisabeth, 280
Kubrick, Stanley, 452, 547
Kulka, Richard, 320
Kumar, Krishna, 340–341
Kurys, Diane, 395

Lacey, Beatrice, 109
Lacey, John, 109
Laird, James, 203
Lamb, Michael, 272–273
Landers, Ann, 171
Lang, Peter, 460–462
Lange, Carl, 36, 115, 200
Language of emotions, 155–156, 156t
Lanzetta, John, 202, 205–206
Larson, John, 242
Laski, Margharita, 329
Laughing gas, 333–334
Lazarus, Richard, 17, 80–83, 85, 97,
    468–469, 483, 498–499, 500, 519
Learned helplessness, 298–301
Learning
    cognitive-learning approaches to
        fear and anxiety, 457–459
    emotions and, 18–19, 57
    observational learning of aggres-
        sion, 370–372
    social learning theory and anger,
        370–381
    and *tabula rasa,* 68–69
Leavitt, Fred, 333
LeBlanc, William, 478
LeBoeuf, A., 471
LeCarré, John, 206, 207
LeDoux, Joseph E., 103–126
Lee, John Alan, 387
Leeper, Robert, 30–31
Leff, J. P., 465
Left hemisphere of brain, 78, 124–
    125, 145, 192–197, 240
Lehman, Darrin, 284
Leisure, 322
Leslie, J. C., 161, 162, 167, 176
Levenson, Robert, 44, 112, 202, 203–
    204, 208–209
Levi, Lennart, 452
Levinger, George, 411
Lewinsohn, Peter, 302
Ley, Robert, 193–194
LH-RF. *See* Luteinizing hormone-
    releasing factor (LH-RF)
Liddy, G. Gordon, 546
Lie-detector tests, 242–244, *245*
Liebowitz, Michael, 396, 398–399
Life Experiences Survey, 482–483
Likert, Rensis, 230
Likert scales, 230–231

Liking. *See* Love
Limbic system, 44, 46–47, *46,* 115,
    118–121, *120,* 132–133, 397
Lindemann, Erich, 280, 282
Lindzey, Gardner, 77
Lingeman, Richard, 334
Lithium, 304–305, 534, 534t
Littman, Richard, 90
Lloyd, Chris Evert, 323
Lloyd, John, 323
Lombroso, Cesare, 493
Lorenz, Konrad, 356, 357
Lorr, Maurice, 236
Losch, Mary, 219
Love
    anatomy of passionate love, 397–
        398
    attachment and adult love, 393–
        394
    chemistry of passionate love, 398–
        400
    cognitive contribution to passionate
        love, 396
    companionate love, 387, 408–427
    decline stage and jealousy in, 421–
        425
    definition of, 387, 403
    emotional interlinkages of, 400–
        402
    end of, 425–427
    equity theory of companionate
        love, 415, 417–420
    erosion of passionate love, 406–
        408, *407*
    gender differences in willingness to
        sacrifice in, 420
    genesis of, 390–393, *391*
    happiness and, 320, 320t, *321*
    initiation and maintenance stages
        of, 411–420
    measurement of, 229–230, 232,
        388–390, 390t, 408–409, 410
    nature of passionate love, 394–400
    passionate love, 387–408
    physiological contribution to pas-
        sionate love, 397
    pleasure and pain in passionate
        love, 402–406
    reinforcement theory and compan-
        ionate love, 412–415, 416
    rewards of, 414–415, 416
    stages of relationships, 411–427
    triangular model of, 387, *388,* 409,
        411
    Watson on, 55
Lowenstein, David, 294
LSD, 334
Lubin, Bernard, 235
Lundberg, Ulf, 137

Lushene, Robert, 14, 236, 459
Luteinizing hormone-releasing factor (LH-RF), 399
Lying
    facial expression and, 188-192
    lie-dectector tests, 242-244, *245*
Lykken, David, 243

MAACL. *See* Multiple Affect Adjective Checklist (MAACL)
MacLean, Paul, 41, 44-47, 58, 118-119, 120, 127, 141, 331
Maddi, Salvatore, 501
Mandler, George, 4-5, 200, 490-491, 499
Manic-depressive disorders, 288, 534, 534t
Manifest Anxiety Scale (MAS), 459, 459t
Mann, Thomas, 85, 387-388
Manning, Horace, 90
MAOIs. *See* Monoamine oxidase inhibitors (MAOIs)
Marijuana, 334, 541-542
Marks, Isaac, 547
Marriage. *See also* Companionate love; Love
    children's impact on, 408
    companionate love and, 407-408, *407*
    happiness and, 320-321, 320t, *321*
    passionate love and, 406-407, *407*
Marsella, Anthony, 289
Marshall, Gary, 88
Martin, Leonard, 204
Martin, Steve, 322
Martzke, Jeffrey, 215
MAS. *See* Manifest Anxiety Scale (MAS)
Masking, 174-175
Masks
    cultural masks, 184-188, 186t, 187t, *188*
    in Greek theatre, 182
Maslach, Christina, 88
Maslow, Abraham, 318-319, 413-414
Mason, John, 478
Masserman, Jules, 170, 446
Maugham, Somerset, 53, 54
Max coding system, 256, 257
May, Rollo, 433
McFarlane, Bud, 529
McNally, Richard, 144
Mead, Margaret, 422, 464
Measurement of emotion
    adjective checklists, 234, 235-238
    aggression, 367, 369, 370
    in animals, 250-254
    anxiety, 459-464

behavioral measures, 249-259
    in children, 255-257, 256t
    in the clinic, 257-259
cognitive approaches to, 87-88
depression, 294, 297
emotional intensity, 219
ethological observations, 253-254
through facial expression, 213-221, *214, 216, 218,* 255
fear, 459-464
happiness, 314-317, 317t
in humans, 255-259
Jung's approach to, 76-77
laboratory studies, 251-253
lie-detector tests, 242-244, *245*
love, 388-390, 390t, 408-409, 410
multi-perspective approach to, 259
multiple emotional assessment, 234-238
physiological measures, 77, 239-241
positive versus negative emotions, 213-217, *214, 216, 218*
psychometric principles, 228-233
psychophysiological measures, 238-249, *245,* 245t, *248*
sadness, 265-267
scales, 228-233
self-report measures, 227-238
social psychophysiological measurement, 213-221, *214, 216, 218*
stress, 479-485, 481t
subjective measures, 227-238
word association, 76
Meczek, Klaus, 169
Medial forebrain bundle (MFB), 332
Meditation, 553-554
Meehan, Henry, 136
Meehan, John, 136
Meichenbaum, Donald, 457, 523, 525-526, 528
Melancholy. *See* Depression
Melzack, Ronald, 506-507
Memory, state-dependent, 91-94, 95
Mental illness. *See* Abnormal emotional behavior
MFB. *See* Medial forebrain bundle (MFB)
Micro-expressions, and lying, 191
Midler, Bette, 488
Millenson, J. R., 55, 150, 160, 161-177
Miller, George, 401
Miller, Lyle, 449
Miller, Neal, 367, 368, 455-456
Milner, Peter, 123, 331-332
Mimicry. *See* Motor mimicry
Mind. *See* Brain; Cognition
Mintz, Norbett, 413-414
Mittleman, Bela, 450

Modeling, 375-377
Monoamine oxidase inhibitors (MAOIs), 304, *305,* 398, 532-533, 533t
Mood Adjective Checklist (MACL), 235-237
Mood congruence, 95
Moods, definition of, 15. *See also* Emotion; Feelings
Moral anxiety, 34, 445
Morgan, Michael, 374
Morphine, 334
Morrow, Lisa, 197
Morse, W. H., 169
Moscovitch, Morris, 195
Moss, Howard, 272
Mothers. *See* Caretakers
Motivational theories, 29-36, 29t, 30t, 64
Motivations
    emotions compared with, 29-31, 29t, 30t
    Freud on, 31-36, 33t
Motor mimicry, 204-206, *205*
Mound, 217
Mowrer, O. Hobart, 17-18, 55, 453-454, 468
Moyer, Kenneth, 351
Müller, Johannes, 184
Multiple Affect Adjective Checklist (MAACL), 235
Murder, probability of, 379, 379t
Murnen, S. K., 414
Murphy, Lois, 268-269, 311, 312
Muscle tension, and fear, 450-451
Myerscough, Rodney, 541

Nader, George, 536
Nation, Carry, 539, 540
Negative reinforcement, 57
Neocortex, 44, 46, 115, 123, 125
Nervous system. *See* Brain; Central nervous system; Peripheral nervous system
Nesdale, Andrew, 369
Neural inhibition, and anger, 353
Neuroanatomy, 44, 351-354
Neurochemistry, 37
Neuroendocrine theory of emotion
    of anger, 128, *129,* 132-134, 135
    archetypes and, 141-144
    bases of negative emotions, 128-138, *129*
    of depression, 128, *129,* 135-138
    of elation, 128, *130,* 140-141
    of fear, 128, *129,* 134-135
    general model of, 127-128, *127*
    perception of control, 129-132

of serenity, 128, *130*, 138–139, *139*
Neurological approaches to emotion, 37, 41–48
Neurophysiological theory of emotion
  central nervous system, 115–126, *116–118*
  peripheral nervous system and, 103–115, *104*, 105t, *107*
Neurophysiology, 44, 351–354
Neuroses, 436–437
Neurotic anxiety, 34, 445
Neurotransmitters, 106, 108, 303, 486, 508. *See also* names of specific neurotransmitters
Newton, Isaac, 21
Nicotine, 334
Nitrous oxide, 333–334
Nixon, Richard, 476, 495
Nolen-Hoeksema, Susan, 291
Nominal scaling, 228–229, 232
Noradrenaline, 108, 355
Norepinephrine, 108, 133–134, 135, 138, 302, 303, 452, 486, 488
Norwood, Robin, 539
Nowlis, Helen, 235
Nowlis, Vincent, 235, 236
Noyes, Russell, 257–258

Objective anxiety, 34, 445
Obrist, Paul, 449
Observational learning, and aggression, 370–372
Obsessions, 440–441
Obsessive-compulsive disorder, 440–441
Olds, James, 123, 331–332
Olds, Janet, 195
O'Neill, George, 423
O'Neill, Nena, 423
Operant aggression, 364
Operant conditioning, 453, 549–552
Operants, 57
Opiates, 334
Opium, 334
Opponent process theory of joy, 336–339, *338*
Ordinal scaling, 229, 232
Ornstein, Robert, 45–47
Ostfeld, Adrian, 495
Overeating, 489–490
Owens, David, 374

Pain
  behavioral methods of pain control, 511–513
  brain mechanisms for, 508–509
  cognition and, 510

cognitive methods of pain control, 511–513
  control of, 510–514
  emotion and, 504–505
  gate control theory of, 506–507
  physiological methods of pain control, 511
  physiology of, 505–508
  purposes of, 505
Palliation, 81–82
Panic disorder, 439–440
Papez, James W., 115–118, *118*, 119–120
Papez loop, 115–118, *118*
Parasympathetic nervous system, 106, 108–109
Parents. *See* Caretakers
Parke, Ross, 375
Parker, Bob, 141
Parkes, C. Murray, 282, 495
Passionate love
  anatomy of, 397–398
  attachment and, 393–394
  chemistry of, 398–400
  children and, 391–393, *394*
  cognitive contribution to, 396
  definition of, 387, 403
  emotional interlinkages of, 400–402
  emotionally neutral arousal and, 405–406
  erosion of, 406–408, *407*
  genesis of, 390–393, *391*
  measurement of, 388–390, 390t, 409, 410
  nature of, 53, 54, 394–400
  negative emotions and, 403–405
  physiological contribution to, 397
  pleasure and pain in, 402–406
  positive emotions and, 403
  self-esteem and, 395
Passionate Love Scale (PLS), 388–390, 390t
Passive coping, 449
Patel, Chandra, 138
Patterson, Gerald, 376, 549–550
Pavlov, Ivan, 251
Pavlovian conditioning, 163, 453, 543–549
PEA. *See* Phenylethylamine (PEA)
Pekala, Ronald, 340–341
Peplau, Anne, 404
Peripheral nervous system (PNS)
  classification of peripheral nerves, 105, 105t
  LeDoux's approach to, 103–115, *104*, 105t, *107*
  somatic versus autonomic nervous systems, 106

structure of, 103, *104*
Perlman, Daniel, 404
Persky, Harold, 354
Persona, 70
Personal unconscious, 67
Personality. *See also* Temperament
  attitudes and, 72
  Freud's approach to, 34
  functions and, 72–77
  introverts versus extraverts, 72
  Jung's approach to, 65–72
  Jung's psychological types, 72–77
  Plutchik's approach to, 158, 159
  stress and, 500, 501–502
Personality traits, 158, 159
Peterson, Christopher, 301
Petty, Richard, 213, 214, 215, 219, 220
Phenylethylamine (PEA), 398
Phobic disorder, 144, 437–438, 438t
Physical illnesses
  atherosclerosis, 494–496
  cancer, 298
  cardiovascular disease, 493–497
  essential hypertension, 496–497
  immunity and, 497–498
  Millenson on, 177
  psychosomatic disorders, 41, 177
  stress and, 491–498
  ulcers, 492–493
Physiological methods
  for dealing with fear and anxiety, 468
  of emotional control, 528–542
  of pain control, 511
Physiological processes
  of emotion, 29t, 36–48, 77
  of fear and anxiety, 447–453
  measurement of, 77, 239–241, 245t, 266–267
  of pain, 505–508
  processing of responses, 245–246
  recording of responses, 246–247
  of sadness, 266–267
  of stress, 486–488, *486*
Picard, R. S., 498
Pituitary gland, 130–131, 133, 134, 136, 302, 488, 509
Plato, 336–337, 359, 360
Pleasure center of brain, 332, 398
Plomin, Robert, 273, 274
PLS. *See* Passionate Love Scale (PLS)
Plutchik, Robert, 13, *15*, 16, 21, 53, 54, 69, 137, 150, 151–160, 165, 169, 234, 253, 311
PMS. *See* Premenstrual syndrome (PMS)
PNS. *See* Peripheral nervous system (PNS)

Poe, Edgar Allan, 211
Polygraph, *214*, 242–244, *245*, 246
POMS. *See* Profile of Mood States (POMS)
Positive attitude, and stress, 502–503
Positive reinforcement, 57
Post-traumatic stress disorder (PTSD), 441–443
Potter, William, 302
Preconscious, 67
Premenstrual syndrome (PMS), 142, 143
Primary anxiety, 444–445
Primary appraisals, 80–81
Problem-solving skills, and stress, 503
Profile of Mood States (POMS), 556
Proprioceptors, 105
Protection responses, 151–152
Prototype emotions, 152
Proust, Marcel, 119
Proxmire, William, 11, 229–230
Prozac, 533
Psyche, 66
Psychoanalysis, 35
Psychobiologic program, 127
Psychodynamic theories
    of aggression, 358–359
    of depression, 291–294, 295
    of fear and anxiety, 444–447, 455–457
    overview of, 29–36, 29t, 30t, 64
    psychodynamic behavior theory of fear and anxiety, 455–457
Psychoevolutionary synthesis
    diagnostic concepts of, 158, 160
    emotion solid, 154–155, *154*
    emotional mixtures, 156–158
    language of emotions, 155–156, 156t
    personality traits, 158, 159
    structure of emotions, 153–158
    theoretical postulates of, 151–153
Psychometric principles of measurement, 228–233
Psychophysiological measures, 238–249, *245*, 245t, *248*, 460–462
Psychophysiology, 36–41
Psychosomatic disorders, 41, 177
Psychotherapy. *See* Treatment
Psychotic depression, 288
PTSD. *See* Post-traumatic stress disorder (PTSD)
Puccetti, Mark, 501

Questionnaires, self-report, 234–238

Rachman, Stanley, 454, 455
Radical behaviorism, 56
Rado, Sandor, 30

Rahe, Richard, 479, 480, 481, 483
Raphael, Beverley, 281
Rapson, Richard, 287–288, 557
Ratio scaling, 229–230, 231–233
Rational-emotive therapy (RET), 523–525
Raush, Harold, 378
Reaction formation, 446
Reagan, Ronald, 378, 529
Reality anxiety, 34
Reappraisal, 81
Reber, Arthur, 6, 29–30, 31, 433
Reflexes, 57
Rehm, Lynn, 301
Reik, Theodor, 406, 558
Reinforcement, 57
Reinforcement theory
    aggression and, 377–381, 377t
    companionate love and, 412–415, 416
Relationships. *See* Love
Relaxation, 470–471, 513, 531, 553–554
Repression, 32, 33, 33t, 35
Reproduction responses, 152
Research, state of, 10–12. *See also* Measurement of emotion
Resistance stage of stress, 478, 487–488
Respiration rate, 77
RET. *See* Rational-emotive therapy (RET)
Reynolds, George, 543
Ricks, David, 315
Ride, Sally, 143
Right hemisphere of brain, 78, 125, 192–197, 240
Riklin, Franz, 76
Robinson, John, 318
Rolls, Edmund, 124
Romantic love. *See* Passionate love
Rosenblatt, Paul, 53–54
Rosenman, Ray, 494
Rosenthal, Robert, 192
Rousseau, Serge, 289
Roussin, Michelle, 289
Rubenstein, Carin, 393
Rubin, Zick, 230–231, 408–409
Rufus of Ephesus, 491–492
Rule, Brendan Gail, 369
Rushdie, Salman, 346, 368
Ruskin, John, 386
Rycroft, Charles, 444

Sackheim, Harold, 194–195, 197
Sacks, Oliver, 201, 329–331, 480
Sadness
    in adults, 277–280

antecendents and responses to, 277–278
assessment of, 265–267
in children, 266, 267
definition of, 264
description of, 265
functions of, 279–280
St. Martin, Alexis, 207–208
Salapatek, Philip, 463
Sarason, Irwin, 482
Sarnoff, Irving, 433, 434–435
Sarton, May, 559
Savitsky, Jeffrey, 279
Saxe, Leonard, 244
Scales and scaling procedures, 228–233
Scarr, Sandra, 463
Schachter, Stanley, 83–88, 97, 113, 125, 208
Schaefer, Catherine, 483
Schaefer, Earl, 160
Scheff, Thomas, 359
Scherer, Klaus, 21
Schlor, K. H., 133
Schlosberg, Harold, 13, *14*
Schneiderman, Neil, 478
Scholes, Robert, 196, 197
Schreuder, Frances, 372, 373
Schultz, Duane, 68
Schwartz, Gary, 450
Schwarz, J. Conrad, 393, 394
SCR. *See* Skin conductance response (SCR)
SDS. *See* Self-Rating Depression Scale (SDS)
Sears, Robert, 366–367
Sechrest, L., 464
Secondary appraisal, 81
Selective filtering, 92
Selective retrieval, 92–93
Self-esteem, and passionate love, 395
Self-Rating Depression Scale (SDS), 289
Self-report measures, 227–238, 459–460, 459t
Seligman, Martin, 298–299
Selye, Hans, 111–112, 477–478, 483, 486, 489, 492
Separation anxiety, 446–447
Serenity, 128, *130*, 138–139, *139*
Serotonin, 302, 303, 332, 399
Serviceable associated habits, principle of, 49–50
Shadow, 71
Shaver, Philip L., 315, 318, 327, 393
Sherif, Carolyn, 143
Shmavonian, Barry, 449
Shore, Parkhurst, 452
Shyness, 550–551

Siegel, Judith, 482
Signal anxiety, 445
Signorielli, Nancy, 374
Sim, Marguerite, 279
Similarity, of emotions, 154
Singer, Jerome, 85–88, 208
Skin. *See* Galvanic skin response (GSR)
Skin conductance, 241, 449–450
Skin conductance response (SCR), 241
Skin potential response (SPR), 241
Skin temperature, and fear, 450
Skinner, B. F., 55, 56–58, 150, 167, 173, 176, 249
Smith, Adam, 204–205
Smith, Iola, 236
Smith, Keith, 354
Smith, L. G., 424–425
Snap judgments, 93
Sociability, as component of temperament, 274
Social judgments, 93–94
Social learning theory, and anger, 370–381
Social psychophysiologists, 213
Social psychophysiology, of facial expression, 212–221, *214, 216, 218*
Social Readjustment Rating Scale (SRRS), 479–482, 481t
Social referencing, 185
Social skills, and stress, 503
Social support, and stress, 503–504
Sociobiological perspective on aggression, 356–358
Solomon, Richard, 153, 336–339
Somatic nervous system, 106
Somatic palliation, 82
Spielberger, Charles, 14, 236, 459
Spike, 217
Spitz, Rene, 295, 312
SPR. *See* Skin potential response (SPR)
SRRS. *See* Social Readjustment Rating Scale (SRRS)
STAI. *See* State-Trait Anxiety Inventory (STAI)
State dependence, 95
State-dependent memory, 91–94, 95
State-Trait Anxiety Inventory (STAI), 233–234, 236, 459–460, 465
States, emotional, 14
Steiner, Jacob, 185, 268, 312
Steinmetz, Suzanne, 371–372, 378, 560
Stephens, Patricia M., 127, 129, 130–132, 141
Stepper, Sabine, 204
Sternbach, Richard, 505
Sternberg, Craig, 79
Sternberg, Robert, 387, 408, 409

Steroids, 133
Stewart, Lawrence, 72
Stewart, Louis, 78
Stimulus evaluation and reward, 121–124
Stock, G., 133
Stone, L., 364
Stoyva, Johann, 259
Strack, Fritz, 204
Straus, Murray, 371–372, 374
Stress
    aggression and, 490
    alarm stage of, 478, 486–487
    atherosclerosis and, 494–496
    autonomic nervous system and, 111–112
    behavioral responses to, 488–489
    cardiovascular disease and, 493–497
    cognitive appraisal, 81
    cognitive responses to, 490–491
    coping with, 498–504
    death by, 480
    diseases of, 491–498
    early contributions to study of, 477–479
    emotional responses to, 485–491
    essential hypertension and, 496–497
    exhaustion stage of, 478, 488
    hardiness and, 500, 501–502
    hassles and, 483–485, 485t
    health and energy and, 500
    immunity and, 497–498
    major stressors, 479–483, 481t
    material resources and, 504
    measurement of, 479–485, 481t
    overeating and, 489–490
    personality factors and, 500, 501–502
    physiological responses to, 486–488, *486*
    positive beliefs and, 502–503
    problem-solving skills and, 503
    resistance stage of, 478, 487–488
    social skills and, 503
    social support and, 503–504
    sources of, 479–485, 481t, 485t
    stages of, 478, 486–488
    ulcers and, 492–493
Stress Inoculation Training, 523, 525–526
Strickland, Bonnie, 503
Stroebe, Margaret, 281, 283
Stroebe, Wolfgang, 281, 283
Subjective language, of emotions, 155, 156, 156t
Subjective (self-report) measures of emotion, 227–238

Superego, 34, 445
Swain, Mary Ann, 378
Sympathetic nervous system, 106, 108–109
Systematic desensitization, 470, 544–545, *548*
Szucko, Julian, 243

Talkington, J., 302
Tassinary, Louis, 213, 215, 219
Taylor, Shelley, 485
Taylor, Stuart, 541
Taylor Manifest Anxiety Scale (MAS), 459, 459t
TCAs. *See* Tricyclics (TCAs)
Television violence, 374–375
Tellegen, Auke, 340
Temperament. *See also* Personality
    consistency of, 275
    definition of, 273
    traits involved in, 273–274
Temperature. *See* Skin temperature
Temporal lobe, 44
Tennov, Dorothy, 396
TENS unit. *See* Transcutaneous stimulator (TENS unit)
Testosterone, 128, 133, 135, 140, 354, 399, 488
Thalamus, 42, 115, 116, 119, 123, 508, 511
Tharp, Roland, 550
Theory, state of, 10–12. *See also* names of specific theories
Therapy. *See* Treatment
Thermistor, 241
Theroux, Paul, 285–286
Thibaut, John, 323–324, 327
Thinking. *See* Brain; Cognition
Thomas, Alexander, 275
Thompson, Richard, 45–47
Thompson, Ross, 272–273
Timing, and lying, 192
Tinbergen, Nikolas, 356
Tomkins, Silvan, 16, 78, 185, 199–200, 279–280
Tosheff, Julij, 488
Traits, emotional, 14
Tranquilizers, 534–535, 535t
Transcutaneous stimulator (TENS unit), 511
Transpersonal unconscious, 67–68
Traupmann, Jane, 418, 420
Treatment. *See also* Drug therapy
    behavioral therapies, 468–471, 543–552
    cognitive therapies, 468, 511–513, 522–528
    for control of fear, 466–471
    of depression, 296–298, 303–306

for pain control, 510–514
Tresemer, David, 466
Triangulation, 259
Tricyclics (TCAs), 303–304, *304,* 532–533, 533t, 535t
Two-process approaches to fear and anxiety, 453–455

UCS. *See* Unconditioned fear stimulus (UCS)
Ulcers, 492–493
Unconditioned fear stimulus (UCS), 163
Unconscious, 32, 67–68, 71–72
Unemployment, 321–322
Unipolar depression, 288
Unlearned fear response, 163
Uplifts Scale, 483

Valins, Stuart, 89
Vaughan, Katherine, 205–206
Veroff, Joseph, 314, 320
Vincent, John, 414
Violence. *See* Aggression
Vrtunski, Bart, 197

Wall, Patrick, 506–507
Wallace, Russell, 49
Wallach, Jeffrey, 478

Wallis, Claudia, 505
Walster, G. William, 328, 349, 387, 403, 420
Walter, W. Grey, 238
Walters, R. H., 371
Ward, Ingeborg, 142
Warhol, Andy, 542–543
Watson, David, 550
Watson, John B., 13, 55–56, 58, 150, 152, 163, 166, 444, 543
Watson, Robert, 196, 197
Webb, Eugene, 259, 464
Weidner, Gerdi, 403
Weill, Kurt, 71
Weiss, Jay, 131, 177
Weiss, Robert, 404, 414
Weisz, Judith, 142
Weldon, Fay, 362, 519–521
Wenger, Marion, 36, 41, 200
Wernicke's aphasia, 196
Wernicke's area, 196
Wessman, Alden, 315
Wheeler, Ladd, 87
Whitman, Charles, 352–353
Willers, R. R., 363
Williams, Allan, 284
Wilson, Edward O., 53, 356–357
Wilson, John, 490
Wilson, Warner, 314, 318, 322

Witt, David, 322
Wolf, Katherine, 312
Wolf, S., 44, 492
Wolfe, Tom, 447–448
Wolff, Harold, 44, 450, 492
Wolff, Peter, 312
Wolff, Werner, 194
Woods, Clayton C., 310
Woodward, Bob, 336
Woodworth, Robert, 13
Woolf, Virginia, 294, 296, 439–440
Word association, 76
Work, and happiness, 321–322
Wortman, Camille, 284
Wundt, Wilhelm, 13

Yalom, Irvin, 441
Yeager, Chuck, 82, 83
Yerkes, Robert, 490
Yerkes-Dodson principle, 490
Young, Paul, 36

Zajonc, Robert, 88–91, 97
Zeisset, Ray, 258
Zimbardo, Philip, 88, 433, 434–435, 550–551
Zuckerman, Marvin, 235
Zuckerman, Miron, 192
Zung, William, 289, 463

Permissions and Acknowledgments

ON THE COVER

MATISSE, Henri (1869–1954). *Icarus,* Plate VIII from *Jazz.* Paris, Teriade, 1947. Pochoir, printed in color, composition: 16¼ x 10¾". Collection, The Museum of Modern Art, New York. The Louis E. Stern Collection. Photograph copyright 1992 The Museum of Modern Art, New York.

CHAPTER 1

Figure 1.1 (p. 3): MATISSE, Henri. *Dance (first version).* (1909, early) Oil on canvas, 8' 6½" x 12' 9½". Collection, The Museum of Modern Art, New York. Gift of Nelson A. Rockefeller in honor of Alfred H. Barr, Jr.

Figure 1.2 (p. 14): Schlosberg, H. (1954). Three dimensions of emotion. *Psychological Review, 61,* p. 81f. Public domain.

CHAPTER 2

Figure 2.1 (p. 26): *Dance of Life (Livets dans).* Edvard Munch. Copyright Oslo Kommunes Kunstsamlinger, Munch-Museet.

Excerpt from *Savage Grace* (p. 28): Copyright 1985 by Steven M.L. Aronson and Natalie Robins. By permission of William Morrow and Company, Inc.

Figure 2.3 (p. 40): Copyright 1966, The Society for Psychophysiological Research. Reprinted with permission of the publisher from *Psychophysiology;* Table 7 (adapted) from "Studies of Autonomic Balance: A Summary," by M.A. Wenger, 1966, *2,* p. 173–186; and data from "Some Effects of Spinal Cord Lesions on Experienced Emotional Feelings," by G.W. Hohmann, 1966, *3,* p. 143–156.

Box 2.2 and Figures 2.5 through 2.8 (pp. 45–47): From *The Amazing Brain,* by Robert Ornstein and Richard Thompson. Text copyright © 1984 by Robert Ornstein and Richard A. Thompson. Illustration copyright © 1984 by David A. Macaulay. Reprinted by permission of Houghton Mifflin Company.

CHAPTER 3

Figure 3.1 (p. 62): KLEE, Paul. *Cat and Bird (Katze und Vogel).* 1928. Oil and ink on gessoed canvas, mounted on wood, 15 x 21". Collection, The Museum of Modern

Art, New York. Sidney and Harriet Janis Collection Fund and gift of Suzy Prudden and Joan H. Meijer in memory of F.H. Hirschland.

Figure 3.2 (p. 97): Adapted from "The Persistent Problems of Emotion," by D.K. Candland. In *Emotion*, by D.K. Candland, et al. (Eds.). Copyright © 1977 by Wadsworth Publishing Company, Inc. Reprinted by permission of Brooks/Cole Publishing Company, Pacific Grove, CA 93950.

CHAPTER 4

Figure 4.1 (p. 100): *Consolation*. Edvard Munch. Copyright Oslo Kommunes Kunstsamlinger, Munch-Museet.

Figure 4.2 (p. 104): From *Psychology: Science, Behavior and Life*, by R. Crooks and J. Stein, copyright © 1988 by Holt, Rinehart and Winston, Inc., reprinted by permission of the publisher.

Table 4.1 (p. 105): From *Mind and Brain: Dialogues in Cognitive Neuroscience*, by J.E. LeDoux and W. Hirst, published by Cambridge University Press.

Figure 4.3 (p. 107): in *Dynamics of Health and Wellness*, by J. Green and R. Shellenberger, copyright © 1991 by Holt, Rinehart and Winston, Inc., reprinted by permission of the publisher.

Figure 4.4 (p. 115): Reprinted with permission of Macmillan Publishing Company from *Sleep: An Experimental Approach*, by W.B. Webb. Copyright © 1968 by Wilse B. Webb.

Figure 4.5 (p. 116): From *Introduction to Psychology*, Sixth Edition, by E.R. Hilgard and R.L. Atkinson, copyright © 1975 by Harcourt Brace Jovanovich, Inc., reprinted by permission of the publisher.

Figure 4.7 (p. 120): From *Emotion: A Psychoevolutionary Synthesis*, by Robert Plutchik. Copyright © 1980 by Individual Dynamics, Inc. Reprinted by permission of HarperCollins Publishers.

Figure 4.8 (p. 127): Material from Henry, J.P., and Stephens, P.M. (1977). *Stress, Health, and the Social Environment: A Sociobiologic Approach to Medicine*. New York: Springer-Verlag.

Figures 4.9, 4.10 (pp. 129, 130): Material from Henry, J.P. (1986). Neuroendocrine patterns of emotional response. In R. Plutchik and H. Kellerman (Eds.), *Emotion: Theory, Research and Experience*, Volume 3 (pp. 37–60). New York: Academic Press.

Figure 4.11 (p. 138): Reprinted with permission from *Social Science and Medicine, 16*. Henry, J.P., The relation of social to biological processes in disease (1982). Pergamon Press, plc.

CHAPTER 5

Figure 5.1 (p. 148): *Separation*. Edvard Munch. Copyright Oslo Kommunes Kunstsamlinger, Munch-Museet.

Plutchik's Postulates (pp. 151–153): Excerpts from *Emotion: A Psychoevolutionary Synthesis*, by Robert Plutchik. Copyright © 1980 by Individual Dynamics, Inc. Reprinted by permission of HarperCollins Publishers.

Figure 5.2 (p. 154): Excerpts from *Emotion: A Psychoevolutionary Synthesis*, by Robert Plutchik. Copyright © 1980 by Individual Dynamics, Inc. Reprinted by permission of HarperCollins Publishers.

Tables 5.1 through 5.3 (pp. 155, 156, 159): Excerpts from *Emotion: A Psychoevolutionary Synthesis*, by Robert Plutchik. Copyright © 1980 by Individual Dynamics, Inc. Reprinted by permission of HarperCollins Publishers.

Table 5.4 (p. 165): Reprinted by permission of Macmillan Publishing Company from *Principles of Behavioral Analysis*, Second Edition, by J.R. Millenson and Julian C. Leslie. Copyright © 1979 by J.R. Millenson.

CHAPTER 6

Figure 6.1 (p. 180): *Jealousy*. Edvard Munch. Copyright Oslo Kommunes Kunstsamlinger, Munch-Museet.

Figure 6.2 (p. 183): Cacioppo, J.T., Martzke, J.S., Petty, R.E., and Tassinary, L.G. Specific forms of facial EMG response index emotions during an interview. *Journal of Personality and Social Psychology*, Volume 54, No. 4, pp. 592–604. Copyright 1988 by the American Psychological Association. Reprinted by permission of the publisher and author.

Table 6.1 (p. 186): From "Constants Across Cultures in the Face and Emotion," by Paul Ekman and Wallace V. Friesen. *Journal of Personality and Social Psychology*, *17*, pp. 124–129 (1971). Copyright 1971 by the American Psychological Association. Reprinted by permission.

Figures 6.5, 6.6 (pp. 209, 210): Reprinted with permission from *Science*, Volume 221, pages 1208–1210, 16 September 1983; "Autonomic Nervous System Activity Distinguishes Among Emotions," Ekman, R.E., Levenson, R.W., and Friesen, W.V. Copyright 1983 by the AAAS.

Figure 6.8 (p. 216): Cacioppo, J.T., Petty, R.E., Losch, M.E., and Kim, H.S. (1986). Electromyographic activity over facial muscle regions. *Journal of Personality and Social Psychology*, *50*, pp. 260–268. Copyright 1986 by the American Psychological Association. Reprinted by permission of the author.

Figure 6.9 (p. 218): Cacioppo, J.T., Martzke, J.S., Petty, R.E., and Tassinary, L.G. Specific forms of facial EMG response index emotions during an interview. *Journal of Personality and Social Psychology*, Volume 54, No. 4, pp. 592–604. Copyright 1988 by the American Psychological Association. Reprinted by permission of the publisher and author.

CHAPTER 7

Figure 7.1 (p. 224): *Lovers in Waves*. Edvard Munch. Copyright Oslo Kommunes Kunstsamlinger, Munch-Museet.

Box 7.1 (p. 232): From Berschied, E., and Hatfield (Walster), E., *Interpersonal Attraction*, Second Edition (1978). Reprinted with permission of McGraw-Hill, Inc.

Box 7.2 (p. 237): Mood Adjective Check List from Nowlis, V., and Nowlis, H.H. (1956). The description and analysis of mood. *Annals of the New York Academy of Science*, *65*, pp. 345–355.

Figure 7.3 (p. 248): Reprinted by permission of Elsevier Science Publishing Co., Inc., from "Gradients of Physiological Arousal in Parachutists as a Function of an Approaching Jump," by Fenz, W.D., and Epstein, S., in *Psychosomatic Medicine*, Volume 29, pp. 33–51. Copyright 1967 by the American Psychosomatic Society, Inc.

Table 7.3 (p. 256): From The Bayley Scales of Infant Development. Copyright ©

1969 by The Psychological Corporation. Reproduced by permission. All rights reserved.

CHAPTER 8

Figure 8.1 (p. 262): van GOGH, Vincent. *Sorrow.* (1882, November) Transfer lithograph, printed in black, composition: 15³/₈ x 11³/₁₆″. Collection, The Museum of Modern Art, New York. Purchase.

Box 8.5 (p. 295): Reprinted from *Psychoanalytic Study of the Child,* Volume 22, by R.A. Spitz, by permission of International Universities Press, Inc. Copyright 1946 by International Universities Press.

CHAPTER 9

Figure 9.1 (p. 308): Hals, Frans (after 1580–1666). *Merrymakers at Shrovetide (The Merry Company).* Oil on canvas. 51³/₄ x 39¹/₄ in. (131.5 x 99.7 cm.). The Metropolitan Museum of Art, Bequest of Benjamin Altman, 1913. (14.40.605) All rights reserved, The Metropolitan Museum of Art, New York.

Box 9.2 (p. 323): From "Is That All There Is?" (news article); copyright © 1986 by The New York Times Company. Reprinted by permission.

Figure 9.3 (p. 325): "Peanuts" cartoon by Charles Schulz reprinted by permission of UFS, Inc.

Figure 9.4 (p. 338): From Solomon, R.L., and Corbit, J.D. (1974). An opponent-process theory of motivation: I. Temporal dynamics of affect. *Psychological Review, 81,* pp. 119–145. Copyright 1974 by the American Psychological Association. Reprinted by permission.

CHAPTER 10

Table 10.2 (p. 356): From Averill, J. (1938), Studies on anger and aggression: Implications for theories of emotion. *American Psychologist, 38,* pp. 1145–1160. Reprinted by permission of the publisher and author.

Box 10.3 (p. 366): From *The Needle's Eye,* by Margaret Drabble. Copyright © 1972 by Margaret Drabble. Reprinted by permission of Alfred A. Knopf, Inc.

Table 10.3 (p. 372): From Table 4 in *Behind Closed Doors,* by M.A. Straus, R.J. Gelles, and S.K. Steinmetz. Copyright © 1980 by M.A. Straus and R.J. Gelles. Reprinted by permission of Doubleday, a division of Bantam/Doubleday/Dell Publishing Group, Inc.

Box 10.6 (p. 373): Excerpted from *Nutcracker,* by Shana Alexander. Copyright © 1985 by Shana Alexander. Reprinted by permission of Doubleday, a division of Bantam/Doubleday/Dell Publishing Group, Inc.

Table 10.5 (p. 379): From Lloyd Shearer, *Parade Magazine.*

CHAPTER 11

Figure 11.1 (p. 384): LICHTENSTEIN, Roy. *Drowning Girl.* 1963. Oil and synthetic polymer paint on canvas, 67⁵/₈ x 66³/₄″. Collection, The Museum of Modern Art, New York. Philip Johnson Fund.

Figure 11.2 (p. 388): From "Triangulating Love" (p. 121–122), by Robert J. Sternberg, in *The Psychology of Love,* edited by R.J. Sternberg and M.L. Barnes (1988). New Haven, Conn.: Yale University Press. Copyright 1988 by Yale University Press. Reprinted by permission.

Figure 11.3 (p. 391): Photograph property of Primate Behavior Laboratory: SUNY/ HSCB.

Figure 11.5 (p. 405): "Peanuts" cartoon by Charles Schulz reprinted by permission of UFS, Inc.

CHAPTER 12

Figure 12.1 (p. 430): *The Scream. (Geschrei: Ich fühlte das grosse Geschrei durch die Natur.)* Edvard Munch. Copyright Oslo Kommunes Kunstsamlinger, Munch-Museet.

Excerpt from Virginia Woolf's diary (pp. 439–440): Excerpted from *The Diary of Virginia Woolf,* Volume 4, by Virginia Woolf. Copyright © 1982 by Quentin Bell and Angelica Garnett. Reprinted by permission of Harcourt Brace Jovanovich, Inc.

Quotation from L. Borton (pp. 442–443): Copyright © 1988 by The New York Times Company. Reprinted by permission.

Figure 12.2 (p. 451): Photograph by Anita Henderson / *Beloit Daily News* / Associated Press.

CHAPTER 13

Figure 13.1 (p. 474): *Les Baigneuses.* Pablo Picasso. Cliché des Musées Nationaux, Paris. Service photographique de la Réunion des musées nationaux. 89, avenue Victor Hugo, 75116 Paris. Copyright © Photo R.M.N./SPADEM.

Box 13.1 (p. 480): From Sacks, Oliver (1976). *Awakenings.* New York: Vintage Books.

Table 13.1 (p. 481): Reprinted with permission from *Journal of Psychosomatic Research, 11.* Holmes, T., and Rahe, R., The social readjustment scale (1967). Pergamon Press, plc.

Box 13.2 (p. 484): From Kanner, A.D., Schaffer, J.C., and Lazarus, R.S. (1981). *Journal of Behavioral Medicine, 4.* Plenum Publishing Corporation.

CHAPTER 14

Figure 4.1 (p. 516): *Guernica.* Pablo Picasso. Spanish, 1881–1973. May 1–June 4, 1937. Oil on canvas, 11' 5½" x 25' 5¾". Collection of the Museo Nacional Del Prado, Calle de Felipe IV, Madrid, Spain. On extended loan to The Museum of Modern Art, New York. Copyright 1991 ARS, N.Y./SPADEM.

Table 14.2 (p. 534): From Baldessarini, R.J., *Chemotherapy in Psychiatry,* Revised and Enlarged Edition (1985), Table 27, p. 108. Cambridge, Mass.: Harvard University Press.

Box 14.3 (p. 536): From *Rock Hudson,* by Rock Hudson and Sara Davidson. Copyright © 1986 by Rock Hudson AIDS Research Foundation. By permission of William Morrow and Company, Inc.

Figure 14.3 (p. 538): Copyright 1974 Time, Inc. All rights reserved. Reprinted by permission from TIME.

Box 14.5 (p. 546): From *Will: The Autobiography of G. Gordon Liddy,* by G. Gordon Liddy (1980). New York: St. Martin's Press, Inc. Copyright © 1980 by G. Gordon Liddy.

Figure 14.4 (p. 548): Reprinted with permission from *Journal of Behavior Therapy and*

Experimental Psychiatry, 10; Van Hasselt, B.B., Herson, M., Bellack, A.S., Rosenbloom, N., and Lamparski, D. (1979). Tripartite assessment of the effects of systematic densensitization in a multiphobic child: An experimental analysis. Pergamon Press, plc.

Box 14.7 (p. 559): Reprinted from *Anger,* A Novel, by May Sarton, by permission of W.W. Norton & Company, Inc. Copyright © 1982 by May Sarton.